American Casebook Series
Hornbook Series and Basic Legal Texts
Black Letter Series and Nutshell Series

of

WEST PUBLISHING COMPANY
P.O. Box 64526
St. Paul, Minnesota 55164–0526

Accounting

FARIS' ACCOUNTING AND LAW IN A NUT-SHELL, 377 pages, 1984. Softcover. (Text)

FIFLIS' ACCOUNTING ISSUES FOR LAWYERS, TEACHING MATERIALS, , 706 pages, 1991. Teacher's Manual available. (Casebook)

SIEGEL AND SIEGEL'S ACCOUNTING AND FINANCIAL DISCLOSURE: A GUIDE TO BASIC CONCEPTS, 259 pages, 1983. Softcover. (Text)

Administrative Law

AMAN AND MAYTON'S HORNBOOK ON ADMINISTRATIVE LAW, Approximately 750 pages, 1992. (Text)

BONFIELD AND ASIMOW'S STATE AND FEDERAL ADMINISTRATIVE LAW, 826 pages, 1989. Teacher's Manual available. (Casebook)

GELLHORN AND LEVIN'S ADMINISTRATIVE LAW AND PROCESS IN A NUTSHELL, Third Edition, 479 pages, 1990. Softcover. (Text)

MASHAW, MERRILL, AND SHANE'S CASES AND MATERIALS ON ADMINISTRATIVE LAW—THE AMERICAN PUBLIC LAW SYSTEM, Third Edition, approximately 950 pages, September 1992 Pub. (Casebook)

ROBINSON, GELLHORN AND BRUFF'S THE ADMINISTRATIVE PROCESS, Third Edition, 978 pages, 1986. (Casebook)

Admiralty

HEALY AND SHARPE'S CASES AND MATERIALS ON ADMIRALTY, Second Edition, 876 pages, 1986. (Casebook)

MARAIST'S ADMIRALTY IN A NUTSHELL, Second Edition, 379 pages, 1988. Softcover. (Text)

SCHOENBAUM'S HORNBOOK ON ADMIRALTY AND MARITIME LAW, Student Edition, 692 pages, 1987 with 1992 pocket part. (Text)

Agency—Partnership

DEMOTT'S FIDUCIARY OBLIGATION, AGENCY AND PARTNERSHIP: DUTIES IN ONGOING BUSINESS RELATIONSHIPS, 740 pages, 1991. Teacher's Manual available. (Casebook)

FESSLER'S ALTERNATIVES TO INCORPORATION FOR PERSONS IN QUEST OF PROFIT, Third Edition, 339 pages, 1991. Softcover. (Casebook)

HENN'S CASES AND MATERIALS ON AGENCY, PARTNERSHIP AND OTHER UNINCORPORATED BUSINESS ENTERPRISES, Second Edition, 733 pages, 1985. Teacher's Manual available. (Casebook)

REUSCHLEIN AND GREGORY'S HORNBOOK ON THE LAW OF AGENCY AND PARTNERSHIP, Second Edition, 683 pages, 1990. (Text)

SELECTED CORPORATION AND PARTNERSHIP STATUTES, RULES AND FORMS. Softcover. Revised 1991 Edition, approximately 950 pages.

STEFFEN AND KERR'S CASES ON AGENCY-PARTNERSHIP, Fourth Edition, 859 pages, 1980. (Casebook)

STEFFEN'S AGENCY-PARTNERSHIP IN A NUTSHELL, 364 pages, 1977. Softcover. (Text)

Agricultural Law

MEYER, PEDERSEN, THORSON AND DAVIDSON'S AGRICULTURAL LAW: CASES AND MATERIALS,

Agricultural Law—Cont'd
931 pages, 1985. Teacher's Manual available. (Casebook)

Alternative Dispute Resolution
KANOWITZ' CASES AND MATERIALS ON ALTERNATIVE DISPUTE RESOLUTION, 1024 pages, 1986. Teacher's Manual available. (Casebook) 1990 Supplement.

NOLAN–HALEY'S ALTERNATIVE DISPUTE RESOLUTION IN A NUTSHELL, Approximately 300 pages, 1992. Softcover. (Text)

RISKIN AND WESTBROOK'S DISPUTE RESOLUTION AND LAWYERS, 468 pages, 1987. Teacher's Manual available. (Casebook)

RISKIN AND WESTBROOK'S DISPUTE RESOLUTION AND LAWYERS, Abridged Edition, 223 pages, 1987. Softcover. Teacher's Manual available. (Casebook)

RISKIN'S DISPUTE RESOLUTION FOR LAWYERS VIDEO TAPES, 1992. (Available for purchase by schools and libraries.)

American Indian Law
CANBY'S AMERICAN INDIAN LAW IN A NUTSHELL, Second Edition, 336 pages, 1988. Softcover. (Text)

GETCHES AND WILKINSON'S CASES AND MATERIALS ON FEDERAL INDIAN LAW, Second Edition, 880 pages, 1986. (Casebook)

Antitrust—see also Regulated Industries, Trade Regulation
BARNES AND STOUT'S ECONOMIC FOUNDATIONS OF REGULATION AND ANTITRUST LAW, Approximately 150 pages, 1992. Softcover. Teacher's Manual available. (Casebook)

FOX AND SULLIVAN'S CASES AND MATERIALS ON ANTITRUST, 935 pages, 1989. Teacher's Manual available. (Casebook)

GELLHORN'S ANTITRUST LAW AND ECONOMICS IN A NUTSHELL, Third Edition, 472 pages, 1986. Softcover. (Text)

HOVENKAMP'S BLACK LETTER ON ANTITRUST, 323 pages, 1986. Softcover. (Review)

HOVENKAMP'S HORNBOOK ON ECONOMICS AND FEDERAL ANTITRUST LAW, Student Edition, 414 pages, 1985. (Text)

POSNER AND EASTERBROOK'S CASES AND ECONOMIC NOTES ON ANTITRUST, Second Edition, 1077 pages, 1981. (Casebook) 1984–85 Supplement.

SULLIVAN'S HORNBOOK OF THE LAW OF ANTITRUST, 886 pages, 1977. (Text)

Appellate Advocacy—see Trial and Appellate Advocacy

Architecture and Engineering Law
SWEET'S LEGAL ASPECTS OF ARCHITECTURE, ENGINEERING AND THE CONSTRUCTION PROCESS, Fourth Edition, 889 pages, 1989. Teacher's Manual available. (Casebook)

Art Law
DUBOFF'S ART LAW IN A NUTSHELL, 335 pages, 1984. Softcover. (Text)

Banking Law
BANKING LAW: SELECTED STATUTES AND REGULATIONS. Softcover. 263 pages, 1991.

LOVETT'S BANKING AND FINANCIAL INSTITUTIONS LAW IN A NUTSHELL, Third Edition, approximately 500 pages, 1992. Softcover. (Text)

SYMONS AND WHITE'S BANKING LAW: TEACHING MATERIALS, Third Edition, 818 pages, 1991. Teacher's Manual available. (Casebook)

Statutory Supplement. *See Banking Law: Selected Statutes*

Business Planning—see also Corporate Finance
PAINTER'S PROBLEMS AND MATERIALS IN BUSINESS PLANNING, Second Edition, 1008 pages, 1984. (Casebook) 1990 Supplement.

Statutory Supplement. *See Selected Corporation and Partnership*

Civil Procedure—see also Federal Jurisdiction and Procedure
AMERICAN BAR ASSOCIATION SECTION OF LITIGATION—READINGS ON ADVERSARIAL JUSTICE: THE AMERICAN APPROACH TO ADJUDICATION, 217 pages, 1988. Softcover. (Coursebook)

CLERMONT'S BLACK LETTER ON CIVIL PROCEDURE, Second Edition, 332 pages, 1988. Softcover. (Review)

COUND, FRIEDENTHAL, MILLER AND SEXTON'S CASES AND MATERIALS ON CIVIL PROCEDURE, Fifth Edition, 1284 pages, 1989. Teacher's

Civil Procedure—Cont'd

Manual available. (Casebook)

COUND, FRIEDENTHAL, MILLER AND SEXTON'S CIVIL PROCEDURE SUPPLEMENT. 476 pages, 1991. Softcover. (Casebook Supplement)

FEDERAL RULES OF CIVIL PROCEDURE—EDUCATIONAL EDITION. Softcover. Approximately 775 pages, 1992.

FRIEDENTHAL, KANE AND MILLER'S HORNBOOK ON CIVIL PROCEDURE, 876 pages, 1985. (Text)

KANE AND LEVINE'S CIVIL PROCEDURE IN CALIFORNIA: STATE AND FEDERAL 1992 Edition, approximately 550 pages. Softcover. (Casebook Supplement)

KANE'S CIVIL PROCEDURE IN A NUTSHELL, Third Edition, 303 pages, 1991. Softcover. (Text)

KOFFLER AND REPPY'S HORNBOOK ON COMMON LAW PLEADING, 663 pages, 1969. (Text)

LEVINE, SLOMANSON AND WINGATE'S CALIFORNIA CIVIL PROCEDURE, CASES AND MATERIALS, . 546 pages, 1991. Teacher's Manual available. (Casebook)

MARCUS, REDISH AND SHERMAN'S CIVIL PROCEDURE: A MODERN APPROACH, 1027 pages, 1989. Teacher's Manual available. (Casebook) 1991 Supplement.

MARCUS AND SHERMAN'S COMPLEX LITIGATION—CASES AND MATERIALS ON ADVANCED CIVIL PROCEDURE, Second Edition, approximately 1050 pages, 1992. Teacher's Manual available. (Casebook)

PARK AND MCFARLAND'S COMPUTER-AIDED EXERCISES ON CIVIL PROCEDURE, Third Edition, 210 pages, 1991. Softcover. (Coursebook)

SIEGEL'S HORNBOOK ON NEW YORK PRACTICE, Second Edition, Student Edition, 1068 pages, 1991. Softcover. (Text) 1992 Supplemental Pamphlet.

Commercial Law

BAILEY AND HAGEDORN'S SECURED TRANSACTIONS IN A NUTSHELL, Third Edition, 390 pages, 1988. Softcover. (Text)

EPSTEIN, MARTIN, HENNING AND NICKLES' BASIC UNIFORM COMMERCIAL CODE TEACHING MATERIALS, Third Edition, 704 pages, 1988.

Teacher's Manual available. (Casebook)

HENSON'S HORNBOOK ON SECURED TRANSACTIONS UNDER THE U.C.C., Second Edition, 504 pages, 1979, with 1979 pocket part. (Text)

MEYER AND SPEIDEL'S BLACK LETTER ON SALES AND LEASES OF GOODS, Approximately 400 pages, October 1992 Pub. Softcover. (Review)

NICKLES' BLACK LETTER ON COMMERCIAL PAPER, 450 pages, 1988. Softcover. (Review)

NICKLES, MATHESON AND DOLAN'S MATERIALS FOR UNDERSTANDING CREDIT AND PAYMENT SYSTEMS, 923 pages, 1987. Teacher's Manual available. (Casebook)

NORDSTROM, MURRAY AND CLOVIS' PROBLEMS AND MATERIALS ON SALES, 515 pages, 1982. (Casebook)

NORDSTROM, MURRAY AND CLOVIS' PROBLEMS AND MATERIALS ON SECURED TRANSACTIONS, 594 pages, 1987. (Casebook)

RUBIN AND COOTER'S THE PAYMENT SYSTEM: CASES, MATERIALS AND ISSUES, 885 pages, 1989. Teacher's Manual Available. (Casebook)

SELECTED COMMERCIAL STATUTES. Softcover. 1897 pages, 1992.

SPEIDEL, SUMMERS AND WHITE'S COMMERCIAL LAW: TEACHING MATERIALS, Fourth Edition, 1448 pages, 1987. Teacher's Manual available. (Casebook)

SPEIDEL, SUMMERS AND WHITE'S COMMERCIAL PAPER: TEACHING MATERIALS, Fourth Edition, 578 pages, 1987. Reprint from Speidel et al., Commercial Law, Fourth Edition. Teacher's Manual available. (Casebook)

SPEIDEL, SUMMERS AND WHITE'S SALES: TEACHING MATERIALS, Fourth Edition, 804 pages, 1987. Reprint from Speidel et al., Commercial Law, Fourth Edition. Teacher's Manual available. (Casebook)

SPEIDEL, SUMMERS AND WHITE'S SECURED TRANSACTIONS: TEACHING MATERIALS, Fourth Edition, 485 pages, 1987. Reprint from Speidel et al., Commercial Law, Fourth Edition. Teacher's Manual available. (Casebook)

STOCKTON AND MILLER'S SALES AND LEASES OF GOODS IN A NUTSHELL, Third Edition,

Commercial Law—Cont'd

approximately 425 pages, 1992. Softcover. (Text)

STONE'S UNIFORM COMMERCIAL CODE IN A NUTSHELL, Third Edition, 580 pages, 1989. Softcover. (Text)

WEBER AND SPEIDEL'S COMMERCIAL PAPER IN A NUTSHELL, Third Edition, 404 pages, 1982. Softcover. (Text)

WHITE AND SUMMERS' HORNBOOK ON THE UNIFORM COMMERCIAL CODE, Third Edition, Student Edition, 1386 pages, 1988. (Text)

Community Property

MENNELL AND BOYKOFF'S COMMUNITY PROPERTY IN A NUTSHELL, Second Edition, 432 pages, 1988. Softcover. (Text)

VERRALL AND BIRD'S CASES AND MATERIALS ON CALIFORNIA COMMUNITY PROPERTY, Fifth Edition, 604 pages, 1988. (Casebook)

Comparative Law

BARTON, GIBBS, LI AND MERRYMAN'S LAW IN RADICALLY DIFFERENT CULTURES, 960 pages, 1983. (Casebook)

FOLSOM, MINAN AND OTTO'S LAW AND POLITICS IN THE PEOPLE'S REPUBLIC OF CHINA IN A NUTSHELL, Approximately 450 pages, 1992. Softcover. (Text)

GLENDON, GORDON AND OSAKWE'S COMPARATIVE LEGAL TRADITIONS: TEXT, MATERIALS AND CASES ON THE CIVIL LAW, COMMON LAW AND SOCIALIST LAW TRADITIONS, 1091 pages, 1985. (Casebook)

GLENDON, GORDON AND OSAKWE'S COMPARATIVE LEGAL TRADITIONS IN A NUTSHELL. 402 pages, 1982. Softcover. (Text)

Computers and Law

MAGGS, SOMA AND SPROWL'S COMPUTER LAW—CASES, COMMENTS, AND QUESTIONS, 731 pages, 1992. Teacher's Manual available. (Casebook)

MAGGS AND SPROWL'S COMPUTER APPLICATIONS IN THE LAW, 316 pages, 1987. (Coursebook)

MASON'S USING COMPUTERS IN THE LAW: AN INTRODUCTION AND PRACTICAL GUIDE, Second Edition, 288 pages, 1988. Softcover. (Coursebook)

Conflict of Laws

CRAMTON, CURRIE AND KAY'S CASES–COMMENTS–QUESTIONS ON CONFLICT OF LAWS, Fourth Edition, 876 pages, 1987. (Casebook)

HAY'S BLACK LETTER ON CONFLICT OF LAWS, 330 pages, 1989. Softcover. (Review)

SCOLES AND HAY'S HORNBOOK ON CONFLICT OF LAWS, Student Edition, 1160 pages, 1992. (Text)

SIEGEL'S CONFLICTS IN A NUTSHELL, 470 pages, 1982. Softcover. (Text)

Constitutional Law—Civil Rights—see also First Amendment and Foreign Relations and National Security Law

ABERNATHY'S CIVIL RIGHTS AND CONSTITUTIONAL LITIGATION, CASES AND MATERIALS, Second Edition, 753 pages, 1992. (Casebook)

BARNES AND STOUT'S THE ECONOMICS OF CONSTITUTIONAL LAW AND PUBLIC CHOICE, Approximately 150 pages, 1992. Softcover. Teacher's Manual available. (Casebook)

BARRON AND DIENES' BLACK LETTER ON CONSTITUTIONAL LAW, Third Edition, 440 pages, 1991. Softcover. (Review)

BARRON AND DIENES' CONSTITUTIONAL LAW IN A NUTSHELL, Second Edition, 483 pages, 1991. Softcover. (Text)

ENGDAHL'S CONSTITUTIONAL FEDERALISM IN A NUTSHELL, Second Edition, 411 pages, 1987. Softcover. (Text)

FARBER AND SHERRY'S HISTORY OF THE AMERICAN CONSTITUTION, 458 pages, 1990. Softcover. Teacher's Manual available. (Text)

FISHER AND DEVINS' POLITICAL DYNAMICS OF CONSTITUTIONAL LAW, 333 pages, 1992. Softcover. (Casebook Supplement)

GARVEY AND ALEINIKOFF'S MODERN CONSTITUTIONAL THEORY: A READER, Second Edition, 559 pages, 1991. Softcover. (Reader)

LOCKHART, KAMISAR, CHOPER AND SHIFFRIN'S CONSTITUTIONAL LAW: CASES–COMMENTS–QUESTIONS, Seventh Edition, 1643 pages, 1991. (Casebook) 1992 Supplement.

LOCKHART, KAMISAR, CHOPER AND SHIFFRIN'S THE AMERICAN CONSTITUTION: CASES AND MATERIALS, Seventh Edition, 1255 pages,

Constitutional Law—Civil Rights—Cont'd

1991. Abridged version of Lockhart, et al., Constitutional Law: Cases–Comments–Questions, Seventh Edition. (Casebook) 1992 Supplement.

LOCKHART, KAMISAR, CHOPER AND SHIFFRIN'S CONSTITUTIONAL RIGHTS AND LIBERTIES: CASES AND MATERIALS, Seventh Edition, 1333 pages, 1991. Reprint from Lockhart, et al., Constitutional Law: Cases–Comments–Questions, Seventh Edition. (Casebook) 1992 Supplement.

MARKS AND COOPER'S STATE CONSTITUTIONAL LAW IN A NUTSHELL, 329 pages, 1988. Softcover. (Text)

NOWAK AND ROTUNDA'S HORNBOOK ON CONSTITUTIONAL LAW, Fourth Edition, 1357 pages, 1991. (Text)

ROTUNDA'S MODERN CONSTITUTIONAL LAW: CASES AND NOTES, Third Edition, 1085 pages, 1989. (Casebook) 1992 Supplement.

VIEIRA'S CONSTITUTIONAL CIVIL RIGHTS IN A NUTSHELL, Second Edition, 322 pages, 1990. Softcover. (Text)

WILLIAMS' CONSTITUTIONAL ANALYSIS IN A NUTSHELL, 388 pages, 1979. Softcover. (Text)

Consumer Law—see also Commercial Law

EPSTEIN AND NICKLES' CONSUMER LAW IN A NUTSHELL, Second Edition, 418 pages, 1981. Softcover. (Text)

SELECTED COMMERCIAL STATUTES. Softcover. 1897 pages, 1992.

SPANOGLE, ROHNER, PRIDGEN AND RASOR'S CASES AND MATERIALS ON CONSUMER LAW, Second Edition, 916 pages, 1991. Teacher's Manual available. (Casebook)

Contracts

BARNES AND STOUT'S THE ECONOMICS OF CONTRACT LAW, Approximately 150 pages, 1992. Softcover. Teacher's Manual available. (Casebook)

CALAMARI AND PERILLO'S BLACK LETTER ON CONTRACTS, Second Edition, 462 pages, 1990. Softcover. (Review)

CALAMARI AND PERILLO'S HORNBOOK ON CONTRACTS, Third Edition, 1049 pages, 1987. (Text)

CALAMARI, PERILLO AND BENDER'S CASES AND

PROBLEMS ON CONTRACTS, Second Edition, 905 pages, 1989. Teacher's Manual Available. (Casebook)

CORBIN'S TEXT ON CONTRACTS, One Volume Student Edition, 1224 pages, 1952. (Text)

FESSLER AND LOISEAUX'S CASES AND MATERIALS ON CONTRACTS—MORALITY, ECONOMICS AND THE MARKET PLACE, 837 pages, 1982. Teacher's Manual available. (Casebook)

FRIEDMAN'S CONTRACT REMEDIES IN A NUTSHELL, 323 pages, 1981. Softcover. (Text)

FULLER AND EISENBERG'S CASES ON BASIC CONTRACT LAW, Fifth Edition, 1037 pages, 1990. (Casebook)

HAMILTON, RAU AND WEINTRAUB'S CASES AND MATERIALS ON CONTRACTS, Second Edition, 916 pages, 1992. Teacher's Manual available. (Casebook)

KEYES' GOVERNMENT CONTRACTS IN A NUTSHELL, Second Edition, 557 pages, 1990. Softcover. (Text)

SCHABER AND ROHWER'S CONTRACTS IN A NUTSHELL, Third Edition, 457 pages, 1990. Softcover. (Text)

SUMMERS AND HILLMAN'S CONTRACT AND RELATED OBLIGATION: THEORY, DOCTRINE AND PRACTICE, Second Edition, 1037 pages, 1992. Teacher's Manual available. (Casebook)

Copyright—see Patent and Copyright Law

Corporate Finance—see also Business Planning

HAMILTON'S CASES AND MATERIALS ON CORPORATION FINANCE, Second Edition, 1221 pages, 1989. (Casebook)

OESTERLE'S THE LAW OF MERGERS, ACQUISITIONS AND REORGANIZATIONS, 1096 pages, 1991. (Casebook) 1992 Supplement.

Corporations

HAMILTON'S BLACK LETTER ON CORPORATIONS, Third Edition, approximately 550 pages, 1992. Softcover. (Review)

HAMILTON'S CASES AND MATERIALS ON CORPORATIONS—INCLUDING PARTNERSHIPS AND LIMITED PARTNERSHIPS, Fourth Edition, 1248 pages, 1990. Teacher's Manual available. (Casebook) 1990 Statutory Supplement.

Corporations—Cont'd

HAMILTON'S THE LAW OF CORPORATIONS IN A NUTSHELL, Third Edition, 518 pages, 1991. Softcover. (Text)

HENN'S TEACHING MATERIALS ON THE LAW OF CORPORATIONS, Second Edition, 1204 pages, 1986. Teacher's Manual available. (Casebook)

Statutory Supplement. *See Selected Corporation and Partnership*

HENN AND ALEXANDER'S HORNBOOK ON LAWS OF CORPORATIONS, Third Edition, Student Edition, 1371 pages, 1983, with 1986 pocket part. (Text)

SELECTED CORPORATION AND PARTNERSHIP STATUTES, RULES AND FORMS. Softcover. Revised 1991 Edition.

SOLOMON, SCHWARTZ AND BAUMAN'S MATERIALS AND PROBLEMS ON CORPORATIONS: LAW AND POLICY, Second Edition, 1391 pages, 1988. Teacher's Manual available. (Casebook) 1992 Supplement.

Statutory Supplement. *See Selected Corporation and Partnership*

Corrections

KRANTZ' THE LAW OF CORRECTIONS AND PRISONERS' RIGHTS IN A NUTSHELL, Third Edition, 407 pages, 1988. Softcover. (Text)

KRANTZ AND BRANHAM'S CASES AND MATERIALS ON THE LAW OF SENTENCING, CORRECTIONS AND PRISONERS' RIGHTS, Fourth Edition, 619 pages, 1991. Teacher's Manual available. (Casebook)

Creditors' Rights

BANKRUPTCY CODE, RULES AND OFFICIAL FORMS, LAW SCHOOL EDITION. Approximately 900 pages, 1992. Softcover.

EPSTEIN'S DEBTOR-CREDITOR LAW IN A NUTSHELL, Fourth Edition, 401 pages, 1991. Softcover. (Text)

EPSTEIN, LANDERS AND NICKLES' CASES AND MATERIALS ON DEBTORS AND CREDITORS, Third Edition, 1059 pages, 1987. Teacher's Manual available. (Casebook)

EPSTEIN, NICKLES AND WHITE'S HORNBOOK ON BANKRUPTCY, Approximately 1000 pages, November, 1992 Pub. (Text)

LOPUCKI'S PLAYER'S MANUAL FOR THE DEBTOR-CREDITOR GAME, 123 pages, 1985. Soft-cover. (Coursebook)

NICKLES AND EPSTEIN'S BLACK LETTER ON CREDITORS' RIGHTS AND BANKRUPTCY, 576 pages, 1989. (Review)

RIESENFELD'S CASES AND MATERIALS ON CREDITORS' REMEDIES AND DEBTORS' PROTECTION, Fourth Edition, 914 pages, 1987. (Casebook) 1990 Supplement.

WHITE AND NIMMER'S CASES AND MATERIALS ON BANKRUPTCY, Second Edition, approximately 775 pages, 1992. Teacher's Manual available. (Casebook)

Criminal Law and Criminal Procedure—see also Corrections, Juvenile Justice

ABRAMS' FEDERAL CRIMINAL LAW AND ITS ENFORCEMENT, 866 pages, 1986. (Casebook) 1988 Supplement.

AMERICAN CRIMINAL JUSTICE PROCESS: SELECTED RULES, STATUTES AND GUIDELINES. 723 pages, 1989. Softcover.

BUCY'S WHITE COLLAR CRIME, CASES AND MATERIALS, Approximately 700 pages, 1992. Teacher's Manual available. (Casebook)

DIX AND SHARLOT'S CASES AND MATERIALS ON CRIMINAL LAW, Third Edition, 846 pages, 1987. (Casebook)

GRANO'S PROBLEMS IN CRIMINAL PROCEDURE, Second Edition, 176 pages, 1981. Teacher's Manual available. Softcover. (Coursebook)

HEYMANN AND KENETY'S THE MURDER TRIAL OF WILBUR JACKSON: A HOMICIDE IN THE FAMILY, Second Edition, 347 pages, 1985. (Coursebook)

ISRAEL, KAMISAR AND LAFAVE'S CRIMINAL PROCEDURE AND THE CONSTITUTION: LEADING SUPREME COURT CASES AND INTRODUCTORY TEXT. Approximately 700 pages, 1992 Edition. Softcover. (Casebook)

ISRAEL AND LAFAVE'S CRIMINAL PROCEDURE—CONSTITUTIONAL LIMITATIONS IN A NUTSHELL, Fourth Edition, 461 pages, 1988. Softcover. (Text)

JOHNSON'S CASES, MATERIALS AND TEXT ON CRIMINAL LAW, Fourth Edition, 759 pages, 1990. Teacher's Manual available. (Casebook)

JOHNSON'S CASES AND MATERIALS ON CRIMI-

Criminal Law and Criminal Procedure—Cont'd

NAL PROCEDURE, 859 pages, 1988. (Casebook) 1992 Supplement.

KAMISAR, LaFAVE AND ISRAEL'S MODERN CRIMINAL PROCEDURE: CASES, COMMENTS AND QUESTIONS, Seventh Edition, 1593 pages, 1990. (Casebook) 1992 Supplement.

KAMISAR, LaFAVE AND ISRAEL'S BASIC CRIMINAL PROCEDURE: CASES, COMMENTS AND QUESTIONS, Seventh Edition, 792 pages, 1990. Softcover reprint from Kamisar, et al., Modern Criminal Procedure: Cases, Comments and Questions, Seventh Edition. (Casebook) 1992 Supplement.

LaFAVE'S MODERN CRIMINAL LAW: CASES, COMMENTS AND QUESTIONS, Second Edition, 903 pages, 1988. (Casebook)

LaFAVE AND ISRAEL'S HORNBOOK ON CRIMINAL PROCEDURE, Second Edition, 1309 pages, 1992. (Text)

LaFAVE AND SCOTT'S HORNBOOK ON CRIMINAL LAW, Second Edition, 918 pages, 1986. (Text)

LOEWY'S CRIMINAL LAW IN A NUTSHELL, Second Edition, 321 pages, 1987. Softcover. (Text)

LOW'S BLACK LETTER ON CRIMINAL LAW, Revised First Edition, 443 pages, 1990. Softcover. (Review)

SALTZBURG AND CAPRA'S CASES AND COMMENTARY ON AMERICAN CRIMINAL PROCEDURE, Fourth Edition, approximately 1350 pages, 1992. Teacher's Manual available. (Casebook) 1992 Supplement.

SUBIN, MIRSKY AND WEINSTEIN'S THE CRIMINAL PROCESS: PROSECUTION AND DEFENSE FUNCTIONS, Approximately 450 pages, October, 1992 Pub. Softcover. Teacher's Manual available. (Text)

VORENBERG'S CASES ON CRIMINAL LAW AND PROCEDURE, Second Edition, 1088 pages, 1981. Teacher's Manual available. (Casebook) 1990 Supplement.

Domestic Relations

CLARK'S HORNBOOK ON DOMESTIC RELATIONS, Second Edition, Student Edition, 1050 pages, 1988. (Text)

CLARK AND GLOWINSKY'S CASES AND PROBLEMS ON DOMESTIC RELATIONS, Fourth Edition. 1150 pages, 1990. Teacher's Manual available. (Casebook) 1992 Supplement.

KRAUSE'S BLACK LETTER ON FAMILY LAW, 314 pages, 1988. Softcover. (Review)

KRAUSE'S CASES, COMMENTS AND QUESTIONS ON FAMILY LAW, Third Edition, 1433 pages, 1990. (Casebook)

KRAUSE'S FAMILY LAW IN A NUTSHELL, Second Edition, 444 pages, 1986. Softcover. (Text)

KRAUSKOPF'S CASES ON PROPERTY DIVISION AT MARRIAGE DISSOLUTION, 250 pages, 1984. Softcover. (Casebook)

Economics, Law and—see also Antitrust, Regulated Industries

BARNES AND STOUT'S CASES AND MATERIALS ON LAW AND ECONOMICS, Approximately 550 pages, 1992. Teacher's Manual available. (Casebook)

GOETZ' CASES AND MATERIALS ON LAW AND ECONOMICS, 547 pages, 1984. (Casebook)

MALLOY'S LAW AND ECONOMICS: A COMPARATIVE APPROACH TO THEORY AND PRACTICE, 166 pages, 1990. Softcover. (Text)

Education Law

ALEXANDER AND ALEXANDER'S THE LAW OF SCHOOLS, STUDENTS AND TEACHERS IN A NUTSHELL, 409 pages, 1984. Softcover. (Text)

YUDOF, KIRP AND LEVIN'S EDUCATIONAL POLICY AND THE LAW, Third Edition, 860 pages, 1992. (Casebook)

Employment Discrimination—see also Gender Discrimination

ESTREICHER AND HARPER'S CASES AND MATERIALS ON THE LAW GOVERNING THE EMPLOYMENT RELATIONSHIP, Second Edition, approximately 975 pages, 1992. Teacher's Manual available. (Casebook) Statutory Supplement.

JONES, MURPHY AND BELTON'S CASES AND MATERIALS ON DISCRIMINATION IN EMPLOYMENT, (The Labor Law Group). Fifth Edition, 1116 pages, 1987. (Casebook) 1990 Supplement.

PLAYER'S FEDERAL LAW OF EMPLOYMENT DISCRIMINATION IN A NUTSHELL, Third Edition, 338 pages, 1992. Softcover. (Text)

Employment Discrimination—Cont'd

PLAYER'S HORNBOOK ON EMPLOYMENT DIS-CRIMINATION LAW, Student Edition, 708 pages, 1988. (Text)

PLAYER, SHOBEN AND LIEBERWITZ' CASES AND MATERIALS ON EMPLOYMENT DISCRIMINATION LAW, 827 pages, 1990. Teacher's Manual available. (Casebook)

Energy and Natural Resources Law—see al-so Oil and Gas

LAITOS' CASES AND MATERIALS ON NATURAL RESOURCES LAW, 938 pages, 1985. Teach-er's Manual available. (Casebook)

LAITOS AND TOMAIN'S ENERGY AND NATURAL RESOURCES LAW IN A NUTSHELL, 554 pages, 1992. Softcover. (Text)

SELECTED ENVIRONMENTAL LAW STATUTES—EDUCATIONAL EDITION. Softcover. Approx-imately 1270 pages, 1992.

Environmental Law—see also Energy and Natural Resources Law; Sea, Law of

BONINE AND MCGARITY'S THE LAW OF ENVI-RONMENTAL PROTECTION: CASES—LEGISLA-TION—POLICIES, Second Edition, 1042 pages, 1992. (Casebook)

FINDLEY AND FARBER'S CASES AND MATERI-ALS ON ENVIRONMENTAL LAW, Third Edition, 763 pages, 1991. Teacher's Manual avail-able. (Casebook)

FINDLEY AND FARBER'S ENVIRONMENTAL LAW IN A NUTSHELL, Third Edition, 355 pages, 1992. Softcover. (Text)

PLATER, ABRAMS AND GOLDFARB'S ENVIRON-MENTAL LAW AND POLICY: NATURE, LAW AND SOCIETY, 1039 pages, 1992. Teacher's Manual available. (Casebook)

RODGERS' HORNBOOK ON ENVIRONMENTAL LAW, 956 pages, 1977, with 1984 pocket part. (Text)

SELECTED ENVIRONMENTAL LAW STATUTES—EDUCATIONAL EDITION. Softcover. Ap-proximately 1270 pages, 1992.

Equity—see Remedies

Estate Planning—see also Trusts and Es-tates; Taxation—Estate and Gift

LYNN'S INTRODUCTION TO ESTATE PLANNING IN A NUTSHELL, Fourth Edition, approxi-mately 350 pages, 1992. Softcover. (Text)

Evidence

BERGMAN'S TRANSCRIPT EXERCISES FOR LEARNING EVIDENCE, 273 pages, 1992. Teacher's Manual available. (Coursebook)

BROUN AND BLAKEY'S BLACK LETTER ON EVI-DENCE, 269 pages, 1984. Softcover. (Re-view)

BROUN, MEISENHOLDER, STRONG AND MOS-TELLER'S PROBLEMS IN EVIDENCE, Third Edi-tion, 238 pages, 1988. Teacher's Manual available. Softcover. (Coursebook)

CLEARY, STRONG, BROUN AND MOSTELLER'S CASES AND MATERIALS ON EVIDENCE, Fourth Edition, 1060 pages, 1988. (Casebook)

FEDERAL RULES OF EVIDENCE FOR UNITED STATES COURTS AND MAGISTRATES. Soft-cover. Approximately 650 pages, 1992.

FRIEDMAN'S THE ELEMENTS OF EVIDENCE, 315 pages, 1991. Teacher's Manual avail-able. (Coursebook)

GRAHAM'S FEDERAL RULES OF EVIDENCE IN A NUTSHELL, Third Edition, 486 pages, 1992. Softcover. (Text)

LEMPERT AND SALTZBURG'S A MODERN AP-PROACH TO EVIDENCE: TEXT, PROBLEMS, TRANSCRIPTS AND CASES, Second Edition, 1232 pages, 1983. Teacher's Manual available. (Casebook)

LILLY'S AN INTRODUCTION TO THE LAW OF EVIDENCE, Second Edition, 585 pages, 1987. (Text)

MCCORMICK, SUTTON AND WELLBORN'S CASES AND MATERIALS ON EVIDENCE, Seventh Edi-tion, 932 pages, 1992. Teacher's Manual available. (Casebook)

MCCORMICK'S HORNBOOK ON EVIDENCE, Fourth Edition, Student Edition, approxi-mately 1200 pages, 1992. (Text)

ROTHSTEIN'S EVIDENCE IN A NUTSHELL: STATE AND FEDERAL RULES, Second Edition, 514 pages, 1981. Softcover. (Text)

Federal Jurisdiction and Procedure

CURRIE'S CASES AND MATERIALS ON FEDERAL COURTS, Fourth Edition, 783 pages, 1990. (Casebook)

CURRIE'S FEDERAL JURISDICTION IN A NUT-SHELL, Third Edition, 242 pages, 1990. Softcover. (Text)

FEDERAL RULES OF CIVIL PROCEDURE—EDU-

Federal Jurisdiction and Procedure—Cont'd

CATIONAL EDITION. Softcover. Approximately 775 pages, 1992.

REDISH'S BLACK LETTER ON FEDERAL JURISDICTION, Second Edition, 234 pages, 1991. Softcover. (Review)

REDISH'S CASES, COMMENTS AND QUESTIONS ON FEDERAL COURTS, Second Edition, 1122 pages, 1989. (Casebook) 1992 Supplement.

VETRI AND MERRILL'S FEDERAL COURTS PROBLEMS AND MATERIALS, Second Edition, 232 pages, 1984. Softcover. (Coursebook)

WRIGHT'S HORNBOOK ON FEDERAL COURTS, Fourth Edition, Student Edition, 870 pages, 1983. (Text)

First Amendment

GARVEY AND SCHAUER'S THE FIRST AMENDMENT: A READER, Approximately 530 pages, 1992. Softcover. (Reader)

SHIFFRIN AND CHOPER'S FIRST AMENDMENT, CASES—COMMENTS—QUESTIONS, 759 pages, 1991. Softcover. (Casebook) 1992 Supplement.

Foreign Relations and National Security Law

FRANCK AND GLENNON'S FOREIGN RELATIONS AND NATIONAL SECURITY LAW, 941 pages, 1987. (Casebook)

Future Interests—see Trusts and Estates

Gender Discrimination—see also Employment Discrimination

KAY'S TEXT, CASES AND MATERIALS ON SEX-BASED DISCRIMINATION, Third Edition, 1001 pages, 1988. (Casebook) 1992 Supplement.

THOMAS' SEX DISCRIMINATION IN A NUTSHELL, Second Edition, 395 pages, 1991. Softcover. (Text)

Health Law—see Medicine, Law and

Human Rights—see International Law

Immigration Law

ALEINIKOFF AND MARTIN'S IMMIGRATION: PROCESS AND POLICY, Second Edition, 1056 pages, 1991. (Casebook)

Statutory Supplement. *See Immigration and Nationality Laws*

IMMIGRATION AND NATIONALITY LAWS OF THE

UNITED STATES: SELECTED STATUTES, REGULATIONS AND FORMS. Softcover. Approximately 525 pages, 1992.

WEISSBRODT'S IMMIGRATION LAW AND PROCEDURE IN A NUTSHELL, Third Edition, approximately 350 pages, 1992. Softcover. (Text)

Indian Law—see American Indian Law

Insurance Law

DEVINE AND TERRY'S PROBLEMS IN INSURANCE LAW, 240 pages, 1989. Softcover. Teacher's Manual available. (Coursebook)

DOBBYN'S INSURANCE LAW IN A NUTSHELL, Second Edition, 316 pages, 1989. Softcover. (Text)

KEETON'S COMPUTER-AIDED AND WORKBOOK EXERCISES ON INSURANCE LAW, 255 pages, 1990. Softcover. (Coursebook)

KEETON AND WIDISS' INSURANCE LAW, Student Edition, 1359 pages, 1988. (Text)

WIDISS AND KEETON'S COURSE SUPPLEMENT TO KEETON AND WIDISS' INSURANCE LAW, 502 pages, 1988. Softcover. Teacher's Manual available. (Casebook)

WIDISS' INSURANCE: MATERIALS ON FUNDAMENTAL PRINCIPLES, LEGAL DOCTRINES AND REGULATORY ACTS, 1186 pages, 1989. Teacher's Manual available. (Casebook)

YORK AND WHELAN'S CASES, MATERIALS AND PROBLEMS ON GENERAL PRACTICE INSURANCE LAW, Second Edition, 787 pages, 1988. Teacher's Manual available. (Casebook)

International Law—see also Sea, Law of

BUERGENTHAL'S INTERNATIONAL HUMAN RIGHTS IN A NUTSHELL, 283 pages, 1988. Softcover. (Text)

BUERGENTHAL AND MAIER'S PUBLIC INTERNATIONAL LAW IN A NUTSHELL, Second Edition, 275 pages, 1990. Softcover. (Text)

FOLSOM'S EUROPEAN COMMUNITY LAW IN A NUTSHELL, 423 pages, 1992. Softcover. (Text)

FOLSOM, GORDON AND SPANOGLE'S INTERNATIONAL BUSINESS TRANSACTIONS—A PROBLEM-ORIENTED COURSEBOOK, Second Edition, 1237 pages, 1991. Teacher's Manual available. (Casebook) 1991 Documents Supplement.

International Law—Cont'd

FOLSOM, GORDON AND SPANOGLE'S INTERNATIONAL BUSINESS TRANSACTIONS IN A NUTSHELL, Fourth Edition, approximately 540 pages, 1992. Softcover. (Text)

HENKIN, PUGH, SCHACHTER AND SMIT'S CASES AND MATERIALS ON INTERNATIONAL LAW, Second Edition, 1517 pages, 1987. (Casebook) Documents Supplement.

JACKSON AND DAVEY'S CASES, MATERIALS AND TEXT ON LEGAL PROBLEMS OF INTERNATIONAL ECONOMIC RELATIONS, Second Edition, 1269 pages, 1986. (Casebook) 1989 Documents Supplement.

KIRGIS' INTERNATIONAL ORGANIZATIONS IN THEIR LEGAL SETTING, 1016 pages, 1977. Teacher's Manual available. (Casebook) 1981 Supplement.

WESTON, FALK AND D'AMATO'S INTERNATIONAL LAW AND WORLD ORDER—A PROBLEM-ORIENTED COURSEBOOK, Second Edition, 1335 pages, 1990. Teacher's Manual available. (Casebook) Documents Supplement.

Interviewing and Counseling

BINDER AND PRICE'S LEGAL INTERVIEWING AND COUNSELING, 232 pages, 1977. Softcover. Teacher's Manual available. (Coursebook)

BINDER, BERGMAN AND PRICE'S LAWYERS AS COUNSELORS: A CLIENT–CENTERED APPROACH, 427 pages, 1991. Softcover. (Coursebook)

SHAFFER AND ELKINS' LEGAL INTERVIEWING AND COUNSELING IN A NUTSHELL, Second Edition, 487 pages, 1987. Softcover. (Text)

Introduction to Law—see Legal Method and Legal System

Introduction to Law Study

HEGLAND'S INTRODUCTION TO THE STUDY AND PRACTICE OF LAW IN A NUTSHELL, 418 pages, 1983. Softcover. (Text)

KINYON'S INTRODUCTION TO LAW STUDY AND LAW EXAMINATIONS IN A NUTSHELL, 389 pages, 1971. Softcover. (Text)

Judicial Process—see Legal Method and Legal System

Jurisprudence

CHRISTIE'S JURISPRUDENCE—TEXT AND READINGS ON THE PHILOSOPHY OF LAW, 1056 pages, 1973. (Casebook)

Juvenile Justice

FOX'S JUVENILE COURTS IN A NUTSHELL, Third Edition, 291 pages, 1984. Softcover. (Text)

Labor and Employment Law—see also Employment Discrimination, Workers' Compensation

FINKIN, GOLDMAN AND SUMMERS' LEGAL PROTECTION OF INDIVIDUAL EMPLOYEES, (The Labor Law Group). 1164 pages, 1989. (Casebook)

GORMAN'S BASIC TEXT ON LABOR LAW—UNIONIZATION AND COLLECTIVE BARGAINING, 914 pages, 1976. (Text)

LESLIE'S LABOR LAW IN A NUTSHELL, Third Edition, 388 pages, 1992. Softcover. (Text)

NOLAN'S LABOR ARBITRATION LAW AND PRACTICE IN A NUTSHELL, 358 pages, 1979. Softcover. (Text)

OBERER, HANSLOWE, ANDERSEN AND HEINSZ' CASES AND MATERIALS ON LABOR LAW—COLLECTIVE BARGAINING IN A FREE SOCIETY, Third Edition, 1163 pages, 1986. Teacher's Manual available. (Casebook) Statutory Supplement. 1991 Case Supplement.

RABIN, SILVERSTEIN AND SCHATZKI'S LABOR AND EMPLOYMENT LAW: PROBLEMS, CASES AND MATERIALS IN THE LAW OF WORK, (The Labor Law Group). 1014 pages, 1988. Teacher's Manual available. (Casebook) 1988 Statutory Supplement.

Land Finance—Property Security—see Real Estate Transactions

Land Use

CALLIES AND FREILICH'S CASES AND MATERIALS ON LAND USE, 1233 pages, 1986. (Casebook) 1991 Supplement.

HAGMAN AND JUERGENSMEYER'S HORNBOOK ON URBAN PLANNING AND LAND DEVELOPMENT CONTROL LAW, Second Edition, Student Edition, 680 pages, 1986. (Text)

WRIGHT AND GITELMAN'S CASES AND MATERIALS ON LAND USE, Fourth Edition, 1255 pages, 1991. Teacher's Manual available.

Land Use—Cont'd

(Casebook)

WRIGHT AND WRIGHT'S LAND USE IN A NUT-SHELL, Second Edition, 356 pages, 1985. Softcover. (Text)

Legal History—see also Legal Method and Legal System

PRESSER AND ZAINALDIN'S CASES AND MATER-IALS ON LAW AND JURISPRUDENCE IN AMERI-CAN HISTORY, Second Edition, 1092 pages, 1989. Teacher's Manual available. (Case-book)

Legal Method and Legal System—see also Legal Research, Legal Writing

ALDISERT'S READINGS, MATERIALS AND CASES IN THE JUDICIAL PROCESS, 948 pages, 1976. (Casebook)

BERCH, BERCH AND SPRITZER'S INTRODUCTION TO LEGAL METHOD AND PROCESS, Second Edition, approximately 600 pages, 1992. Teacher's Manual available. (Casebook)

BODENHEIMER, OAKLEY AND LOVE'S READ-INGS AND CASES ON AN INTRODUCTION TO THE ANGLO-AMERICAN LEGAL SYSTEM, Second Edition, 166 pages, 1988. Softcover. (Casebook)

DAVIES AND LAWRY'S INSTITUTIONS AND METHODS OF THE LAW—INTRODUCTORY TEACHING MATERIALS, 547 pages, 1982. Teacher's Manual available. (Casebook)

DVORKIN, HIMMELSTEIN AND LESNICK'S BE-COMING A LAWYER: A HUMANISTIC PERSPEC-TIVE ON LEGAL EDUCATION AND PROFESSION-ALISM, 211 pages, 1981. Softcover. (Text)

KEETON'S JUDGING, 842 pages, 1990. Soft-cover. (Coursebook)

KELSO AND KELSO'S STUDYING LAW: AN IN-TRODUCTION, 587 pages, 1984. (Coursebook)

KEMPIN'S HISTORICAL INTRODUCTION TO AN-GLO-AMERICAN LAW IN A NUTSHELL, Third Edition, 323 pages, 1990. Softcover. (Text)

MEADOR'S AMERICAN COURTS, 113 pages, 1991. Softcover. (Text)

REYNOLDS' JUDICIAL PROCESS IN A NUTSHELL, Second Edition, 308 pages, 1991. Soft-cover. (Text)

Legal Research

COHEN AND OLSON'S LEGAL RESEARCH IN A NUTSHELL, Fifth Edition, approximately 500 pages, 1992. Softcover. (Text)

COHEN, BERRING AND OLSON'S HOW TO FIND THE LAW, Ninth Edition, 716 pages, 1989. (Text)

COHEN, BERRING AND OLSON'S FINDING THE LAW, 570 pages, 1989. Softcover reprint from Cohen, Berring and Olson's How to Find the Law, Ninth Edition. (Course-book)

Legal Research Exercises, 4th Ed., for use with Cohen, Berring and Olson, 253 pages, 1992. Teacher's Manual availa-ble.

ROMBAUER'S LEGAL PROBLEM SOLVING—ANALYSIS, RESEARCH AND WRITING, Fifth Edition, 524 pages, 1991. Softcover. Teacher's Manual with problems availa-ble. (Coursebook)

STATSKY'S LEGAL RESEARCH AND WRITING, Third Edition, 257 pages, 1986. Softcover. (Coursebook)

TEPLY'S LEGAL RESEARCH AND CITATION, Fourth Edition, approximately 465 pages, 1992. Softcover. (Coursebook)

Student Library Exercises, Fourth Edi-tion, approximately 290 pages, 1992. Answer Key available.

Legal Writing and Drafting

CHILD'S DRAFTING LEGAL DOCUMENTS: PRIN-CIPLES AND PRACTICES, Second Edition, ap-proximately 425 pages, 1992. Softcover. Teacher's Manual available. (Coursebook)

DICKERSON'S MATERIALS ON LEGAL DRAFT-ING, 425 pages, 1981. Teacher's Manual available. (Coursebook)

FELSENFELD AND SIEGEL'S WRITING CON-TRACTS IN PLAIN ENGLISH, 290 pages, 1981. Softcover. (Text)

GOPEN'S WRITING FROM A LEGAL PERSPEC-TIVE, 225 pages, 1981. (Text)

MARTINEAU'S DRAFTING LEGISLATION AND RULES IN PLAIN ENGLISH, 155 pages, 1991. Softcover. Teacher's Manual available. (Text)

MELLINKOFF'S DICTIONARY OF AMERICAN LE-GAL USAGE, Approximately 700 pages, 1992. Softcover. (Text)

Legal Writing and Drafting—Cont'd

MELLINKOFF'S LEGAL WRITING—SENSE AND NONSENSE, 242 pages, 1982. Softcover. Teacher's Manual available. (Text)

PRATT'S LEGAL WRITING: A SYSTEMATIC APPROACH, 468 pages, 1990. Teacher's Manual available. (Coursebook)

RAY AND COX'S BEYOND THE BASICS: A TEXT FOR ADVANCED LEGAL WRITING, 427 pages, 1991. Softcover. Teacher's Manual available. (Text)

RAY AND RAMSFIELD'S LEGAL WRITING: GETTING IT RIGHT AND GETTING IT WRITTEN, 250 pages, 1987. Softcover. (Text)

SQUIRES AND ROMBAUER'S LEGAL WRITING IN A NUTSHELL, 294 pages, 1982. Softcover. (Text)

STATSKY AND WERNET'S CASE ANALYSIS AND FUNDAMENTALS OF LEGAL WRITING, Third Edition, 424 pages, 1989. Teacher's Manual available. (Text)

TEPLY'S LEGAL WRITING, ANALYSIS AND ORAL ARGUMENT, 576 pages, 1990. Softcover. Teacher's Manual available. (Coursebook)

WEIHOFEN'S LEGAL WRITING STYLE, Second Edition, 332 pages, 1980. (Text)

Legislation—see also Legal Writing and Drafting

DAVIES' LEGISLATIVE LAW AND PROCESS IN A NUTSHELL, Second Edition, 346 pages, 1986. Softcover. (Text)

ESKRIDGE AND FRICKEY'S CASES AND MATERIALS ON LEGISLATION: STATUTES AND THE CREATION OF PUBLIC POLICY, 937 pages, 1988. Teacher's Manual available. (Casebook) 1992 Supplement.

NUTTING AND DICKERSON'S CASES AND MATERIALS ON LEGISLATION, Fifth Edition, 744 pages, 1978. (Casebook)

STATSKY'S LEGISLATIVE ANALYSIS AND DRAFTING, Second Edition, 217 pages, 1984. Teacher's Manual available. (Text)

Local Government

FRUG'S CASES AND MATERIALS ON LOCAL GOVERNMENT LAW, 1005 pages, 1988. (Casebook) 1991 Supplement.

MCCARTHY'S LOCAL GOVERNMENT LAW IN A NUTSHELL, Third Edition, 435 pages, 1990. Softcover. (Text)

REYNOLDS' HORNBOOK ON LOCAL GOVERNMENT LAW, 860 pages, 1982, with 1990 pocket part. (Text)

VALENTE AND MCCARTHY'S CASES AND MATERIALS ON LOCAL GOVERNMENT LAW, Fourth Edition, 1158 pages, 1992. Teacher's Manual available. (Casebook)

Mass Communication Law

GILLMOR, BARRON, SIMON AND TERRY'S CASES AND COMMENT ON MASS COMMUNICATION LAW, Fifth Edition, 947 pages, 1990. (Casebook)

GINSBURG, BOTEIN AND DIRECTOR'S REGULATION OF THE ELECTRONIC MASS MEDIA: LAW AND POLICY FOR RADIO, TELEVISION, CABLE AND THE NEW VIDEO TECHNOLOGIES, Second Edition, 657 pages, 1991. (Casebook) Statutory Supplement.

ZUCKMAN, GAYNES, CARTER AND DEE'S MASS COMMUNICATIONS LAW IN A NUTSHELL, Third Edition, 538 pages, 1988. Softcover. (Text)

Medicine, Law and

FISCINA, BOUMIL, SHARPE AND HEAD'S MEDICAL LIABILITY, 487 pages, 1991. Teacher's Manual available. (Casebook)

FURROW, JOHNSON, JOST AND SCHWARTZ' HEALTH LAW: CASES, MATERIALS AND PROBLEMS, Second Edition, 1236 pages, 1991. Teacher's Manual available. (Casebook)

FURROW, JOHNSON, JOST AND SCHWARTZ' BIOETHICS: HEALTH CARE LAW AND ETHICS, Reprint from Furrow et al., Health Law, Second Edition. Softcover. Teacher's Manual available. (Casebook)

FURROW, JOHNSON, JOST AND SCHWARTZ' THE LAW OF HEALTH CARE ORGANIZATION AND FINANCE,Reprint from Furrow et al., Health Law, Second Edition. Softcover. Teacher's Manual available.

FURROW, JOHNSON, JOST AND SCHWARTZ' LIABILITY AND QUALITY ISSUES IN HEALTH CARE, Reprint from Furrow et al., Health Law, Second Edition. Softcover. Teacher's Manual available. (Casebook)

HALL AND ELLMAN'S HEALTH CARE LAW AND ETHICS IN A NUTSHELL, 401 pages, 1990. Softcover (Text)

Medicine, Law and—Cont'd

JARVIS, CLOSEN, HERMANN AND LEONARD'S AIDS LAW IN A NUTSHELL, 349 pages, 1991. Softcover. (Text)

KING'S THE LAW OF MEDICAL MALPRACTICE IN A NUTSHELL, Second Edition, 342 pages, 1986. Softcover. (Text)

SHAPIRO AND SPECE'S CASES, MATERIALS AND PROBLEMS ON BIOETHICS AND LAW, 892 pages, 1981. (Casebook) 1991 Supplement.

Military Law

SHANOR AND TERRELL'S MILITARY LAW IN A NUTSHELL, 378 pages, 1980. Softcover. (Text)

Mining Law—see Energy and Natural Resources Law

Mortgages—see Real Estate Transactions

Natural Resources Law—see Energy and Natural Resources Law, Environmental Law

Negotiation

GIFFORD'S LEGAL NEGOTIATION: THEORY AND APPLICATIONS, 225 pages, 1989. Softcover. (Text)

TEPLY'S LEGAL NEGOTIATION IN A NUTSHELL, 282 pages, 1992. Softcover. (Text)

WILLIAMS' LEGAL NEGOTIATION AND SETTLEMENT, 207 pages, 1983. Softcover. Teacher's Manual available. (Coursebook)

Office Practice—see also Computers and Law, Interviewing and Counseling, Negotiation

HEGLAND'S TRIAL AND PRACTICE SKILLS IN A NUTSHELL, 346 pages, 1978. Softcover (Text)

MUNNEKE'S LAW PRACTICE MANAGEMENT: MATERIALS AND CASES, 634 pages, 1991. Teacher's Manual available. (Casebook)

Oil and Gas—see also Energy and Natural Resources Law

HEMINGWAY'S HORNBOOK ON THE LAW OF OIL AND GAS, Third Edition, Student Edition, 711 pages, 1992. (Text)

KUNTZ, LOWE, ANDERSON AND SMITH'S CASES AND MATERIALS ON OIL AND GAS LAW, 857 pages, 1986. Teacher's Manual available. (Casebook) Forms Manual. Revised.

LOWE'S OIL AND GAS LAW IN A NUTSHELL, Second Edition, 465 pages, 1988. Softcover. (Text)

Partnership—see Agency—Partnership

Patent and Copyright Law

CHOATE, FRANCIS AND COLLINS' CASES AND MATERIALS ON PATENT LAW, INCLUDING TRADE SECRETS, COPYRIGHTS, TRADEMARKS, Third Edition, 1009 pages, 1987. (Casebook)

HALPERN, SHIPLEY AND ABRAMS' CASES AND MATERIALS ON COPYRIGHT, Approximately 675 pages, 1992. (Casebook)

MILLER AND DAVIS' INTELLECTUAL PROPERTY—PATENTS, TRADEMARKS AND COPYRIGHT IN A NUTSHELL, Second Edition, 437 pages, 1990. Softcover. (Text)

NIMMER, MARCUS, MYERS AND NIMMER'S CASES AND MATERIALS ON COPYRIGHT AND OTHER ASPECTS OF ENTERTAINMENT LITIGATION—INCLUDING UNFAIR COMPETITION, DEFAMATION, PRIVACY, ILLUSTRATED, Fourth Edition, 1177 pages, 1991. (Casebook) Statutory Supplement. See *Selected Intellectual Property Statutes*

SELECTED INTELLECTUAL PROPERTY AND UNFAIR COMPETITION STATUTES, REGULATIONS AND TREATIES. Softcover.

Products Liability

FISCHER AND POWERS' CASES AND MATERIALS ON PRODUCTS LIABILITY, 685 pages, 1988. Teacher's Manual available. (Casebook)

PHILLIPS' PRODUCTS LIABILITY IN A NUTSHELL, Third Edition, 307 pages, 1988. Softcover. (Text)

Professional Responsibility

ARONSON, DEVINE AND FISCH'S PROBLEMS, CASES AND MATERIALS IN PROFESSIONAL RESPONSIBILITY, 745 pages, 1985. Teacher's Manual available. (Casebook)

ARONSON AND WECKSTEIN'S PROFESSIONAL RESPONSIBILITY IN A NUTSHELL, Second Edition, 514 pages, 1991. Softcover. (Text)

LESNICK'S BEING A LAWYER: INDIVIDUAL CHOICE AND RESPONSIBILITY IN THE PRACTICE OF LAW, Approximately 400 pages, 1992. Softcover. (Coursebook)

MELLINKOFF'S THE CONSCIENCE OF A LAW-

Professional Responsibility—Cont'd

YER, 304 pages, 1973. (Text)

PIRSIG AND KIRWIN'S CASES AND MATERIALS ON PROFESSIONAL RESPONSIBILITY, Fourth Edition, 603 pages, 1984. Teacher's Manual available. (Casebook)

ROTUNDA'S BLACK LETTER ON PROFESSIONAL RESPONSIBILITY, Third Edition, 492 pages, 1992. Softcover. (Review)

SCHWARTZ, WYDICK AND PERSCHBACHER'S PROBLEMS IN LEGAL ETHICS, Third Edition, approximately 350 pages, September, 1992 Pub. (Coursebook)

SELECTED STATUTES, RULES AND STANDARDS ON THE LEGAL PROFESSION. Softcover. Approximately 925 pages, 1992.

SMITH AND MALLEN'S PREVENTING LEGAL MALPRACTICE, 264 pages, 1989. Reprint from Mallen and Smith's Legal Malpractice, Third Edition. (Text)

SUTTON AND DZIENKOWSKI'S CASES AND MATERIALS ON PROFESSIONAL RESPONSIBILITY FOR LAWYERS, 839 pages, 1989. Teacher's Manual available. (Casebook)

WOLFRAM'S HORNBOOK ON MODERN LEGAL ETHICS, Student Edition, 1120 pages, 1986. (Text)

WYDICK AND PERSCHBACHER'S CALIFORNIA LEGAL ETHICS, Approximately 430 pages, 1992. Softcover. (Coursebook)

Property—see also Real Estate Transactions, Land Use, Trusts and Estates

BARNES AND STOUT'S THE ECONOMICS OF PROPERTY RIGHTS AND NUISANCE LAW, Approximately 75 pages, 1992. Softcover. Teacher's Manual available. (Casebook)

BERNHARDT'S BLACK LETTER ON PROPERTY, Second Edition, 388 pages, 1991. Softcover. (Review)

BERNHARDT'S REAL PROPERTY IN A NUTSHELL, Second Edition, 448 pages, 1981. Softcover. (Text)

BOYER, HOVENKAMP AND KURTZ' THE LAW OF PROPERTY, AN INTRODUCTORY SURVEY, Fourth Edition, 696 pages, 1991. (Text)

BROWDER, CUNNINGHAM, NELSON, STOEBUCK AND WHITMAN'S CASES ON BASIC PROPERTY LAW, Fifth Edition, 1386 pages, 1989. Teacher's Manual available. (Casebook)

BRUCE, ELY AND BOSTICK'S CASES AND MATERIALS ON MODERN PROPERTY LAW, Second Edition, 953 pages, 1989. Teacher's Manual available. (Casebook)

BURKE'S PERSONAL PROPERTY IN A NUTSHELL, 322 pages, 1983. Softcover. (Text)

CUNNINGHAM, STOEBUCK AND WHITMAN'S HORNBOOK ON THE LAW OF PROPERTY, Student Edition, 916 pages, 1984, with 1987 pocket part. (Text)

DONAHUE, KAUPER AND MARTIN'S CASES AND MATERIALS ON PROPERTY, AN INTRODUCTION TO THE CONCEPT AND THE INSTITUTION, Third Edition, approximately 1500 pages, October, 1992 Pub. Teacher's Manual available. (Casebook)

HILL'S LANDLORD AND TENANT LAW IN A NUTSHELL, Second Edition, 311 pages, 1986. Softcover. (Text)

JOHNSON, JOST, SALSICH AND SHAFFER'S PROPERTY LAW, CASES, MATERIALS AND PROBLEMS, 908 pages, 1992. Teacher's Manual available. (Casebook)

KURTZ AND HOVENKAMP'S CASES AND MATERIALS ON AMERICAN PROPERTY LAW, 1296 pages, 1987. Teacher's Manual available. (Casebook) 1991 Supplement.

MOYNIHAN'S INTRODUCTION TO REAL PROPERTY, Second Edition, 239 pages, 1988. (Text)

Psychiatry, Law and

REISNER AND SLOBOGIN'S LAW AND THE MENTAL HEALTH SYSTEM, CIVIL AND CRIMINAL ASPECTS, Second Edition, 1117 pages, 1990. (Casebook)

Real Estate Transactions

BRUCE'S REAL ESTATE FINANCE IN A NUTSHELL, Third Edition, 287 pages, 1991. Softcover. (Text)

MAXWELL, RIESENFELD, HETLAND AND WARREN'S CASES ON CALIFORNIA SECURITY TRANSACTIONS IN LAND, Fourth Edition, 778 pages, 1992. (Casebook)

NELSON AND WHITMAN'S BLACK LETTER ON LAND TRANSACTIONS AND FINANCE, Second Edition, 466 pages, 1988. Softcover. (Review)

NELSON AND WHITMAN'S CASES AND MATERIALS ON REAL ESTATE TRANSFER, FINANCE

Real Estate Transactions—Cont'd

AND DEVELOPMENT, Fourth Edition, approximately 1350 pages, 1992. (Casebook)

NELSON AND WHITMAN'S HORNBOOK ON REAL ESTATE FINANCE LAW, Second Edition, 941 pages, 1985 with 1989 pocket part. (Text)

Regulated Industries—see also Mass Communication Law, Banking Law

GELLHORN AND PIERCE'S REGULATED INDUSTRIES IN A NUTSHELL, Second Edition, 389 pages, 1987. Softcover. (Text)

MORGAN, HARRISON AND VERKUIL'S CASES AND MATERIALS ON ECONOMIC REGULATION OF BUSINESS, Second Edition, 666 pages, 1985. (Casebook)

Remedies

DOBBS' HORNBOOK ON REMEDIES, Second Edition, December, 1992 Pub. (Text)

DOBBS' PROBLEMS IN REMEDIES. 137 pages, 1974. Teacher's Manual available. Softcover. (Coursebook)

DOBBYN'S INJUNCTIONS IN A NUTSHELL, 264 pages, 1974. Softcover. (Text)

FRIEDMAN'S CONTRACT REMEDIES IN A NUTSHELL, 323 pages, 1981. Softcover. (Text)

LEAVELL, LOVE AND NELSON'S CASES AND MATERIALS ON EQUITABLE REMEDIES, RESTITUTION AND DAMAGES, Fourth Edition, 1111 pages, 1986. Teacher's Manual available. (Casebook)

O'CONNELL'S REMEDIES IN A NUTSHELL, Second Edition, 320 pages, 1985. Softcover. (Text)

SCHOENBROD, MACBETH, LEVINE AND JUNG'S CASES AND MATERIALS ON REMEDIES: PUBLIC AND PRIVATE, 848 pages, 1990. Teacher's Manual available. (Casebook) 1992 Supplement.

YORK, BAUMAN AND RENDLEMAN'S CASES AND MATERIALS ON REMEDIES, Fifth Edition, 1270 pages, 1992. Teacher's Manual available. (Casebook)

Sea, Law of

SOHN AND GUSTAFSON'S THE LAW OF THE SEA IN A NUTSHELL, 264 pages, 1984. Softcover. (Text)

Securities Regulation

HAZEN'S HORNBOOK ON THE LAW OF SECURITIES REGULATION, Second Edition, Student Edition, 1082 pages, 1990. (Text)

RATNER'S SECURITIES REGULATION IN A NUTSHELL, Fourth Edition, approximately 320 pages, 1992. Softcover. (Text)

RATNER AND HAZEN'S SECURITIES REGULATION: CASES AND MATERIALS, Fourth Edition, 1062 pages, 1991. Teacher's Manual available. (Casebook) Problems and Sample Documents Supplement.

Statutory Supplement. *See Securities Regulation, Selected Statutes*

SECURITIES REGULATION, SELECTED STATUTES, RULES, AND FORMS. Softcover. 1361 pages, 1992.

Sports Law

SCHUBERT, SMITH AND TRENTADUE'S SPORTS LAW, 395 pages, 1986. (Text)

Tax Practice and Procedure

GARBIS, RUBIN AND MORGAN'S CASES AND MATERIALS ON TAX PROCEDURE AND TAX FRAUD, Third Edition, 921 pages, 1992. Teacher's Manual available. (Casebook)

MORGAN'S TAX PROCEDURE AND TAX FRAUD IN A NUTSHELL, 400 pages, 1990. Softcover. (Text)

Taxation—Corporate

KAHN AND GANN'S CORPORATE TAXATION, Third Edition, 980 pages, 1989. Teacher's Manual available. (Casebook) 1991 Supplement.

SCHWARZ AND LATHROPE'S BLACK LETTER ON CORPORATE AND PARTNERSHIP TAXATION, 537 pages, 1991. Softcover. (Review)

WEIDENBRUCH AND BURKE'S FEDERAL INCOME TAXATION OF CORPORATIONS AND STOCKHOLDERS IN A NUTSHELL, Third Edition, 309 pages, 1989. Softcover. (Text)

Taxation—Estate & Gift—see also Estate Planning, Trusts and Estates

MCNULTY'S FEDERAL ESTATE AND GIFT TAXATION IN A NUTSHELL, Fourth Edition, 496 pages, 1989. Softcover. (Text)

PEAT AND WILLBANKS' FEDERAL ESTATE AND GIFT TAXATION: AN ANALYSIS AND CRITIQUE, 265 pages, 1991. Softcover. (Text)

PENNELL'S CASES AND MATERIALS ON INCOME TAXATION OF TRUSTS, ESTATES, GRANTORS

Taxation—Estate & Gift—Cont'd

AND BENEFICIARIES, 460 pages, 1987. Teacher's Manual available. (Casebook)

Taxation—Individual

DODGE'S THE LOGIC OF TAX, 343 pages, 1989. Softcover. (Text)

GUNN AND WARD'S CASES, TEXT AND PROBLEMS ON FEDERAL INCOME TAXATION, Third Edition, approximately 800 pages, 1992. Teacher's Manual available. (Casebook)

HUDSON AND LIND'S BLACK LETTER ON FEDERAL INCOME TAXATION, Fourth Edition, approximately 400 pages, 1992. Softcover. (Review)

MCNULTY'S FEDERAL INCOME TAXATION OF INDIVIDUALS IN A NUTSHELL, Fourth Edition, 503 pages, 1988. Softcover. (Text)

POSIN'S HORNBOOK ON FEDERAL INCOME TAXATION, Student Edition, 491 pages, 1983, with 1989 pocket part. (Text)

ROSE AND CHOMMIE'S HORNBOOK ON FEDERAL INCOME TAXATION, Third Edition, 923 pages, 1988, with 1991 pocket part. (Text)

SELECTED FEDERAL TAXATION STATUTES AND REGULATIONS. Softcover. Approximately 1700 pages, 1993.

Taxation—International

DOERNBERG'S INTERNATIONAL TAXATION IN A NUTSHELL, 325 pages, 1989. Softcover. (Text)

KAPLAN'S FEDERAL TAXATION OF INTERNATIONAL TRANSACTIONS: PRINCIPLES, PLANNING AND POLICY, 635 pages, 1988. (Casebook)

Taxation—Partnership

BERGER AND WIEDENBECK'S CASES AND MATERIALS ON PARTNERSHIP TAXATION, 788 pages, 1989. Teacher's Manual available. (Casebook) 1991 Supplement.

BISHOP AND BROOKS' FEDERAL PARTNERSHIP TAXATION: A GUIDE TO THE LEADING CASES, STATUTES, AND REGULATIONS, 545 pages, 1990. Softcover. (Text)

BURKE'S FEDERAL INCOME TAXATION OF PARTNERSHIPS IN A NUTSHELL, 356 pages, 1992. Softcover. (Text)

SCHWARZ AND LATHROPE'S BLACK LETTER ON CORPORATE AND PARTNERSHIP TAXATION, 537

pages, 1991. Softcover. (Review)

Taxation—State & Local

GELFAND AND SALSICH'S STATE AND LOCAL TAXATION AND FINANCE IN A NUTSHELL, 309 pages, 1986. Softcover. (Text)

HELLERSTEIN AND HELLERSTEIN'S CASES AND MATERIALS ON STATE AND LOCAL TAXATION, Fifth Edition, 1071 pages, 1988. (Casebook)

Torts—see also Products Liability

BARNES AND STOUT'S THE ECONOMIC ANALYSIS OF TORT LAW, Approximately 150 pages, 1992. Softcover. Teacher's Manual available. (Casebook)

CHRISTIE AND MEEKS' CASES AND MATERIALS ON THE LAW OF TORTS, Second Edition, 1264 pages, 1990. (Casebook)

DOBBS' TORTS AND COMPENSATION—PERSONAL ACCOUNTABILITY AND SOCIAL RESPONSIBILITY FOR INJURY, 955 pages, 1985. Teacher's Manual available. (Casebook) 1990 Supplement.

KEETON, KEETON, SARGENTICH AND STEINER'S CASES AND MATERIALS ON TORT AND ACCIDENT LAW, Second Edition, 1318 pages, 1989. (Casebook)

KIONKA'S BLACK LETTER ON TORTS, 339 pages, 1988. Softcover. (Review)

KIONKA'S TORTS IN A NUTSHELL, Second Edition, 449 pages, 1992. Softcover. (Text)

PROSSER AND KEETON'S HORNBOOK ON TORTS, Fifth Edition, Student Edition, 1286 pages, 1984 with 1988 pocket part. (Text)

ROBERTSON, POWERS AND ANDERSON'S CASES AND MATERIALS ON TORTS, 932 pages, 1989. Teacher's Manual available. (Casebook)

Trade Regulation—see also Antitrust, Regulated Industries

MCMANIS' UNFAIR TRADE PRACTICES IN A NUTSHELL, Third Edition, approximately 475 pages, December, 1992 Pub. Softcover. (Text)

SCHECHTER'S BLACK LETTER ON UNFAIR TRADE PRACTICES, 272 pages, 1986. Softcover. (Review)

WESTON, MAGGS AND SCHECHTER'S UNFAIR TRADE PRACTICES AND CONSUMER PROTECTION, CASES AND COMMENTS, Fifth Edition,

Trade Regulation—Cont'd

957 pages, 1992. Teacher's Manual available. (Casebook)

Trial and Appellate Advocacy—see also Civil Procedure

APPELLATE ADVOCACY, HANDBOOK OF, Second Edition, 182 pages, 1986. Softcover. (Text)

BERGMAN'S TRIAL ADVOCACY IN A NUTSHELL, Second Edition, 354 pages, 1989. Softcover. (Text)

BINDER AND BERGMAN'S FACT INVESTIGATION: FROM HYPOTHESIS TO PROOF, 354 pages, 1984. Teacher's Manual available. (Coursebook)

CARLSON'S ADJUDICATION OF CRIMINAL JUSTICE: PROBLEMS AND REFERENCES, 130 pages, 1986. Softcover. (Casebook)

CARLSON AND IMWINKELRIED'S DYNAMICS OF TRIAL PRACTICE: PROBLEMS AND MATERIALS, 414 pages, 1989. Teacher's Manual available. (Coursebook) 1990 Supplement.

CLARY'S PRIMER ON THE ANALYSIS AND PRESENTATION OF LEGAL ARGUMENT, 106 pages, 1992. Softcover. (Text)

DESSEM'S PRETRIAL LITIGATION IN A NUTSHELL, Approximately 375 pages, 1992. Softcover. (Text)

DESSEM'S PRETRIAL LITIGATION: LAW, POLICY AND PRACTICE, 608 pages, 1991. Softcover. Teacher's Manual available. (Coursebook)

DEVINE'S NON-JURY CASE FILES FOR TRIAL ADVOCACY, 258 pages, 1991. (Coursebook)

GOLDBERG'S THE FIRST TRIAL (WHERE DO I SIT? WHAT DO I SAY?) IN A NUTSHELL, 396 pages, 1982. Softcover. (Text)

HAYDOCK, HERR, AND STEMPEL'S FUNDAMENTALS OF PRE-TRIAL LITIGATION, Second Edition, 786 pages, 1992. Softcover. Teacher's Manual available. (Coursebook)

HAYDOCK AND SONSTENG'S TRIAL: THEORIES, TACTICS, TECHNIQUES, 711 pages, 1991. Softcover. (Text)

HEGLAND'S TRIAL AND PRACTICE SKILLS IN A NUTSHELL, 346 pages, 1978. Softcover. (Text)

HORNSTEIN'S APPELLATE ADVOCACY IN A NUTSHELL, 325 pages, 1984. Softcover. (Text)

JEANS' HANDBOOK ON TRIAL ADVOCACY, Student Edition, 473 pages, 1975. Softcover. (Text)

LISNEK AND KAUFMAN'S DEPOSITIONS: PROCEDURE, STRATEGY AND TECHNIQUE, Law School and CLE Edition. 250 pages, 1990. Softcover. (Text)

MARTINEAU'S CASES AND MATERIALS ON APPELLATE PRACTICE AND PROCEDURE, 565 pages, 1987. (Casebook)

NOLAN'S CASES AND MATERIALS ON TRIAL PRACTICE, 518 pages, 1981. (Casebook)

SONSTENG, HAYDOCK AND BOYD'S THE TRIALBOOK: A TOTAL SYSTEM FOR PREPARATION AND PRESENTATION OF A CASE, 404 pages, 1984. Softcover. (Coursebook)

WHARTON, HAYDOCK AND SONSTENG'S CALIFORNIA CIVIL TRIALBOOK, Law School and CLE Edition. 148 pages, 1990. Softcover. (Text)

Trusts and Estates

ATKINSON'S HORNBOOK ON WILLS, Second Edition, 975 pages, 1953. (Text)

AVERILL'S UNIFORM PROBATE CODE IN A NUTSHELL, Second Edition, 454 pages, 1987. Softcover. (Text)

BOGERT'S HORNBOOK ON TRUSTS, Sixth Edition, Student Edition, 794 pages, 1987. (Text)

CLARK, LUSKY AND MURPHY'S CASES AND MATERIALS ON GRATUITOUS TRANSFERS, Third Edition, 970 pages, 1985. (Casebook)

DODGE'S WILLS, TRUSTS AND ESTATE PLANNING—LAW AND TAXATION, CASES AND MATERIALS, 665 pages, 1988. (Casebook)

MCGOVERN'S CASES AND MATERIALS ON WILLS, TRUSTS AND FUTURE INTERESTS: AN INTRODUCTION TO ESTATE PLANNING, 750 pages, 1983. (Casebook)

MCGOVERN, KURTZ AND REIN'S HORNBOOK ON WILLS, TRUSTS AND ESTATES—INCLUDING TAXATION AND FUTURE INTERESTS, 996 pages, 1988. (Text)

MENNELL'S WILLS AND TRUSTS IN A NUTSHELL, 392 pages, 1979. Softcover. (Text)

SIMES' HORNBOOK ON FUTURE INTERESTS, Second Edition, 355 pages, 1966. (Text)

TURANO AND RADIGAN'S HORNBOOK ON NEW

Trusts and Estates—Cont'd

YORK ESTATE ADMINISTRATION, 676 pages, 1986 with 1992 pocket part. (Text)

UNIFORM PROBATE CODE, OFFICIAL TEXT WITH COMMENTS. 863 pages, 1991. Softcover.

WAGGONER'S FUTURE INTERESTS IN A NUTSHELL, 361 pages, 1981. Softcover. (Text)

Water Law—see also Energy and Natural Resources Law, Environmental Law

GETCHES' WATER LAW IN A NUTSHELL, Second Edition, 459 pages, 1990. Softcover. (Text)

SAX, ABRAMS AND THOMPSON'S LEGAL CONTROL OF WATER RESOURCES: CASES AND MATERIALS, Second Edition, 987 pages, 1991. Teacher's Manual available. (Casebook)

TRELEASE AND GOULD'S CASES AND MATERIALS ON WATER LAW, Fourth Edition, 816 pages, 1986. (Casebook)

Wills—see Trusts and Estates

Workers' Compensation

HOOD, HARDY AND LEWIS' WORKERS' COMPENSATION AND EMPLOYEE PROTECTION LAWS IN A NUTSHELL, Second Edition, 361 pages, 1990. Softcover. (Text)

LITTLE, EATON AND SMITH'S CASES AND MATERIALS ON WORKERS' COMPENSATION, Approximately 525 pages, September, 1992 Pub. (Casebook)

BEING A LAWYER:

INDIVIDUAL CHOICE AND RESPONSIBILITY IN THE PRACTICE OF LAW

By

Howard Lesnick
Jefferson B. Fordham Professor of Law
University of Pennsylvania

AMERICAN CASEBOOK SERIES®

WEST PUBLISHING CO.
ST. PAUL, MINN., 1992

American Casebook Series, the key symbol appearing on the front
cover and the WP symbol are registered trademarks of West Publishing
Co. Registered in the U.S. Patent and Trademark Office.

COPYRIGHT © 1992 By WEST PUBLISHING CO.
                    610 Opperman Drive
                    P.O. Box 64526
                    St. Paul, MN 55164–0526
Library of Congress Cataloging-in-Publication Data

Lesnick, Howard, 1931–
    Being a lawyer : individual choice and responsibility in the
practice of ⅂w / by Howard Lesnick.
      p.   cm. — (American casebook series)
    ISBN 0–314–00916–7
    1. Legal ethics—United States. 2. Lawyers—United States.
3. Practice of law—United States. I. Title, II. Series.
KF306.L47 1992
174'.3'0973—dc20   92–16679
                                                   CIP

ISBN 0–314–00916–7

May the One that is Most Compassionate
bless my father who taught me
and my mother who taught me

Grace After Meals

This book is dedicated

to the memory of my father

GEORGE L. LESNICK
1903–1959

who taught me, by his life, to respect my own labor,
and that of every other person

and to my mother

SADIE ROVNER BARON

who is teaching me, by her life, how to grow older

*

In spite of your reproaches, Callicles, there can be no finer subject for discussion than the question what a man should be like and what occupation he should engage in and how . . . he should pursue it, both in earlier and later life.

Socrates

I do not say with Socrates that the unexamined life is not worth living — that is unnecessarily harsh. However, when we guide our lives by our own pondered thoughts, it then is *our* life that we are living, not someone else's. In this sense, the unexamined life is not lived as fully.

Robert Nozick

You will say, Christ saith this, and the apostles say this; but what canst thou say?

George Fox

*

Preface

This book is designed to be used with Elizabeth Dvorkin, Jack Himmelstein, & Howard Lesnick, *Becoming a Lawyer: A Humanistic Perspective on Legal Education and Professionalism* (West 1981). In addition, one class session is based on a reading of Plato's *Gorgias*. (Any translation will do.) Relevant excerpts from the American Bar Association's *Model Code of Professional Responsibility* and *Model Rules of Professional Conduct* are contained in an Appendix to this book, p. 407, below.

Footnotes have been deleted from edited material without notation of it; where footnotes are included, they bear the original footnote numbers. Footnotes that I have added to a text are headed by asterisks.

The quotations in the Frontispiece, p. v, are, respectively, from Plato's *Gorgias,* pp. 487–488 in the standard "Stephanus" pagination; Robert Nozick's *The Examined Life: Philosophical Meditations* 15 (1989); and the "Testimony of Margaret Fox . . .," in the 1831 edition of *The Works of George Fox* 1:50 (reprinted by AMS Press, New York, 1975).

Acknowledgments

I am grateful for various forms of encouragement and support, in what has often seemed to be a quixotic endeavor: Carrie Menkel-Meadow, Joy Schless, and Carolyn Schodt encouraged me, at different critical moments, to take the project (and myself) seriously; Gary Friedman, Alan Lerner, and Jeffrey Pasek have provided, through their own law practices, continuing reminders of the reality of the possibilities for choice; Roger Cramton, Emily Fowler Hartigan, and Thomas Shaffer have illuminated my path by their writings. I benefited from the summer financial support of the Raymond Pearlstine Fund of the University of Pennsylvania Law School.

I thank the following holders of copyrights for permission to excerpt copyrighted work.

American Bar Association, Model Code of Professional Responsibility, copyright © 1982 by the American Bar Association, and Model Rules of Professional Conduct, copyright © 1989, with errata and amendments copyright © 1991, by the American Bar Association. Copies of these publications may be obtained from Order Fulfillment, American Bar Association, 750 North Lake Shore Drive, Chicago, IL 60611.

Sidney Callahan, The Role of Emotion in Ethical Decisionmaking, 18 Hastings Center Report 9 (1988). Copyright © 1988 The Hastings Center.

HOWARD LESNICK

Philadelphia, Pa.
April 22, 1992

Summary of Contents

III. THE CONTOURS OF AN ALTERNATIVE SYNTHESIS

APPENDICES

Table of Contents

This Table of Contents incorporates by reference, at the places noted, the following works, with which this book is designed to be used: Plato's *Gorgias* (any translation), and Elizabeth Dvorkin, Jack Himmelstein, & Howard Lesnick, *Becoming a Lawyer: A Humanistic Perspective on Legal Education and Professionalism* (West 1981).

III. THE CONTOURS OF AN ALTERNATIVE SYNTHESIS

APPENDICES

*

Table of Cases

The principal cases are in bold type. Cases cited or discussed in the text are roman type. References are to pages. Cases cited in principal cases and within other quoted materials are not included.

*

Table of Model Rules, Model Code Provisions and ABA Formal Opinions

Table of Secondary Authorities

References are to Pages

*

BEING A LAWYER:

INDIVIDUAL CHOICE AND RESPONSIBILITY IN THE PRACTICE OF LAW

*

INTRODUCTION

> It is not in heaven, that you should say, Who shall go up for us to heaven, and bring it to us, and make us to hear it that we may do it? Neither is it beyond the sea, that you should say, Who shall go over the sea, and bring it to us, and make us to hear it, that we may do it? But the word is very near to you, in your mouth, and in your heart, that you may do it.
>
> *Deuteronomy*, XXX:12.

As I was about to become a teacher, a wise friend said to me that, although most teachers use people to teach things, teaching is using things to teach people. I have set out in this book *not* to treat Professional Responsibility as the thing that I am teaching, that is, as a body of knowledge or ideas that I am transmitting or imparting to students. My intention is rather to use Professional Responsibility, both doctrinal development and theoretical critiques, to evoke in students their own responses to some fundamental questions about themselves as emergent lawyers, to teach students to ask themselves: Who am I? In my work as a lawyer, what will I be doing in the world? What do I want to be doing in the world?

These questions—which I will call here questions of identity—are without doubt far from easy to address in a law school course or classroom. Beyond that difficulty, however, many teachers and students question whether they are appropriate to consider. The dilemma is that if a teacher does not want to consider as part of legal education how students (and teachers) answer such questions for themselves, he or she will answer them simply by not asking them. It is not possible to talk or think about questions of lawyering without one's thoughts or statements reflecting a set of answers to the questions of identity. For there is in our culture and our polity a prevailing set of responses to these questions, embedded in our thinking about law and lawyering, but ordinarily not acknowledged; and failure to address the questions of identity as questions to be considered reinforces that embedding process. If, therefore, we as teachers do not invite students to ask themselves the questions I have put, if we seek simply to teach a subject, we in fact answer the questions implicitly, without discussing our answers, without espousing them, without putting the issue on the table. There is, quite literally, no exit.*

---

* Some of what is written in this Introduction is a revision of portions of an un- published paper that I delivered some years ago, excerpts from which are quoted

1

The content of the prevailing answers is not easily summarized in a few sentences, and can be given many variant formulations. The following sketch is one version of the propositions that, I believe, we implicitly communicate to students when we do not invite them to make their life choices part of their explicit agenda:

- Each of you is here (that is, in the world) to get ahead in the world.

- You are here (in law school) to learn a job, one that will help you get ahead in the world.

- Your job will be to help your clients get ahead in the world.

- People can relate to each other only instrumentally, as objects, in a world that is accurately described primarily as one of separateness, competition, and scarcity.

- Justice, which is a basic aspiration, is obtained by fair procedures, by following the rules of the game (not lying, for example), and by seeking mutually beneficial exchanges.

- Justice *is* obtained, by and large; the interaction of individuals seeking to advance themselves produces a reasonably harmonious and legitimate social order.

The failing in this answer is not that it is untrue; there obviously is much truth in it. I believe, however, that it is only part of the truth, and is experienced as more than that. Moreover, because of the implicit quality of its avowal, the fact that it is not on the learning agenda, it is being put forward as true without an acknowledgement that it is contestable, without an acknowledgement that it is being addressed, indeed, as an undiscussible answer to a set of nonaddressable questions. Should an attempt be made to question the felt answer, the response is that this is no longer college, this is law school, that such questions are a private matter, for private consideration, not appropriate to take up in class. The result of this dynamic is that what is sometimes justified as respecting students' (and teachers') autonomy, by not "indoctrinating" them about values and politics, in reality does exactly what it says it wants to avoid. A message is being put forward, and any effort to engage with it is repressed.

The alternative to which I am drawn is not to avow a contrary message as the (whole) truth, but to avow the appropriateness of asking the questions and of engaging with whatever answers the questions call forth. **Teaching, to me, is evoking that engagement.** Imparting information, whether about the questions of identity or any answers to them, a fortiori about the law of Professional Responsibility, is of value as teaching as it tends to aid that process, as it often can; but it is a positive interference with teaching when it tends to shut that process down, as it often does.

or paraphrased in Roger Cramton, Beyond
the Ordinary Religion, 37 J.Leg.Educ. 509
(1987).

As I hope is clear, I do not deny my responsibility to assure students the means of learning "the law of lawyering." My goal is that knowledge of the law be "imparted" as a result of the central enterprise described in the text, not for its own sake. (My view is close to that articulated by Edwin Chemerinsky, Training the Ethical Lawyer: a Rejoinder to Schneyer, 1986 A.B.F.Res.J. 959 (1985)). My hope and belief is that such knowledge will be obtained through grappling with the themes and materials presented here. But by focusing on *individual* responsibility, I hope to offset the tendency, to which we are all subject, to abstract the issues from our own decisionmaking, and more to argue and ponder them as questions of law or "public policy" than to approach them as questions the answers to which give content to our own emergent lives as lawyers.

This book begins by setting out the ingredients of what I will call "the traditional concept of advocacy," as they are manifested in doctrinal development or commentary, and to present some of the major theoretical perspectives by which they are sought to be justified or questioned. My hypothesis is that, within wide parameters of difference, most students will experience the traditional concept as both axiomatically sound and significantly problematic. The major value, in my view, of your learning this body of law and critique is its triggering your own engagement with your emergent professional stance, your asking yourself the question: What concept of lawyering do *I* propose to follow in my professional life?

We will not ignore the question whether it is realistic or appropriate to regard questions of professional responsibility as matters of individual choice. Indeed, after looking at some of the controversies that have arisen with respect to several aspects of the traditional concept of advocacy, we will seek to articulate and examine a number of elements that constitute powerful barriers to taking seriously the possibility of formulating an alternative concept. Some of these barriers are in "the law" or the legal system, and some are endemic in the wider world in which we live. We will take these barriers—of which the experience of lack of choice is a leading example—seriously, but we will not assume *a priori* that individual choice plays or should play little part.

Finally, the book will attempt to articulate some aspects of what I will term an alternative synthesis. My hope is that this effort will not be thought of as a proposed "answer," but as a concept to be engaged with, just as I hope you will engage with the traditional concept.

I. THE TRADITIONAL CONCEPT
OF ADVOCACY

By the "traditional concept of advocacy," I have in mind three major principles: First, for the most part, only lawyers may do advocates' work, even though lawyers may be unavailable to individuals needing advocacy services. Second, attorney dominance over clients is regarded as legitimate, in recognition of the expertise and craft autonomy of the lawyer, notwithstanding that in consequence people who turn to legal representation to enhance their power of self-determination in the face of threats from powerful public or private actions may find that their advocate becomes in many ways yet another threatening force. Third, lawyers are expected to give near-total primacy to their clients' interests—without regard to their social utility, without regard to the relative ability of those adversely affected to protect themselves, without regard to the advocate's own personal beliefs or human reactions.

There is much ferment about the soundness of these principles, but I believe that there is general agreement that they have been the prevailing norms and that they continue to be widely defended, although also strongly questioned. This section of the book will first present, and examine the premises of, three judicial decisions, each applying one of the three principles. It will thereafter examine both the meaning and the justification of the second and third principles in greater depth.*

1. SOME ILLUSTRATIVE DECISIONS

(a) *Professional Monopolization*

HACKIN v. STATE

Supreme Court of Arizona, 1967.
102 Ariz. 218, 427 P.2d 910.

PER CURIAM.

Defendant H. Samuel Hackin, was charged in the Justice Court of West Phoenix of violating A.R.S. § 32–261, prohibiting any person from

---

* This book was initially developed for use at the University of Pennsylvania Law School, where students are required to take a course in The Legal Profession and Professional Responsibility in their first year. Students using this book in an introductory course should familiarize themselves with the terminology, evolution and status of the Model Code of Professional Responsibility and the Model Rules of Professional Conduct, by reading Section 2.6, "The Lawyer Codes," of Charles Wolfram, *Modern Legal Ethics* 48–63 (student ed. 1986).

The text of those codes provisions not quoted in full relevant part may be found in the Appendix, p. 407, below.

4

practicing law in this state unless he is an active member of the state bar. A jury found him guilty of the charge. Defendant then appealed to the Superior Court of Maricopa County where his conviction was upheld and he was sentenced to fifteen (15) days in the Maricopa County jail. The matter comes to this court on a petition for a writ of habeas corpus in accordance with A.R.S. § 13–2001.

On October 24, 1966 the defendant represented one Jasper Winnegar in a hearing upon a petition for habeas corpus, conducted in the Superior Court of Maricopa County. The defendant is not now, nor was he then, a licensed attorney. Defendant was advised at the time by a deputy county attorney that should he insist on representing Winnegar in court he would be subject to prosecution for violation of a state law ... prohibiting the illegal practice of law. However, because the court refused upon defendant's request to appoint counsel for Winnegar, the defendant chose to conduct the hearing on Winnegar's behalf. Thereafter the charges for which he stands convicted were brought against defendant.

A.R.S. § 32–261 provides:

"A. No person shall practice law in this state unless he is an active member of the state bar in good standing as defined in this chapter.

"B. A person who, not being an active member of the state bar, or who after he has been disbarred, or while suspended from membership in the state bar, practices law, is guilty of a misdemeanor."

The prohibition of this provision is, however, subject to the following limitation set out in A.R.S. § 13–2002:

"Application for the writ [writ of habeas corpus, A.R.S. § 13–2001] shall be made by verified petition, signed either by the party for whose relief it is intended or by some person in his behalf...."

The state concedes that this statute allows one not an attorney to file an application for a writ of habeas corpus on behalf of another. It would concede also, perhaps, that the filing of such verified petition could properly be considered the "practice [of] law," within A.R.S. § 32–261. What the state does not concede, however, is that A.R.S. § 13–2002 should be extended to permit a nonlawyer, other than the petitioner who has filed an application with the court, to then go into open court and argue the merits of the application. It is with this primary question that we must therefore deal.

. . .

The provision embodied in A.R.S. § 13–2002 permitting any person acting on behalf of the prisoner to file an application for a writ of habeas corpus ... safeguards the protection that the writ was designed to provide. It is a practical realization that one confined to a cell, without ready access to a lawyer, often must depend on his family or friends to have "his body brought before the court" (i.e. "habeas corpus") to determine the legality of his incarceration.

Once before the court, however, the purpose of the writ and the statute has been served. No longer is it necessary for the prisoner's family or friends to act in his behalf. The matter is then in the hands of the court which is well acquainted with the law, and whose duty it is to determine the legality of the petitioner's detention. See A.R.S. § 13–2010. It is true that a lawyer to represent the petitioner may well be helpful to the court in its legal consideration of the matter, but this is due to a lawyer's special training and knowledge of the law. He can provide a service which a layman cannot, the very reason why a person is required to be licensed before he is permitted to practice law.... We are not prepared, therefore, to say that a layman is any more able to represent a person in a habeas corpus proceeding than he is in any other legal proceeding. A layman has done his deed by assisting the petitioner to get before the court.

That we have held in Palmer v. State, 99 Ariz. 93, 407 P.2d 64, that an indigent is not entitled to court appointed counsel in habeas corpus proceedings, does not alter our view of this matter. It in no way affects our determination that one layman is unsuited to represent another layman in a legal proceeding. We take the opportunity to note here, however, that our decision in Palmer does not in any way deny the court's power to appoint counsel, and to assert that this power should be exercised freely, taking into account the Public Defender and Legal Aid programs that have been established in our state.

Whether counsel should be appointed as a matter of course in habeas corpus proceedings, however, is not in issue here. We limit ourselves to the question of whether defendant's acts in representing Jasper Winnegar can be justified in the face of A.R.S. § 32–261. We hold that they cannot. The "exception" provided in A.R.S. § 13–2002 serves a specific purpose, and that purpose is fulfilled once the incarcerated prisoner is brought before the court.

[The court's discussion of defendant's constitutional claims of vagueness and interference with freedom of speech, is omitted. In the course of addressing the vagueness contention, the court spoke about the meaning of the prohibition on the "practice [of] law."]

"[T]he practice of law" is normally considered to include "those acts, whether performed in court or in a law office, which lawyers have customarily carried on from day to day through the centuries...." [citation omitted] It cannot be disputed that one who represents another in court, be he an indigent or not, is, under our adversary process, going to the very core of the practice of law, a fact which even the most uninformed persons are well aware.

Writ denied.

On Appeal to the Supreme Court of the United States

HACKIN v. ARIZONA

389 U.S. 143, 88 S.Ct. 325, 19 L.Ed.2d 347 (1967).

PER CURIAM.

The motion to dispense with printing the jurisdictional statement is granted. The motion to dismiss is granted and the appeal is dismissed for want of a substantial federal question.

MR. JUSTICE DOUGLAS, dissenting.

Appellant, who is not a licensed attorney, appeared in a state court habeas corpus proceeding on behalf of an indigent prisoner. The indigent prisoner was being held for extradition to Oklahoma, where he had been convicted of murder and had escaped from custody. Appellant had previously attempted to secure for the prisoner appointed counsel to argue in court the prisoner's contention that his Oklahoma conviction was invalid due to denial of certain constitutional rights. But in Arizona an indigent has no right to appointed counsel at habeas corpus proceedings [1] ... including habeas corpus proceedings that are part of the extradition process.... Unable to obtain counsel for the indigent, appellant chose to represent him himself and was convicted of a misdemeanor....

Appellant ... is no stranger to the law. He graduated from an unaccredited law school but was refused admission to the Arizona Bar. See Hackin v. Lockwood, 361 F.2d 499 (C.A. 9th Cir.), cert. denied, 385 U.S. 960, 87 S.Ct. 396, 17 L.Ed.2d 305.

The claim that the statute deters constitutionally protected activity is not frivolous. Whether a State, under guise of protecting its citizens from legal quacks and charlatans, can make criminals of those who, in good faith and for no personal profit, assist the indigent to assert their constitutional rights is a substantial question this Court should answer.

Rights protected by the First Amendment include advocacy and petition for redress of grievances ..., and the Fourteenth Amendment ensures equal justice for the poor in both criminal and civil actions.... But to millions of Americans who are indigent and ignorant—and often members of minority groups—these rights are meaningless. They are helpless to assert their rights under the law without assistance. They suffer discrimination in housing and employment, are victimized by shady consumer sales practices, evicted from their homes at the whim of the landlord, denied welfare payments, and endure domestic strife

---

1. Appellant's conviction for unauthorized practice of law would seem to be the result of Arizona's restrictive reading of Gideon v. Wainwright, 372 U.S. 335, 83 S.Ct. 792, 9 L.Ed.2d 799. In State v. Bost, 2 Ariz.App. 431, 409 P.2d 590, the court held Gideon inapplicable to extradition proceedings because they were ministerial rather than judicial in nature.... Had Arizona courts [not] approached the problem [as one of] selecting between the labels "ministerial" and "judicial," they might have concluded that indigents in the position of the prisoner whom appellant aided here are entitled to counsel under *Gideon.*

without hope of the legal remedies of divorce, maintenance, or child custody decrees.

If true equal protection of the laws is to be realized, an indigent must be able to obtain assistance when he suffers a denial of his rights. Today, this goal is only a goal. Outside the area of criminal proceedings . . . counsel is seldom available to the indigent. As this Court has recognized, there is a dearth of lawyers who are willing, voluntarily, to take on unprofitable and unpopular causes. NAACP v. Button, 371 U.S., at 443, 83 S.Ct. 328. . . .

    . . .

There is emerging . . . a type of organization styled to bring a new brand of legal assistance to the indigent. These groups, funded in part by the federal Office of Economic Opportunity [the predecessor of the Legal Services Corporation], characteristically establish neighborhood offices where the poor can come for assistance. They attempt to dispense services on a comprehensive integrated scale, using lawyers, social workers, members of health professions, and other nonlawyer aides. These new and flexible approaches to giving legal aid to the poor recognize that the problems of indigents—although of the type for which an attorney has traditionally been consulted—are too immense to be solved solely by members of the bar. The supply of lawyer manpower is not nearly large enough.[5] . . .

The so-called "legal" problem of the poor is often an unidentified strand in a complex of social, economic, psychological, and psychiatric problems. Identification of the "legal" problem at times is for the expert. But even a "lay" person can often perform that function and mark the path that leads to the school board, the school principal, the welfare agency, the Veterans Administration, the police review board, or the urban renewal agency.[7] If he neither solicits nor obtains a fee for his services, why should he not be free to act? Full-fledged representation in a battle before a court or agency requires professional

---

5. See Cahn & Cahn, What Price Justice: The Civilian Perspective Revisited, 41 Notre Dame Law. 927 (1966). "Finally, with respect to manpower, we have created an artificial shortage by refusing to learn from the medical and other professions and to develop technicians, nonprofessionals and lawyer-aides—manpower roles to carry out such functions as: informal advocate, technician, counsellor, sympathetic listener, investigator, researcher, form writer, etc." (P. 934.) "[The] possibility of advancing the cause of justice through increasing lay involvement in fact finding, adjudication and arbitration, should not be sacrificed a priori out of fear of abuse." (P. 951.) . . .

7. See Frankel, Experiments in Serving the Indigent, in National Conference on Law and Poverty Proceedings 69, 75–76 (1965): "[We] lawyers must certainly con-

front constructively the idea that what we have traditionally regarded as legal business cannot permanently be so regarded. The needs of the poor for services in matters that are somehow legal appear pretty clearly to be enormous. Among those needs are many kinds of matters that are narrow, that are specialized, and can be routinized. Matters related to housing, to workmen's compensation, to consumer problems are a few that one could name. . . . [We] should attempt to create a class of legal technicians who can handle, under lawyers' supervision, some of the problems that have thus far seemed to us to be exclusively the province of the lawyer. I think we have an important creative function to perform in trying to mark out these areas where lawyers are not really needed." . . .

skills that laymen lack; and therefore the client suffers, perhaps grievously, if he is not represented by a lawyer....

Moreover, what the poor need, as much as our corporate grants, is protection before they get into trouble and confront a crisis. This means "political leadership" for the "minority poor." Id., at 351. Lawyers will play a role in that movement; but so will laymen. The line that marks the area into which the layman may not step except at his peril is not clear. I am by no means sure the line was properly drawn by the court below where no lawyer could be found and this layman apparently served without a fee.

Legal representation connotes a magic it often does not possess—as for example, the commitment procedure in Texas, where, by one report, 66 seconds are given to a case, the lawyer usually not even knowing his client and earning a nice fee for passive participation. Weihofen, Mental Health Services for the Poor, 54 Calif.L.Rev. 920, 938–939 (1966). If justice is the goal, why need a layman be barred here?

Broadly phrased unauthorized-practice-of-law statutes such as that at issue here could make criminal many of the activities regularly done by social workers who assist the poor in obtaining welfare and attempt to help them solve domestic problems.[9] Such statutes would also tend to deter programs in which experienced welfare recipients represent other, less articulate, recipients before local welfare departments.

[S]tatutes with the broad sweep of the Arizona provision now before this Court would appear to have the potential to "freeze out" the imaginative new attempts to assist indigents realize equal justice, merely because lay persons participate.... Certainly the States have a strong interest in preventing legally untrained shysters who pose as attorneys from milking the public for pecuniary gain.... But it is arguable whether this policy should support a prohibition against charitable efforts of nonlawyers to help the poor.... It may well be that until the goal of free legal assistance to the indigent in all areas of the law is achieved, the poor are not harmed by well-meaning, charitable assistance of laymen. On the contrary, for the majority of indigents, who are not so fortunate to be served by neighborhood legal offices, lay assistance may be the only hope for achieving equal justice at this time.

9. "Social workers in public assistance may already be required to practice law as substantially as if they were in a courtroom. In making an initial determination of an applicant's eligibility, the public assistance worker must complete the applicant's financial statement. 'Every question, or nearly every question, on the financial statement, is a legal question. When the social worker advises, or even discusses the questions or answers, he may very likely be giving legal advice.' The private social worker who advises an applicant that he should apply, how to apply, what to answer and how to appeal if the application is rejected is also giving 'legal' advice. When he argues with the public worker on behalf of the applicant, he is giving representation. When and if he goes to a hearing on behalf of the applicant, he is surely engaging in advocacy." Sparer, Thorkelson & Weiss, [The Lay Advocate, 43 U.Det.L.J. 493,] 499–500....

In sum, I find the questions posed in this appeal both timely and troublesome; and it would appear that appellant has standing to raise the indigent's First Amendment rights of advocacy and petition of redress and of equal justice.... Accordingly, I would hear this appeal.

Note on Hackin: "Unauthorized practice"
or "professional monopolization"?

1. The prohibition of lay practice of law is contained in the statute laws, rather than the codes of professional responsibility, because it is addressed to persons who are not members of the bar.* Model Rule 5.5(b), however, specifically provides that an attorney:

> shall not assist a person who is not a member of the bar in the performance of activity that constitutes the unauthorized practice of law.

This provision deters lawyers from cooperating with programs that teach or advise lay people in the handling of "legal" problems (except where the attorney is doing no more than helping one or more lay persons to act "pro se," that is, on his or her own behalf, without legal or lay representation).

2. (a) Choosing whether to refer to restrictions on lay practice of law as "unauthorized practice" law or as "professional monopolization" seems to signal a person's judgment about the legitimacy of such restrictions. Presumably, the label should be chosen as the result, and not as an attempted justification, of one's conclusion regarding the question of legitimacy.

Do you come to that question—whether restrictions on lay practice of law, whatever they are called, are legitimate—with a *supportive* or a *skeptical* state of mind?

(b) As you think about the question further, what factors are significant in judging the question of legitimacy? Justice Douglas' opinion tells us many facts that the Arizona court did not regard as significant to the question, but which his opinion suggests are relevant. Some are specific to the case at bar, and were apparently not a matter of dispute: Hackin was a law school graduate, he did not charge a fee, Winnegar knew that Hackin was not admitted to the Arizona bar, and Winnegar had sought without success to have counsel appointed for him. Others are contestable propositions of "social" or "legislative" fact: the propositions that many people, especially poor people, cannot obtain legal representation in the market to

---

* Federal (nonconstitutional) law sets some significant restrictions on the state rules of unauthorized practice. The most important of these is derived from the Social Security Act, which permits those claiming benefits under the public assistance or related programs to have the aid of representatives of their own choosing in administrative hearings, see 45 C.F.R. Section 205.10(a)(3)(iii), and thereby displaces any state law of unauthorized practice that might otherwise limit such representation

to attorneys. On the principle of federal supremacy, see Sperry v. Florida ex rel. Florida Bar, 373 U.S. 379, 384–85, 83 S.Ct. 1322, 1325–26, 10 L.Ed.2d 428 (1963), dealing with the specific context of Patent Attorneys.

For a thorough survey and critique of contemporary unauthorized-practice law, see Deborah Rhode, Policing the Professional Monopoly: A Constitutional and Empirical Analysis of Unauthorized Practice Prohibitions, 34 Stan.L.Rev. 1 (1981).

assist them with disputes that affect their important interests; that many actions that constitute "the practice of law" can be competently performed by lay people; and that much legal representation is carried on by attorneys in a routinized and hurried manner.

Do any of these facts or propositions affect your own view on the question of legitimacy? Should they?

(c) Am I wrong in suggesting that the legitimacy of the "unauthorized practice" principle, and of its application to this case, seems to become more disputable as more facts are admitted into consideration of the issue? There seems to be a connection between the abstract quality of the State court opinion and its "celebratory" tone, and also a connection between Justice Douglas' interest in pursuing the factual context so fully and the "troubled" tone of his opinion. Is this so?

3. Traditional legal analysis would suggest that there should not be such a connection, that the proper way to consider the question which view of unauthorized practice law is sound is, first, to decide the "relevance" of the factual elements on which Justice Douglas relies and, if they are deemed to be relevant, to consider whether they are "true." Questions like the correctness of a "celebratory" or a "troubled" stance are thought to be ideological, political, etc., and not properly taken into account in neutral, "legal" decisionmaking.

Yet neither the Arizona court nor Justice Douglas *discusses* the question of relevance, or takes any notice of the fact that one acts as if the facts in question are irrelevant, while the other obviously thinks them highly relevant. The independent input seems to be one's adoption of a "celebratory" or a "troubled" stance, rather than the extent of one's receptivity to the factual context. By this I mean that the Arizona court is reluctant to look into the factual context *because* it seems to dispute or undermine the "celebratory" stance that it deems right, while Justice Douglas appears eager to consider the factual context *because* it is likely to confirm his "troubled" stance on the question of legitimacy. Is this reading of the opinions correct, in your view?

If so, the consequence seems to be that, in order to *explain* the existence of differences of opinion—whether within the judiciary, as in the *Hackin* litigation or within any group of lawyers or law students—over the legitimacy of the idea of professional monopolization one should look, not to differences of view about the factual propositions that Justice Douglas relies on, but to differences over the appropriateness of a "celebratory" or a "troubled" stance toward the legitimacy of the law of unauthorized practice. Is this conclusion sound?

4. What is the relation, if any, between the adoption of a "celebratory" or a "troubled" stance toward the law of unauthorized practice and one's stance toward the legal system as a whole? In this regard, consider the structure of the Arizona opinion, specifically, the answers that the court gives to the following questions:

• If a lay person is permitted to file a petition for a writ of habeas corpus, why was Hackin at fault here?

- If a person facing incarceration, and financially unable to retain counsel, is constitutionally entitled to have counsel appointed for him or her, why was Winnegar properly denied counsel?

- If it was right for him to be denied counsel, why could a lay person not represent him?

- Since Hackin was a law school graduate, why is he to be deemed a lay person?

- What does "practicing law" mean?

What is the court's evident level of satisfaction with the answers to these questions? What about Justice Douglas?

Do your answers to these two last questions tend to suggest that the adoption of a "celebratory" or a "troubled" stance toward the legitimacy of the law of unauthorized practice is embedded in one's belief that the legal system overall, and not merely the law of unauthorized practice, tends to produce results that one should celebrate or be troubled over?

5. Consider now the direction toward which you lean:

- on the question of the legitimacy of the idea of unauthorized practice;

- on the relevance of the facts, whether about Hackin and Winnegar or about the overall need for advocacy services in our society, to the question;

- on the overall praiseworthiness of the legal order.

Are your choices on the three preceding questions *related?* Is so, how?

Begin to think, too, about the probable *sources* of your "leanings."

(b) *Professional Dominance*

JONES v. BARNES

Supreme Court of the United States, 1983.
463 U.S. 745, 103 S.Ct. 3308, 77 L.Ed.2d 987.

CHIEF JUSTICE BURGER delivered the opinion of the Court.

We granted certiorari to consider whether defense counsel assigned to prosecute an appeal from a criminal conviction has a constitutional duty to raise every nonfrivolous issue requested by the defendant.

. . .

In 1976, Richard Butts was robbed at knifepoint by four men in the lobby of an apartment building; he was badly beaten and his watch and money were taken. Butts informed a Housing Authority detective that he recognized one of his assailants as a person known to him as "Froggy," and gave a physical description of the person to the detective. The following day the detective arrested respondent David Barnes, who is known as "Froggy."

Respondent was charged with first- and second-degree robbery, second-degree assault, and third-degree larceny. The prosecution rested primarily upon Butts' testimony and his identification of respondent.

During cross-examination, defense counsel asked Butts whether he had ever undergone psychiatric treatment; however, no offer of proof was made on the substance or relevance of the question after the trial judge sua sponte instructed Butts not to answer. At the close of trial, the trial judge declined to give an instruction on accessorial liability requested by the defense. The jury convicted respondent of first- and second-degree robbery and second-degree assault.

The Appellate Division of the Supreme Court of New York, Second Department, assigned Michael Melinger to represent respondent on appeal. Respondent sent Melinger a letter listing several claims that he felt should be raised. Included were claims that Butts' identification testimony should have been suppressed, that the trial judge improperly excluded psychiatric evidence, and that respondent's trial counsel was ineffective. Respondent also enclosed a copy of a pro se brief he had written.

In a return letter, Melinger accepted some but rejected most of the suggested claims, stating that they would not aid respondent in obtaining a new trial and that they could not be raised on appeal because they were not based on evidence in the record. Melinger then listed seven potential claims of error that he was considering including in his brief, and invited respondent's "reflections and suggestions" with regard to those seven issues. The record does not reveal any response to this letter.

Melinger's brief to the Appellate Division concentrated on three of the seven points he had raised in his letter to respondent: improper exclusion of psychiatric evidence, failure to suppress Butts' identification testimony, and improper cross-examination of respondent by the trial judge. In addition, Melinger submitted respondent's own pro se brief. Thereafter, respondent filed two more pro se briefs, raising three more of the seven issues Melinger had identified.

At oral argument, Melinger argued the three points presented in his own brief, but not the arguments raised in the pro se briefs. [T]he Appellate Division affirmed by summary order.... The New York Court of Appeals denied leave to appeal ...

[Between 1978 and 1980, Barnes unsuccessfully sought collateral review of his conviction, first from federal, then from State, court].

[O]n March 31, 1980, he filed a petition in the New York Court of Appeals for reconsideration of that court's denial of leave to appeal. In that petition, respondent for the first time claimed that his appellate counsel, Melinger, had provided ineffective assistance. The New York Court of Appeals denied the application ...

Respondent then returned to United States District Court for the second time, with a petition for habeas corpus based on the claim of ineffective assistance by appellate counsel. The District Court concluded that respondent had exhausted his state remedies, but dismissed the petition, holding that the record gave no support to the claim of ineffective assistance of appellate counsel.... The District Court concluded:

> "It is not required that an attorney argue every conceivable issue on appeal, especially when some may be without merit. Indeed, it is his professional duty to choose among potential issues, according to his judgment as to their merit and his tactical approach." ...

A divided panel of the Court of Appeals reversed....[3] Laying down a new standard, the majority held that when "the appellant requests that [his attorney] raise additional colorable points [on appeal], counsel must argue the additional points to the full extent of his professional ability." Id., at 433 (emphasis added). In the view of the majority, this conclusion followed from Anders v. California, 386 U.S. 738, 87 S.Ct. 1396, 18 L.Ed.2d 493 (1967). In Anders, this Court held that an appointed attorney must advocate his client's cause vigorously and may not withdraw from a nonfrivolous appeal. The Court of Appeals majority held that, since Anders bars counsel from abandoning a nonfrivolous appeal, it also bars counsel from abandoning a nonfrivolous issue on appeal.

The court concluded that Melinger had not met the above standard in that he had failed to press at least two nonfrivolous claims: the trial judge's failure to instruct on accessory liability and ineffective assistance of trial counsel. The fact that these issues had been raised in respondent's own pro se briefs did not cure the error, since "[a] pro se brief is no substitute for the advocacy of experienced counsel." The court reversed and remanded, with instructions to grant the writ of habeas corpus unless the State assigned new counsel and granted a new appeal.

. . .

[I]n Griffin v. Illinois, 351 U.S. 12, 18, 76 S.Ct. 585, 590, 100 L.Ed. 891 (1956), and Douglas v. California, 372 U.S. 353, 83 S.Ct. 814, 9 L.Ed.2d 811 (1963), the Court held that if an appeal is open to those who can pay for it, an appeal must be provided for an indigent. It is also recognized that the accused has the ultimate authority to make certain fundamental decisions regarding the case, as to whether to plead guilty, waive a jury, testify in his or her own behalf, or take an appeal, see Wainwright v. Sykes, 433 U.S. 72, 93, n. 1, 97 S.Ct. 2497, 2509 n. 1, 53 L.Ed.2d 594 (1977) (BURGER, C.J., concurring); ABA Standards for Criminal Justice 4–5.2, 21–2.2 (2d ed. 1980). In addition, we have held that, with some limitations, a defendant may elect to act as his or her own advocate, Faretta v. California, 422 U.S. 806, 95 S.Ct. 2525, 45 L.Ed.2d 562 (1975). Neither Anders nor any other decision of this Court suggests, however, that the indigent defendant has a constitutional right to compel appointed counsel to press nonfrivolous points request-

---

3. By this time, at least 26 state and federal judges had considered respondent's claims that he was unjustly convicted for a crime committed five years earlier; and many of the judges had reviewed the case more than once. Until the latest foray, all courts had rejected his claims.

ed by the client, if counsel, as a matter of professional judgment, decides not to present those points.[4]

This Court, in holding that a State must provide counsel for an indigent appellant on his first appeal as of right, recognized the superior ability of trained counsel in the "examination into the record, research of the law, and marshalling of arguments on [the appellant's] behalf," Douglas v. California, supra, at 358, 83 S.Ct. 817. Yet by promulgating a per se rule that the client, not the professional advocate, must be allowed to decide what issues are to be pressed, the Court of Appeals seriously undermines the ability of counsel to present the client's case in accord with counsel's professional evaluation.

Experienced advocates since time beyond memory have emphasized the importance of winnowing out weaker arguments on appeal and focusing on one central issue if possible, or at most on a few key issues....

. . .

There can hardly be any question about the importance of having the appellate advocate examine the record with a view to selecting the most promising issues for review. This has assumed a greater importance in an era when oral argument is strictly limited in most courts— often to as little as 15 minutes—and when page limits on briefs are widely imposed.... Even in a court that imposes no time or page limits, however, the new per se rule laid down by the Court of Appeals is contrary to all experience and logic. A brief that raises every colorable issue runs the risk of burying good arguments—those that, in the words of the great advocate John W. Davis, "go for the jugular," Davis, The Argument of an Appeal, 26 A.B.A.J. 895, 897 (1940)—in a verbal mound made up of strong and weak contentions. See generally, e.g., Godbold, Twenty Pages and Twenty Minutes—Effective Advocacy on Appeal, 30 Sw.L.J. 801 (1976).[6]

---

4. The record is not without ambiguity as to what respondent requested. We assume, for purposes of our review, that the Court of Appeals majority correctly concluded that respondent insisted that Melinger raise the issues identified, and did not simply accept Melinger's decision not to press those issues.

6. The ABA Model Rules of Professional Conduct provide:

"A lawyer shall abide by a client's decisions concerning the objectives of representation ... and shall consult with the client as to the means by which they are to be pursued.... In a criminal case, the lawyer shall abide by the client's decision, ... as to a plea to be entered, whether to waive jury trial and whether the client will testify." Model Rules of Professional Conduct, Proposed Rule 1.2(a) (Final Draft 1982) (emphasis added).

With the exception of these specified fundamental decisions, an attorney's duty is to take professional responsibility for the conduct of the case, after consulting with his client.

Respondent points to the ABA Standards for Criminal Appeals, which appear to indicate that counsel should accede to a client's insistence on pressing a particular contention on appeal, see ABA Standards for Criminal Justice 21–3.2, p. 21.42 (2d ed. 1980). The ABA Defense Function Standards provide, however, that, with the exceptions specified above, strategic and tactical decisions are the exclusive province of the defense counsel, after consultation with the client. See id., 4–5.2. See also ABA Project on Standards for Criminal Justice, The Prosecution Function and The Defense Function § 5.2 (Tent.Draft 1970). In any event, the fact that the ABA may

This Court's decision in Anders, far from giving support to the new per se rule announced by the Court of Appeals, is to the contrary. Anders recognized that the role of the advocate "requires that he support his client's appeal to the best of his ability." 386 U.S., at 744, 87 S.Ct., at 1400. Here the appointed counsel did just that. For judges to second-guess reasonable professional judgments and impose on appointed counsel a duty to raise every "colorable" claim suggested by a client would disserve the very goal of vigorous and effective advocacy that underlies Anders. Nothing in the Constitution or our interpretation of that document requires such a standard ...

JUSTICE BLACKMUN, concurring in the judgment.

I do not join the Court's opinion, because ... I agree with Justice Brennan, and the American Bar Association, ABA Standards for Criminal Justice 21–3.2, Comment, p. 21.42 (2d ed. 1980), that, as an ethical matter, an attorney should argue on appeal all nonfrivolous claims upon which his client insists. Whether or not one agrees with the Court's view of legal strategy, it seems to me that the lawyer, after giving his client his best opinion as to the course most likely to succeed, should acquiesce in the client's choice of which nonfrivolous claims to pursue.

... I agree with the Court, however, that neither my view, nor the ABA's view, of the ideal allocation of decisionmaking authority between client and lawyer necessarily assumes constitutional status where counsel's performance is "within the range of competence demanded of attorneys in criminal cases," McMann v. Richardson, 397 U.S. 759, 771, 90 S.Ct. 1441, 1449, 25 L.Ed.2d 763 (1970), and "assure[s] the indigent defendant an adequate opportunity to present his claims fairly in the context of the State's appellate process," Ross v. Moffitt, 417 U.S. 600, 616, 94 S.Ct. 2437, 2446, 41 L.Ed.2d 341 (1974). I agree that both these requirements were met here.

JUSTICE BRENNAN, with whom JUSTICE MARSHALL joins, dissenting.

The Sixth Amendment provides that "[i]n all criminal prosecutions, the accused shall enjoy the right ... to have the Assistance of Counsel for his defence" (emphasis added). I find myself in fundamental disagreement with the Court over what a right to "the assistance of counsel" means. The import of words like "assistance" and "counsel" seems inconsistent with a regime under which counsel appointed by the State to represent a criminal defendant can refuse to raise issues with arguable merit on appeal when his client, after hearing his assessment of the case and his advice, has directed him to raise them. I would remand for a determination whether respondent did in fact insist that his lawyer brief the issues that the Court of Appeals found were not frivolous.

have chosen to recognize a given practice as desirable or appropriate does not mean that that practice is required by the Constitution.

It is clear that respondent had a right to the assistance of counsel in connection with his appeal. "As we have held again and again, an indigent defendant is entitled to the appointment of counsel to assist him on his first appeal...." Entsminger v. Iowa, 386 U.S. 748, 751, 87 S.Ct. 1402, 1403, 18 L.Ed.2d 501 (1967) (citations omitted).[2] ...

The Constitution does not on its face define the phrase "assistance of counsel," but surely those words are not empty of content. No one would doubt that counsel must be qualified to practice law in the courts of the State in question, or that the representation afforded must meet minimum standards of effectiveness. See Powell v. Alabama, 287 U.S. 45, 71, 53 S.Ct. 55, 65, 77 L.Ed. 158 (1932). To satisfy the Constitution, counsel must function as an advocate for the defendant, as opposed to a friend of the court. Anders v. California, supra, at 744, 87 S.Ct., at 1400; Entsminger v. Iowa, supra, at 751, 87 S.Ct., at 1403. Admittedly, the question in this case requires us to look beyond those clear guarantees. What is at issue here is the relationship between lawyer and client—who has ultimate authority to decide which nonfrivolous issues should be presented on appeal? I believe the right to "the assistance of counsel" carries with it a right, personal to the defendant, to make that decision, against the advice of counsel if he chooses.

. . .

[T]he right to counsel is more than a right to have one's case presented competently and effectively. It is predicated on the view that the function of counsel under the Sixth Amendment is to protect the dignity and autonomy of a person on trial by assisting him in making choices that are his to make, not to make choices for him, although counsel may be better able to decide which tactics will be most effective for the defendant....

The right to counsel ... is not an all-or-nothing right, under which a defendant must choose between forgoing the assistance of counsel altogether or relinquishing control over every aspect of his case beyond its most basic structure (i.e., how to plead, whether to present a defense, whether to appeal). A defendant's interest in his case clearly extends to other matters. Absent exceptional circumstances, he is bound by the tactics used by his counsel at trial and on appeal.... He may want to press the argument that he is innocent, even if other stratagems are more likely to result in the dismissal of charges or in a reduction of punishment. He may want to insist on certain arguments for political reasons. He may want to protect third parties. This is just as true on appeal as at trial, and the proper role of counsel is to assist him in these efforts, insofar as that is possible consistent with the lawyer's conscience, the law, and his duties to the court.

---

2. Both indigents and those who can afford lawyers have this right. However, with regard to issues involving the allocation of authority between lawyer and client, courts may well take account of paying clients' ability to specify at the outset of their relationship with their attorneys what degree of control they wish to exercise, and to avoid attorneys unwilling to accept client direction.

I find further support for my position in the legal profession's own conception of its proper role. The American Bar Association has taken the position that:

> "when, in the estimate of counsel, the decision of the client to take an appeal, or the client's decision to press a particular contention on appeal, is incorrect[, c]ounsel has the professional duty to give to the client fully and forcefully an opinion concerning the case and its probable outcome. Counsel's role, however, is to advise. The decision is made by the client." ABA Standards for Criminal Justice 21–3.2, Comment, p. 21.42 (2 ed. 1980)....

The Court disregards this clear statement of how the profession defines the "assistance of counsel" at the appellate stage of a criminal defense by referring to standards governing the allocation of authority between attorney and client at trial. See ... ABA Standards for Criminal Justice 4–5.2 (2 ed. 1980). In the course of a trial, however, decisions must often be made in a matter of hours, if not minutes or seconds. From the standpoint of effective administration of justice, the need to confer decisive authority on the attorney is paramount with regard to the hundreds of decisions that must be made quickly in the course of a trial. Decisions regarding which issues to press on appeal, in contrast, can and should be made more deliberately, in the course of deciding whether to appeal at all.

The Court's opinion seems to rest entirely on two propositions. First, the Court observes that we have not yet decided this case. This is true in the sense that there is no square holding on point, but ... the mere fact that a constitutional question is open is no argument for deciding it one way or the other. Second, the Court argues that good appellate advocacy demands selectivity among arguments. That is certainly true—the Court's advice is good. It ought to be taken to heart by every lawyer called upon to argue an appeal in this or any other court, and by his client. It should take little or no persuasion to get a wise client to understand that, if staying out of prison is what he values most, he should encourage his lawyer to raise only his two or three best arguments on appeal, and he should defer to his lawyer's advice as to which are the best arguments. The Constitution, however, does not require clients to be wise, and other policies should be weighed in the balance as well.

It is no secret that indigent clients often mistrust the lawyers appointed to represent them. See generally Burt, Conflict and Trust Between Attorney and Client, 69 Geo.L.J. 1015 (1981); Skolnick, Social Control in the Adversary System, 11 J. Conflict Res. 52 (1967). There are many reasons for this, some perhaps unavoidable even under perfect conditions—differences in education, disposition, and socioeconomic class—and some that should (but may not always) be zealously avoided. A lawyer and his client do not always have the same interests. Even with paying clients, a lawyer may have a strong interest in having judges and prosecutors think well of him, and, if he is working for a flat fee—a common arrangement for criminal defense attorneys—or if his fees for court appointments are lower than he would receive for other work, he has an obvious financial incentive to conclude cases on his criminal docket swiftly. Good lawyers undoubtedly recognize these temptations and resist them, and they endeavor to convince their clients that they will. It would be naive, however, to suggest that they always succeed in either task. A constitutional rule that encourages lawyers to disregard their clients' wishes without compelling need can only exacerbate the clients' suspicion of their lawyers.... In the end, what the Court hopes to gain in effectiveness of appellate representation by the rule it imposes today may well be lost to decreased effectiveness in other areas of representation.

. . .

Finally, today's ruling denigrates the values of individual autonomy and dignity central to many constitutional rights, especially those Fifth and Sixth Amendment rights that come into play in the criminal process. Certainly a person's life changes when he is charged with a crime and brought to trial. He must, if he harbors any hope of success, defend himself on terms—often technical and hard to understand—that are the State's, not his own. As a practical matter, the assistance of counsel is necessary to that defense. See Johnson v. Zerbst, 304 U.S., at 463, 58 S.Ct., at 1022.... The role of the defense lawyer should be above all to function as the instrument and defender of the client's autonomy and dignity in all phases of the criminal process.

... The Court subtly but unmistakably adopts a different conception of the defense lawyer's role—he need do nothing beyond what the State, not his client, considers most important. In many ways, having a lawyer becomes one of the many indignities visited upon someone who has the ill fortune to run afoul of the criminal justice system.

I cannot accept the notion that lawyers are one of the punishments a person receives merely for being accused of a crime. Clients, if they wish, are capable of making informed judgments about which issues to appeal, and when they exercise that prerogative their choices should be respected unless they would require lawyers to violate their consciences, the law, or their duties to the court. On the other hand, I would not presume lightly that, in a particular case, a defendant has disregarded his lawyer's obviously sound advice.... The Court of Appeals, in reversing the District Court, did not address the factual question whether respondent, having been advised by his lawyer that it would not be wise to appeal on all the issues respondent had suggested, actually insisted in a timely fashion that his lawyer brief the nonfrivolous issues identified by the Court of Appeals.... If he did not, or if he was content with filing his pro se brief, then there would be no deprivation of the right to the assistance of counsel. I would remand for a hearing on this question.

Note on Jones v. Barnes: "Professional expertise"
or "professional dominance"?

1. *Who's coercing whom?* Chief Justice Burger describes the rule that he refuses to adopt* as one that would permit the client "to compel" counsel to raise issues against his or her professional judgment, while Justice Brennan sees the majority's rule as subjecting a defendant to "restrictions on individual autonomy." Each sees the side that he favors as seeking to avoid coercion by the other. This observation may suggest that lawyer autonomy and client autonomy are engaged in a zero-sum struggle, a tug of war, in which one can be honored only at the expense of the other. To the extent that is so, the issue cannot be resolved, can it, simply by taking a stand in favor of autonomy and against coercion.

Neither Justice, however, seems to see it that way. Each writes as if he were simply favoring autonomy over coercion. Is the solution to be found in the following set of observations? Justice Brennan's opinion asserts that the majority decision requires Barnes to "relinquish control over ... his own case," suggesting that what Barnes sought to control was *his own,* and that he was therefore not coercing his lawyer any more than I would be coercing you by using force to keep *your* foot off *my* neck. Chief Justice Burger, on the other hand, at one point asserts that the Brennan position "seriously undermines the ability of counsel to present the client's case in accord with counsel's professional evaluation," suggesting that there is a relevant sense in which "counsel's professional evaluation" *belongs* to counsel, in which event a client would be "coercing" counsel to surrender control over something that was personal to counsel. The inference is that the answer to the question whether an "anti-coercion" stance points to one result or the other depends on the answer to the question, "Whose case is it?"

2. *Whose case is it?* What factors channel one's answer to this question? Consider, first, the *instrumental* consequences of lawyer or client control over the issue of choice of grounds for appeal, that is, which rule is likely to produce better litigative outcomes: Do Chief Justice Burger and Justice Brennan differ in their evaluation of those consequences? Do they differ in their view of the relevance of such an evaluation? In that connection, think about what Justice Brennan says about client mistrust of their attorneys, especially, indigent clients' mistrust of assigned counsel. Describe the differing ways in which Justice Brennan and Chief Justice Burger apparently think the law should respond to the existence of such mistrust.

Consider, second, the client's and the attorney's *autonomy* interests. What are those interests, with respect to the issue in question? To what extent are they legitimate, to what extent are they of substantial weight? Do the Justices differ, or (since the opinions are not explicit here) seem to differ, on this issue too?

---

* The case is complicated by the presence of an important issue—the scope of federal habeas corpus review of state-court judgments of conviction—that is not relevant to the subject of this book, but is of great salience to the Justices, and on which they differ significantly from one another. For purposes of considering the light that the opinions cast on the question of professional expertise and professional dominance, I will not take this factor further into account.

How would *you* weigh the strength and legitimacy of the autonomy interests of lawyer and client here?

3. *The politics of legal reasoning.* (a) To what extent, and in what ways, do the Justices' (or your) overall "celebratory" or "troubled" stance toward the legal system, referred to in the Note on the *Hackin* decision, *supra,* play a significant role in affecting their (or your) thinking here too?

- Note the high level of comfort with the workings of the judicial system evidenced in the Chief Justice's opinion, beginning with his inclusion early in his opinion of the (legally irrelevant) facts tending to suggest that Barnes was clearly guilty, and his reference, in n. 3, to his habeas corpus petition as a "foray"; compare Justice Brennan's reference, toward the end of his dissenting opinion, to the defendant as having had the "ill fortune" to "run afoul" of the legal system. Are there other, more substantive manifestations of the connection suggested by the opening question?

- Whatever may be true of the Justices, is there a significant connection between *your* basic "stance" toward the legal system and your reaction to the legal issues and competing arguments presented in the *Jones v. Barnes* opinions?

(b) Compare the opinions in *Jones v. Barnes* with those in *Hackin* with respect to the differing modes of legal reasoning that the Justices employ. Chief Justice Burger enumerates several specific areas in which the law has adopted the view that the client, and not the lawyer, has decisional authority, and notes that they do not apply to the question of choice of argument on appeal. Justice Brennan seeks to give the constitutional term, "assistance of counsel," meaning in light of the underlying values that he believes should shape the law. The former view is obviously less hospitable, the other more hospitable, to previously unrecognized claims.

- Is it fair to say that the Justices probably adopt one or the other mode of legal reasoning *because of* that "hospitability" effect?

- If so, is the extent of one's hospitability to hospitality yet another manifestation of one's "celebratory" or "troubled" stance toward the legal system?

Test the truth of the contentions made in the two preceding sentences by reflecting on *your* preferred style of legal reasoning, and the probable sources of that preference.

(c) *Professional Role-Differentiation*

[T]he function and responsibility of a law firm . . . was to serve and represent each client as an individual, whether the client was a corporate malefactor or a presumably saintly civil libertarian. Once a client had been accepted, the lawyer's course was clear. If the interest of the client required the lawyer to advocate a position or seek a result which he personally disliked or even which he considered contrary to society's welfare, it was the lawyer's duty to do so with all his mind and heart, subject only to the restrictions and proprieties which the rules and conventions impose. Ezra Pound, the Grand Kleagle of the Ku Klux Klan, a cigarette company, a rapist, a great corporation which polluted the streams, a government typist—all were entitled to and received the same total commitment and dedication, once their cause had been undertaken. And the social implications of the position to be taken on the client's behalf were submerged by the lawyer's dedication to the value of the legal and constitutional system as he saw it, to the duty of the advocate, and to the obligations of advocacy in an adversary system.

Justice Abe Fortas*

SPAULDING v. ZIMMERMAN
Supreme Court of Minnesota, 1962.
263 Minn. 346, 116 N.W.2d 704.

THOMAS GALLAGHER, JUSTICE.

Appeal from an order of the District Court of Douglas County vacating and setting aside a prior order of such court dated May 8, 1957, approving a settlement made on behalf of David Spaulding on March 5, 1957, at which time he was a minor of the age of 20 years; and in connection therewith, vacating and setting aside releases executed by him and his parents, a stipulation of dismissal, an order for dismissal with prejudice, and a judgment entered pursuant thereto.

. . .

On appeal defendants contend that the court was without jurisdiction to vacate the settlement solely because their counsel then possessed information, unknown to plaintiff herein, that at the time he was suffering from an aorta aneurysm which may have resulted from the accident, because [among other grounds] no duty rested upon them to disclose information to plaintiff which they could assume had been disclosed to him by his own physicians; . . . .

---

* Fortas, Thurman Arnold and the The-   (1970).
atre of the Law, 79 Yale L.J. 988, 996

After the accident, David's injuries were diagnosed by his family physician, Dr. James H. Cain, as a severe crushing injury of the chest with multiple rib fractures; a severe cerebral concussion, probably with petechial hemorrhages of the brain; and bilateral fractures of the clavicles. At Dr. Cain's suggestion, on January 3, 1957, David was examined by Dr. John F. Pohl, an orthopedic specialist, who made X-ray studies of his chest. Dr. Pohl's detailed report of this examination included the following:

> "... The lung fields are clear. The heart and aorta are normal."

Nothing in such report indicated the aorta aneurysm with which David was then suffering....

In the meantime, on February 22, 1957, at defendants' request, David was examined by Dr. Hewitt Hannah, a neurologist. On February 26, 1957, the latter reported to Messrs. Field Arvesen & Donoho, attorneys for defendant John Zimmerman, as follows:

> "The one feature of the case which bothers me more than any other part of the case is the fact that this boy of 20 years of age has an aneurysm, which means a dilatation of the aorta and the arch of the aorta. Whether this came out of this accident I cannot say with any degree of certainty and I have discussed it with the Roentgenologist and a couple of Internists. ... Of course an aneurysm or dilatation of the aorta in a boy of this age is a serious matter as far as his life. This aneurysm may dilate further and it might rupture with further dilatation and this would cause his death.

> "It would be interesting also to know whether the X-ray of his lungs, taken immediately following the accident, shows this dilatation or not. If it was not present immediately following the accident and is now present, then we could be sure that it came out of the accident."

Prior to the negotiations for settlement, the contents of the above report were made known to counsel for defendants Florian and John Ledermann.

The case was called for trial on March 4, 1957, at which time the respective parties and their counsel possessed such information as to David's physical condition as was revealed to them by their respective medical examiners as above described. It is thus apparent that neither David nor his father, the nominal plaintiff in the prior action, was then aware that David was suffering the aorta aneurysm but on the contrary believed that he was recovering from the injuries sustained in the accident.

On the following day an agreement for settlement was reached wherein, in consideration of the payment of $6,500, David and his father agreed to settle in full for all claims arising out of the accident.

Richard S. Roberts, counsel for David, thereafter presented to the court a petition for approval of the settlement, wherein David's injuries were described as:

"... severe crushing of the chest, with multiple rib fractures, severe cerebral concussion, with petechial hemorrhages of the brain, bilateral fractures of the clavicles."

Attached to the petition were affidavits of David's physicians, Drs. James H. Cain and Paul S. Blake, wherein they set forth the same diagnoses they had made upon completion of their respective examinations of David as above described. At no time was there information disclosed to the court that David was then suffering from an aorta aneurysm which may have been the result of the accident. Based upon the petition for settlement and such affidavits of Drs. Cain and Blake, the court on May 8, 1957, made its order approving the settlement.

Early in 1959, David was required by the army reserve, of which he was a member, to have a physical checkup. For this, he again engaged the services of Dr. Cain. In this checkup, the latter discovered the aorta aneurysm. He then reexamined the X rays which had been taken shortly after the accident and at this time discovered that they disclosed the beginning of the process which produced the aneurysm. He promptly sent David to Dr. Jerome Grismer for an examination and opinion. The latter confirmed the finding of the aorta aneurysm and recommended immediate surgery therefor. This was performed by him at Mount Sinai Hospital in Minneapolis on March 10, 1959.

Shortly thereafter, David, having attained his majority, instituted the present action for additional damages due to the more serious injuries including the aorta aneurysm which he alleges proximately resulted from the accident. As indicated above, the prior order for settlement was vacated. In a memorandum made a part of the order vacating the settlement, the court stated:

"...

"The mistake concerning the existence of the aneurysm was not mutual. For reasons which do not appear, plaintiff's doctor failed to ascertain its existence. By reason of the failure of plaintiff's counsel to use available rules of discovery, plaintiff's doctor and all his representatives did not learn that defendants and their agents knew of its existence and possible serious consequences. Except for the character of the concealment in the light of plaintiff's minority, the Court would, I believe, be justified in denying plaintiff's motion to vacate, leaving him to whatever questionable remedy he may have against his doctor and against his lawyer.

"That defendants' counsel concealed the knowledge they had is not disputed.... There is no doubt of the good faith of both defendants' counsel. There is no doubt that during the course of the negotiations, when the parties were in an adversary relationship, no rule required or duty rested upon defendants or their representatives to disclose this knowledge. However, once the agreement to settle was reached, it is difficult to characterize the parties' relationship as adverse. At this point all parties were interested in securing Court approval....

" ...

"When the adversary nature of the negotiations concluded in a settlement, the procedure took on the posture of a joint application to the Court, at least so far as the facts upon which the Court could and must approve settlement is concerned. It is here that the true nature of the concealment appears, and defendants' failure to act affirmatively, after having been given a copy of the application for approval, can only be defendants' decision to take a calculated risk that the settlement would be final....

"To hold that the concealment was not of such character as to result in an unconscionable advantage over plaintiff's ignorance or mistake, would be to penalize innocence and incompetence and reward less than full performance of an officer of the Court's duty to make full disclosure to the Court when applying for approval in minor settlement proceedings."

... The principles applicable to the court's authority to vacate settlements made on behalf of minors and approved by it appear well established....

...

... From the foregoing it is clear that in the instant case the court did not abuse its discretion in setting aside the settlement which it had approved on plaintiff's behalf while he was still a minor.... The seriousness of this disability ... was known by counsel for both defendants but was not disclosed to the court at the time it was petitioned to approve the settlement. While no canon of ethics or legal obligation may have required them to inform plaintiff or his counsel with respect thereto, or to advise the court therein, it did become obvious to them at the time that the settlement then made did not contemplate or take into consideration the disability described. This fact opened the way for the court to later exercise its discretion in vacating the settlement and under the circumstances described we cannot say that there was any abuse of discretion on the part of the court in so doing....

Note on Spaulding: "Role differentiation" or "hired gun"?

1. Defendants argued on appeal that counsel "could assume" that the information had been disclosed to plaintiff by his own physicians, even though it was conceded that counsel knew that it had not been disclosed, indeed, that plaintiff's physicians were unaware of the existence of the aneurysm. The argument was that defendants' counsel should be free to act *as if* plaintiff and his attorney knew facts that in actuality they did not

know. The inadequacies of plaintiff's doctors, who did not discover the aneurysm, and his lawyer, who did not seek to obtain defendants' medical report through discovery, should not, on this view, affect the professional responsibility of defendants' lawyers.

Spell out, as fully as you can, the premises underlying this position.

2. It is clear from Model Rule 1.6 and DR 4–101(B) of the Model Code—both adopted long after the decision in *Spaulding*—that the drafters of the professional codes not only agree with the *Spaulding* court that a lawyer in the position of defendants' counsel should have no duty to disclose the fact of the aneurysm during settlement negotiations with counsel for plaintiff, but that he or she should have a duty *not* to do so. Comments 1 through 4 and 9 to MR 1.6 attempt to provide a rationale for this position. To what extent, if at all, does that rationale seem to you sufficient to explain the requirement of nondisclosure?

3. Is your own view similar to or different from those reflected in *Spaulding* and the preceding Notes? What would *you* hope to have done had you been counsel for defendants during the settlement negotiations? Would you have:

- concluded that any problem was the responsibility of plaintiff's attorney and his doctor, not yours or your client's?

- counseled your clients that they should authorize you to make disclosure, but left the decision to the clients?

- advised the clients that, unless they authorized disclosure, you would not continue to act as counsel in the case?

- advised the clients that, should they refuse to authorize disclosure, you would not only withdraw but would advise plaintiff or his counsel of the facts about the aneurysm?

Ask yourself what the *sources* of your responses are. Specifically (but not exclusively), to what extent does your self-identification as a "celebrator" or "doubter" of the overall justice of the legal system, as described in the Notes following *Hackin* and *Jones v. Barnes,* seem a significant part of your answer here?

4. Compare with *Spaulding* the circumstances of Zabella v. Pakel, 242 F.2d 452 (7th Cir.1957).

Defendant Pakel is President and Manager of the Chicago Savings and Loan Association. In the 1920s he was a contractor. For a time during that period, Zabella worked for him as a carpenter. From time to time defendant borrowed money from plaintiff. None of it was repaid, but defendant executed new notes for the amounts due plus interest. The note given on September 1, 1931 for $4,577.00 and which is the subject of this suit, included amounts due on previous notes and was the last note received by plaintiff from defendant.

Under date of December 28, 1929 defendant and his wife executed three warranty deeds in which plaintiff and his wife were named as grantees. Two of the conveyances covered vacant lots. The third deed covered property where defendant resided. Each of these conveyances was sent or brought to the Recorder's office of Cook County and was recorded on December 30, 1929. A notation on each deed shows that it was returned to the defendant.

The plaintiff testified he knew nothing of these deeds until 1952. In that year, one Gaw desired to purchase a vacant lot which was described in one of the deeds from Pakel to plaintiff. [Pakel aided Zabella in selling this lot, and suggested to him that he "come back and see me again. I have some more property in your name"]. Plaintiff testified that two months later he visited Pakel again, at which time Pakel had a large number of deeds and papers in a desk drawer. He picked out two deeds and gave them to plaintiff, telling him to see if he could get anything out of them.

The debt was not repaid, and Zabella brought suit. Defendant asserted that the claim was barred by both the 10–year statute of limitations and by a discharge in bankruptcy that he had obtained in 1937. The court upheld these defenses, and held that the transactions in 1952 were not sufficient to imply a new promise to pay the balance so as to revive the discharged debt or recommence the running of the period of limitations. The court concluded:

> Of course, the jury was justified in thinking that defendant who then was in a position of some affluence and was the Chief Executive Officer of the Chicago Savings and Loan Association should feel obligated to pay an honest debt to his old friend, employee and countryman. Nevertheless, we are obliged to follow the law.... The ... suggestion that payments would be made under certain vague conditions that might obtain in the future [was] not a sufficient basis for the jury's verdict favorable to the plaintiff.

———

(a) Assume that you had been consulted by Pakel regarding Zabella's claim. Consider these three related but differing questions:

- How would you have advised Pakel?
- Assuming that Pakel would not pay the claim voluntarily, would you have agreed to represent him in the lawsuit?
- If so, would you have consented to plead the statute of limitations?

As part of your consideration of these questions, compare the situation with that facing counsel for the Zimmermans. In what ways is *Pakel* an easier case for giving primacy to the client's interest? Is it in any way a harder case?

(b) What answers to the three questions that are presented at the beginning of sub-section (a), above, are suggested by Model Rule 1.2? Does the Model Code—see EC 7–8, and compare DR 7–101(A)(1) with DR 7–101(B)(1)—differ from the Rules in approach or outcome?

Sub-section (a) also asks whether there are ways in which the question presented to Pakel's lawyer was an easier one than that facing the Zimmermans' lawyer. Note that, under the Model Rules and the

Model Code, any such differences would be irrelevant. (Why do I say that?) Why would the professional norms take such a position? Do you agree or disagree with that position?

(c) Abraham Lincoln, then a practicing lawyer, once answered a question similar to that presented by *Pakel* in these terms:

> Yes, we can doubtless gain your case for you; we can set a whole neighborhood at loggerheads; we can distress a widowed mother and her six fatherless children and thereby get you six hundred dollars to which you seem to have a legal claim, but which rightfully belongs, it appears to me, as much to the woman and her children as it does to you. You must remember that some things legally right are not morally right. We shall not take your case, but will give a little advice for which we will charge you nothing. You seem to be a sprightly, energetic man; we would advise you to try your hand at making six hundred dollars in some other way.

W.H. Herndon & J.W. Weik, Life of Lincoln 279 (1942).

- What is your reaction?

- Were you to find yourself inclined to act as Lincoln did, what thoughts would the professional codes prompt in you? Consider Rule 1.2 (including Comments 3 and 4) and its Code analogues (including EC 7–8).

2. THE BASIC QUESTION OF JUSTIFICATION

The preceding section has presented some examples of the principal components of what this book terms "the traditional concept of advocacy." The question that immediately arises has been stated by Richard Wasserstrom as "whether there is adequate justification for the kind of moral universe that comes to be inhabited by the lawyer as he or she goes through professional life." Wasserstrom, Lawyers as Professionals: Some Moral Issues, 5 Human Rights 1 (1975) (ABA Section of Individual Rights and Responsibilities). The question may not be turned aside, Charles Fried has observed, by the assertion that "anyone whose conscience is so tender that he cannot fulfill the prescribed obligations of a professional should not undertake those obligations. [T]his suggestion merely pushes the inquiry back a step. We must ask then not how a decent lawyer may behave, but whether a decent, ethical person can ever be a lawyer." Fried, The Lawyer as Friend: The Moral Foundations of the Lawyer–Client Relation, 85 Yale L.J. 1060, 1062 (1976).

The materials in this section are designed to trigger your own engagement with this question. The initial reading will demonstrate, among other matters, that the question is no latter-day consequence of recent changes in the practice of law.

(a) *The Question Posed Socratically*

PLATO, GORGIAS

Read *The Gorgias*. Any edition will do; I have found the Penguin Classics edition (Hamilton trans., 1960) easy to use in several ways. You might read the following Note prior to reading the work, although you should read it afterward in any event.

Note on The Gorgias: The lawyer as panderer

1. Gorgias was an orator, and teacher of rhetoric; this book is about being a lawyer: Why *The Gorgias?*

Socrates engages Gorgias in conversation in order to ask him "what the power of his art consists in and what it is that he professes and teaches" (447 *). Gorgias' answer is that the art of oratory is the ability to produce conviction in the mind of the hearer. About what? —about questions of right and wrong. How? —through persuasion or belief, rather than knowledge. Its appeal as a profession, Gorgias asserts, is that it gives its practitioner influence over one's fellow-countrymen, advancement in public life, and the "great comfort" of being able "to meet specialists in all the other arts on equal terms without going to the trouble of acquiring more than this single one" (459). In light of these responses, can what follows be thought *not* applicable to the practice of law?

2. To Socrates, Gorgias' profession is not an art at all, but merely a "knack," the knack of "producing a kind of gratification and pleasure"; it is a variety of "pandering" (462–63), requiring only "a shrewd and bold spirit together with a natural aptitude for dealing with men" (463).

- According to Socrates, why is so harsh a judgment warranted?

- Do his reasons (whatever their merit) appear applicable to the practice of law, in particular, to the concepts of role-differentiation and professional expertise as they are reflected in the materials studied thus far in this book?

3. Gorgias, Polus, and Callicles each in turn attempt to offer a justification for the profession of oratory. Consider:

    (a) the content of the three responses, and the ways in which they differ from one another;

    (b) Socrates' answer to each;

    (c) the extent to which the voices of Gorgias, Polus, and Callicles can be heard today, in law schools, the legal profession, the larger society, and your own mind;

    (d) your own reactions.

4. Callicles not only seeks to answer Socrates' charge; he questions the value of spending much time over the issue of justification, and urges Socrates to give up dwelling on matters appropriate only for adolescents, to "learn the accomplishments of active life" (486), and to model his life on

---

* This and succeeding references are to the "Stephanus" pagination, to be found in the margins of most editions of Plato's *Dialogues.*

"those who have a good livelihood and reputation and many other blessings" (*id.*). Socrates continues to insist:

> [T]here can be no finer subject for discussion than the question what a man [sic] should be like and what occupation he should engage in and how ... he should pursue it, both in earlier and later life. (487–88)

Callicles' challenge (which I encourage you to reread at this point; see 484–86) rings loudly today in all aspects of our society, and especially so in professional education. This book is premised on my belief that Callicles is wrong on this score, that his challenge is a siren song whose power needs to be acknowledged so that it can be resisted. To what extent do you and I part company at the outset on this fundamental question? If we do (part company), I ask that you revisit this question from time to time as you go through the book.

5. Consider finally a question regarding Socrates' use of the "socratic method." Socrates insists that his purpose in asking questions is not "to win a verbal victory" (457–58), that he is seeking to persuade no one but the person with whom he is speaking (see especially 471–72 and 474 for eloquent expressions of his method as he perceives it); and that he is "not speaking dogmatically from the certainty of assured knowledge; [he is] simply your fellow-explorer in the search for truth" (506). Yet his interlocutors view him as manipulative and a "bully" (505), "always set upon victory" (515), and the Dialogue ends in a prolonged monologue.

- Perhaps this dissonance is simply a product of the participants' personalities, or of Socrates' style of discourse. Try your hand, for example, at discerning the sleight of hand in his argument about the relative pain involved in doing and in suffering wrong, at page 475.

- Even so, do you think that there may be more than this, something of general significance, at work here?

- Is your experience of the "socratic method" in law school relevant to your response to this last question?

(b) *The Question in Modern Dress*

Note: Being a lawyer as acting in a role

1. The core of the concept of role-defined behavior is that the answers to questions like those posed with respect to the attorneys for Pakel and Zimmerman are determined *a priori*, rather than situationally: "*As* a lawyer, I do not divulge information harmful to my client without his or her informed consent"; "*as* a lawyer, I am obliged (and therefore entitled) to assist a client who wishes to avoid a just debt by legally available means."

The concept of role is of course not limited to lawyering—"as a worker, I am not interested in the use to which the product on which I work is put"; "as a student, I allow my teachers to decide what I need to learn"; "as a wife, I put my husband's career ahead of my own"; "as a corporate director, my sole responsibility is to the shareholders"—and it may be that the ready acceptance that the power of role has won in lawyering simply mirrors its similar prevalence in our society generally.

Two aspects of these additional examples of role are worthy of note: First, in each example the concept serves to justify or require a response to the situation at hand that is relatively detached or passive, in the sense that, except for the one concern about which it cares strongly (client, wages, husband's career, shareholders), it is indifferent to what is at stake in a given situation. Is that so simply because of the examples I have chosen, or is the observation generally apt with respect to the role of role? Second, the appropriateness of a strong concept of role in each of the above contexts has been seriously disputed, in part because of the quality of passivity or detachment associated with it.

2. What is the *content* of the lawyer's role? While no catalogue can be complete and useful, the following paragraphs attempt to articulate some fundamental aspects of the prevailing answer. Think about the consistency of this summary with the ways in which you have observed lawyers act or have heard it suggested that they should act. Your observations may have been grounded in cases you have read, in first-hand contact that you have had with lawyers, or in approving or disapproving statements that you have heard. Recall that what follows is meant to describe what, in the dominant model, is prescribed; it is presented to raise, and not to foreclose, the question whether, as a prescription, you find it justified.

(a) *A lawyer is not responsible for the consequences of his or her work, so long as they do not flow from his or her unlawful acts or from incompetence.* A legendary aphorism summing up this principle is attributed to Justice Holmes, who, on being dropped off one day at the Supreme Court building, is said to have responded to a departing sally of Judge Learned Hand's: "Do justice," with the reply, "That's not my job, sonny. My job is to play the game according to the rules." The traditional "rule" of professional responsibility is succinctly stated—as a rule of *non*responsibility—in Rule 1.2(b) of the Model Rules: "A lawyer's representation of a client ... does not constitute an endorsement of the client's political, economic, social or moral views or activities."

The ethic that one does not judge one's client's aims or methods finds a parallel in the principle that one does not get "over-involved" in them either. Professional zeal and professional detachment are complementary, rather than competing, norms. That the client loses is no more *your* problem (assuming that it was not on account of your lack of skill or judgment) than that your client wins. Someone else decides what the rules should be, and applies them. Your attempt to influence that process on your client's behalf does not implicate you in the outcome, one way or the other.

(b) *One's personal values are an inappropriate input to decision-making as a lawyer.* Professional detachment extends to detachment from one's own, as well as the client's, priorities and values. It is not only permissible to separate oneself from one's client and his or her objectives and tactics, it is inappropriate not to do so, and inappropriate to "intrude" one's own concerns into the representation. Note the narrowness of the Model Code's formulations, for example: A lawyer may (but need not) counsel a client in ways that take account of moral as well as legal consequences, EC 7–8; he or she may, "where permissible [*sic*], ... fail to assert a [client's] right or position," DR 7–101(B)(1); and a lawyer may (but need not) "refuse to aid in conduct that he believes to be unlawful," although the illegality is not clearly established, DR 7–101(B)(2). The inference is, is it not, that refusal to aid is appropriate only in cases of *unlawful* client conduct. Withdrawal from the representation is permitted, where the client is acting contrary to the lawyer's "judgment and advice," *only* if the matter is not pending before a tribunal, DR 2–110(C)(1)(e), and is in any event not required unless the lawyer "knows or it is obvious" that the client's position is designed "merely for the purpose of harassing or maliciously injuring" another person, DR 2–110(B)(1). The overall tone is plainly that a client is entitled to have the services of a lawyer's legal talents, free of encumbrance by other things that he or she cares about.

There is presumably a freer discretion to decline to accept a client in the first place on "personal" grounds than there is to withdraw from or limit it. However, the prevalent structure of law practice tends to make the availability of a financially attractive representational opportunity the major criterion of choice of client. Going where the money is is deemed to be a neutral choice; placing any other consideration on the scales bears a burden, sometimes a significant burden, of explanation and justification.

(c) *A lawyer tends to be profoundly skeptical about values, viewing truth and justice as essentially subjective, manipulable concepts.* To what extent does your experience of legal education support this conclusion of Roger Cramton?

> Modern dogmas entangle legal education—a moral relativism tending toward nihilism, a pragmatism tending toward amoral instrumentalism, a realism tending toward cynicism, [and] an individualism tending toward atomism . . . .

Cramton, The Ordinary Religion of the Classroom, 29 J.Leg.Educ. 247, 262 (1978).

To the extent that this perception is accurate, it may not be attributable solely to the personalities of teachers or lawyers, but may also be a product of the system of partisan advocacy and its attendant faith in procedural fairness as a means of achieving just results. With each side claiming truth, justice, and fundamental values as support for its position, it is easy to come to view them as merely rhetorical devices. This tendency is reinforced, is it not, by the traditional lawyer's emphasis on proof and skepticism; again, Justice Holmes captured the prevailing philosophical approach in another famous one-liner: "The truth is what I can't help believing."

(d) *A lawyer acts as the guardian of mistrust, whose most significant task is to protect the client from an indifferent or hostile world.* Legal representation is associated with conflict, actual or potential; our dominant political and legal preferences place a great value on autonomy, defined as being free of having to do what others want one to do. The role of a lawyer is in these circumstances readily seen as to structure a transaction—a contract between people whose interests are not perceived as hostile, no less than a fiercely contested litigation—so as to leave his or her client as free as possible to do what he or she pleases, and to make it as difficult as possible for the other person(s) to take action not to the client's liking. The lawyer's experience reminds him or her of the many ways in which amicable relations can turn hostile, and in which self-interest can overcome collaboration, friendship, even love; and those reminders seem more salient than any contrary ones that might be available to the lawyer. Excessive suspicion can "kill a deal" that would have been to the client's advantage, and excessive trust that another person will not take advantage of the client can aid in making a deal that leaves the client insufficiently protected should the relationship turn sour in some significant respect: Both are failures in lawyering, but to err in the former direction is a minor vice, simply succumbing to an occupational hazard of the job, while the latter failing is a betrayal.

(e) *The effective practice of law rests on power and control. A good lawyer is one who dominates a situation.* The ready analogy is to military and athletic competitions. Winning is the aim, tactics and strategy the tools of achieving it.

Recall the question that preceded the foregoing catalogue: To what extent is the above an accurate portrayal of the prevalent conception of what it is to be a lawyer?

BECOMING A LAWYER: A HUMANISTIC PERSPECTIVE ON LEGAL EDUCATION AND PROFESSIONALISM
E. Dvorkin, J. Himmelstein, & H. Lesnick
West Pub. Co., 1981.

Read pages 1–26.*

Note: Role and identity

1. A central theme in several of the excerpts from *Becoming a Lawyer* is the distinction between role and identity.

- As you think about yourself as a lawyer, does that distinction seem to have validity?

- What was there about being a lawyer that drew you to that career choice?

- What, among those things, seems to have been reinforced by what you have learned about a lawyer's role?

- What seems to have been pushed into the background?

2. The Wasserstrom excerpt, *Becoming a Lawyer*, pp. 19–25, questions both the role-differentiation and the professional dominance of lawyers, while the traditional concept supports both. The former idea appears to place client preferences ahead of those of the lawyer, while the second appears to do the opposite. Is this paradoxical, or is there a reason why the two ideas are in harmony rather than in tension?

---

* The assigned pages in *Becoming a Lawyer* include the first of three sets of excerpts assigned in that book from Robert Bolt's study of Sir Thomas More, *A Man* *for All Seasons.* While the excerpts are intelligible for the purposes of this course, I encourage you to read the play, if you have not already done so, as it was written.

3. In questioning the justification for the traditional concept of advocacy, one might focus on its felt lack of a moral basis, on the personal costs to the lawyer, or on the social costs.

- Socrates' critique of oratory is an example of the first emphasis, questioning the value accorded persuasion rather than teaching, the advocate's lack of an underlying commitment to his or her own beliefs about truth, justice, and the common good.

- The above-noted pages in *Becoming a Lawyer* emphasize the personal costs to the lawyer. Try to identify those that seem suggested to you by the readings.

- Finally, one might focus on the social costs. Consider, in that connection, the following view:

    [W]hen professional action is estranged from ordinary moral experience, the lawyer's sensitivity to the moral costs in both ordinary and extraordinary situations tends to atrophy. The ideal of neutrality permits, indeed requires, that the lawyer regard his professional activities and their consequences from the point of view of the uninvolved spectator. One may abstractly regret that the injury is done, but this regret is analogous to the regret one feels as a spectator to [a] traffic accident ... This has troubling consequences: without a proper appreciation of the moral costs of one's actions one cannot make effective use of the faculty of practical judgement.... As Bernard Williams argued, "only those who are [by practice] reluctant or disinclined to do the morally disagreeable when it is really necessary have much chance of not doing it when it is not necessary...."

Gerald Postema, Moral Responsibility in Professional Ethics, 55 N.Y.U.L.Rev. 63, 79–80 (1980).

Which set of concerns (if any) seems most salient to you, based on your own experience of legal education and—first- or second-hand—of lawyering?

4. The question whether the traditional concept of a lawyer's role is justified or is seriously flawed can be addressed at several levels. The most familiar one is to ask whether it would be a good or a bad idea for the profession, the courts, or the legislatures to make changes in the official expressions of that concept. The controversy that has accompanied the drafting and proposed adoption or amendment of the Model Rules as a successor to the Model Code, first within the organized Bar and then within each State, is a recent, ongoing instance of such an approach; the current effort by the American Law Institute to restate "the law of lawyering" is another. In these examples, the issue is posed as one of public policy.

Another approach is for each of us to ask ourselves: "What concept of lawyering do *I* want to follow in my professional life? As discussed in the Introduction, this book takes this second approach. Its effort is not so much to aid you in thinking about the question whether (for example) Model Rule so-and-so should be amended in one or another respects, as it is to trigger your own engagement with your emergent professional stance. We will not ignore the question whether individual choice does or should exist with respect to questions of professional responsibility. Indeed, after looking at some of the controversies that have arisen with respect to several aspects of the traditional concept of advocacy, we will examine carefully several factors that operate for many as powerful barriers to attempts to articulate an alternative concept. For the present, I ask that you not assume *a priori* that individual choice plays or should play little part. My aim is for you to take to heart the thought that underlies the admonition attributed to George Fox, the 17th Century founder of the Religious Society of Friends (Quakers):

> You will say, Christ saith this, and the apostles say this; but what canst thou say?

THE LAWYER AS FRIEND: THE MORAL FOUNDATIONS OF THE LAWYER–CLIENT RELATION

Charles Fried
85 Yale L.J. 1060 (1976).

Advocatus sed non ladro,
Res miranda populo . . . .
Medieval anthem
honoring St. Ives

Can a good lawyer be a good person? The question troubles lawyers and law students alike. They are troubled by the demands of loyalty to one's client and by the fact that one can win approval as a good, maybe even great, lawyer even though that loyalty is engrossed by over-privileged or positively distasteful clients. How, they ask, is such loyalty compatible with that devotion to the common good characteristic of high moral principles? And whatever their views of the common good, they are troubled because the willingness of lawyers to help their clients use the law to the prejudice of the weak or the innocent seems morally corrupt. The lawyer is conventionally seen as a professional devoted to his client's interests and as authorized, if not in fact required, to do some things (though not anything) for that client which he would not do for himself.[1] In this essay I consider the

---

1. See, e.g., J. Auerbach, Unequal Justice (1976); M. Green, The Other Government (1975).

Lord Brougham stated the traditional view of the lawyer's role during his defense of Queen Caroline:

[A]n advocate, in the discharge of his duty, knows but one person in all the world, and that person is his client. To save that client by all means and expedients, and at all hazards and costs to other persons, and, among them, to himself, is his first and only duty; and in performing this duty he must not regard the alarm, the torments, the destruction which he may bring upon others. Separating the duty of a patriot from that of an advocate, he must go on reckless of consequences, though it should be his unhappy fate to involve his country in confusion.

Trial of Queen Caroline 8 (J. Nightingale ed. 1821). A sharply contrasting view was held by law professors at the University of Havana who said that "the first job of a revolutionary lawyer is not to argue that his client is innocent, but rather to determine if his client is guilty and, if so, to seek the sanction which will best rehabilitate him." Berman, The Cuban Popular Tribunals, 69 Colum.L.Rev. 1317, 1341

compatibility between this traditional conception of the lawyer's role and the ideal of moral purity—the ideal that one's life should be lived in fulfillment of the most demanding moral principles, and not just barely within the law. So I shall not be particularly concerned with the precise limits imposed on the lawyer's conduct by positive rules of law and by the American Bar Association's *Code of Professional Responsibility* except as these provide a background. I assume that the lawyer observes these scrupulously. My inquiry is one of morals: Does the lawyer whose conduct and choices are governed only by the traditional conception of the lawyer's role, which these positive rules reflect, lead a professional life worthy of moral approbation, worthy of respect—ours and his own?

. . .

Two frequent criticisms of the traditional conception of the lawyer's role attack both its ends and its means. First, it is said that the ideal of professional loyalty to one's client permits, even demands, an allocation of the lawyer's time, passion, and resources in ways that are not always maximally conducive to the greatest good of the greatest number. Interestingly, this criticism is leveled increasingly against doctors as well as lawyers. Both professions affirm the principle that the professional's primary loyalty is to his client, his patient. A "good" lawyer will lavish energy and resources on his existing client, even if it can be shown that others could derive greater benefit from them. The professional ideal authorizes a care for the client and the patient which exceeds what the efficient distribution of a scarce social resource (the professional's time) would dictate.

That same professional ideal has little or nothing to say about the initial choice of clients or patients. Certainly it is laudable if the doctor and lawyer choose their clients among the poorest or sickest or most dramatically threatened, but the professional ideal does not require this kind of choice in any systematic way—the choice of client remains largely a matter of fortuity or arbitrary choice. But once the client has been chosen, the professional ideal requires primary loyalty to the client whatever his need or situation. Critics contend that it is wasteful and immoral that some of the finest talent in the legal profession is devoted to the intricacies of, say, corporate finance or elaborate estate plans, while important public and private needs for legal services go unmet. The immorality of this waste is seen to be compounded when the clients who are the beneficiaries of this lavish attention use it to avoid their obligations in justice (if not in law) to society and to perpetuate their (legal) domination of the very groups whose greater needs these lawyers should be meeting.

(1969). And a Bulgarian attorney has been quoted as saying, " 'In a Socialist state there is no division of duty between the judge, prosecutor and defense counsel ... the defense must assist the prosecution to find the objective truth in a case.' " J. Kaplan, Criminal Justice: Introductory Cases and Materials 264–65 (1973).

The second criticism applies particularly to the lawyer. It addresses not the misallocation of scarce resources, which the lawyer's exclusive concern with his client's interests permits, but the means which this loyalty appears to authorize, tactics which procure advantages for the client at the direct expense of some identified opposing party. Examples are discrediting a nervous but probably truthful complaining witness or taking advantage of the need or ignorance of an adversary in a negotiation. [Further discussion of this "second criticism" is omitted].

In this essay I will consider the moral status of the traditional conception of the professional. The two criticisms of this traditional conception, if left unanswered, will not put the lawyer in jail, but they will leave him without a moral basis for his acts. The real question is whether, in the face of these two criticisms, a decent and morally sensitive person can conduct himself according to the traditional conception of professional loyalty and still believe that what he is doing is morally worthwhile.

It might be said that anyone whose conscience is so tender that he cannot fulfill the prescribed obligations of a professional should not undertake those obligations. He should not allow his moral scruples to operate as a trap for those who are told by the law that they may expect something more. But of course this suggestion merely pushes the inquiry back a step. We must ask then not how a decent lawyer may behave, but whether a decent, ethical person can ever be a lawyer. Are the assurances implicit in assuming the role of lawyer such that an honorable person would not give them and thus would not enter the profession? And, indeed, this is a general point about an argument from obligation: It may be that the internal logic of a particular obligation demands certain forms of conduct (e.g., honor among thieves), but the question remains whether it is just and moral to contract such obligations.

I will argue in this essay that it is not only legally but also morally right that a lawyer adopt as his dominant purpose the furthering of his client's interests—that it is right that a professional put the interests of his client above some idea, however valid, of the collective interest. I maintain that the traditional conception of the professional role expresses a morally valid conception of human conduct and human relationships, that one who acts according to that conception is to that extent a good person. Indeed, it is my view that, far from being a mere creature of positive law, the traditional conception is so far mandated by moral right that any advanced legal system which did not sanction this conception would be unjust.

The general problem raised by the two criticisms is this: How can it be that it is not only permissible, but indeed morally right, to favor the interests of a particular person in a way which we can be fairly sure is either harmful to another particular individual or not maximally conducive to the welfare of society as a whole?

The resolution of this problem is aided, I think, if set in a larger perspective. Charles Curtis made the perspicacious remark that a lawyer may be privileged to lie for his client in a way that one might lie to save one's friends or close relatives.[17] I do not want to underwrite the notion that it is justifiable to lie even in those situations, but there is a great deal to the point that in those relations—friendship, kinship—we recognize an authorization to take the interests of particular concrete persons more seriously and to give them priority over the interests of the wider collectivity. One who provides an expensive education for his own children surely cannot be blamed because he does not use these resources to alleviate famine or to save lives in some distant land. Nor does he blame himself. Indeed, our intuition that an individual is authorized to prefer identified persons standing close to him over the abstract interests of humanity finds its sharpest expression in our sense that an individual is entitled to act with something less than impartiality to that person who stands closest to him—the person that he is. There is such a thing as selfishness to be sure, yet no reasonable morality asks us to look upon ourselves as merely plausible candidates for the distribution of the attention and resources which we command, plausible candidates whose entitlement to our own concern is no greater in principle than that of any other human being. Such a doctrine may seem edifying, but on reflection it strikes us as merely fanatical.

This suggests an interesting way to look at the situation of the lawyer. As a professional person one has a special care for the interests of those accepted as clients, just as his friends, his family, and he himself have a very general claim to his special concern. But I concede this does no more than widen the problem. It merely shows that in claiming this authorization to have a special care for my clients I am doing something which I do in other contexts as well.

. . .

Consider for a moment the picture of the human person that would emerge if the utilitarian claim were in fact correct. It would mean that in all my choices I must consider the well-being of all humanity—actual and potential—as the range of my concern. Moreover, every actual or potential human being is absolutely equal in his claims upon me. Indeed, I myself am to myself only as one of this innumerable multitude. And that is the clue to what is wrong with the utilitarian vision. Before there is morality there must be the person. We must attain and maintain in our morality a concept of personality such that it makes sense to posit choosing, valuing entities—free, moral beings. But the picture of the moral universe in which my own interests disappear and are merged into the interests of the totality of humanity is incompati-

17. .... Analogizing the lawyer to a friend raises a range of problems upon which I shall not touch. These have to do with the lawyer's benevolent and sometimes not so benevolent tyranny over and imposition on his client, seemingly authorized by the claim to be acting in the client's interests. Domineering paternalism is not a normal characteristic of friendship....

ble with that, because one wishes to develop a conception of a responsible, valuable, and valuing agent, and such an agent must first of all be dear to himself. It is from the kernel of individuality that the other things we value radiate. The Gospel says we must love our neighbor as ourselves, and this implies that any concern for others which is a *human* concern must presuppose a concern for ourselves. The human concern which we then show others is a concern which first of all recognizes the concrete individuality of that other person just as we recognize our own.

. . .

Therefore, it is not only consonant with, but also required by, an ethics for human beings that one be entitled first of all to reserve an area of concern for oneself and then to move out freely from that area if one wishes to lavish that concern on others to whom one stands in concrete, personal relations. Similarly, a person is entitled to enjoy this extra measure of care from those who choose to bestow it upon him without having to justify this grace as either just or efficient. We may choose the individuals to whom we will stand in this special relation, or they may be thrust upon us, as in family ties. . . .

In explicating the lawyer's relation to his client, my analogy shall be to friendship, where the freedom to choose and to be chosen expresses our freedom to hold something of ourselves in reserve, in reserve even from the universalizing claims of morality. These personal ties and the claims they engender may be all-consuming, as with a close friend or family member, or they may be limited, special-purpose claims, as in the case of the client or patient. The special-purpose claim is one in which the beneficiary, the client, is entitled to all the special consideration *within* the limits of the relationship which we accord to a friend or a loved one. It is not that the claims of the client are less intense or demanding; they are only more limited in their scope. After all, the ordinary concept of friendship provides only an analogy, and it is to the development of that analogy that I turn.

. . .

How does a professional fit into the concept of personal relations at all? He is, I have suggested, a limited-purpose friend. A lawyer is a friend in regard to the legal system. He is someone who enters into a personal relation with you—not an abstract relation as under the concept of justice. That means that like a friend he acts in your interests, not his own; or rather he adopts your interests as his own. I would call that the classic definition of friendship. To be sure, the lawyer's range of concern is sharply limited. But within that limited domain the intensity of identification with the client's interests is the same. It is not the specialized focus of the relationship which may make the metaphor inapposite, but the way in which the relation of legal friendship comes about and the one-sided nature of the ensuing "friendship."

. . .

The claims that are made on the doctor or lawyer are made within a social context and are defined, at least in part, by social expectations. Most strikingly, in talking about friendship the focus of the inquiry is quite naturally upon the free gift of the donor; yet in professional relationships it is the recipient's need for medical or legal aid which defines the relationship. So the source of the relationship seems to be located at the other end, that of the recipient. To put this disquiet another way, we might ask how recognizing the special claims of friendship in any way compels society to allow the doctor or the lawyer to define his role on the analogy of those claims. Why are these people not like other social actors designated to purvey certain, perhaps necessary, goods? Would we say that one's grocer, tailor, or landlord should be viewed as a limited-purpose friend? Special considerations must be brought forward for doctors and lawyers.

A special argument is at hand in both cases. The doctor does not minister just to any need, but to health. He helps maintain the very physical integrity which is the concrete substrate of individuality. To be sure, so does a grocer or landlord. But illness wears a special guise: it appears as a critical assault on one's person. The needs to which the doctor ministers usually are implicated in crises going to one's concreteness and individuality, and therefore what one looks for is a kind of ministration which is particularly concrete, personal, individualized. Thus, it is not difficult to see why I claim that a doctor is a friend, though a special purpose friend, the purpose being defined by the special needs of illness and crisis to which he tends.

But what, then, of the lawyer? Friendship and kinship are natural relations existing within, but not defined by, complex social institutions. Illness too is more a natural than social phenomenon. The response here requires an additional step. True, the special situations—legal relations or disputes—in which the lawyer acts as a limited-purpose friend are themselves a product of social institutions. But it does not follow that the role of the lawyer, which is created to help us deal with those social institutions, is defined by and is wholly at the mercy of the social good. We need only concede that at the very least the law must leave us a measure of autonomy, whether or not it is in the social interest to do so. Individuals have rights over and against the collectivity....

It is because the law must respect the rights of individuals that the law must also create and support the specific role of legal friend. For the social nexus—the web of perhaps entirely just institutions—has become so complex that without the assistance of an expert adviser an ordinary layman cannot exercise that autonomy which the system must allow him. Without such an adviser, the law would impose constraints on the lay citizen (unequally at that) which it is not entitled to impose explicitly. Thus, the need which the lawyer serves in his special-purpose friendship ... is a need which has a moral grounding analogous to the need which the physician serves: the need to maintain one's integrity as a person. When I say the lawyer is his client's legal friend,

I mean the lawyer makes his client's interests his own insofar as this is necessary to preserve and foster the client's autonomy within the law. This argument does not require us to assume that the law is hostile to the client's rights. All we need to assume is that even a system of law which is perfectly sensitive to personal rights would not work fairly unless the client could claim a professional's assistance in realizing that autonomy which the law recognizes.

The lawyer acts morally because he helps to preserve and express the autonomy of his client vis-à-vis the legal system. It is not just that the lawyer helps his client accomplish a particular lawful purpose. Pornography may be legal, but it hardly follows that I perform a morally worthy function if I lend money or artistic talent to help the pornographer flourish in the exercise of this right. What is special about legal counsel is that whatever else may stop the pornographer's enterprise, he should not be stopped because he mistakenly believes there is a legal impediment. There is no wrong if a venture fails for lack of talent or lack of money—no one's rights have been violated. But rights *are* violated if, through ignorance or misinformation about the law, an individual refrains from pursuing a wholly lawful purpose. Therefore, to assist others in understanding and realizing their legal rights is always morally worthy. Moreover, the legal system, by instituting the role of the legal friend, not only assures what it in justice must—the due liberty of each citizen before the law—but does it by creating an institution which exemplifies, at least in a unilateral sense, the ideal of personal relations of trust and personal care which (as in natural friendship) are good in themselves.

. . . The lawyer does work for pay. Is there not something odd about analogizing the lawyer's role to friendship when in fact his so-called friendship must usually be bought? If the lawyer is a public purveyor of goods, is not the lawyer-client relationship like that underlying any commercial transaction? My answer is "No." The lawyer and doctor have obligations to the client or patient beyond those of other economic agents. A grocer may refuse to give food to a customer when it becomes apparent that the customer does not have the money to pay for it. But the lawyer and doctor may not refuse to give additional care to an individual who cannot pay for it if withdrawal of their services would prejudice that individual. Their duty to the client or patient to whom they have made an initial commitment transcends the conventional quid pro quo of the marketplace. It is undeniable that money is usually what cements the lawyer-client relationship. But the content of the relation is determined by the client's needs, just as friendship is a response to another's needs. It is not determined, as are simple economic relationships, by the mere coincidence of a willingness to sell and a willingness to buy. So the fact that the lawyer works for pay does not seriously undermine the friendship analogy.

. . .

Another possible objection to my analysis concerns the lawyer in government or the lawyer for a corporation. My model posits a duty of exclusive concern (within the law) for the interests of the client. This might be said to be inappropriate in the corporate area because larger economic power entails larger social obligations, and because the idea of friendship, even legal friendship, seems peculiarly far-fetched in such an impersonal context. After all, corporations and other institutions, unlike persons, are creatures of the state. Thus, the pursuit of their interests would seem to be especially subject to the claims of the public good. But corporations and other institutions are only formal arrangements of real persons pursuing their real interests. If the law allows real persons to pursue their interests in these complex forms, then why are they not entitled to loyal legal assistance, "legal friendship," in this exercise of their autonomy just as much as if they pursued their interests in simple arrangements and associations?

. . .

It is time to apply the concept of legal friendship to the first of the two criticisms with which this essay began: that the lawyer's ethic of loyalty to his client and his willingness to pick clients for any and every reason (usually, however, for money) result in a maldistribution of a scarce resource, the aid of counsel. . . .

The lawyer-client relation is a personal relation, and legal counsel is a personal service. This explains directly why, once the relation has been contracted, considerations of efficiency or fair distribution cannot be allowed to weaken it. The relation itself is not a creature of social expediency (though social circumstances provide the occasion for it); it is the creature of moral right, and therefore expediency may not compromise the nature of the relation. . . . The relation must exist in order to realize the client's rights against society, to preserve that measure of autonomy which social regulation must allow the individual. But to allow social considerations—even social regulations—to limit and compromise what by hypothesis is an entailment of the original grant of right to the individual is to take away with the left hand what was given with the right. Once the relation has been taken up, it is the client's needs which hold the reins—legally and morally. . . . But what of the initial choice of client? Must we not give some thought to efficiency and relative need at least at the outset, and does this not run counter to the picture of purely discretionary choice implicit in the notion of friendship? The question is difficult, but before considering its difficulties we should note that the preceding argumentation has surely limited its impact. We can now affirm that whatever the answer to this question, the individual lawyer does a morally worthy thing whomever he serves and, moreover, is bound to follow through once he has begun to serve. . . . So if there is fault here it is a limited fault. What would be required for a lawyer to immunize himself more fully from criticism that he is unjust in his allocation of care? Each lawyer would have to consider at the outset of his career and during that career where the greatest need for his particular legal talents lies.

He would then have to allocate himself to that area of greatest need. Surely there is nothing wrong in doing this (so long as loyalty to relations already undertaken is not compromised); but is a lawyer morally at fault if he does not lead his life in this way? It is at this point too that the metaphor of friendship and the concept of self as developed above suggest the response. But this time they will be viewed from another perspective—the lawyer's as opposed to the client's rights and liberties.

Must the lawyer expend his efforts where they will do the most good, rather than where they will draw the largest fee, provide the most excitement, prove most flattering to his vanity, whatever? Why must he? If the answer is that he must because it will produce the most good, then we are saying to the lawyer that he is merely a scarce resource. But a person is not a resource. He is not bound to lead his life as if he were managing a business on behalf of an impersonal body of stockholders called human society. It is this monstrous conception against which I argued earlier. Justice is not all; we are entitled to reserve a portion of our concern and bestow it where we will. We may bestow it entirely at our discretion as in the case of friendship, or we may bestow it at what I would call "constrained discretion" in the choice and exercise of a profession. That every exercise of the profession is morally worthwhile is already a great deal to the lawyer's credit. Just as the principle of liberty leaves one morally free to choose a profession according to inclination, so within the profession it leaves one free to organize his life according to inclination. The lawyer's liberty—moral liberty—to take up what kind of practice he chooses and to take up or decline what clients he will is an aspect of the moral liberty of self to enter into personal relations freely.

I would not carry this idea through to the bitter end. It has always been accepted, for instance, that a court may appoint an available lawyer to represent a criminal defendant who cannot otherwise find counsel. Indeed, I would be happy to acknowledge the existence of some moral duty to represent any client whose needs fit one's particular capacities and who cannot otherwise find counsel. This is not a large qualification to the general liberty I proclaim. The obligation is, and must remain, exceptional; it cannot become a kind of general conscription of the particular lawyer involved. And the obligation cannot compromise duties to existing clients. Furthermore, I would argue that this kind of representation should always be compensated— the duty to the client who cannot afford representation is initially a duty of society, not of the individual lawyer. . . .

But surely I must admit that the need for legal representation far exceeds what such an unstructured, largely individualistic system could supply. Are there not vast numbers of needy people with a variety of legal problems who will never seek us out, but must be sought out? And what of the general responsibility that just laws be passed and justly administered? These are the obligations which the traditional conception of the lawyer, with his overriding loyalty to the paying client, is thought to leave unmet. At this point I yield no further. If the lawyer is really to be impressed to serve these admitted social needs, then his independence and discretion disappear, and he does indeed become a public resource cut up and disposed of by the public's needs. There would be no justice to such a conception. If there are really not enough lawyers to care for the needs of the poor, then it is grossly unfair to conscript the legal profession to fill those needs. If the obligation is one of justice, it is an obligation of society as a whole. It is cheap and hypocritical for society to be unwilling to pay the necessary lawyers from the tax revenues of all, and then to claim that individual lawyers are morally at fault for not choosing to work for free. In fact, as provision of legal services has come to be seen as necessary to ensure justice, society has indeed hired lawyers in an effort to meet that need.

Finally, I agree that the lawyer has a moral obligation to work for the establishment of just institutions generally, but entirely the wrong kind of conclusions have been drawn from this. Some of the more ecstatic critics have put forward the lawyer as some kind of anointed priest of justice—a high priest whose cleaving to the traditional conception of the lawyer's role opens him to the charge of apostasy. But this is wrong. In a democratic society, justice has no anointed priests. Every citizen has the same duty to work for the establishment of just institutions, and the lawyer has no special moral responsibilities in that regard. . . .

THE LAWYER'S AMORAL ETHICAL ROLE: A DEFENSE, A PROBLEM, AND SOME POSSIBILITIES
Stephen L. Pepper
1986 A.B.F. Res.J. 613.

. . .

The premise with which we begin is that law is a public good available to all. Society, through its "lawmakers"—legislatures, courts, administrative agencies, and so forth—has created various mechanisms to ease and enable the private attainment of individual or group goals. The corporate form of enterprise, the contract, the trust, the will, and access to civil court to gain the use of public force for the settlement of private grievance are all vehicles of empowerment for the individual or group; all are "law" created by the collectivity to be generally available for private use. In addition to these structuring mechanisms are vast amounts of law, knowledge of which is intended to be generally available and is empowering: landlord/tenant law, labor law, OSHA, Social Security—the list can be vastly extended. Access to both forms of law increases one's ability to successfully attain goals.

The second premise is a societal commitment to the principle of individual autonomy. This premise is founded on the belief that liberty and autonomy are a moral good, that free choice is better than constraint, that each of us wishes, to the extent possible, to make our own choices rather than to have them made for us. This belief is incorporated into our legal system, which accommodates individual autonomy by leaving as much room as possible for liberty and diversity. Leaving regulatory law aside for the moment (and granting that it has grown immensely, contributing to the legalization to be mentioned below), our law is designed (1) to allow the private structuring of affairs (contracts, corporations, wills, trusts, etc.) and (2) to define conduct that is intolerable. The latter sets a floor below which one cannot go, but leaves as much room as possible above that floor for individual decision making. It may be morally wrong to manufacture or distribute cigarettes or alcohol, or to disinherit one's children for marrying outside the faith, but the generality of such decisions are left in the private realm. Diversity and autonomy are preferred over "right" or "good" conduct. The theory of our law is to leave as much room as possible for private, individual decisions concerning what is right and wrong, as opposed to public, collective decisions.

   ... The third step is that in a highly legalized society such as ours, autonomy is often dependent upon access to the law. Put simply, first-class citizenship is dependent on access to the law. And while access to law—to the creation and use of a corporation, to knowledge of how much overtime one has to pay or is entitled to receive—is formally available to all, in reality it is available only through a lawyer. Our law is usually not simple, usually not self-executing. For most people most of the time, meaningful access to the law requires the assistance of a lawyer. Thus the resulting conclusion: First-class citizenship is frequently dependent upon the assistance of a lawyer. If the conduct which the lawyer facilitates is above the floor of the intolerable—is not unlawful—then this line of thought suggests that what the lawyer does is a social good. The lawyer is the means to first-class citizenship, to meaningful autonomy, for the client.

   For the lawyer to have moral responsibility for each act he or she facilitates, for the lawyer to have a moral obligation to refuse to facilitate that which the lawyer believes to be immoral, is to substitute lawyers' beliefs for individual autonomy and diversity. Such a screening submits each to the prior restraint of the judge/facilitator and to rule by an oligarchy of lawyers.... If the conduct is sufficiently "bad," it would seem that it ought to be made explicitly unlawful. If it is not that bad, why subject the citizenry to the happenstance of the moral judgment of the particular lawyer to whom each has access? If making the conduct unlawful is too onerous because the law would be too vague, or it is too difficult to identify the conduct in advance, or there is not sufficient social or political concern, do we intend to delegate to the individual lawyer the authority for case-by-case legislation and policing?

   An example may help. Professor Wasserstrom implies that a lawyer ought to refuse to draft a will disinheriting a child because of the child's views concerning the war in Nicaragua. ... Ought we to have a law on the issue? If not, why screen use of the legal device of testacy either through the diverse consciences of lawyers or through the collective conscience of the profession? And if the law is clear but contrary to the lawyer's moral beliefs, such as a tax loophole for the rich or impeachment-oriented cross-examination of the truthful witness, why allow (let alone require) that the lawyer legislate for this particular person or situation?

It is apparent that a final significant value supporting the first-class citizenship model is that of equality. If law is a public good, access to which increases autonomy, then equality of access is important. For access to the law to be filtered unequally through the disparate moral views of each individual's lawyer does not appear to be justifiable. Even given the current and perhaps permanent fact of unequal access to the law, it does not make sense to compound that inequality with another. If access to a lawyer is achieved (through private allocation of one's means, public provision, or the lawyer's—or profession's—choice to provide it), should the extent of that access depend upon individual lawyer conscience? The values of autonomy and equality suggest that it should not; the client's conscience should be superior to the lawyer's. One of the unpleasant concomitants of the view that a lawyer should be morally responsible for all that she does is the resulting inequality: unfiltered access to the law is then available only to those who are legally sophisticated or to those able to educate themselves sufficiently for access to the law, while those less sophisticated—usually those less educated—are left with no access or with access that subjects their use of the law to the moral judgment and veto of the lawyer.

. . .

. . . Up to this point in the discussion, access to the law as the primary justification for the amoral professional role has been presented with relatively little focus on what "the law" refers to.

. . . The implication has been that the law is existent and determinable, that there is "something there" for the lawyer to find (or know) and communicate to the client. The "thereness" of the law is also the assumption underlying the commonly understood limit on the amoral role: the lawyer can only assist the client "within the bounds of the law." This accords with the usual understanding of the law from the lay or client point of view, but not from the lawyer's point of view. The dominant view of law inculcated in the law schools, which will be identified here as "legal realism," approaches law without conceiving of it as objectively "out there" to be discovered and applied. A relatively little explored problem is the dynamic between the amoral professional role and a skeptical attitude toward law.

By "legal realism" I mean a view of law which stresses its open-textured, vague nature over its precision; its manipulability over its certainty; and its instrumental possibilities over its normative content. From "positivism" modern legal education takes the notion of the separation of law and morality: in advising the client, the lawyer is concerned with the law as an "is," a fact of power and limitation, more than as an "ought." From "legal realism" it takes the notion of law as a prediction of what human officials will do, more than as an existent, objective, determinable limit or boundary on client behavior. From "process jurisprudence" it takes an emphasis on client goals and private structuring, an instrumental use of law that deemphasizes the determination of law through adjudication or the prediction of the outcome of adjudication. These three views of "the law" are mutually reinforcing rather than conflicting. To the extent that legal education inculcates these views, "the law" becomes a rather amorphous thing, dependent upon the client's situation, goals, and risk preferences. What is the interaction between this view of the law and the view of the lawyer as an amoral servant of the client whose assistance is limited only by "the law"?

The apt image is that of Holmes's "bad man." The modern lawyer is taught to look at the law as the "bad man" would, "who cares only for the material consequences." The lawyer discovers and conveys "the law" to his client from this perspective and then is told to limit his own assistance to the client based upon this same view of "the law." The modern view of contract law, for example, deemphasizes the normative obligation of promises and views breach of contract as a "right" that is subject to the "cost" of damages. Breach of contract is not criminal and, normally, fulfillment of a contractual obligation is not forced on a party (not "specifically enforced," in contract law terminology). The client who comes in with a more normative view of the obligation of contracts (whether wishing the lawyer to assist in structuring a trans-action through a prospective contract or in coping with the unwelcome constraints of a past contract) will be educated by the competent lawyer as to the "breach as cost" view of "the law." Similarly, modern tort law has emphasized allocation of the "costs" of accidents, as opposed to the more normative view of 19th- and early 20th-century negligence law. Thus, negligence law can be characterized as establishing a right to a nonconsensual taking from the injured party on the part of the tort-feasor, subject once again to the "cost" of damages. An industrial concern assessing and planning conduct which poses risks of personal injury or death to third parties will be guided by a lawyer following this view away from perceiving the imposition of unreasonable risk as a "wrong" and toward perceiving it as a potential cost.

There are, of course, variations in the extent to which legal realism will be encountered in a lawyer's office. One is more likely to find the cost-predictive view presented in relation to a contract problem than a tort problem,[50] and it is more likely to come from a lawyer advising a

---

50. Viewing law in terms of "cost" entails perceiving enforcement as a part of the law. This is clear with Holmes's "bad man" view, and in his view that a contractual obligation entails only an obligation to pay damages for breach. It becomes more problematic when the lawyer is dealing with a potential criminal violation, rather than with contract or tort. ... Nonetheless, advice about enforcement has been

large corporate enterprise than one advising an individual. But it is valid as a general suggestive model that most clients, most of the time, (1) will enter the lawyer's office thinking of law as more normative and more certain than does the lawyer, and (2) will go out having been influenced toward thinking of the law in terms of possible or probable costs more than they would have had they not consulted a lawyer.

From the perspective of fully informed access to the law, this modification of the client's view is good because it accords with the generally accepted understanding of the law among those who are closest to its use and administration—lawyers and judges. It is accurate; it is useful to the client. From the perspective of the ethical relationship between lawyer and client, it is far more problematic. First, the lawyer is to be an amoral technician who serves rather than judges the client. The lawyer is not the repository of moral limits on the client's behavior. Second, the law itself, as presented by the lawyer, also is not a source of moral limits. Rather, it is presented from the lawyer's technical, manipulative stance as a potential constraint, as a problem, or as data to be factored into decisions as to future conduct. Finally, in determining how far he or she can go in helping the client, the lawyer is instructed to look to that same uncertain, manipulable source: "the law." "Within the bounds of the law" sounds like an objective, knowable moral guide. Any second-year law student knows that as to any but the most obvious (and therefore uninteresting) questions, there will probably be no clear line, no boundary, but only a series of possibilities. Thus, if one combines the dominant "legal realism" understanding of law with the traditional amoral role of the lawyer, *there is no moral input or constraint in the present model of the lawyer-client relationship.*

Again, from the premises of the first-class citizenship model, this is as it should be. The client's autonomy should be limited by the law, not by the lawyer's morality. And if "the law" is manipulable and without clear limits on client conduct, that aspect of the law should be available to the client. If moral limits are not provided by the law and are not imposed by the lawyer, their source will be where it ought to be: the client. Morality is not to be inserted in the lawyer's office, its source either the lawyer or the law. Morality comes through the door as part of the client.

This shifts our focus from the lawyer and the law to the client. It should come as no surprise that many clients will come through the door without much internal moral guidance. Common sources of moral guidance are on the decline: religion, community, family. In a secularized society such as ours, religion no longer functions as the authoritative moral guide it once was. Geographic mobility and divorce have robbed many of the multigenerational moral guidance that families can

considered part of the advice about "law"   lawyer function....
in general, and thus has been an accepted

provide. Small, supportive, usually contiguous and homogenous moral communities are the experience of fewer and fewer people. The rural town, the ethnic neighborhood, the church attended for several generations, the local business or trade community (the chamber of commerce or the grocers' trade association)—all are the experience of a far smaller segment of the population than before. Even the role of the public school in inculcating values may have declined. For many, law has replaced alternative sources of moral guidance.

Our problem now posits: (1) a client seeking access to the law who frequently has only weak internal or external sources of morality; (2) a lawyer whose professional role mandates that he or she not impose moral restraint on the client's access to the law; (3) a lawyer whose understanding of the law deemphasizes its moral content and certainty, and perceives it instead as instrumental and manipulable; and (4) law designed as (*a*) neutral structuring mechanisms to increase individual power (contracts, the corporate form, civil litigation), (*b*) a floor delineating minimum tolerable behavior rather than moral guidance, and (*c*) morally neutral regulation. From this perspective, access to the law through a lawyer appears to systematically screen out or deemphasize moral considerations and moral limits. The client who consults a lawyer will be guided to maximize his autonomy through the tools of the law—tools designed and used to maximize freedom, not to provide a guide to good behavior. . . .

. . .

Note on Fried and Pepper: Autonomy, friendship, citizenship, and the politics of question-begging

1. The concepts of autonomy, citizenship, and friendship are central, are they not, to the arguments that Fried and Pepper advance. Consider the question of the meaning that they may be thought to have.

(a) Contrast, for example, Pepper's concept of "citizenship" with the following definition, from a standard reference:

> [C]itizens enjoy a certain reciprocity of rights against, and duties toward, the community. . . . One of [the elements of the modern concept of citizenship] is the concept of membership in a political unit, involving cooperation in public decisions as a right and sharing of public burdens, chiefly military service and taxation, as a duty.

Ency. Soc. Sci., *Citizenship,* p. 471 (1930). Compare Danis and Churchill, Autonomy and the Common Weal, Hastings Center Rep. 25 (Jan.–Feb. 1991), emphasizing the "social aspect of citizenship" to balance the traditional emphasis on the "private and individual facet": "Citizens are persons who perceive allegiances as extending beyond self-interest. . . . Citizens both enjoy the rights and protections of [the sociopolitical] order and incur responsibilities for its maintenance and well-being." *Id.* at 27.

(b) As for autonomy, James Boyd White has expressed a concept of "autonomy" starkly different from that assumed by Fried and Pepper to be the meaning of the term:

> [T]o reduce the ideas of voluntary action, autonomy, and liberty to mere freedom from restraint ... is deeply impoverishing. For us political liberty has not meant merely freedom from restraint but enablement or capacitation, and this is always social and communal in character. The question is not only how far people are free or restrained in their exercise of dominion over the assets that nature and society give them, but far more importantly, what our community enables its people to do or to become. What range of responsibilities and participations, what opportunities for self-development and education what roles in self-government, does this community offer its members? These are the serious questions about liberty—defining the kind of liberty one could imagine fighting and perhaps dying for, liberty as an aspect of community.

White, Economics and Law: Two Cultures in Tension, 54 Tenn.L.Rev. 161, 179–80 (1986). The philosopher Alan Goldman has described autonomy in these words:

> To be morally autonomous is to assume moral responsibility for one's own actions, not simply to act out of narrow self-interest.

A. Goldman, The Moral Foundations of Professional Ethics 126 (1980).* Compare also the following:

> By moral autonomy I do not mean the radical independence that rejects any conditioning of individual judgment. Moral autonomy involves the willingness to accept insight from other persons and to submit one's own judgment to scrutiny. All persons have foundational values. A reflection on specific actions demonstrates how one examines a decision in reference to intention, result, and the foundation values which may have occasioned one act rather than another. Moral autonomy has reference, then, to the capacity of the self to act authentically and consistently in relation to foundational principles.

Donald Campbell, Doctors, Lawyers, Ministers: Christian Ethics in Professional Practice 62–63 (1982).

(c) Finally, consider William Simon's view of the essential ingredients of the concept of friendship:

> The classic definition of friendship emphasizes, not the adoption by one person of another's ends, but rather the sharing by two people of common ends. Moreover, the classical notion of friendship includes a number of other qualities foreign to the relation Fried describes. These missing qualities include affection, admiration, intimacy, and vulnerability.... Fried's lawyer is a friend in the same sense that your Sunoco dealer is "very friendly" or that Canada Dry Ginger Ale "tastes like love."

Simon, The Ideology of Advocacy: Procedural Justice and Professional Ethics, 1978 Wis.L.Rev. 30, 108–09.

---

* Compare Socrates' description of the duty of one who "cares for" one who "does wrong," in the *Gorgias,* p. 480).

2. Consider the significance of these sharp contrasts in under-
standings of the meanings of terms that are agreed to be important values.

(a) Am I right in suggesting that Fried's and Pepper's failure to
recognize or acknowledge that the words in question do not have but one,
self-evident meaning is not simply an analytic "gaffe" on their part, but
manifests a characteristic hazard of a justificatory approach? Professor
Phyllis Goldfarb suggests a reason why this might be so:

> Not surprisingly, those whose experiences are reflected in the law ...
> are likely to view the law as neutral, objective, and sound. Those
> whose experiences are at odds with the dominant position embedded in
> the doctrine can see more easily the particularity and partiality of the
> law and its implicit assumptions about how the world works and about
> whose perspectives count.

Goldfarb, A Theory–Practice Spiral: The Ethics of Feminism and Clinical
Education, 75 Minn.L.Rev. 1599, 1642–43 (1991).

(b) Would it be right to suggest, further, that, although Fried and
Pepper use the concepts of autonomy, citizenship, and friendship to justify
their defense of the traditional concept of advocacy, it is their justificatory
stance toward the traditional concept that prompts their adoption of the
particular meanings that they give those terms?

(c) If the preceding suggestion is sound, does it then follow that one's
choice between or among fundamentally conflicting meanings of the fundamental values of autonomy, citizenship, and friendship is less a question of
"professional ethics" as it is one of political philosophy? Note, in that
regard, Professor Fried's assertion, made in response to a published criticism of his essay, that "it is immoral for society to constrain anyone from
informing another what [the] limits on [an]other's autonomy are." Fried,
Author's Reply, 86 Yale L.J. 584, 586 (1977). Try to articulate what the
source is of the moral code on which Fried is apparently relying.

(d) Does it not then, finally, follow that there should not be an
authoritative answer, at the level of the profession or the state, to the
question of justification?

3. (a) How would *you* decide what meaning you find in the terms,
citizenship, friendship, and autonomy?

(b) What is your present response to the basic question of justification?

(c) What are the *sources* of your responses to these questions?

3. PROFESSIONAL DETACHMENT: THE DICHOTOMIZATION OF THE PROFESSIONAL AND THE PERSONAL

THE ETHICS OF ADVOCACY

Charles P. Curtis
4 Stanf.L.Rev. 1 (1951).

I want first of all to put advocacy in its proper setting. It is a
special case of vicarious conduct. A lawyer devotes his life and career
to acting for other people. So too does the priest, and in another way

the banker. The banker handles other people's money. The priest handles other people's spiritual aspirations. A lawyer handles other people's troubles.

But there is a difference. The loyalty of a priest or clergyman runs, not to the particular parishioner whose joys or troubles he is busy with, but to his church; and the banker looks to his bank. It is the church or the bank, not he, but he on its behalf, who serves the communicant or the borrower. Their loyalties run in a different direction than a lawyer's....

Not so the lawyer in private practice. His loyalty runs to his client. He has no other master. Not the court? you ask. Does not the court take the same position as the church or the bank? Is not the lawyer an officer of the court? Why doesn't the court have first claim on his loyalty? No, in a paradoxical way. The lawyer's official duty, required of him indeed by the court, is to devote himself to the client. The court comes second by the court's, that is the law's, own command.

Lord Brougham, in his defense of Queen Caroline, in her divorce case, told the House of Lords: "I once before took occasion to remind your Lordships, which was unnecessary, but there are many whom it may be needful to remind, that an advocate, by the sacred duty which he owes his client, knows in the discharge of that office but one person in the world—that client and no other.... Nay, separating even the duties of a patriot from those of an advocate, and casting them if need be to the wind, he must go on reckless of the consequences, if his fate it should unhappily be to involve his country in confusion for his client's protection."

Lord Brougham was a great advocate, and when he made this statement he was arguing a great case, the divorce of Queen Caroline from George IV before the House of Lords. Plainly he was exerting more than his learning and more than his legal ability. Years later he explained to William Forsythe, the author of a book on lawyers called *Hortensius,* who had asked him what he meant. Before you read Brougham's reply, let me remind you that the king, George IV, was the one who was pressing the divorce, which Brougham was defending, and that George had contracted a secret marriage, while he was heir apparent, with Mrs. Fitzherbert, a Roman Catholic. Brougham knew this, and knew too that it was enough to deprive the king of his crown under the Act of Settlement. Brougham wrote:

> The real truth is, that the statement was anything rather than a deliberate and well-considered opinion. It was a menace, and it was addressed chiefly to George IV, but also to wiser men, such as Castlereagh and Wellington. I was prepared, *in case of necessity,* that is, in case the Bill passed the Lords, to do two things—first, to resist it in the Commons *with the country at my back;* but next, if need be, to dispute the King's title, to show he had forfeited the crown by marrying a Catholic, in the words of the Act, "as if he were naturally dead." What I said was fully understood by Geo.

IV; perhaps by the Duke and Castlereagh, and I am confident it would have prevented them from pressing the Bill beyond a certain point.

Lord Brougham's menace has become the classic statement of the loyalty which a lawyer owes to his client, perhaps because being a menace it is so extreme. And yet the Canons of Ethics is scarcely more moderate, "... entire devotion to the interest of the client, warm zeal in the maintenance and defense of his rights and the exertion of his utmost learning and ability...."

. . .

The person for whom you are acting very reasonably expects you to treat him better than you do other people, which is just another way of saying that you owe him a higher standard of conduct than you owe to others. This goes back a long way. It is the pre-platonic ethics which Socrates had disposed of at the very outset of the *Republic;* that is that justice consists of doing good to your friends and harm to your enemies. A lawyer, therefore, insensibly finds himself treating his client better than others; and therefore others worse than his client. A lawyer, or a trustee, or anyone acting for another, has lower standards of conduct toward outsiders than he has toward his clients or his beneficiaries or his patrons against the outsiders. He is required to treat outsiders as if they were barbarians and enemies. The more good faith and devotion the lawyer owes to his client, the less he owes to others when he is acting for his client. It is as if a man had only so much virtue, and the more he gives to one, the less he has available for anyone else. The upshot is that a man whose business it is to act for others finds himself, in his dealings on his client's behalf with outsiders, acting on a lower standard than he would if he were acting for himself, and lower, too, than any standard his client himself would be willing to act on, lower, in fact, than anyone on his own.

You devote yourself to the interests of another at the peril of yourself. Vicarious action tempts a man too far from himself. Men will do for others what they are not willing to do for themselves— nobler as well as ignoble things....

The problem presented to a lawyer when he is asked to defend a man he knows is guilty or to take a case he knows is bad is perplexing only to laymen. Brandeis said, "As a practical matter, I think the lawyer is not often harassed by this problem, partly because he is apt to believe at the time in most of the cases that he actually tries, and partly because he either abandons or settles a large number of those he does not believe in."

It is profoundly true that the first person a lawyer persuades is himself. A practicing lawyer will soon detect in himself a perfectly astonishing amount of sincerity. By the time he has even sketched out his brief, however skeptically he started, he finds himself believing more and more in what it says, until he has to hark back to his original opinion in order to orient himself. And later, when he starts arguing the case before the court, his belief is total, and he is quite sincere about it. You cannot very well keep your tongue in your cheek while you are talking. He believes what he is saying in a way that will later astonish himself as much as now it does others.

Not that he cares how much we are astonished. What he does care is whether we are persuaded, and he is aware that an unsound argument can do much worse than fall flat. For it may carry the implication that he has no better one. He will not want to make it unless he really has no better.

This sort of self-sown sincerity, however, is seldom deep-rooted in lawyers, and it had better not be. If what Justice Darling said was cynical, it is also true. "I think," he said, "that most Counsel would be better advocates did they content themselves with simulating the belief instead of actually embracing it. The manifest appearance of a believer is all that is wanted; and this can well be acted after a little study, and will not interfere with that calmness of judgment which it is well to preserve in the midst of uncertainties, and which does not appear to be consistent with much faith."

We want to make it as easy as we can for a lawyer to take a bad case, and one of the ways the bar helps go about it is the canon of ethics which says, "It is improper for a lawyer to assert in argument his personal belief in his client's innocence or in the justice of his cause." It is called improper just so that the lawyer may feel that he does not have to. This, I think, must be its only purpose, for it is honored in no other way.

. . .

[H]ere is a canon which calls improper something which the most proper lawyers do. I suggest that its only purpose is to relieve lawyers of the necessity of expressing their opinion, so that they may never need express it unless they want to express it, and keep it to themselves whenever they choose. The canon gives a lawyer an excuse when his client wants him to espouse his cause, when all the lawyer wants to take is a case.

No, there is nothing unethical in taking a bad case or defending the guilty or advocating what you don't believe in. It is ethically neutral. It's a free choice. There is a Daumier drawing of a lawyer arguing, a very demure young woman sitting near him, and a small boy beside her sucking a lollypop. The caption says, "He defends the widow and the orphan, unless he is attacking the orphan and the widow." And for every lawyer whose conscience may be pricked, there is another whose virtue is tickled. Every case has two sides, and for every lawyer on the wrong side, there's another on the right side.

I am not being cynical. We are not dealing with the morals which govern a man acting for himself, but with the ethics of advocacy. We are talking about the special moral code which governs a man who is acting for another. Lawyers in their practice—how they behave elsewhere does not concern us—put off more and more of our common morals the farther they go in a profession which treats right and wrong, vice and virtue, on such equal terms. Some lawyers find nothing to take its place. There are others who put on new and shining raiment.

I will give you as good an example as I know that a lawyer can make a case as noble as a cause. I want to tell you how Arthur D. Hill came into the *Sacco–Vanzetti Case*. It was through Felix Frankfurter, and it is his story. Frankfurter wrote some of it in the newspapers shortly after Arthur's death, and he told it to me in more detail just after the funeral.

When the conviction of Sacco and Vanzetti had been sustained by the Supreme Judicial Court of Massachusetts, there was left an all but hopeless appeal to the federal courts, that is, to the Supreme Court. "It was at this stage," Felix Frankfurter said, "that I was asked if I would try to enlist Arthur Hill's legal services to undertake a final effort, hopeless as it seemed, by appeal to the Federal Law."

Frankfurter called Arthur Hill up and said that he had a very serious matter to discuss with him. "In that case," said Arthur Hill, "we had better have a good lunch first. I will meet you at the Somerset Club for lunch and afterwards you will tell me about it." They lunched together at the Somerset Club, and after lunch they crossed Beacon Street and they sat on the bench in Boston Common overlooking the Frog Pond. And Frankfurter asked Arthur Hill if he would undertake this final appeal of the *Sacco–Vanzetti Case* to the Supreme Court.

Arthur Hill said, "If the president of the biggest bank in Boston came to me and said that his wife had been convicted of murder, but he wanted me to see if there was any possible relief in the Supreme Court of the United States and offered me a fee of $50,000 to make such an effort, of course I would take the retainer, as would, I suppose, everybody else at the bar. It would be a perfectly honorable thing to see whether there was anything in the record which laid a basis for an appeal to the Federal Court.

"I do not see how I can decline a similar effort on behalf of Sacco and Vanzetti simply because they are poor devils against whom the feeling of the community is strong and they have no money with which to hire me. I don't particularly enjoy the proceedings that will follow, but I don't see how I can possibly refuse to make the effort."

If any of you have read Morgan and Joughin's book, you will know that Arthur Hill was hired. He did get a fee. Arthur Hill took it as a law case. To him it was a case, not a cause. He was not the partisan, he was the advocate. I want to add just one other thing, that Arthur Hill said to me, years later. It sets a sort of seal upon his conduct in the case.

I used to meet him fairly often walking downtown, because we both often stopped at the Boston Athenaeum and we would go on downtown together. One morning I was stupid enough to ask him an indiscreet question. I had expressed my own opinion on the guilt or innocence of Sacco and Vanzetti. I said I thought that on the whole it seemed to me probable that they had been guilty, and I asked Arthur what he thought. Arthur looked at me, it was years later, twenty years later, and he smiled and said, "I have never said, and I cannot say, what I think on that subject because, you see, Charlie, I was their counsel."

. . .

Let us now go back and reconsider, and perhaps reconstruct, in the light of my examples and our discussion, this "entire devotion" which a lawyer owes to his client.

The fact is, the "entire devotion" is not entire. The full discharge of a lawyer's duty to his client requires him to withhold something. If a lawyer is entirely devoted to his client, his client receives something less than he has a right to expect. For, if a man devotes the whole of himself to another, he mutilates or diminishes himself, and the other receives the devotion of so much the less. This is no paradox, but a simple calculus of the spirit.

Good lawyers know this. It was true of Brandeis. His appointment to the Supreme Court was opposed for his sharp practices at the bar, for being a ruthless and unscrupulous advocate, for taking cases against former clients. So his opponents said. And yet Austen G. Fox, who led the fight against his confirmation by the Senate before the Senate subcommittee is quoted as saying, "The trouble with Mr. Brandeis is that he never loses his judicial attitude toward his clients. He always acts the part of a judge toward his clients instead of being his client's lawyer, which is against the practices of the Bar." This remark loses nothing in Fox's obvious disapproval. Frederick P. Fish would never own any stock in a client's corporation. He said that he "never invested in a client." He would no more do that than a judge would hold stock in a corporation which was a party in a case before him....

. . .

Fish and Brandeis ... knew that they could not give their clients the full measure of their services if they did not keep themselves detached. Thereby they were able to offer their clients what they had come to get—advice and counsel from someone above the turmoil of their troubles or at least far enough away from them to look at them. By not putting their emotions as well as their minds up for hire, they saved, for the clients as well as for themselves, the waste of spirit which some lawyers confuse with devotion.

There is authority for such detachment. It is not Christian. Nor is the practice of law a characteristically Christian pursuit. The practice of law is vicarious, not altruistic, and the lawyer must go back of Christianity to Stoicism for the vicarious detachment which will permit him to serve his client.

E.R. Bevan, in his *Stoics and Sceptics,* summarized the Stoic faith as follows: "The Wise Man was not to concern himself with his brethren ... he was only to serve them. Benevolence he was to have, as much of it as you can conceive; but there was one thing he must not have, and that was love.... He must do everything which it is possible for him to do, shrink from no extreme of physical pain, in order to help, to comfort, to guide his fellow men, but whether he succeeds or not must be a matter of pure indifference to him. If he has done his best to help you and failed, he will be perfectly satisfied with having done his best. The fact that you are no better off for his exertions will not matter to him at all. Pity, in the sense of a painful emotion caused by the sight of other men's suffering, is actually a vice.... In the service of his fellow men he must be prepared to sacrifice his life; but there is one thing he must never sacrifice: his own eternal calm."

. . .

A lawyer should treat his cases like a vivid novel, and identify himself with his client as he does with the hero or the heroine in the plot. Then he will work with "the zest that most people feel under their concern when they assist at existing emergencies, not actually their own; or join in facing crises that are grave, but for somebody else." . . .

How is a lawyer to secure this detachment? There are two ways of doing it, two devices, and all lawyers, almost all, are familiar with one or the other of them.

One way is to treat the whole thing as a game. I am not talking about the sporting theory of justice. I am talking about a lawyer's personal relations with his client and the necessity of detaching himself from his client. Never blame a lawyer for treating litigation as a game, however much you may blame the judge. The lawyer is detaching himself. A man who has devoted his life to taking on other people's troubles, would be swamped by them if he were to adopt them as his own. He must stay on the upland of his own personality, not only to protect himself, but to give his client the very thing that his client came for, as Brandeis and Fish and Cravath and Montaigne so well understood.

I must refer again to the Stoics. In Gilbert Murray's small book, *The Stoic Philosophy,* he says, "Life becomes, as the Stoics more than once tell us, like a play which is acted or a game played with counters. Viewed from outside, the counters are valueless; but to those engaged in the game their importance is paramount. What really and ultimately matters is that the game shall be played as it should be played. God, the eternal dramatist, has cast you for some part in His drama, and hands you the role. It may turn out that you are cast for a triumphant king; it may be for a slave who dies of torture. What does that matter to the good actor? He can play either part; his only business is to accept the role given him, and to perform it well. Similarly, life is a game of counters. Your business is to play it in the right way. He who set the board may have given you many counters; he may have given you few. He may have arranged that, at a particular point in the game, most of your men shall be swept accidentally off the board. You will lose the game; but why should you mind that? It is your play that matters, not the score that you happen to make. He is not a fool to judge you by your mere success or failure. Success or failure is a thing he can determine without stirring a hand. It hardly interests Him. What interests Him is the one thing which He cannot determine—the action of your free and conscious will." ...

The other way is a sense of craftmanship. Perhaps it comes to the same thing, but I think not quite. There is a satisfaction in playing a game the best you can, as there is in doing anything else as well as you can, which is quite distinct from making a good score.

. . .

A lawyer may have to treat the practice of law as if it were a game, but if he can rely on craftsmanship, it may become an art, and "Art, being bartender, is never drunk; and Magic that believes itself, must die".... I wonder if there is anything more exalted than the intense pleasure of doing a job as well as you can irrespective of its usefulness or even of its purpose. At least it's a comfort.

Note on Curtis: Attachment to detachment?

1. What is your reaction to Curtis' vision of good lawyering? * What aspects of it, if any, do you find attractive? What, if any, are repellent to you?

2. Curtis makes two different but related assertions:

(a) The principal one is that the measure of detachment that he espouses is necessary in order to do right by one's client: "[I]f a man [*sic*] devotes the whole of himself to another, he mutilates or diminishes himself, and the other receives the devotion of so much the less."

- Is this an empirical observation, a psychological insight, or a philosophical position? Does it *matter* what the answer to this question is?

- Is the observation inevitably true, usually true, or (simply) a hazard to bear in mind in one's practice?

(b) The second assertion is that such detachment is necessary for the lawyer's own sake as well: "A man who has devoted his life to taking on other people's troubles, would be swamped by them were he to adopt them as his own."

---

* Charles Curtis, lawyer and author, was a quintessential Boston Brahmin, from a world now largely gone—a world in which gentlemen walked to their offices, and practiced law in a spirit that was much of a piece with that in which they visited Boston's great cultural establishments and fine private clubs. To some extent, certainly, the tone of his essay reflects that context, which to most readers today will seem quaint at best and often downright offensive. What he wrote, however, is simply a "purer" statement of a point of view that is widely held about professionalism, and I encourage you to consider your reaction to his thesis apart from your reaction to his sub-culture.

• This is a familiar theme, is it not, not only in lawyering, but in all professions that deal with people in need or trouble. To what extent is *your* conception of the role that detachment should play in your own professional stance a response to concerns of this second sort?

• What are the sources, and the validating experiences, underlying any such concerns?

3. Two additional questions are raised:

(a) To what extent does the stance that Curtis espouses present hazards of its own, either to the quality of the representation a lawyer gives or to the quality of his or her life?

(b) Is there a way in which one can take seriously *both* the hazards that concern Curtis *and* the polar hazards to which the last question is addressed?

4. The additional readings in this section are designed to shed some light on these questions. I suggest that you return to them after completing the readings.

A CRIMINAL LAWYER'S INNER DAMAGE
Seymour Wishman
N.Y. Times, July 18, 1977.

I surprised my client near the end of his testimony by confronting him with the photographs of his two-year-old daughter lying naked on a slab, her little body showing whipping scars, cigarette burns and pieces of flesh torn away.

"Did you do this? Did you do this to your own daughter?" I asked accusatorially.

"Some of the marks. Yes. My wife also beat her."

"How could you do such a thing?"

"She kept crying. She'd mess in her pants, things like that. I had to teach her," he answered tentatively, taken aback by my anger. "I thought that's what you're supposed to do."

From the far end of the courtroom, my voice charged with emotion, I screamed, "Did you love her?"

"Yes," he said softly, looking at the jury, "I loved her very much."

The jury, at last, heard barely restrained pain and remorse from my client. The male foreman of the jury wept. It was very effective.

One cost of the administration of criminal justice is the damage it does to the emotional and spiritual life of the lawyers. The criminal process is, surely, worse for defendants, and still worse for victims; but I am concerned here with lawyers like me who have, over a period of years, tried too many cases like this one, and are, I believe, scarred by the process.

My world is filled with deceit, incompetence, aggression, and violence. I've had to adjust.

Many of my clients are monsters who have done monstrous things. Although occasionally not guilty of the crime charged, nearly all my clients have been guilty of something. To deal with shocking behavior, the mind creates a separating distance. In my murder case with the little girl, I constantly resisted calling her "it" in front of the jury, but "it" was usually what I thought.

It seems, at times, that everyone lies to me. Virtually every client has, at some point, lied to me. But not only criminals lie; witnesses, paid experts such as psychiatrists, prosecutors, even some judges lie. Many cops, I suspect, can no longer identify the truth.

As a result, I have grown more distrustful of people. I automatically search for motives and reflexively recall all prior inconsistent statements, however trivial—good habits for a criminal lawyer, if only they didn't carry over, insidiously, into my personal life.

I am surrounded by incompetence. On one side are the clients, each a failed burglar, rapist, murder, or whatever. If they had been successful, they wouldn't have needed me. On the other side there is an astounding array of professional incompetents. The client accused of killing his daughter was acquitted of murder because the cops had improperly searched his apartment, the police photographer had lost the most gruesome close-ups, and the medical examiner could barely speak English.

To be effective in court I must act forcefully, and, often, brutally, I must frequently, for example, discredit witnesses, destroy them if possible. Surely not every witness I have humiliated was as despicable as I had tried to portray them. Yet, to function successfully, and with less guilt, I began years ago to regard the cross-examination as an art form, nothing personal, and I have been complimented by judges for my skill.

The successes also make it difficult to leave behind in the courtroom the arrogance and inflated sense of control over people. The trial itself is ritualized aggression between combatants. Fighting as vigorously and resourcefully as possible to win for one's client is in the highest tradition of the profession. The less worthy the client, the more noble the effort.

But this "professionalism" that makes a virtue out of noninvolvement with the client fosters an attitude of dissociation that can distort other parts of your life.

The detachment needed to function dispassionately widens the distance between one's natural emotional and intellectual reactions. This detachment is exacerbated when intellectual judgments require conjuring up emotional reactions in the courtroom that are deceits in themselves. When too many contrived emotions, these deceits, are successful, emotions in other contexts become suspect.

. . .

Question:

An easy reaction to Wishman is to say that the problem he describes arises only in the defense of criminal cases, or perhaps in their prosecution as well. To what extent do you believe that to be the case?

BECOMING A LAWYER: A HUMANISTIC PERSPECTIVE ON LEGAL EDUCATION AND PROFESSIONALISM

E. Dvorkin, J. Himmelstein, & H. Lesnick
West Pub. Co., 1981.

Read pages 33–43, 146–52.

THE ROLE OF EMOTION IN ETHICAL DECISIONMAKING

Sidney Callahan
18 Hastings Ctr Rep. 9 (1988).

What is the moral significance of my feelings when I hear that newly dead human bodies are used in car crashes for research on automobile safety? What should I make of the emotions aroused by the news that dying old persons will have their food and water withdrawn, or in other instances, be straitjacketed and forcibly fed? And does my emotional response to the dilemmas presented by AIDS or surrogate motherhood count? Everyone agrees that bioethical decisions, involving as they often do matters of life, death, sex, reproduction, and familial and professional loyalties, can arouse emotional responses. What is *not* agreed upon is whether, or how, one should weigh emotions when trying to resolve an ethical dilemma.

A completely rationalist view dismisses the role of emotions with the assertion that "arguments are one thing, sentiments another, and nothing fogs the mind so thoroughly as emotion." Adherents of this negative estimate of emotion would advise a person confronting an ethical dilemma to arrive at a decision using rational considerations alone....

Other philosophers may begrudgingly admit the inevitability of emotive intuitions, or gut feelings in moral argumentation but vigorously resist employing them. As James Rachels puts it, "The idea cannot be to avoid reliance on unsupported 'sentiments' (to use Hume's word) altogether—that is impossible. The idea is always to be suspicious of them, and to rely on as few as possible, only after examining them critically, and only after pushing the arguments and explanations as far as they will go without them."

. . .

I propose a model for the mutual interaction of thinking and feeling in ethical decisionmaking. Certainly, reason should monitor reason as in traditional philosophical critiques, and reason should tutor the emotions.... But I would also claim that emotion should tutor reason and that emotion should monitor emotion. The ideal goal is to come to an ethical decision through a personal equilibrium in which emotion and reason are both activated and in accord.

. . .

[T]he emotions are particularly important in moral and ethical functioning.... Studies of psychopaths indicate that they are below average or deficient in emotional responsiveness. A lack of anxiety, guilt, empathy, or love devastates moral functioning. Persons may have a high I.Q. and be able to articulate verbally the culture's moral rules, but if they cannot feel the emotional force of inner obligation, they can disregard all moral rules or arguments without a qualm.

Emotions energize the ethical quest. A person must be emotionally interested enough and care enough about discerning the truth to persevere despite distractions. Even more, a person who wrestles with moral questions is usually emotionally committed to doing good and avoiding evil. A good case can be made that what is specifically moral about moral thinking, what gives it its imperative "oughtness," is personal emotional investment. When emotion infuses an evaluative judgment, it is transformed into a prescriptive moral judgment of what ought to be done.

. . .

The working model of moral conflict has been that of emotion warring against reason, with only reason's mastery offering trustworthy guidance.... Rational tutoring of self or others assesses the inappropriate responses and substitutes others. Reasoning can affect mood and emotions as stoic strategies, psychotherapy, and ordinary self-control regularly prove.

Rational persons may have a more difficult time noticing and assessing those less dramatic but equally disabling disorders consisting of deficits of emotion. In philosophical arguments the problem of such deficits is regularly ignored and that of excessive emotion emphasized. Yet in our technological culture perhaps the greatest moral danger arises not from sentimentality, but from devaluing feeling and not attending to or nurturing moral emotions. Numbness, apathy, isolated disassociations between thinking and feeling are also moral warning signals. Psychopaths, persons under stress, persons who have coped by ignoring or denying their emotions, suffer from deficit problems in moral emotions.

Some persons are too "burned out" from stress to see or care about moral dilemmas. Others are so accustomed to isolating and not attending to their emotions that when they inadvertently must confront feeling, they are overwhelmed by what seems to them an alien external force. They are all the more susceptible to moral collapse and making poor ethical decisions.

. . .

But the more controversial claim being made here is that just as reason tutors and monitors emotion, so too can our emotions tutor reason. Why so? And how? ...

As we think through moral options or pursue arguments there can arise negative emotional responses ranging from mild feelings of aversion to intense feelings of repugnance. A rational argument without any apparent logical flaws may be presented—in, for instance, proposals for using torture, or harvesting neomorts, or refusing to treat AIDS—but our moral emotions prevent us from giving assent. When we feel strongly and persistently that this is wrong, wrong, wrong, but we can't articulate why, we withhold assent. Our discomfort induces us to continue looking beyond the proposed arguments, to keep searching and broaden the review. Later we may be able to understand the emotional reaction and feel profoundly grateful that we were not carried away by abstractions.

Emotions also tutor moral reasoning in positive ways. Much of our creativity in moral thinking emerges as ideas and emotions are activated in memory and produce new reverberations. Many moral revolutions have been initiated by empathy felt for previously excluded groups: slaves, women, workers, children, the handicapped, experimental subjects, patients in institutions. As I emotionally respond to another person or group, I may be forced to confront a conflicting moral attitude concerning the group. Novel emotional responses of sympathy clash with previously accepted moral principles, an inconsistency and unsettling discrepancy that can then prompt a creative moral readjustment.

The emotion of love, defined minimally as joyful interest with a predisposition to approach and attachment, most aptly tutors reason. Love engenders attention and concern, and minimizes fear and indifference. It motivates the resistance necessary to withstand automatic dismissals. At the other end of the emotional spectrum, anger, especially vicarious anger, can also tutor moral reasoning. Since the time of the Old Testament prophets, the experience of indignation or anger has moved persons to call for a drastic revision of their moral ideas. Present experiences of anger at what happens to an AIDS patient, a dying old person, or the mentally retarded in institutions, may cause a drastic reappraisal of moral thinking.

In a more subtle process, even more difficult to elucidate or articulate, one emotion can monitor and tutor another. Love and sympathy neutralize many negative emotions, as for instance when in the treatment of the diseased or handicapped, sympathy overcomes disgust. Love can quell anger or mitigate contempt for a person's moral lapse or betrayal. On the other hand, anger can transform sadness, depression, and apathy into active assertion or aspiration....

Loving attachments to virtuous persons influence and tutor my own emotions and moral sentiments. In ethical decisionmaking, I can assess an emotional response by comparing it to the response of those I admire and love. Their moral authority and persuasiveness arise from my emotional response to their goodness. In the same way, my emotional aversion to a person's life and moral being can make me distrust their reactions to a moral dilemma.

Our trust in the moral sentiments of those we hold to be good is not irrational, but neither is it infallible, since they too can be mistaken. Nonetheless, we are drawn even more persuasively to those we think to be rationally acute as well as good. If emotion and reason are inevitably intertwined, then the traditionally acclaimed guidance of persons communally held to be wise and good is most to be trusted....

If one would decide wisely and well, the best strategy would include both trusting and skeptical awareness of all of one's capacities and reactions. An individual is far too complex and personal consciousness (and preconsciousness) operates too instantaneously, for simple linear processing. It is essential to engage in fully extended, fully inclusive, circular, parallel processing of the dynamic interplays of consciousness.

While I am assessing my reasoning and arguments by rational criteria, I should pay attention to emotions, even those fleeting negative feelings that may be most in danger of defensive suppression. In the same process my emotional responses are in turn being rationally and emotionally assessed for appropriateness, or for their infantile or qualitative characteristics. Deficits and numbness should also be considered. As rational argument proceeds I can seek to enrich the process with emotional intuitions and associations, imagined moral scenarios, and the testimony of the wise and good. Can these emotions become universal, can they produce good consequences, are these feelings consistent with my other best emotions? Communication about my feelings with others would be a further test. Certainly, I should also continually compare my rational arguments to the critical reasoning of reflective experts, as found, say, in analytic articles or ethical guidelines. New ideas, arguments, or emotions should be continually checked and mutually adjusted.

. . .

As one wrestles with an ethical decision the goal is an emotively grounded reflective equilibrium in which all systems are integrated, all tests are satisfied, and a wholehearted decision can be made. The person as knower or whole self has done the best he or she can after a fully personal engagement. But one may still have to deal with further conflict arising from disagreements with others, either as personal individuals or collective professional groups or institutions. What about other persons and their differing moral sentiments? Their lack of emotion, or different emotions combined with different reasoning may lead to very different resolutions in direct conflict with my own. What then? Must I resign, resist, persuade, sue, or politically organize? Since such social conflicts and challenges present new ethical dilemmas, I may have to repeat my whole decision-making process again to deal with the consequences of an ethical decision.

One conclusion I would have to draw, however, is that I must respect the differing moral sentiments of others. Just as in my reasoning I would be open to correction from better arguments, so I should be open to the possibility that the moral emotions of others may be more valid and morally sound than my own.... I would be especially slow to label the moral sentiments or responses of others as squeamishness, or sentimentality, or irrationality. I would be especially aware that graver moral danger arises from a deficit of moral emotion than from emotional excess.

Even if a person cannot articulate or defend his or her emotions philosophically, that would not necessarily prove them wrong. The requirement that everyone must be able to articulate and defend rationally their moral sentiments seems excessive. This requirement may be hard even for moral philosophers, and might be beyond many people's resources. Since emotions and moral sentiments arise partially from non-verbally encoded interpersonal experiences that a person may not quickly retrieve from memory, persons with developed intuitive emotional responses may still lack the vocabulary or skill to compete in philosophical or political debate....

Note on Callahan: Emotions, rationality, and judgment

1. Compare Professor Michael Moore's observation:

[T]he emotions are not invaders of our processes of reasoned deliberations, nor are they preemptors of such processes. Rather, our emotions are both products and causes of the judgments we make as we decide what to do. When we get angry, for example, our anger can itself be caused by judgment: e.g., that an innocent person has just suffered undeserved punishment. Further, such anger at unjust treatment need not make reasoned choice more difficult. It may instead make choice easier by highlighting what we otherwise might have missed. Anger at injustice is at least as effective as reciting Kant when keeping the priority of justice before one's mind as one decides how to respond.

Moore, Choice, Character, and Excuse, 7 Soc.Phil. & Pol'y 29, 38–39 (1990).

2. Barbara Bezdek asserts (*Becoming a Lawyer,* p. 40) that "for me everything does start with my caring."

•What does she mean by "start" in that context?

•Is *this* statement a psychological insight, or a philosophical position?

•To what extent, if at all, is it true of you?

3. (a) Look again at the questions posed in the Note following the Curtis excerpt, p. 58, above, in light of all of the readings that followed it. What responses to those questions are suggested by the readings?

(b) What effect, if any, do they have on your own reaction to Curtis?

4. THE MEANING AND VALUE OF CLIENT AUTONOMY

As we have seen, a major ingredient of the justification for the emphasis on role-differentiation in the traditional concept of advocacy is its asserted responsiveness to the value of client autonomy. This section examines three related questions raised by that assertion:

(a) To what extent, if any, is it appropriate for a lawyer to influence (perhaps unintentionally) a client's understanding of the client's own goals in seeking legal representation?

(b) To what extent, if any, is it appropriate for a lawyer to limit or influence a client's choices on the basis of the lawyer's professional skill, knowledge or judgment?

(c) Does a practice carried on in the spirit of the traditional concept of advocacy tend to answer these questions in a manner that contradicts its own premises or justification?

(a) *The Identification of Client Priorities*

Problem

Assume that it is a year or two from now. You have just left your bar-admission certificate at the framing store, when you happen to run into a friend of yours who is a resident at a local hospital. He seems as serious and weighed down as you are cheerful and relaxed. On your asking "what's up," he says: "You know, maybe it's fate that I met you now. I think I need some legal advice—at least, I was urged, just an hour ago, to talk to a lawyer—and I certainly could use some sort of advice, or something. If you have a few minutes now, I'd like to tell you about it."

You agree, and the two of you repair to a suitable place to talk. He tells you that the other day he was working in the Emergency Room, and saw a two-month old baby whose parents brought her in for a check-up because they were concerned that she wasn't gaining enough weight and she seemed to have a cold or something. He examined the baby, and found no illness or any other problem, reassured the parents, and sent them all home. Six hours later, the baby was dead. She died while asleep, suddenly and noiselessly, from a cause which cannot be identified in advance through a clinical examination nor explained afterward through an autopsy. (In fact, the autopsy establishes the "cause" of death, and gives it a name—Sudden Infant Death Syndrome—by ruling out all observable causes of infant death.)

"You can imagine how I felt," he goes on, "trying to coax a heartbeat out of that baby when I was looking at her for the second time that day, and trying to explain to the parents how they didn't do anything to cause the death, that there was nothing they or anyone could have done to prevent it. *I* am one of those 'anyones,' and the bewilderment, guilt and anger which the parents feel—and which I tried to help them cope with—has an echo in my own. I want to call the parents, to see how they're doing, to give them another chance to talk with me; if they are agreeable,

I'd like to go to the baby's funeral tomorrow, to let go of it all a little more gradually than we usually do. Everyone at the hospital tells me I'm crazy, and shouldn't do any of those things, that I'm getting overinvolved and unprofessional, and am letting my own needs come before the parents' or my job. I don't see it that way, but just an hour ago someone said, 'For God's sake, before you do all that, talk to a lawyer, and see what he'd say.' I don't know if I'd have done it, or *what* I'll do, but seeing you, like I say, maybe it was fate.

"What do you think I should do?"

Just at this point, your friend's beeper goes off, and while he is on the telephone, you have a chance to think about your response.

He's back now, and doesn't have to leave.

Note:

In answering any question, one first decides what the question is. Often, that process does not appear to require conscious thought; sometimes, however, that appearance can be misleading. Before answering your friend's question, therefore, ask yourself specifically: What is he asking you? In answering *that* question, consider these questions:

- •To what extent do traditional presuppositions about professionalism—both of lawyers and of doctors—influence your perception regarding the question?

- •To what extent might they influence *his* perception of what it is that he wants to learn from you?

Now consider how you would answer your friend's question. To what extent is your answer to this question influenced by your own concept of professionalism?

THE IDEOLOGY OF ADVOCACY: PROCEDURAL JUSTICE AND PROFESSIONAL ETHICS
William Simon
1978 Wisc.L.Rev.

This excerpt from Professor Simon's article is reprinted on pages 26 to 32 of *Becoming a Lawyer*. Read it there.

THE PURSUIT OF A CLIENT'S INTEREST
Warren Lehman
77 Mich.L.Rev. 1078 (1979).

. . .

This paper is concerned with [the lawyer-client] relation. It was written while I was unaware of all [the] recent work on the subject. There are some losses as a result of that innocence; there are, however, enough advantages to justify my leaving the Article essentially as I wrote it. It would certainly have been more difficult to write and probably much longer, for no reason but to inflate my ego or improve my image, had I been tempted to turn the Article into a contribution to a debate. It would also, I think, have been a worse Article. It has been hard enough to put together in straightforward fashion what I want to say. Equally important, the tone would have changed from meditation to argument. That, too, would have been a loss. We are dealing with the most difficult problems of the interior and virtuous life. Ethical dilemmas do not resolve under the assault of argument. We must speak more gently to the spirit. I have not found the way to score points gently.

Clients come to lawyers for help with important decisions in their business and private lives. How do lawyers respond to these requests, and how ought they? Doubtless many clients, thinking they know what they want—or wishing to appear to know—encourage the lawyer to believe he is consulted solely for a technical expertise, for a knowledge of how to do legal things, for his ability to interpret legal words, or for the objective way he looks at legal and practical outcomes. It is as if the lawyer were being invited to join the client in a conspiracy of silence; the point of the conspiracy is that in silence neither shall question the assumption that the means can be truly separated from the end and that the end is the client's sole problem and solely his. . . .

It is not self-evident that the transactions of lawyers and their clients are as I have stated, so let me say a little more. The view of the lawyer as a technician in service of a client-principal we may call instrumentalism: the lawyer is an instrument of his client's purposes. . . .

The instrumentalists' view fails not only because the lawyer cannot avoid being a party to the client's decision, but because the client has no decision before he sees his lawyer. It is required by the instrumentalist view that a client have, when he comes to the lawyer's office, a clear set of preferences, intransigent to discussion or circumstances. But there is no such set of preferences inside an individual that he can trot out when he gets to the lawyer's office. There is, then, no clear will of which the lawyer can be the simple instrument. The client may say, to take an obvious example, "I want a divorce." That goal of the client is a result, usually of his feeling trapped, hurt, and hopeless of any other way of coming to terms with his wife. It is not in any profound sense what he wants. If a lawyer could magically return that marriage to a happy state, we should certainly call him a fool or worse if he were to bypass that opportunity on the ground that the client, having said, "I want a divorce," had defined beyond question the scope of the lawyer's obligation. The best that can be said of a divorce is that it is not what the client wants, but only that which at the moment seems to him most likely to move him toward that interior state of comfort or satisfaction that all of us ultimately seek.

In fact, everything we want to achieve we want ultimately because of the connection we suppose it to have to a desired feeling. Therefore, what we want is not the things we say we want, but the feelings we suppose they will produce. The list a client brings to a lawyer's office is not a ranking of desired states, but only of what the client supposes may produce them. Our judgment on issues of that sort is especially likely to be bad at the crucial time we go to a lawyer. We say we want justice when we want love. We say we were treated illegally when we hurt. We insist upon our rights when we have been snubbed or cut. We want money when we feel impotent. We are likely to act most sure of ourselves when most desperately we want a simple, human response. If this is true, the lawyer presenting himself as an uncritical mirror is not a satisfaction but a disappointment. The lawyer is in the deeper sense not then doing what the client wants. It may well be that in a given situation a lawyer can do no more than accept a particular client's statement of his desires. But that is not because he ought to be his client's tool or because he must be. . . .

The problem of all—client, lawyer, judge—is the choice of acts: which to do, which to advise to do, what to say of those that have been done. I have adopted the traditional view that all people seek the good, or happiness, which is achieved in living and doing in the world. The relation between particular acts that might be done or things that might be gotten in the world and that interior state of being called happiness is not a necessary or simple one. Logic does not tell us which acts will produce that state; that is the subject matter of what Aristotle and St. Thomas Aquinas called practical wisdom. Practical wisdom, the virtue of those who know how to live well, is the poorly understood product of age and experience. Through time and with sensitivity we may learn to recognize what in a given situation will most advance us toward that inner comfort that is *the* good and the sum of what we want.

The lawyer is consulted as a man of practical wisdom. People, despite an insistent undercurrent of distrust of the profession, widely look to lawyers as worthy advisers and take seriously what they have to say. Surely every lawyer has at some time dissuaded a client from some wasteful or destructive pursuit. Every lawyer, no matter what he says of the rhetoric of instrumentalism, has at some time recognized and taken advantage of a client's being malleable in his preferences, getting him to drop a personally malicious suit, or to settle rather than fight and thereby to reestablish a friendship, a business relation, or a marriage. The occasions may be few, but they are sufficient to demonstrate that the simple instrumentalist view does not describe a necessary reality. A lawyer can obtrude a personal judgment upon the wisdom of a client's expressed desires, and the client can change his mind.

I suspect that many adopt the instrumentalist view less because of any very firm belief that it describes what the lawyer ought to do than because it is so difficult to broach with the client a touchy moral or emotional issue. For most of us such moral and personal points are hard to make under any circumstances. How much harder to risk making such a point with an apparently self-confident stranger. How do I tell him it is small to pursue a petty claim, unbecoming to maneuver an advantage, destructive to organize one's life around the hope of a successful suit? How do I say to an alcoholic client that he ought to suffer the penalty for a drunk driving charge, rather than be gotten off, or tell a sex offender that he ought to be committed for treatment?

There is the problem. I do not think I like what this client wants to do, but I would feel very uncomfortable raising the issue. What, then, do I as a lawyer do? Here is the difficult answer: I admit to myself that I cannot talk to a particular client who is off-putting or overwhelming or cock-sure, and that I would probably be a better person and lawyer if I could. This seems costly because it requires first that I take the trouble to discover in each case what I ought to do, and second that I recognize that, like every other human being, I cannot do everything. Neither the introspection nor the confession is comfortable. It is no wonder we are tempted to avoid them. And seemingly we can. We can attempt to rationalize our engaging upon a distasteful course chosen by a client on the ground that what is to be done is the client's decision and we are but tools. That way we try to persuade ourselves that internal discomforts can be safely ignored.

It only *seems* easier to adopt the instrumentalist rationalization for proceeding unquestioningly in courses we do not really like. But it certainly does seem easier, for there is much in the culture to support such a decision: Everything tells us to isolate our own feelings and to respect even the most obviously riddled barrier the client may have erected. Certain issues are personal. It is in bad taste to explore them. Delicacy urges us not to make a client face his cupidity. Better we be its tool. Reason is trustworthy; feelings are not. Judgments of this sort are mere matters of taste. Taste is idiosyncratic and personal. What right have we to impose our tastes upon others? A becoming modesty urges us not to assert any view that might discomfort another. Everyone needs space to grow, yes, even to make mistakes. We ought stand in no one's way, do nothing to influence the natural course of a personality's flowering according to its own inner motive (a version of the error of the unchangeable set of preferences). And I have not yet touched the rhetoric of the adversary system or of liberal proceduralism. The point is that we are invited by both ideology and apparent convenience into a psychic trap. Instrumentalism offers us an argument with which to bludgeon such feelings as aversion or sympathy, which might lead us to respond as humans to our clients' predicaments. It seems an attractive alternative to the intimidating prospect of living with our clients as judging fellow men. But, as the economist says, there is no free lunch. We pay for such uneasy peace of mind as instrumentalism offers us. If feeling may be influenced by persuasive reflection, it is not talked out of existence by rationality. It is there and accumulates in the form of distaste with ourselves and what we are doing. The consequences of accumulating distaste can be personally disastrous: alcoholism, hypertension, an early heart attack, even suicide.

On one side of the table an attorney, trying to hide, both from his own feelings and the client's, behind a wall called instrumentalism; on the other side a client, anxious, even if he will not admit it, for any hint he can get from the lawyer of how to be a good client, a good person, and happy. For the ordinary, infrequent user of lawyers, the approach to one is likely to be an important event in exciting, sometimes dangerous, sometimes hopeful circumstances: criminal indictment, divorce, home buying, injury, accident, business expectations, estate matters, or dealing with obtrusive and threatening regulatory agencies. The client does not know the substance of his problem or perhaps even what to expect from his lawyer. It is in large measure up to the lawyer to define what the relation is going to be. It is his ethical responsibility. The client will find judgments in the lawyer's behavior no matter how the lawyer attempts, in the act of protecting himself, to avoid judging. The client will find his guidance, if the attorney is silent, in that silence. As the silent mind approves the errant will, so the compliant attorney approves the client's.

I suppose the effect of silence is clear enough. What may be less evident is that the *way* the lawyer approaches even that narrow range of questions which the instrumentalist will admit are within his expertise will influence the client and involve both in a major moral commitment. The lawyer's style will almost certainly be utilitarian. Utilitarian ethical thinking has been so successful and become so much a part of our culture that we think in the way recommended by utilitarians without our even realizing that we are thinking ethically, let alone that we have made a commitment to an ideology....

Part of utilitarianism's appeal may be the result of a peculiar fact. Utilitarianism is originally an ethical theory, a theory by which it is supposed to be possible to discover the morally right act—as a matter either of public policy or of private behavior. Yet a utilitarian demonstration is viewed as a morally neutral, supremely practical guide to action. Where one would not dare urge that an act is morally right or wrong, one would feel quite free to comment upon its utility. Utility is socially acceptable; morality is not. If pressed, we suppose, though there is no proof, that long-run utilities are moral, that consideration of the long run will lead us to avoid bad behavior. Therefore, when we want to influence people to act in the manner we believe right, we are likely to try to persuade them of the long-run utility of doing so. ("Let us save the environment for our future, despite apparent short-run gains from ransacking it," but not "A good man would so use the world that it is none the worse for his having been here.") The practical utilitarian, therefore, thinks he can have it both ways; he has a moral guide to behavior without the taint of being a moralist or the possibility of ever discomfiting anyone. He is supremely reasonable. But once again, the price of self-delusion can be high.

. . .

One of the ways a client and lawyer are likely to be corrupted by utilitarianism is the result of its being not a closed but an open system—a fact easily overlooked. What I mean is that utilitarianism is not sufficient without more to answer a moral question. Before we can weigh outcomes, we need to know how they are to be valued. If a public policy under consideration would result in greater egg production, we do not know whether it is a good policy unless we know—from somewhere else—whether we want more or fewer eggs. Utilitarianism does not answer that question. It says only that we should ask it.

One reason we seldom notice the open character of utilitarianism is because to make decisions we normally consider only noncontroversial outcomes. The general presumption would be that more eggs is a good. So long as all agree upon the advantage of perpetually increasing the gross national product, the limits of public debate will be narrow, and the impression will be sustainable that we are engaged simply in minor problems of assessing the utilities. Utilitarianism collapses, however, when the consensus that is its necessary support collapses, as when a significant minority becomes committed to environmental protection. There is no utilitarian resolution to the argument between the paper manufacturers who emit wastes and the fisherman and others who do not want mercury in the Wisconsin River.

Much of what the lawyer does may seem to be based upon consensus and hence to raise no such difficult question, but often it is only the force of the lawyer's experience and position that makes a real conflict disappear. The substantive ethical act that the lawyer cannot avoid, even through instrumentalism, is the act of filling in the blanks in the utilitarian calculus. And there is the rub. The values or ends the lawyer chooses are likely to be equivalents in private life of a greater gross national product in public debate, the readily assumed, the safe, the self-evident: more money, freedom from incarceration or procedural delay. Yet for many clients, such goods are neither what they want nor what they need. Hardly anyone will dispute that the goods a utilitarian seeks are desirable. The getting of money is generally a good. So is freedom, so is time. . . .

. . . Yet the real client may in some sense want or need that seemingly less attractive result. What I want to discuss in the balance of this Article is how utilitarianism in specific kinds of familiar counseling situations leads to giving clients bad advice, advice that sacrifices their humanity in the name of seemingly self-evident goods.

. . .

A practicing lawyer, call him Doe, who also teaches client counseling, said that he is very concerned, in doing estate matters, with the possibility that a client will be overborne by information about tax consequences. His tactic to avoid that result is to persuade his client—before there is any mention of those consequences—to expand in as much detail as possible upon what it is he wants to do. Only after that does Doe point out costs and mention ways the client's plan could be changed to save money. In teaching as well as in practice, Doe is trying to take account of the power a lawyer has to impress upon a client the importance of his lawyerly considerations. The progress represented by Doe's concerned approach is the recognition that the client's values may not be the lawyer's, or more precisely, that the real, live client's interests may not match those of the "standard client" for whom lawyers are wont to model their services.

. . .

I told Doe of a friend of mine, a widow recovering from alcoholism, who is fifty-four years old. Her house has become a burden to her, perhaps even a threat to her sobriety, although it might seem overly dramatic to say as much to a stranger. If she waits until she is fifty-five, the better part of a year, the large capital gain on the house will be tax free. She decided she did not want to go to a lawyer for fear he might talk her into putting off the sale. I asked Doe if that were realistic. He said her fear was well grounded; a lawyer might well give her the impression that another year in the house ought to be suffered for the tax saving. . . .

One possible analysis of these cases is that suggested by Doe: that the lawyer needs to be careful to discover what it is the client is really about, to give fullest possible opportunity for her interests to be explored, and to avoid the over-bearing assertion of simple money saving. . . .

The problem being described occurs because utilitarian analysis is incomplete until someone fills in the price tags of costs and benefits. When the lawyer's standard array of price tags doesn't quite work, the first solution is to pass the buck to the client. Give him some uncolored information and let him decide. Modifying the sequence in which information is presented can be at best palliative, no more effective than most other efforts to make people free and wise by manipulating information, whether by pressing it on people, withholding it from them, or shaping the circumstances in which it is passed on. . . .

The problem of the lawyer . . . is to assure that only rational influences play upon those in their charge so that the presumed internal preferences will be able to realize themselves freely by the best light of reason. (As we have said, there is no such fixed core of the self.) Rational behavior is, as we are wont to see it, the maximization of egoistic self-interest (which is presumably the will's real preference). Our great intellectual problem is to account for altruism. The only time we are sure that people are behaving rationally is when they are behaving badly. We are, therefore, driven to give people the opportunity to behave so, because we are a free society. Life follows art and they misbehave. The only cure for antisocial behavior consistent with freedom is information addressed to reason. If, after the administration of more information, the subject still decides egoistically or in a self-destructive way, we who gave the information claim no responsibility. That is our model of the political order, of how to deal with cigarette smoking, the integrity of politicians and judges, the doctor-patient relation when a serious medical procedure is under consideration, fair campaign practices, medical experimentation, legal education, the relation between the police and the arrestee, and so on, and on and on.

. . .

Indeed, the only way, finally, that a lawyer can deal with the problem is to cease to deal with it. It is impossible so to organize my behavior that it is not manipulative. It is impossible to act so as to make another man free. Whether I plan to say my piece on the tax advantages of deferral first or last or in the middle, loudly or softly, with deprecation or enthusiasm, my influence will be corrupting and destructive. The only thing the lawyer can do for his client is be free himself, which means free to be honest in saying exactly what he thinks and feels, to confront himself. It is transcendence for a lawyer to say to a client: "I am fearful of influencing you unduly in this matter. The tax saving is there. It may be important to you to save the money. If so, by all means defer the gift. But money saving is not everything. One should hardly organize one's life around a revenue code. I will think none the less of you whether you choose to defer or not. Some people, I suspect, may be embarrassed—odd as it may sound—to ignore an apparent financial advantage, for to do so sounds irrational. Let me assure you, I would respect most highly a man who will do now what seems right to him now. What sounds rational is not always humanly reasonable...." The important thing about any such message is not that it be calculated to neutralize the legal-rational bias, the legal influence, but that it be honest and not intended to manipulate. Sometimes a side benefit of the speaker's honesty is a shock in the listener that shakes him loose and helps him be free.

... We continually give things to each other to generate in ourselves the sense of rightness that comes from the alternating experiences of gratitude as recipient and gratitude as donor. In the exchange we find most of the psychological support we need to survive as content people: the feelings of worth, of effectiveness, of loving and being loved. The external product, the by-product as it were, is a web of good feelings and obligation. Indeed, one may say that the exchange of gifts, kindnesses, service, and hospitality are, if not the substance, at least the warp and woof of all social life. The need for ties even at the price of rationality is demonstrated by the widespread practice of men alternately buying drinks for each other. Such gifting pairs are to be found in every bar, for the inclination to enter them is profound.

The rhythm of gift-giving has its own rules, so that relations do not become one-sided and oppressive or so infrequent as to fall apart. The art of leadership lies in the timely and measured distribution of rewards (gifts) for services. So does the art of friendship. These are matters far too important to be controlled by the Internal Revenue

Code. They are also matters that have supremely to do with the way we apprehend a present situation, not with the calculation of outcomes.

It might at first appear otherwise. Reciprocal transactions are functionally necessary and, in a sense, as obligatory as contracts; in the functional anthropologist's sense, we engage in them instrumentally, for the purpose of creating ties and obligations. But the workability of the system depends upon the actions being taken in a nonmanipulative, non-self-conscious way for the pure satisfaction that arises from the act of giving. We are well advised not to let our one hand know what the other does....

But in a way it is peculiar to describe the nonmanipulative ignoring of consequences as disinterested. It is really an important change in the focus of interestedness from the future to the present, to doing what is right in the present because it feels good in the present because it is consonant with our best definition of ourselves. It is a completely interested, completely self-interested, completely present state of mind, in which all I do for another is, after all, for myself right now, to make me feel good about myself. And it is a state of mind in which the question is the character of the act, not the outcome. This is the traditional and proper focus of ethical inquiry. It is difficult to deal with because in a real case, being sui generis, the problem of how to act cannot be rationally answered. Rationality has nothing to do with the individual, for it is inherently statistical. That means we have no certain guides, no clear answers, but must find our way as best we can.

Among those who first hear what I have to say, it is obvious that I hit some nerve. What I say is appealing. It is the way we would want the world to be. It is common also for readers to say, that may all be well and good in some limited situation; in private life, but not in public life; or in dealing with a naive client, but not with an experienced one; or for old lawyers but not for young ones; or where the client is human but not when it is a corporate entity.

There is no doubt that it is more difficult for a young man than for an old man to be old. But we must all act according to the light we have. If because of youth we have nothing to say, it is no problem to us that we do not say it. If because of youth it is harder to say what we have to say, we had better confess it than pretend to ourselves that we ought not say it because that is not our role or our duty. The sophisticated client and the naive represent really the same problem as the young or old lawyer: the balance of personal power between the client and the attorney. And the answer is no different, because, after all, the ones to be saved are ourselves.

. . .

Note on Simon and Lehman: Who is aiming the hired gun?

1. Reconsider the questions posed in the Note following the Problem that begins this sub-section, p. 67, above. What do the Simon and Lehman excerpts say that bears on those questions?

2. (a) Simon levels at what he calls the positivist conception of lawyering a charge of self-contradiction, in that it rests on the assertions that values are subjective and personal, and that a lawyer can at the same time safely assume that what the client values most is maximizing his or her wealth and freedom of action. A "simple country lawyer" might respond to Simon by saying that the idea that values are subjective doesn't mean that they are distributed randomly throughout the population; certainly, *most* clients come to lawyers because their wealth or freedom of action has been impaired or is threatened, and what they want from the lawyer is help in ending that situation. To what extent does such a response undermine Simon's argument?

Were Lehman to reply to the simple country lawyer, he would emphasize the embryonic, emergent quality of the client's priorities: "[T]he client has no decision before he sees his lawyer.... There is ... no clear will of which the lawyer can be the simple instrument"; and the powerful shaping effect of the lawyer's words and actions on them: "The client will find judgments in the lawyer's behavior no matter how the lawyer attempts ... to avoid judging. The client will find his guidance, if the lawyer is silent, in that silence."

Before evaluating them, try to spell out, as fully as you can, the bases of Lehman's views in this respect: Why, according to Lehman, is this so?

(b) In evaluating the strength of Lehman's thesis, consider the following factors:

- the *accuracy* of his portrayal of the process of lawyer-client interaction by which the client's understanding of his or her own priorities is shaped:
  - Is it seriously exaggerated?
  - Is there nonetheless a substantial core of truth in it?
  - Separating these questions, and putting them in this form, helps us to realize that the answers to *both* may be in the affirmative. Is it fair to say that the traditional concept of advocacy tends to assume that an affirmative answer to the first question warrants dismissing the second?

- the *implications* of his portrayal: To avoid influencing a client's perception of what he or she wants, a lawyer, according to Lehman, should "be honest in saying exactly what he thinks and feels," should "confront himself." If youth, or discomfort, or a feeling of relative lack of power or authority get in our way as lawyers in being candid with a client, we should "admit to" ourselves that it is true; we should "confess it [rather] than pretend to ourselves that we ought not say it because that it is not our role or our duty." Where we *are* able to speak fully, we should (for example, in counseling about courses of action with tax consequences) say this:

  I am fearful of influencing you unduly in this matter. The tax saving is there. It may be important to you to save the money. If so, by all means defer the gift. But ... I will think none the less of you whether you choose to defer or not. Some people may be embarrassed—odd as it may sound—to ignore an apparent financial advantage.... I would respect most highly a man who will do now what seems right to him now....

- Assuming that Lehman has identified a serious problem in lawyer-client interaction, are his responses a solution to it?

- Deferring for a moment the question whether they are *acceptable* responses, are they likely to be sufficient?

- If not, are there better ones?

- Suppose one were to conclude that the problem is to a significant degree unsolvable: What would be the implications of such a conclusion for the validity of Lehman's critique? —for the validity of the traditional concept of advocacy?

- the *merit* of his alternative. In the passages quoted in this Note, and elsewhere in the article, Lehman calls for an attorney-client dialogue characterized by an honest acknowledgment of the power dynamics at work between lawyer and client. Is this goal seriously objectionable, in (among others) either of the following respects?

  - Are there circumstances in which pursuit of such a goal would itself constitute or legitimate a form of attorney domination of the client?

  - Is such pursuit inconsistent to a significant degree with the value of professional detachment, examined in the preceding section of this book?

If so, which value should take precedence?

3.   The attraction of corporate practice is, for some, attributable in part to the expectation that the problems with which this sub-section are concerned are rarely encountered there. (A similar expectation also may account in part for the aversion to corporate practice for others). To what extent is that expectation soundly based?

(b) *Professional Expertise and Client Autonomy*

The value of client autonomy interacts in complex ways with the idea of the lawyer as a skilled and knowledgeable professional. This sub-section asks three fundamental questions about that interaction:

1.   Is the lawyer often better able than the client to judge what courses of action will best advance the client's own goals?

2.   Does the lawyer often have substantial autonomy interests of his or her own in exercising an informed discretion in carrying on professional work?

3.   Is it appropriate for the lawyer-client relation to reflect the idea that the lawyer has a responsibility to serve a governmental interest in maintaining public confidence in the administration of justice?

As we saw in connection with *Jones v. Barnes* earlier in this section, one aspect of the traditional concept of advocacy is a belief that these questions should be answered in the affirmative. As you read what follows, consider, among other questions:

- how you believe each question should be answered;
- whether you agree with my observation that the answers of the traditional concept of advocacy are (once again) bound up with its adoption of a "celebratory" rather than a "troubled" stance toward the justness of the legal system.

FARETTA v. CALIFORNIA
Supreme Court of the United States, 1975.
422 U.S. 806, 95 S.Ct. 2525, 45 L.Ed.2d 562.

MR. JUSTICE STEWART delivered the opinion of the Court.

The Sixth and Fourteenth Amendments of our Constitution guarantee that a person brought to trial in any state or federal court must be afforded the right to the assistance of counsel before he can be validly convicted and punished by imprisonment. This clear constitutional rule has emerged from a series of cases decided here over the last 50 years. The question before us now is whether a defendant in a state criminal trial has a constitutional right to proceed without counsel when he voluntarily and intelligently elects to do so. Stated another way, the question is whether a State may constitutionally hale a person into its criminal courts and there force a lawyer upon him, even when he insists that he wants to conduct his own defense. It is not an easy question, but we have concluded that a State may not constitutionally do so.

Anthony Faretta was charged with grand theft in an information filed in the Superior Court of Los Angeles County, Cal. At the arraignment, the Superior Court Judge assigned to preside at the trial appointed the public defender to represent Faretta. Well before the date of trial, however, Faretta requested that he be permitted to represent himself. Questioning by the judge revealed that Faretta had once represented himself in a criminal prosecution, that he had a high school education, and that he did not want to be represented by the public defender because he believed that that office was "very loaded down with . . . a heavy case load." The judge responded that he believed Faretta was "making a mistake" and emphasized that in further proceedings Faretta would receive no special favors. Nevertheless, after establishing that Faretta wanted to represent himself and did not want a lawyer, the judge, in a "preliminary ruling," accepted Faretta's waiver of the assistance of counsel. The judge indicated, however, that he might reverse this ruling if it later appeared that Faretta was unable adequately to represent himself.

Several weeks thereafter, but still prior to trial, the judge sua sponte held a hearing to inquire into Faretta's ability to conduct his own defense, and questioned him specifically about both the hearsay rule and the state law governing the challenge of potential jurors.[3] After consideration of Faretta's answers, and observation of his de-

3. The colloquy was as follows:

"THE COURT: In the Faretta matter, I brought you back down here to do some reconsideration as to whether or not you should continue to represent yourself.

"How have you been getting along on your research?

"THE DEFENDANT: Not bad, your Honor.

"Last night I put in the mail a 995 motion and it should be with the Clerk within the next day or two.

"THE COURT: Have you been preparing yourself for the intricacies of the trial of the matter?

"THE DEFENDANT: Well, your Honor, I was hoping that the case could possibly be disposed of on the 995.

"Mrs. Ayers informed me yesterday that it was the Court's policy to hear the pretrial motions at the time of trial. If possible, your Honor, I would like a date set as soon as the Court deems adequate after they receive the motion, sometime before trial.

"THE COURT: Let's see how you have been doing on your research.

"How many exceptions are there to the hearsay rule?

"THE DEFENDANT: Well, the hearsay rule would, I guess, be called the best evidence rule, your Honor. And there are several exceptions in case law, but in actual statutory law, I don't feel there is none.

"THE COURT: What are the challenges to the jury for cause?

"THE DEFENDANT: Well, there is twelve peremptory challenges.

"THE COURT: And how many for cause?

"THE DEFENDANT: Well, as many as the Court deems valid.

"THE COURT: And what are they? What are the grounds for challenging a juror for cause?

"THE DEFENDANT: Well, numerous grounds to challenge a witness—I mean, a juror, your Honor, one being the juror is perhaps suffered, was a victim of the same type of offense, might be prejudiced toward the defendant. Any substantial ground that might make the juror prejudice[d] toward the defendant.

"THE COURT: Anything else?

"THE DEFENDANT: Well, a relative perhaps of the victim.

"THE COURT: Have you taken a look at that code section to see what it is?

"THE DEFENDANT: Challenge a juror?

"THE COURT: Yes.

"THE DEFENDANT: Yes, your Honor. I have done—

"THE COURT: What is the code section?

"THE DEFENDANT: On voir diring a jury, your Honor?

"THE COURT: Yes.

"THE DEFENDANT: I am not aware of the section right offhand.

"THE COURT: What code is it in?

"THE DEFENDANT: Well, the research I have done on challenging would be in Witkins Jurisprudence.

"THE COURT: Have you looked at any of the codes to see where these various things are taken up?

"THE DEFENDANT: No, your Honor, I haven't.

"THE COURT: Have you looked in any of the California Codes with reference to trial procedure?

"THE DEFENDANT: Yes, your Honor.

"THE COURT: What codes?

"THE DEFENDANT: I have done extensive research in the Penal Code, your Honor, and the Civil Code.

"THE COURT: If you have done extensive research into it, then tell me about it.

"THE DEFENDANT: On empaneling a jury, your Honor?

"THE COURT: Yes.

"THE DEFENDANT: Well, the District Attorney and the defendant, defense counsel, has both the right to 12 peremptory challenges of a jury. These 12 challenges are undisputable. Any reason that the defense or prosecution should feel that a juror would be inadequate to try the case or to rule on a case, they may then discharge that juror.

"But if there is a valid challenge due to grounds of prejudice or some other grounds, that these aren't considered in the 12 peremptory challenges. There are numerous and the defendant, the defense and the prosecution both have the right to make any inquiry to the jury as to their feelings toward the case."

meanor, the judge ruled that Faretta had not made an intelligent and knowing waiver of his right to the assistance of counsel, and also ruled that Faretta had no constitutional right to conduct his own defense. The judge, accordingly, reversed his earlier ruling permitting self-representation and again appointed the public defender to represent Faretta. Faretta's subsequent request for leave to act as co-counsel was rejected, as were his efforts to make certain motions on his own behalf. Throughout the subsequent trial, the judge required that Faretta's defense be conducted only through the appointed lawyer from the public defender's office. At the conclusion of the trial, the jury found Faretta guilty as charged, and the judge sentenced him to prison.

In the federal courts, the right of self-representation has been protected by statute since the beginnings of our Nation. Section 35 of the Judiciary Act of 1789, 1 Stat. 73, 92, enacted by the First Congress and signed by President Washington one day before the Sixth Amendment was proposed, provided that "in all the courts of the United States, the parties may plead and manage their own causes personally or by the assistance of ... counsel...." The right is currently codified in 28 U.S.C. § 1654.

With few exceptions, each of the several States also accords a defendant the right to represent himself in any criminal case. The Constitutions of 36 States explicitly confer that right. Moreover, many state courts have expressed the view that the right is also supported by the Constitution of the United States.

This Court has more than once indicated the same view....

The United States Courts of Appeals have repeatedly held that the right of self-representation is protected by the Bill of Rights....

This Court's past recognition of the right of self-representation, the federal-court authority holding the right to be of constitutional dimension, and the state constitutions pointing to the right's fundamental nature form a consensus not easily ignored. "[T]he mere fact that a path is a beaten one," Mr. Justice Jackson once observed, "is a persuasive reason for following it." We confront here a nearly universal conviction, on the part of our people as well as our courts, that forcing a lawyer upon an unwilling defendant is contrary to his basic right to defend himself if he truly wants to do so.

This consensus is soundly premised. The right of self-representation finds support in the structure of the Sixth Amendment, as well as in the English and colonial jurisprudence from which the Amendment emerged.

The Sixth Amendment includes a compact statement of the rights necessary to a full defense:

"In all criminal prosecutions, the accused shall enjoy the right ... to be informed of the nature and cause of the accusation; to be confronted with the witnesses against him; to have compulsory process for obtaining witnesses in his favor, and to have the Assistance of Counsel for his defence."

Because these rights are basic to our adversary system of criminal justice, they are part of the "due process of law" that is guaranteed by the Fourteenth Amendment to defendants in the criminal courts of the States. . . .

The Sixth Amendment does not provide merely that a defense shall be made for the accused; it grants to the accused personally the right to make his defense. It is the accused, not counsel, who must be "informed of the nature and cause of the accusation," who must be "confronted with the witnesses against him," and who must be accorded "compulsory process for obtaining witnesses in his favor." Although not stated in the Amendment in so many words, the right to self-representation—to make one's own defense personally—is thus necessarily implied by the structure of the Amendment. The right to defend is given directly to the accused; for it is he who suffers the consequences if the defense fails.

The counsel provision supplements this design. It speaks of the "assistance" of counsel, and an assistant, however expert, is still an assistant. The language and spirit of the Sixth Amendment contemplate that counsel, like the other defense tools guaranteed by the Amendment, shall be an aid to a willing defendant—not an organ of the State interposed between an unwilling defendant and his right to defend himself personally. To thrust counsel upon the accused, against his considered wish, thus violates the logic of the Amendment. In such a case, counsel is not an assistant, but a master;[16] and the right to make a defense is stripped of the personal character upon which the Amendment insists. It is true that when a defendant chooses to have a lawyer manage and present his case, law and tradition may allocate to the counsel the power to make binding decisions of trial strategy in many areas. . . . This allocation can only be justified, however, by the defendant's consent, at the outset, to accept counsel as his representative. An unwanted counsel "represents" the defendant only through a tenuous and unacceptable legal fiction. Unless the accused has acquiesced in such representation, the defense presented is not the defense guaranteed him by the Constitution, for, in a very real sense, it is not his defense.

The Sixth Amendment, when naturally read, thus implies a right of self-representation. This reading is reinforced by the Amendment's roots in English legal history.

---

16. Such a result would sever the concept of counsel from its historic roots. The first lawyers were personal friends of the litigant, brought into court by him so that he might "take 'counsel' with them" before pleading. 1 F. Pollock & F. Maitland, The History of English Law 211 (2d ed. 1909).

Similarly, the first "attorneys" were personal agents, often lacking any professional training, who were appointed by those litigants who had secured royal permission to carry on their affairs through a representative, rather than personally. Id., at 212–213.

In the long history of British criminal jurisprudence, there was only one tribunal that ever adopted a practice of forcing counsel upon an unwilling defendant in a criminal proceeding. The tribunal was the Star Chamber. That curious institution, which flourished in the late 16th and early 17th centuries, was of mixed executive and judicial character, and characteristically departed from common-law traditions. For those reasons, and because it specialized in trying "political" offenses, the Star Chamber has for centuries symbolized disregard of basic individual rights. The Star Chamber not merely allowed but required defendants to have counsel. The defendant's answer to an indictment was not accepted unless it was signed by counsel. When counsel refused to sign the answer, for whatever reason, the defendant was considered to have confessed. Stephen commented on this procedure: "There is something specially repugnant to justice in using rules of practice in such a manner as to debar a prisoner from defending himself, especially when the professed object of the rules so used is to provide for his defence." 1 J. Stephen, A History of the Criminal Law of England 341–342 (1883). The Star Chamber was swept away in 1641 by the revolutionary fervor of the Long Parliament. The notion of obligatory counsel disappeared with it.

By the common law of that time, it was not representation by counsel but self-representation that was the practice in prosecutions for serious crime. At one time, every litigant was required to "appear before the court in his own person and conduct his own cause in his own words" [Pollock & Maitland, supra, n. 16, at 211]. While a right to counsel developed early in civil cases and in cases of misdemeanor, a prohibition against the assistance of counsel continued for centuries in prosecutions for felony or treason. Thus, in the 16th and 17th centuries the accused felon or traitor stood alone, with neither counsel nor the benefit of other rights—to notice, confrontation, and compulsory process—that we now associate with a genuinely fair adversary proceeding.... As harsh as this now seems, at least "the prisoner was allowed to make what statements he liked...." [Holdsworth, A History of English Law, 195–196].

... The ban on counsel in felony cases, which had been substantially eroded in the courts, was finally eliminated by statute in 1836. In more recent years, Parliament has provided for court appointment of counsel in serious criminal cases, but only at the accused's request. At no point in this process of reform in England was counsel ever forced upon the defendant. The common-law rule ... has evidently always been that "no person charged with a criminal offence can have counsel forced upon him against his will." ...

In the American Colonies the insistence upon a right of self-representation was, if anything, more fervent than in England.

The colonists brought with them an appreciation of the virtues of self-reliance and a traditional distrust of lawyers. When the Colonies were first settled, "the lawyer was synonymous with the cringing

Attorneys–General and Solicitors–General of the Crown and the arbitrary Justices of the King's Court, all bent on the conviction of those who opposed the King's prerogatives, and twisting the law to secure convictions" [C. Warren, A History of the American Bar 7 (1911)]. This prejudice gained strength in the Colonies where "distrust of lawyers became an institution" [D. Boorstin, The Americans; The Colonial Experience 197 (1958)]. Several Colonies prohibited pleading for hire in the 17th century.... The years of Revolution and Confederation saw an upsurge of antilawyer sentiment, a "sudden revival, after the War of the Revolution, of the old dislike and distrust of lawyers as a class" [Warren, supra, at 212]. In the heat of these sentiments the Constitution was forged.

This is not to say that the Colonies were slow to recognize the value of counsel in criminal cases. Colonial judges soon departed from ancient English practice and allowed accused felons the aid of counsel for their defense. At the same time, however, the basic right of self-representation was never questioned. We have found no instance where a colonial court required a defendant in a criminal case to accept as his representative an unwanted lawyer. Indeed, even where counsel was permitted, the general practice continued to be self-representation.

The right of self-representation was guaranteed in many colonial charters and declarations of rights. These early documents establish that the "right to counsel" meant to the colonists a right to choose between pleading through a lawyer and representing oneself.[37] After the Declaration of Independence, the right of self-representation, along with other rights basic to the making of a defense, entered the new state constitutions in wholesale fashion. The right to counsel was clearly thought to supplement the primary right of the accused to defend himself,[39] utilizing his personal rights to notice, confrontation, and compulsory process. And when the Colonies or newly independent

37. See, e.g., the Massachusetts Body of Liberties, Art. 26 (1641) ..., [and] the Concessions and Agreements of West New Jersey [1677]....

The Pennsylvania Frame of Government of 1682, perhaps "the most influential of the Colonial documents protecting individual rights," 1 B. Schwartz, The Bill of Rights: A Documentary History 130 (1971) ..., provided:

"That, in all courts all persons of all persuasions may freely appear in their own way, and according to their own manner, and there personally plead their own cause themselves; or, if unable, by their friends...."

That provision was no doubt inspired by William Penn's belief that an accused should go free if he could personally persuade a jury that it would be unjust to convict him. In England, 12 years earlier, Penn, after preaching a sermon in the street, had been indicted and tried for disturbing the peace. Penn conceded that he was "unacquainted with the formality of the law," but requested that he be given a fair hearing and the "liberty of making my defence." The request was granted, Penn represented himself, and although the judges jailed him for contempt, the jury acquitted him of the charge....

39. The Founders believed that self-representation was a basic right of a free people. For example, Thomas Paine, arguing in support of the 1776 Pennsylvania Declaration of Rights, said:

"Either party ... has a natural right to plead his own cause; this right is consistent with safety, therefore it is retained; but the parties may not be able, ... therefore the civil right of pleading by proxy, that is, by a council, is an appendage to the natural right [of self-representation]...."

States provided by statute rather than by constitution for court appointment of counsel in criminal cases, they also meticulously preserved the right of the accused to defend himself personally.

. . .

In sum, there is no evidence that the colonists and the Framers ever doubted the right of self-representation, or imagined that this right might be considered inferior to the right of assistance of counsel. To the contrary, the colonists and the Framers, as well as their English ancestors, always conceived of the right to counsel as an "assistance" for the accused, to be used at his option, in defending himself. The Framers selected in the Sixth Amendment a form of words that necessarily implies the right of self-representation. That conclusion is supported by centuries of consistent history.

There can be no blinking the fact that the right of an accused to conduct his own defense seems to cut against the grain of this Court's decisions holding that the Constitution requires that no accused can be convicted and imprisoned unless he has been accorded the right to the assistance of counsel. . . . For it is surely true that the basic thesis of those decisions is that the help of a lawyer is essential to assure the defendant a fair trial. And a strong argument can surely be made that the whole thrust of those decisions must inevitably lead to the conclusion that a State may constitutionally impose a lawyer upon even an unwilling defendant.

But it is one thing to hold that every defendant, rich or poor, has the right to the assistance of counsel, and quite another to say that a State may compel a defendant to accept a lawyer he does not want. The value of state-appointed counsel was not unappreciated by the Founders, yet the notion of compulsory counsel was utterly foreign to them. And whatever else may be said of those who wrote the Bill of Rights, surely there can be no doubt that they understood the inestimable worth of free choice.

It is undeniable that in most criminal prosecutions defendants could better defend with counsel's guidance than by their own unskilled efforts. But where the defendant will not voluntarily accept representation by counsel, the potential advantage of a lawyer's training and experience can be realized, if at all, only imperfectly. To force a lawyer on a defendant can only lead him to believe that the law contrives against him. Moreover, it is not inconceivable that in some rare instances, the defendant might in fact present his case more effectively by conducting his own defense. Personal liberties are not rooted in the law of averages. The right to defend is personal. The defendant, and not his lawyer or the State, will bear the personal consequences of a conviction. It is the defendant, therefore, who must be free personally to decide whether in his particular case counsel is to his advantage. And although he may conduct his own defense ultimately to his own detriment, his choice must be honored out of "that respect for the individual which is the lifeblood of the law." Illinois v. Allen, 397 U.S.

337, 350–351, 90 S.Ct. 1057, 1064, 25 L.Ed.2d 353 (BRENNAN, J., concurring).[46]

When an accused manages his own defense, he relinquishes, as a purely factual matter, many of the traditional benefits associated with the right to counsel. For this reason, in order to represent himself, the accused must "knowingly and intelligently" forgo those relinquished benefits. Johnson v. Zerbst, 304 U.S., at 464–465, 58 S.Ct., at 1023.... Although a defendant need not himself have the skill and experience of a lawyer in order competently and intelligently to choose self-representation, he should be made aware of the dangers and disadvantages of self-representation, so that the record will establish that "he knows what he is doing and his choice is made with eyes open." Adams v. United States ex rel. McCann, 317 U.S., at 279, 63 S.Ct., at 242.

Here, weeks before trial, Faretta clearly and unequivocally declared to the trial judge that he wanted to represent himself and did not want counsel. The record affirmatively shows that Faretta was literate, competent, and understanding, and that he was voluntarily exercising his informed free will. The trial judge had warned Faretta that he thought it was a mistake not to accept the assistance of counsel, and that Faretta would be required to follow all the "ground rules" of trial procedure. We need make no assessment of how well or poorly Faretta had mastered the intricacies of the hearsay rule and the California code provisions that govern challenges of potential jurors on voir dire. For his technical legal knowledge, as such, was not relevant to an assessment of his knowing exercise of the right to defend himself.

. . .

MR. CHIEF JUSTICE BURGER, with whom MR. JUSTICE BLACKMUN and MR. JUSTICE REHNQUIST join, dissenting.

.... As the Court seems to recognize ..., the conclusion that the rights guaranteed by the Sixth Amendment are "personal" to an accused reflects nothing more than the obvious fact that it is he who is on trial and therefore has need of a defense. But neither that nearly trivial proposition nor the language of the Amendment, which speaks in uniformly mandatory terms, leads to the further conclusion that the right to counsel is merely supplementary and may be dispensed with at

---

46. We are told that many criminal defendants representing themselves may use the courtroom for deliberate disruption of their trials. But the right of self-representation has been recognized from our beginnings by federal law and by most of the States, and no such result has thereby occurred. Moreover, the trial judge may terminate self-representation by a defendant who deliberately engages in serious and obstructionist misconduct. See Illinois v. Allen, 397 U.S. 337, 90 S.Ct. 1057, 25 L.Ed.2d 353. Of course, a State may—even over objection by the accused—appoint a "standby counsel" to aid the accused if and when the accused requests help, and to be available to represent the accused in the event that termination of the defendant's self-representation is necessary....

The right of self-representation is not a license to abuse the dignity of the courtroom. Neither is it a license not to comply with relevant rules of procedural and substantive law. Thus, whatever else may or may not be open to him on appeal, a defendant who elects to represent himself cannot thereafter complain that the quality of his own defense amounted to a denial of "effective assistance of counsel."

the whim of the accused. Rather, this Court's decisions have consistently included the right to counsel as an integral part of the bundle making up the larger "right to a defense as we know it." ...

The reason for this hardly requires explanation. The fact of the matter is that in all but an extraordinarily small number of cases an accused will lose whatever defense he may have if he undertakes to conduct the trial himself. The Court's opinion in Powell v. Alabama, 287 U.S. 45, 53 S.Ct. 55, 77 L.Ed. 158 (1932), puts the point eloquently:

> "Even the intelligent and educated layman has small and sometimes no skill in the science of law. If charged with crime, he is incapable, generally, of determining for himself whether the indictment is good or bad. He is unfamiliar with the rules of evidence. Left without the aid of counsel he may be put on trial without a proper charge, and convicted upon incompetent evidence, or evidence irrelevant to the issue or otherwise inadmissible. He lacks both the skill and knowledge adequately to prepare his defense, even though he have a perfect one. He requires the guiding hand of counsel at every step in the proceedings against him. Without it, though he be not guilty, he faces the danger of conviction because he does not know how to establish his innocence. If that be true of men of intelligence, how much more true is it of the ignorant and illiterate, or those of feeble intellect." Id., at 69, 53 S.Ct., at 64.

Obviously, these considerations do not vary depending upon whether the accused actively desires to be represented by counsel or wishes to proceed pro se. Nor is it accurate to suggest, as the Court seems to later in its opinion, that the quality of his representation at trial is a matter with which only the accused is legitimately concerned.... Although we have adopted an adversary system of criminal justice ..., the prosecution is more than an ordinary litigant, and the trial judge is not simply an automaton who insures that technical rules are adhered to. Both are charged with the duty of insuring that justice, in the broadest sense of that term, is achieved in every criminal trial.... That goal is ill-served, and the integrity of and public confidence in the system are undermined, when an easy conviction is obtained due to the defendant's ill-advised decision to waive counsel. The damage thus inflicted is not mitigated by the lame explanation that the defendant simply availed himself of the "freedom" "to go to jail under his own banner...." United States ex rel. Maldonado v. Denno, 348 F.2d 12, 15 (CA2 1965). The system of criminal justice should not be available as an instrument of self-destruction.

In short, both the "spirit and the logic" of the Sixth Amendment are that every person accused of crime shall receive the fullest possible defense; in the vast majority of cases this command can be honored only by means of the expressly guaranteed right to counsel, and the trial judge is in the best position to determine whether the accused is capable of conducting his defense. True freedom of choice and society's interest in seeing that justice is achieved can be vindicated only if the trial court retains discretion to reject any attempted waiver of counsel and insist that the accused be tried according to the Constitution. This discretion is as critical an element of basic fairness as a trial judge's discretion to decline to accept a plea of guilty....

    . . .

MR. JUSTICE BLACKMUN, with whom THE CHIEF JUSTICE and MR. JUSTICE REHNQUIST join, dissenting.

    [T]he Court holds that any defendant in any criminal proceeding may insist on representing himself regardless of how complex the trial is likely to be and regardless of how frivolous the defendant's motivations may be. I cannot agree that there is anything in the Due Process Clause or the Sixth Amendment that requires the States to subordinate the solemn business of conducting a criminal prosecution to the whimsical—albeit voluntary—caprice of every accused who wishes to use his trial as a vehicle for personal or political self-gratification.

    The Court seems to suggest that so long as the accused is willing to pay the consequences of his folly, there is no reason for not allowing a defendant the right to self-representation.... That view ignores the established principle that the interest of the State in a criminal prosecution "is not that it shall win a case, but that justice shall be done." Berger v. United States, 295 U.S. 78, 88, 55 S.Ct. 629, 633, 79 L.Ed. 1314 (1935).... For my part, I do not believe that any amount of pro se pleading can cure the injury to society of an unjust result, but I do believe that a just result should prove to be an effective balm for almost any frustrated pro se defendant.

    . . .

    If there is any truth to the old proverb that "one who is his own lawyer has a fool for a client," the Court by its opinion today now bestows a constitutional right on one to make a fool of himself.

Note on Faretta: The lawyer as padrone

    1. In what sense did the trial judge mean that Faretta had not made an "intelligent and knowing waiver" of his right to counsel? What, according to the Supreme Court majority, was erroneous about this conclusion?

    2. Consider the difference of opinion within the Court with respect to the following factors:

    (a) Are defendants better off having than waiving counsel?

    • Do the Justices differ in their view of the instrumental value of having counsel?

    • in their notion of what "better off" means?

    (b) How should the law respond to the phenomenon that clients (especially criminal defendants who prefer to proceed *pro se*), sometimes mistrust their attorneys? Justice Stewart, for the majority, notes that "to force a lawyer on a defendant can only lead him to believe that the law contrives against him." To Justice Blackmun, "a just result should prove to be an effective balm for almost any frustrated pro se defendant."

• What does "should" mean in this latter sentence?

• How would you articulate the difference between the Justices on this issue? Compare Note 2 following *Jones v. Barnes,* p. 20, above.

(c) How do they differ in their expectations of the bases on which some defendants will insist on proceeding to trial without counsel if they are allowed the choice? What response to Justice Blackmun's portrayal of defendants acting pro se out of "whimsical caprice" and "folly" is implicit in the majority opinion?

(d) How do the Justices differ in their understanding of the purpose(s) of the Sixth Amendment guarantee? What response does the Court's opinion suggest to Chief Justice Burger's assertion that "the quality of his representation at trial is [not] a matter with which only the accused is legitimately concerned"?

3. Justice Stewart supports his doctrinal conclusion regarding the meaning of the Sixth and Fourteenth Amendments with traditional interpretative aids: the constitutional language, the history of the rights to have counsel and to appear pro se, the contemporaneous understanding of those rights in the colonial and post-colonial periods, and the pattern of judicial opinion over the years. The dissenters do not find these factors sufficient to compel them to adopt a position that they find absurd and unfair.

(a) Am I correct in suggesting that it is the difference of opinion on the questions put in Note 2, above, rather than on the constitutional language and history, that accounts for the majority's acceptance, and the dissents' rejection, of that language and history as dispositive? Is that true of your own view?

(b) Consider, too, the possible *sources* of one's views (including your views) on the questions in Note 2. Am I over-using the idea of "celebratory" and "troubled" stances toward the justness of the legal system in suggesting, once again, that as a foundational source? Does the idea have explanatory power, in your judgment, as you think about some of the above questions with it in mind?

4. Are the issues presented in *Faretta* at all relevant in considering the proper mode of attorney-client interaction in circumstances where a person *is* represented by counsel?

(a) Look again at *Jones v. Barnes,* page 12, in the introductory section of this chapter. Five of the seven Justices participating in both *Faretta* and *Barnes* were in the majority in only one of them, dissenting in the other.* The New Jersey Supreme Court has read *Faretta* in a manner that suggests (with Justices White and Powell) that the two decisions can stand together. "*Faretta* recognized that when a defendant chooses to have a lawyer represent him at trial, ordinarily such counsel controls trial strate-

---

* Perhaps Justice Blackmun, who concurred only in the result in *Barnes,* should be counted as disagreeing with *both* majority opinions.

gy." State v. Pratts, 71 N.J. 399, 365 A.2d 928, 929 (1976) (decision not to call a witness who counsel believed would harm defendant's case).

On what grounds might you nonetheless conclude, with Justice Brennan, that *Barnes* is inconsistent with *Faretta* ?

(b) In 1967, the Supreme Court held that, should an assigned appellate counsel conclude that the appeal is frivolous, he or she may not simply seek leave of the court to withdraw, but must include with the motion to withdraw a statement referring to anything in the record that might arguably support an appeal. Anders v. California, 386 U.S. 738, 87 S.Ct. 1396, 18 L.Ed.2d 493 (1967). In McCoy v. Court of Appeals, 486 U.S. 429, 108 S.Ct. 1895, 100 L.Ed.2d 440 (1988), the Court upheld a Wisconsin Supreme Court rule requiring an attorney filing an "*Anders* " statement to include in it "a discussion of why the issue lacks merit." The Wisconsin requirement, the Court reasoned:

> provides an additional safeguard against mistaken conclusions by counsel that the strongest arguments he or she can find are frivolous. . . .
> [It] may forestall some motions to withdraw and will assist the court in passing on the soundness of the lawyer's conclusion that the appeal is frivolous.

Justice Brennan, in dissent, relied in part on an asserted difference between the situation of assigned counsel and that of retained counsel, who is obliged to withdraw if he or she can find no arguable merit in an appeal but can do so without announcing that conclusion to the court, and in part on the legitimacy of assigning counsel a role as aid to the court itself:

> Our disagreement boils down to whether defense counsel who details for a court why he believes his client's appeal is frivolous befriends the client or the court. The Court looks at Wisconsin's regime and sees a friend of the client who "assur[es] that the constitutional rights of indigent defendants are scrupulously honored." . . . I look at the same regime and see a friend of the court whose advocacy is so damning that the prosecutor never responds. See Trans. of Oral Arg. 13–14, 30. Either way, with friends like that, the indigent criminal appellant is truly alone.

Why "either way"? Why does Justice Brennan think that a lawyer who "assures" that his or her client's rights are honored is no friend to the client?

(c) Is there an appropriate charge of inconsistency to be made against supporters of the traditional concept of advocacy, on the ground that they reject any notion that an attorney has a responsibility toward the legal system (going beyond compliance with the law itself) when considering the question of role-differentiation, but rely on it in considering questions like those raised by *Faretta* and *McCoy* ?

Can a similar charge be justly laid against those who reject the traditional concept, who seem simply to reverse positions (while retaining the inconsistency)?

5. The remaining materials in this sub-section address the three questions with which it began, in the context of representation in civil matters.

LAWYER AND CLIENT: WHO'S IN CHARGE?

Douglas Rosenthal
Chapters 1, 6 (1974).

There are two ideas about the proper distribution of power in professional consulting relationships. The traditional idea is that both parties are best served by the professional's assuming broad control over solutions to the problems brought by the client. The contradictory view is that both client and consultant gain from a sharing of control over many of the decisions arising out of the relationship. The traditional view has been more systematically elaborated as part of a larger theory of professional service—especially by sociologists specializing in the study of professionalization in medicine. This view is traditional in the sense that it has been the prevailing view since the time of Hippocrates. Even Plato, who argued that free men are entitled to the care of physicians who spend time hearing their patients out and explaining and justifying their diagnosis and proposed remedies, viewed the physician as retaining the position of dominance, using the art of persuasion as a technique of control. . . .

Sociologist Howard Becker has characterized what I call the traditional approach in the following terms:

Professionals, in contrast to members of other occupations, claim and are often accorded complete autonomy in their work. Since they are presumed to be the only judges of how good their work is, no layman or other outsider can make any judgment of what they can do. If their activities are unsuccessful, only another professional can say whether this was due to incompetence or to the inevitable workings of nature or society by which even the most competent practitioner would have been stymied. This image of the professional justifies his demand for complete autonomy and his demand that the client give up his own judgment and responsibility, leaving everything in the hands of the professional.

. . .

Underlying each approach is a relatively consistent, usually implicit model of how professionals and clients should interact and the justifications for these forms of interaction. Not only does each model lead to different positions on the larger issue of power but to different ideas about how the professional-client relationship should be conducted in specific details. These disagreements can be seen in the contrasting answers that a supporter of each approach would give to the following six questions:

1. How active should clients be in trying to understand their problem and in trying to influence its solution?

2. Do professionals usually give effective service?

3. Do client problems have a single best routine and technical solution inaccessible to lay understanding?

4.   Do professionals give disinterested service?

5.   Are high professional standards set and maintained by professional associations and the courts?

6.   How accessible is effective professional service to paying clients?

[T]he two contrasting sets of answers [can be] stated as six basic elements of each model.

. . .

	Question	Traditional Answer	Participatory Answer
1.	Proper client behavior?	It consists of little effort at understanding; passive, trusting delegation of responsibility; and following of instructions.	It involves an active, skeptical effort to be informed and to share responsibility, making mutually agreeable choices.
2.	Effectiveness of professional service?	Ineffective professional service is rare.	Ineffective professional service is common.
3.	Nature of professional problems?	They are routine and technical, having a best solution inaccessible to lay understanding.	They involve open, unpredictable individualized choices, understandable to a layman, for which there is no single best answer.
4.	Disinterested service?	Professionals can and do make the client's interest their own.	Disinterested professional service is virtually impossible.
5.	Professional standards?	High standards are set and maintained by the professions themselves and by the courts.	Standards are neither clearly set nor effectively enforced by either the professions or the courts.
6.	Accessibility of effective professional service to paying clients?	Effective professional service is accessible to all paying clients.	Many paying clients have difficulty finding effective professional service.

HOW ACTIVE SHOULD CLIENTS BE IN TRYING TO UNDERSTAND THEIR PROBLEM AND IN TRYING TO INFLUENCE ITS SOLUTION?

According to the traditional theory the client who is passive, follows instructions, and trusts the professional without criticism, with few questions or requests, is preferable and will do better than the difficult client who is critical and questioning. It is of paramount importance that the interaction between client and professional be stable and free of conflict. This stability requirement is one of the justifications cited for demanding complete client confidence in the professional consultant. Without such confidence the client may disrupt the consultation and undercut the effectiveness of the professional's service. . . .

The participatory theory promotes an active strategy assuming that it is primarily the client's own responsibility to grapple with the problem. Instead of delegating responsibility to the professional and leaving the decisions to him while being kept only minimally informed, the participating client seeks information to help him define his problem and what he wants to accomplish, rather than waiting to be told how to proceed. Periodically he reviews and reevaluates the steps already taken, and the professional's performance, by questioning and by appraising the consistency and accuracy of the professional's answers. He is aware that there are open choices to be made in solving his problem and expects to have his concerns reflected in the choices made.

. . .

The passive client's delegation of responsibility and control detaches him from the problem solving process. Only repeated or dramatic evidence of professional nonperformance or misconduct leads to an active reevaluation of the delegation—and the decision whether or not to fire the first professional and delegate responsibility to a second one.

Of course, the active strategy is costly. From the client, it demands energy, intelligence, and judgment. From the professional it demands patience and tolerance built on recognition of an obligation to earn the client's cooperation. The passive strategy makes fewer demands on both parties, but if the professional in fact makes a mistake, it may not be noticed in time to be corrected.

Traditionalists find the notion of an active strategy naïve and possibly dangerous. Take away the professional's role of decision responsibility and the client is more likely to be frightened and resentful. Traditionalists are convinced in fact that people would reject an active problem-solving role even if it were offered to them by an unusually self-sacrificing and foolhardy professional. While participationists concede that most people presently do not push to assert an active role, they contend that clients have never received any real encouragement. On the contrary, they say, clients have been socialized by the traditional theory to think it mistrustful to want influence—mistrust being an illegitimate client response. In the participationist view, if clients don't want decision-making responsibility once it has been effectively offered to them, they can knowingly waive it. But even the chance to forego participatory opportunities is an improvement over the norm of nonparticipation. Traditionalists respond with skepticism about the capacities of most people to make *knowing* waivers. The traditional model implies that there are only two choices for a client: complete trust or uncompromising hostility. The participating model rejects such a clean-cut distinction. . . . It has been argued that in fact people never do fully trust strangers, even if they are profession-als, and that, as with a treaty negotiation between suspicious diplomats, stable and efficient collaborative effort can be maintained between mutually suspicious professionals and clients for extended periods about matters of great delicacy and importance.

Do Professionals Usually Give Effective Service?

Traditionalists believe that passive client trust is warranted by the consistently high standards of performance of virtually all certified professionals. As part of a broad and impressionistic survey of the legal profession conducted after World War II, Phillips and McCoy concluded that,

> on the whole, the service which the Bar renders to the community is immeasureable. That it should be rendered with so little justi-fied criticism is a splendid tribute to the maintenance of lofty standards by men whose only restriction is their own conscience and whose only guide is the high tradition of their profession.
>
> . . .

... To the extent that professional failure is not rare, it becomes more urgent for clients to make the effort to participate actively in solving their problem. On the other hand, if professional problem solving is effective in virtually all situations, client activity to monitor, appraise, and supplement professional conduct is less necessary.

Do Client Problems Have a Single Best Routine and Technical Solution Accessible to Lay Understanding?

. . .

The traditional theory rests heavily on the need for trust because it is believed that lay clients do not have and cannot feasibly obtain sufficient knowledge for even partial self-diagnosis and remedy. As Alexander Pope observed, "a little learning is a dangerous thing"; the client who thinks he knows better will inflict greater harm upon himself by rejecting good advice than by accepting it unquestioningly. Participationists are more optimistic....

Participationists are suspicious about the professionals wittingly or unwittingly maintaining client uncertainty and client feelings of incom-petence as a means of increasing their own indispensability—their power over the client.

. . .

Many traditionalists would not deny that professionals frequently avoid informing their clients, but they feel that most clients prefer it this way. As they see it, clients want simple, reassuring answers. They are afraid of knowing too much lest some news be bad news. Illustrative of traditional thinking is the following advice offered to lawyers by the Wisconsin Bar Association:

Get at the client's problem immediately and stick to it. Don't bother to explain the reasoning processes by which you arrive at your advice. The client expects you to be an expert. This not only prolongs the interview, but generally confuses the client. The client will feel better and more secure if told in simple straightforward language what to do and how to do it, without an explanation of *how* you reached your conclusions.

The participationist counters that people have a greater capacity for confronting reality than they are given credit for—especially when the risks of avoiding reality are made clear to them.

The traditional model assigns the determination of how much information the client should be given about his problem and the possible ways of dealing with it to the discretion of each professional. The professional's judgment may be based on a case-by-case assessment of what each client wants to hear, how much trouble the client is likely to make for the professional in added demands, how much time and energy it is worth spending on the case, how easy it is to communicate with the client, and related factors.

A participatory view of the problem-solving relationship gives explicit and extensive disclosure a central place. Since it is the client who will have to live with the outcome, he should be informed about the risks and benefits of alternative courses of action even if the choice is obvious to the professional and even if the client does not fully comprehend what he is being told. It is not enough to leave the amount of disclosure to the discretion of the professional. The client should be entitled to this information as a matter of course. This information will not only provide psychological reassurance, but will provide a basis for the client's appraisal of the professional's competence to help him. Furthermore, it can be used as a means for sharing decision responsibility with the client. Full disclosure will facilitate the client's ratification of the action taken, thus minimizing the grounds for subsequent client grievances. The discipline of having to hear and understand the information will help the client to feel less estranged from the profession and professional jargon....

Do Professionals Give Disinterested Service?

The concept of disinterested service is a hallmark of the traditional model. The competent professional is able to see what is in the best interests of his client—and to make those interests his own....

Critics of the traditional theory find it serving an important ideological function for the professional: to justify his freedom from criticism and control. The theory encourages both popular respect for the professions and practitioner self-respect: public relations and self-esteem. Participationists are suspicious that traditionalists may be engaging in self-delusive propaganda more than in realistic analysis. They feel traditionalists give insufficient attention to the possibility of the professional's bias in determining the client's interest.

. . .

. . . The point relevant to a participatory theory is that the professional has self-interests, of which he himself may be unaware, that may compete with the objective interests of his clients. Without sufficient self-awareness, the professional is not likely to be disinterested. Traditionalists doubt that these unconscious needs play a significantly negative part in interaction between mature adults over nonpsychiatric "technical" matters.

. . .

ARE HIGH PROFESSIONAL STANDARDS SET AND MAINTAINED BY PROFESSIONAL ASSOCIATIONS AND THE COURTS?

Traditionalists are impressed with the way legal and medical professionals are "socialized into the world of work"—the way they are trained in the norms of ethical and skilled practice and meet self-imposed high standards. One book introducing the layman to the law states:

> The standards of the American lawyer are high. He must meet rigid character and educational requirements established by the courts in order to become a member of the legal profession, and in daily practice he must conform to a rigorous code of principles and practice.

. . .

In recent scholarship, the traditional view has been disputed. Davis and Blake have argued that social rules themselves are frequently in conflict, that feared sanctions frequently conflict with and prove less influential than social rules, and that for many of the circumstances of life and work, specific social guidelines do not exist. Jerome Carlin has conducted research suggesting that certain social pressures within the professional community of New York City lawyers actually reinforce unethical conduct; Carlin's findings have been replicated by Kenneth Reichstein in a concurrent study of the Chicago Bar, and disputed by Joel Handler, at least as applied to nonmetropolitan areas of the midwest. If in fact there is a high degree of unethical and incompetent conduct among professionals, it argues for more active client scrutiny and involvement in the hired professional's performance.

HOW ACCESSIBLE IS EFFECTIVE PROFESSIONAL SERVICE TO PAYING CLIENTS?

Two studies of how patients find doctors report the existence of "lay referral systems," relatively structured social contacts with lay influentials which paying patients use to identify medical problems, find doctors, and appraise their ability. The concept of a lay referral system implies that clients know enough about how to find professional help to obtain it when they need it. Access to effective service is traditionally recognized as a problem mainly for the nonpaying poor. Whether clients have adequate access to effective service is tied to the general question about competency among certified professionals. Many traditionalists say that,

> Today the requirements for becoming a lawyer in most states are quite stringent. You may be *quite sure* [italics mine] that the man you are dealing with has the minimum qualifications.

If they are right, virtually any lawyer approached can be relied upon to give at least adequate service.

The contrary view is not only that adequate minimum qualifications are not often met, but that the problem of access is primarily one of clients' not being informed about when and to whom to go for help.

> . . .

Even if a layman knows that he should consult a professional, what criteria of selection does he use? Traditionally, a professional's reputation among his colleagues has been considered the most effective criterion a client can use to choose a consultant. There is a widespread assumption that the higher a professional's status within the professional community, the more ethical and competent he is likely to be. . . .

With the participatory approach, it is important that clients have access to information relevant to choosing among professional consultants. Yet, given both the problems that a layman has in determining an expert's professional reputation and in appraising the appropriateness of that reputation, it is recognized that important criteria accessible to the client in the choice of a professional are responsiveness to the client's wants and a manner that shows promptness, clear thinking, attention to details, and knowledgeability in responding to questions. Liking a professional and feeling at ease with him is part of this assessment.

[The core of the book is an empirical study of a group of tort claimants. The results tend to suggest that plaintiffs whose interaction with their attorneys fits the "participatory" model did better, as measured by the amount of the settlement, than those represented in accordance with the "traditional" model.]

Some will accept the validity and the generalizability of the evidence presented in this book and yet be unwilling to abandon the traditional model as the ideal pattern of behavior for the professional and client. This is a position justifiable according to at least two concepts of human nature—one conservative and one reformist. The conservative position would be founded on skepticism about the potential for improvement of institutions so dependent upon the frailties of human nature. If men are to rise above their limitations, so the argument goes, it is only by giving them a higher ideal of nobility and selflessness to which to aspire, an ideal which can lift, at best, a few above the pull of human temptations. This higher ideal is admirably provided by the traditional model. The desirability of, as well as the potential for, extensive professional reform is questioned by many of this disposition. They tend to have a view of the development of social institutions such as professional-client relationships which sees existing institutions as a reflection of the desires and needs of those who live and work within these institutions and which mistrusts the ultimate constructiveness of basic institutional reform. "The relationship of authority-dependency between professional and client has developed as it has because that is the way people want it to be." If clients choose a relationship of dependency and if this dependency entails certain risks because of the limitations of professionals and because of the uncertain nature of professional problems then, in the words of Dostoyevski's Grand Inquisitor, it is because "man has no more agonizing anxiety than to find someone to whom he can hand over with all speed the gift of freedom with which the unhappy creature is born."

The reformist defense of the traditional ideal sees it as a potential source of tremendous good. Can it be doubted that many distinguished doctors, lawyers, scientists, teachers, and others have been inspired to careers of extraordinary generosity, probity, and responsibility by the traditional professional ideal? At no time in the past, one may argue, have professionals performed so well, has professional service been more accessible or professional conduct so well defined and policed; it is not the ideals that have outlived their usefulness as ideals but an improvable failure of will and initiative in implementing these ideals.

. . .

I do not accept the appropriateness of the conservative defense of the traditional model because it relies, I believe, on an unduly pessimistic view of human nature, and undue willingness to tolerate what is wrong with existing institutions, and an unduly fearful attitude about the possibilities of constructive social innovation. Nor do I accept the reformist defense which asks too much from educated professionals and too little from educated laymen. Professionals are asked, under the traditional ideal, to make uncertain problems appear certain, to neutralize their passions, to be uncompromising toward the failings of their colleagues, and to surrender the special privileges of a preferred status. Lay clients, however, are assumed to be virtually helpless in coping with complex personal problems, to be nuisances when they try to involve themselves in the experts' province, and to be incapable of accepting effective decision making responsibility. It seems unfair and unrealistic to ask so much more of professionals than is asked of nonprofessionals. A participatory model which looks to the professional and the lay client more nearly as equals capable of joint collaboration takes a more properly balanced view of human nature. To paraphrase Paul Ramsey's paraphrase of Reinhold Niebuhr's defense of democracy, on both positive and negative grounds, "Man's capacity to become joint adverturers (sic) in a common cause makes the participatory relation possible; man's propensity to overreach his joint adverturer even in a good cause makes the participatory relation necessary."

. . .

The participatory model implies that citizens should have an opportunity to learn more than they presently know about problems likely to be important to them during the course of their lives—possibly even learning about these problems before they reach adulthood. For many years the public schools have taught courses in civics on the assumption that it is desirable in a democratic society to have politically sophisticated citizens. If the participatory model is appropriate, adolescents might also be given the opportunity to take problem-oriented courses in being sophisticated consumers of professional services, sophisticated personal problem solvers, capable of confronting difficult problems and working with trained professionals to cope with them. Problems for consideration in such a course might include some of the following: dealing with serious physical illness, possibly requiring surgery; dealing with a serious emotional problem; dealing with the death of a close relative; bringing a lawsuit for damages arising out of a serious accident; finding a job; planning one's estate; being charged with the commission of a crime; investing money; or buying a home. There are large issues for profitable consideration if one looks closely and imaginatively at prosaic matters.

. . .

There is more that can be said to justify the normative claims of the participatory model and its use as a paradigm for new patterns of governance of professional-client relationships than merely that it appears more realistically to account for the process of personal injury problem solving. . . .

The participatory model promotes the dignity of citizens as clients. The desire of human beings to be their own master has been described by Sir Isaiah Berlin:

> I wish my life and decisions to depend on myself, not on external forces of whatever kind. I wish to be the instrument of my own not of other men's, acts of will. I wish to be a subject, not an object; to be moved by reasons, by conscious purposes, which are my own, not by causes which affect me, as it were, from outside. I wish to be somebody, not nobody; a doer—deciding, not being decided for, self-directed and not acted upon by external nature or by other men as if I were a thing, or an animal, or a slave incapable of playing a human role, that is, of conceiving goals and policies of my own and realizing them. This is at least part of what I mean when I say that I am rational, and that it is my reason that distinguishes me as a human being from the rest of the world. I wish, above all, to be conscious of myself as a thinking, willing, active being, bearing responsibility for my choices and able to explain them by references to my own ideas and purposes.

Client participation in problem solving makes the client a doer, responsible for his choices. The traditional model, on the other hand, encourages passivity, dependence, and an absence of responsibility for choices.

The participatory model increases the chances for client satisfaction in at least two respects. Client participation not only yields satisfactions which comes with achieving a measure of control over one's life but participation also reduces excessive anxieties which are the product of uninformed fears and unexpected stress. Dealing with difficult personal problems is a task requiring an individual's intellectual and emotional preparation. A client is faced with a previously unexperienced situation, the perils of which can be magnified out of true proportion unless controlled by a realistic assessment of what may be encountered and the likelihood of experiencing various anticipated dangers. Active collaboration with the professional invites the client to obtain the information necessary to anticipate and cope with the real strains of the problem. Evidence continues to accumulate that client satisfactions are increased by meaningful access to full information about their problems.

The main innovative finding of the research reported in this book is that active participation can actually promote effective problem solving. The traditional model is incapable of explaining this finding. Evidence drawn from the personal injury claims process indicates that clients can supplement the specialized knowledge of professionals, fill gaps, catch mistakes, and provide criteria relevant for decision. Conversely, the collaborative task of having to explain and discuss the problem with the client can help the professional avoid mistakes and focus on the relevant aspects of the problem. While this book does not prove that client participation promotes rational decision, it establishes a prima facie case requiring clear and convincing contrary evidence before it can be rejected.

The participatory model . . . reduces the burdens imposed upon the professional by the paternal role. . . . It also brings professional-client relationships into congruence with this society's abiding commitment to democratic values which values are necessarily challenged by the existence within our society of paternalistic institutions.

The participatory model . . . promotes public sophistication about service institutions which increases a true appreciation of their indispensability and invites the more extensive use of these professional services.

Finally, and perhaps most surprisingly to those who see the participatory model as a threat to professionals, it can actually increase the satisfactions of professional practice by freeing professionals both from impossible standards which are bound to be undershot, thereby inevitably disappointing large segments of the public and from the excessive burdens of full responsibility for the solving of the personal problems of individuals. The participatory model invites the professional to assume a broader counseling role than he frequently now assumes and to share in the personal satisfactions and experiences of his clients. It invites personal contact in a society becoming increasingly impersonal. The participatory model liberates the professional from the impossible ideal that he be neutral, disinterested, and passionless. It permits him to articulate and lobby for professional standards and institutions which meet his needs without having necessarily to defend himself against the charges of being selfish, venal, and corrupt. For this freedom, the professional of course pays a price. His preferences are less automatically realized than in a low-visibility vacuum of monopoly professional control. They must win out in the public marketplace of ideas, where they will be challenged by the often competing interests of clients. But this is only fair because clients too must pay a price for the advantages to be gained from participation.

So far, this chapter has presented an unabashedly one-sided argument that client participation in professional decision merits serious consideration as a viable alternative to the traditional ideal of professional control. Several concrete suggestions have been offered for implementing the norms of client participation; benefits to be gained from the promotion of client participation have been proposed. Now, let us consider the burdens client participation entails.

First, confronting complex and uncertain problems with heavy risks is threatening to all of us, professionals and laymen alike. Many clients may find this threat to be too heavy a price to pay for the benefits of participation....

Most clients want their lawyer to command their respect by showing an authoritative and businesslike manner; but this can be overdone. They also want him to treat them respectfully, as equals, demonstrating patience, emotional concern, and courtesy. Clients are in conflict. They both want and don't want to be dependent. Clients are also in conflict about the values implied in their passive behavior. Most are aware of and feel obliged to accept the traditional ideals of professional service; they should trust the lawyer, not be critical and not hold back cooperation. But at the same time they want to be self-reliant and responsible. Too heavy a reliance may imply weakness.

The participatory model assumes that most clients are able to cope with the emotional stress of responsible participation, especially when the risks of nonparticipation are disclosed. They remain free to be passive, responsible only for the consequences of their passivity. It is one thing to say that all clients are tempted to passivity and that some clients need to be passive. It is quite another to say that most clients need to be passive. Furthermore, it is not necessary that clients be active participants in dealing with every one of their personal problems.

A second difficulty in implementing the participatory model is that even with it the professional retains disproportionate resources for manipulating the professional-client relationship to deny the client effective collaboration. This power is enhanced not only by his more extensive knowledge and experience but by the social setting in which the relationship takes place. Face-to-face interaction between two people is frequently stressful. Feeling the other person out and trying to manage the impression one is making is difficult work, in which professionals have more experience than most clients. The first interview almost always takes place in the professional's office. His position of authority as the professional helper is reinforced by the physical setting. He frequently sits behind a desk, the seat of authority in the room. The client has come to see him in a place where he bosses people (e.g. a secretary, a young associate). Other clients are waiting to see him. He gives the impression of being busy. The interview is interrupted by telephone calls or by a colleague's request for advice. "Clearly," the less confident client thinks, "this is an important man. He is doing me a favor by giving me his valuable time. I had better not ask too many questions or I will appear stupid, better not make any demands that could offend him."

But this is only one side of the story. The reaction of many men to someone seeking their paternalism would be to reject the role. Many professionals, however, seem to need and gain pleasure from being paternalistic and dominating. One negligence specialist I interviewed said,

> The truth is, the client is ignorant. He is the last person to know whether or not his lawyer is doing a good job for him.... Because the client is ignorant, I don't let my clients think. If you look for guff from your clients you'll get it.

The attitude is, "Put them in their place or they will walk over you." A litigator with 15 years of experience commented to me:

> I tell the client that I will do all the worrying about the case— period! ... A little education is a dangerous thing. Just let the client know that the problem is in the hands of an extremely competent counsel.

> ...

A third limitation upon the realistic application of the participatory model is the pervasive public acceptance of the traditional model at the present time. The traditional model performs the function of a self-fulfilling prophecy. Because many clients believe it is proper to trust a professional (whose interests, they believe, never conflict with their own) without the necessity for him to earn that trust, because they believe it is mistrustful to ask too many questions and talk to other professionals "behind the back" of their consultant, and because clients believe that professional problems are too complicated to understand and have a single best technical solution, they think it impossible that their participation could be productive, and they think it is wrong for a client to want to participate. Unquestionably, if client participation is to be given a meaningful chance, clients as well as professionals are going to have to reexamine and alter certain deeply rooted attitudes. It is worth reasserting that this book has marshalled evidence not lightly dismissed, which indicates that we should revise our ideas about the appropriateness of behavior that is proper in general social situations, being appropriate for the special situations of professional-client problem solving.

. . .

A fourth limitation upon the participatory model's implementation is the inability of some clients to deal with the complexities of technical language and uncertain, multifaceted decisions.... Unquestionably, full client collaboration will require that citizens routinely possess more information about the nature of their personal problems and about the opportunities available for coping with them than most now do. We have hardly begun the effort to educate the public about these matters.

A fifth limitation upon the participatory model's implementation is our relative ignorance about the proper scope and form disclosure leading to informed consent should take. In theory it should be possible to develop effective techniques and standards of relevance for disclosure which neither waste the time of the participants, unduly confuse the client, nor unduly threaten him. Experience in developing such techniques and standards, are needed, it would appear, for all professions, save perhaps psychiatry and psychological counseling.

A sixth limitation upon the implementation of the participatory model is that it may well be expensive. Professionals will probably be required to spend more time with individual clients than they do now. Active clients may insist upon receiving more and better services than passive clients are willing to accept. In the law, active clients may prove to be more litigious, thus resulting in extra burdens for the courts. This too is obviously a matter for further investigation.... In any event, before one concludes that client participation is too expensive to be encouraged, it should be borne in mind that there are substantial hidden costs of traditional professional practice which deserve to be reflected in any economic cost-benefit accounting. What are the costs in ineffective service of processing more clients more rapidly, of taking shortcuts in serving them, of discouraging them from seeking the best possible solution they can obtain? The stories of several of the clients interviewed in this study suggest that the hidden costs of client nonparticipation may be tremendous.

A seventh limitation is the limitation of time itself. Active client participation is time consuming as well as expensive. The participatory model will not alter the fact of everyday life that people, consciously or unconsciously, have to establish their own priorities of importance among their personal concerns. Active participation as a client strategy will be used, even by the most committed, selectively. What the model does is add to the repertory of possible responses by a layman to his personal problems, the response of active participation. At the present time, this is not part of the repertory of most laymen, even in crisis situations.

A final limitation inherent in the participatory model is that in reducing the professional's domination of the professional-client relationship, professionals will probably lose some of the ability they now have to restrain clients from taking immoral, illegal, or simply unfortunate actions in coping with their problems....

The costs of pursuing the participatory model are I believe tolerable, especially when weighed against the advantages to be gained from client participation. We can only learn if, as both professionals and as clients, we make a serious effort to test the participatory model in our daily conduct.

LAWYERING AND CLIENT DECISIONMAKING: INFORMED CONSENT AND THE LEGAL PROFESSION

Mark Spiegel
128 U.Pa.L.Rev. 41 (1979).

Lawyers created the doctrine of informed consent for the medical profession. This Article examines the possibility and wisdom of turning that lawyers' creation back on the lawyers themselves.

. . .

Unless the client chooses to delegate decisionmaking authority to the lawyer, the client should be presumed to have control over all aspects of his case. The very label "his case" is suggestive. A claim, a case, or a problem belongs to the client; this claim of ownership gives the client a presumptive right of control.

. . .

[T]he legal system is a representational system for the substantive claims of clients. The system assumes that a client's claim is his, just as the political system assumes that a citizen's vote is his. Indeed, access to the legal system is an a priori assumption of the proper functioning of economic and political institutions. If the legal system is intended to facilitate client autonomy and self-determination in spheres outside that system, it would be anomalous if choosing a representative in order to gain access to the legal system entailed surrender of control.

. . .

The traditional model of professional-client relationships does not explicitly deny that clients have the presumptive right to make decisions, but argues instead that clients consent to professional decisionmaking. By choosing a lawyer (or a physician), this argument goes, clients elect to delegate the authority to make decisions on their cases or problems.

Richard Epstein, writing about physicians, recently offered a variant of this view. He argues that, in general, medical malpractice problems should be approached as questions of contract: "[T]he basic rules governing the relationship between physician and patient are then best understood as approximations of the rules which the parties themselves would choose to govern their own relationship." A doctrine such as informed consent should be rejected, Epstein says, because it is "at war with the mutual expectations of the parties."

. . .

Epstein's assertion that informed-consent doctrine may be at war with the expectations of the parties is not based on any empirical data. His conclusion seems to follow from the fact that the custom of the profession is narrower than the legal obligation to obtain informed consent. He assumes that, if consumers desired deviations from these customs, they would have demanded such changes, and market forces eventually would have produced them.

This reasoning reflects more faith in the market than most commentators on professional-client relationships have expressed. Beside the general objections to the economic argument that the status quo reflects people's desires, such reasoning is not descriptive of professional-client relationships, even if acceptable in other contexts.

The major difficulty is that the lawyer and client do not have equal information about the possible structuring of the relationship and about the decisions that are involved. Indeed, a client often comes to a lawyer because he lacks such information. At least at the beginning of the relationship, therefore, the buyer-client cannot realistically be expected to tell the seller-lawyer what decisions he wants to control. But, by Epstein's reasoning, failure to do so indicates acceptance of the customs of the profession.

Second, clients may not perceive the issue of allocation of decision-making authority to be a legitimate item on the agenda for discussion. Today's "customs" regarding that agenda are to some extent a result of laws and expectations created in the past. If, as appears likely, professionals have exerted disproportionate control over these past laws and expectations, then clients' "true expectations" cannot be ascertained until the past set of laws, customs, and expectations has been changed.

Third, even when clients perceive control to be an issue, status and power differences between themselves and their lawyers may lead them to accept less information and control than they might like. To the extent this is true, the status quo may in some sense reflect the "expectations" of the parties, but those expectations should not be controlling.

. . .

Perhaps, though, I have been taking Epstein too literally. Regardless of whether the client's silence indicates agreement with traditional decisionmaking roles, Epstein's insight that the parties contract over decisionmaking may be useful. Epstein ends his discussion of informed consent by suggesting that the burden should be placed on the professional to make explicit the terms of the agreement. This proposal has the virtue of requiring the more knowledgeable party to place decision-making on the agenda, but it does not by itself solve the information and transaction-cost problems.   Absent a more demanding rule, professionals would likely draft form contracts in order to fulfill the requirement of making explicit the issue of decisionmaking authority.   These forms would reduce the costs of individualized negotiation but would usually retain for the professional control over the terms. . . .

. . .

If, however, individualized bargaining is required regarding some or all decisionmaking issues, the solution begins to resemble a contractual version of the informed-consent doctrine.   Indeed, as long as both parties are free to choose whether to enter the relationship, and as long as the client's right to make decisions can be waived, the informed-consent solution seems to mirror Epstein's contractual bargaining.   Yet a significant difference remains.   Epstein seems to assume that decisionmaking authority will be allocated at the beginning of the relationship, whereas informed-consent doctrine postpones this dialogue until particular decisions become necessary.   The latter does not permit blanket waivers of the right to make decisions; any waiver must be substantially contemporaneous with the relevant decision.

Postponement of the decision about decisions is more likely to facilitate realistic client decisionmaking.   The client is least able to evaluate the right to decide certain issues at the beginning of the relationship.   Instead of concrete terms, the client may be left to weigh only the vague proposition that the lawyer can do his best if left alone.   Indeed, the professional himself may lack sufficient knowledge at that time to predict the future with any accuracy.   Postponement of the decision enables the client to learn more about the significance of decisionmaking and about the extent to which the particular professional is worthy of his trust.

In contrast, a one-time contractual solution compresses the burden of information transmittal and evaluation into one short time span.   It thereby minimizes the client's chances of making informed choices.   This solution also seems to assume . . . that the whole future of the relationship can be expressed in the first meeting.   If client involvement in decisionmaking is to be anything more than ratification of decisions already made, or the signing of prepared forms, it must be part of the continuing relationship between professional and client.

. . .

Another major justification for professional decisionmaking is that it produces better results for the client.   From the clients' perspective, if delegation of decisions to lawyers produces better results, the assumption that clients consent to professional control becomes more reasonable.   From the lawyer's and society's perspectives, proof of better results introduces the possibility of justifying professional decisionmaking on paternalistic grounds.   Although paternalism can be attacked directly, this Article will not attempt that task.   Instead, it will explore whether delegation of all or most decisions to the professional actually does produce better results.   If the answer to that question is negative or unclear, then, given the arguments in the preceding sections, decisionmaking authority should be allocated to the client.

Whether the lawyer or the client is the better decisionmaker depends on who has superior information and who can better use that information to make decisions. The lawyer presumably has superior legal knowledge, and his training and experience may give him superior competence to make decisions about a particular case.

For two reasons, however, these professional skills might not lead to better results for the client. First, although the professional is better equipped to use the relevant information, one who is not completely loyal to his client might not use that information for the client's benefit. Second, the client has superior knowledge of the facts of his case and of the relation between his values and objectives and those facts.

. . .

Although professionals are presumed to be loyal, that presumption is cast aside when a particular professional faces a conflict of interest. The requirement that settlement decisions be made by the client may be rooted in fears of professional disloyalty and potential conflicts of interest. In a contingent-fee case, the lawyer's prediction of the verdict may make a trial seem beneficial for either the lawyer or the client, but not necessarily both.[181] In a criminal case, in which the lawyer works for a fixed fee, the economic temptation to plea-bargain is strong, notwithstanding the client's interest. In legal-services work, with its usually heavy case load, the lawyer may place a much greater value than does the client on expeditious disposition of a case. Even in

---

181. The lawyer's decision turns on his estimate of the expected recovery if the case proceeds to trial, the amount of additional lawyer time necessary to prepare for and conduct a trial, the alternative uses of his time, and his valuation of risk. Assuming that the lawyer is risk-neutral and that the alternative use of his time is worth $50, his economic interest is to proceed to trial if the number of hours necessary to achieve a particular result multiplied by $50 is less than the difference between the expected recovery at trial (the likelihood of winning times recovery) and the settlement figure. If the difference between trial value and settlement is less than the cost of his time, his interest lies in settlement. The client's interest in settlement may well diverge from the lawyer's. For example, if the expected recovery at trial is $1,800, if the settlement offer is $1,000, and if the additional expenses associated with trial are less than $800, then, assuming risk-neutrality, the client would elect to proceed to trial. The lawyer hired for a contingent fee of ⅓ will realize an additional $277 from trial. If preparing for and

doing a trial exceeds five and one-half hours, the lawyer would prefer to settle. . . .

The model above is overly simplistic, of course. The lawyer probably cannot calculate expected recovery too precisely. Even if he can, there is probably a range of expected recoveries. The choices are not always binary—they may include settle, attempt further negotiations, or go to trial. The timing of the settlement offer is important. The question of associated costs is more complex. Furthermore, the client's and the lawyer's valuations of risk are likely to diverge. The client is a one-shot player in a lottery, while the lawyer has a portfolio of claims. Most likely, therefore, the client will be more risk-averse than the lawyer. Thus, the client might want to accept a smaller settlement, while the lawyer might want to gamble on a larger recovery at trial. . . .

But these complexities do not change the basic point—the lawyer's and the client's economic incentives to settle do not necessarily converge. . . .

corporate practice, lawyers' and clients' incentives for settlement may diverge.[184]

Problems of professional disloyalty are not limited to the settlement context. In many of the decisions a lawyer makes on behalf of his client, there is a potential divergence of the lawyer's and client's interests.[185] For example, the decision not to seek out a witness may involve a trade-off between the lawyer's use of his time and the client's desire for that witness's testimony. The choice of the forum may involve a trade-off between the lawyer's convenience and the client's. The lawyer's decision to present a novel legal argument or his decision not to offer a foolish one also may involve a trade-off between the lawyer's and client's needs.

All this would merely be interesting footnote material if society could control disloyal behavior through its usual mechanisms—the market, legal regulation, and systems of norms. Both theoretical and empirical evidence suggests, however, that these mechanisms do not effectively control the behavior of lawyers.

. . .

The superior knowledge of lawyers is the generalized technical information and the experience brought to bear on their clients' problems. The client possesses superior knowledge of another sort—knowledge of the facts and circumstances of his case. To the extent that this information is historical, the lawyer may elicit it through skillful interviewing. The client, however, also possesses unique knowledge regarding his goals and values as related to his case, information that even a skillful interviewer may not be able to elicit.

Settlement, a decision allocated to the client by present law, illustrates this point. The relatively simple decision to accept or reject a settlement offer of $2,000 in a personal-injury case involves the valuation and comparison of monetary and nonmonetary factors, including the risk that the client will lose at trial. The client must compare an immediate payment of $2,000 with a future payment that may be greater or less than $2,000. How the client will value the

---

184. The hourly fee, although it removes the financial incentive for the lawyer to select a particular settlement that diverges from the client's interests, does not guarantee that the lawyer will put the appropriate time and effort into a case.... In addition, anecdotal evidence suggests that corporate lawyers tend to over-deliver services relative to the client's interests.

185. See Anderson, Conflicts of Interest: Efficiency, Fairness and the Corporate Structure, 25 U.C.L.A.L.Rev. 738, 739–53, 758 (1978), for development of the thesis that all exchange transactions inherently involve problems of disloyalty because one side can take advantage of the other by providing lower quality work than bargained for by doing less work (shirking), or

by doing unneeded work. These problems are particularly prevalent in service transactions in which expertise is an integral part of the service.

The analysis offered here is not limited to economically motivated disloyalty, although such disloyalty constitutes a large part of the problem. [citations omitted throughout this note] Disloyalty may also arise because of differing ideological views, because of differing needs to deal with the legal system on an ongoing basis, because control is a potential conflict issue, and because the professional and client possess different systems of values which influence the way they view the world....

future payment will depend on when he would receive it, on the spread of the possible outcomes, and on his degree of risk aversion. For example, assume his lawyer tells him that, if he refuses the offer, he has a sixty-percent chance of receiving $4,000 and a forty-percent chance of receiving nothing. The value of this sixty-percent lottery to the client depends upon the client's attitude towards risk. A client who is strongly risk-averse may prefer the certain $2,000; one who prefers risk may take the chance of getting $4,000.

Other factors to be considered include the client's feelings about going to trial. Does he place positive value on "telling his story," or is he concerned about feeling foolish? What does settlement mean for his self-image—"chickening out," vindication, or a "wise" tendency not to prolong a dispute unnecessarily?

A sensitive lawyer might, through appropriate probing, uncover the values at stake in his client's settlement decision. More difficult will be eliciting the precise weights the client attaches to each of the factors governing that decision.... The client will always know more than he can tell.

What is the significance of the client's superior knowledge of his own values? Perhaps this knowledge is merely another reason why settlement decisions belong to the client. Such decisions frequently require the weighing of almost incomparable values. Because the lawyer cannot know the relative weights of the competing values for his client, he cannot be sure that his decision will satisfy his client's real needs.

The same difficulty can arise in connection with other tactical choices. The decision to seek a continuance may involve a trade-off between the client's tolerance of anxiety and an opportunity for greater gains. Whether to call a particular witness may involve more than technical questions of evidence: the client may want to avoid subjecting the witness to a public attack on his credibility or to harrassment at the hands of the opposition. The decision to try a case to judge or jury may involve not only considerations of which decisionmaker will be more favorable, but also client preference regarding the audience for his story. In addition to technical questions of jurisdiction and venue, choice of forum may also be affected by the client's convenience and tolerance of delay.

The basic problem is that the division between subject matter and procedure is inevitably artificial. It is based upon a false view of an ends/means dichotomy. A client in a civil suit may want money, but he may want that money at the least cost in terms of personal embarrassment and delay. A criminal defendant may want liberty, but he may also want to tell his story, obtain absolution, or protect a friend. These other ends may not rise to consciousness at the time of the initial lawyer-client consultation. They may not occur to the client, or to the lawyer, until particular means are selected for achieving the ostensibly primary end of money or freedom.

Further, a client often comes to a lawyer without fixed, unambiguous ends in mind. Just as patients may approach physicians with nothing more than generalized demands for improved health, clients may approach lawyers with nothing more than the desire for advice about their problems. For such clients, the formulation of concrete goals will depend upon what they are told they can get, which in turn depends upon the lawyer's assessment of what means are appropriate for their situations. That judgment is likely to be influenced by the lawyer's values and his sense of role. For example, a client who receives an eviction notice may come to a lawyer for help about "this." Whether "this" comes to mean defending the eviction, finding housing, obtaining more time to move, or resolving the dispute with the landlord may depend as much on the lawyer's selection of means as on the client's fixed ends. Allocating the choice of means to the lawyer can, in effect, determine the ends that the client will pursue.

As discussed above, even a lawyer who recognizes the existence of subsidiary ends would be hampered in making satisfactory procedural decisions by the client's inability fully to communicate his values to the lawyer. Beyond this difficulty is another problem akin to the "dwarfing of soft values" problem, which occurs in cost-benefit analysis. In theory, emotion-laden or subjective goals can, and perhaps will, be taken into account; in practice, however, the separation between subject matter and procedure discourages consideration of these ends. The separation of decisionmaking authority along artificial means/ends lines may communicate an implicit value judgment that "procedural" decisions do not implicate legitimate client ends.

. . .

Whether the informed-consent model can serve as the basis of the lawyer-client relationship depends on the client's receipt of reliable information and ability to make the necessary decisions. Although, at the start of the lawyer-client relationship, most clients lack the information and expertise to value decisionmaking control and to evaluate the lawyer's promised performance, they are not therefore unable to fulfill their role in a relationship based on informed consent. Informed-consent doctrine does not require that the client actually make the final decisions. It does require that, at the proper time, a decision be brought to the client and that the information needed for evaluation be disclosed. The client then chooses whether to delegate the decision to the professional, seek further consultation, or make the decision himself. Thus, the client becomes the monitor of the lawyer's actions.

. . .

A more important consideration is the educative value of the lawyer-client relationship. At the beginning of the relationship, an inexperienced client operates in a void. He cannot be expected to evaluate the whole of a relationship that may involve many decisions and stretch over a long period of time. Informed-consent doctrine allows the client to receive information in small doses and to make less global decisions. Informed consent, if it leads to periodic meetings between lawyer and client, can help bridge the information gap between them. Thus, over time, the client's ability to monitor the lawyer's progress and to make decisions should improve.

. . .

Of course, the switch to a rule of informed consent would involve certain costs: the costs of increased lawyer and client time discussing decisionmaking and making collaborative decisions; the costs of enforcing the client's right to information; the possible costs of limiting lawyer autonomy; and, if increased client control prolongs hearings, the costs of increased court time. These costs may be substantial, but perhaps not as large as expected. Multiplication of the cost of the initial meeting between lawyer and client by the number of subsequent meetings almost certainly would overstate the total cost in terms of the lawyer's and client's time. As the relationship progresses, the client should become more familiar with the lawyer, the case, and the legal process. The exchanges between lawyer and client should thus become more efficient and less time-consuming. Furthermore, a rule of informed consent might encourage lawyers to become more skilled at conducting decisionmaking discussions with clients. Clients too might have an incentive to educate themselves about the legal process. Both developments ultimately could reduce the costs of informed consent.

Moreover, cost alone should not be determinative. Clients do not currently make informed choices between cost and other values, and some system must therefore be devised for educating clients about the value of decisionmaking authority. Such a system inevitably has costs. The question, then, is not whether the costs exist, but whether they are justifiable. . . .

Using . . . the example of a client deciding whether to file in state or federal court, a discussion . . . might take a half hour of a lawyer's time. Clients might well be willing to pay a minimum of twenty-five to fifty dollars for the opportunity to decide whether they wish to incur delays of up to five years before trial. The present system usually does not give them the opportunity to make that choice. Informed consent, by contrast, affords clients the option of deciding that participating in any given decision is worth the cost. The relevant question, at least in cost-benefit terms, is whether the cost of discussing this option should be imposed upon every client in order to insure that some clients have the choice.[295]

295. The costs of discussing the option would be much lower than the costs of making the decision. [For example:]

Lawyer: We now have to decide what court to file in. Choosing state court would mean a long delay but might mean a better chance of winning. If you leave the decision to me, I will go to state court, but if the delay is important to you, we can discuss it. This is your decision, if you wish, but if we do discuss it, it may take a half hour or so, which, as you know, costs $25 of my time. What do you want to do?

This discussion would take a few minutes. It may not be all that a "rational" decision-maker would want to know in order to decide whether to engage in further discus-

. . .

Because the lawyer is his client's agent, his only legitimate interest is arguably serving the best interests of his client. Decisionmaking problems, then, would arise only when a client decided on an action which the lawyer judged to be contrary to the client's best interests. This narrow view of the lawyer's interest seems misguided in two respects. A system of rules that ignores the lawyer's own interests may have little chance of adoption. Moreover, if the lawyer does have legitimate interests, ignoring them would be as objectionable as ignoring those of the client.

What are these legitimate interests? The lawyer has an interest in autonomy; an interest in his identity as a lawyer; a craft interest in not being forced to do substandard work; and an interest in not being forced to violate his own standards of professional responsibility or those of the profession.

. . .

A professional's control over the way he performs his work may . . . be justified by considerations of autonomy. The literature on work and workers contrasts control over the decision to do a particular task with control over the decisions involved in performing that task. Controlling the latter decisions greatly curbs a worker's discretion. Although specifying the task to be performed can likewise have that effect, it frequently leaves the worker large discretion over choices of techniques, over ordering of subtasks, and so on. Discretion and autonomy are not synonymous; at some point, however, limits on discretion interfere with a worker's autonomy in a very basic way.

First, meticulous control over how a worker does a task denies his capacity to do the job. To an auto mechanic, for example, a knowledgeable car owner might not merely say, "The car is not running; please fix it," but might specify both the task he wanted performed—"Fix the carburetor"—and how to perform that task—"First, turn that screw, then remove that part and soak it in oil, . . ." At some point, the specificity of the instructions infringes the mechanic's sense of being a mechanic. He is then justified in asserting that the owner does not want a mechanic, but merely a tool. The mechanic may choose to be such a tool, but that is a choice the mechanic should have; society should not impose it on him.

Second, the more external control exerted over the way one does a task, the closer such control comes to dictating one's physical movements, at some point becoming control over the worker's body. Because control over one's body is a fundamental aspect of the notion of autonomy, maintaining control over the way one does a task is similarly fundamental.

Finally, being told how to do a task with great specificity is reminiscent of childhood, denying the adult potential for competence.

sion, but it sufficiently conveys the nature
of the decision involved. . . .

Being told to do a particular task may be distasteful, but, in some sense, it affirms one's ability to do the task.

The distinction between being ordered to do a task and being told how to do it does not correlate precisely with the absence or existence of autonomy. But the closer a rule comes to prescribing the exact steps a worker must take, the more the prescription infringes the worker's sense of autonomy. Thus, despite its definitional difficulties, the distinction between task and performance of task is, by and large, a useful tool. The notion of task has a certain core that resists endless subdivision; it implies something that potentially involves more than one action.

. . .

The lawyer's third major interest in controlling decisions is to protect his sense of self-esteem as a lawyer. Although related to both autonomy and ethical interests, this interest is distinct from both. It stems from a sense of craft and pride in one's work. The lawyer, directed by his client to make an argument the lawyer deems untenable, may feel that the instruction infringes his autonomy, and he may feel morally bound not to present frivolous arguments. But he also has an interest in not being compelled to produce what he considers substandard work.

Finally, the lawyer has an interest in not being forced to make decisions that conflict with either the profession's or his own code of professional responsibility. Expansion of the role of client decision-making might increase the number of instances in which a lawyer will be asked to violate these sets of rules.

Assume a case in which a lawyer does not want to present the testimony of a witness because he believes the testimony would be false. Assume further that the Code does not prohibit presentation of the evidence, but leaves the decision to the lawyer's discretion. Present case law suggests that the lawyer need not ask the client whether to offer the testimony. If, however, informed-consent doctrine allocated the decision to the client, he could insist that the witness be called. Informed consent may therefore create additional ethical conflicts for the lawyer.

Informed consent, however, would not necessarily require presentation of the testimony. Under that doctrine, after discussing the issue with the client, the lawyer could decide not to call the witness because of suspected perjury. He would then have to justify that conclusion to the client. If the latter insisted on calling the witness, the lawyer could be allowed to withdraw. . . .

. . . Respect for an individual's autonomy requires an open exchange of views, although not necessarily acquiescence in anything that person desires.

. . .

THE NEW MODEL RULES OF PROFESSIONAL CONDUCT: LAWYER–CLIENT DECISION MAKING AND THE ROLE OF RULES IN STRUCTURING THE LAWYER–CLIENT DIALOGUE

Mark Spiegel
1980 Am.Bar Found.Res.J. 1003.

. . .

In order to meaningfully affect decision-making patterns between lawyer and client there has to be more than an exchange of paper or words going from lawyer to client. The exchange has to involve qualities of participation and involvement that enable the client to genuinely understand the decision to be made. In addition, part of the value of clients being more involved in decision making is the effect such involvement might have on the quality of the lawyer-client relationship. Howard Lesnick states:

> I've come to a curious conclusion. I honestly do not think it matters which position the attorney takes—to leave the final decision with the client or insist on keeping it—so much as I think it matters whether the attorney makes either decision in a way which respects the concerns of both attorney and client, and treats the client as an understanding independent person, with interests and sensibilities separate from the attorney, and the ability and obligation to assume responsibility for his or her decisions.

. . .

If this view is correct, that the spirit and quality of the interchange between lawyer and client is of utmost significance, then the usefulness of mandatory rules is open to serious question. Indeed, there are some who would argue not only that mandatory rules are unlikely to improve the quality of the lawyer-client relationship, but also that the adoption of rules such as those proposed in the Model Rules will affect the relationship adversely.

Those who argue that rules will affect the relationship adversely seem to reach this conclusion from one of two perspectives. According to the first perspective, because the Rules acknowledge the possibility that a lawyer might deceive a client or lack commitment to the client's best interests, the Rules will breed distrust in the client. This view confuses the normative goal of trust with the question of how one creates trust. Ignoring the reality of conflict will not create trust; at best it will only create the image of trust.

According to the second perspective, lawyers may regard the rules as mere formalities that can be manipulated. Indeed it has been argued that the clearer the rule the more it will seem to have only formal qualities whose underlying spirit can justifiably be evaded. Moreover, it is argued that this evasion in the Model Rules' provisions regarding disclosure to the client will take the form of perfunctory disclosures similar to the *Miranda* warnings read by the police. The atmosphere created by these *Miranda* -type warnings will then breed distrust.

. . .

The possibility . . . that lawyers may take evasive actions is a serious one. This possibility raises a second general set of arguments about rules and relationships, whether they work. They cannot work if lawyers find formal ways of compliance that evade the real meaning of the rules. There is, however, a deeper problem. Coerced actions of community do not have the same subjective meaning as voluntary actions. Hence the fact that a rule exists that is being complied with changes the meaning of the actions for both parties. Therefore, to the extent the rules are intended to improve a relationship, they can never work.

The above argument then suggests that, at best, rules involving allocating decision-making authority between lawyer and client can only have nominal formal effect, thus bringing into question the whole effort.

. . . The rules must either limit themselves to those areas where formal compliance is sufficient or encompass areas where rules will not work, with the attendant risks of causing disrespect for the whole effort. Aspirational ethics, on the other hand, resolve this dilemma by allowing the expression of the sentiment while avoiding the pretense of enforcement.

. . .

Those who consider it important to separate aspirational ethics from rules usually argue that the distinction is necessary to prevent intolerable coercion.[41] Our problem today, however, is to move beyond this point to one where, rather than keeping these dualities separate, we allow them both to express themselves.

How to do this is, of course, the problem. . . . The problems of the effects of rules on relationships are real . . . [I]s there a way of thinking about rules and relationships that moves us beyond a separation of aspirational ethics from rules but does not relegate us to having simply formal requirements? . . . If one views the provisions regarding lawyer and client as structures that create dialogue, rather than as scripts that prescribe, there may be possibilities in rules that can at least partially contribute toward building relationships.

---

41. It has been my experience both as lawyer and teacher that discussions of professional responsibility issues oscillate between these poles of rules and ethics. First, the problem is viewed as one of rules and the lawyers' games of statutory construction and line drawing dominate the discussion. The discussion then swings to the other pole—the ethics pole—and invariably ends with some expression that it is all subjective and therefore each individual has to make up his own mind. What is lacking is a mode of discourse that encompasses both poles in a satisfactory manner. . . .

This approach tries to encompass both substance and process, recognizing that "pure substance" has the problems of rigidity, with its consequent rebellion against rules, and that "pure process" has the problem of being simply an empty vessel.... The solution to the problem of lawyer domination is not necessarily to allow client domination; the solution to the dilemma of rules is not necessarily to eliminate rules. To deny the lawyer some of his professional authority is not to claim there is no authority of expertise that the lawyer can and should exercise.

. . .

Moreover, ... the structural approach suggests there may be virtue in the Model Rules not allocating specific decisions to either lawyer or client but instead using a more ambiguous directive that admonishes the lawyers to allow clients to make decisions that clients have a legitimate interest in making. Similarly, the notion of face-to-face encounter suggests why the Model Rules' present requirement of pre-representation agreements is not desirable. There is a need for dialogue at that time, but there is also a need for dialogue later. Finally, it is important to identify which elements of professional authority lawyers wish to preserve. Therefore, it is important that the rules attempt to give recognition to legitimate lawyer interests.

Of course, the notion of structure is not a panacea. It can collapse into the emptiness of pure process or be viewed as rigid rules that should be evaded. Moreover, it is uncertain what rules by themselves can accomplish without changes in the world outside. Still, perhaps because I am a lawyer, I hold onto the belief that the insight that rules do not determine conduct does not make rules irrelevant. And what better place to test the possible relevance of rules to relationships than with the rules that govern ourselves as lawyers....

Note on Rosenthal and Spiegel: The lawyer as co-venturer

1. In considering the several questions that Rosenthal's work raises, it is helpful, I believe, to begin with your responses to three questions:

(a) Are you attracted to, or wary of, the "participatory model"?

(b) How would you tend to answer the six questions that Rosenthal suggests at the outset underlie one's preference for the traditional or participatory models of lawyer-client interaction?

(c) Do you believe that, as Rosenthal suggests at the outset, that your answers to the six questions *explain* your reaction to the traditional and participatory models?

2. Rosenthal seems to suggest (p. 96, above) that one's preference for the traditional or participatory model of lawyering rests on beliefs about far more basic matters, which he describes as "concepts of human nature." Am I wrong in thinking that this is a very different statement than the one that finds explanatory force in one's answers to the six questions? Note that, in form, only the first of those questions, using the word "should," is

avowedly normative; the remainder use the word "do," "is," or "are," and appear to be empirical. But consider whether I am wrong in suggesting that:

(a) the answers that you or I give to the six questions rest not on empirical but on normative beliefs;

(b) in either event, our "concepts of human nature" are not driven by our beliefs about the practice of law; it is rather the other way round. By that, I mean that one's empirical perceptions (as well as one's normative ideas) about the lawyer-client relation do not align one's concepts of human nature, but rather are aligned by them.

If these perceptions seem right to you, two further questions arise:

(c) What are the implications for the legitimacy of any profession-wide answer (via a professional code) to the question, "who's in charge"? (Compare a similar question raised in Note 2(d) of the Note on Fried and Pepper, above, page 51).

(d) What are the implications, for the importance of your becoming aware of your own conception of the proper model of lawyering, of its connection with fundamental aspects of your professional identity, and of the ways in which your practice choices can be an affirmation, or a denial, of that conception?

3. To what extent *is there* a profession-wide answer? The codes find it easier to address the substantive question whether lawyer or client has decisional authority over an issue, than the deeper question how a lawyer should interact with a client in reaching a decision (if the question is for the lawyer to decide) or in helping a client to reach one (if the decision is the client's).

(a) What answers to the first of these questions are suggested by MR 1.2(a), including Comment 1, and by EC 7–7 and 7–8?

(b) As to the second, MR 1.4(b) purports to require a lawyer to "explain a matter to the extent reasonably necessary to permit the client to make informed decisions"; see further Comment 2.

• Does this formulation supply any meaningful guidance?

• Does it lean, with respect to matters that are for the client to decide, toward either the traditional or the participatory model?

• Does it imply that, as to matters that are for the lawyer to decide, no explanation is called for?

(c) The second Spiegel article suggests that the relative "failure" of the codes to speak to the process of attorney-client decisionmaking may be all to the good. Why? Do you agree?

4. What is your reaction to Spiegel's emphasis on "dialogue" as a value in legal representation?

(a) Consider the relative weight that he, and you, would give to:

• the ways in which clients have more salient knowledge about their cases than do their lawyers;

• the extent to which lawyers have real and legitimate craft and autonomy interests in making decisions;

• the extent to which cost and efficiency concerns should be a serious barrier to dialogue.

(b) Am I right to suggest that differences among us about the weight to be given these factors have much of their source in differing ideas about what it is that makes legal representation worthwhile, and what it is that makes being a lawyer worthwhile?

For most of us, these ideas are largely implicit and unstated; to test my hypothesis, begin to articulate, as well as you can, some of *your* thoughts about what it was in the practice of law that drew you to it as an occupational choice.

(c) *Role-Orientation and Client Autonomy*

THE ETHICS OF ARGUMENT: PLATO'S *GORGIAS* AND THE MODERN LAWYER

James Boyd White
50 U.Chi.L.Rev. 849 (1983).

[This article is written in the form of an imagined conversation between Socrates and two successful attorneys. Following is a portion of that conversation.]

Socrates: What I really want to know is who you are and what you do. I know you are called a "lawyer," but what I want to know is this: what do you do in the world that makes you what you are?

Euerges*: I would put it this way: I give advice to people who seek it from me about their legal rights and duties, and I represent them in legal proceedings.

Socrates: In whose interests are you acting when you do these things?

Euerges: In the interests of my clients, of course. And in the interest of the law as well, for in my work I help see to it that the law is obeyed and adhered to, and that legal institutions function as they are intended to.

Socrates: Let us take the client first. How does what you do serve his interests?

Euerges: By increasing what can be called his power over the world: his range of choices for action, his liberty, and his wealth. Those are all good things and my clients show by their appreciation that they know this is true. I use the law to help them get what they want. I am their friend in the law.

Socrates: But is it always in someone's interest to increase what you call his "power"? I suppose you would agree that people some-

* ["Euerges means 'good doer'." See 50 U.Chi.L.Rev., at 872 n. 33].

times use their "power" in ways that are self-destructive, and in such cases to increase their power is not a help, but an injury?

Euerges: That is a theoretical possibility, I suppose, but, as the world goes, not a real one. My clients are intelligent, practical people who know what they want and are satisfied by my efforts to help them get it. If what you mean is that it might in some way be better for one of my clients to do something else with his time and energy and money, to become a South Seas missionary, for example, or to write the novel he has always talked about, that is, I suppose, possibly so, though I do not often think about such things. I am not even sure what it would mean to say that such a course was "better" for one of my clients, since everyone is entitled to his own views on such personal matters. Anyway, who am I to make such a judgment about someone else, especially when I know so few of the relevant facts?

Socrates: But it remains true that you do not after all serve your client's interests, as you originally said, but instead what appear to him to be his interests, that is, his wants or desires. Isn't that right? And in what you have just said you do not deny this but seek to explain or justify it, by pointing to the supposed competence of your clients (and your own supposed incompetence) at deciding what is good for them, and to the allegedly uncertain character of that judgment, whoever makes it. Strictly speaking, then, is it true that you serve not your client's interests but his wishes or his wants?

Euerges: Strictly speaking, that is true.

Socrates: If so, you are in this respect no different from the keeper of one of those Pleasure Ranches they have out West, who sells his customers whatever they desire, however bad for them it might be: too much food and liquor and drugs, and every kind of sex. In both cases it is not the client's interests that are catered to but his desires, and in the case of the law the desire in question is more dangerous than any other, for it is the desire for power.

Euerges: This is nonsense! Don't you know that an important part of the practice of law is talking with one's client about the wisdom of one course of action over another, in a mutual attempt to determine what his true interests require? We are constantly teaching our clients that they cannot have everything they want and advising them to pursue what is more important to them and to forgo what is less important. We help them to discover their true interests and to shape their wants to suit those interests.

Socrates: If that is so, the present conversation can come to an end, for I have no differences with you, and we should begin on another subject: how do you do what you have just described? For nothing could be more wonderful than to discover a person who knows not only what is best for himself and for others, but also how to teach others what their true interests really are. But I imagine that not every lawyer would make such a claim and that many of those who did would mean by it nothing more than this: that they advised their clients how they could gratify their desires the most—as a really expert keeper of a Pleasure Ranch might do, telling his customers not to drink to incapacitation, or not to combine drug A and drug B, and so on—but having no concern at all for their true interests. Shall I tell you what I would say to such a lawyer? If you permit me, I will make a speech to him, and you can tell me when I am done whether you and I are wrong, or he is.

Here is what I would say: by reason of your training and natural capacities you have what is commonly called a great power, the power of persuading those who have power of a different kind, political and economic power, to do what you wish them to do. Of course your power is not absolute, for there are limits to what even you can achieve. And properly speaking, this is not a true power unless it is exercised in your true interests, but it is a real force, as your record of success and the fees you receive demonstrate, and we can speak as others do and call it a "power" too, though putting it in quotation marks.

Your professional aim is to present your case, whatever its merits, so that those with control over economic and political forces will decide for your client, and you most succeed when you most prevail. You use your mind, as we used to say of the sophists, to make the weaker argument appear the stronger. Your goal in all of this is to get the most, first for your client, but ultimately for yourself, for what you do with your "power" of persuasion is to sell it, getting in exchange another "power," that of money. Of course neither the power of money nor the power of persuasion is a good thing of itself; that depends upon whether they are used to advance or injure one's interests, and that is no concern of yours, with respect to your client or apparently to yourself.

You say you are your client's friend, but you do not serve his interests; in truth you are not his friend, but his flatterer, which is to be his enemy. For your concern is not with his real interests, but with assisting him to attain whatever it is he may desire. If it should happen that what you do does advance his true interests and thus tends to make him happy rather than unhappy, that still does not make you his friend, because for you that result is accidental, of no interest or consequence. Not having been your object it can be no ground for your satisfaction. Likewise, you are no friend to the law, for you will always say that justice requires whatever it is that your client wishes, and you use all your skill and art to make it seem that this is so.

In all of this you are least of all friend to yourself, for in return for money that you cannot take the time to learn how to spend, you give yourself the mind and character of one who does these things. You never ask yourself in a serious way what fairness and justice require in a particular case for to do that would not leave time for what you do. In fact you incapacitate yourself for the pursuit of such a question by giving yourself the mind of the casemaker and brief-writer, of one who looks ceaselessly for the characterization, the turn of phrase, or the line of argument, that will make your client's case, however weak, seem the stronger.   To persuade those whom you must persuade you devote yourself with the attention of a lover to the ways in which they can be pleased, to the tricks of voice and manner and tone, to the kinds of argument, that will persuade this jury or that judge, this tax official or that fellow lawyer.

The art of rhetoric is in fact the art of ministration to the pleasures of another, really a species of prostitution.   As the sexual responses and energies of a prostitute are debased and debasing by the way they are employed, so also are your intellectual energies and responses, your ways of seeing things and describing them, your ways of making appeals and claims and arguments, the very workings of your mind and the feelings of your heart.   When you represent an unjust client you are in the position of actually wanting an unjust result.   And what do you get in return?   A prostitute's pay.   Like other flatterers you tend to become like the object of your flattery, but since you have so many and various objects of attention what you really give yourself is the character of none but that of the chameleon, who appears to be whatever suits the moment.   In your trade you lose yourself.

Well, Euerges, what do you say of my speech?   Is it fair or not?   I speak not of you, of course, but of those lawyers who serve a client's wants rather than his interests.

. . .

Note on White: Socrates Unbound

1.   To what extent do you regard this modern-language restatement of the *Gorgias* as a fair indictment of the practice of law?

(a) First, is it an accurate description (of law practice, not necessarily of the *Gorgias*)?   If you regard it as "over-stated," what would be a fair restatement?

(b) Even if accurate, what is your response to the condemnatory quality of the description?

2.   Is the attempt to represent a client's "interests" rather than his or her "wants or desires" itself illegitimate?   If so, on what ground?   (Compare the issue raised in the concluding paragraph of Note 2 of the Note on Simon and Lehman, page 77, above).

3.   Compare the analysis of philosopher Alan Goldman:

To the claim that the moral autonomy of the client is at stake in his ability to find a strong legal advocate for his interest, several further replies are in order.   First, ... the client may in fact lose his own sense of moral responsibility when he sees his most partisan interest warmly embraced and given institutional respectability by his lawyer.   Certainly the many technicalities and rituals of legal maneuvering tend to alienate all but the most sophisticated corporate clients from participation in the achievement of their own supposed legal objectives.   The encounter with a special professional ethics seemingly oblivious to ordinary notions of moral responsibility can add to that sense of moral alienation. If the client were required instead to justify his objective to his lawyer, or at least claim a moral right to pursue it in highly questionable cases, this might restore a sense of moral responsibility and autonomy rather than squash it. To be morally autonomous is to assume moral responsibility for one's own actions, not simply to act out of narrow self-interest. Moral rights create space for individual values and the development of autonomy in this sense as well. Features of the legal system that lessen the sense of moral responsibility might diminish the sense of autonomy within the system too, for clients as well as lawyers. Extreme partisanship is one such feature.

Goldman, The Moral Foundations of Professional Ethics 126 (1980).

(a) Am I right to suggest that the difference between Goldman's approach and White's derives from the differing *meaning* that each gives to the concept of (client) autonomy?

(b) Am I right to suggest also that they differ too in their view of the *legitimacy* of a lawyer's influencing a client's understanding of his or her interests?

(c) Are the two preceding suggestions consistent with one another?

(d) On what ground do the preceding questions suggest a basis on which one might regard Goldman as less vulnerable than White (or Socrates) to a charge of paternalism?

THE IDEOLOGY OF ADVOCACY: PROCEDURAL JUSTICE AND PROFESSIONAL ETHICS

William H. Simon.
1978 Wisc.L.Rev.

This excerpt is reprinted on pages 188 to 196 of *Becoming a Lawyer*. Read it there, along with the Comment following it.

Note on "non-professional advocacy": Vision or nightmare?

1. (a) In what ways does Simon's approach differ from, in what ways is it similar to, those of White and Goldman, with respect to the issues raised in Note 2 of the preceding Note?

(b) To what extent is Simon's approach, whatever its overall merit, open to the objection of paternalism? Why?

2. Is your initial reaction to Simon's prescription one of attraction or repulsion? Can you (for the moment) separate your response at the level of practicality, difficulty, cost, and the like, from that at the level of his objective or animating values, that is, whether a lawyer-client relation such as he describes, assuming arguendo that it could be implemented, would be a good thing? Consider, among others, the following elements:

(a) Simon is at pains to make clear that his call for decisionmaking as a matter of "personal ethics" does not mean that a lawyer should help a client only to gain ends that he or she approves of; there can be, Simon asserts, a morally acceptable relation of lawyer and client "in the absence of a coincidence of ends."

• Articulate, as fully as you can, the principles that he suggests for guidance.

• How would they apply in cases like *Spaulding* and *Zabella?* (Compare Thomas Morgan's treatment of *Zabella,* concluding that it "came out about right—morally as well as legally." Morgan, Thinking about Lawyers as Counsellors, 42 Fla.L.Rev. 439, 448–50 (1990). Morgan has more difficulty coming to an answer about *Spaulding;* see id. at 454–55).

• Are the principles that Simon articulates sufficient to meet your concerns?

(b) Simon applies to the moral sphere a dialogic approach similar to that espoused by Spiegel for questions of tactics.

• Are your reactions to the two similar?

• How, if at all, are the two contexts different?

(c) What are the values that animate Simon's vision of "non-professional advocacy"? *   What is your reaction to the espousal of such values:

• in light of your overall political philosophy?

• in light of what it is that attracted you to the practice of law as a career?

3.   Returning now to questions of practicality and the like, to what extent are your answers regarding such matters influenced by your views on the more fundamental question of value? To the extent that they are, discussion of matters of practicality is not likely to be fruitful, is it?

5.   THE ADVERSARIAL FRAME OF MIND

DR 7–101, entitled "Representing a client zealously," states the basic norm of adversariness in sub-section (A)(1):

A lawyer shall not intentionally fail to seek the lawful objectives of his client through reasonably available means permitted by law and the Disciplinary Rules ....

There are a number of limitations and exceptions, some permissible and others mandatory, and you should examine the text of DR's 7–101 and 7–102 at this point.

The language quoted above, and the title to DR 7–102, suggest that it is positive law that sets the principal, and perhaps the only obligatory, boundary on zealousness. Permissible boundaries shrink or expand according to an individual's underlying outlook. They may also be

---

* Professor Simon has since recanted his use of the term, "non-professional" advocacy, recognizing that his critique does not require "abandoning the lawyer's professional role." Simon, Ethical Discretion in Lawyering, 101 Harv.L.Rev. 1083, 1084 n. 1 (1988). This article is in part an attempt to develop further the approach suggested in The Ideology of Advocacy.

influenced, consciously and otherwise, by the prevalent mindset of the profession. A major object of this book is to encourage you to make conscious such matters of outlook and influence.

The traditional concept of advocacy tends to read the language of professional codes in the light of the far less measured statement of the norm of adversariness made by Lord Brougham in 19th century England:

> [A]n advocate, in the discharge of his duty, knows but one person in all the world, and that person is his client. To save that client by all means and expedients, and at all other hazards and costs to other persons ... is his first and only duty; and in performing this duty he must not regard the alarm, the torments, the destruction which he may bring upon others. Separating the duty of a patriot from that of an advocate, he must go on reckless of consequences, though it should be his unhappy fate to involve his country in confusion.

The attraction of this formulation for many lawyers is evidenced by its use in two of the essays (those by Fried and Curtis) that you have previously encountered in this book.

This section will set forth several less lurid and more common applications of the ways in which lawyers deal with the interests of individuals or groups—opposing parties and counsel, the court, third persons, and portions of the public at large—that may be harmed by a client's acts or by lawyer conduct on a client's behalf. It will raise, among others, the question whether there is room for a lawyer to seek to accommodate client interests to the lawyer's own sense of how he or she wants to act in the world.

VALDEZ v. ALLOWAY'S GARAGE

This account of a negotiation settling a wrongful death suit is widely available on videotape, and you should watch it at this point.* George Beach represents Mr. and Mrs. Valdez, whose son was killed in an automobile accident allegedly caused by the negligence of one of Alloway's mechanics in failing to tighten a lug nut properly. Sam Kepler represents defendant's insurer.

Note on Valdez: Law practice as fox hunting

1. It is important, I believe (postponing consideration of Beach's conduct until the next Note), to distinguish three questions regarding Kepler:

- To what extent, if at all, were Kepler's actions *justified?*
- To what extent, if at all, were Kepler's actions *required?*

---

* If it is not available to you in that medium, you will find the transcript reprinted in Gary Bellow and Bea Moulton, The Lawyering Process 586–91 (Foundation Press, 1979).

• *Why* did Kepler act as he did?

2. Consider, first, what the professional codes appear to say about the matter:

(a) The words of DR 7–101(A)(1), set forth at the outset of this sub-section, appear to impose an affirmative duty on Kepler "not [to] fail" to do what he did (unless the Disciplinary Rules forbid it). The Model Rules have no similar language.

(b) In your view, did Kepler misrepresent the *law* when he said that "the facts appear to relieve [the defendant] of liability," or when he allowed Beach's statement that plaintiffs' contributory negligence would bar recovery to go uncorrected?

Did he misrepresent the *facts* when he said that:

• "[Rossini's] deposition is solidly on our side";

• defendant's "policy [was] to try the case" rather than settle, he doubted "very seriously" whether it would consider "*any* offer," and substantially more than two thousand dollars would be regarded by defendant as a "very high figure";

• he had "laid all [his] cards on the table"; or

• it was the practice to deduct litigation expenses from the settlement?

Model Rule 4.1 sharply distinguishes between making a false statement and nondisclosure of the truth. It prohibits an attorney from making a "knowingly ... false statement of material fact or law to a third person," that is, one other than a client; it prohibits failure to disclose "only when disclosure is necessary to avoid assisting a criminal or fraudulent act by a client," and then only to the extent permitted by the confidentiality requirements of Rule 1.6. Comment 2, however, says that, "under generally accepted conventions in negotiation, certain types of statements ordinarily are not taken as statements of material fact"; an example is "a party's intentions as to an acceptable settlement of a claim."

MR 3.3(a), which applies only to statements made "to a tribunal," imposes a duty to disclose to the court adverse controlling legal authority; it also prohibits the making of a materially false statement of fact or law, requiring disclosure of material facts only when necessary to avoid assisting a client's crime or fraud.

(c) Did Kepler violate DR 7–105, which prohibits threats "to present criminal charges" to settle a civil matter? The Model Rules have no analogous prohibition.

(d) Is it an accurate summary to conclude that the language of the professional codes, far from prohibiting anything that Kepler did, actually appear to prohibit him from acting other than as he did? (For an analysis of this question as it applies to the Code (it predates the adoption of the Rules), see Bellow & Moulton, op. cit. supra, at 591–96).

3. What relevance, if any, does the preceding section of this Note shed on the questions whether what Kepler did was justified or required? Consider these factors:

(a) Am I right to suggest that the professional codes cannot be a dispositive source of an affirmative answer to the question of justification? In Charles Fried's words, quoted earlier in this book, reliance on supposed "prescribed obligations of a professional . . . merely pushes the inquiry back a step. We must ask then not how a decent lawyer may behave, but whether a decent, ethical person can ever be a lawyer." Fried, The Lawyer as Friend: The Moral Foundations of the Lawyer–Client Relation, 85 Yale L.J. 1060, 1062 (1976), quoted at p. 28, above.

The function of a norm like DR 7–101 is, I believe, to separate the question of justification for being a lawyer from that of acting as Kepler did in a specific context like the Valdez negotiation; the former decision is necessarily an abstract one, and the concreteness of the second is turned aside by that process of separation. The result can become that it is either too early, or too late, to consider the question of justification.

Compare the admonition of George Sharswood, Chief Justice of Pennsylvania and the University of Pennsylvania's first Professor of Law, who in 1854 wrote one of the profession's earliest ethical codes. Having given a classic defense of attorney role-differentiation, that it is for the court and not the lawyer to judge the rightness of a client's cause, he thought it appropriate to go on:

> As an answer to any sweeping objection made to the profession in general, the view thus presented may be quite satisfactory. It by no means follows, however, as a principle of private action for the advocate, that all causes are to be taken by him indiscriminately, and conducted with a view to one single end, *success*.

G. Sharswood, An Essay on Professional Ethics 84 (5th ed. 1907).

(b) Is it in any event accurate to infer from the language of DR 7–101 that adversarial conduct like Kepler's *is* in fact mandatory? Such an inference would need to rest, would it not, on a belief that Kepler would probably suffer some sanction, whether through disciplinary or malpractice liability or through a loss of stature among his peers, for failing to act as he did? Am I wrong to suggest that such a belief would lack any substantial basis? Compare Charles Curtis' assertion, p. 54, above—made with reference to the supposed imperative of professionalism that a lawyer not express a personal belief in the justice of a client's cause—that an apparent prohibition in fact only "gives a lawyer an excuse" to do what he or she wants to do.

(c) If the latter assertion is "on point" in the present context, the existence of discretion is being masked by the language of the rule. What follows from bringing it into the open? In an Orwellian world, everything not forbidden is compulsory; an attorney is required to do everything for a client that he or she is allowed to do. The epithet of Orwellianism apart, should there be such a rule, or should there be a substantial discretionary zone in which lawyers are permitted but not required to act harshly to their clients' adversaries?

• Would it be a benefit or a detriment to you as a lawyer to have such a zone of discretion?

• Does a negative answer to the question of the desirability of discretion tend to correlate with an affirmative answer to that of justification? If it does, does that suggest that the function of discretion is to open up the question of justification, and that the function of obligation is to close it off?

• David Wilkins has argued that a rule should be relatively inhospitable to the existence of discretion, to offset the tendency that the goals of predictability, uniformity, and enforcement will be "likely to be undervalued by individuals attempting to decide how they should act in specific cases." Wilkins, Legal Realism for Lawyers, 104 Harv. L.Rev. 468, 510 (1990). He criticizes an approach to the scope of discretion that "tend[s] to move freely between arguments addressed to individual lawyers and those addressed to officials responsible for creating the regulatory structure." Id. at 508. Does Wilkins' view, if accepted, tend to support or to undermine the position suggested by this Note?

4. There was little question, given the recent abrogation of the state's contributory negligence rule, that Mr. and Mrs. Valdez were entitled to recover a substantial amount. Was it unjustified for Kepler, in deciding whether to engage in the practices at issues in these examples, not to have given weight to the substantive merits of the claim against his client? Consider the response of Judge Sharswood to this question:

[T]here may and ought to be a difference in the mode of conducting a defense against what is believed to be a righteous, and what is believed to be an unrighteous claim..... Counsel ... may and even ought to refuse to act ... to defeat what he believes to be an honest and just claim, by insisting upon the slips of the opposite party, by sharp practice, or special pleading—in short, by any other means than a fair trial on the merits in open court. There is no professional duty ... to secure success in any cause, just or unjust; and when so instructed, if he believes it to be intended to gain an unrighteous object, he ought to throw up the cause, and retire from all connection with it, rather than thus be a participator in other men's sins.

G. Sharswood, op. cit. supra, at 98–99.

The professional codes, whatever else they may say on the questions raised by *Valdez,* seem to give no support to the Sharswood position. (Why do I say that?) Why do you think that his approach has been eclipsed?

5. Should the size of the gap between Kepler's competence and diligence and that of Beach (plaintiffs' attorney) have any effect on the justification for Kepler's conduct?

(a) The traditional concept of advocacy tends to answer this question in the negative. (Compare the issue raised in *Spaulding v. Zimmerman* by defendants' contention, see p. 22, above, that their attorney "could assume" that plaintiff had information which he knew plaintiff did not have). Does that answer square with or differ from your own?

(b) Am I wrong in suggesting that one's response to the question is primarily a manifestation of one's fundamental political outlook, not of factors specific to the practice of law? Specifically, my hypothesis is that one who tends to share traditional individualist perceptions or values regarding the legitimacy of inequality in society, and the limited nature of one's responsibility to others, will tend to answer the question in the negative, while one who regards serious inequality as a major social evil, and an augmented sense of mutual responsibility as a social good, will tend to give the question an affirmative answer. As you consider your own views, and those of others, is that hypothesis borne out or undermined?

6. (a) Are there other factors that seem relevant to the question of justification?

(b) What would *you* want to do, were you in Kepler's position in a negotiation like *Valdez*?

7. Note that a conclusion that Kepler's actions were justified cannot answer the question why he acted as he did.

(a) Which of the following factors might have contributed to his decision, conscious or otherwise, to act as he did:

• his personality;

• random factors, such as the kind of day he was having;

• his political outlook with respect to tort plaintiffs;

• his political outlook with respect to undocumented aliens;

• his decision to specialize in insurance defense work;

• his decision to become a litigator;

• his decision to become a lawyer?

(b) Several of the above factors—his political outlook and his personality—have to do with aspects of Kepler that go beyond his being a lawyer. The last question asked whether they were a *cause* of his acting as he did in the Valdez negotiation: To what extent might the causal influence run in the other direction, that is, might his personality or political outlook be a consequence, rather than (or in addition to) a cause, of his work?

(c) What are the implications of your responses to the immediately preceding question:

• for the question whether professional norms should leave a zone of discretion with regard to actions like those of Kepler's?

• for the question whether *you* would want to act as Kepler did?

8. (a) As we have seen—see Comment 2 to MR 4.1, partially quoted above—the Model Rules expressly legitimate the making of certain kinds of knowingly untrue statements, by asserting that they are conventionally understood not to be statements of fact at all. (Geoffrey Hazard, the Reporter for the Model Rules Project, explaining the bases for the norm of trustworthiness in instrumental terms—in a section of his article entitled, "The Uses of Trustworthiness"—has defined the word as "truthfulness in statements made as representations." Hazard, The Obligation to be Trustworthy, 33 So.Car.L.Rev. 181, 182–85 (1981)).

To what extent, if at all, does this approach correspond to your own norms of truthtelling? If those norms have a foundation that is not instrumental, and if they lead you to view statements of the sort contemplated by the Comment to MR 4.1 not as "mere puffery" but as lying, which you would engage in (if at all) only in far more pressing circumstances than an everyday negotiation over money, is there a response that you can make when your adversary asks you (for example) whether your client is interested in a settlement, or what his or her "bottom line" is, and you believe that a truthful answer will hurt your client?

(b) Do you find helpful the following conclusion to Gerald Wetlaufer's essay, The Ethics of Lying in Negotiations, 75 Iowa L.Rev. 1219, 1272–73 (1990)?

> Effectiveness in negotiations is central to the business of lawyering and a willingness to lie is central to one's effectiveness in negotiations. Within a wide range of circumstances, well-told lies are highly effective. Moreover, the temptation to lie is great not just because lies are effective, but also because the world in which most of us live is one that honors instrumental effectiveness above all other things. Most lawyers are paid not for their virtues but for the results they produce. Our clients, our partners and employees, and our families are all counting on us to deliver the goods. Accordingly, and regrettably, lying is not the province of a few "unethical lawyers" who operate on the margins of the profession. It is a permanent feature of advocacy and thus of almost the entire province of law.

> Our discomfort with that fact has, I believe, led us to create and embrace a discourse on the ethics of lying that is uncritical, self-justificatory and largely unpersuasive. Our motives in this seem reasonably clear. Put simply, we seek the best of both worlds. On the one hand, we would capture as much of the available surplus as we can. In doing so, we enrich our clients and ourselves. Further, we gain for ourselves a reputation for personal power and instrumental effectiveness. And we earn the right to say we can never be conned. At the same time, on the other hand, we assert our claims to a reputation for integrity and personal virtue, to the high status of a profession, and to the legitimacy of the system within which we live and work. Even Gorgias, for all his powers of rhetoric, could not convincingly assert both of these claims. Nor can we.

> Somehow we must stop kidding ourselves about these matters. We must grant a place to ethics, first in our discourse and then in our actions. There are, I think, several concrete steps that might be taken. First, we might acknowledge that we have a personal stake in the existing discourse concerning the relationship between effectiveness and ethics. As a result of that personal stake, we have shown a strong disposition in favor not just of self-justification but also of the conclusion that there are no hard choices to be made, no price to be paid in the name of ethics. Second, we might admit that, in a wide range of circumstances, lying works. Third, we might become more critical of our self-serving claims about what is not a lie and about what lies are ethically permissible. This involves acknowledging, for instance, that many lies are ethically impermissible even though they effectively serve our interests and those of our clients—and even though they are not forbidden either by law or by our codes of professional self-

regulation. It also involves giving up our claim that all our lies are justified by the rules of the game or by our duties to our clients. It entails accepting the proposition that ethics and integrity are things for which a price may have to be paid. Fourth, we might clearly define winning in a way that leaves room for ethics. It might, for instance, be understood not as "getting as much as we can" but as "winning as much as possible without engaging in unacceptable behavior" and "unacceptable behavior" might then be understood to exclude not just those things that are stupid or illegal but also those other things that are unethical. And finally, we might give up our claim that this is all too hard, that we have no choice in these matters and that we are not responsible for the choices we make and the harm we inflict upon others.

Short of all this, we can, even those who disagree with most or all of what I have said, make our own contributions to this continuing conversation. In that way, we can do our best to understand and confront the choices we must make between the harsh individualistic reality of instrumental effectiveness and the elusive possibilities of ethics, integrity, reciprocity, and community.

CHANGING THE BALANCE OF
LITIGATING POWER
Stuart Israel
New Directions in Legal Services, July–August 1977.

... Consider the case of Peter Collinson, a member of Laborers' Local 423.

Two days before Christmas, Collinson became a debtor at a downtown jewelry store where he bought a diamond ring for his wife. He signed a pre-printed contract form provided by the jewelry salesman who filled in the blank spaces with the specifics of the transaction. Collinson became obligated to pay the $840 credit price in 21 monthly installments beginning in January. Buying on credit, Collinson agreed to pay an annual interest rate of over 15% which added more than $100 to the cash price.

Because the ring was expensive, Collinson decided to buy it only after careful consideration. The salesman pointed out that Collinson was entitled to a union member discount and that the diamond was a good buy from an investment standpoint. The salesman recognized that the construction industry had been depressed and work for laborers had been scarce, but, he said, things were bound to get better. Besides, Collinson could take close to two years to pay. Collinson knew his wife would be thrilled by the ring. He decided he would be able to meet the payment schedule by making a few sacrifices.

Collinson was right about his wife's reaction to the ring but he was wrong about his ability to meet the payment schedule. He made payments for two and a half months and then, out of work, was able to pay no more.

The jewelry store's credit manager telephoned Collinson and explained that he was obligated to make monthly payments whether or not he was working. The credit manager pointed out that the acceleration clause in the contract gave him a right to sue Collinson immediately for the entire contract balance because Collinson had defaulted on his obligation by missing payments. The credit manager's interpretation of the contract was somewhat surprising to Collinson. Still, whatever the contract said, for Collinson the matter was a simple one: no paycheck, no payments. He promised to resume payment as soon as he found work.

The credit manager made increasingly insistent phone calls to Collinson for the next several months. Finally, impatient with promises, the credit manager gave the account to the jewelry store's collections lawyer, ironically at about the same time that Collinson found work.

Collections lawyers file lawsuits on behalf of retailers and other creditors to recover outstanding debts, often in return for healthy percentages of the amounts recovered. Many base the economics of their law practices on the generally accurate assumption that a large percentage of debtors will not contest lawsuits so that most suits will end with default judgments. The assumption is generally accurate because so many debtors cannot afford legal services or cannot find lawyers willing or able to undertake consumer litigation involving relatively small amounts of money. Because they rarely are challenged, collections lawyers have been able to dominate the litigation process.

The collections lawyer for the jewelry store filed a mimeographed form complaint to initiate a lawsuit against Collinson in county court. Typed on the form was a demand for the contract balance and contractual late charges, a total of $758, plus interest and court costs. The store's lawyer anticipated a default judgment which would have permitted him to proceed against Collinson's wages and house. Collinson didn't wait for the default period to elapse; he brought the complaint to Local 423 Legal Service, the Laborers prepaid law office.

Collinson and the Legal Service discussed contesting the lawsuit and raising counterclaims but Collinson decided to try to end the unpleasant experience as fairly and rapidly as possible by offering a settlement. The Legal Service wrote, and then phoned, the jewelry store's lawyer and presented the offer: Collinson would pay the arrearage immediately and would make future payments on schedule until the contract price was paid. In return, Collinson asked that the lawsuit against him be dismissed.

The store's lawyer rejected the offer on the phone....

[The Legal Service moved to dismiss the complaint, on the basis of several technical errors in it, which could easily have been corrected by amendment].

Inexplicably, the store's lawyer did not amend the complaint. Still annoyed, he telephoned the Legal Service and opined, "whoever wrote this motion doesn't understand what this simple contract case is all about." The county judge disagreed. Confronted with the uncorrected errors in the complaint, the judge granted the motion to dismiss.

The lawsuit was dismissed without prejudice to the store's claim. The lawyer for the store could have corrected the complaint, paid a second filing fee to the court, and reinitiated the suit against Collinson. Before he could do so, the Legal Service took the offensive by filing, on behalf of Collinson, a suit against the jewelry store in federal court. The suit charged that the store had violated the Truth In Lending Act by inaccurately disclosing to Collinson the credit terms in the contract.[5] The complaint requested $213 in statutory damages, a reasonable lawyer fee, interest and court costs.

The jewelry store hired another lawyer to represent its interests in federal court. The new lawyer answered the federal complaint by denying the substance of Collinson's claims. The Legal Service sought additional information on the denial by serving the store's lawyer with detailed interrogatories and requests for admissions. In response, the lawyer telephoned the Legal Service and offered Collinson a $213 settlement in return for a dismissal of the lawsuit. Perhaps he did so to save the store the cost of litigation, perhaps he was persuaded of the merits of Collinson's claims. In any event, Collinson accepted the offer and a check. By agreement, the suit was dismissed with prejudice, which precluded both parties from reinitiating the suit.

The benefit of the dismissal agreement to Collinson was greater than the amount of the store's check. The store's lawyer had not raised the claim for the contract balance in federal court though he should have done so to preserve it. The contract claim was a compulsory counterclaim under federal procedural rules as it arose out of the transaction that was the subject matter of the federal suit. By agreeing to the dismissal without preserving the contract claim, the store lost the right to sue Collinson on the contract in both federal and state courts.

Several weeks after the dismissal, the credit manager phoned the Legal Service and asked when Collinson would resume contract payments. He was unaware of the consequence of the disposition of the federal suit. He was referred to his lawyer for a discussion of compulsory counterclaims and procedural rules....

Note on Israel's tale: The lawyer as Robin Hood

1. Can one be critical of Kepler's conduct in *Valdez*, and at the same time be accepting of the conduct of Collinson's lawyer? What differences,

---

5. The Legal Service alleged eight errors under the Truth In Lending Act, federal consumer credit disclosure legislation. Among them: the annual interest percentage rate was understated, the initial payment due date was not indicated, the description of the subject of the transaction, the ring, in which a security interest was taken and other disclosures in the contract were illegible, the "discount" was inappropriately disclosed.

if any, are there between the two contexts? Do any such differences seem sufficient to you?

(a) The jewelry store's entitlement to recover the contract price of the ring sold to Collinson was as clear, was it not, as was the Valdez' right to recover notwithstanding their contributory negligence (unless the federal statute not only imposed certain obligations on vendors but made their contracts of sale unenforceable as a remedy for non-compliance).

- Should this factor be given greater weight here than in the *Valdez* situation?

- Is there a sense in which you can responsibly assert that the seller's claim was *not* (to use Judge Sharswood's terminology, p. 126, above) "honest and just"?

(b) Are there any other bases on which you can distinguish the Collinson from the Valdez situation?

(c) For an analysis that takes questions like these seriously, and attempts to think through and articulate the considerations that, in the author's view, ought to be considered in resolving them, see William Simon, Ethical Discretion in Lawyering, 101 Harv.L.Rev. 1088, 1090–1113 (1988).

2. Compare now the approach of Collinson's lawyer, with that not of Kepler but of Beach, the Valdez' lawyer.

(a) Consider:

- his attitude toward his clients;

- his attitude toward his practice;

- the form of his practice.

(b) What factors, these or others, might account for the difference?

(c) What inferences do you draw from thinking about these questions?

THE CORPORATE LAWYER'S OBLIGATION TO THE PUBLIC INTEREST

John M. Ferren

33 Business Lawyer 1253 (1978).

Trireme Aluminum Co., a closely held corporation manufacturing alloys primarily used by the aircraft industry, has developed a new, higher strength aluminum alloy especially for use in light planes. Largely because of significant demand for this one product, Trireme has turned around a three-year earnings deficit and is well into a second profitable year.

One evening over dinner, the company's chief engineer confided to Trireme's outside counsel, who was an old college friend, that he feared the worst. The engineer said that although the new alloy had met all applicable safety standards and design requirements when officially tested, the company lab's recent tests had convinced him that the alloy would crack at extremely cold temperatures; that the potential danger to the public had increased as Trireme marketed the alloy for use in larger planes flying at higher altitudes; and that he had kept the company president informed of this research but had been told not to discuss it with anyone else. He added that his conscience had bothered him for not telling anyone, but that for a number of reasons he was unwilling to "surface" with this information. Primarily, it appeared, he was afraid of losing his job. He told counsel to use this information as needed, but not to mention his name. He reasoned that his identity would be safe because the entire ten-member engineering staff was aware of the problem and most of them agreed with him; no one would immediately think that he was the source.

Counsel preserved his informant's anonymity, but mentioned what he had heard to the company president the next day. The president insisted that despite a majority view of the engineering staff that there was, in fact, a danger, a substantial minority of the more experienced members of that staff believed that the tests showed no danger or at worst were inconclusive. More important, he said, was the fact that the alloy unquestionably met established minimum design requirements and safety standards. He added, finally, that adjustments in the alloy formula were in the process of being tested, so that in due course any problem—which he believed not to exist anyway—would undoubtedly be resolved.

Counsel raised the possibilities of informing Trireme's customers and of suggesting the recall of planes. He also suggested that Trireme consider repurchase of all inventory in the field. The president sharply rebuked him with references not only to the conflicting opinions about the tests themselves but also to the recent turnaround in company fortunes because of the alloy, the fact that 25 percent of company sales were now dependent on the alloy, and that employment in the local community, which had been depressed for years, would suffer severely if there were any break in production.

Counsel informed the board of directors about these conversations at the next regular meeting, but the board unanimously agreed with the president and informed counsel that the matter should be considered closed.

A month later a medium-range, higher altitude plane made of the alloy, the Roton S–12, crashed during a charter flight, killing everyone aboard. The investigation did not conclusively determine the cause; it stated that pilot error appeared to be the principal factor. A portion of the report, however, referred to unusual fractures in the aileron and elevator spars. One investigator questioned the ductility of the basic metal; another surmised that the particular assembly was defective—essentially human error rather than a deficiency in design.

No investigator had contacted Trireme. Without further evidence, however, the National Transportation Safety Board made a most unusual recommendation with respect to such ambiguous facts: that the FAA summarily issue an "Airworthiness Directive" (AD) suspending use of the new alloy until further investigation could take place, and grounding all Roton S–12s and other aircraft made of the alloy. The FAA did so. Trireme's president asked ... counsel to join Roton Corp.'s counsel in a challenge to the suspension by going first to the FAA and, if necessary, to court.

Counsel agreed. Trireme and Roton prevailed in court, which ordered revocation of the AD solely on the basis of the government's scanty, ambiguous documentation. Trireme's counsel had successfully moved to quash government subpoenas of company records and employees on the ground of irrelevance, arguing that the FAA's summary issuance of the AD must be judged solely by reference to its prima facie case. The court held that, given the investigative report's emphasis on human error, the AD had been issued arbitrarily on purely speculative grounds. The government filed a notice of appeal and sought a stay of the trial court's action. Without waiting for completion of the judicial process, a Congressional subcommittee, upset by this rebuff to the FAA's authority when the public safety was involved, immediately announced an investigation, issuing subpoenas to company officials and to the engineering staff. The Trireme board of directors has asked to meet with ... counsel.

     . . . .

This particular hypothetical case is intended to present an ethical dilemma where resignation by the lawyer when a corporate client resists his advice may not be enough by itself to satisfy a responsibility he may have to the public at-large. In other words, the principal question is whether, under these circumstances, the lawyer's duty to keep his client's confidences and secrets arguably becomes subordinate, at some point, to an obligation not only to resign from the representation but also to reveal to public authorities what he has learned from the chief engineer about the alloy's probable danger.

One has to bear in mind, of course, that a central feature of our adversary system is the confidentiality inherent in the lawyer-client relationship. If a client has reason to believe he cannot deal in confidence with his attorney, he is likely to withhold information vital to the rendering of sound legal and practical advice; counsel will not even have an opportunity to argue a legal position, let alone a moral one. Furthermore, any obligation of an attorney to "turn in" a client will create a conflict of interest between lawyer and client that may cause the lawyer not only to compromise his legal advice but also to act principally in his own interest, to avoid any possible disciplinary proceeding.

In summary, the very integrity of our system is based on a premise of complete confidentiality, subject to the most limited of exceptions that are clearly understood by lawyer and client alike. The public interest is almost always served best when the client is encouraged, through the promise of confidentiality, to consult freely with counsel, and the lawyer is protected, without fear of reprisal, in giving advice as the law and his conscience suggest. This paper explores the question whether, if ever, this principle need not be honored in view of a higher public interest.

AT THE BOARD MEETING

The first question concerns the extent of counsel's duty to make sure that the board is completely informed about the matter. Given the potential harm to the public if the chief engineer's analysis were correct, [what] should counsel have advised ...?

"Advice of a lawyer to his client need not be confined to purely legal considerations." [EC 7–8] Counsel is free—and possibly required—to say exactly what he thinks should be done. "In assisting his client to reach a proper decision, it is often desirable for a lawyer to point out those factors which may lead to a decision that is morally just as well as legally permissible" [ibid.] (or impermissible). Given counsel's own beliefs about the present danger, he might well advise that the company, as a matter of basic fairness, ought to inform its alloy customers, issue a public warning, and even recall inventories in the field. If he also were to conclude, however, that such disclosure, based on the evidence to date, were not *legally* required, he would be obliged, of course, to make that legal position clear to the company. If the Trireme board then decided, finally, to follow the president's recommendation, counsel apparently must accept that decision or withdraw from representation. "In the final analysis, ... the lawyer should always remember that the decision whether to forego legally available objectives or methods because of non-legal factors is ultimately for the client and not for himself. In the event that the client in a non-adjudicatory matter insists upon a course of conduct that is contrary to the judgment and advice of the lawyer but not prohibited by Disciplinary Rules, the lawyer may withdraw from the employment." [ibid.]

Is there a persuasive argument that counsel has some other step to consider at this point beyond withdrawal from employment to satisfy his professional conscience or obligation? For example, given the engineering staff's majority view, is counsel on notice that his client, Trireme, may be guilty of criminal negligence or recklessness, opening the possibility that counsel may be permitted if not obliged to reveal the test data to the authorities, pursuant to DR 4–101(C)(3), on the ground that the client has an "intention ... to commit a crime"? *

On the facts to this point in the case, a lawyer probably would be stretching it to perceive reportable criminal "intent" within the meaning of DR 4–101(C)(3), even if he were to find the client negligent or even reckless. To the contrary, in fact, if counsel were to decide that

---

* [DR 4–101 prohibits disclosure by a lawyer of a "confidence" or a "secret" of a client, subject to specified exceptions, one of which permits (but does not require) disclosure of "the intention of [the] client to commit a crime and the information necessary to prevent the crime." A confidence is defined as "information protected by the attorney-client privilege," and a secret as any information "gained in the professional relationship ... disclosure of which ... would be likely to be detrimental to the client."]

his client was *not* pursuing an illegal course of conduct, counsel might conclude that he was not even in a position to withdraw, let alone disclose the test data. Arguably, if the client were to resist its counsel's proposed resignation, only a very strong conviction about the immorality of the Trireme board's decision would justify the lawyer's withdrawal, for despite the permissive provisions of DR 2–110(C), no withdrawal can be accomplished until the lawyer "has taken reasonable steps to avoid foreseeable prejudice to the rights of his client. . . ." Given his tenure as counsel to the company, the pendency of other serious matters about which he has detailed knowledge, and the strong feelings by board members that they very much depend on *him,* he may feel he has little if any *choice* about staying with the company—for the time being.

Probably, however, this argument questioning the propriety of counsel's withdrawal is overstated. Rarely, if ever, will a matter be beyond the competence of successor counsel, assuming the time to find and adequately brief a new lawyer. Furthermore, a client's resistance to counsel's proposed resignation should not be equated with "prejudice" to the rights of the client; such a reading would take the determination of what constitutes prejudice entirely out of the hands of counsel and put him at the mercy of the client. If counsel in good faith believes that there will be no real prejudice to the client, counsel should be entitled to withdraw from the representation even if the client were to insist that he remain.

There is, of course, the problem of what the resigning lawyer can tell substitute counsel about the client. To the extent that there is applicable authority, it would appear that resigning counsel is precluded from volunteering information about the client. [T]he Committee on Professional Ethics [has] held that an attorney who learned that a client had not resided in the state long enough to procure a divorce and thus declined the case cannot properly reveal that fact to the court or to successor counsel who apparently filed for the divorce on the basis of the client's false statements about residency. Given the rationale of this opinion, namely, the supremacy of the lawyer's obligation to keep a confidence, there is no reason to believe that the ABA Committee would permit counsel to reveal such information (absent the client's permission) even if his successor, before taking on the client, had specifically *requested* the grounds for resignation. More recently, however, the Council of the Law Society in England reached the opposite conclusion: its Professional Purposes Committee concluded that a solicitor ought to disclose to the new solicitor a client's attempt to suppress the fact of a decedent's marriage, in an effort to prevent the widow's inheritance.

To me, the British view is correct. Resigning counsel should be free to communicate fully with successor counsel about the client, with such communication retaining a privileged status as to other third parties. Clients should not find it easy to shop for a lawyer (after the first time!) using false or misleading information. Conceivably, of course, a distressed resigning counsel could unfairly tarnish a client, but surely that is no basis for withholding information from new counsel, who should be expected to make his own objective evaluation. Nevertheless, if Opinion 268 remains the preferred view, there is a proper way around it—i.e., assuming that a prospective counsel's ethical standards are as high as his predecessor's. Successor counsel, as a matter of practice, should undertake no representation without obtaining the client's consent to a comprehensive interview with prior counsel, who should be expressly relieved by such consent of any obligation to withhold information as privileged. In the *Trireme* case, if outside counsel chooses to withdraw when the Board rejects his advice, any prospective successor counsel should find out why and evaluate whether, in good conscience, he can uphold Trireme's position.

Immediately after the crash, should counsel have advised calling a Trireme board meeting to discuss whether to make the company's test data available to the investigators? What should counsel have recommended to the board at this point, prior to issuance of the investigative report?

Keep in mind that once there has been a crash, counsel will know that a government investigation by the National Transportation Safety Board is inevitable, followed by likely involvement of the FAA. Should he have expected, therefore, on the facts of this case, that the Safety Board, the FAA, or government counsel would seek testimony from the Trireme officers and engineering staff during the course of the investigation? If that were the most reasonable expectation, would counsel have been justified in viewing his case from the moment of the crash strictly as an adversary of the public authorities, leaving it to *them* to initiate requests for all information to be supplied?

Once the inconclusive investigative report had been issued without any consultation with Trireme, would it have become more reasonable for counsel to assume (before issuance of the AD) that the government would never obtain the Trireme test data unless the company proffered it? If so, does that place a greater ethical burden on counsel than he faces in a clearly adversary context?

Assume that counsel had the engineering staff review the investigative report, and that the staff unanimously agreed that the crash evidenced a likely defect in the Trireme alloy. Should counsel have recommended to the board that the company turn over its test data to the authorities and/or Trireme's customers (assuming no clear legal obligation to do so)? Could counsel have properly threatened to withdraw if the company refused to follow such advice? Could he properly have threatened to turn over the test data himself?

Whether counsel is in an adversary situation or not, he is confronted with a number of ethical restraints on the zealousness of his advocacy.

DR 7–102. Representing a Client Within the Bounds of the Law.

(A) In his representation of a client, a lawyer shall not:

(1) File a suit, assert a position, conduct a defense, delay a trial, or take other action on behalf of his client when he knows that it is obvious that such action would serve merely to harass or maliciously injure another.

. . .

(3) Conceal or knowingly fail to disclose that which he is required by law to reveal.

. . .

(7) Counsel or assist his client in conduct that the lawyer knows to be illegal or fraudulent.

. . .

(B) A lawyer who receives information *clearly establishing* that:

(1) His client has, in the course of the representation, *perpetrated a fraud upon a person or tribunal,* shall promptly call upon his client to rectify the same, and if his client refuses or is unable to do so, he shall reveal the fraud to the affected person or tribunal, *except when the information is protected as a privileged communication.* [Emphasis added.]

. . .

"*. . . perpetrated a fraud . . .*"

When the public authorities have not yet targeted Trireme through investigative demands or issuance of the AD, counsel has to resolve whether his client conceivably could have "perpetrated a fraud upon a person or tribunal," through the *failure* to proffer information that unquestionably is relevant to a substantial, immediate concern about the public safety. The threshold question is whether Trireme has misrepresented a fact, or has omitted disclosure of a fact in a fiduciary context. Possibly there will have been such a misrepresentation or omission if Trireme was principally responsible for establishing the design requirements and/or safety standards on which the FAA relied. Additional facts may be determinative as well, such as evasion of inquiries by Roton Corp. about the possible meaning of the investigator's reference to unusual fractures of the alloy. Conceivably, too, Trireme's warranty of the alloy explicitly or implicitly required disclosure of this most recent test data to Roton Corp. Absent such misrepresentation (or omission under fiduciary circumstances), Trireme will not have committed fraud.

Second, in making the judgment about possible fraud, counsel will have to consider whether there has been conduct "clearly establishing" an "intent to deceive." Given the majority viewpoint of the engineering staff, reinforced by the crash, that the alloy presented a public danger, and also given the fact that the principal, if not the only, reason why the Trireme board still insisted on withholding the test data was a concern for the company income statement, is counsel now actually faced with the requisite *scienter?*

"*. . . upon a person or tribunal . . .*"

Counsel's obligation under DR 7–102(B)(1) is further limited to disclosure of fraud on a "person," defined as a distinct individual or entity (as distinguished from the public-at-large), or fraud on a "tribunal," defined as an adjudicative body (as distinguished, for example, from an investigative agency). It would appear, therefore, that counsel would not be required to announce a client's fraud to an unidentifiable class of prospective airplane passengers.

Probably this limitation requiring the disclosure of fraud only on tribunals and other identifiable entities, but not fraud on the public generally, has been derived from the traditional notion of privity: i.e., the act (or omission) must be specifically directed at someone, where the injury is clear, before the lawyer is permitted, let alone required, to break a confidential relationship. This is not a meaningful limitation, however, on counsel's duty in our hypothetical case. The term "person," which includes any "legal entity," is broad enough to cover a specific governmental investigative agency, acting on behalf of the general public. Thus, the limitation of the term "tribunal" to an adjudicative body should not be construed to exclude other governmental agencies from the category of "persons" covered by DR 7–102(B)(1).

There can be little doubt, therefore, that if (but only if) Trireme's conduct were "clearly" fraudulent at some point toward the Safety Board, the FAA, and/or Trireme's customers, then they were defrauded "persons," as defined by the Code.

"*. . . except when the information is protected as a privileged communication . . .*"

The final hurdle in deciding whether a lawyer must disclose a client's fraud is the admonition in DR 7–102(B)(1) against revelation of even a fraud "when the information is protected as a privileged communication."

There is little if any authority that affords substantial help here; analyses of the principles involved have been confined for the most part to relatively simple situations of clear-cut perjury or fraud. [H]owever, the lawyer's duty to break a client confidence in certain situations has probably been more broadly recognized under the previous Canons and under the Code as originally promulgated in 1969 than it is under the Code today, as amended in 1974.

[Judge Ferren here summarizes the evolution of ABA approaches, leading up to the issuance of Formal Opinion 341, p. 147, below]

In the hypothetical case before us, the question whether Trireme's persistent refusal to disclose the test data to its customers or to the government during the period after the crash arguably puts increasingly severe strain on counsel's judgment that his client is not committing a fraud. Moreover, if fraud is involved, the significance of distinctions based on past versus prospective conduct, or on civil versus criminal fraud, becomes blurred at best. In any event, a lawyer may be hard-pressed to conclude that avoidance of an investigation into an airplane crash through failure to disclose material facts will not have criminal law consequences, especially if he realizes that his client's insistence on nondisclosure may amount to reckless, if not intentional, disregard of life, and that a subsequent crash very likely would reveal that the alloy caused it.

In summary, prior to issuance of the AD, counsel will have to choose one of two courses of action, embracing different views of the facts. Would it be more appropriate to conclude that fraud is not involved, or that even if fraud is involved it cannot be disclosed under DR 7–102(B)(1) because it is not necessarily criminal (ongoing or intended) and counsel learned of it on a "confidential" or "secret" basis? Or would counsel be better advised to tell the investigative authorities about the test data, based on a conclusion that Trireme is perpetrating a fraud, and that even if Trireme's conduct is not technically criminal, it is ethically tantamount to criminal fraud in view of the reckless disregard of life suggested by the circumstances?

AFTER ISSUANCE OF THE AIRWORTHINESS DIRECTIVE

After issuance of the AD, company counsel was thrust more directly into an adversary relationship with the public authorities and clearly faced the prospect—and responsibility—of appearing before a tribunal. Does the fact that the FAA has now targeted Trireme, and thus assumed the burden of developing relevant information, suggest that company counsel has less responsibility than before the AD was issued to urge his client to volunteer the test data to the government, and even to Trireme's customers?

This question presupposes, of course, that there was no obligation to disclose prior to issuance of the AD. Moreover, since the AD already has been issued, the question more precisely is this: can counsel properly fight the AD on behalf of Trireme solely on the ground of arbitrary and capricious agency action, without disclosing the test data to its customer co-plaintiff, Roton Corp., or to the court? When government counsel subpoenas Trireme documents and employees as part of the proceeding, can company counsel properly attempt to quash the subpoenas on the ground of irrelevance, given an AD on its face unsupported by sufficient investigative evidence?

My own sense of it is that this post-AD phase adds little, if anything, to counsel's ethical situation. If he were justified in withholding the test data from the investigators or Trireme's customers prior to the court proceeding, there does not appear to be a new obligation to disclose just because the court is now involved; DR 7–102(B)(1) governs counsel's conduct in both phases of the case. On the other hand, if counsel had been obliged to reveal the data prior to his date in court, he merely would be adding a "tribunal" to the "persons" defrauded by Trireme's conduct—compounding an earlier violation of the Code.

THE CONGRESSIONAL INVESTIGATION

Again, nothing appears to be added here, except still another opportunity for counsel to decide whether he properly can attempt to quash a subpoena, perhaps on the ground that the matter is still before the court and Congressional interference is thus unwarranted.

I assume, however, that despite counsel's efforts, sooner or later the company's test data will be forced into the open by Congress or the courts, with all the attendant embarrassment. After all, there is no suggestion in this case that the test data itself is privileged against discovery in a proper proceeding. Surely as a practical if not ethical matter, therefore, counsel should have been able to convince his client that failure to disclose the test data after the crash was likely to be counterproductive.

. . .

Note on Trireme: Ethics as following the rules

1. What strikes me most about Judge Ferren's discussion is not any of his answers to this hypothetical professional-responsibility problem, but the way that he so completely—and without any discussion—treats ethical problems as legal issues. The question is whether certain action constitutes fraud, whether the FAA constitutes a tribunal, whether a statement is a privileged communication, whether withdrawal would prejudice the client, et cetera. To Ferren, it seems self-evident that this is the proper approach. Why? (Compare the issues raised in Section 3 of the Note on *Valdez,* p. 125, above). I have elsewhere posed the issue raised in these terms:

> [W]e are talking about an unusual source of law. The Model Code is something between the Ten Commandments and a press release. The American Bar Association is a private organization, and its pronouncements have no legal force. Of course, in one form or another the Code is—or was—law, in the sense that the Supreme Court of every state promulgated it, but if you ask why we have to follow it, the going gets a bit slippery. One answer could be that one who violates the Code may get into trouble. Some discussions say that explicitly: Would you be "in trouble," considering the language of DR "X" in light of ABA Opinion "Y"? The accurate answer is that you very likely will not be in trouble no matter what you do. Very few lawyers are ever disciplined, and especially not in mind-boggling, agonizing matters like the Trireme problem. You really do not have to worry on that account.[14]

> Perhaps (of course), the point refers to the moral basis of the Code. There was a time when many lawyers did view the Code as something

---

14. Recent years have seen a partial erosion of the relative insulation of attorneys from the risk of discipline in a case such as Trireme, although the "discipline" is more likely to take the form of [malpractice] litigation ... than that of a disciplinary proceeding itself. I do not think that that trend has as yet progressed far enough to explain the phenomenon under discussion in the text, which of course long antedated it in any event.

like the Ten Commandments.[15] I do not think that many lawyers believe that today.   Richard Abel has observed that the change in names—from Canons of Ethics to Code of Responsibility to Rules of Conduct—expresses a "progressive decline in normativity." [Abel, Why Does the ABA Promulgate Ethical Rules?, 59 Tex.L.Rev. 939, 686 n. 257 (1981)] One of the by-products of the controversy over the drafting and adoption of the Model Rules is that both the Code and the Rules are now even more than previously viewed simply as positive law, as open to criticism, avoidance, or evasion as any other act of a lawmaking body.

Lesnick, Infinity in a Grain of Sand: The World of Law and Lawyering as Portrayed in the Clinical Teaching Implicit in the Law School Curriculum, 37 U.C.L.A. L.Rev. 1157, 1166–67 (1990).

2.   What are some of the consequences of viewing the problem in legal terms?   Consider the following responses to that question:

(a) If "whistle-blowing" (or other action inconsistent with a client's wishes or interests) is required by the Code, a lawyer must blow the whistle, and if it is not required by the Code he or she may not, because the duty of loyalty fills up all the rest of the space.... In this environment, problems of ethics or responsibility—What action do I choose to take, or feel called upon to take?—come to be viewed as problems of advocacy: What actions can I justify as permissible (or, better yet, obligatory)?

Lesnick, supra, at 1167.

(b) [A]s the process of legal analysis continues, it acquires accelerating complexity.   A relatively simple problem—not simple in its solution, but simple factually—becomes a multi-layered law review article.   There are six crucial words of the Code that need construction; there are several Bar Association Opinions that need reconciliation. By the time that one is finished, ... a decision to do nothing seems comfortable.   After all, what does one do after reading ten pages of dense legal analysis about a moral problem?   One says, 'Well, that's a hard question and who knows what is right,' and goes on to something else, not having engaged with the moral or existential dimension of the problem and channeled toward a response that avoids the need to do so.

Id., at 1167–68.

(c) Great attention is paid to the questions of disclosure and withdrawal, but none to the fact that the attorney is asked to move from passively aiding or protecting the company by silence, to actively seeking to keep the planes flying by filing motions designed to fend off the FAA.   The explanation for this priority, I believe, is nothing more than the fact that filing motions is thought to raise ethical problems

---

15. A lawyer once said to me explicitly, with reference to the 1974 ABA amendment regarding group legal services (one of the controversial and short-lived "Houston" amendments). When I respond- ed that it has never been reported that the Ten Commandments were amended by a vote of 140 to 117, his reply was to shrug; he did not care, he viewed the Code as per se morally authoritative.

only when they are substantively groundless [See DR 7–102(A); MR 3.1].

Id., at 1167 n. 17.

(d) Seeing the moral or existential question as a legal issue, and multiplying the complexity and subtlety of the legal issues, remove from thought [what to me is] the real question ...: What do you do if you, an autonomous professional genuinely concerned about the danger but recognizing that you do not really know whether it is a substantial one, are told by this powerful, successful, fairly aggressive person whom you represent not to worry about it? You are reluctant to drop the matter, because you are afraid that the company president may not really be open to hearing the problem, and part of your job, as well as your responsibility to yourself, is to worry. On the other hand, he is intimidating you and might fire you or lose confidence in you. More than that, you respect him: He knows more about this matter than you do, and if you have been representing him you probably think that he is doing an admirable job under dreadful circumstances. When the president tells you not to worry about it, that he knows all about it and has decided it is all right, it is not just lust for the client and money that keeps you quiet; all that is reinforced (if you have any sense) by some humility about whether he may be right. Trust me, he says, and says it with a smile and with a fist. And both of them are effective.

... The problem is transformed from a painful to a stimulating one by viewing it as a series of legal complexities. By the time the panelists finish analyzing all the issues, everyone is ready to shake hands all around, say that this has been a very useful discussion—no one could possibly remember which Code provision he or she thinks has been the crucial one—and go off thinking: "Well, I'll just pick up the next matter in my 'in' box and go on with my work." The intellectual challenges of wrestling with a hard problem in professional responsibility provide a cathartic release from the grip of the problem as it would otherwise be experienced.

... Thus, the analysis both illustrates the way, and reinforces the process by which, our selves become removed from the legal problems we work on as lawyers. Personal conflicts—whether over conflicts between loyalty to client interest and concern over public harms, or the conflict between one's self-image as an independent professional and the power imbalance vis-a-vis the company president—are abstracted from the activity of lawyering.

Id., at 1168–69.

Ask yourself (with respect to this list of consequences):

• Is it accurate as a description, or is it overdrawn in some significant ways?

• To the extent it is accurate, that is, to the extent that one or more of the phenomena noted do seem to you to be consequences of the approach that Judge Ferren's discussion manifests, which (if any) of these consequences appear to you to be troubling?

3.   Assume that a colleague seeks to explain his or her agreement with Judge Ferren's approach to the problem in one of the following ways:

- "I read the Code as *requiring* me to keep everything confidential, whether I would want to or not, unless it either allows or requires disclosure in this case. So, I look at the Code to see whether I have any choice in the matter, and that means looking at it as a statute."

- "I would *want* to keep everything that I learned in the representation confidential, and would therefore look to the Code to see whether I must disclose in this case. That's why I treat the Code as a statute."

(a) What premises does each of these responses rest on?

(b) What is your reaction to them?

4.   Are there viable alternative approaches to a problem like Trireme? Consider this question in two contexts:

(a) Looking first at the question as one of *individual decisionmaking*, if you were inclined to adopt an approach that did not lean so heavily on the professional codes, what considerations would be most important to you in deciding what to do? How would you want to have acted, were you to have been counsel in that situation?

(b) Addressing now the question whether the *professional norm itself* should be less "legalistic" in its approach, consider both the diagnosis and the prescription contained in the following excerpt, asking yourself:

- how it differs from the critique suggested by this Note;

- in what ways, in light of that difference, it might find the prescription suggested by this Note (or this book) to be an inadequate solution to the problem it identifies;

- to what extent you agree with both its diagnosis and prescription.

THE TROUBLE WITH LEGAL ETHICS
William H. Simon
41 J.Leg.Educ. 65 (1991).

Legal ethics is a disappointing subject. From afar, it seems exciting; it promises to engage the central normative commitments that make lawyering a profession and that account for much of the nonpecuniary appeal of the lawyer's role. . . .

But close up, legal ethics usually turns out to be dull and dispiriting. At most law schools, students find the course in legal ethics or professional responsibility boring and insubstantial. . . . Bar association ethics discussions rarely generate interest over the kind of basic questions of value that the view from afar associates with legal ethics. The reason that legal ethics is so consistently disappointing is that the prevailing conceptions of the subject fail to respond to the aspirations that draw people to it.

There are two prevailing conceptions of legal ethics or professional responsibility. The first conflates legal ethics with the disciplinary rules of the codes—rules promulgated under state-delegated authority and enforced by punitive sanctions. Under this conception, the subject might better be called "Regulation of Lawyers," a name in fact used by one of the legal ethics textbooks, in the same way that the study of the rules governing the practice of transportation companies is called "Regulation of Common Carriers." The second conception conflates legal ethics with the private or personal moralities of individual lawyers. Here the core concerns are the constraints of role on self-expression and the legitimacy of requiring the individual lawyer to perform actions in role that conflict with her personal values.

The disciplinary rule conception is the dominant one among lawyers and law teachers. Most law school courses and bar association discussions of legal ethics are devoted largely to such rules. The professional responsibility component of bar exams consists entirely of a test of such rules. The personal morality conception is the dominant one among philosophers and psychologists concerned with lawyering, and it has influenced a minority of law teachers and practitioners as well, including most of those with the more original and ambitious approaches to legal ethics. These people try to help lawyers become more self-conscious and articulate about their personal values and to provide some psychological support for such values against the pressures of role.

Each of these conceptions disappoints an important part of the expectations that lead people to legal ethics or professional responsibility. The trouble with the disciplinary rule conception is that it does not have much to do with ethics or responsibility; the trouble with the personal morality conception is that there is nothing especially legal or professional about it. The first treats legal ethics as merely a set of rules; the second as purely individual values.

But one of the most distinctive and appealing implications of the ideal of professional role is that professional practice is simultaneously a form of social commitment and self-expression. In theory this happens because the practitioner is personally committed to the profession's norms, but also more fundamentally, because he participates in elaborating them. The most important participation occurs not through the formal organizational processes of the bar but through the lawyer's day-to-day practice in the form of a distinctive kind of judgment. As the *Code of Professional Responsibility* puts it, the "essence of the professional judgment of the lawyer is his educated ability to relate the general body and philosophy of law to the specific legal problem of the client."

Because the general legal norms do not mechanically apply themselves to specific circumstances, this judgment requires creative effort. Because the general norms express the normative commitments of the legal system and the profession, the effort to apply them to specific circumstances can be experienced as direct participation in the normative life of the community. This type of creative, normatively charged judgment is the distinctive ethical component of the ideal of professionalism. In my view, it accounts for the moral appeal of the lawyering role. The attractive implication of this notion of professionalism is that lawyers, not just in exceptional moments of public service, but in their everyday practice, participate directly in furthering justice....

[The field] of professional responsibility, however, ... consists predominantly of exegesis of the two disciplinary codes, and these days, primarily the *Model Rules*. Now one might object that the focus on the codes implies that the lawyer's main concern is avoiding sanctions, which seems inconsistent with the kind of internalized disposition to serve justice that one associates with professionalism. But this is not the most important objection to the disciplinary rule conception.... The critical objection is that the codes obviate complex, creative judgment and thus subvert the vital aspirations of professionalism.

The codes replicate within themselves the two dominant conceptions described earlier. On the one hand, there are norms designed for disciplinary enforcement prohibiting specified conduct. Although the drafters of the *Model Rules* describe these norms as "rules of reason," most of them in fact have a rigid, categorical character that leaves little room for judgment, and in fact these norms were designed, as one drafter put it, "to provide a black letter rule for every case." On the other hand, we find a set of norms that effectively grant broad, unreviewable autonomy to lawyers to consult their personal values. These norms are typically contentless; they make no effort to suggest how the decisions that fall under them might be made other than in terms of the lawyer's subjective predispositions.

... Perhaps the two most important norms in the *Model Rules* are those concerning confidentiality and withdrawal. The first is an example of the rigid, mechanical disciplinary rule. The lawyer is forbidden to disclose adverse client information except in two narrowly specified exceptional situations. Outside the exceptions, the lawyer has no authority to balance considerations that favor disclosure against the values of confidentiality, even when confidentiality perpetuates grotesque injustice. The withdrawal rule is an example of a contentless norm that simply defers to personal values. With a few narrowly specified exceptions, the lawyer is authorized to withdraw whenever he finds the client's objective "repugnant." The lawyer has no obligation to consider the extent to which withdrawal would cause injustice.

(In passing, we should note the political consequences of the *Model Rules* on confidentiality and withdrawal: the general prohibition of disclosure cements the lawyer's subordination to wealthy clients by depriving her of the only effective leverage she has to curb unjust conduct by the client, while the relegation of withdrawal issues to personal morality enables her to dominate poor clients by authorizing the lawyer to condition continued representation on compliance with her wishes.)

Although the confidentiality rule is primarily disciplinary in character, it also incorporates the personal morality perspective. The rigid disciplinary prohibitions are accompanied by two types of exception, one permitting disclosure when necessary for some interest of the lawyer herself and the other permitting it when necessary to save a third person from "death or substantial bodily injury" resulting from a client's criminal act. This second exception, which covers some of the most compelling ethical issues, does not give rise to an obligation to disclose or even to consider doing so. The rules simply give the lawyer permission to disclose; they state that she "may" do so but provide no criteria for such decisions and make clear that the decisions are not subject to disciplinary review. . . .

My point is not that the relegation of legal ethical issues to mechanical rules on the one hand and personal morality on the other results in relatively poor decisions on such issues (though in fact I think this is the case). Rather, the point for now is that this practice accounts for the failure of legal ethics to respond to the aspirations people bring to it. For the practice leaves no role in confronting the most compelling issues of legal ethics for the kind of complex, creative judgment that people associate with fulfilling aspects of professionalism.

The important aspect of this judgment is not just that it is demanding or intellectually challenging but that in linking particular technical concerns to broad social values, it enables the practitioner to experience the resolution of particular problems as vindicating universal interests. In contrast, under a regime of alternatively mechanical and subjective norms the practitioner repeatedly experiences his client's and his own concerns as alien from more general social interests.

FORMAL OPINION 341
ABA Committee on Ethics and Professional Responsibility (1975).

This opinion is made in response to several inquiries regarding the effect of the February 1974 amendment to DR 7–102(B), which presently reads:

"(B) A lawyer who receives information clearly establishing that

"(1) His client has, in the course of the representation, perpetrated a fraud upon a person or tribunal shall promptly call upon his client to rectify the same, and if his client refuses or is unable to do so, he shall reveal the fraud to the affected person or tribunal, <u>except when the information is protected as a privileged communication</u>." [<u>Underscored</u> language added by amendment February 1974.]

The derivation of DR 7–102(B)(1) is informative.

The . . . preliminary Draft of the Code of Professional Responsibility (January 1969) did not contain a Disciplinary Rule requiring a lawyer to reveal misconduct of a client. Perhaps the omission was due to the committee's consideration of the high fiduciary duty owed by lawyer to client and consideration of the firm support found in the law of evidence for the attorney-client privilege. The Preliminary Draft contained a Disciplinary Rule virtually identical to present DR 4–101(C), forbidding a lawyer, with certain exceptions, from knowingly revealing a confidence or secret of his client. Some lawyers objected, however, to the Preliminary Draft .... The result was the addition to the Code of Professional Responsibility, at that time, of DR 7–102(B).

When DR 7–102(B) was added to the Code of Professional Responsibility prior to its adoption in August 1969, the full significance of DR 4–101(C) apparently was not appreciated, even though the Preliminary Draft contained a virtually identical provision stating that "[a] lawyer may reveal ... [c]onfidences or secrets when permitted [under] Disciplinary Rules or required by law or court order." That provision of DR 4–101(C), while quite proper in the Preliminary Draft, had the unacceptable result when combined with new DR 7–102(B)(1) of requiring a lawyer in certain instances to reveal privileged communications which he also was duty-bound not to reveal according to the law of evidence. The amendment of February 1974 was necessary in order to relieve lawyers of exposure to such diametrically opposed professional duties.

A similar impasse arising under the prior Canons of Professional Ethics was considered by this committee in Formal Opinion 287 (1953). Then Canon 37 required a lawyer to "preserve his client's confidences" although Canon 29 required a lawyer to reveal perjury to the prosecuting authorities and Canon 41 required a lawyer to inform against his client in certain circumstances in regard to "fraud or deception." The situation in Opinion 287 was that of a client who had committed perjury ... during the trial of his divorce action. Three months later the client sought advice from the same lawyer who had represented him in the divorce action. The advice was sought in regard to a dispute with his former wife over support money; in connection with this consultation the client told the lawyer that he had given false material testimony in the divorce action in which he had been represented by the same lawyer. Tracing the background of the evidentiary law concerning the attorney-client privilege, this committee held that the duty of the lawyer to preserve his client's confidences prevailed over the duty under Canon 41 to reveal fraud or deception, and over the duty under Canon 29 to bring knowledge of perjury to the attention of others. In Opinion 287 it was said that the lawyer, "despite Canons 29 and 41, should not disclose the facts to the court or to the authorities."

One effect of the 1974 amendment to DR 7–102(B)(1) is to reinstate the essence of Opinion 287 which had prevailed from 1953 until 1969. It was as unthinkable then as now that a lawyer should be subject to disciplinary action for failing to reveal information which by law is not to be revealed without the consent of the client and the lawyer is not now in that untenable position. The lawyer no longer can be confronted with the necessity of either breaching his client's privilege at law or breaching a disciplinary rule.

. . .

. . . The conflicting duties to reveal fraud and to preserve confidences have existed side-by-side for some time.

However, it is clear that there has long been an accommodation in favor of preserving confidences either through practice or interpretation. Through the Bar's interpretation in practice of its responsibility to preserve confidences and secrets of clients, and through its interpretations like Formal Opinion 287, significant exceptions to any general duty to reveal fraud have been long accepted. Apparently, the exceptions were so broad or the policy underlying the duty to reveal so weak that the earlier drafts of the Code of Professional Responsibility omitted altogether the concept embodied in Canon 41. Nonetheless, DR 7–102(B) is a part of the Code of Professional Responsibility and must be given some meaning. . . .

. . .

The tradition (which is backed by substantial policy considerations) that permits a lawyer to assure a client that information (whether a confidence or a secret) given to him will not be revealed to third parties is so important that it should take precedence, in all but the most serious cases, over the duty imposed by DR 7–102(B). . . .

The balancing of the lawyer's duty to preserve confidences and to reveal frauds is best made by interpreting the phrase "privileged communication" in the 1974 amendment to DR 7–102(B) as referring to those confidences and secrets that are required to be preserved by DR 4–101.

Such an interpretation does not wipe out DR 7–102(B), because DR 7–102(B) applies to information received from any source, and it is not limited to information gained in the professional relationship as is DR 4–101. Under the suggested interpretation, the duty imposed by DR 7–102(B) would remain in force if the information clearly establishing a fraud on a person or tribunal and committed by a client in the course of representation were obtained by the lawyer from a third party (but not in connection with his professional relationship with the client), because it would not be a confidence or secret of a client entitled to confidentiality. . . .

Note: Confidentiality as the summum bonum of the bar

1. The authors of the Opinion acknowledge that, by their interpretation of the 1974 amendment to DR 7–102(B)(1),* the body of it applies only to the case of information obtained "from a third party (but not in connection with [the lawyer's] professional relationship with the client)." What are the "substantial policy considerations" that support so skewed an interpretation? To what extent should we credit the assertion that the reason lies in the "diametrically opposed" requirement of the law of evidence?

---

* The 1974 amendment was adopted in less than one-half of the States.

2. *The Model Rules and the limits of confidentiality.* Amid substantial criticism that the Bar had gone too far in upholding confidentiality as a supreme value, the early drafts of the Model Rules proposed substantial limits on the obligation to keep silent in the face of client conduct threatening harm to others or seriously misrepresenting the truth. The relevant rules were those dealing directly with the duty of confidentiality, and those seeking to impose a duty of truthfulness in dealings with third persons.

(a) Initially, the proposed confidentiality rule would have *mandated* disclosure when necessary "to prevent the client from committing an act that would seriously endanger the life or safety of another person, result in wrongful detention or incarceration of a person or wrongful destruction of substantial property, or corrupt judicial or governmental procedure," and would have *permitted* disclosure when necessary "to prevent or rectify the consequences of a deliberately wrongful act in which the lawyer's services are or were involved" (for example, when a contract of sale had been prepared by a lawyer on the basis of a deliberate misrepresentation by the seller-client, of which the lawyer learned prior to the closing). 1979 Unofficial Pre-circulation Draft.

The 1980 Discussion Draft limited mandatory disclosure to cases of threats of "death or serious bodily harm." The 1981 Proposed Final Draft retreated significantly further, abandoning mandatory disclosure altogether, and limiting discretionary disclosure to "criminal or fraudulent act[s]," while broadening the type of harms to include threats of "substantial injury to the financial interest or property of another." Permissible disclosure to prevent or rectify would have been limited to "criminal or fraudulent" acts.

The Rules as officially promulgated in 1983 reflected the belief of the ABA House of Delegates that the principle of confidentiality needed still further protection. Rule 1.6(b) provides for permissible disclosure only "to prevent the client from committing a criminal act that the lawyer believes is likely to result in imminent death or substantial bodily harm...." Disclosure to rectify has been removed completely.

Identify:

- the differing ideas expressed about the proper limits of the norm of confidentiality by the language of these several versions; and

- the extent to which the replacement of the Code with the Rules (as ultimately adopted) expanded, rather than narrowed, the reach of the requirement of confidentiality.

(b) The evolution of MR 4.1 followed an analogous course. The 1980 Draft required disclosure of material facts known to the lawyer, when necessary to "correct a manifest misapprehension ... resulting from a previous representation made by the lawyer or known by the lawyer to have been made by the client...." This was narrowed in the 1981 Draft, to apply only to non-disclosure that assisted "a criminal or fraudulent act by a client." The 1982 Draft specified that the duty to disclose would apply "even if compliance requires disclosure of information otherwise protected by Rule 1.6," but the final version of Rule 4.1 makes the opposite move, explicitly providing that disclosure is required "unless ... prohibited by Rule 1.6."

(c) A large number of States have adopted revised versions of the Rules, which do not carry so far the primacy accorded the interest in confidentiality. The primary points of divergence concern the limitation of the exception to criminal acts, the requirement that the threat of death be of "imminent" death, and the exclusion of serious economic harm as a ground of permissible disclosure. As a result, there are significant inter-state variations in the applicable rules governing disclosure. (For a tabulation of State-to-State variations, see S. Gillers & R. Simon, Regulation of Lawyers: Statutes and Standards 54–56 (1992)).

(d) The intensity of the controversy over the contours of Rule 1.6 should not cause you to lose sight of the narrow range within which the debate has been carried on. Consider the following recent description of "the law governing lawyers" presented to the American Law Institute:

> *Conflict between protection of confidential client information and other values....* The broad prohibition against divulging confidential client information comes at a cost to both lawyers and society. Lawyers sometimes learn of information that cannot be disclosed ... but that would be highly useful if it could be made known to other persons. On occasion, those may include persons whose personal plight and character might be much more sympathetic to the lawyer and to the public at large than that of the lawyer's client. Those may also include persons who are in a position to accomplish great public good or avoid great public detriment if the information could be shared with them. Moreover, the personal interest of lawyers in being free to speak and publish information is compromised by a broad rule of confidentiality, a rule which to that extent impinges on their normal opportunity of free expression. Nonetheless, although the confidentiality rule sometimes imposes burdens on third persons and society and silence on the part of lawyers, it reflects a considered judgment that high net social value justifies the rule.

Illustration:

> 1. Lawyer is appointed to represent Client, a person who has been accused of murder. During confidential conferences between them, Client informs Lawyer that Client in fact committed the murder charged as well as two others. Client gives Lawyer confirming details of all three murders, in sufficient detail to confirm beyond question that Client's story is true. The two other murders involve victims whose bodies have not yet been discovered. Lawyer takes further steps to confirm Client's story while preparing a possible defense of insanity. Because of similarities between the circumstances of the charged murder and the circumstances of the disappearance of the other victims, parents of one of the victims approach Lawyer and beg Lawyer for any information about their child. Lawyer realizes the personal anguish of the victim's parents and the peace the information that he knows could bring them. Unless Client consents to disclosure ..., Lawyer must respond that he has no information that he can give them.

American Law Institute, Restatement of the Law Governing Lawyers § 111 Comment *b* (Tent. Draft No. 3, 1990).

In thinking about the effect of a statement like this on your own lawyering decisionmaking, try to separate out the weights that you would want to give these differing inputs:

- a felt pressure to act in conformity to the professional norm, out of concern over the sanction that might flow from nonconformity;

- a felt obligation to act so, out of a belief that you *should* conform to norms reflecting a professional consensus in preference to your personal norms;

- a judgment that adherence to the norm is right, out of a belief that competing values cannot be weighed *ad hoc* without undermining the objectives of the confidentiality principle and introducing excessive role conflicts into your professional work;

- an individual decision that the "other values" at stake in a particular case or type of case are not strong enough to override the value of confidentiality.

(e) In considering what the "professional norm" actually is, perhaps the rule should not be taken at face value. Consider these actions of the Restaters:

- Following MR 1.6, Tentative Draft No. 3 of the proposed *Restatement* (1990) allows disclosure of confidential client information in certain cases where "the client intends to commit a crime ... that threatens to cause death or serious bodily injury" (Sec. 117A). Illustration 1 is as follows:

    At a meeting with engineers employed by Client Corporation, Lawyer learns that one of the engineers has violated a criminal statute by releasing a toxic substance into a city's sewer drainage system. From information available, Lawyer reasonably believes that the discharge will cause death or serious bodily injury, that the lawyer's disclosure of the discharge will permit authorities to remove that threat or lessen the number of its victims, that the need to take preventive action is immediate, and that efforts to persuade responsible Client Corporation personnel to take corrective action would be unavailing. Although the act creating the threat has already occurred, Lawyer has discretion to use or disclose under this Section for the purpose of preventing the consequences of the act.

Am I wrong in suggesting that this proposed response is flatly at variance with the language of the proposed blackletter, and with MR 1.6?

- Tentative Draft No. 2 (1989), Sec. 132, dealt with the "crime/fraud" exception to the attorney-client privilege. Comment *e* asserts that "past client wrongs, no matter how serious their nature," remain privileged. "The law accepts the possible social costs of denying access in litigation to relevant evidence in order to realize the advantages of enhanced legality and fairness that confidentiality fosters." Illustration 4 was as follows:

Client informs Lawyer that Client has killed Victim. The communication occurs under circumstances such that the attorney-client privilege ... applies. Thereafter, the state indicts X for the murder of Victim. The lawyer for X seeks to call Lawyer as a defense witness to testify to Client's confession. Despite the importance of the testimony to X's defense, Lawyer is required ... to assert the attorney-client privilege. Because Client's communication with Lawyer concerned a past act, the crime-fraud exception recognized by this Section does not apply.

At a stormy session of the American Law Institute, bitter objection was made to the illustration, and the Institute voted to delete it from the Draft. No proposal was made, however, to amend Comment *e* or the proposed rule on which it was based. 5 ABA/BNA Lawyers' Manual on Professional Conduct 159 (1989).

How do you explain these examples of a refusal to apply the confidentiality norm in cases thought to be compellingly extreme, combined with a refusal to relax the extremity of the norm itself? Compare (again) Charles Curtis' comment about the rule against the expression of personal belief in the client's cause, p. 54, above.

3. *Withdrawal and the prompting of client consent to disclosure.* A decision that disclosure without client consent would be improper does not end the matter, since the further question is presented, whether a lawyer who believes strongly that the information in question should be revealed may justifiably refuse to continue as counsel unless the client consents to (or makes) disclosure. If so, the further question is whether the lawyer may justifiably *fail* to refuse to continue.

(a) The language of the Code contains a general prohibition of withdrawal except in specified cases, one of which is the situation in which the client:

insists, in a matter not pending before a tribunal, that the lawyer engage in conduct that is contrary to the judgment and advice of the lawyer ...

DR 2–110(C)(1)(e). See also EC 7–8 (withdrawal permitted "in a non-adjudicatory matter").

The Rules are significantly broader with respect to permissible withdrawal, approving it when a client "insists on pursuing an objective that the lawyer considers repugnant or imprudent," MR 1.16(b)(3), even if there is "material adverse effect on the interests of the client," MR 1.16(b), so long as the lawyer "take[s] steps to the extent reasonably practicable to protect a client's interests," MR 1.16(d). (This last-quoted proviso refers to such matters as advance notice, passing on papers and property, and refunding advance payments of fees). Does this language broadly permit threats to withdraw over disputes concerning client refusals to waive confidentiality?

(b) Two polar questions arise from this language:

• If the applicable rule suggests that you may *not* threaten to withdraw, is that the end of the matter? This question is very similar to those posed at the end of Section 2(d) of this Note.

• If the applicable rule suggests that withdrawal *is* permissible, can a decision not to use the threat of withdrawal as a means of inducing the client to make or authorize disclosure be justified by the confidentiality norm itself? The client has, to be sure, the "right" to confidentiality, but the lawyer equally has the "right" to withdraw: Does the answer to one control the other? If so, why? If not, by what criteria would you decide whether to insist on disclosure as a condition of your continued representation of the client?

4. *Client perjury: the summum malum?* While the ABA was responding to pressures to limit the norm of confidentiality by strengthening it, even in cases involving client fraud or criminal acts, it was moving in exactly the opposite direction with respect to one situation, acknowledged perjury by a client.

(a) Opinion 287 (1953) involved a criminal context in addition to the divorce setting referred to in Opinion 341, p. 147, above. It posed the situation of a defendant at sentencing, whom the judge proposed to place on probation on the ground that he had no prior convictions. His attorney knew that the court records, on which the judge was relying, were in error, and that there was a prior conviction. The opinion held that the attorney was required to remain silent (unless it appeared that the judge was specifically looking to him for confirmation of the fact), and that the same conclusion would follow even if the client, in response to a question from the judge about his lack of a record, lied about it.

(b) In 1970, notwithstanding the recent adoption by the ABA of the Model Code—with its exception to the requirement of confidentiality for "the intention of his client to commit a crime" (DR 4–101(C)(3)) and the (as yet unamended) requirement of disclosure of client fraud (DR 7–102(B)(1))—an ABA project suggested that disclosure was forbidden even when a client admitted guilt, the admission was confirmed by the lawyer's independent investigation, and the client insisted on taking the stand and denying his or her guilt. The lawyer was to withdraw (or seek leave of the court in the case of appointed counsel), but if withdrawal was "not feasible" or not allowed, the lawyer was to remain silent about the perjury, but not to "lend any aid" to it by questioning the defendant in the usual manner or arguing in summation that the false testimony should be credited. American Bar Association, Project on Standards for Criminal Justice, Standards Relating to the Defense Function Section 7.7 (1970).

(c) In a widely discussed and intensely controversial article, Monroe Freedman, a public-interest lawyer later a law school teacher and dean, argued in 1966 that only by maintaining silence and doing nothing to signal disbelief in the client's testimony could the lawyer live up to the norm of adequate representation. His conclusion was based on an argument that saw all alternative responses as invalid:

> Criminal defense lawyers do not win their cases by arguing reasonable doubt. Effective trial advocacy requires that the attorney's every word, action, and attitude be consistent with the conclusion that his client is innocent. As every trial lawyer knows, the jury is certain that the defense attorney knows whether his client is guilty. The jury is therefore alert to, and will be enormously affected by, any indication

by the attorney that he believes the defendant to be guilty. Thus, the plea of not guilty commits the advocate to a trial, including a closing argument, in which he must argue that "not guilty" means "not guilty in fact."

It is also argued that a defense attorney can remain selectively ignorant. He can insist in his first interview with his client that, if his client is guilty, he simply does not want to know. It is inconceivable, however, that an attorney could give adequate counsel under such circumstances. How is the client to know, for example, precisely which relevant circumstances his lawyer does not want to be told? The lawyer might ask whether his client has a prior record. The client, assuming that this is the kind of knowledge that might present ethical problems for his lawyer, might respond that he has no record. The lawyer would then put the defendant on the stand and, on cross-examination, be appalled to learn that his client has two prior convictions for offenses identical to that for which he is being tried.

Of course, an attorney can guard against this specific problem by telling his client that he must know about the client's past record. However, a lawyer can never anticipate all of the innumerable and potentially critical factors that his client, once cautioned, may decide not to reveal. In one instance, for example, the defendant assumed that his lawyer would prefer to be ignorant of the fact that the client had been having sexual relations with the chief defense witness. The client was innocent of the robbery with which he was charged, but was found guilty by the jury—probably because he was guilty of fornication, a far less serious offense for which he had not even been charged.

The problem is compounded by the practice of plea bargaining. It is considered improper for a defendant to plead guilty to a lesser offense unless he is in fact guilty. Nevertheless, it is common knowledge that plea bargaining frequently results in improper guilty pleas by innocent people. For example, a defendant falsely accused of robbery may plead guilty to simple assault, rather than risk a robbery conviction and a substantial prison term. If an attorney is to be scrupulous in bargaining pleas, however, he must know in advance that his client is guilty, since the guilty plea is improper if the defendant is innocent. Of course, if the attempt to bargain for a lesser offense should fail, the lawyer would know the truth and thereafter be unable to rationalize that he was uncertain of his client's guilt.

If one recognizes that professional responsibility requires that an advocate have full knowledge of every pertinent fact, it follows that he must seek the truth from his client, not shun it. This means that he will have to dig and pry and cajole, and, even then, he will not be successful unless he can convince the client that full and confidential disclosure to his lawyer will never result in prejudice to the client by any word or action of the lawyer....

... the truth can be obtained only by persuading the client that it would be a violation of a sacred obligation for the lawyer ever to reveal a client's confidence. Beyond any question, once a lawyer has persuaded his client of the obligation of confidentiality, he must respect that obligation scrupulously.

. . .

Is it proper to put a witness on the stand when you know he will commit perjury? Assume, for example, that the witness in question is the accused himself, and that he has admitted to you, in response to your assurances of confidentiality, that he is guilty. However, he insists upon taking the stand to protest his innocence. There is a clear consensus among prosecutors and defense attorneys that the likelihood of conviction is increased enormously when the defendant does not take the stand. Consequently, the attorney who prevents his client from testifying only because the client has confided his guilt to him is violating that confidence by acting upon the information in a way that will seriously prejudice his client's interests.

Perhaps the most common method for avoiding the ethical problem just posed is for the lawyer to withdraw from the case, at least if there is sufficient time before trial for the client to retain another attorney. The client will then go to the nearest law office, realizing that the obligation of confidentiality is not what it has been represented to be, and withhold incriminating information or the fact of his guilt from his new attorney. On ethical grounds, the practice of withdrawing from a case under such circumstances is indefensible, since the identical perjured testimony will ultimately be presented. More important, perhaps, is the practical consideration that the new attorney will be ignorant of the perjury and therefore will be in no position to attempt to discourage the client from presenting it. Only the original attorney, who knows the truth, has that opportunity, but he loses it in the very act of evading the ethical problem.

. . . The perjury in question may not necessarily be a protestation of innocence by a guilty man. Referring to the [case of a] defendant wrongly accused of a robbery at 16th and P, the only perjury may be his denial of the truthful, but highly damaging, testimony of [a] corroborating witness who placed him one block away from the intersection five minutes prior to the crime. Of course, if he tells the truth and thus verifies the corroborating witness, the jury will be far more inclined to accept the inaccurate testimony of the principal witness, who specifically identified him as the criminal.[16]

If a lawyer has discovered his client's intent to perjure himself, one possible solution to this problem is for the lawyer to approach the bench, explain his ethical difficulty to the judge, and ask to be relieved, thereby causing a mistrial. This request is certain to be denied, if only because it would empower the defendant to cause a series of mistrials

---

16. One lawyer, who considers it clearly unethical for the attorney to present the alibi in this hypothetical case, found no ethical difficulty himself in the following case. His client was prosecuted for robbery. The prosecution witness testified that the robbery had taken place at 10:15, and identified the defendant as the criminal. However, the defendant had a convincing alibi for 10:00 to 10:30. The attorney presented the alibi, and the client was acquitted. The alibi was truthful, but the attorney knew that the prosecution witness had been confused about the time, and that his client had in fact committed the crime at 10:45.

in the same fashion. At this point, some feel that the lawyer has avoided the ethical problem and can put the defendant on the stand. However, one objection to this solution, apart from the violation of confidentiality, is that the lawyer's ethical problem has not been solved, but has only been transferred to the judge. Moreover, the client in such a case might well have grounds for appeal on the basis of deprivation of due process and denial of the right to counsel, since he will have been tried before, and sentenced by, a judge who has been informed of the client's guilt by his own attorney.

A solution even less satisfactory than informing the judge of the defendant's guilt would be to let the client take the stand without the attorney's participation and to omit reference to the client's testimony in closing argument. The latter solution, of course, would be as damaging as to fail entirely to argue the case to the jury, and failing to argue the case is "as improper as though the attorney had told the jury that his client had uttered a falsehood in making the statement."

Therefore, the obligation of confidentiality, in the context of our adversary system, apparently allows the attorney no alternative to putting a perjurious witness on the stand without explicit or implicit disclosure of the attorney's knowledge to either the judge or the jury....

Freedman, Professional Responsibility of the Criminal Defense Lawyer: The Three Hardest Questions, 64 Mich.L.Rev. 1469 (1966).*

(d) The project to replace the Code with the Model Rules presented the Bar with the opportunity, and the need, to resolve this question. Consider, at this point, what in your view the answer should have been.

- Does Freedman persuade you? If not, at what point in his argument do your views diverge from his?

- Which of the alternatives seems best to you?

- Does your answer differ depending on whether the perjury pertains to the ultimate issue of guilt or (in a civil case) liability, or is intended by a client who is innocent (or has a meritorious civil case)?

(e) Model Rule 3.3(a)(4), adopted in 1983, specifies that a lawyer:

shall not knowingly ... offer evidence that the lawyer knows to be false. If a lawyer has offered evidence and comes to know of its falsity, the lawyer shall take reasonable remedial measures.

Comment 11 specifies that a lawyer in this circumstance "should make disclosure to the court." ABA Formal Opinion 87–353 (1987) goes a bit further than the language of the Rule and Comments, and mandates

---

* This article was based on a speech given to a group of lawyers in the District of Columbia. As a result, Warren Burger, then Chief Judge of the Court of Appeals (later Chief Justice) and a number of other lawyers, lodged a complaint against Freedman with the local grievance committee. After a significant inquiry, it was decided not to proceed further with disciplinary proceedings. See Freedman, supra, at 1469 n. 1.

Professor Freedman discusses the alternatives in greater depth, and also analyzes the relevant Model Code and Model Rules provisions, in his text, Understanding Lawyers' Ethics 87–141 (1990).

disclosure when the perjury is "known" to the lawyer and has already occurred.

Note the breadth, as well as the limits, of mandated disclosure: The rule applies to all perjury, not only to admissions of guilt, indeed, to civil as well as criminal cases. At the same time, it does not apply to merely suspected perjury, no matter how strong the grounds for suspicion, nor to statements of intention to commit perjury; Opinion 87–353 specifies that knowledge of perjury is "ordinarily based on admissions the client has made.... The lawyer's suspicions are not enough." †

Comments 7 to 10 of Rule 3.3 attempt to justify the position taken by the Model Rules, with respect to criminal cases. What is your judgment on the question of justification?

(f) Nix v. Whiteside, 475 U.S. 157, 106 S.Ct. 988, 89 L.Ed.2d 123 (1985), upheld the constitutionality of a conviction obtained after a lawyer induced his client not to testify to a fact that the client had formerly told the lawyer was untrue, by threatening to withdraw otherwise. The prosecution was for murder, the defense was self-defense, and the false statement was that defendant had seen "something metallic" (presumably a gun) in his assailant's hand just before stabbing him. Defendant testified that he was convinced that his assailant was reaching for a gun (under a pillow), but he feared that the jury would not believe him if he did not say that he had actually seen a gun. (His fear proved quite well founded, for he was convicted). The Court unanimously rejected the constitutional claim of ineffective assistance of counsel, with a five-Justice majority joining Chief Justice Burger's opinion asserting that "centuries of accepted standards" of professional responsibility supported a rule of compelled disclosure. Four Justices objected to the gratuitous "essay" (Justice Brennan's word) on a question of State professional responsibility law.

5.   (a) How do you explain:

- the simultaneous reinforcement of the norm of confidentiality in most circumstances, as evidenced by the evolution of Rule 1.6, and the broad rejection of it with respect to the crime of perjury?

- the contours of Rule 3.3, prohibiting presentation of perjured testimony in defense of an innocent person, while allowing presentation of testimony strongly believed by counsel to be perjured?

(b) Does the idea of a "celebratory" stance toward the justness of the legal system point toward an explanation?

Consider, in that regard, the opinion in People v. Berrios, 28 N.Y.2d 361, 321 N.Y.S.2d 884, 270 N.E.2d 709 (1971), in which the Court of Appeals of New York was presented with five appeals from convictions for posses-

---

† Except perhaps in defense of a criminal case—compare United States v. Long, 857 F.2d 436, 444–45 (8th Cir.1988), with People v. Bartee, 208 Ill.App.3d 105, 566 N.E.2d 855 (1991)—a "lawyer may refuse to offer evidence that the lawyer reasonably believes is false," MR 3.3(c), but the lawyer need not so refuse. This authorization of a departure from client-orientation is justified by the ABA, not on the ground of concern over contributing to an erroneous verdict, but on the ground that "offering such proof may reflect adversely on the lawyer's ability to discriminate in the quality of evidence and thus impair the lawyer's effectiveness as an advocate." MR 3.3, Comment 14.

sion of heroin, in all of which "arresting officers testified that glassine envelopes containing narcotics were dropped on the ground as the defendants were approached by the police." Appellants asked the court to rule that, "in these 'dropsy' cases," the burden on a motion to suppress should be shifted to the prosecution to prove the lawfulness of the search, on the ground that "police testimony in these cases is inherently untrustworthy and the product of fabrication. . . ." What was especially noteworthy about the appeal was that the District Attorney of New York County *joined* in this request.

In rejecting it nonetheless, the Court of Appeals relied in part on the fact that a shift in the burden of proof would still leave the question essentially one of the respective credibility of the defendant and the arresting officer. However, it preceded that observation with the following response:

> The several appellants herein and the New York County District Attorney seek a change in these rules of burden of proof. It is argued that the present rule is inadequate to cope with the problem of perjured testimony. . . . We have been told that with the advent of Mapp v. Ohio, 367 U.S. 643, 81 S.Ct. 1684, 6 L.Ed.2d 1081 [requiring the States to exclude illegally seized evidence], there has been a great incidence of "dropsy" testimony by police officers. Hence, this court has been asked to infer that the police are systematically evading the mandate of *Mapp* by fabricating their testimony. We cannot embrace this *post hoc ergo propter hoc* reasoning for as the then Judge Warren Burger observed in Bush v. United States, 375 F.2d 602, 604, "it would be a dismal reflection on society to say that when the guardians of its security are called to testify in court under oath, their testimony must be viewed with suspicion." Thus, we reject this frontal attack on the integrity of our entire law enforcement system.

Judge Fuld, dissenting, relied on the submission of the New York District Attorney, Frank Hogan, that police testimony was subject to question in a "substantial . . . percentage of dropsy cases," and on the experience and "objective studies" of "commentators and judges" (see citations, 270 N.E.2d at 715 nn. 2, 3); he concluded that the traditional rule "does not sufficiently take into account the danger of false testimony." "The integrity of the judicial process demands that there be a reallocation of the burden of proof," which would allow a trial judge to grant a motion to suppress when he is "unable to make up his mind as to who is telling the truth."

How, if at all, does this episode shed light on the question posed at the beginning of this section of this Note?

6. (a) Although Model Rule 3.8 deals with the "special responsibilities of a prosecutor," it does not speak to the question of presenting evidence known or believed to be false. Recall Rule 3.3(c), permitting a lawyer to refuse to offer evidence that the lawyer "reasonably believes" is false. Why is this an inadequate response to the problem of police perjury (whether the problem is viewed from the perspective of the prosecutor's dilemma, the defendant's rights, or the credibility of the system)?

(b) Would the burden-of-proof rule proposed in *Berrios* have had any effect on the situation facing an Assistant District Attorney in "dropsy" cases? How do you explain the decision of District Attorney Hogan to support the proposed rule?

THE CRIMINAL LAWYER'S "DIFFERENT MISSION": REFLECTIONS ON THE "RIGHT" TO PRESENT A FALSE CASE

Harry I. Subin
1 Geo.J.Leg. Ethics 125 (1987).

... Should the criminal lawyer be permitted to represent a client by putting forward a defense the lawyer knows is false? I limit my inquiry to criminal practice because this field is most frequently cited to justify the use of truth defeating devices for the higher purpose of preserving the adversary system, our defense against overreaching by the state. Some use the criminal law to illustrate what they believe justifies all attorneys to obstruct truth finding. Others assert that while most lawyers should have a greater concern for the truth, there is an exception for the criminal lawyer. In either case, civil lawyers ride the ethical coattails of the criminal lawyer on this issue. If, as I shall argue, the criminal lawyer should not be permitted to impede arriving at a truthful verdict to the extent he or she can today, then similar claims by civil lawyers would be weaker still.

Presenting a "false defense," as used here, means attempting to convince the judge or jury that facts established by the state and known to the attorney to be true are not true, or that facts known to the attorney to be false are true. While this can be done by criminal means—e.g., perjury, introduction of forged documents, and the like—I exclude these acts from the definition of false defense used here. I am not concerned with them because such blatant criminal acts are relatively uninteresting ethically, and both the courts and bar have rejected their use.

My concern, instead, is with the presently legal means for the attorney to reach a favorable verdict even if it is completely at odds with the facts. The permissible techniques include: (1) cross-examination of truthful government witnesses to undermine their testimony or their credibility; (2) direct presentation of testimony, not itself false, but used to discredit the truthful evidence adduced by the government, or to accredit a false theory; and (3) argument to the jury based on any of these acts. One looks in vain in ethical codes or case law for a definition of "perjury" or "false evidence" that includes these acts, although they are also inconsistent with the goal of assuring a truthful verdict.

To the extent that these techniques of legal truth-subversion have been addressed at all, most authorities have approved them.

[The proposition] ... that it is proper to destroy a truthful government witness when essential to provide the defendant with a defense, and that failure to do so would violate the lawyer's duty under the *Model Code of Professional Responsibility* to represent the client zealously, [has been expressed, in a "most emphatic form," by Justice White, in his opinion in United States v. Wade, 388 U.S. 218, 87 S.Ct. 1926, 18 L.Ed.2d 1149 (1967)]....

> [D]efense counsel has no ... obligation to ascertain or present the truth. Our system assigns him a different mission. He must be and is interested in preventing the conviction of the innocent, but ... we also insist that he defend his client whether he is innocent or guilty. The State has the obligation to present evidence. Defense counsel need present nothing, even if he knows what the truth is. He need not furnish any witnesses to the police, or reveal any confidences of his client, or furnish any other information to help the prosecution's case. If he can confuse a witness, even a truthful one, or make him appear at a disadvantage, unsure or indecisive, that will be his normal course. Our interest in not convicting the innocent permits counsel to put the State to its proof, to put the State's case in the worst possible light, regardless of what he thinks or knows to be the truth. Undoubtedly there are some limits which defense counsel must observe but more often than not, defense counsel will cross-examine a prosecution witness, and impeach him if he can, even if he thinks the witness is telling the truth, just as he will attempt to destroy a witness who he thinks is lying. In this respect, as part of our modified adversary system and as part of the duty imposed on the most honorable defense counsel, we countenance or require conduct which in many instances has little if any, relation to the search for truth.

Emanating from such an impeccable source, the concept of the defense attorney's special relation to the truth seeking process may well have a self-evident status. I suspect that it did for me when I first read it twenty years ago. Now it strikes me as excessive. It is true that in our system the prosecution has the burden of proving guilt, and the defense the corresponding right to remain completely passive in the presentation of facts to the jury. It is true that the defense attorney has the right, and the obligation, to challenge the government's proof to assure its accuracy. The question is whether it should also be the "duty" of the "most honorable" defense attorney to take affirmative steps to subvert the government's case when he or she knows it is accurate. I shall argue that the attorney can perform his or her duty fully even if not permitted to act in this way, and that if stricter limits on truth-subversion were instituted, the rights of persons accused of crimes generally would be enhanced.

About fifteen years ago I represented a man charged with rape and robbery. The victim's account was as follows: Returning from work in the early morning hours, she was accosted by a man who pointed a gun at her and took a watch from her wrist. He told her to go with him to a nearby lot, where he ordered her to lie down on the ground and disrobe. When she complained that the ground was hurting her, he took her to his apartment, located across the street. During the next hour there, he had intercourse with her. Ultimately, he said that they had to leave to avoid being discovered by the woman with whom he lived. The complainant responded that since he had gotten what he wanted, he should give her back her watch. He said that he would.

As the two left the apartment, he said he was going to get a car. Before leaving the building, however, he went to the apartment next door, leaving her to wait in the hallway. When asked why she waited, she said that she was still hoping for the return of her watch, which was a valued gift, apparently from her boyfriend.

She never did get the watch. When they left the building, the man told her to wait on the street while he got the car. At that point she went to a nearby police precinct and reported the incident. She gave a full description of the assailant that matched my client. She also accurately described the inside of his apartment. Later, in response to a note left at his apartment by the police, my client came to the precinct, and the complainant identified him. My client was released at that time but was arrested soon thereafter at his apartment, where a gun was found. No watch was recovered.

My client was formally charged, at which point I entered the case. At our initial interview and those that followed it, he insisted that he had nothing whatever to do with the crime and had never even seen the woman before. He stated that he had been in several places during the night in question: visiting his aunt earlier in the evening, then traveling to a bar in New Jersey, where he was during the critical hours. He gave the name of a man there who would corroborate this. He said that he arrived home early the next morning and met a friend. He stated that he had no idea how this woman had come to know things about him such as what the apartment looked like, that he lived with a woman, and that he was a musician, or how she could identify him. He said that he had no reason to rape anyone, since he already had a woman, and that in any event he was recovering from surgery for an old gun shot wound and could not engage in intercourse. He said he would not be so stupid as to bring a woman he had robbed and was going to rape into his own apartment.

I felt that there was some strength to these arguments, and that there were questionable aspects to the complainant's story. In particular, it seemed strange that a man intending rape would be as solicitous of the victim's comfort as the woman said her assailant was at the playground. It also seemed that a person who had just been raped would flee when she had the chance to, and in any case would not be primarily concerned with the return of her watch. On balance, however, I suspected that my client was not telling me the truth. I thought the complaining witness could not possibly have known what she knew about him and his apartment, if she had not had any contact with him. True, someone else could have posed as him, and used his apartment. My client, however, could suggest no one who could have done so.

Moreover, that hypothesis did not explain the complainant's accurate description of him to the police. Although the identification procedure used by the police, a one person "show up," was suggestive, the woman had ample opportunity to observe her assailant during the extended incident. I could not believe that the complainant had selected my client randomly to accuse falsely of rape. By both her and my client's admission, the two had not had any previous association.

That my client was probably lying to me had two possible explanations. First, he might have been lying because he was guilty and did not see any particular advantage to himself in admitting it to me. It is embarrassing to admit that one has committed a crime, particularly one of this nature. Moreover, my client might well have feared to tell me the truth. He might have believed that I would tell others what he said, or, at the very least, that I might not be enthusiastic about representing him.

He also might have lied not because he was guilty of the offense, but because he thought the concocted story was the best one under the circumstances. The sexual encounter may have taken place voluntarily, but the woman complained to the police because she was angry at my client for refusing to return the valued wrist watch, perhaps not stolen, but left, in my client's apartment. My client may not have been able to admit this, because he had other needs that took precedence over the particular legal one that brought him to me. For example, the client might have felt compelled to deny any involvement in the incident because to admit to having had a sexual encounter might have jeopardized his relationship with the woman with whom he lived. Likewise, he might have decided to "play lawyer," and put forward what he believed to be his best defense. Not understanding the heavy burden of proof on the state in criminal cases, he might have thought that any version of the facts that showed that he had contact with the woman would be fatal because it would simply be a case of her word against his.

At this point the case was in equipoise for me. I had my suspicions about both the complainant's and the client's version of what had occurred, and I supposed a jury would as well. That problem was theirs, however, not mine. All I had to do was present my client's version of what occurred in the best way that I could.

Or was that all that was required? Committed to the adversarial spirit reflected in Justice White's observations about my role, I decided that it was not. The "different mission" took me beyond the task of presenting my client's position in a legally correct and persuasive manner, to trying to untrack the state's case in any lawful way that occurred to me, regardless of the facts.

With that mission in mind, I concluded that it would be too risky to have the defendant simply take the stand and tell his story, even if it were true. Unless we could create an iron-clad alibi, which seemed unlikely given the strength of the complainant's identification, I thought it was much safer to attack the complainant's story, even if it were true. I felt, however, that since my client had persisted in his original story I was obligated to investigate the alibi defense, although I was fairly certain that I would not use it. My students and I therefore interviewed everyone he mentioned, traveled and timed the route he said he had followed, and attempted to find witnesses who may have seen someone else at the apartment. We discovered nothing helpful. The witness my client identified as being at the bar in New Jersey could not corroborate the client's presence there. The times the client gave were consistent with his presence at the place of the crime when the victim claimed it took place. The client's aunt verified that he had been with her, but much earlier in the evening.

Because the alibi defense was apparently hopeless, I returned to the original strategy of attempting to undermine the complainant's version of the facts. I demanded a preliminary hearing, in which the complainant would have to testify under oath to the events in question. Her version was precisely as I have described it, and she told it in an objective manner that, far from seeming contrived, convinced me that she was telling the truth. She seemed a person who, if not at home with the meanness of the streets, was resigned to it. To me that explained why she was able to react in what I perceived to be a nonstereotypical manner to the ugly events in which she had been involved.

I explained to my client that we had failed to corroborate his alibi, and that the complainant appeared to be a credible witness. I said that in my view the jury would not believe the alibi, and that if we could not obtain any other information, it might be appropriate to think about a guilty plea, which would at least limit his exposure to punishment. The case, then in the middle of the aimless drift towards resolution that typifies New York's criminal justice system, was left at that.

Some time later, however, my client called me and told me that he had new evidence; his aunt, he said, would testify that he had been with her at the time in question. I was incredulous. I reminded him that at no time during our earlier conversations had he indicated what was plainly a crucial piece of information, despite my not too subtle explanation of the elements of an alibi defense. I told him that when the aunt was initially interviewed with great care on this point, she stated that he was not with her at the time of the crime. Ultimately, I told him that I thought he was lying, and that in my view even if the jury heard the aunt's testimony, they would not believe it.

Whether it was during that session or later that the client admitted his guilt I do not recall. I do recall wondering whether, now that I knew the truth, that should make a difference in the way in which the case was handled. I certainly wished that I did not know it and began to understand, psychologically if not ethically, lawyers who do not want to know their clients' stories.

I did not pause very long to ponder the problem, however, because I concluded that knowing the truth in fact did not make a difference to my defense strategy, other than to put me on notice as to when I might be suborning perjury. Because the mission of the defense attorney was to defeat the prosecution's case, what I knew actually happened was not important otherwise. What did matter was whether a version of the "facts" could be presented that would make a jury doubt the client's guilt.

Viewed in this way, my problem was not that my client's story was false, but that it was not credible, and could not be made to appear so by legal means. To win, we would therefore have to come up with a better theory than the alibi, avoiding perjury in the process. Thus, the defense would have to be made out without the client testifying, since it would be a crime for him to assert a fabricated exculpatory theory under oath. This was not a serious problem, however, because it would not only be possible to prevail without the defendant's testimony, but it would probably be easier to do so. Not everyone is capable of lying successfully on the witness stand, and I did not have the sense that my client would be very good at it.

There were two possible defenses that could be fabricated. The first was mistaken identity. We could argue that the opportunity of the victim to observe the defendant at the time of the original encounter was limited, since it had occurred on a dark street. The woman could be made out to have been in great emotional distress during the incident.[36] Expert testimony would have [to] be adduced to show the hazards of eyewitness identification.[37] We could demonstrate that an unreliable identification procedure had been used at the precinct.[38] On the other hand, given that the complainant had spent considerable time with the assailant and had led the police back to the defendant's apartment, it seemed doubtful that the mistaken identification ploy would be successful.

---

36. This would be one of those safe areas in cross-examination, where the witness was damned no matter what she answered. If she testified that she was distressed, it would make my point that she was making an unreliable identification; if she testified that she was calm, no one would believe her. Perhaps this is why cross-examination has been touted as "beyond any doubt the greatest legal engine ever invented for the discovery of truth." 5 J. Wigmore, Evidence § 1367 (J. Chadbourn rev. ed. 1974). Another commentator makes similar claims for his art, and while he acknowledges in passing that witnesses might tell the truth, he at no point suggests what the cross-examiner should do when faced with such a situation. F. Wellman, The Art of Cross–Examination 7 (4th ed. 1936). The cross-examiner's world, rather, seems to be divided into two types of witnesses: those whose testimony is harmless, and those whose testimony must be destroyed on pain of abandoning "all hope for a jury verdict." Id. at 9.

37. On the dangers of misidentification, see, e.g., United States v. Wade, 388 U.S. 218 (1967). The use of experts to explain the misidentification problem to the jury is well established.

38. See Watkins v. Sowders, 449 U.S. 341 (1981) (identification problems properly attacked during cross-examination at trial; no per se rule compelling judicial determination outside presence of jury concerning admissibility of identification evidence).

The second alternative, consent, was clearly preferable. It would negate the charge of rape and undermine the robbery case.[39] To prevail, all we would have to do would be to raise a reasonable doubt as to whether he had compelled the woman to have sex with him. The doubt would be based on the scenario that the woman and the defendant met, and she voluntarily returned to his apartment. Her watch, the object of the alleged robbery, was either left there by mistake or, perhaps better, was never there at all.

The consent defense could be made out entirely through cross-examination of the complainant, coupled with argument to the jury about her lack of credibility on the issue of force. I could emphasize the parts of her story that sounded the most curious, such as the defendant's solicitude in taking his victim back to his apartment, and her waiting for her watch when she could have gone immediately to the nearby precinct that she went to later. I could point to her inability to identify the gun she claimed was used (although it was the one actually used), that the allegedly stolen watch was never found, there was no sign of physical violence, and no one heard screaming or any other signs of a struggle. I could also argue as my client had that even if he were reckless enough to rob and rape a woman across the street from his apartment, he would not be so foolish as to bring the victim there. I considered investigating the complainant's background, to take advantage of the right, unencumbered at the time, to impeach her on the basis of her prior unchastity.[40] I did not pursue this, however, because to me this device, although lawful, was fundamentally wrong. No doubt in that respect I lacked zeal, perhaps punishably so.[41]

Even without assassinating this woman's character, however, I could argue that this was simply a case of a casual tryst that went awry. The defendant would not have to prove whether the complainant made the false charge to account for her whereabouts that evening, or to explain what happened to her missing watch. If the jury had reason to doubt the complainant's charges it would be bound to acquit the defendant.

How all of this would have played out at trial cannot be known. Predictably, the case dragged on so long that the prosecutor was forced to offer the unrefusable plea of possession of a gun. As I look back, however, I wonder how I could justify doing what I was planning to do had the case been tried. I was prepared to stand before the jury posing as an officer of the court in search of the truth, while trying to fool the jurors into believing a wholly fabricated story, i.e., that the woman had

---

39. Consent is a defense to a charge of rape.... While consent is not a defense to a robbery charge, if the complainant could be made out to be a liar about the rape, there was a good chance that the jury would not believe her about the stolen watch either.

40. When this case arose it was common practice to impeach the complainant in rape cases by eliciting details of her prior sexual activities. Subsequently the rules of evidence were amended to require a specific showing of relevance to the facts of the case....

41. ... Model Code DR 7–101(A)(1) suggests this omission violated the *Model Code.*

consented, when in fact she had been forced at gunpoint to have sex with the defendant. I was also prepared to demand an acquittal because the state had not met its burden of proof when, if it had not, it would have been because I made the truth look like a lie. If there is any redeeming social value in permitting an attorney to do such things, I frankly cannot discern it.

Others have discerned it, however, and while they have been criticized, they seem clearly to represent the majority view. They rely on either of two theories. The first is that the lawyer cannot possibly be sufficiently certain of the truth to impose his or her view of it on the client's case. The second is that the defense attorney need not be concerned with the truth even if he or she does know it. Both are misguided.

A principal argument in favor of the propriety of asserting a "false" defense is that there is, for the lawyer, no such thing. The "truth," insofar as it is relevant to the lawyer, is what the trier of fact determines it to be.[48] The role of the lawyer in the adversary system is not to interpose his or her own belief about what the facts are. Instead, the truth will emerge through a dialectical process, in which the vigorous advocacy of thesis and antithesis will equip the neutral arbiter to synthesize the data and reach a conclusion.

The appeal of this approach to truth seeking is very great among lawyers, perhaps in large part because of the way they were indoctrinated in law school: the so-called Socratic method is heavily oriented toward argument of this kind over legal doctrine. To the law student, who is largely oblivious to the fact finding process (facts are always already found in casebooks), it may be the only valid method of analysis.

Whether the dialectical approach is as useful in resolving what facts are as it may be in determining what would be a sound policy is debatable. Even conceding the utility of the method, however, it makes sense to characterize what emerges as "truth" only if information, rather than "disinformation," is presented to the arbiter. Insofar as the jury's finding of fact is based upon fiction, it cannot be said that "truth" emerges from the adversary process in any meaningful sense of the word.

My rape case exemplifies how the dialectic theory can be applied and misapplied as a means to learn the "truth." Under the New York rape law at the time this case arose, it was necessary for the state to corroborate the victim's allegation. The same was not true of the crime of robbery. However irrational and discriminatory this may have been, I was faced with the situation in which the uncorroborated testimony of the victim about two crimes committed as part of the same transaction

---

48. See M. Frankel, Partisan Justice, ... at 24. Judge Frankel, who is critical of this theory, quotes the famous answer of Samuel Johnson to the question how he can represent a bad cause: "Sir, you do not know it to be good or bad till the judge determines it." Id. ...

would lead to an acquittal as a matter of law on one, and could justify a conviction on the other. I challenged this result by arguing that while a robbery charge did not ordinarily require corroboration, it should be held to do so when the crime was allegedly committed in the course of a rape. The problem with the argument was first, that there was nothing in the rape legislation, or its history, to support it; and second, that it had in several virtually identical cases been authoritatively rejected by the state courts.

This did not matter, though, because as long as I did not attempt to fabricate legal authority for my position, I was free to advance it, hoping that some court would find that my argument was the "true" one. This approach was entirely consistent with good and ethical lawyering.

It is quite another thing to apply this method of analysis to the question of determining whether in fact there was corroboration of the woman's charge that the intercourse was forced. Suppose, for example, that I had interviewed the neighbor into whose apartment the defendant had gone following the rape—and who was unknown to the police. Suppose that he had told me that at the time of the incident he heard screams, and the sound of a struggle, and that my client had made incriminating remarks to him about what had occurred. It may be that there are reasons of policy that permit me to conceal these facts from the prosecution. It is ludicrous to assert, however, that because I can conceal them I do not know them. It is also ludicrous to suggest that if in addition I use my advocacy skills—and rights—to advance the thesis that there were no witnesses to the crime, I have engaged in a truth finding process.[57]

The argument that the attorney cannot know the truth until a court decides it fails. Either it is sophistry, designed to simplify the moral life of the attorney, or it rests on a confusion between "factual truth" and "legal truth." The former relates to historical fact. The latter relates to the principle that a fact cannot be acted upon by the legal system until it is proven in accordance with legal rules. Plainly one can know the factual truth, for example, that one's client forced a woman to have sex with him, without or before knowing the legal truth that he is punishable for the crime of rape. The question is not whether an attorney can know the truth, but what standards should be applied in determining what the truth is.

. . .

We confront at last the "Different Mission" argument we set out initially to examine. It is that the defense attorney has a broader function than protecting the innocent against wrongful conviction.

---

57. My "proof" that there were no witnesses to the crime would come in the form of an "accrediting" cross-examination of the complainant and/or a police officer who testified. I could inquire of both concerning whether they saw or otherwise became aware of the presence of any witnesses, and then argue to the jury that their negative answers established that there were none.

Equally important is the task of protecting the factually guilty individual against overreaching by the state. The defense attorney may well be able to know the truth, but can be indifferent to it because it is the state's case, not the client's with which he or she is concerned. Professor Freedman puts it this way:

> The point ... is not that the lawyer cannot know the truth, or that the lawyer refuses to recognize the truth, but rather that the lawyer is told: "You, personally, may very well know the truth, but your personal knowledge is irrelevant. In your capacity as an advocate (and, if you will, as an officer of the court) you are forbidden to act upon your personal knowledge of the truth, as you might want to do as a private person, because the adversary system could not function properly if lawyers did so."

> . . .

The extravagant notion of the right to put on a defense is the fallacy in the argument supporting a right to assert a false defense. Again, a moment's reflection on prevailing penal law limitations on advocacy will demonstrate that the defendant is not entitled to gain an acquittal by any available means. Unless we abandon completely the notion that verdicts should be based upon the truth, we must accept the fact that there may simply be no version of the facts favorable to the defense worthy of assertion in a court. In such cases, the role of the defense attorney should be limited to assuring that the state adduces sufficient legally competent evidence to sustain its burden of proof.

This limitation on the defense function is consistent with the notion that a factually guilty person has a right to a defense. That subject has provoked a good deal of commentary, probably more than it deserves. It is fundamental to our system of justice that the guilty as well as the innocent client be accorded the right to put the state to its proof and have the assistance of counsel in doing so. It is morally appropriate for the attorney who knows that the defendant is guilty to assist the defendant in making that challenge, since otherwise the system's promise of due process of law would be empty.

The question is not, however, whether a "guilty" person has a right to a defense, but what kind of defense can be advanced on behalf of anyone, whether known to be guilty or not, or even if known to be innocent. Here what the defense attorney knows should be crucial to what he or she does.

It may help to explain this position by positing the defense function as consisting of two separate roles, usually intertwined but theoretically distinct. One enlists the attorney as the "monitor" of the state's case, whose task it is to assure that a conviction is based on an adequate amount of competent and admissible evidence. The lawyer as monitor is a kind of quality inspector, with no responsibility for developing a different product, if you will, to "sell" to the jury. The other attorney role involves the attorney as the client's "advocate," whose task is to present that different product, by undermining the state's version of the facts or presenting a competing version sufficient at least to establish a reasonable doubt about the defendant's guilt. The monitor's role is to assure that the state has the facts to support a conviction. The advocate attempts to demonstrate that the state's evidence is not fact at all. Where, as in most cases, the facts are in doubt, or where the state's case is believed or known to be based upon mistaken perceptions or lies, the defense attorney quite properly plays both roles. Having monitored the state's case and found it factually and legally sound, however, should he or she be permitted to act as advocate and attempt to undermine it? I submit that the answer to that is no, and that the defendant's rights in cases of this kind extend only as far as the monitoring role takes the attorney. The right in question, to have the state prove guilt beyond a reasonable doubt, can be vindicated if the attorney is limited to good faith challenges to the state's case; to persuading the jury that there are legitimate reasons to doubt the state's evidence. It may on occasion be more effective for the attorney to use his or her imagination to create doubts; but surely there cannot be a right to gain an acquittal whenever the imagination of one's attorney is good enough to produce one.

. . .

I propose a system in which the defense attorney ... who knew there were no facts to contest would be limited to the "monitoring" role. Assuming that a defendant in my client's situation wanted to assert his right to contest the evidence against him, the attorney would work to assure that all of the elements of the crime were proven beyond a reasonable doubt, on the basis of competent and admissible evidence. This would include enforcing the defendant's rights to have privileged or illegally obtained evidence excluded: The goal sought here is not the elimination of all rules that result in the suppression of truth, but only those not supported by sound policy. It would also be appropriate for the attorney to argue to the jury that the available evidence is not sufficient to sustain the burden of proof. It would not, however, be proper for the attorney to use any of the presently available devices to refute testimony known to be truthful. I wish to make clear, however, that this rule would not prevent the attorney from challenging *inaccurate* testimony, even though the attorney knew that the defendant was guilty. Again, the truth-seeking goal is not applicable when a valid policy reason exists for ignoring it. Forcing the state to prove its case is such a reason.

Applying these principles to my rape case, I would engage fully in the process of testing the admissibility of the state's evidence, moving to suppress testimony concerning the suggestive "show-up" identification at the precinct, and the gun found in the defendant's apartment after a warrantless search, should the state attempt to offer either piece of evidence. At the trial, I would be present to assure that the complainant testified in accordance with the rules of evidence.

Assuming that she testified at trial as she had at the preliminary hearing, however, I would not cross-examine her, because I would have no good faith basis for impeaching either her testimony or her character, since I "knew" that she was providing an accurate account of what had occurred.[113]   Nor would I put on a defense case.   I would limit my representation at that stage to putting forth the strongest argument I could that the facts presented by the state did not sustain its burden. In these ways, the defendant would receive the services of an attorney in subjecting the state's case to the final stage of the screening process provided by the system to insure against unjust convictions.   That, however, would be all that the defense attorney could do.

There are several commonly raised questions concerning the procedure proposed here that I have yet to address.   The first is whether interposing the attorney as a judge of the client's guilt creates an unacceptable risk that defendants deserving a fuller day in court will be deprived of it.   I do not think that would be so. . . .   [T]he presumption in favor of the defendant on the question of the truth of his or her story is a heavy one, and will permit the attorney to proceed with that story in most cases.   It is necessary to emphasize this point: I am concerned here with a class of cases which is at the edge, not the core of the defense attorney's world, the case where the facts are clear and not where legitimately held doubts exist.   It is in these clear cases that the attorney would not be permitted to do what I had planned to do, which was to substitute the defendant's story for a better one.

. . .

If this proposal seems radical, consider that it is essentially an adaptation of what today is the principal function of the defense attorney in every criminal justice system of significance in this nation. That function is not to create defenses out of whole cloth to present to juries, but to guide the defendant through a process that will usually end in a guilty plea.   It will so end, at least when competent counsel are involved, very frequently because the defense attorney has concluded after thorough analysis that there is no answer to the state's case.

---

113. I recently made an informal presentation of this position to a group of my colleagues, who beseiged me with hypotheticals, the most provocative of which were these: (A) A witness not wearing her glasses, identifies my client as having been at a certain place.   If my client were in fact at that place, could I cross-examine the witness on the grounds that she was not wearing her glasses?   The answer is yes: The witness' ability to perceive affects the quality of the state's proof, and the fact that she happened to be correct is irrelevant. (B) In the same situation, except here I knew that the witness was wearing her glasses.   Could I cross-examine the witness in an effort to show that she was not?   The answer is no: The state had adduced reliable evidence, and that is all that it was required to do.

I was also asked whether I would apply the same truth based rule and refuse, in the situation described in (B), to impeach the witness if I knew that my client were innocent.   My first response was something of a dodge: If I knew that, it was difficult for me to see why I would have to impeach this witness.   Ultimately (albeit tentatively) I would conclude that it was too dangerous to adopt the notion that even these ends justified subverting the truth, and I would not cross-examine on that point.

If that role can be played in out of court resolution of the matter there seems to be no reason why it cannot be played in court, when the defendant insists upon his right to a trial. The important point is that the right to a trial does not embody the right to present to the tribunal any evidence at all, no matter how fictitious it is.

. . .

Note on Subin: Can an advocate care about the truth?

1.   Presumably, a lawyer who decided to act as Subin suggests would feel obliged to inform his or her client of that decision, at which point either the client will consent or counsel will resign or (in the case of appointed counsel) seek leave to withdraw. The latter motion could not be fully explained to the court, and is likely to be denied. At that point, which of the following responses is appropriate (from a perspective sympathetic to Subin's position)?

- "I met my obligation to my client by trying to withdraw. The court wouldn't let me out, and now I can fulfill my responsibility not to try to convince a jury to disbelieve testimony that I know is correct. I won't try to impeach the complaining witness' testimony."

- "I met my obligation not to participate in trying to mislead the jury by first seeking my client's consent, and then moving for leave to withdraw. The court wouldn't let me out, and now I can fulfill my responsibility to give my client full adversarial representation. I will try to impeach the complaining witness' testimony."

2.   Subin refuses to draw a morally significant line between facilitating perjury and seeking to persuade the trier of fact to reach a conclusion known to the lawyer to be false. In this respect, he agrees with Monroe Freedman, differing in that Freedman would give controlling weight to service of the client's interest while Subin would prefer the lawyer's fidelity to the truth.

Freedman's position requires a degree of adversariness that can be fueled by a strongly individualistic political stance, which tends to accept institutional reasons for not being seriously troubled by the social consequences of one's own actions. It can also reflect a very different political stance, one which finds social value in protecting even guilty defendants from the consequences of conviction. Subin seems implicitly to reject the sufficiency of both varieties of "political stance." Do you? Does your answer to that question seem to explain your response to Freedman and Subin?

The prevalent position, rejecting both Freedman and Subin, essentially accepts the adversarial stance, but draws the line at the facilitation of perjury. It has a certain practicality, both in its giving deference to the weight of judicial condemnation of the practice and in its giving some recognition to both poles of the Freedman–Subin axis. In both aspects, it may be thought at the same time to lack a certain integrity that both Freedman and Subin have.

- Is this observation accurate?

• If so, do you view it more as a criticism or as a justification for the prevalent position?

3. Another line with arguable moral significance is that between a guilty and an innocent client. When the client is known to be guilty, truth and justice may be allies, but when the client is innocent, in danger of being wrongly convicted (by a verdict that is neither true nor just) because the trier will be unduly influenced by a particular bit of evidence, aggressive cross-examination of a truthful witness may serve the end of justice. Should Subin's view apply to an attempt to impeach truthful testimony in defense of an *innocent* client? Consider this excerpt from Freedman's article:

> Is it proper to cross-examine for the purpose of discrediting the reliability or the credibility of a witness whom you know to be telling the truth? Assume the following situation. Your client has been falsely accused of a robbery committed at 16th and P Streets at 11:00 p.m. He tells you at first that at no time on the evening of the crime was he within six blocks of that location. However, you are able to persuade him that he must tell you the truth and that doing so will in no way prejudice him. He then reveals to you that he was at 15th and P Streets at 10:55 that evening, but that he was walking east, away from the scene of the crime, and that, by 11:00 p.m., he was six blocks away. At the trial, there are two prosecution witnesses. The first mistakenly, but with some degree of persuasion, identifies your client as the criminal. At that point, the prosecution's case depends on this single witness, who might or might not be believed. Since your client has a prior record, you do not want to put him on the stand, but you feel that there is at least a chance for acquittal. The second prosecution witness is an elderly woman who is somewhat nervous and who wears glasses. She testifies truthfully and accurately that she saw your client at 15th and P Streets at 10:55 p.m. She has corroborated the erroneous testimony of the first witness and made conviction virtually certain. However, if you destroy her reliability through cross-examination designed to show that she is easily confused and has poor eyesight, you may not only eliminate the corroboration, but also cast doubt in the jury's mind on the prosecution's entire case. On the other hand, if you should refuse to cross-examine her because she is telling the truth, your client may well feel betrayed, since you knew of the witness's veracity only because your client confided in you, under your assurance that his truthfulness would not prejudice him.

Freedman, supra, 64 Mich.L.Rev. at 1474.

Recall that the Model Rules do not make ultimate guilt or liability relevant, whether disclosure (as in the case of perjury) or vigorous advocacy (as in the case of impeachment of a truthful witness) is required.

4. Compare the case of prosecution testimony known to defense counsel (but not to the prosecutor) to be in error, which enables counsel to present truthful testimony tending, because of the error, to exonerate a defendant known by counsel to be guilty. An example is that given in the earlier excerpt from the Freedman article, page 156 n. 16 above.

What is your reaction to the following response?

A defense attorney can present any evidence that is truthful; if the ethical rule was otherwise it would mean that a defendant who confessed guilt to his counsel would never be able to have an active defense at trial. . . . The victim's mistake concerning the precise time of the crime results in a windfall defense [but] it must be remembered that litigation involves the independent testing by an impartial trier of fact of events recalled by human beings.

Michigan State Bar Committee on Professional and Judicial Ethics, Opinion CI–1164, 3 ABA/BNA Lawyers' Manual on Professional Conduct 44 (1987).

5. We have been speaking of "guilt," that is, the context of criminal cases. If Subin's position is sound, does it have no bite in civil matters? Assume that you represent an employer in an unfair labor practice proceeding. An employee has been discharged after committing a violation of a company rule, but it is acknowledged to you that the supervisor who initiated the discharge probably would not have done so but for the person's activities in support of a union (which under applicable law renders the discharge unlawful). The discharge was approved largely to back up supervisory authority, and now the company is unwilling to take the person back. It asks you to do your best to undermine the NLRB General Counsel's case, by impeaching the charging party's credibility and by emphasizing other cases where employees not engaged in union activities were discharged.

Although a leading treatise expresses great "doubt" that the norm permitting the impeachment of testimony known to be accurate "should be extended to civil cases," C. Wolfram, Modern Legal Ethics 651 (1986), many lawyers would not find anything problematic in taking on such a representation.

(a) *Should* it be more seriously questioned? Are Subin's concerns inapt? If so, why?

(b) If not, is the proper conclusion that a substantially more far-reaching change in professional norms is called for, or is it that the very breadth of that implication is sufficient reason for rejecting Subin's position altogether?

(c) To what extent, if at all, does the idea suggested in the second paragraph of Note 2 of this Note, p. 172, above, imply that your response might depend on the particular context, e.g., labor cases, tort cases, debt collections, etc., that is, that "civil cases" is too broad a category?

OPINION 314
ABA Committee on Professional Ethics.
(1965).

The Committee has received a number of specific inquiries regarding the ethical relationship between the Internal Revenue Service and lawyers practicing before it.

. . .

Certainly a lawyer's advocacy before the Internal Revenue Service must be governed by "the same principles of ethics which justify his appearance before the Courts". But since the service, however fair and impartial it may try to be, is the representative of one of the parties, does the lawyer owe it the same duty of disclosure which is owed to the courts? Or is his duty to it more nearly analogous to that which he owes his brother attorneys in the conduct of cases which should be conducted in an atmosphere of candor and fairness but are admittedly adversary in nature? An analysis of the nature of the Internal Revenue Service will serve to throw some light upon the answer to these questions.

The Internal Revenue Service is neither a true tribunal, nor even a quasi-judicial institution. It has no machinery or procedure for adversary proceedings before impartial judges or arbiters, involving the weighing of conflicting testimony of witnesses examined and cross-examined by opposing counsel and the consideration of arguments of counsel for both sides of a dispute. While its procedures provide for "fresh looks" through departmental reviews and informal and formal conference procedures, few will contend that the service provides any truly dispassionate and unbiased consideration to the taxpayer. Although willing to listen to taxpayers and their representatives and obviously intending to be fair, the service is not designed and does not purport to be unprejudiced and unbiased in the judicial sense.

. . .

The problem arises when, in the course of his professional employment, the attorney acquires information bearing upon the strength of his client's claim. . . .

For example, what is the duty of a lawyer in regard to disclosure of the weaknesses in his client's case in the course of negotiations for the settlement of a tax case?

Negotiation and settlement procedures of the tax system do not carry with them the guarantee that a correct tax result necessarily occurs. The latter happens, if at all, solely by reason of chance in settlement of tax controversies just as it might happen with regard to other civil disputes. In the absence of either judicial determination or of a hypothetical exchange of files by adversaries, counsel will always urge in aid of settlement of a controversy the strong points of his case and minimize the weak; this is in keeping with Canon 15, which does require "warm zeal" on behalf of the client. Nor does the absolute duty not to make false assertions of fact require the disclosure of weaknesses in the client's case and in no event does it require the disclosure of his confidences, unless the facts in the attorney's possession indicate beyond reasonable doubt that a crime will be committed. A wrong, or indeed sometimes an unjust, tax result in the settlement of a controversy is not a crime.

Similarly, a lawyer who is asked to advise his client in the course of the preparation of the client's tax returns may freely urge the statement of positions most favorable to the client just as long as there is reasonable basis for those positions. Thus where the lawyer believes there is a reasonable basis for a position that a particular transaction does not result in taxable income, or that certain expenditures are properly deductible as expenses, the lawyer has no duty to advise that riders be attached to the client's tax return explaining the circumstances surrounding the transaction or the expenditures.

. . .

Note on Opinion 314: Adversarial self-assessment?

1. (a) The proposition, that a tax return need not disclose the facts regarding a transaction that the taxpayer knows or believes the Internal Revenue Service would challenge, has two somewhat different justifying antecedents:

- One is the proposition that a taxpayer may take a position on its return that the IRS would (perhaps successfully) challenge;

- the other that parties to a negotiation need not volunteer information that would likely harm their position.

Is there any logical connection between each of these antecedent propositions and the case for non-disclosure?

(b) Logic apart, what is the fit between the rationale of Opinion 314 and the practicalities of tax administration? Consider the analysis put forth in James R. Rowen, When May a Lawyer Advise a Client that he May Take a Position on his Tax Return?, 29 Tax Lawy. 237 (1970):

> If a tax return is regarded as like a submission in an adversary proceeding, then Ethical Considerations 7–3 and 7–4 are strong authority for the Opinion 314 view that an attorney may advise that a position may be taken on a return if there is a reasonable basis therefor, regardless of whether the attorney believes it to be correct. This appears to be the rationale of Opinion 314.

> Assuming that a tax return is like a submission in an adversary proceeding, one may still question the statement in Opinion 314 that there is no duty to attach a rider to the return noting doubtful items. If a tax return is like a submission in an adversary proceeding, and if, in an adversary proceeding before a tribunal, an attorney should point out authority directly adverse to his position, it may be argued that the taxpayer should point out on the return where his position is inconsistent with existing authority. It may be further argued that regulations and revenue rulings should be considered existing authority.

> Opinion 314 rejects such an argument on the basis that the tax return is submitted to the Internal Revenue Service and that the Service is not an impartial tribunal. The premise of Opinion 314 is that the Service generally takes an adversary attitude in auditing returns, and that "few will contend that the Service provides any truly dispassionate and unbiased consideration to the taxpayer." (Is this correct, or do not most agents try to determine what the law provides?) The Opinion notes that it is not necessary to cite adverse authority to opposing counsel in an adversary proceeding and suggests that the taxpayer has no greater obligation of disclosure in a tax return than an

attorney has in dealing with such opposing counsel. Assuming, arguendo, that there is some basis for taking this view with respect to submissions to an agent in the course of audit, should this view apply to the return itself? . . .

Even if one accepts the premise of Opinion 314 that a tax return is like a brief in an adversary proceeding, one may question whether the ordinary rules of adversary litigation should apply to the tax return. The rationale of the adversary system is that justice may best be reached between contending parties when each contending party, represented by counsel, presents his argument to an independent tribunal. As applied to the tax return system, the premise would be that the taxpayer is presenting his position as to his tax liability. The government then has an opportunity to audit the taxpayer's return and to present its position on the tax liability. When there is a conflict, each side, more or less equally represented by counsel, can then present its position to an independent tribunal, which can then make a rational decision. This is fine in theory, but in practice the government is not able to audit most returns effectively:

(a) The government does not have enough personnel to audit more than a small fraction of the returns that are filed.

(b) The auditing agents who do audit a taxpayer usually do not have the time to make a thorough audit to uncover all possible questions. To uncover doubtful questions requires a great deal of digging and considerable knowledge of taxpayer's business; it is difficult for an auditing agent to acquire such knowledge in the limited time available to him.

(c) The law is so complicated that in many areas it takes a lawyer or accountant of considerable training and intelligence to understand the problem. While the government has many able agents, it is unrealistic to think that the government can adequately instruct all of its agents in the complexities of the law in such a manner that they can uncover most doubtful questions.

The premise of the adversary system, that the two adversaries will be in an equal position to uncover and present the facts, is unrealistic as applied to the current tax system. While the government's disadvantage is overcome somewhat by the rule that places the burden of proof on the taxpayer, this rule only applies when an issue has been raised; it does not help the government to uncover the issue.

If one considers the filing of a tax return as an act of conduct required by the government, rather than as a submission in an adversary proceeding, Canon 7 does not give much support to Opinion 314. If the lawyer is advising on required conduct, rather than acting as advocate, Ethical Considerations 7–3 through 7–5 do not say that the lawyer can advise a course of conduct on the grounds that there is a "reasonable basis" that it is legal. . . .

2. Twenty years later, at the request of the Section of Taxation, the ABA Standing Committee on Ethics and Professional Responsibility reconsidered the "reasonable basis" test of Opinion 314. In *Opinion 85–352*

(1986), it rejected the view that "any colorable claim on a tax return [would] justify exploitation of the lottery of the tax return audit selection process," but reaffirmed that a lawyer could take a position on a return notwithstanding that he or she expected it to be rejected if challenged and litigated, so long as the claim was made in "good faith," which it described as requiring "some realistic possibility" of success if litigated.

An accompanying Report of the Special Task Force on Formal Opinion 85–352, 39 Tax Lawy. 635 (1986), specified that "a position having only 5% or 10% likelihood of success, if litigated, should not meet the new standard. A position having a likelihood of success closely approaching one-third should meet the standard...." A final admonitory paragraph is titled, "Tax Returns are not Adversarial Proceedings," but begins by acknowledging that "the taking of aggressive positions on tax returns may be the first step in development of an adversarial relationship between the client and the Internal Revenue Service," so long as there is the requisite attorney good faith as defined above.

(a) To what extent, if at all, has there been a change in the governing norm?

(b) Why did the ABA make so modest a change?

(c) Why did it make any change at all?

3. Is it fair to say that neither the question of the permissibility of taking a relatively weak position on a return, nor the question of nondisclosure of the transaction in question, has anything to do with the norm of confidentiality? Rather, the issue is one of the broader norm of *adversariness*.

Why do I say that?

For a discussion of the Treasury Department's controversial effort to hold practitioners to a higher standard than that of Opinion 85–352, see 1 Wolfman, Holden, and Harris, Standards of Tax Practice 474–78 (CCH Tax Trans.Lib. 1991).

The question of the depth of a lawyer's adversarial stance vis-a-vis a public agency like IRS, and a public law program like the Internal Revenue Code, is a central one, in my view. The following fictional account of a dispute between two lawyers in the same firm is illustrative.

THE AVOIDANCE DYNAMIC: A TALE OF TAX PLANNING, TAX ETHICS, AND TAX REFORM

George Cooper
80 Colum.L.Rev. 1553 (1980).

[Note: This article was written prior to a number of significant changes in the tax law, in particular the abolition of the preferential treatment of capital gains, and the transactions discussed in it no longer have the tax consequences described. Please bear in mind too that you are asked to read it, not for the substantive legal questions it addresses, but for the light it sheds on the world-views of the two lawyers, and the relevance of those world-views to the ways in which each sees his professional responsibilities.]

. . .

Memorandum from Mr. Younger to Mr. Senior, dated March 1, 1980.

Re: Income Tax Planning for Sally Songriter

Ms. Songriter is a composer of popular songs and ballads who has recently achieved some measure of success. Her earned income for 1980 will be approximately $200,000, derived mostly from royalties on her musical compositions. In a few instances Ms. Songriter has sold movie rights to a ballad for a lump sum, and Ms. Songriter's agents foresee much wider exploitation of this subsidiary rights market in the future, including, for example, a possible television series based on the characters in a ballad. Ms. Songriter's income is expected to be at least at the current year's level for the next several years and may be much more than that, but it could (and very likely will) fall drastically, depending on the vagaries of commercial success.

Supplementing her professional earnings, Ms. Songriter receives interest and dividends on $200,000 in savings, which is invested in a variety of bonds, stocks, and money market funds. This currently produces approximately $24,000 in annual income.

Ms. Songriter is unmarried and has no legal dependents, although Mr. Greenshade discreetly advises that she has lived for several years with a man in an apparently stable relationship. This man is a musician who earns little at present (less than $5,000, says Mr. Greenshade). Ms. Songriter is 35 years old and is a resident of New York City. She conducts her profession from her home, where she has a studio equipped with a piano, a typewriter, and other necessary paraphernalia. She employs no one except a part-time secretary. In addition to the usual personal expenses, Ms. Songriter is paying $10,000 per year to her 65–year–old widowed mother to augment the mother's small pension and Social Security benefits.

. . .

Five basic themes have been explored: (1) making tax-favored investments, (2) using trusts to shift taxable income to a lower bracket, (3) making use of pension and retirement planning opportunities provided under the Code for deferring taxation on a portion of current income, (4) making use of a personal corporation as a tax-reduction/tax-deferral device, and (5) converting the ordinary income from Ms. Songriter's profession into capital gains.

Our conclusion is that Ms. Songriter's tax burden can be reduced very substantially through use of a combination of these techniques. A plan is outlined using techniques that, for the most part, are available to any self-employed professional (such as a doctor or lawyer) and that would reduce her effective federal income tax burden from 48.1% to only 17.5%, without taking into account the tax saving opportunities available through itemized deductions.

. . .

As an uncomplicated investment, tax-exempt bonds seem as good as anything. The return on these bonds has traditionally run at the level to attract taxpayers in the 30% to 40% brackets (i.e., the return is approximately 60% to 70% that of a taxable security), which provides a nice windfall to someone in Ms. Songriter's bracket. For example, an 8% exempt return (the rate currently prevailing) is, for her, the equivalent of 32% taxable interest. This is as good a rate of net after-tax return as on more elaborate tax shelter investments, when all the risks and recapture paybacks are taken into account. Indeed, the logic of the marketplace is that the tax benefits of shelters will become factored into their prices, making them competitive with alternative investments.

A detailed examination of some fancy tax shelter investment proposals bears this out. [discussion omitted].

If exempt bonds seem too quiet and staid an investment for Ms. Songriter, and she wants risk, an alternative is the oldest tax preference in existence—direct investment in long-term growth assets such as real estate or growth stocks. From a tax viewpoint, the favoritism extended to these assets is difficult to beat. No tax at all is payable on accrued gains until they are "realized" and "recognized." The gains can be drawn out without tax through borrowing; the assets can, in many instances, be exchanged for others without tax; and thanks to Congress's recent action reinstating "stepped-up basis" for assets transferred at death, the gains will be permanently excluded from tax if not realized during life. If for any reason it ever becomes necessary to realize gains, they will never be taxed at more than 28%. And all of these tax benefits are solid and unchallengeable. Of course, these investments entail greater risk than exempt bonds, but this is ordinary investment risk, and it can turn out positively as well as negatively. For taxpayers who have plenty of capital to diversify investments, and enough current income from other sources to enable them to hold for the long haul, there is little doubt that they can come out well ahead and pay little or no tax. . . .

. . .

One obvious technique for reducing the tax on Ms. Songriter's earned income is to transfer some of that income to a lower-bracket taxpayer.

Wealthy taxpayers do this all the time with investment income. They create trusts to pay such expenses as their children's college educations and fund the trusts with assets generating substantial dividend or interest income. So long as the trusts meet certain minimum requirements, which are carefully spelled out in the Code, this income is transferred to and taxed to the trust or the beneficiary, either of which is presumably in a much lower tax bracket than the parents.

Briefly stated, to accomplish this tax purpose, a trust must run for at least ten years (except that it can terminate on the death of the income beneficiary if that is earlier), § 673; none of the income for that period can be held for or diverted to the grantor of the trust or to his or her spouse, either directly or in satisfaction of legal obligations of support, § 677; and the grantor cannot reserve unfettered discretionary powers to manipulate the benefits from the income among beneficiaries, §§ 674, 677. But a variety of powers can be given either to the grantor or to a friendly and compliant trustee who is not a close relative or employee—such as an attorney—which maintain the grantor's control over the income in critical respects. For example, the grantor (or any other person) can have power to choose when, how, and for what purpose income is to be expended on behalf of a beneficiary, § 674(b)(6). A lawyer-trustee can be given unfettered discretionary powers to decide whether to accumulate or pay out income, to spray any income distributions as he wishes among designated beneficiaries, and to distribute corpus as he chooses among designated beneficiaries, § 674(c), with the grantor holding a power to remove the trustee and substitute another nonrelative, nonemployee, Treas.Reg. § 1.674(d)–2(a).

Ms. Songriter does not have any children, but she is supporting her mother, which, for tax purposes, is almost as good. If a trust were set up and funded with property generating sufficient income, the mother's expenses could be paid out of income subject to her tax bracket rather than Ms. Songriter's. Because all of the mother's Social Security benefits are nontaxable, as may be a portion of her pension, she is likely to be in a relatively low bracket, probably around 20%. The difference between this rate and Ms. Songriter's tax rate would, in effect, become a little government-funded welfare program to help with the support of the mother. This trust could be unconditional for the mother's remaining lifetime, or it could be terminable at the end of ten years. Ms. Songriter could also reserve the powers, as trustee, to decide how the money is to be invested and to decide when and how to expend the earnings on the mother's behalf. These proposed powers would probably give Ms. Songriter all the continuing control she would wish, and make broader powers in an unrelated trustee unnecessary.

. . .

The trust for Ms. Songriter is only one potential use of short-term trusts to save tax money for our prospective client. As we get to know her better and get more information there may well be additional possibilities. In general, there is little reason for a wealthy taxpayer to spend after-tax dollars on behalf of anyone else except to the extent that he or she is satisfying a legal support obligation. All else can be handled through trusts, with significant tax saving. Thus, a trust for Ms. Songriter's boyfriend could be used to pay his living expenses, which are now being paid by her directly, at less than half the current out-of-pocket cost. The drawback is that boyfriends, unlike mothers, change from time to time. But we should be clever enough, using the broad powers that can be given to an unrelated trustee, to build in some provisions that will keep a trust up-to-date with Ms. Songriter's romantic inclinations.[h]

. . .

Ms. Songriter is plainly authorized to set up a Keogh plan and put aside $7,500 per year in a tax-deferred retirement plan. See § 404(e). She would pay no current income tax on this amount, and the earnings it produced while invested would also be tax-deferred until such time (after age 59½) as she drew the money out. While such a plan is attractive, the deferrable amount is unimpressive for a taxpayer at Ms. Songriter's income level. Much more appealing are the benefits available to a corporate employee, for whom 25% of salary, up to an annual dollar contribution limit, could be set aside in a qualified defined-contribution retirement plan. This dollar contribution limit was initially set at a fairly generous $25,000, and it, unlike the much lower Keogh plan limit, has been automatically adjusted upward for inflation each year, pursuant to existing law. § 415(d)(1)(B). For 1980, $36,875 could be set aside for Ms. Songriter in a corporate defined-contribution plan. . . .

Ms. Songriter is not now a corporate employee. If, however, she created a wholly-owned corporation, it could hire her and establish the requisite retirement plan. The retirement plan tax savings are certainly substantial enough to be considered seriously. In five years, assuming funding of $36,875 per year and 12% annual interest, the plan would be worth $262,373, while savings of the same income without a plan would produce only $84,692. To be fair, this comparison overlooks one significant disadvantage of the plan: the accumulation will be taxed as ordinary earned income when drawn out, while the nonplan accumulation is fully tax-paid.[k] . . . [The discussion of this problem is omitted.]

h. For example, we might think about a trust with discretionary powers to accumulate income or to spray it to and among a class consisting of Ms. Songriter's mother, her boyfriend, any future-born children, and selected charities. As these powers would be discretionary, this trust would need a nonrelative, nonemployee trustee, but either we or Mr. Greenshade would qualify and would be happy to oblige. The trustee would, naturally, pay careful attention to Ms. Songriter's interests and wishes in exercising the discretion, particularly since she could have the power to remove one trustee and substitute another (with the same nonrelatedness) if she wished. Payments could be made to Ms. Songriter's mother and her boyfriend as needed and so long as they maintained pleasant relations with Ms. Songriter. If, at any time, it appeared that she would no longer favor payments to the boyfriend, the trustee could (in his "discretion," of course) pay it all, income and/or corpus, to the mother or accumulate it for possible future children. Eventual charitable disposition would be the last resort if income or corpus were never needed by the mother or children. Corpus, less accumulated income, could be returned to Ms. Songriter after ten years.

k. In addition, although Ms. Songriter is a bit young to be thinking about such things, some mention should be made of the estate planning bonanza available for monies accumulated in a qualified pension plan. It is possible, under § 2039(c), to

It should also be noted that the use of a corporation offers some other income tax fringe benefits, most notably the ability to deduct all medical expenses through a corporate medical reimbursement plan, without the need first to exceed the floor of 3% of the employee's gross income. . . .

. . . They are known as "loan-out" corporations because the usual form of operation is for the individual to contract with the corporation to loan out his or her services to third parties, in return for a salary based on the revenues the corporation earns from loaning these services. . . .   Given the tax benefits available from the retirement plan, such a corporation is difficult to resist in any situation where a taxpayer has substantial current earned income in excess of his or her current consumption needs.   Ms. Songriter fits this description.

As might be expected, these one-person corporations are not the darlings of the IRS, and the Service has a variety of weapons to use against them.   However, there is a persuasive and, I think, legally correct, defense to any attack the Service might make on a corporation set up by Ms. Songriter.   For your information, I have summarized the tax problems that might arise and evaluated them in an Appendix to this memorandum.   A salient feature of this evaluation is that there is little real downside risk.   Even if the IRS should attack and succeed (both improbable), Ms. Songriter is unlikely to wind up worse off for tax purposes than if she had not incorporated at all.   Given this bottom line, the corporate opportunity seems one not to be missed.   The popularity of these corporations among doctors, entertainers, and other professionals indicates that I am not alone in this view and, in a sense, bespeaks a Service quiescence regarding them.

In recommending formation of a one-person, loan-out corporation for Ms. Songriter to take advantage of retirement plan benefits we assumed that all the net income of the corporation, after deducting plan contributions, would be passed through to Ms. Songriter as salary.

There is an important reason why such a complete flowthrough is normally essential.   To the extent the earnings of the corporation are royalties from copyrights in works produced by Ms. Songriter or are compensation for her "loaned out" personal services, the earnings will be classified as personal holding company income, making the corporation a personal holding company.   § 543(a)(4), (7).   Such a company must pay not only the regular corporate income tax on its retained earnings but also a 70% penalty tax.   Retained earnings must therefore be scrupulously avoided unless strategies can be developed to avoid personal holding company status.

Although the rules on personal holding companies are quite complex, in general the undesirable status can be avoided if more than 40%

pass these accumulations on to heirs and legatees entirely free of estate tax.   This could produce a tax saving of many hundreds of thousands of dollars.   For example, the estate tax on a $2,000,000 accumulation would normally be more than $780,000, but would be zero if qualified under § 2039(c).

of gross income is derived from sources not classified as personal holding company income. If this goal is achieved, the tax situation changes drastically. Earnings can then be retained subject to the regular corporate income tax, which, thanks to the recent generosity of Congress in cutting rates for "small" corporations, is only 17% on the first $25,000 annually and only 20% on the next $25,000. The top corporation rate is only 46%, which is less than Ms. Songriter's 50%, and that rate is not hit until $100,000 of income. (These rates reflect federal taxes only.)

A technique exists for converting the earnings from copyrights into non-personal-holding-company income. Since section 543(a)(4) applies only to "royalties," and not to the proceeds from a sale of a copyright or a portion thereof, earnings derived from the sale of Ms. Songriter's copyrights would go toward protecting the corporation from falling into the unwanted personal holding company category. Rev.Rul. 75–202, 1975–1 C.B. 170.

The process of "selling" rather than licensing does not require that Ms. Songriter give up all continuing interest in profits from her works. Rather, she could sell in return for a lump sum guarantee plus a percentage override.[m] Moreover, Ms. Songriter need not sell all rights in a package. It will suffice if she sells rights to "exploit a copyrighted work in a particular medium." Rev.Rul. 54–409, 1954–2 C.B. 174, *modified,* Rev.Rul. 60–226, 1960–1 C.B. 26. . . . Thus, if the deal were set up correctly, it would seem possible for Ms. Songriter's corporation to sell defined subsidiary rights, such as the right to make a movie or a television series, and treat the proceeds of such sales, even if they include royalty-like percentage arrangements, as non-personal-holding-company income. . . .

If she wished to pursue this technique for producing non-personal-holding-company income, Ms. Songriter would refrain from seeking salary payments from the corporation as to some or all of the copyrights transferred to it. Instead, she would transfer these copyrights in a tax-free section 351 exchange, giving the corporation her low basis and shifting all the profitability to it. Or she could enter into a compensatory arrangement that allowed the corporation to keep a portion of sales proceeds in return for bona fide agency, promotional, and financial services. If done before any contract for exploitation of the copyright is negotiated, these transfers should not raise assignment of income problems.

. . .

m. In Rev.Rul. 75–202, 1975–1 C.B. 170, an author transferred his copyrights to a wholly-owned corporation, which in turn "sold" the rights to an unrelated publishing company for (1) a minimum lump sum plus (2) a percentage of retail prices for sales of the work if in excess of the minimum. Despite the fact that this arrangement seems impossible to distinguish from a usual guaranteed advance against royalties, the IRS ruled that it constituted a sale and did not produce royalty income within the meaning of § 543(a)(4).

There is also an opportunity open to Ms. Songriter to avoid personal holding company income status for the earnings derived from corporate "loan out" of her services. The relevant statutory provision, § 543(a)(7), covers only loan-out contracts in which she is specifically "designated" to perform work or in which a third party is given the "right to designate" her. The Service has interpreted this provision narrowly, requiring an actual contractual obligation rather than an expectation (even one soundly grounded) to constitute a designation. Most striking, the Service takes this position even if a sole owner is the only employee of a corporation and the corporation renders professional services, such as medical services, in such a manner that its clients clearly know who they are dealing with and whose services they are receiving. Does a patient really have to designate Dr. Sawbones to perform services when he goes to the office where Dr. Sawbones is the only doctor, in order for the fees to be personal service income to the doctor? Apparently the government thinks so [p] and, as a consequence, the way would seem open to avoid the personal holding company onus on income earned from corporate loan-out of Ms. Songriter's services through careful contract drafting.

. . .

The oldest tax minimization game in town is transmuting [ordinary income (OI)] to long-term [capital gain (CG)]. [L]ong-term capital gains are taxed at 28% (40% of the 70% rate on investment OI) rather than the 50% she pays on earned OI (federal rates only).

One might expect the capital gains rate to apply to gains from sales of properties such as copyrights, suggesting the possibility of Ms. Songriter's selling off her copyrights rather than holding them and earning ordinary income royalties. . . .

Unfortunately, however, capital gain treatment is specifically denied to anyone who profits from sale of copyrights in works that she herself has produced. § 1221(3). That clearly bars Ms. Songriter from the most direct route to capital gain.

. . .

There is, however, a very sophisticated alternative open to Ms. Songriter that will generate deductions to shelter her professional income from current ordinary taxation and transform it into long-term capital gain taxable at the new 28% maximum rate, all without involving her in surrender of her copyrights or in a risky commitment of her capital. The source of this tax marvel is straddles in treasury bill futures.

---

p. In Rev.Rul. 75–67, 1975–1 C.B. 169, a medical service corporation employed only one doctor, the corporation's owner. Patients going to the office wanted and naturally expected to receive services from that doctor, but the Service ruled that unless a "designation" was actually made, § 543(a)(7) would not apply, and the corporation would not have personal holding company income. Accord, Rev.Rul. 75–250, 1975–1 C.B. 172 (accountants); Private Ruling 7934092 (1979) (engineering consultant).

A T-bill future is a contract to buy or to sell an agreed face amount of treasury bills at an agreed price in some determined future month. Without going into detail, the basic arrangement in a straddle is to buy (go long) and sell (go short) "matched" pairs of T-bill futures, which are traded on several recognized exchanges. The term "matched" is used advisedly, because some spread between the pairs of buy and sell contracts, and therefore imperfect matching, is necessary to avoid problems with the sham transaction doctrine and associated statutes, *see* §§ 165, 1233; . . . .

The usual "mismatch" in these transactions is to have the buy and sell contracts fall due from one to three months apart. As market interest rates change, one leg of a pair will go up in value and the other leg will go down in a generally offsetting manner. The trick of this transaction is getting an ordinary loss deduction for the loss leg and long-term capital gain treatment for the gain leg.

[The "trick" is made possible because the Internal Revenue Code specified that gain or loss on a T-bill is "ordinary" rather than "capital," contrary to the treatment of other securities or commodities in like circumstances, while the Internal Revenue Service had ruled that gain or loss on a futures contract (as distinguished from the bill itself) receives "capital" treatment. The memorandum proposes differing steps to be taken, with respect to the "buy" and the "sell" half of the straddle, depending on whether each produces a gain or a loss. The following table summarizes this portion of the memorandum:

	If the price rises	If the price falls
Brought future	1. Realize capital gain by contracting to sell an "off-setting future" (same commodity, same month of maturity). The Exchange will treat the two futures as cancelling one another, which terminates both transactions and produces gain on the prior purchase.	3. Realize ordinary loss by taking delivery of the bill at maturity, and selling it at current market price.
Sold future	2. Realize ordinary loss by buying a bill at current market price, and delivering it to the buyer of the "future."	4. Contracting to purchase an off-setting future (as in above, left) would produce short-term, rather than long-term, gain, which is taxed as ordinary income. Instead, buy a new straddle maturing in the next taxable year, in a large enough amount that the loss portion can be terminated (as above) in the current year to produce loss sufficient to

<u>If the price rises</u>   <u>If the price falls</u>
                                                offset the gain on the origi-
                                                nal "future." Replace the
                                                loss portion to create a new
                                                "straddle" with the gain
                                                portion. Repeat the entire
                                                process the following year.]

    T-bill straddles are not entirely free of investment risk since the price movement of the two contracts constituting the straddle is not perfectly linked. Indeed, the existence of some risk, including a reasonable possibility of gain as well as loss, is critical to the argument that this is not merely a tax artifice that can be ignored by the Commissioner.... But the risk in any straddle is inherently quite limited because of the tendency of one half of the pair to offset the other.[t]

    These T-bill manipulations also are not, of course, without tax risk. In addition to the risk of imposition of the tax artifice doctrine, there is also a tax risk that the attempt to shift the loss leg of the straddle from capital to ordinary by making or taking delivery of an actual T-bill might not work.[u] Beyond these latent tax risks there is also a published ruling that threatens one aspect of the transactions. Rev.Rul. 77–185, 1977–1 C.B. 48, deals with an attempt to use commodity straddles to defer gain from one year to another by closing out the loss half of the straddle in one year and postponing realization of the gain half until the next year. The ruling takes the position that a straddle is a "sham," despite a disparity in the pairings, and is not a closed transaction until both legs have been settled. It is not clear what application, if any, this ruling would have to us if interest rates fell and we were able to bring the entire transaction to an end in one year. Nor would the ruling seem to apply if we had accrued losses on other investments, which we could use to offset short-term gains and thereby bring our straddling to an end within a calendar year. If we are forced to use straddles to defer gain to later years we would run smack up against the ruling, but its reasoning is questionable, and it has been rejected by most commentators. See Barbakoff & Sabin, Are All Silver Transactions Created Equal?—An Analysis of Revenue Ruling 77–185, 56 Taxes 3 (1978); Goldfein & Hochberg, An Analysis of IRS' Ruling that Straddle Transactions Lack Requisite Profit Motive, 47 J. Tax. 142 (1977); Note, Tax Treatment of Treasury Bill Futures, 52 S.Cal.L.Rev. 1555 (1979).

    Aggressive tax planning is always a parlous game. I believe we can keep the tax peril to a minimum by avoiding excessively close

---

t. Since both contracts cover the same face amount of U.S. Treasury bills and will differ only in the delivery date by a month or two, their prices move generally in tandem, but there is always some differential fluctuation....

u. Even though the loss is realized on sale or purchase of the T-bill, the Service could argue, with obvious justification, that the loss is really a loss on the future rather than a loss on the T-bill. However, this argument would run counter to longstanding rulings that making or taking delivery on a future is not a taxable event in itself but rather is a step in determining gain or loss on the commodity taken or delivered.

matching of our pairs, thus leaving ourselves with an important investment risk, and by otherwise turning square corners and structuring the transactions carefully. Certainly we can muster a reasonable argument in defense of our position and one that I think is technically correct.

All in all, the chances of winning a contest with the Service over straddles are difficult to assess. Depending on how this transaction goes, I would say we have somewhere between a 25% and an 85% probability of success if the issue is raised on audit. However, Ms. Songriter has not been audited yet, and there is a good chance that she will continue to slip by or that this issue will not even be raised if she is audited. The actual fact of straddling is not even reported on a return, which simply shows gains and loss[es] from closed or terminated transactions.

We can even suggest to Ms. Songriter that she improve the possibilities of nondiscovery by using a number of brokers and various commodities exchanges. She might also engage in a good bit of other commodity trading during the year, thus masking the tax straddle transactions.

Putting together our chances of nondiscovery and our chances of success even if discovered, the overall odds on succeeding with these T-bill manipulations are surely better than 50–50. Moreover, the downside threat, even if we lose entirely, is not all that bad. There are basically two remedies that the IRS could pursue. First, the Service could seek to have the straddle ignored for tax purposes, treating it as a meaningless sham, or it could seek to have the ordinary loss denied and treated as capital. Either of these would merely result in payment of the ordinary income tax that would have been due anyhow, with deductible interest at the rate of 12%. Assuming we can earn a rate of return as good as that or better, this is no great burden. It simply puts us in the tax position we would have been in anyway, with a little sweetener if we can beat the Treasury's interest rate. Second, the Service could seek to deny deductions for the expenses of engaging in the straddles. However, the only expenses are small. . . .

Overall, we roughly break even on these manipulations at the very worst, and the odds are excellent that we will do very well, particularly since it is unlikely that the transactions will be discovered. In view of this favorable cost-benefit analysis, the T-bill straddle technique is one that Ms. Songriter should seriously consider.

     . . . .

It is interesting to see the cumulative effect of the various tax saving suggestions discussed in this memorandum, and I have prepared [the following] Table to illustrate them. As you can see, assuming Ms. Songriter has $200,000 of royalty income and $24,000 before-tax return on her investments, these proposals will cut her federal tax from $107,720 to only $39,273, including an implicit "tax" of $8,000 in the form of reduced interest on tax-exempt bonds. This is a reduction in her effective rate of federal taxation from 48.1% to 17.5%, and because only slight use is being made so far of the tax saving possibilities of corporate retained earnings, the plan can maintain this low rate of taxation even if Ms. Songriter's income rises substantially....

FEDERAL INCOME TAX BURDENS
OF SALLY SONGRITER

Before and After Implementation of
Tax Saving Proposals

Before Proposals:	Pretax Income	Federal Tax *	Net After Tax
Professional Income	$200,000	$ 91,174	$108,826
Investments	24,000	16,546	7,454
Totals	$224,000	$107,720	$116,280

After Proposals:

	Pretax Income	Federal Tax	Net After Tax
Salary	$147,500	$ 28,242 **	$119,258
Retirement Plan	36,875	—	36,875
Corporate Retained Earnings	3,125	531	2,594
Trust (for mother)	12,500	2,500	10,000
Tax-exempt Investments	24,000 ***	8,000 ***	16,000
Totals	$224,000	$ 39,273	$184,727

(Less Total Net Before Proposals)	($116,280)
Overall Tax Benefit From Proposals	$ 68,447

APPENDIX

Summary Evaluation of Legal Grounds for Challenging a One–Person Corporation Established for Ms. Songriter

(1) Coverage of Employee—Ms. Songriter uses a part-time secretary to help with her work. If this secretary is an "employee" within the meaning of the tax law, it may be necessary to include her in the pension plan (and the medical reimbursement plan) on nondiscriminatory terms. For example, if the pension plan covers Ms. Songriter with annual contributions equal to 25% of her salary (the maximum percentage allowed by law, of which we are likely to avail ourselves), the same percentage might have to be contributed for the secretary.

* All calculations assume a $1,000 personal exemption, a $2,300 zero bracket amount, and no other deductions except as generated by T-bill manipulation. See note ** below.

** This figure assumes a T-bill manipulation to transform $125,000 of salary into long-term capital gain, and allows $2,000 for transaction costs of this manipulation as an implicit "tax" on it.

*** This figure assumes all savings are invested in tax-exempt bonds which are subject to an implicit "tax" of $8,000 in the form of reduced interest income.

If this raises a problem for Ms. Songriter, there are ways around it. The most obvious avoidance technique, hiring the secretary as a personal, noncorporate employee, has been precluded by section 414(b) and (c), which requires, in effect, that such noncorporate employees be included in the pension plan. However, since the secretary is only part-time the problem could be solved by imposing a minimum service requirement for plan eligibility. Employees who work less than half-time can be excluded.

If a secretary is needed more than half-time, the alternative of obtaining services from an office temporary agency could be explored. A secretary obtained in this fashion would be an employee of the agency, not of Ms. Songriter. This would not require Ms. Songriter simply to take pot luck with a temporary from week to week. Specialized firms have been set up to supply support personnel to professional corporations of doctors and lawyers under arrangements carefully tailored to satisfy the employment needs of these professionals while avoiding damaging "employer" status for pension plan purposes. . . .

If neither of these techniques for excluding the secretary is used, the pension contributions for him or her can in any event be substantially reduced through use of permitted provisions for delaying plan eligibility until an employee has worked for several years, for deferring vesting of pension accumulations, and for integrating the plan with Social Security (reducing contributions with regard to earnings subject to FICA tax). In one way or another, if Ms. Songriter wants to shortchange her secretary on pension contributions, she should be able to do so.

On the other hand, if, as is likely, Ms. Songriter has a friendly relationship with the secretary and wishes to maximize benefits for her, it would be beneficial to all simply to include the secretary within plan coverage. The secretary would then benefit from the opportunity for tax-deferred savings, which is useful even in low brackets. To the extent the secretary had current needs for the money, the plan could include loan provisions that would effectively allow her to get current use of much of her accumulation.

(2) Excessive compensation—In a situation where a wholly-owned corporation pays a large salary to its shareholder, where that salary is contingent on the actual earnings of the corporation, and where the corporation pays no dividends—all of which would be true in Ms. Songriter's case—the claim can be made that the salary is, in part, a disguised dividend. If the IRS should make this argument and prevail, the tax implications would be quite serious. . . . The risk of this happening, however, seems minor. The law (§ 162) permits payment of "reasonable" compensation to a corporate officer. Here, all the earnings of the corporation that would fund Ms. Songriter's salary would be produced by her services and those services would be valued by the arm's length copyright sales or licenses and loan out contracts with third parties. The IRS would be hard pressed to support an argument

of unreasonableness. Why should Ms. Songriter be paid any less than the full value of what she produces?

Moreover, the Service has recently moderated its position on unreasonable compensation in an important respect, which is favorable to Ms. Songriter. In Rev.Rul. 79–8, 1979–1 C.B. 92, the IRS ruled that, contrary to past practice, the absence of dividend payments will not in itself create a presumption of unreasonable compensation in a closely-held corporation. My research reveals only one case where the Service has even attempted to challenge the reasonableness of compensation in a situation similar to Ms. Songriter's, and there unsuccessfully. In this case, an architect in a one-man corporation paid himself a salary equal to almost all the earnings of his corporation, and no dividends, and succeeded in defending his salary as reasonable. *Eduardo Catalano, Inc.*, 38 T.C.M. (CCH) 763 (1979). Experienced practitioners seem to see no problem with this compensation issue in a loan-out corporation. . . .

[The remainder of this memorandum is omitted.]

PART II. TAX ETHICS

Memorandum from Mr. Senior to Mr. Younger, dated March 4, 1980.

Re: Yours re: Sally Songriter

I am impressed and disturbed by your memo. Impressed by the ideas you have come up with for Ms. Songriter, but disturbed at your approach in doing so, particularly in regard to the T-bill proposal. I am still reviewing the memo and may get back to you later with specific comments and questions. In the meantime, however, I wish that you could address yourself to some basic and transcendent issues.

When I used to be active in tax law (years ago, it is true, when things were simpler), I was taught that the job of the tax lawyer was, in the words of Randolph Paul, "one of the hardest in the world." As Paul put it, "he must wash all his conclusions with the cynical acid of distrust," and he "must watch for inarticulate law," for "the function of the tax advisor is systematized prediction." Paul, The Responsibilities of the Tax Adviser, 63 Harv.L.Rev. 377 (1950). Taking those words to heart, I used to agonize over an obscure provision until I thought I knew the right interpretation. And I would advise the client accordingly, encouraging him to conduct his affairs so that he would fare well under what I detected to be the probable legal result, and steering him away from schemes, no matter how alluring their song, that depended on an unsound interpretation. More than that, I thought there was some mix in my duty. It was not unalloyed avoidance-seeking, but had at least a measure of allegiance to the fisc and to higher principle. Some things were wrong, even if they worked.

How much easier it seems for you. There is in your memo no quest to sort out right from wrong, much less any attempt to determine the correct legal result under complex provisions. Instead your stance seems to be: let's find an argument for the taxpayer and, having found it, let's carry it as far as we can, so long as the downside risk is not too bad, while freely factoring the possibility of nondiscovery into the risk assessment.

I suppose that may be the modern way. Cost-benefit analysis is all. But I still see more to the *profession* of law than that. Take the centerpiece of your scheme—T-bill manipulations. Maybe that can work under existing law. I instinctively doubt it, but the courts are sometimes strange in their views. If it does work, however, it is surely mad to allow it and Congress would have to respond promptly with corrective legislation, which would add a new layer of complexity to the law. Otherwise we would have a system where the rich, who could afford to go into these manipulations, could freely convert ordinary income to capital gain and move income around from year to year as they saw fit. They could, I suppose, even avoid any income taxation at all, by deferring all gains until death. It has to be a long shot to put any reliance on the expectation that you can get away with a manipulation having these implications. That means, as you seem to admit, that the probability of nondiscovery is critical to your recommendation. There is nothing new or clever in seeing that playing this so-called audit lottery is a winning game for the taxpayer. A generation ago, Jacob Rabkin counseled that a "tremendous amount of self-restraint on the part of the tax bar is required" in order to refrain from exploiting this possibility. Ethical Problems of Tax Practitioners, 8 Tax L.Rev. 1, 29 (1952). I see in you no amount of this self-restraint at all. Worse yet, you seem to think it acceptable to exploit the lottery by reporting transactions on Ms. Songriter's return in a way that may even be directly contrary to a revenue ruling, and not to disclose or reveal this contrariness at all. . . . Indeed, you seek to mask it with other futures trading. May I suggest, my young friend, that your approach goes beyond a lack of self-restraint to openly unethical behavior.

Memorandum from Mr. Younger to Mr. Senior, dated March 6, 1980.

Re: Sally Songriter's Tax Planning

I am sorry you see things the way you do, and I disagree vigorously with the notion that I have done or proposed anything unethical.

It is unethical, I know, to misdate documents, to create false evidence to support a position, or to misstate what has actually been done in reporting it. But I have not suggested anything of the sort. Take the point that seems to have shocked you most, the suggestion that Ms. Songriter conduct and report her futures trading, and even go so far as to engage in additional trading, so as to avoid highlighting a few sensitive transactions. I didn't suggest that she fabricate any additional trading but rather that she actually do it, paying the costs and fees involved and running the risks. There is a world of difference between that and something like a memo to the file making up hypothetical "business needs" for retained earnings to create a section 531 defense, an action to which many of our "ethical" colleagues might stoop. At most, it seems to me, my suggestion is to put the best light on things, which I had always thought was the essence of the lawyer's role.

The view I take regarding additional futures transactions is supported by all the relevant ethical guidelines. Thus, under Canon 7 of the Code of Professional Responsibility a lawyer may not create "false evidence," but there is no bar against creating true evidence. ABA Code of Professional Responsibility, Disciplinary Rule 7–102(A)(4) to (6). Indeed, the relevant Ethical Consideration under this Canon specially authorizes the "*development* and preservation of evidence of existing motive, intent, or desire" where such may have future utility for a client's case. Id., Ethical Consideration 7–6 (emphasis added). Even more to the point is ABA Formal Opinion 314, which deals specifically with the duties of the tax lawyer in relation to the Internal Revenue Service. The only duty of disclosure is "not to mislead ... deliberately and affirmatively, either by misstatements or by silence." ABA Comm. on Professional Ethics, Opinions, No. 314 (1965). I have not suggested any falsehood, half-truth or "overlooking" of relevant facts. Finally, the recently promulgated Guidelines to Tax Practice from the ABA Tax Section support my view. 31 Tax Law. 551 (1978). These guidelines condemn participation in transactions "*entirely lacking* in economic substance and *intended solely* to conceal or mislead," id. at 554 (emphasis added), but say nothing of embarking on bona fide and legitimate transactions that have by-product tax reporting value.

Perhaps I belabor a relatively minor point. Certainly, I did not see the suggestion that Ms. Songriter engage in other futures trading as a central or essential part of my recommendations; it was only an observation in passing. I have gone into some detail regarding the ethical rules on it because that seemed to be the item, minor though it was, that most exercised you, and I agree that it might be thought to be the ethically most questionable item in the memo. My point is that, if this is acceptable under ethical standards, then *a fortiori,* everything else I said is also acceptable.

Let's run down the list of my recommendations. Surely, buying tax-exempt bonds and creating a trust for a widowed mother are not unethical. Nor can I believe you have any ethical doubts about setting up a one-person corporation to capitalize on retirement and medical deduction opportunities. Since retaining corporate earnings has the sanction of published rulings it must be O.K., if you accept that I have in mind a bona fide and truthful plan to avoid a section 531 penalty tax on eventual accumulations, not some trumped-up baloney.

That leaves only the recommendation to transform income with T-bill manipulations. I agree that this plan is walking close to the technical edge, and it is exploiting a "loophole" by any person's definition of the word. But is that unethical? Again, I turn to the ethical guidelines of our profession, which plainly say that loophole-seeking is not merely permitted but is demanded. The Code of Professional Responsibility warns: "A lawyer shall not intentionally ... [f]ail to seek the lawful objectives of his client through reasonably available means permitted by law." ABA Code of Professional Responsibility, Disciplinary Rule 7–101(A)(1) (footnote omitted). Ethical Consideration 7–8 adds that the lawyer must inform his client of relevant considerations and, in so doing, may "point out those factors which may lead to a decision that is morally just as well as legally permissible," but concludes that "[i]n the final analysis, however," the decision is for the client. ABA Code of Professional Responsibility, Ethical Consideration 7–8. And the client's decisions, "if made within the framework of the law, ... are binding on his lawyer." Id., Ethical Consideration 7–7. The route for the supermoral lawyer whose client chooses to pursue a course of action the lawyer finds unpalatable is to withdraw, id., Ethical Considerations 7–8, 7–9, not to hide the option from the client in the first instance.

These general principles in the Code of Professional Responsibility are confirmed in the more specific tax guidelines. Thus, ABA Formal Opinion 314, supra, the tax practitioner's Sermon on the Mount, advises that a lawyer "may freely urge the statement of positions most favorable to the client just as long as there is *reasonable basis* for those positions" (emphasis added), and he has "no duty to advise that riders be attached ... explaining the circumstances surrounding the transaction." This "reasonable basis" standard is confirmed in the ABA Tax Section's new Guidelines to Tax Practice, supra. These Guidelines elaborate the standard a bit further, however. The lawyer should "counsel against" a plan that is "bound to fail if all of the facts become known to the Service," id. at 554 and he should not participate in any plan unless there "is a *substantial likelihood* that the tax consequences will be resolved in favor of the taxpayer," id. (emphasis added). I fully accept and admire these standards. In every instance, the recommendations I have made are supportable by strong legal arguments that easily satisfy anyone's "reasonable basis" or "substantial likelihood" tests. Nothing I have proposed is "bound to fail." My arguments may be technical and legal, not moral, but the shaping of such arguments has long been at the heart of the lawyer's craft. Remember which of Portia's defenses of Antonio won her case?

You suggest that I base my recommendations in part on the betterment of odds provided by the audit lottery, and that this is wrong. If I advanced proposals that had no basis, solely to gain the advantage of the lottery, you would be right. But once I have a "reasonable basis," would I not be derelict in my professional duty if I failed to make a complete evaluation of the risks, and to base my ultimate judgment on all the factors? This seems to be the view of the latest draft of the new Rules for Professional Conduct, proposed to replace the old Code of Professional Responsibility.

> The right to have legal advice extends to persons who have bad motives and purposes as well as those who have good ones. As advisor, a lawyer is required to give an honest opinion about the actual consequences that appear likely to result from a client's

conduct and not an opinion reflecting what society might wish would be the consequences.

ABA Comm. on Evaluation of Professional Standards, *Discussion Draft, Model Rules of Professional Conduct,* comment to Rule 2.3, at 56 (Jan. 30, 1980).

In view of all this, why do you think me unethical?

Memorandum from Mr. Senior to Mr. Younger, dated March 8, 1980.

Re: Tax Law vs. Tax Ethics

You are quite adept at reading the Code, the Internal Revenue Code that is. But the Code of Professional Responsibility is another matter. Its words are not to be picked apart in an attempt to find an angle to justify desired conduct, and mere technical compliance is not an adequate response to it. At some point you must stop being a tax advisor and become a professional. It is the spirit of the professional canons, not their letter, that is all-important.

I admit you build a strong technical case that you are complying with the Code of Professional Responsibility. That is always easy to do so long as one steers clear of downright prevarication, because the responsibility code unavoidably grapples with the tension between duty to the client and duty to something higher—the law or one's conscience. By picking on the client-oriented side of the dilemma you can justify all manner of law conduct. Canon 7, which you take as your text, says: "A Lawyer Should Represent a Client Zealously Within the Bounds of the Law." Taken literally, that means that anything goes so long as it is not openly illegal. Within those bounds, go for it, and zealously. That, I suppose, is your tax lawyer's reading of Canon 7.

I take a different canon as my text. Canon 9: "A Lawyer Should Avoid Even the Appearance of Professional Impropriety." The Ethical Considerations here tell us that the lawyer should act in a manner that "promotes public confidence in the integrity and efficiency of the legal system," ABA Code of Professional Responsibility, Ethical Consideration 9–2, that he should "act as a member of a learned profession" and "reflect credit" on it. Id., Ethical Consideration 9–6. These lofty principles are difficult to put into precise language or to illustrate with specific examples, but I don't think you can read them as telling you to be as clever as you can in beating the system so as to impress your client. That much is clear.

Another aspect of this that the guidelines discuss but you ignore is the distinction between the standard of behavior when the lawyer is an advocate, having been presented with a set of facts that are a *fait accompli,* and when he or she is an advisor. Indeed, I would subdivide the advisor role into two categories: (1) advice on how best from a tax standpoint to carry out a non-tax-motivated transaction that the client has already determined to pursue, and (2) advice on how to save taxes as an end in itself, without any particular transactional objectives in mind. Category (1) advice is of course much closer to the advocacy situation in the sense that the client's predetermined objective is a *fait* proposed to be *accompli*. This inherently assures that the transaction will not be a sham and that tax avoidance is not the sole end in mind. And it gives the lawyer an externally meaningful set of constraints within which he or she must operate. Still, unlike the lawyer in a pure advocacy situation, the lawyer here will have some freedom to shape and define the transaction and even to kill it if the tax implications are disastrous. This raises the temptation to manipulate factual forms to get better tax results from the same substance, which may or may not be legitimate, but at least there is a real dog to which the tax tail is attached. When we turn to category (2) advice, it is all tax tail, and only the lawyer's wisdom and self-restraint stand between the client and the artful construction of transactions. This last category puts the greatest strain on professional standards, and it is, of course, the situation we have in Ms. Songriter's case.

What standards govern our efforts in such a situation? At one extreme, some laymen might believe that there is no proper role for a lawyer at all. Ms. Songriter should simply report the facts and pay the taxes that fall thereon, and any tax-motivated action to reduce those taxes is unethical. That obviously goes too far as a practical matter in a world as tax-ridden as ours. But at the other extreme is the "whatever we can get away with" standard that permeates your memorandum, and that surely goes too far as well.

The Code of Professional Responsibility offers this guidance as a nonbinding "Ethical Consideration": as advocate a lawyer should resolve all doubts in favor of the client, but as advisor a lawyer should "give his professional opinion as to what the ultimate decisions of the courts would likely be." Id., Ethical Consideration 7–3. You surely are not doing that. But, unfortunately, in its binding Disciplinary Rules, the Code relents. While a lawyer cannot "[c]ounsel or assist" in "conduct [he] *knows* to be illegal," id., Disciplinary Rule 7–102(A)(7) (emphasis added), he is free to choose whether or not to offer his assistance in instances of conduct "he believes to be unlawful, even though there is some support for an argument that the conduct is legal." Id., Disciplinary Rule 7–101(B)(2). I suppose this allows a lawyer broad leeway to fit his actions to his conscience except in those cases where conduct is plainly and irretrievably unlawful. See id., Disciplinary Rule 7–102(A)(2).

. . .

. . . All of your proposals, except maybe that for buying tax-exempt bonds, have a little of the "I've found a way to get more than the law intended to allow" quality about them, but I don't suppose that is inherently repugnant. The T-bill deal, however, surely is. I admit that I am at a loss to give a precise definition of repugnancy, but, as they say of other obscenity, I know a bad tax manipulation when I see it, and smell it. There is no doubt that your T-bill deal is obscene. It corrupts the fabric of the tax system, destroying distinctions between ordinary income and capital gain and eliminating the meaning of the accounting year as a tax determinative period. Moreover, it is purely tax motivated—an activity that Ms. Songriter would never think to engage in but for the tax gimmick involved.

Memorandum from Mr. Younger to Mr. Senior, dated March 10, 1980.

Re: Ethical Standards

I appreciate your concern about my ethical standards, and I am as interested as you in conducting myself appropriately. However, perhaps because I am newer at this than you, I do not fully understand what you are saying.

I have tried to find some guidance in the literature on this subject, and I must say it seems to support the view that there are only two unmistakable evils: misleading the government through overt prevarication, half-truths, or deceptive silence; and the taking of absolutely unfounded positions to play the audit lottery. Certainly, there is no duty on a lawyer to preclude clients from lawful schemes because he or she thinks the schemes are "obscene." Randolph Paul, whom you quoted to me, tells us:

> [T]he tax advisor need not worry about his moral position. It is not his function to improve men's hearts.... [I]t is his positive duty to show the client how to avail himself to the full of what the law permits.... [T]he client is entitled to performance unfettered by his attorney's economic and social predilections.

Paul, The Lawyer as Tax Advisor, 25 Rocky Mtn.L.Rev. 412, 417–18 (1953). The only limits Paul recognizes are disguising the real character of a transaction or making factually false claims. Id., at 420. The lawyer should, he says, "avoid anything suggesting concealment or trickery," but the lawyer rarely need volunteer information. Id. at 429.

Several other commentators specifically address the issue of the "gimmicky scheme," and they conclude that there is no moral or ethical duty to avoid it. Some might try to discourage the scheme as "a matter of personal taste," or because the efficacy of the scheme may be questionable, but no ethical imperative exists. See Panel Discussion: What Is Good Tax Practice, 21 N.Y.U. Inst.Fed. Tax, 23, 36–38 (1963); Darrell, The Tax Practitioner's Duty to His Client and His Government, Prac.Law., March 1961, at 23. Though these articles are old, I see nothing different in more recent comments. Thus Corneel, a current champion of higher ethical standards, condemns manufacturing evidence and using complex formalisms that will work only if the truth is not discovered. But he says it is acceptable to "bolster" a tax avoidance transaction, such as a trust to shift income to a child, by setting it up so as not to call attention to the avoidance objective. Corneel, Ethical Guidelines for Tax Practice, 28 Tax L.Rev. 1, 26–28 (1972).

... The reason commentators do not insist on more moral content in their standards becomes clear, I think, when we examine the objections you raise to my proposals. You give two reasons why the T-bill transaction is "obscene." First, you say it corrupts important concepts in the Code, i.e., the capital gain/ordinary income distinction and the accounting year concept. The T-bill manipulations certainly do play games with those concepts, but what is so bad about that? I learned in law school that the definition of "capital gain" was artificial and essentially irrational since, to put it metaphorically, all trees are simply the present discounted value of their fruits. The only legitimate purpose of the capital gain preference—the mitigation of investor lock-in—is served inefficiently. In reality, the preference serves primarily as a loophole through which those with capital income rather than earned income can avoid their fair share of taxes. If this indictment is true, and I believe it is, what is wrong with helping an earner such as Ms. Songriter strike a blow for equity? The corruption in the Code is the capital gains preference, particularly in its newly sweetened form, which is Congress's misdeed, not my modest attempt to exploit it. Similarly, the Code allows holders of capital assets to laugh at the annual accounting year, by deferring tax on their capital gains until they wish to sell the assets. This deferral right, which we owe to Congress, is the unfairness, and I am simply helping Ms. Songriter use it. Another blow for tax justice, if you will. In other words, tax obscenity, as other kinds, is in the eye of the beholder.

Second, you say that this is "purely tax-motivated" activity, as if that is necessarily evil. For one thing, the accusation is not entirely true since, as I stressed in my original memo, we would have to include important nontax risk. But I accept the accusation that this T-bill activity would not be recommended to Ms. Songriter on its merits as an investment activity; the tax objectives are its *raison d'être*. Is that bad? If so, all advice in your second category falls (advice on how to save taxes, in general, apart from transactional goals). For example, the plans to set up a trust and a one-person corporation are as purely tax motivated as the T-bill deal. They are simply the creation of forms that generate tax saving. Moreover, the one-person corporation has the "corrupting" effect of obliterating the distinction between individual income and corporate income, a distinction as central to the Code as the OI–CG one (and as sensible), and it monkeys with the taxable year through pension plan deferrals.

Do you condemn the trust and corporate recommendations in my memo, too? If not, why not? I am at sea, honestly.

Memorandum from Mr. Senior to Mr. Younger, dated March 12, 1980.

Re: Tax Ethics

You raise a tough question, which I will try to answer. Is there any difference between your trust and corporate recommendations and the T-bill manipulations that should make the former ethically accept-able if the latter is not?

I see several significant differences. [This discussion is omitted].

In short, the T-bill manipulation is the quintessential smart aleck's tax gimmick, and no slick arguments can make it into anything else. I would like to think that when anything combines all the negative features this gimmick does, it is unethical for a tax lawyer to promote it.

Unfortunately, when I look to the literature on ethics I have some difficulty finding specific support for my position. There are three ethical principles involved, those regarding factual disclosure, legal disclosure, and advice to clients. First, one must meet a fairly high standard in disclosing facts: as I read the collected wisdom, your proposal of smokescreen-motivated futures dealing violates the ethical injunction against "anything suggesting concealment or trickery," Paul, The Lawyer as Tax Advisor, supra p. 1583, at 429; Graves, Responsibility of the Tax Adviser, 114 J. Acc'y 33 (1962); cf. Discussion Draft, Model Rules of Professional Conduct, . . ., Rule 2.3(a), but I admit the question is muddied by the facts that there is no clear illegality and that these will be real transactions with real risk.

Second, one must meet a somewhat lower standard in disclosing law: the sages disagree about the ethical duty to disclose a questionable legal position. Even when you are acting contrary to a ruling, the consensus seems to be that the duty depends on how strong you think your position is. Some would disclose whenever a ruling was being ignored, Panel Discussion: What is Good Tax Practice, . . . supra at 31; others would do so whenever the lawyer "does not in good faith believe that he has the better of the argument," Panel Discussion on "Question-able Positions," 32 Tax Law. 13, 27–28 (1978); but others believe there is no duty to disclose so long as the taxpayer has a "reasonably tenable" position, Johnson, Does the Tax Practitioner Owe a Dual Responsibility to his Client and to the Government?—The Theory, 15 S.Cal.Tax Inst. 25, 31–32 (1963); and some, as you suggest, see the issue as essentially pragmatic rather than ethical, with the duty to disclose turning on the risk of a fraud accusation, Corneel, Ethical Guidelines for Tax Practice, . . . supra, at 10. Probably, Professor Bittker's standard on the general question of disclosure is the operative one for the average conscientious lawyer: "[I]f the practitioner honestly believes the question *can be* properly resolved in the taxpayer's favor (or has no reason to believe that it cannot be so resolved)," he has no duty of disclosure beyond honest factual reporting, B. Bittker, Professional Responsibility in Federal Tax Practice 270 (1970) (emphasis added). Since you seem to believe, honestly, that your T-bill deal can work, you are off the hook, at least so long as no ruling is being violated. Where there is a ruling on point, I would argue under the proposed Rules of Professional Conduct that this is "law" on the question sufficient to demand openness and disclosure if a challenge is to be made, but I admit that the existing rules are weaker in this regard.

Third, and to my mind more important than these disclosure questions, is the substantive duty to act properly in advising the client, especially when structuring transactions and taking positions that may be undisclosed. But unfortunately, this substantive duty, as an obligation apart from disclosure standards, seems minimal. One cannot structure a transaction deceitfully so as to obscure the factual disclosure he or she does make (but one can "bolster" transactions, as you have noted earlier), and one must have a "reasonable basis" for any legal position taken, but that is the end of the imperatives, and "duty to client" occupies the rest of the obligatory terrain. One can find moral support for a more moral standard, but not commitment to this standard as a workable ethical demand. The commentators lament how abusive transactions lead to remedial legislation, which leaves everyone worse off, see, e.g., Young, Does the Tax Practitioner Owe a Dual Responsibility to his Client and to the Government?—The Practice, 15 S.Cal.Tax Inst. 39, 48 (1963), and, as you indicate, they express their distaste for gimmicky schemes. But they are unwilling to do more than scold those who support and engage in them.

Therefore, if we are talking about "ethics" in the sense of what will get you disbarred, you are probably right, at least under current standards. The T-bill deal may be a new layer of scum on the already polluted waters of tax law, but there is no ethical prohibition against the tax lawyer who wants to put it there. There is, in other words, no enforceable obligation on the tax bar to serve as a protector of the tax environment. However, if the precepts of Canon 9 (avoid even "appearance of impropriety") are to mean anything at all, we must have some self-imposed obligations in this regard. Each of us must necessarily define the scope of those self-imposed obligations for himself, and for me the T-bill deal goes too far. We have to practice law in the world as it is, and if my clients need to swim in already polluted waters I will help them; but I draw the line at adding to the pollution, even if it is technically legal and ethical. Not only does this pollution contribute to unfairness in tax burdens, it is the direct cause of the endless "reforms" that have made our tax code so top-heavy with complexity that it may soon collapse. I cannot, consistent with Canon 9 and my conscience, add to it.

Is this attitude inconsistent with the interests of my clients? I think not. As Darrell has so wisely put it, clients usually are "honest innocents" when it comes to tax manipulations, and the tax advisor "bears a heavy responsibility here, for his standards may become the guiding standards for his client." Darrell, The Tax Practitioner's Duty to his Client and his Government, . . . supra, at 25. It is facile to say that decisions in a technical field such as this are made by the client, when so much depends on how we present the options and what we, as experts, recommend. We have great power to encourage or to discourage transactions, and I read Canon 9 as imploring us to discourage actions that undermine the basic structure of the tax law. There is a great temptation to tout clever dodges, because it makes us look smart, but we serve the law, ourselves, and even our clients better if we accentuate the negative in such deals.

We serve our clients better in this fashion for pragmatic as well as moral reasons. I quote Darrell again:

Cleverness is not competence. The too-clever, overly-enthusiastic tax planner is likely to be either a limited or irresponsible man.

... The difference between the lawyer who encourages grasping at trick loophole opportunities and one who says "Go slow, look ahead," is the difference between the lawyer who wants to keep his client always and the one-shot, in and out, hit and run, advisor.

Responsibilities of the Lawyer in Tax Practice, in B. Bittker, ... supra, at 100–01.

Let's take a harder look at the negative aspects of the T-bill marvel. [Senior's analysis of the financial costs and risks is omitted]

Moreover, in assessing downside risk you have not allowed for the worst possibility—that the IRS will succeed with an extreme attack under § 165 and deny *all* loss deductions on the loss legs while taxing Ms. Songriter on all income from gain legs of her straddles. This is admittedly an outside possibility, but it is a horrendous prospect and not unprecedented. See Knetsch v. United States, 364 U.S. 361, 365 n. 2 (1960); Goldstein v. Commissioner, 364 F.2d 734 (2d Cir.1966).

In other words, this deal, like most other highly touted tax gimmicks, looks good through the rose-colored glasses of a concupiscent tax avoider, but rather bleak through the microscope of a disdainful moralist such as I.

Even your proposal for a corporate retirement plan does not look so good when put under this microscope.... [The discussion of this question is omitted.]

...

I have set up a meeting with Greenshade and Songriter for next Wednesday at 2:00 p.m. I would like you to join us, but you should be forewarned that, while I may mention the T-bill possibility to them so that they are aware we are covering all the bases, I will accentuate the negative. I cannot believe they will be interested in pursuing it. I also plan to be frank about the way I see the other possibilities.

Memorandum from Mr. Younger to Mr. Senior, dated March 14, 1980.

Re: Loopholes for Sally Songriter

I admire the power of your "negative" analysis of the T-bill deal [omitted above], but I think you are unduly pessimistic. For one thing, the Service is neither as astute nor as fast-moving as you suggest. It took them years to get onto the ploy of using straddles to defer capital gain from year to year and turn short gain into long.... They finally attacked it with the 1977 ruling I cited, but I have yet to see a completed prosecution under the ruling, and as I noted, it is doubtful that the ruling will stand up when the case gets to court. The wheels of tax justice grind exceedingly slow as well as not very fine, and any good gimmick has many years before it is knocked out. This is a good one, I think. Maybe I did overstate the benefits a little in my initial enthusiasm, but you still do not convince me that the cost/benefit ratio looks bad. Even with your more conservative projections, there still are tax dollars to be made. Moreover, some of your estimates exaggerate the difficulties. Regarding the "horrendous" possibility that all straddle losses could be denied while all gains are taxed, I think that is off the wall, particularly if we structure our transactions well. See § 183. Note that the IRS has not even tried this extreme argument in its rulings attacking straddle manipulations. Even if we do get challenged by the Service, a possibility you think far more likely than I, Ms. Songriter need not get stuck with big legal fees. More likely there will be others challenged at the same time or earlier, and we can ride on their precedents. In any event, there is ample time, if she is challenged, for Ms. Songriter to decide how much she wants to spend on a fight. She can always throw in the towel with little if any loss.

A fortiori for the rest of my proposals.

Nonetheless, you are the boss. I have marked the Wednesday meeting on my calendar. I promise to be discreet with my personal views.

Letter from Frank Greenshade, C.P.A., to Emanuel Senior, Esq., dated April 16, 1980.

Dear Manny:

I have finally heard from Sally Songriter and gotten her reaction to the meeting we had last month. I am sorry to say she has decided not to pursue the recommendations of your firm.

I am not sure what she is going to do, but to tell the truth, I think she has taken her business to that young man at the meeting who had all those clever ideas. Ms. Songriter said she liked his positive attitude toward her problems.

I gather that this fellow is no longer with your firm. Did he have a gleam in his eye as he rode out of sight?

/s/ Frank Greenshade, C.P.A.

Letter from Emanuel Senior, Esq., to Lawrence Lawyer, Esq., dated April 21, 1980.

Dear Larry:

Enclosed, following up on our telephone conversation, are copies of the intrafirm memoranda in the case I mentioned (with identifying data of course eliminated), which I am sending to you in your capacity as chairman of the Subcommittee on Practice Standards of the bar association Section on Taxation.

As I said, I am bringing this matter to your attention because it illustrates the inadequacies of the ethical standards of our profession in situations such as this. I do not quarrel with Mr. Younger having won the client but rather with the fact that he was able to do so through promotion of schemes that, to my mind, go beyond propriety. I think it would be worthwhile if your committee reviewed ethical standards with cases such as this in mind, to see if some improvement in the situation can be brought about.

/s/ Emanuel Senior, Esq.

Letter from Lawrence Lawyer, Esq., to Emanuel Senior, Esq., dated May 1, 1980.

Dear Manny:

I have now had a chance to review the materials you sent me and have discussed them with members of our Subcommittee on Practice Standards.

The problem you raise is indeed a serious one. As you may recall, a few years ago the section of taxation of the New York State Bar Association sponsored a study of overly complex tax laws, which concluded that such laws create a "Gresham's Law" of tax practice. Bad lawyers drive out good, because the bad lawyers blithely recommend schemes of doubtful legality, and thereby attract clients, while the good lawyers, who naturally have more doubts about schemes, appear to be less fruitful on behalf of their clients. The situation you present seems to be a typical example of this phenomenon.

We have been discussing the idea of upgrading ethical standards to curb such lawyers. This is a matter very current in our thinking because the Treasury Department has been threatening to do something about attorneys who participate in what the General Counsel calls "transaction[s] without any economic purpose other than the generation of tax benefits." However, it is much easier to state this problem than it is to devise a solution.

No responsible tax attorney today goes into transactions that have no economic purpose. Such a transaction would run afoul of the principles set out in *Goldstein v. Commissioner* and *Arnold L. Ginsburg* and would therefore not be effective in accomplishing the tax objectives sought unless one were simply playing the audit lottery, which I think we agree, would be unethical. The *Guidelines to Tax Practice* recently prepared by the Committee on Standards of Tax Practice of the ABA Tax Section, and published in 31 Tax Law. 551 (1978), state that a lawyer is not to participate in transactions "entirely lacking in economic substance," id. at 554.

The real problem, and one that we have difficulty handling under ethical standards, arises in cases where there is economic purpose to a transaction but it nonetheless seems motivated by tax avoidance objectives rather than the economic purpose. The case you sent me falls in this category. The courts have been struggling with this issue for some time, in cases from *Knetsch v. United States* to *Frank Lyon Co. v. United States,* and have not been able to come up with a satisfactory judicial articulation of the line between right and wrong. Until they do so, I do not see how we can or even should (if we could) promulgate an ethical standard that might proscribe participation in a tax avoidance scheme as unethical, when the courts might declare the same scheme to be perfectly proper and effective. Remember that some pretty scurrilous schemes, ... have been sustained.

That does not mean that there are no ethical standards to constrain some of the activities in the case under discussion. It seems to me that the lawyer's professional and fiduciary duty to his or her client requires the lawyer to be not merely open and honest, but fully cautious, in bringing a client into a transaction such as the T-bill deal because of its obviously speculative nature as a tax avoidance device. If the client wants it, the lawyer can set it up. But when he entices an unsuspecting client into it, particularly an unsophisticated client who might not fully appreciate the risks involved even after they have been explained, I think the lawyer could and should be vulnerable to professional sanctions and a malpractice complaint. I, myself, would see it as my duty to warn clients off a scheme such as this, not entice them into it. I would think that the client here might have a well-founded complaint against your young ex-colleague if he actively sells this deal and it is later knocked out on audit. My judgment in this regard is supported by the Guidelines to Tax Practice mentioned earlier. These guidelines call for the lawyer to "counsel against borderline plans," id. at 554.

Moreover, as you have noted, the new Rules of Professional Conduct, in draft, support an argument that openness and disclosure are required whenever a lawyer is challenging IRS interpretations of the Code. We will have to look into the implications of that. You may have heard that the City Bar is critical of the proposed rules for their excessive disclosure requirements.

I think this is as far as we can go with ethical standards at this time.

I hope this has been helpful to you.

/s/ Lawrence Lawyer, Esq.

Letter from Emanuel Senior, Esq., to Lawrence Lawyer, Esq., dated May 5, 1980.

Dear Larry:

Thank you for your letter of May 1, 1980. It seems to me that the ethical principles you quoted from the *Guidelines to Tax Practice* are useful and might have significant impact on the problem I presented, although they are only a modest step and in no sense a complete solution. Unfortunately, these guidelines do not have any binding effect. They are merely exhortations. The binding canons in the Code of Professional Responsibility say nothing whatsoever along these lines and the new Rules of Professional Conduct, now under development, are no improvement except in the one respect you indicate.

You suggest, for example, that my ex-client might have a well-founded complaint against the lawyer if he has "sold" her on a borderline transaction that turns out to be a loser. Maybe so, in a particularly egregious case. But until the bar is willing to take a firm stand and prohibit such promotionism with more than exhortatory guidelines, I do not think that clients have much hope. My doubts on this score are reinforced by the statement in these same *ethical* guidelines that "borderline" transactions can be "justifiable on the basis that the client has much to gain and little to lose," Committee on Standards of Tax Practice, ABA Tax Section, Guidelines to Tax Practice, 31 Tax Law. 551, 554 (1978). When push comes to shove, ethics become nothing but pragmatism.

If you believe in the higher principles set out in your guidelines, why don't you do something about getting teeth put into them? The new Rules of Professional Conduct would be a good place to start. For example, although I have argued that the rule requiring disclosure of possible "illegality" can be read to cover action in violation of a revenue ruling, I have my doubts that such an interpretation will prevail. I suspect that only traditional civil disobedience will be considered within the ambit of this provision. Even in the case of knowing violations of revenue rulings it is likely to be argued successfully that rulings, which are not subject to formal "rulemaking" procedures and are not part of the "legislative" promulgations of the Service or the Treasury, do not invoke any disclosure requirement. Why not modify the proposed rules at least to require disclosure sufficient to advise the agency when any officially promulgated position of a government agency is knowingly violated? Is there some interest in encouraging covert violation? Without this additional requirement, the rule does not really add much to existing standards, and they have not accomplished much.

Another example. You note that the Guidelines call for counseling against borderline transactions. The draft rules also require that a lawyer maintain "adequate communication" with his or her client. Discussion Draft, Model Rules of Professional Conduct, . . ., Rule 1.4. Why not elaborate Rule 1.4 to demand that, in situations where the lawyer has reason to believe that a proposed transaction is likely to be found improper he or she be *required* to plainly and explicitly advise the client of that fact? I would hope that this requirement is implicit in the Rule, but why not make it explicit so that shady promoters know just where they stand and aggrieved clients have a stronger handle for action?[8] ...

Note on Cooper's tale: The wellsprings of adversariness

1. *Counseling as less adversarial lawyering.* Although it is often said that counseling is a less adversarial context than advocacy—especially in litigation but also in negotiation—it should be clear that the *ex parte* nature of the counseling setting has the potential for giving it an even less restrained adversariness. For, if what keeps adversariness within tolerable boundaries is the presence of an equally zealous advocate on the other side, it is expectable, is it not, that where there is no "other side" yet concretely present, the adversarial mindset, honed and legitimated in the litigation and negotiation contexts, will dominate the field.

The Code took virtually no account of this problem, or of the significance of the differing attorney roles. Compare EC 7–4, permitting "the advocate" to take nonfrivolous positions not likely to prevail, with EC 7–5, suggesting that "the advisor" should express his or her belief as to what "the ultimate decision" would be, but is free thereafter to continue to represent a client not following that advice so long as he or she does not take an illegal or frivolous position. And consider the narrowness of the catalogue of forbidden acts in DR 7–102(A). Senior concedes that the Code gives, at best, only nonbinding support for his belief that there is less scope for adversariness in counseling than in advocacy.

The Model Rules contain a separate title on the attorney as counselor. An Introduction to Rule 2.1 in the 1980 Discussion Draft contained these hortatory thoughts:

> In giving advice, a lawyer should consider not only the literal terms of the law but also its purposes and changing course. A lawyer should also take into account equitable and ethical considerations and problems of cost and feasibility.

This language was dropped, and MR 2.1 says the following:

> In rendering advice, a lawyer may refer not only to law but to other considerations such as moral, economic, social and political factors, that may be relevant to the client's situation.

Do the Rules give more, or less, support to Senior's view than the Code?

2. Senior and Younger each see themselves as ethical practitioners, but have radically differing notions of what it means to be an ethical practitioner. Be sure, first, that you articulate as clearly as you can what each lawyer sees as the requisites of professionally responsible behavior and what limits exist or should exist on "aggressive tax planning." In doing so, take care not to oversimplify each lawyer's position: Younger

---

8. Subsequent to Mr. Senior's letter, the Treasury published new proposed regulations designed to force such plain disclosure in "tax shelter opinions" written for use in offerings to persons who are not clients of the attorney writing the opinion. See 45 Fed.Reg. 58,594 (Sept. 4, 1980) (proposed changes in 31 C.F.R. § 10). Under proposed regulation § 10.33(c)(3), however, these rules would have no application to opinions given one's own clients. See generally Sax, Lawyer Responsibility in Tax Shelter Opinions, 34 Tax Law. 5 (1980).

does not assert that anything goes, and Senior does not contend that his role as counsel is to assist only those outcomes that he would regard as consistent with sound tax policy.

3. *Self-imposed obligations and the professional codes.* It is clear, is it not, that Senior's and Younger's disagreement is not primarily accounted for by their differing readings of the language of the Model Code. (The article predates the promulgation of the Model Rules). "Mere technical compliance," Senior insists, "is not an adequate response" to the language of the Code; he acknowledges that, "taken literally, [the words] mean that anything goes as long as it is not openly illegal." To Younger, that his actions are not illegal is the end of the problem; even openness is required only in cases of civil disobedience, and he is "not challenging the law but rather accepting it and exploiting it." The notion of "technical" compliance, to him, is a redundancy, solely an epithet, and existing only "in the eye of the beholder." In replying, Senior is forced to acknowledge his "difficulty finding specific support for [his] position"; the "existing rules are weaker" than he would like, and the commentators are "unwilling to do more than scold."

Senior relies strongly on Canon 9, *A lawyer should avoid even the appearance of impropriety.** It can certainly be read to say that merely following the rules is not necessarily enough. However, there is no Disciplinary Rule saying that; compare the very specific, and narrow, subject matter of the Disciplinary Rules accompanying Canon 9, DR 9–101 and –102. To Younger, as we have seen, that is the end of the matter. If there is no rule forbidding particular conduct, abjuring it may not be insisted on. (Indeed, abjuring it is itself unethical as inconsistent with the rule of zealous representation).

Senior disagrees, and finds in the nonbinding guidance of Canon 9 support for a principle that authorizes him to bind his actions by his own conscience. Further, he finds in that authorization a requirement that he exercise that authority according to his conscience. The fact that professional codes embody a narrower conception of a "requirement" is without significance. Indeed, there would be something of a contradiction in the concept of "self-imposed" restraint that is required by rule, in saying that a rule requires a lawyer to do more than follow the rules.

4. Consider Senior's and Younger's differing attitudes toward the substantive law with which they are dealing, the Internal Revenue Code:

Younger is savagely scornful of the rationality and integrity of the tax law: The exemption of municipal bonds is a "nice windfall"; the use of trusts is a "little government-funded welfare program" to help support the mother of a taxpayer earning $200,000 in a year; it is readily manipulable by a "friendly and compliant trustee," and can be structured in a way that is "clever enough [to] keep a trust up-to-date with Ms. Songriter's romantic inclinations"; retirement planning should take full account of the "estate planning bonanza available" in

---

* The Code followed the practice of preceding each set of Ethical Considerations and Disciplinary Rules with a single sentence, expressed in the hortatory style of the 1908 Canons of Ethics. The Model Rules have no analogue to Canon 9.

the law; the Internal Revenue Service is "striking" in its gullible acceptance of the conclusiveness, notwithstanding the economic realities, of language in paper drafted by taxpayer counsel; legislative efforts to require the inclusion of employees in tax-favored pension plans leave plenty of opportunities to "shortchange" the client's secretary should she be inclined to do so. In sum, the Code is "artificial," "irrational," and "corrupt," and its administration is neither "fast-moving" nor "astute"; "any good gimmick has many years before it is knocked out." Younger is simply helping the firm's client to "strike a blow for equity," the equity of a fair chance to feed at the trough.

Senior, though representing private interests seeking to reduce their taxes, espouses "at least a measure of allegiance to the fisc," a usage that suggests some perception of public good served by the tax law. Adding "a new layer of complexity" to the tax law, or enhancing the ability of "the rich" to manipulate the law, are consequences that he feels responsible to keep in check; "abusive transactions ... leave[ ] everyone worse off." He struggles to find some basis, notwithstanding his acknowledgement that the Code is shot through with tax preferences, for continuing to find integrity in its overall scheme; surely, he asserts, either Congress or the Service will quickly rule the T-bill scheme illegal. In this regime, his "self-imposed obligations" move him to see himself as in part "a protector of the tax environment," and while he will aid his clients "to swim in already polluted waters," he will not add to the pollution.

(a) To what extent do these differences underlie their differences about a tax lawyer's responsibilities?

(b) To the extent that there is a correlation, in which direction is the causal connection? Do one's political views about the Internal Revenue Code and the public good help account for one's views of his or her professional responsibility, or is it the other way round? Compare Section 5(b) of the Note on Valdez v. Alloway's Garage, p. 126 above.

(c) To what extent do Younger's views simply reflect the fact that his practice is the representation of taxpayers seeking to reduce their taxes as much as possible? Senior is a former tax lawyer, now more of a generalist; to some, the moral of Cooper's tale may be that a tax lawyer—especially a junior one seeking to build a practice—*must* take on, or at least act as if he or she has taken on, Younger's world-view. For a thorough, informative, and thought-provoking examination of the validity and reality of the professional ideal that Senior manifests, see Robert Gordon, The Independence of Lawyers, 68 B.U.L.Rev. 1 (1988).

5. Consider the difference in their views of the Internal Revenue Code against the framework of the "celebratory" and "troubled" stances discussed earlier in this book.

(a) Senior fits fairly easily as a "celebrator" of the social value of both the tax law and the private practice of law. It leads him to limit his client-regarding actions and outlook, out of regard for the overlapping factors of the public interest and his sense of himself as a professional.

• To what extent do you regard this stance as justified?

• To what extent do you regard it as one that you would hope to take yourself?

• Is your answer to this last question related in substantial part to your view about the social utility of tax-minimization planning on behalf of wealthy people? In connection with this question, compare Chief Justice Burger's not wholly dissimilar stance in *Jones v. Barnes,* p. 12, above, and Professor Subin's in the article excerpted p. 160, above. Recall your reaction to their positions: Is it related to your views about criminal procedure?

(b) Younger, though certainly not a celebrator of the integrity of the tax law, can scarcely be called "troubled." He draws no discomfort from his Hobbesian vision of the tax law and tax practice. Indeed, it is clear, is it not, that it serves to legitimate, rather than explain or cause, his own and his client's acquisitive inclinations: If tax practice (law practice?) (life?) is simply a scramble for a place at the trough, let's get on with it! Perhaps it is the scramble itself that he celebrates.

(c) What would be the stance of one who shared Senior's *aspirations* for the tax law and for tax practice, but who regarded his perception of them as seriously self-deluded; and saw Younger's *description* of the reality as far more accurate than Senior's, but in no way shared the former's glee at that result?

6. *The perception and construction of reality.* In connection with the last question, consider the following suggestion:

(a) Is the "reality" about which Senior and Younger differ only a datum "out there," simply to be observed, or is there a significant way in which Younger's view is self-fulfilling, in which he is *creating* as well as *observing* the world in which he practices law? What are the bases of this suggestion?

(b) If the suggestion has validity, is it true with respect to Senior as well?

(c) What are the implications of the suggestion for your own preferred stance?

THE ADVERSARY SYSTEM EXCUSE
David Luban
in Luban, ed., *The Good Lawyer* 83–118 (1983)

. . .

Holding forth at table in 1831, Samuel Taylor Coleridge turned to the behavior of lawyers. "There is undoubtedly a limit to the exertions of an advocate for his client," he said, for "the advocate has no right, nor is it his duty, to do that for his client which his client *in foro conscientiae* has no right to do for himself." Thirteen years later, William Whewell elaborated the same point:

[E]very man is, in an unofficial sense, by being a moral agent, a Judge of right and wrong, and an Advocate of what is right....

This general character of a moral agent, he cannot put off, by putting on any professional character.... If he mixes up his character as an Advocate, with his character as a Moral Agent ... he acts immorally. He makes the Moral Rule subordinate to the Professional Rule. He sells to his Client, not only his skill and learning, but himself. He makes it the Supreme Object of his life to be, not a good man, but a successful Lawyer.

Whewell's position is not commonly acknowledged to be valid. George Sharswood, whose 1854 *Legal Ethics* is the great-grandparent of the current ABA Code of Professional Responsibility, wrote: "The lawyer, who refuses his professional assistance because in his judgment the case is unjust and indefensible, usurps the functions of both judge and jury." A lawyer is not to judge the morality of the client's cause; it is irrelevant to the morality of the representation. That, I think, is the official view of most lawyers: the lawyer's morality is distinct from, and not implicated in, the client's.

. . .

[A] more general issue is lurking here, the issue of what I shall call *institutional excuses*. We can state the main question in full generality in this way: can a person appeal to a social institution in which he or she occupies a role in order to excuse conduct that would be morally culpable were anyone else to do it? Plausibly, examples exist in which the answer is yes: we do not call it murder when a soldier kills a sleeping enemy, although it is surely immoral for you or me to do it. There are also cases where the answer is no, as in the job "concentration camp commandant" or "professional strikebreaker." Here, we feel, the immorality of the job is so great that it accuses, not excuses, the person who holds it.

This suggests that an important feature of a successful institutional excuse is that the institution is itself justified. I think that is partly right, but I do not think it is the whole story: I shall argue that the *kind* of justification that can be offered of the institution is germane to the success of the excuses it provides.

[I]t is not just the spectacular examples that are the problem—they only dramatize it. I dare say that all litigators have had cases where, in their heart of hearts, they wanted their client to lose or wished that a distasteful action did not need to be performed. The problem is that (recollecting Brougham's words) "to save that client ... [the lawyer] must not regard the alarm, the torments, the destruction which he may bring upon others." On the face of it, this is as terse a characterization as one could hope to find of amorality; it is reminiscent of Nietzsche's description of the old Teutonic code: "To practice loyalty and, for the sake of loyalty, to risk honor and blood even for evil and dangerous things."

The way it is currently phrased, in the ABA's Code of Professional Responsibility, is this:

> The duty of a lawyer, both to his client and to the legal system, is
> to represent his client zealously within the bounds of the law....
> In our government of laws and not of men, each member of our
> society is entitled ... to seek any lawful objective through legally
> permissible means; and to present for adjudication any lawful
> claim, issue, or defense.

It sounds nicer than [Nietzche's] Zarathustra or Brougham, but in fact
there is no difference: the zealous advocate is supposed to press the
client's interests to the limit of the legal, regardless of the "torments or
destruction" this wreaks on others.

Nor does the phrase "within the bounds of the law" mitigate this.
For the law is inherently double-edged: any rule imposed to limit
zealous advocacy (or any other form of conduct, for that matter) may be
used by an adversary as an offensive weapon. In the words of former
Judge Marvin E. Frankel, "the object always is to beat every plowshare
into a sword." The rules of discovery, for example, initiated to enable
one side to find out crucial facts from the other, are used nowadays to
delay trial or impose added expense on the other side; conversely, one
might respond to an interrogatory by delivering to the discoverer
several tons of miscellaneous documents, to run up their legal bills or
conceal a needle in a haystack.

To take another example: rules barring lawyers from representations involving conflicts of interest are now regularly used by adversaries to drive up the other side's legal costs by having their counsel
disqualified. The general problem of double-edgedness is described by
the novelist Yasunari Kawabata:

> When a law is made, the cunning that finds loopholes goes to work.
> We cannot deny that there is a certain slyness ..., a slyness which,
> when rules are written to prevent slyness, makes use of the rules
> themselves.

It is not just the rules governing lawyer conduct that are double-
edged—double-edgedness is an essential feature of any law because any
restraint imposed on human behavior in the name of just social policy
may be used to restrain behavior when circumstances make this an
unjust outcome. This is the unbridgeable gap between formal and
substantive justice. David Mellinkoff gives these examples:

> The law intended to stop sharpers from claiming money that is
> not owed (the Statute of Frauds) may sometimes defeat a just debt,
> because the claim was not in writing.
>
> The law intended to stop a man from holding off suit until
> defense becomes impossible—memories grown dim, witnesses dead
> or missing—(the Statute of Limitations) may sometimes defeat a
> just suit, because it was not filed fast enough.
>
> The law intended to prevent designing grown-ups from impos-
> ing on children (the defense of infancy) may defeat a just claim,
> because the man who signed the contract was 20 instead of 21.

The law intended to give a man, for all his misfortunes, a new start in life (the bankruptcy laws) may defeat a widow's just claim for the money she needs to live on.

The double-edgedness of law underlines the moral problem involved in representing a client "zealously within the bounds of the law." If on the one hand this means forwarding legal claims that are morally dubious, as in Mellinkoff's examples, on the other, it means pushing claims to the limit of the law and then a bit further, into the realm of what is "colorably" the limit of the law. "Zeal" means zeal at the margin of the legal, and thus well past the margin of whatever moral and political insight constitutes the "spirit" of the law in question. The limits of the law inevitably lie beyond moral limits, and zealous advocacy always means zeal at the margin.

It is at this point that the adversary system looms large, for it provides the institutional excuse for the duty of zealous advocacy. Each side of an adversary proceeding is represented by a lawyer whose sole obligation is to present that side as forcefully as possible; anything less, it is claimed, would subvert the operation of the system. The ABA code states the matter quite clearly: "The duty of a lawyer to his client and his duty to the legal system are the same: to represent his client zealously within the bounds of the law."

Everything rides on this argument. Lawyers have to assert legal interests unsupported by moral rights all the time; asserting legal interests is what they do, and everyone can't be in the right on all issues. Unless zealous advocacy could be justified by relating it to some larger social good, the lawyer's role would be morally impossible. That larger social good, we are told, is justice, and the adversary system is supposed to be the best way of attaining it.

... There are two sorts of arguments: those claiming that the adversary system is the best way of accomplishing various goals (consequentialist arguments), and those claiming that it is intrinsically good (nonconsequentialist arguments). To begin, we shall look at three versions of the former: (1) that the adversary system is the best way of ferreting out truth, (2) that it is the best way of defending people's legal rights, and (3) that by establishing checks and balances it is the best way of safeguarding against excesses....

The question whether the adversary system is, all in all, the best way of uncovering the facts of a case at bar sounds like an empirical question. I happen to think that it is—an empirical question, moreover, that has scarcely been investigated, and that is most likely impossible to answer. This last is because one does not, after a trial is over, find the parties coming forth to make a clean breast of it and enlighten the world as to what *really* happened. A trial is not a quiz show with the right answer waiting in a sealed envelope. We can't learn directly whether the facts are really as the trier determined them because we don't ever find out the facts.

. . .

Given all this, it is unsurprising to discover that the arguments purporting to show the advantages of the adversary system as a fact-finder have mostly been nonempirical, a mix of a priori theories of inquiry and armchair psychology.

Here is one, based on the idea, very similar to Sir Karl Popper's theory of scientific rationality, that the way to get at the truth is a wholehearted dialectic of assertion and refutation. If each side attempts to prove its case, with the other trying as energetically as possible to assault the steps of the proof, it is more likely that all of the aspects of the situation will be presented to the fact-finder than if it attempts to investigate for itself with the help of the lawyers.

This theory is open to a number of objections. First of all, the analogy to Popperian scientific methodology is not a good one. Perhaps science proceeds by advancing conjectures and then trying to refute them, but it does not proceed by advancing conjectures that the scientist knows to be false and then using procedural rules to exclude probative evidence.

The two adversary attorneys, moreover, are each under an obligation to present the facts in the manner most consistent with their client's position—to prevent the introduction of unfavorable evidence, to undermine the credibility of opposing witnesses, to set unfavorable facts in a context in which their importance is minimized, to attempt to provoke inferences in their client's favor. The assumption is that two such accounts will cancel out, leaving the truth of the matter. But there is no earthly reason to think this is so; they may simply pile up the confusion.

This is particularly likely in those frequent cases when the facts in question concern someone's character or state of mind. Out comes the parade of psychiatrists, what Hannah Arendt once called "the comedy of the soul-experts." Needless to say, they have been prepared by the lawyers, sometimes without knowing it. A clinical law teacher explained to a class that when you first contact a psychiatrist and sketch the facts of the case, you mention only the favorable ones. That way, he or she has an initial bias in your favor and tends to discount the unfavorable facts when you finally get around to mentioning them.

The other side, of course, can cross-examine such a witness to get the truth out. Irving Younger, perhaps the most popular lecturer on trial tactics in the country, tells how. Among his famous "Ten Commandments of Cross–Examination" are these:

- Never ask anything but a leading question.
- Never ask a question to which you don't already know the answer.
- Never permit the witness to explain his or her answers.
- Don't bring out your conclusions in the cross-examination. Save them for closing arguments when the witness is in no position to refute them.

Of course, the opposition may be prepared for this; they may have seen Younger's three-hour, $425 videotape on how to examine expert witnesses. They may know, therefore, that the cross-examiner is saving his or her conclusions for the closing argument. Not to worry! Younger knows how to stop an attorney from distorting the truth in closing arguments. "If the opposing lawyer is holding the jury spellbound ... the spell must be broken at all cost[s]. [Younger] suggests the attorney leap to his or her feet and make furious and spurious objections. They will be overruled, but they might at least break the opposing counsel's concentration."

My guess is that this is not quite what Sir Karl Popper had in mind when he wrote, "The Western rationalist tradition ... is the tradition of critical discussion—of examining and testing propositions or theories by attempting to refute them."

A skeptic, in fact, might try this scientific analogy: a beam of invisible electrically charged particles—charge and origin unknown—travels through a distorting magnetic field of unknown strength, then through an opposite field of unknown, but probably different, strength. The beam strikes a detector of undeterminable reliability, from which we are supposed to infer the nature and location of the beam's source. That is the adversary system at its worst.

. . .

[One] premise [is] the idea that truth is served by self-interested rather than disinterested investigation. "The lawyer appearing as an advocate before a tribunal presents, as persuasively as he can, the facts and the law of the case *as seen from the standpoint of his client's interest*" [emphasis added]. The emphasized phrase is accurate, but it gives the game away. For there is all the difference in the world between "the facts seen from X's standpoint" and "the facts seen from the standpoint of X's interest." Of course it is important to hear the former—the more perspectives we have, the better informed our judgment. But to hear the latter is not helpful at all. It is in the murderer's *interest* not to have been at the scene of the crime; consequently, the "facts of the case as seen from the standpoint of [the] client's interest" are that the client was elsewhere that weekend. From the standpoint of my *interest,* the world is my cupcake with a cherry on top; from the standpoint of yours, its streets are paved with gold. Combining the two does not change folly to truth.

All this does not mean that the adversary system may not in fact get at the truth in many hard cases. (Trial lawyers' war stories are mixed.) I suppose that it is as good as its rivals. But, to repeat the point I began with, nobody knows how good that is.

It is sometimes said, however, that the point of the adversary system is *not* that it is the best way of getting at the truth, but rather the best way of defending individuals' legal rights. It is, in the words of the current attorney general of Maryland, "a celebration of other values" than truth. Freedman points out that if the sole purpose of a trial were to get at the truth we would not have our Fourth, Fifth, and Sixth Amendment rights; that improperly obtained evidence cannot be used against us and that we cannot be required to testify against ourselves indicate that our society considers other values more central than truth. And, according to the theory we shall now consider, these other values have to do with legal rights.

The argument is that the best way to guarantee that an individual's legal rights are protected is to provide him or her with a zealous adversary advocate who will further the client's interest.

. . .

. . . The no-holds-barred zealous advocate tries to get everything the law can give (if that is the client's wish) and thereby does a better job of defending the client's legal rights than a less committed lawyer would do.

Put this way, however, it is clear that the argument trades on a confusion. My legal rights are *everything I am in fact legally entitled to,* not *everything the law can be made to give.* For obviously a good lawyer may be able to get me things to which I am not entitled, but this, to call a spade a spade, is an example of infringing my opponent's legal rights, not defending mine. Every lawyer knows tricks of the trade that can be used to do opponents out of their legal deserts—using delaying tactics, for example, to make it too costly for an opponent without much money to prosecute a lengthy suit even though the law is on his or her side.

To this it might be replied that looking at it this way leaves the opponent's lawyer out of the picture. Of course, the reply continues, no one is claiming that a zealous adversary advocate is attempting to *defend* legal rights: he or she is attempting to *win.* The claim is only that the clash of two such adversaries will in fact defend legal rights most effectively.

But what reason do we have to believe this, other than a question-begging analogy to eighteenth-century economic theories of the Invisible Hand, theories that are themselves myth rather than fact? Every skill an advocate is taught is bent to winning cases no matter where the legal right lies. If the opponent manages to counter a lawyer's move with a better one, this has precisely nothing to do with legal rights. In the Middle Ages lawsuits were frequently tried by combat between hired champions. Each was charged with defending the legal right of his employer, but surely the fact that one swordsman successfully fileted the other did not mean that a right was established. Now, of course judicial combat did not involve argument *about* rights. But neither does graymailing, "dollaring to death," driving up an opponent's costs by getting his or her law firm disqualified, peremptorily challenging a juror because he or she seems too smart, or even masking an invalid argument with what Titus Castricius called "the orator's privilege to make statements that are untrue, daring, crafty, deceptive and sophistical, provided they have some semblance of truth and can by any artifice be made to insinuate themselves into the minds of the persons who are to be influenced."

It is obvious that litigators pride themselves on their won-lost record. The *National Law Journal* describes "the world's most successful criminal lawyer—229 murder acquittals without a loss!" and describes the Inner Circle, a lawyer's club whose membership requirement is winning a seven-figure verdict. You never know, of course—maybe each of these cases really had legal right on its side. And when a coin comes up heads 229 times in a row it may be fair, but there *is* another explanation. Lawyers themselves do not see the point of what they do as defending their clients' legal rights, but as using the law to get their clients what they want.

. . .

Let me be clear about what the objection is. It is not that the flaw in the adversary system as a defender of legal rights is overkill on the part of morally imperfect, victory-hungry lawyers. The objection is that under the adversary system an *exemplary* lawyer is required to indulge in overkill to obtain as legal rights benefits that in fact may not be legal rights.

At this point an objection can be raised to my argument. The argument depends on a distinction I have drawn between *what a person is in fact legally entitled to* and *what the law can be made to give.* But this is a suspect distinction because it is based on the notion that there are legal entitlements other than what the law in fact gives. American Realism, the dominant jurisprudential theory of this century, was primarily responsible for throwing cold water on the notion of entitlements-in-themselves floating around in some sort of noumenal never-never land. The law is nothing other than what the courts say it is.

The objection fails, however, for it cuts the ground out from under itself. If legal rights are strictly identical with what the courts decide they are, then it is simply false that the adversary system is the best defender of legal rights. *Any* system whatsoever would defend legal rights equally well, as long as on the basis of that system courts decided cases.

There is, however, a legitimate insight concealed in the Realist objection. Whether or not legal rights are anything beyond what the courts say they are, it is the courts that are charged with adjudicating them. And—the point continues—if lawyers were given discretion to back off from zealous advocacy, they would have to prejudge the case themselves by deciding what the legal rights actually are in order to exercise this discretion. Lawyers would be usurping the judicial function.

Now, it must be said that this insight cannot be used to defend the innumerable tactics lawyers use to force favorable settlements of cases outside of court; if anything, the argument should condemn such practices inasmuch as they preempt the adjudicatory process. Nor does it militate against requiring lawyers to disclose adverse information and arguments, since doing so does not usurp the judicial function. But I do not wish to focus on these points for I think that the insight contains an important argument for the adversary system that we have not yet considered.

This argument is no longer that the excesses of zealous advocacy are excused by appealing to the promotion of truth or the defense of legal rights. Rather, it is that they are excused by what Thomas Nagel calls "ethical division of labor." ...

... The idea is that behavior that looks wrong from the point of view of ordinary morality is justified by the fact that other social roles exist whose purpose is to counteract the excesses resulting from role-behavior. Zealous adversary advocacy is justified by the fact that the other side is also furnished with a zealous advocate; the impartial arbiter provides a further check....

Will this do the trick? The answer, I am afraid, is no. Suppose that a lawyer is about to embark on a course of action that is unjustified from the point of view of ordinary morality, such as attempting to win an unfair, lopsided judgment for a client from a hapless and innocent party.

... A zealous adversary advocate will do whatever he or she can to avoid the opposing counsel's attempt to foil his or her designs. But such an advocate surely cannot claim that the existence of the opposing counsel morally justifies these actions. Certainly the fact that a man has a bodyguard in no way excuses you for trying to kill him, particularly if you bend all your ingenuity to avoiding the bodyguard.

The problem is this. The checks-and-balances notion is desirable because if other parts of the system exist to rectify one's excesses, one will be able to devote undivided attention to the job at hand and do it better. It is analogous to wearing protective clothing in a sport such as fencing: knowing that one's opponent is protected, one is justified in going all out in the match. But in the adversary system the situation is different, since the attorney is actively trying to get around the checks and balances: here the analogy is to a fencer who uses a special foil that can cut through the opponent's protective clothing. To put the point another way, the adversary advocate attempts to evade the system of checks and balances, not rely on it to save his or her opponents.

. . .

[My argument] does not mean that zealous advocacy is immoral, not even when it frustrates the search for truth or violates legal rights. Sometimes frustrating the search for truth may be a morally worthy thing to do, and sometimes moral rights are ill served by legal rights. All I am insisting on is that the standards by which such judgments are made are the same for lawyers and nonlawyers. If a lawyer is permitted to puff, bluff, or threaten on certain occasions, this is not because of the adversary system and the Principle of Nonaccountability, but because, in such circumstances, anyone would be permitted to do these things. Nothing justifies doing them on behalf of a predator....

Note on Luban: *The politics of advocacy*

1. This book has suggested that one's response to specific questions of "professional responsibility" is in significant part a reflection of a fundamental choice between a "celebratory" and a "troubled" stance or perspective toward the overall justness of our legal-political system. Does the suggestion tend to explain your reaction to Luban's critique?

2. It is probably an over-simplification to speak of "a" stance, for there is a full spectrum of attitudes, with most of us having at least some ingredient of the view opposite to that which dominates. My hypothesis is that the traditional concept of advocacy is not neutral with respect to this spectrum, however: It is not only embedded in, and justified by, the celebratory end of the spectrum; it justifies and reinforces that stance, channeling those to whom it seems wrong to repress that reaction.

Is the following brief catalogue a fair (if over-simplified) summary?

(a) The dominant professional norms *permit* you, as a lawyer, to have faith in the justness of the legal system, as a justification for doing acts that cause harm to others, not only in those instances in which that faith does not appear problematic, but in those in which it appears to lack any factual basis (*Spaulding v. Zimmerman* and *Valdez v. Alloway's Garage*, for example) and, so long as neither you nor your client tells an out-and-out lie, even in those in which your actions are designed to undermine the ability of the legal system to serve the ends of truth or justice (*Trireme* and the cross-examination of a truthful witness are examples).

(b) These norms tend also to *require* you to have this faith, or to act as if you did, despite the presence of a substantial basis for doubt, most often in cases like those mentioned in the preceding paragraph, where the harm is done to others, but also in cases where the harm is done to your client, such as that of perjurious testimony that would protect an innocent defendant from being unjustly convicted.

(c) The dominant norms *channel* you away from experiencing the conflict presented by them, by encouraging you to detach yourself from your client, the better to endure harms done *by* your client and *to* your client as well.

3. In considering the merits of this, or Luban's, critique, try to suspend your inclination, as a problem-solving lawyer, to move immediately to a focus on the existence and validity of any alternatives to the traditional concept of advocacy. I have attempted to *begin* by asking you to consider whether or not aspects of that concept are seriously problematic for you as a lawyer. It may be that, even if they are, there is no better alternative. But since one's will to look further is plainly affected by one's judgment about the need to do better, it has seemed to me important to separate the questions. The remaining portions of this book address the question of articulating and applying an alternative conception.

II. ADDRESSING THE BARRIERS TO AN ALTERNATIVE SYNTHESIS

The premise of this section of the book is that the process of articulating alternatives to the traditional concept of advocacy is choked off at the outset by a set of factors—"barriers," I will call them here—that make the traditional concept appear inevitable, and serious dissatisfaction with it impractical, fanciful, or downright dangerous. Unless these barriers are themselves named fully, and addressed frontally, they undermine or distort efforts to articulate an alternative concept; the resulting incomplete or distorted statement of an alternative will appear obviously deficient, and the legitimacy of the traditional concept reinforced, without the substantiality or proper effect of the barriers ever being considered explicitly.

I do not contend that these barriers are only mist, which evaporates on being exposed to daylight air. They are real, and powerful. Indeed, there is a real danger that the process of naming them, and seriously examining their functions and the sources of their power—as I propose to do—will only convince you that they cannot possibly be overborne. My purpose, however, is not to prove the power of the barriers, but to ask whether that power does not tend to be exaggerated, whether it is not possible to address them in ways that leave them real, and entitled to respect, but not the whole of reality—entitled to a voice in shaping the contours of an alternative synthesis, but not to preempt the effort to develop one altogether.

The sections that follow examine some half-dozen factors that appear to me to merit consideration here. The list is not complete, and for any reader some elements will be less salient than others. Ask yourself whether each has operated in your own thought as a significant constraint on the evolution of your self-concept as a lawyer; if it has, what the sources of that constraint have been; and whether there are ways in which you can give those sources their due and at the same time lessen their constraining force.

1. THE IMPLICIT TEACHING OF LEGAL EDUCATION

THE MESSAGES OF LEGAL EDUCATION

Sylvia Law
S. Gillers, ed., Looking at Law School*
Ch. 8 (3d rev. ed. 1990)

. . .

Five characteristics of the first year of law school engender a sense of personal insecurity in students and hinder them from using the study of law as a means of understanding and affecting the world in which we live.

First, the required curriculum of the first year is virtually identical in every law school and has been for most of this century. In contracts, torts, property, and procedure we study disputes between private individuals; criminal and constitutional law focus on issues of public power. Although some teachers attempt to place the cases in a larger social context, the selection of subjects emphasizes the private and the individualistic. All of these courses have a strong common law orientation. All deal, almost exclusively, with the opinions of appellate court judges. The prescribed first-year curriculum plainly does not exhaust that which is interesting in the law. There is no course dealing with the law governing any form of organization—corporations, families, or labor unions. There is no course dealing with the way the legislative and executive branches function; nothing on state and local government; nothing on public taxation or expenditures. We study abstract principles as presented in appellate cases, with little effort to place these abstractions in an empirical and historic context or to connect the principles with the concrete skills and work of lawyers.

The benign explanation for this phenomenal uniformity is simply the weight of history. Many in American legal education today recognize that the content of the first year reflects no eternal verity. But it is much easier to reach a negative consensus than it is to make specific affirmative change. But, whatever the justification, the effect of the present arrangement is to give first-year students a distorted view of what the law is and little training in the skills that lawyers use.

Second, almost all first-year study takes place in very large classes. I find that it is simply not possible to have the sort of exchange I associate with learning in a group of 120 people. The numbers prevent students from knowing each other or developing a sense of community. One justification for the large class is that it is valuable for students to learn to articulate and defend assertions—at the edge of their comprehension—in front of a large group of people. This may be a useful skill, but exclusive reliance on large classes is impossible to justify in educational terms.... The classroom experience generates insecurity and passivity.

A third feature of law school life is that, apart from legal writing, students are evaluated exclusively on the basis of written examinations, graded anonymously. Written exams, however well-designed, test a narrow range of skills, knowledge, and characteristics relevant to the practice of law. More important, the grading process defines a power relationship between grader and graded that is fundamentally inconsistent with true education. Law school purports to encourage students

Teachers (3d rev. ed. 1990) (edited by Stephen Gillers).

to disagree with cases, with professors, and with each other. But our practice says that there is a right answer and that what matters are not the skills of legal practice or an understanding of the way that law shapes social relationships, but rather spotting issues and writing a coherent first draft under pressure. The effect of exams and grading is to take a group of people all of whom were smart and competent when they arrived at law school and to sort them into a pecking order in which almost everyone "fails." The process reinforces the student's sense that it is both inevitable and just that someone else will define your worth, and will find you wanting.

You will quickly learn that the reason exams and grades matter so much is that they are important to the firms. The firms want students sorted into a hierarchy. And legal education is relentless in defining hierarchical relations and persuading people to accept them as just. People in the legal profession believe in the hierarchy of law schools, and believing makes it true. Within each school, grades define the pecking order. Grading is defended as a meritocratic alternative to allocating opportunities through ranking based more directly on race, sex, religion, and family connection. But there are less painful, more effective ways to measure competence in particular subject matter. More important, we should evaluate a much wider range of skills and characteristics—hard work, responsibility, the ability to listen, research and writing skills, persistence—through more cooperative forms of education such as the work that now takes place in clinics and first-year writing programs, and in much legal practice. Law schools should not simply teach technical skills. A complex and troubled society needs people to think deeply about the relations between law and our social arrangements. Even the most practically oriented lawyer will benefit from this kind of thinking. But grading as it is practiced in law schools today does not contribute to either technical competence or reflective thought.

A fourth important feature of life in the first year of law school is that within the first few weeks, before students have a chance to probe the mystery of the law on the most rudimentary level, the placement process begins. The very term *placement* conjures up a static and ordained world in which, if you are good and lucky, you will be "placed," rather than a world that we are creating together. The reality is that it is much more difficult to find a job doing work that is socially useful, or even socially neutral, than it is to find a place in the service of concentrated corporate power. Firms hire months in advance. Public interest organizations and small firms do not have the financial stability that permits such advanced planning, and public interest jobs are more difficult to find. Students interested in pursuing public interest work are often confronted with a choice between a secure, well-paying job offered months in advance, or waiting in the hopes that if they hustle and are lucky they will be able to find a minimally paid position doing socially interesting work. The placement process exacerbates the anxiety of first-year students.

. . .

A fifth and final universal characteristic of the first year of law school is that students are expected to work very hard. . . . The benign explanation for this is that the first year defines the ideology of legal education. It is much easier for a faculty to agree to add something than it is to agree to delete. But the excessive work pressure has the function of making students feel out of control. Law students often feel they must make a choice between school and their friends, the movies, music, and novels. Obsessive work habits and the sense that you lack control over your own life are extremely conducive to encouraging students to pursue particular types of work.

In short, what we do in the first year of law school purports to be a value neutral meritocracy, but it has the effect of generating insecurity and hierarchy, and of pushing students in particular directions. We not only fail to help students to function independently or to work cooperatively, we affirmatively promote the belief that individual worth is defined by individualistic competitive evaluation. We not only fail to help students acquire the concrete skills of legal practice or knowledge of the role of the law in defining concrete institutional arrangements, but we engender a sense of incompetence that encourages the belief that people need an organization of superiors to tell them what to do. Doing well in the insecurity and hierarchy of law school prepares people to accept a place in a firm. The fact that there are common-sense justifications for these arrangements simply makes it more difficult to challenge them.

The intellectual content of the concepts of the law and of the substance of legal education reinforce some of the same messages that are implicitly reflected in the way life is organized in the law school . . .

The formalist theory, which largely informs the study of the first year, conceives the common law as a coherent, principled whole that allows the just settlement of particular disputes to be predicted or derived by a process of logical deduction from a few general principles reflected in the cases that went before. The theory is that once you understand the basic principles of negligence or offer and acceptance, you can then deduce the just result in a particular dispute, or the right answer on a law school exam.

The formalist view of the law embodies commonsense notions of even-handed justice—like cases should be treated alike. It reflects, to a large degree, the way many judges think about their work, though good practitioners are more likely to believe that cases are won or lost on the facts and the lawyer's ability to present a claim as factually and emotionally sympathetic. Its methodology for legal education is convenient because core principles can be understood simply by reading cases; anonymous exams are an appropriate method for determining whether students have grasped the core principles and the process of deduction from those principles.

There are many problems with the formalist approach to the law, which have been explored in depth by the legal realists and pragmatists of the early twentieth century and the contemporary work of the critical scholars. First, the formalist principles incorporate highly controversial value assumptions, often without explicit discussion or acknowledgment. For example, the formalism of the late nineteenth century assumed that the core value of the law is free, individual self-assertion within the context of the free-enterprise system. Torts cases of this period often invoked notions of "progress" or "development" in holding that entrepreneurs could only be held financially responsible for injuries resulting from their activities if the injured person could prove fault. Holmes thought it *self-evident* that "the public generally profits by individual activity. As action cannot be avoided, and tends to the public good, there is obviously no policy in throwing the hazard of what is at once desirable and inevitable upon the actor." It is possible to make radically different assumptions, for example that people should generally be held responsible when their actions cause injury to others. Although few people still blindly accept as universal truth that what's good for General Motors is good for America, the common law that we study in the first year today developed, in a complex way, out of cases accepting this very equation. The formalist approach requires that we accept controversial assumptions as givens from which the fair and consistent result in a particular case can be derived. It discourages probing of these core assumptions.

A second problem with formalism is its failure to recognize that the legal system of a complex society incorporates a large number of core principles, which are often in conflict. For nearly every principle there is an equally well-established counterprinciple.

. . .

In recent years a new version of formalism has appeared in works exploring the connections between law and economics. Such works, which are undeniably fascinating, always begin with certain assumptions.

> (N)o one knows what is best for individuals better than they themselves do . . . (T)he function of the prices of various goods must be to reflect costs to society of producing them, and if prices perform this function properly, the buyer will case an informed vote in making his purchases; thus the best combination of choices available will be achieved.

[G. Calabresi, The Costs of Accidents 69–70 (1970)]. Beginning with assumptions such as these, the analytic tool is then applied to problems in contract, torts, property, and even family or criminal law.

Of course the "model" of the informed consumer casting his vote in the free market election often bears little relationship to reality. It assumes competitive sellers when in fact there are many barriers to free competition, from government regulation to monopoly control. It assumes that the things we want can be purchased individually, when in fact many valuable things such as clean air and safe streets can only be purchased collectively. It assumes that consumers can make informed choices when we all know that is often not possible. It sidesteps all questions about existing and persisting inequalities in the distribution of wealth.

And finally, it encourages the belief that life can be reduced to a series of commodity exchanges. Health care involves not a healing relationship between two people but a transaction in which a medical provider sells a service to an insured. Our visions compete in a "market-place of ideas." Lawyers do not work with others to create a more just society but rather sell their labor for a price.

This new formalism is subtly seductive. With a few unquestionable premises leading to ineluctable conclusions, it offers the potential for an analysis that is consistent and pervasive. But it is also inadequate and misdirected. We cannot analyze complex social problems in terms of a few assumptions about the function and operation of the free market. We cannot come to grips with our common problems, or understand the operation of the law, by simply substituting definitions and deductions for values and facts.

[A] second major approach to the law and to legal education is legal realism or pragmatism. The development of legal realism was a direct response to the inadequacies of the formalist approach. Realist theories reflect a basic mistrust of rules, abstract concepts, deductive logic, and mechanical application of doctrine.

. . .

The problem with the realist approach to the law is that value choices are still unacknowledged. "The metaphor of social engineering substitutes a technocratic slogan for what ought to be a reasoned moral choice. It assumes a bureaucratic perspective within which—once it is fully adopted—there is much less moral choice available."

Both formalist and pragmatic/realist approaches to the law assume a broad-based commitment to shared social values. The formalists make this assumption explicit, whereas the realists make the assumption in more subtle form.... Pragmatism assumes a social consensus—shared value commitments—at least among those who are able to express their opinion. It is increasingly difficult to accept the pragmatic idea that there are widely shared values, within which questions of public policy can be settled by rational technique. The social consensus, if ever there was one, has broken down. There are sharp divisions with respect to basic values, and even sharper conflicts of interest between various groups within the society.

. . .

The point to notice in entering law school is that legal education has not resolved conflicts in social values. Legal education often denies that value conflicts exist. Law school is not going to provide a "coherent system of large ideas" to assist you in resolving the dilemmas that confront a thinking person ...   We all need to develop some sort of philosophy of our lives together with others whose lives and ideas we respect. Law school is not designed to help. It is vital for law students to engage in work on the issues that inspired them to go to law school. Press your school to provide opportunities to expand your knowledge of the areas of human life that you find exciting and important. Do not let the individualist, competitive ideology of the first year discourage you from pursuing more cooperative forms of work that are available....

Note on Law and implicit messages: Legal education as training for hierarchy [1]

1.   (a) Former Dean Roger Cramton has described the ingredients of "the ordinary religion of the classroom" in these terms:

> [A] skeptical attitude toward generalizations; an instrumental approach to law and lawyering; a "tough-minded" and analytical attitude toward legal tasks and professional roles; and a faith that man, by the application of reason and the use of democratic processes, can make the world a better place.

Cramton, The Ordinary Religion of the Classroom, 29 J.Leg.Educ. 247 (1978). Consider this excerpt from Professor Cramton's critique of that set of messages:

> A skeptical attitude toward generalizations, principles and rules is doubtless a desirable attribute of the lawyer. But skepticism that deepens into a belief in the meaninglessness of principles, the relativism of values or the non-existence of an ultimate reality is dangerous and crippling....

> One of the most insistent notions is that there in an unbridgeable chasm between "facts" (which are "real" or "hard" or "tangible") and "values" (which are "subjective" or "soft" or "intangible"). The distinction between the *is* and the *ought*, the legal realists said, was temporary and was designed merely to free legal scholars so they could take a fresh and critical look at how officials actually behaved, all as a preliminary to the main task of reforming legal institutions in the light of the suspended goals. This ideal was rarely achieved; since the divide between *is* and *ought* could not be narrowed by compelling the *is* to conform to the *ought*, the *ought* was permitted to acquiesce in the *is*.

> Instead of transforming society, the functional approach tends to become dominated by society, to become an apologist and technician for established institutions and things as they are, to view change as a form of tinkering rather than a reexamination of basic premises. Surface goals such as "efficiency," "progress," and "the democratic way" are taken at face value and more ultimate questions of value submerged.

---

1.   The sub-title is the title of a well-known article by Duncan Kennedy, the most recent version of which appears in D. Kairys, ed., The Politics of Law 380 (rev. ed. 1990).

... Most law school teaching places the law student in the position of an advocate who is asked to work with existing rules and arguments. The goals underlying the competing rules are adverted to in passing, but are evaluated only rarely. One of the factors which makes it easy to avoid explicit discussion of values and goals in law school is the often less than consciously held idea that the proper role of the lawyer is always merely to take someone else's goals and values—those of the private or public client and "go from there."

...

Today law tends to be viewed in solely instrumental terms and as lacking values of its own, other than a limited agreement on certain "process values" thought to be implicit in our democratic way of doing things. We agree on methods of resolving our disagreements in the public arena, but on little else. Substantive goals come from the political process or from private interests in the community. The lawyer's task, in an instrumental approach to law, is to facilitate and manipulate legal processes to advance the interest of his client.

Id. at 253–57.

(b) Both Law and Cramton are speaking of what has been termed the "implicit curriculum," which I have elsewhere described as "the idea that much of what we [teachers] teach about being a lawyer we transmit by the attitudes and practices that we model." Lesnick, Infinity in a Grain of Sand: The World of Law and Lawyering as Portrayed in the Clinical Teaching Implicit in the Law School Curriculum, 37 U.C.L.A.L.Rev. 1157, 1160 n. 3 (1990). The lessons of these attitudes seem to outrun their explicit content, however; "what we are ... taken to say about being a lawyer is far less measured and qualified than what we may mean to say. Intention is not the end of the matter...." Id., at 1138. Cramton has described in these words the "modern dogmas that entangle legal education":

[A] moral relativism tending toward nihilism, a pragmatism tending toward an amoral instrumentalism, a realism tending toward cynicism, an individualism tending toward atomism, and a faith in reason and democratic processes tending toward mere credulity and idolatry.

Cramton, supra, at 262.

(c) I have suggested that the implicit messages of legal education:

taken as a whole, systematically discourage students (and faculty as well) from inquiring into unspoken premises, whether about the legal system, the larger social order, or the role of lawyers; they inhibit the experience of choice, of human responsibility for the social constructs we call the law and the legal profession....

Lesnick, supra, at 1182. The result is to reinforce powerfully the factors that lead a neophyte lawyer to conceive of his or her task as to fit in, as much as is possible, to things as they are, to view the world as found, not made. Compare Note 6 of the Note on Cooper's Tale, p. 209 above.

(d) To what extent do the themes of these critiques ring true in your own experience or observations of law school?

2. To the extent that this channeling process does exist, in what ways, if any, can it be made the subject of conscious control, by law schools themselves, by individual teachers, by groups of students, or by individual students (e.g., by you)?

(a) The task for law schools as institutions seems daunting. Consider the accuracy of this summary agenda:

> The more general and more fundamental educational purpose ... is to enable students to exercise *responsibility* in the practice of law. The core meaning of the idea of responsibility is the recognition that the choices one makes as a lawyer have an effect on people's lives; from this recognition flows the realization that our work as lawyers can be an affirmation, or a negation, of our values, of the goals that we want our lives to strengthen.

> In my view, the first task of a law school is to help students to explore the fuller meaning and implications of responsibility in law practice. The greater part of our teaching time, however, needs to be devoted to giving students some of what they need in order to be responsible. The law school curriculum should reflect the faculty's effort to give content to these criteria.

> Knowledge of legal doctrine is of course a crucial part of what one needs to be responsible, as is skill at the basic lawyering tasks valued in the traditional curriculum.... Traditional legal education tends to value this skill and knowledge in itself, and it becomes the goal rather than a means toward reaching the goal. As a result, the traditional curriculum often fails to recognize, or to act on the recognition, that a person needs far more than these traditionally-valued skills in order to be a responsible lawyer.

> The "more" includes the wider range of skills associated with clinical teaching in the narrow sense....

> However, these traditional clinical skills do not sufficiently address the need. To practice responsibly, a lawyer must also have acquired several more qualitative skills, primarily those of listening, exercising judgment, and engaging in moral reasoning. Few law schools today seem to consider these skills as central aspects of clinical education.

> Still, however broadened the concept of skill may be, the need goes beyond what may be embraced by the term. The additional qualities central to the education of a responsible lawyer are as simple to state as they are difficult to expand upon, even in a summary fashion: a developing knowledge of oneself and a developing knowledge of the premises of the legal and the social order. The former entails a commitment to experiential learning, feedback, and reflection as primary learning modes; the latter entails a commitment to a substantial integration of legal theory with doctrinal or "skills" study.

> These are obviously demanding goals, very unlikely unreachable in full. But only when they have all been brought within our range of vision as genuine parts of the educational agenda is it time to begin the

difficult work of triage; else, we mask priority decisions as simple imperatives of time pressures.

Lesnick, supra, at 1184–86.

(b) What responses to the problem are open to individual teachers and students? To what extent, if at all, do you believe that the act of making the channeling process conscious can itself enable you to exercise control over it?

(c) Are there other responses that seem promising to you? Consider this evocative, cryptic thought by Roberto Unger:

> The decisive psychological insight that provides the beginning of [a] response is the awareness that the sense of living in history serves as the indispensable prelude.... To live in history means, among other things, to be an active and conscious participant in the conflict over the terms of collective life, with the knowledge that this conflict continues in the midst of the technical and everyday.

R. Unger, The Critical Legal Studies Movement 113 (1983).

- What is Unger saying here?

- Do you find it helpful?

2. CONSTRAINING PATTERNS OF THOUGHT

BECOMING A LAWYER: A HUMANISTIC PERSPECTIVE ON LEGAL EDUCATION AND PROFESSIONALISM

E. Dvorkin, J. Himmelstein, & H. Lesnick
West Pub. Co., 1981.

Read pages 153–74.

Note on Polarities: The role of role revisited

1. The polarization of alternatives is a familiar phenomenon, at times appearing to be a method of carrying on a debate but often a more endemic pattern of thought. Consider, for example, its use by Charles Fried and Charles Curtis, pp. 35 and 51 above. Fried opens his essay by contrasting Lord Brougham's quintessentially undiluted defense of single-minded client-orientation with the wholly undifferentiated ethic of Cuban and Bulgarian defense lawyers; and note his discussion of choosing between "an expensive education for our children" and "sav[ing] lives in some distant land" (p. 38), or between a "purely discretionary choice" of client and considering all through one's career "where the greatest need for [one's] particular talent lies" (p. 42). Curtis, for his part, supports his extreme form of professional detachment by postulating the lawyer's choice as one between "treat[ing] the whole thing as a game" and "devot[ing] his life to taking on other people's troubles ... as his own" (p. 57).

Douglas Rosenthal, p. 90, above, on the other hand, in questioning the traditional concept of professional dominance, acknowledges that "most clients" want an "authoritative and businesslike manner" in their lawyers, but also want to be "self-reliant and responsible." "They both want and don't want to be dependent" (p. 100). And William Simon, in proposing an alternative to the traditional concept of professional role-differentiation, Becoming a Lawyer, pp. 188–96, see p. 121, above, describes conflict, trust, and what Simon terms "procedural considerations," as values that should be given real weight, but never viewed as dispositive a priori.

Is there a connection of some kind between a desire to legitimate the traditional concept of advocacy and a seeming comfort with the polarization of alternatives, and similarly between a desire to challenge the traditional concept and a desire to transcend proffered polarities? If so, the tendency to polarize alternatives is a major underpinning of the traditional concept of advocacy. Why might there be such a connection? What would the connection be?

2.   (a) The foregoing implies that a non-polarized "alternative" to the traditional concept is not a simple "rejection" of it:

> In looking at what an alternative consciousness might be, it is important to begin by considering explicitly the tendency to express a rejection of the traditional in polar terms. What is wrong with the traditional consciousness is that it is incomplete, that it becomes a caricature of reality, a caricature of the human personality. It seeks to protect certain values that are generally important—individual self-expression, for example—and is unwilling to respect other values out of a fear that can be done only at the cost of the first set.... Upon realizing the limited nature of the traditional consciousness, it is easy to react by becoming caught in its polar opposite, which, although fashioned on opposite values than the traditional, is similarly undimensional and partial....

> A non-polar alternative consciousness seeks to incorporate the traditional in a broader view, holding to what is worth holding to, but insisting on a more situational consideration of consequences and the possibility of respecting the aims of apparently inconsistent values. The hoary academic debate, between rigor and values or intellect and emotion in studying cases, is a classic example of this polarized form of thinking. We are usually required to decide which pole repels us the most, so that we can cling desperately to the opposite one. Rigor and values are conflicting only from a linear perspective; in "rejecting" rigor, we are rejecting only the claim of completeness for it, in order to seek a broader value, one that includes values as well.

> An alternative consciousness of lawyering expresses a view that attempts to go beyond both the traditional adversary consciousness and a polar rejection of it. The central theme is not the rejection of role, but a dynamic relation between role and self ...

Lesnick, The Integration of Responsibility and Values: Legal Education in an Alternative Consciousness of Law and Lawyering, 10 Nova L.J. 633, 639–40 (1986).

(b) A non-polarized approach to each of the major ingredients of the traditional concept of advocacy is available:

- Rosenthal's treatment of the question of *professional dominance* is one example.

- Regarding the question of *professional detachment,* consider the difference between Curtis' view and that taken by Anthony Kronman in the following discussion:

A legal counselor advises his clients on business and personal matters. To be technically competent, he must know the law in detail and be skilled at devising strategies. . . . Technical competence, however, does not by itself constitute practical wisdom. The practically wise counselor is able [among other things] to act, toward his client, as a kind of critical friend. Like a friend, he takes his client's interests as his own and devotes his time and energy to helping the client realize them. To do this, he must be compassionate or sympathetic in the sense [that] he must be able to put himself in his client's position and see things from the point of view of his concerns. At the same time, however, it is the counselor's responsibility to be a *critical* friend, one who pushes the client to interrogate and clarify his own ends, questioning, challenging, and, in extreme cases, simply rejecting the client's own statement or defense of his ambitions. In order to function as a effective critic, it is necessary for the counselor to maintain some distance from his client and to retain a measure of objectivity regarding the client's situation. Strangers do not take one another's interests as their own; lovers and intimate friends often do so to such a degree that they lose the capacity (and the will) to judge one another from an independent point of view. As a critical friend, the legal counselor must be simultaneously sympathetic and detached; he must see his client's situation bifocally, both from within and from without. The counselor who is able to do this neither feels indifferent toward this client's interest—regarding them in the same disinterested way he would those of a complete stranger—nor takes the client's own account of his interest at face value, simply accepting what he has to say and proceeding from there. . . .

. . . These requirements are not only different, . . . but seem actually to pull in opposite directions. We may say therefore that a judge [or wise counselor] must not only possess the seemingly opposite qualities of sympathy and detachment, but must also have the capacity to endure the tension between them.

Kronman, Practical Wisdom and Professional Character, 4 Soc. Phil. & Pol'y 203, 224–25, 221 (1986).

- Simon's concept of "non-professional advocacy," developed in the excerpt from *Becoming a Lawyer* referred to at the beginning of this Note, is an example of an effort to articulate a non-polarized approach to the question of *professional role-differentiation.* Consider also, in this respect, the following attempt at a reassessment of the role of role.

MORAL RESPONSIBILITY IN PROFESSIONAL ETHICS

Gerald Postema
55 N.Y.U.L.Rev. 63 (1980).

. . .

. . . . The requirements of professional ethics can sometimes move some distance from the concerns of private or ordinary morality, a phenomenon we might call *moral distance*. The range of practical considerations which alone are relevant to a proper ethical decision in a professional role is the *moral universe* of that role. For many professional roles the moral universe of the role is considerably narrower than that of ordinary morality, and, when the two overlap, they often assign different weights to the same set of considerations.

. . .

. . . the moral dilemmas facing a lawyer generally cannot be reduced to a single perspective. Our personal and professional concerns do not have the collective uniformity necessary for the construction of a general scheme of principles and priority rules. On the contrary, our concerns are characterized by a complexity and a variety which resist reduction to a uniform scale.[16] As Thomas Nagel has argued, we are subject to moral and other motivational claims of very different kinds, because we are able to view the world from a variety of perspectives, each presenting a different set of claims. Nagel maintains that conflicts between perspectives

> [c]annot . . . be resolved by subsuming either of the points of view under the other, or both under a third. Nor can we simply abandon any of them. There is no reason why we should. The capacity to view the world simultaneously from the point of view of one's relations to others, from the point of view of one's life extended through time, from the point of view of everyone at once, and finally from the detached viewpoint often described as the view *sub specie aeternitatis* is one of the marks of humanity. This complex capacity is an obstacle to simplification.

Are we left without any rational means for resolving this conflict? Nagel rightly resists this skeptical response. The conflict Nagel describes shows only that it may be futile to search for a general reductive method or a clear set of priority rules to structure our basic concerns. There is always likely to be a significant gap between general practical theory and actual decision and practice.

---

16. Perhaps one of the most serious general objections to Utilitarianism is that, although it professes to give full respect to all sources of value, it creates its simple normative structure by reducing all such values to a single dimension. The net effect is that either it distorts radically the world of human concerns, or it limits its scope to that range of values in which its simplifying assumptions are most natural. . . .

In Aristotle's view, this gap is bridged by the faculty of *practical judgment*—what he called practical wisdom. Our ability to resolve conflicts on a rational basis often outstrips our ability to enunciate general principles. In doing so, we exercise judgment. Judgment is neither a matter of simply applying general rules to particular cases nor a matter of mere intuition. It is a complex faculty, difficult to characterize, in which general principles or values and the particularities of the case both play important roles. The principles or values provide a framework within which to work and a target at which to aim. But they do not determine decisions. Instead, we rely on our judgment to achieve a coherence among the conflicting values which is sensitive to the particular circumstances. Judgment thus involves the ability to take a comprehensive view of the values and concerns at stake, based on one's experience and knowledge of the world. And this involves awareness of the full range of shared experience, beliefs, relations, and expectations within which these values and concerns have significance.

In professional contexts there is much need for practical judgment in this Aristotelian sense. Judgment, however, is both a disposition—a trait of character—and a skill which must be learned and continually exercised. It is important, then, if we are seriously to consider matters of moral responsibility in professional contexts, that we pay attention to the conditions of development of this disposition and the exercise of this skill.

The ... current approach to questions raised by the conflict between private and professional moralities ... rests on a mistaken view of moral judgment and moral experience. Practical moral reasoning is wrongly viewed as strictly analogous to theoretical reasoning, the central objective of which is to arrive at correct answers to specific problems. This view of moral reasoning and experience is too narrow, for moral reasoning is not so singularly outcome-determinative. Our evaluations of ourselves and our actions depend not only on getting our moral sums right, but also on having the appropriate attitudes and reactions to the moral situation in which we act. Let me illustrate.

Consider the truck driver who, through no fault of his own, hits and seriously injures a child. It may be correct to say that, since he drove with care and could not have avoided hitting the child, the driver is guilty of no wrong and thus is not blameworthy. However, consider the accident and the driver's involvement in it from his point of view. There is a very important difference between the driver's likely reaction and that of an uninvolved spectator. Both may feel and express regret, but the nature and behavioral expression of this regret will be quite different. The driver's direct, personal (albeit unintentional) involvement in the accident alters the structure of the moral situation and the driver's attitude toward it. The difference in the emotional responses of the driver and the spectator will be reflected in the way these feelings are expressed. The driver may attempt to make restitution in the hope that he can repair the injury he caused. The spectator may offer help, or contribute money for hospital bills, or even visit the child, but these actions would be understood (by him and by us) as expressions of pity, kindly concern, or perhaps generosity. From the driver, these same actions would be intended and understood as expressions of a special form of regret. Suppose, however, that the driver takes the attitude of the uninvolved spectator, perhaps expressing detached regret, but feeling no need to make restitution. He can rightly argue that he was not to be blamed for the accident, that he had done no wrong. In doing so, he could perhaps be rightly said to have gotten his moral sums right. But in asserting this defense quite sincerely and too quickly, he would reveal a defect of character—a defect much deeper and more serious than a lack of generosity. Morality seems to require not only that one be able to apply moral principles properly to one's own or another's conduct, but also that one be able to appreciate the moral costs of one's actions, perhaps even when those actions are unintentional. By "moral costs" I mean those features of one's action and its consequences touching on important concerns, interests, and needs of others that, in the absence of special justification, would provide substantial if not conclusive moral reasons against performing it.[22]

Similarly, in cases in which obligations to other persons are correctly judged to be overridden by weightier moral duties, with the result that some injury is done, it is not enough for one to work out the correct course of action and pursue it. It is also important that one appreciate the moral costs of that course of action. This appreciation will be expressed in a genuine reluctance to bring about the injury, and a sense of the accompanying loss or sacrifice. It may even call for concrete acts of reparation: explaining and attempting to justify the action to the person injured, or making up the loss or injury to some extent. This is one way in which the moral status of the principle or right which was violated is acknowledged, and the moral relations between the parties affirmed and, when necessary, repaired.

Moral sentiments are an essential part of the moral life. The guilt or remorse one feels after mistreating a person is not merely a personal sanction one imposes on oneself after judging the action to have been wrong; it is the natural and most appropriate expression of this judgment. Similarly, the outrage we feel at injustice done to another and the resentment we feel at wrong done to ourselves are not just the emotional coloring of detached moral judgments, but the way in which

22. One aspect of the failure of professionals in law to appreciate the moral costs of their actions is captured by G.K. Chesterton:

> [T]he horrible thing about all legal officials, even the best, about all judges, magistrates, barristers, detectives, and policemen, is not that they are wicked (some of them are good), not that they are stupid (several of them are quite

intelligent), it is simply that they have got used to it.

> Strictly they do not see the prisoner in the dock; all they see is the usual man in the usual place. They do not see the awful court of judgment; they only see their own workshop.

Chesterton, The Twelve Men, in Tremendous Trifles 57–58 (1955).

we experience and express these judgments. Thus, morality is not merely a matter of getting things right—as in solving a puzzle or learning to speak grammatically—but a matter of relating to people in a special and specifically human way.

. . .

For these reasons, we must approach the problems of professional ethics from a perspective that recognizes the importance of practical judgment and moral sentiment. The notion of professional responsibility should take on a different and broader meaning. The primary concern is not with the definition, structuring, and delimitation of a lawyer's professional *responsibilities* (his official concerns and duties), nor with those situations in which the lawyer is to be held professional *responsible* (i.e., liable to blame or sanction). Rather, the concern is with responsibility as a virtue or trait of character. The focus, then, is on the notion of a *responsible* person—or perhaps better, on the notion of a person's *sense of responsibility*. . . .

. . .

The central problem I am concerned with is whether, given the fact of moral distance, it is possible to retain and act out of a mature sense of responsibility in a professional role. In this section, I argue that because of particular social and psychological features of professional roles, the pressures and tensions of acting and deliberating within such roles pose a serious threat to responsible professional behavior. In addition, I hope to show that the atrophy of the professional's sense of general moral responsibility is a serious and costly matter. If this argument is correct, we have discovered an important reason for radically rethinking the standard conception of the lawyer's role.

. . .

Since the lawyer often acts as an extension of the legal and moral personality of the client, the lawyer is under great temptation to refuse to accept responsibility for his professional actions and their consequences. Moreover, except when his beliefs coincide with those of his client, he lives with a recurring dilemma: he must engage in activities, make arguments, and present positions which he himself does not endorse or embrace. The lawyer's integrity is put into question by the mere exercise of the duties of his profession.

To preserve his integrity, the lawyer must carefully distance himself from his activities. Publicly, he may sharply distinguish statements or arguments he makes for the client and statements on which he stakes his professional honor. The danger in this strategy is that a curious two-stage distancing may result. First, the lawyer distances himself from the argument: it is not his argument, but that of his client. His job is to construct the arguments; the task of evaluating and believing them is left to others. Second, after detaching himself from the argument, he is increasingly tempted to identify with this stance of detachment. What first offers itself as a device for distancing oneself from personally unacceptable positions becomes a defining feature of one's professional self-concept. This, in turn, encourages an uncritical, uncommitted state of mind, or worse, a deep moral skepticism. When such detachment is defined as a professional ideal, as it is by the standard conception, the lawyer is even more apt to adopt these attitudes.

. . .

Consider first the personal costs the lawyer must pay to act in this detached manner. . . .

. . . . In a large portion of his daily experience, in which he is acting regularly in the moral arena, he is alienated from his own moral feelings and attitudes and indeed from his moral personality as a whole. Moreover, in light of the strong pressures for role identification, it is not unlikely that the explicit and conscious adoption of the minimal identification strategy involves a substantial element of self-deception.

The social costs of cutting off professional deliberation and action from their sources in ordinary moral experience are even more troubling. First, . . .

Second, the lawyer's practical judgment, in the Aristotelian sense, is rendered ineffective and unreliable. [I have] argued that, because human values are diverse and complex, one is sometimes thrown back on the faculty of practical judgment to resolve moral dilemmas. This is as true within the professional context as outside of it. To cut off professional decisionmaking from the values and concerns which structure the moral situation, thereby blocking appeal to a more comprehensive point of view from which to weigh the validity of role morality, is to risk undermining practical judgment entirely.[46]

Third, and most importantly, when professional action is estranged from ordinary moral experience, the lawyer's sensitivity to the moral costs in both ordinary and extraordinary situations tends to atrophy. The ideal of neutrality permits, indeed requires, that the lawyer regard his professional activities and their consequences from the point of view of the uninvolved spectator. One may abstractly regret that the injury is done, but this regret is analogous to the regret one feels as a spectator to [a] traffic accident . . .; one is in no way personally implicated. The responses likely from a mature sense of responsibility appear morally fastidious and unprofessional from the perspective of the present Code. This has troubling consequences: without a proper appreciation of the moral costs of one's actions one cannot make effective use of the faculty of practical judgment. In fact, a proper perspective of the moral costs of one's action has both intrinsic and

---

46. This may explain, in part, the attitude of "ethical minimalism" among lawyers which many, both within and outside the profession, deplore. This minimalism is an understandable reaction, in light of the fact that there are few fixed and settled rules in the Code and the lawyer is effectively cut off from the resources needed to resolve the indeterminacies unavoidably left by the Code.

instrumental value. The instrumental value lies in the added safeguard that important moral dilemmas will receive appropriate reflection. As Bernard Williams argued, "only those who are [by practice] reluctant or disinclined to do the morally disagreeable when it is really necessary have much chance of not doing it when it is not necessary. . . . [A] habit of reluctance is an essential obstacle against the happy acceptance of the intolerance." [48]

But this appreciation is also important for its own sake. To experience sincere reluctance, to feel the need to make restitution, to seek the other's pardon—these simply are appropriate responses to the actual feature of the moral situation. In this way, the status and integrity of important moral principles are maintained in compromising circumstances, and the moral relations between persons are respected or restored.

Finally, the moral detachment of the lawyer adversely affects the quality of the lawyer-client relationship. Unable to draw from the responses and relations of ordinary experience, the lawyer is capable of relating to the client only as a client. He puts his moral faculties of reason, argument, and persuasion wholly at the service of the client, but simultaneously disengages his moral personality. He views himself not as a moral actor but as a legal technician. In addition, he is barred from recognizing the client's moral personality. The moral responsibilities of the client are simply of no interest to him. Thus, paradoxically, the combination of partisanship and neutrality jeopardizes client autonomy and mutual respect (two publicly stated objectives of the standard conception), and yields instead a curious kind of impersonal relationship.

It is especially striking, then, that Charles Fried, the most sophisticated defender of these central ideals of the standard conception, should describe the lawyer as a "special purpose" friend. Indeed, it is the contrast between the standard conception of the lawyer-client relationship and the characteristics of a relationship between friends which, on reflection, is likely to make the deepest impression. The impersonalism and moral detachment characteristic of the lawyer's role under the standard conception are not found in relations between friends. Loyalty to one's friend does not call for disengagement of one's moral personality. When in nonprofessional contexts we enter special relationships and undertake special obligations which create duties of loyalty or special concern, these special considerations must nevertheless be integrated into a coherent picture of the moral life as a whole. Often we must view our moral world from more than one perspective simultaneously. As Goffman points out, roles are often structured with

---

48. Williams, Politics and Moral Character, in Private and Public Morality 64 (S. Hampshire ed. 1978). Milgram's well-known experiments underscore the commonplace that the more we are able to distance ourselves (often literally) from the consequences of our actions, the more we are able to inflict pain and suffering on others without moral qualms. See generally S. Milgram, Obedience to Authority: An Experimental View 32–43 (1974).

the recognition that persons occupying the role fill other roles which are also important to them. Room is left for the agent to integrate his responsibilities from each role into a more or less coherent scheme encompassing his entire moral life.

But it is precisely this integrated conception of the moral personality that is unavailable to the professional who adopts either the minimal or the maximal identification strategy. Either the moral personality is entirely fragmented or compartmentalized, or it is shrunk to fit the moral universe defined by the role. Neither result is desirable.

The unavoidable social costs of the standard conception of professional legal behavior argue strongly for a radical rethinking of the lawyer's role. One alternative ... is to recognize the unavoidable discontinuities in the moral landscape and to bridge them with a unified conception of moral personality. Achieving any sort of bridge, however, requires that lawyers significantly alter the way they view their own activities. Each lawyer must have a conception of the role that allows him to serve the important functions of that role in the legal and political system while integrating his own sense of moral responsibility into the role itself. Such a conception must improve upon the current one by allowing a broader scope for engaged moral judgment in day-to-day professional activities while encouraging a keener sense of personal responsibility for the consequences of these activities.[52]

The task of forging a concrete alternative conception is a formidable one. To begin, however, it may be useful to contrast two conceptions of social roles: the fixed role and the recourse role. In a fixed role, the professional perceives the defining characteristics of the role— its basic rules, duties, and responsibilities—as entirely predetermined. The characteristics may be altered gradually through social evolution or more quickly by profession-wide regulatory legislation, but as far as the individual practitioner is concerned, the moral universe of his role is an objective fact, to be reckoned with, but not for him to alter....

In contrast, in a recourse role, one's duties and responsibilities are not fixed, but may expand or contract....

---

52. David Hoffman, a nineteenth century legal educator in Maryland, offered a conception of lawyering in which the lawyer's sense of responsibility was central. 2 D. Hoffman, A Course of Legal Study (2d ed. 1836)....   Hoffman wrote: "My client's conscience, and my own, are distinct entities: and though my vocation may sometimes justify my maintaining as facts, or principles, in doubtful cases, what may be neither one nor the other, I shall ever claim the privilege of solely judging to what extent to go"....   Furthermore, he insisted that:

Should my client be disposed to insist on captious requisitions, or frivolous and

vexatious defences, they shall be neither enforced nor countenanced by me....   If, after duly examining a case, I am persuaded that my client's claim or defence ... cannot, or rather ought not, to be sustained, I will promptly advise him to abandon it. To press it further in such a case, with the hope of gleaning some advantage by an extorted compromise, would be lending myself to a dishonourable use of legal means, in order to gain a *portion* of that, the *whole* of which I have reason to believe would be denied to him both by law and justice.

... A recourse role conception forces the lawyer to recognize that the exercise of his role duties must fully engage his rational and critical powers, and his sense of moral responsibility as well. Although not intended to obliterate the moral distance between professional and private moralities, a recourse role conception bridges that gap by integrating to a significant degree the moral personality of the individual with the performance of role responsibilities. Most significantly, this conception prevents the lawyer from escaping responsibility by relying on his status as an agent of the client or an instrument of the system. He cannot consider himself simply a legal technician, since his role essentially involves the exercise of his *engaged* moral judgment....

. . .

... The recourse role conception is not paternalistic even in the very broad sense that the lawyer is encouraged to make the client's moral decisions for him. The moral judgments that the lawyer makes are made on his own behalf; he does not make the client's decisions. Indeed, it is an advantage of my proposal, in contrast to the standard conception, that it enables both lawyer and client to recognize and respect the moral status of the other. The lawyer-client relationship should not be any more paternalistic than a relationship between friends.

Note on Postema and the integration of polarities: Some markers on the path

1. Is there generalizable wisdom in Charles Hampden–Turner's treatment of the values of courage and caution, altruism and self-interest (Becoming a Lawyer, p. 161)?

> Whichever [quality] is manifested at one moment is constrained and contained by its latent opposite, which in turn becomes manifest and is contained by *its* opposite.... There is nothing inherently good or bad in the fact of risk-taking alone. Vice or virtue lies in the manner in which different degrees of risk-taking have been sequentially organized and optimally related.

2. Consider, more broadly, the soundness and relevance of the following:

> Logical contradiction is a property of propositions. A logical contradiction involves two terms, a proposition and its logical denial. For example, if P is a proposition, then a logical contradiction is involved in asserting simultaneously that P and not-P are both true. A conceptual opposition, on the other hand, is a property of a relation between concepts in a particular context—it therefore need not involve a logical contradiction between propositions....
>
> If we say that red and green are opposite colors in a traffic light, we are not saying that they logically contradict each other. Rather, they are opposed with respect to the meanings these colors are given in traffic signals. The context of conventions concerning traffic signals makes them opposites. In another context, they may be seen as

similar to each other. For example, red and green are both colors of the natural spectrum, or colors associated with Christmas, while lavender and brown are not....

Conceptual oppositions are thus intimately related to questions of similarity and difference....

... The problem arises because we often forget that what produces a conceptual opposition is context and relation and not logical contradiction. This mistake is easy to make because many conceptual oppositions look and act like logical contradictions in particular contexts. Our cultural practices make red and green conceptual opposites in the context of a traffic light. It is also true that the same object cannot be at the same time wholly green and wholly red. Thus it appears as if statements of the form "This object is red" and "This object is green" might be logically contradictory, and that to predicate both properties (red and green) of the same object might involve logical contradiction.

Nevertheless, [it] is not true that everything must be either green or red, nor is it true that nothing can be both green and red. Green and red are mutually exclusive in some contexts, but they do not use up the entire spectrum of color—a sweater can be purple or grey. And in still other contexts green and red are not even mutually exclusive, for a green and red striped sweater can be both green and red. Thus, conceptual oppositions like red and green only give rise to statements of logical contradiction in specific contexts.

... The contextuality of similarity and difference means that conceptual oppositions are only opposed in certain contexts. In other contexts, the terms of the opposition have similarities and are not opposed.

... A nested opposition is a conceptual opposition each of whose terms contains the other, or each of whose terms shares something with the other....

Deconstruction makes a basic claim about the logic of similarity and difference: All conceptual oppositions can be reinterpreted as some form of nested opposition. This follows from the contextual and relational nature of conceptual oppositions. Because opposition depends upon context and relation, recontextualization of a conceptual opposition may reveal similarities where before we saw only differences, or historical or conceptual dependence where before we saw only differentiation. Thus, to deconstruct a conceptual opposition is to reinterpret it as a nested opposition. It is to observe simultaneously the similarity and difference, the dependence and differentiation, involved in a relation between concepts....

...

One might well wonder whether deconstructive theory really claims that *all* conceptual oppositions can be reinterpreted as nested opposition. Such a translation would not be possible if there were a conceptual opposition where neither pole bore any element of similarity or conceptual or historical dependence with respect to its opposite.

However, it is always possible to create a context, no matter how artificial, in which two things are said to be alike in some respects.[24] Indeed, we might note that the very fact that we see the two concepts as opposed, rather than as completely irrelevant to each other, indicates some basis of similarity or some conceptual relation between them.[25]

It is important to understand that the deconstructive claim that all conceptual opposition can be reinterpreted as nested opposition is not a claim that all conceptual opposition are incoherent or false opposition. For this involves a confusion of similarity with identity. To say that A and B form a nested opposition is not to say that A is identical with B, or that it is impossible to tell A and B apart in a particular context. Indeed, the concept of a nested opposition only makes sense if we assume that there are points of a difference between A and B; otherwise we could not see these concepts as opposed. Therefore it is a misuse of deconstructive argument to claim that one can abolish all distinctions and demonstrate that all forms of intellectual endeavor lack coherence. For deconstructive argument itself rests upon the very possibility of those distinctions and those coherences.

Jack M. Balkin, Nested Oppositions, 99 Yale L.J. 1669, 1674–77 (1990).

How, if at all, does this analysis inform the search for a non-polarized approach to advocacy?

3. There is a critical difference between simply compromising between, or laminating together, two "competing" values, and a genuine integration of both. The Pirsig and Schumacher excerpts (Becoming a Lawyer, pp. 153, 166) suggest that what makes such an integration possible is a *quality of being,* rather than a prescription of one sort or another: It is only from "out in front of the train" (Pirsig, p. 155) that both poles can be seen in relation to one another and to their underlying values; it is only through "faculties of a higher order than those required for any policy" (Schumacher, p. 168) that conflicting values can "cease to be opposites" (p. 169).

Is this a mystification, or a beam of light?

The concluding sub-section of this book, pp. 355 et seq., below, attempts to apply an "alternative synthesis" to several lawyering contexts.

---

24. For example, even logical contradictions, such as that between P and not-P, can be interpreted as nested opposition, if we shift our focus from the opposed meanings of the two propositions to the opposition between the propositions themselves. We might note that both propositions have in common the property of being propositions, both involve a statement about a state of affairs P, and each is dependent for its truth value upon the truth value assigned to the opposite proposition.

25. Nevertheless, this answer suggests that at least some reinterpretations of conceptual opposition as nested opposition will be trivial or uninteresting. We might then ask if there is any way of demarcating in advance those conceptual opposition that will produce interesting forms of nested opposition from those that will produce only trivial or uninteresting ones. But we cannot compile such a list in advance, for triviality and interest, like similarity and difference, are highly contextual properties. In other words, although deconstructive techniques can be explained formulaically, the actual practice of deconstruction is not formulaic—it requires sensitivity and creativity on the part of the deconstructor in discovering interesting or relevant points of similarity or conceptual dependence between conceptual opposites.

4. Practicing law in a responsible manner seems a significantly more demanding activity, morally and emotionally, than—to take Postema's example—driving without seriously injuring pedestrians. The capacity "to endure the tension" between competing pulls (Kronman), and to possess and act on "a comprehensive and integrated concept of [one's] activities both within and outside the role" of lawyer (Postema), is not acquired and consistently acted on without substantial effort.

(a) By what processes is the possession or acquisition of this capacity derived? Specifically:

- To what extent is it a matter of one's personality?
- To what extent is it a matter of having sufficient motivation or engaging one's will?
- To what extent may it be both?

(b) What factors seem to you to fuel that motivation, what seem to inhibit it?

- What answer to the first part of this question is suggested by Simon, The Trouble with Legal Ethics, p. 144, above?
- What other responses, if any, do you have?

3. THE DENIAL OF CHOICE AND RESPONSIBILITY

BECOMING A LAWYER: A HUMANISTIC PERSPECTIVE ON LEGAL EDUCATION AND PROFESSIONALISM

E. Dvorkin, J. Himmelstein, & H. Lesnick
West Pub. Co., 1981.

Read pages 91–120, 125–45.

Note on choice and responsibility: A non-polarized understanding

> It is not your duty to complete the work, but neither are you free to desist from it.*

1. The excerpts from *Becoming a Lawyer* present an extensive catalogue of the sources of the tendency to deny choice and responsibility:

- Choice is denied by reference to authority of one kind or another, whether of a group norm or of the necessities of "the times"; by the experience of oneself as victim; by the preeminence that security needs seem to demand; and by the perception that the only alternative to acceding to that demand is martyrdom.
- Responsibility is denied by its division among actors, none of whom is solely responsible, and by its equation with guilt, leading either to its

---

* Ethics of the Fathers 2:16, in The Baby-   Aboth 24 (Soncino Ed.1935).
lonian Talmud 4 Order Nezikin, Tractate

righteous rejection or to a spurious acceptance in the form of self-flagellation.

• These ideas are powerfully reinforced by the array of difficulties that immediately come into view (if not entirely into awareness) once their hold is questioned: the difficulty of finding answers, the tension of continually searching for answers, the elusiveness of self-knowledge, the fear of loss of mastery, of being wrong, of acknowledging vulnerability.

Consider the specific ideas or incidents contained in the excerpts from *Becoming a Lawyer,* as they bear on each of these sources:

• To what extent, if at all, do they ring true in your own experience?

• To what extent do you think that they are reinforced:

   • in the culture of legal education?

   • in the culture of law practice?

   • in the larger society in which we grew up and live?

2.   The excerpts from *Becoming a Lawyer* also contain several ideas that are intended to address the question how awareness of the reality of this barrier can lead to a weakening, rather than a strengthening, of the power of its hold on our consciousness.   To what extent, if at all, do the following factors contribute to this "weakening" process?

• the avoidance of polarization of alternatives: "Weakening" is not "evaporation";

• recognition of the costs of continued denial of choice and responsibility, and of the ways in which those costs tend to be masked;

• acknowledgement of internal conflict over the identification of one's own norms, and over decisionmaking in light of them;

• thinking of choice and responsibility in non-polarized ways: What would it mean to *accept* responsibility, or to *exercise* choice? What do those ideas *not* mean?

3.   The Christian theologian H. Richard Niebuhr explores "the meaning of responsibility" in his book, The Responsible Self (1963).   To Niebuhr, the concept of responsibility begins with the idea of *response,* "the action of a self [in] response to interpreted action" (p. 61) upon one, but includes the crucial element of *accountability:*

Our actions are responsible not only insofar as they are reactions to interpreted actions upon us but also insofar as they are made in anticipation of answers to our answers. An agent's action is like a statement in a dialogue. Such a statement not only seeks to meet, as it were, or to fit into, the previous statement to which it is an answer, but is made in anticipation of reply. It looks forward as well as backward; it anticipates objections, confirmations, and corrections. It is made as part of a total conversation that leads forward and is to have meaning as a whole.

Id. at 64.

4. Is the emphasis on "responsibility" simply an indirect way of promoting values that the traditional concept of advocacy tends to devalue? Is it, on the other hand, simply a contentless appeal to be "authentic"? Consider the soundness and sufficiency of this response:

To teach students what it means to be responsible is to attempt to empower to do so those who would choose to do so. That effort is importantly different from teaching students that they *ought* to be responsible, in a way that bears on the central question whether the emphasis on responsibility has any values implication. To the extent that it does not—that it is simply asking people to act out of authenticity, in congruence with their own values, whatever they may be—it seems woefully incomplete, and oriented only to a narrow form of personal fulfillment. To the extent that there is substantive values content in the idea of responsibility, there is concern ... that its legitimacy is open to question and that students are being manipulated or indoctrinated in an institutionally determined value orthodoxy.

My hypothesis is that a fully developed concept of responsibility can resolve the dilemma between these two poles, that the idea of responsibility is far more demanding than it is often viewed, that it has values content in a way that respects individual choice.... Our tendency is to see the choice as polar. Either responsibility is the key, or values are. Either there is a values content to responsibility, or there is not. In both dilemmas, each pole has serious flaws....

The dilemma is often posed in a static way: Suppose a student tells you that he or she is in law school simply to learn the rules, get the certificate, and head out to become a "happy rich person." Do you kick the student out, write him or her off as free to do it but bound for hell, or adopt some other unhappy variation on either oppression or surrender? My response is that we continually *invite* the student to engage with us over his or her choice, its implications, and the decision to take responsibility for it. If we *continually* ask students to take responsibility, do it over time, ask them to interact with one another and with the question, ... we come into touch with our connection with others; not as a role, not as a moral imperative, not as political pressure—and not in the same way for all—but as an authentic part of us. Once that happens to me (as student or teacher), I can choose to put the realization aside, not act on it. However, it is now partly *me* that I am putting aside, and if the question keeps coming up, in an endless variety of ways, it has to be continually put aside.

Once our connections with others is acted on rather than put aside, even in a minor context, there has been an important shift, which makes new shifts possible. Experiencing choice where it did not seem to exist before makes it more readily seem to exist the next time. This process is not linear, and in some individuals will never take hold. But that is not to say that it does not have enormous significance, looking at a group of ... people over three years. And overall the shift *has* a values content, it is not simply that each of us becomes more himself or herself, whatever that may happen to be. In our society, there is a systematic strengthening of some parts of the self as we grow up, and a systematic weakening of others, and the process of taking responsibility and becoming more fully oneself strengthens the delegitimated parts. They tend to be the values of the alternative consciousness: the emphasis on equality, on relationship, on caring.

Lesnick, The Integration of Responsibility and Values: Legal Education in an Alternative Consciousness of Law and Lawyering, 10 Nova L.J. 633, 641–43 (1986).

To what extent, if at all, does this analysis seem helpful?

4. THE EXPERIENCE OF MEANINGLESSNESS

BECOMING A LAWYER: A HUMANISTIC PERSPECTIVE ON LEGAL EDUCATION AND PROFESSIONALISM

E. Dvorkin, J. Himmelstein, & H. Lesnick
West Pub. Co., 1981.

Read pages 47–90.

Note on Tolstoy, Jonah, and Sir Thomas More: The lawyer as mortal

1. The practice of law constantly places a lawyer in a fiduciary role, acting for someone else, and the traditional concept of advocacy places a dominant emphasis on role-differentiation and professional detachment, justifying and prescribing the removal of the lawyer's self from his or her actions and words. The result can readily be what I have termed a "moot court" view of lawyering: "[L]awyers are all simply doing technical work, and a 'good' legal job implicates such major matters as one's tangible conditions of employment and such minor matters as the length of one's commute to and from home." Lesnick, Infinity in a Grain of Sand, supra, 37 U.C.L.A.L.Rev. at 1163. Elizabeth Dvorkin contends (Becoming a Lawyer, pp. 56–57) that a central premise of the traditional concept too easily leads to the belief "that legal representation is a meaningless business," suppressing the tendency to ask oneself: "What sort of work [as a lawyer] is consistent with my vision of what is most important to my life?"

The readings in the opening portion of the above-noted portion of *Becoming a Lawyer* suggest that the result can be the denial of a need that is deep-seated in us as human beings. Does that seem true?

2. The remaining excerpts suggest several factors that tend to explain why the preceding question is a difficult one for most of us even to think seriously about, and certainly to talk about, especially in a public setting, especially in the context of preparing oneself for being a professional. The fears of acting juvenile, of becoming or appearing pretentious, of placing at risk what seems important to hold on to, and of being engulfed in negative emotions, are hardly matters that a sensible person ignores.

• Which of these concerns seems to you most salient?

• Is there (again) a way past the barrier of these concerns, which does not ignore them, but which does not see them as wholly dispositive, and gives them only their due?

5.   THE LEGAL CONSCIOUSNESS OF WORK

While most thinking and writing about the practice of law emphasize its unique aspects, it is important to recognize that being a lawyer is one variety of work, and that what our culture and our law teach us about what it means to work will have some significant applicability to the work of a lawyer. This section attempts to demonstrate how there is much in the dominant consciousness of work that interacts in a mutually supportive way with the traditional concept of advocacy, and to suggest that a serious attempt to articulate an alternative concept can be made only in the context of an attempt to articulate an alternative consciousness of work itself.

(a) *The professional as worker, under common law principles of employment "at will"*

GEARY v. UNITED STATES STEEL CORP.

Supreme Court of Pennsylvania, 1974.
456 Pa. 171, 319 A.2d 174.

Opinion By Mr. Justice Pomeroy.

The complaint avers that appellant, George B. Geary, was continuously employed by appellee, United States Steel Corporation (hereinafter "company"), from 1953 until July 13, 1967, when he was dismissed from his position. Geary's duties involved the sale of tubular products to the oil and gas industry. His employment was at will. The dismissal is said to have stemmed from a disagreement concerning one of the company's new products, a tubular casing designed for use under high pressure. Geary alleges that he believed the product had not been adequately tested and constituted a serious danger to anyone who used it; that he voiced his misgivings to his superiors and was ordered to "follow directions", which he agreed to do; that he nevertheless continued to express his reservations, taking his case to a vice-president in charge of sale of the product; that as a result of his efforts the product was reevaluated and withdrawn from the market; that he at all times performed his duties to the best of his ability and always acted with the best interests of the company and the general public in mind; and that because of these events he was summarily discharged without notice....[3]

Appellant candidly admits that he is beckoning us into uncharted territory. No court in this Commonwealth has ever recognized a non-

---

3. The company in its brief denies that the new product was withdrawn from the market as a result of Geary's efforts, and has offered to prove that it has been marketed successfully without incident for several years. This factual contention is irrelevant at the preliminary objection stage.

statutory cause of action for an employer's termination of an at-will employment relationship. What scant authority there is on the subject points the other way....

The Pennsylvania law is in accordance with the weight of authority elsewhere. Absent a statutory or contractual provision to the contrary, the law has taken for granted the power of either party to terminate an employment relationship for any or no reason. This power of termination is explicitly recognized in the Restatement of Torts, § 762, Privilege of Selecting Persons for Business Relations:

> One who causes intended or unintended harm to another merely by refusing to enter into a business relation with the other or to continue a business relation terminable at his will is not liable for that harm if the refusal is not (a) a breach of the actor's duty to the other arising from the nature of the actor's business or from a legislative enactment, or (b) a means of accomplishing an illegal effect on competition, or (c) part of a concerted refusal by a combination of persons of which he is a member.

We recognize that economic conditions have changed radically.... The huge corporate enterprises which have emerged in this century wield an awesome power over their employees. It has been aptly remarked that

> We have become a nation of employees. We are dependent upon others for our means of livelihood, and most of our people have become completely dependent upon wages. If they lose their jobs they lose every resource, except for the relief supplied by the various forms of social security. Such dependence of the mass of the people upon others for all of their income is something new in the world. For our generation, the substance of life is in another man's hands.

[F. Tannenbaum, A Philosophy of Labor 9 (1951)]. Against the background of these changes, the broad question to which appellant invites our attention is whether the time has come to impose judicial restrictions on an employer's power of discharge.

. . .

Appellant's final argument is an appeal to considerations of public policy. Geary asserts in his complaint that he was acting in the best interests of the general public as well as of his employer in opposing the marketing of a product which he believed to be defective. Certainly, the potential for abuse of an employer's power of dismissal is particularly serious where an employee must exercise independent, expert judgment in matters of product safety, but Geary does not hold himself out as this sort of employee. So far as the complaint shows, he was involved only in the sale of company products. There is no suggestion that he possessed any expert qualifications, or that his duties extended to making judgments in matters of product safety. In essence, Geary argues that his conduct should be protected because his intentions were good. No doubt most employees who are dismissed from their posts can make the same claim. We doubt that establishing a right to litigate every such case as it arises would operate either in the best interest of the parties or of the public.

[We have considered] the possible impact of such suits on the legitimate interests of employers in hiring and retaining the best personnel available. The ever-present threat of suit might well inhibit the making of critical judgments by employers concerning employee qualifications.[13]

The problem extends beyond the question of individual competence, for even an unusually gifted person may be of no use to his employer if he cannot work effectively with fellow employees. Here, for example, Geary's complaint shows that he bypassed his immediate superiors and pressed his views on higher officers, utilizing his close contacts with a company vice president. The praiseworthiness of Geary's motives does not detract from the company's legitimate interest in preserving its normal operational procedures from disruption. In sum, while we agree that employees should be encouraged to express their educated views on the quality of their employer's products, we are not persuaded that creating a new non-statutory cause of action of the sort proposed by appellant is the best way to achieve this result. On balance, whatever public policy imperatives can be discerned here seem to militate against such a course.

. . .

DISSENTING OPINION BY MR. JUSTICE ROBERTS:

I cannot accept the view implicit in the majority's decision that today's jurisprudence is so lacking in awareness and vitality that our judicial process is incapable of affording relief to a responsible employee for an arbitrary and retaliatory discharge from employment. I dissent.

. . .

As a salesman, Geary was required to know intimately the products he was selling. He represented United States Steel and it was

---

13. Professor Blades has analyzed some of the difficulties in this area:

> Ordinarily, where both sides present equally credible versions of the facts, the plaintiff will have failed to carry his burden. However, there is the danger that the average jury will identify with, and therefore believe, the employee. This possibility could give rise to vexatious lawsuits by disgruntled employees fabricating plausible tales of employer coercion. If the potential for vexatious suits by discharged employees is too great, employers will be inhibited in exercising their best judgment as to which employees should or should not be re-

tained.... Compromise of the employer's power to make such judgments about professional, managerial or other high-ranking employees ... is especially undesirable. The higher ranking the employee, the more important to the success of the business is his effective performance.... Blades, [Employment at Will vs. Individual Freedom: On Limiting the Abusive Exercise of Employer Power, 67 Colum.L.Rev. 1404,] 1428–9 [(1967)].

Professor Blades nevertheless favors judicial intervention to protect employees at all levels from abusive discharge....

expected that he would be alert to protect his employer's reputation. Likewise, it was natural that he would seek to shield himself and his employer from the consequences of a dangerous product. When he correctly recognized that the defective steel pipe had strong potential for causing injury and damage, he immediately notified his superiors. His reward for loyalty was dismissal....

. . .

[A]ppellant as an employee was "subject to a duty to use reasonable efforts to give his [employer] information which is relevant to affairs entrusted to him, and which, as the [employee] has notice, the [employer] would desire to have and which can be communicated without violating a superior duty to a third person." Restatement (Second) of Agency § 381 (1958). Had Geary refrained from notifying his superiors of the defective product, he could have been discharged for violating this duty to come forward with information. No responsible policy is served which permits an employee to be discharged solely for obeying his legal duty to communicate information to his superiors. Indeed, the policy underlying this duty to communicate is frustrated by denying Geary the opportunity to present his case to the court.

. . .

Our society has long been apprehensive of the arbitrary dismissal power of employers, and has sought through various solutions to remedy the problem. To countervail employers' dismissal power, unions were created.[7] Congress has sought to safeguard certain classes of employees from wrongful and capricious discharges.[8] And our Legislature has decided that certain state employees must be guarded from the abuses of arbitrary discharge.[9]

Yet, under the majority's view, unorganized employees remain unprotected.... In my view this Court should take this first step and protect Geary and unorganized employees from arbitrary and retaliatory discharges.

PIERCE v. ORTHO PHARMACEUTICAL CORP.
Supreme Court of New Jersey, 1980.
84 N.J. 58, 417 A.2d 505.

The opinion of the Court was delivered by POLLOCK, J.

7. See American Steel Foundries v. Tri-City Central Trades Council, 257 U.S. 184, 209 ... (1921).

"A single employee was helpless in dealing with an employer. He was dependent ordinarily on his daily wage for the maintenance of himself and family. If the employer refused to pay him the wages that he thought fair, he was nevertheless unable to leave the employ and to resist arbitrary and unfair treatment. Union was essential to give laborers opportunity to deal on equality with their employer."

8. E.g., The Automobile Dealer Franchise Act of 1956, 15 U.S.C. §§ 1221–25 (1970).

9. The Civil Service Act provides that "[no] regular employe in the classified service shall be removed except for just cause." 71 P.S. § 741.807 (Supp.1973)....

The Civil Service Act further requires that every state employee covered by the Act be given notice of "any personnel action taken with respect to him," id. § 741.950, and that he be provided an opportunity to appeal to and appear publicly before the Civil Service Commission. Id. § 741.951.

This case presents the question whether an employee at will has a cause of action against her employer to recover damages for the termination of her employment following her refusal to continue a project she viewed as medically unethical....

Plaintiff, Dr. Grace Pierce, sued for damages after termination of her employment with defendant, Ortho Pharmaceutical Corporation. The trial judge granted defendant's motion for summary judgment....

Since the matter involves a motion for summary judgment, we glean the facts from the pleadings, affidavits, and depositions before the court on the motion, giving plaintiff the benefit of all reasonable inferences that may be drawn in her favor....

Ortho specializes in the development and manufacture of therapeutic and reproductive drugs. Dr. Pierce is a medical doctor who was first employed by Ortho in 1971 as an Associate Director of Medical Research. She signed no contract except a secrecy agreement, and her employment was not for a fixed term. She was an employee at will. In 1973, she became the Director of Medical Research/Therapeutics, one of three major sections of the Medical Research Department. Her primary responsibilities were to oversee development of therapeutic drugs and to establish procedures for testing those drugs for safety, effectiveness, and marketability. Her immediate supervisor was Dr. Samuel Pasquale, Executive Medical Director.

In the spring of 1975, Dr. Pierce was the only medical doctor on a project team developing loperamide, a liquid drug for treatment of diarrhea in infants, children, and elderly persons. The proposed formulation contained saccharin. Although the concentration was consistent with the formula for loperamide marketed in Europe, the project team agreed that the formula was unsuitable for use in the United States. An alternative formulation containing less saccharin might have been developed within approximately three months.

By March 28, however, the project team, except for Dr. Pierce, decided to continue with the development of loperamide. That decision was made apparently in response to a directive from the Marketing Division of Ortho. This decision meant that Ortho would file an investigational new drug application (IND) with the Federal Food and Drug Administration (FDA), continue laboratory studies on loperamide, and begin work on a formulation. FDA approval is required before any new drug is tested clinically on humans. 21 U.S.C. § 355; 21 C.F.R. §§ 310.3 et seq. Therefore, loperamide would be tested on patients only if the FDA approved the saccharin formulation.

Dr. Pierce knew that the IND would have to be filed with and approved by the FDA before clinical testing could begin. Nonetheless, she continued to oppose the work being done on loperamide at Ortho. On April 21, 1975, she sent a memorandum to the project team expressing her disagreement with its decision to proceed with the development of the drug. In her opinion, there was no justification for seeking FDA permission to use the drug in light of medical controversy over the safety of saccharin.

Dr. Pierce met with Dr. Pasquale on May 9 and informed him that she disagreed with the decision to file an IND with the FDA. She felt that by continuing to work on loperamide she would violate her interpretation of the Hippocratic oath. She concluded that the risk that saccharin might be harmful should preclude testing the formula on children or elderly persons, especially when an alternative formulation might soon be available.

Dr. Pierce recognized that she was joined in a difference of "viewpoints" or "opinion" with Dr. Pasquale and others at Ortho concerning the use of a formula containing saccharin. In her opinion, the safety of saccharin in loperamide pediatric drops was medically debatable. She acknowledged that Dr. Pasquale was entitled to his opinion to proceed with the IND. On depositions, she testified concerning the reason for her difference of opinion about the safety of using saccharin in loperamide pediatric drops:

Q That was because in your medical opinion that was an unsafe thing to do. Is that so?

A No. I didn't know. The question of saccharin was one of potential harm. It was controversial. Even though the rulings presently look even less favorable for saccharin it is still a controversial issue.

After their meeting on May 9, Dr. Pasquale informed Dr. Pierce that she would no longer be assigned to the loperamide project. On May 14, Dr. Pasquale asked Dr. Pierce to choose other projects. After Dr. Pierce returned from vacation in Finland, she met on June 16 with Dr. Pasquale to discuss other projects, but she did not choose a project at that meeting. She felt she was being demoted, even though her salary would not be decreased. Dr. Pierce summarized her impression of that meeting in her letter of resignation submitted to Dr. Pasquale the following day. In that letter, she stated:

Upon learning in our meeting June 16, 1975, that you believe I have not 'acted as a Director', have displayed inadequacies as to my competence, responsibility, productivity, inability to relate to the Marketing Personnel, that you, and reportedly Dr. George Braun and Mr. Verne Willaman consider me to be non-promotable and that I am now or soon will be demoted, I find it impossible to continue my employment at Ortho.

The letter made no specific mention of her difference of opinion with Dr. Pasquale over continuing the work on loperamide. Nonetheless, viewing the matter most favorably to Dr. Pierce, we assume the sole reason for the termination of her employment was the dispute over the loperamide project. Dr. Pasquale accepted her resignation.

In her complaint, which was based on principles of tort and contract law, Dr. Pierce claimed damages for the termination of her employment. Her complaint alleged:

> The Defendant, its agents, servants and employees requested and demanded Plaintiff follow a course of action and behavior which was impossible for Plaintiff to follow because of the Hippocratic oath she had taken, because of the ethical standards by which she was governed as a physician, and because of the regulatory schemes, both federal and state, statutory and case law, for the protection of the public in the field of health and human well-being, which schemes Plaintiff believed she should honor.

However, she did not specify that testing would violate any state or federal statutory regulation. Similarly, she did not state that continuing the research would violate the principles of ethics of the American Medical Association. She never contended her participation in the research would expose her to a claim for malpractice.

Ortho moved for summary judgment on two theories. The first was that Dr. Pierce's action for wrongful discharge was barred because she resigned. The trial judge denied the motion on that ground because he found that there was a fact question whether Ortho induced Dr. Pierce's resignation. However, the trial court granted Ortho's motion on the alternative ground that because Dr. Pierce was an employee at will, Ortho could end her employment for any reason....

. . .

Under the common law, in the absence of an employment contract, employers or employees have been free to terminate the employment relationship with or without cause....

The rule temporarily attained constitutional magnitude in Adair v. United States, 208 U.S. 161, 175 ... (1907), where the United States Supreme Court held unconstitutional a federal statute making it illegal for an employer to prohibit an employee from joining a union. See also Coppage v. Kansas, 236 U.S. 1, 13–14 ... (1914) ... As a corollary of the development of legislation, administrative regulation, and judicial decisions, the rule has since lost its constitutional protection. See NLRB v. Jones & Laughlin Steel Corp., 301 U.S. 1 ... (1937).

In the last century, the common law developed in a laissez-faire climate that encouraged industrial growth and approved the right of an employer to control his own business, including the right to fire without cause an employee at will.... The twentieth century has witnessed significant changes in socioeconomic values that have led to reassessment of the common law rule. Businesses have evolved from small and medium size firms to gigantic corporations in which ownership is separate from management. Formerly there was a clear delineation between employers, who frequently were owners of their own businesses, and employees. The employer in the old sense has been replaced by a superior in the corporate hierarchy who is himself an employee. We are a nation of employees. Growth in the number of employees has been accompanied by increasing recognition of the need for stability in labor relations.

Commentators have questioned the compatibility of the traditional at will doctrine with the realities of modern economics and employment practices. See, e.g., Blades, Employment at Will vs. Individual Freedom: On Limiting the Abusive Exercise of Employer Power, 67 Colum.L.Rev. 1404 (1967) [hereinafter cited as Blades]. The common law rule has been modified by the enactment of labor relations legislation. See, e.g., NLRB v. Jones & Laughlin Steel Corp., supra. The National Labor Relations Act and other labor legislation illustrate the governmental policy of preventing employers from using the right of discharge as a means of oppression. . . . Consistent with this policy, many states have recognized the need to protect employees who are not parties to a collective bargaining agreement or other contract from abusive practices by the employer.

Recently those states have recognized a common law cause of action for employees at will who were discharged for reasons that were in some way "wrongful". The courts in those jurisdictions have taken varied approaches, some recognizing the action in tort, some in contract. . . . Nearly all jurisdictions link the success of the wrongfully discharged employee's action to proof that the discharge violated public policy.

In Geary v. United States Steel Corp., 456 Pa. 171, 319 A.2d 174 (1974), a salesman employed at will was discharged after he expressed to the management his opinion that a new product was defective and dangerous. The court sustained the dismissal of the complaint because it revealed only that "there was a dispute over the merits of the new product," and because no public policy is violated when a company discharges an employee who is not qualified to make technical judgments for making "a nuisance of himself." 319 A.2d at 178–179. However, the court suggested that an action in tort might exist if a "clear mandate of public policy is violated." Id. at 180. See [cases cited, upholding the claims of employees fired for taking time off for jury duty or refusal to take a polygraph test].

In Monge v. Beebe Rubber Co., 114 N.H. 130, 316 A.2d 549 (1974), the court allowed an at will employee to sue for breach of contract when she was dismissed after she refused to date the foreman. Balancing the employee's interest in maintaining employment, the employer's interest in running a business, and the public interest, the court held that termination motivated by bad faith or malice is not in the public interest and constitutes a breach of the employment contract. 316 A.2d at 551. See [case upholding the claim of an employee discharged to avoid paying a bonus].

Employees have recovered damages for wrongful discharge in a variety of contexts. It is well established that an employee has a cause of action where he is discharged in retaliation for filing a worker's compensation claim, even if the worker's compensation statute does not provide such a remedy....

[The court also cited cases upholding claims of employees discharged for refusal to participate in an illegal scheme to fix retail prices; for refusal to give false answers to a legislative committee; for refusing to submit to a lie detector test, where a statute prohibited conditioning employment on the taking of such tests; and for trying to convince an employer to comply with the consumer credit laws.]

. . .

In evaluating claims for wrongful discharge, courts have been careful not to interfere with the employer's right to make business decisions and to choose the best personnel for the job. In Lampe v. Presbyterian Medical Center, 590 P.2d 513 (Colo.App.1979), a nurse was discharged after refusing to reduce her staff's overtime as requested. She felt that the reduction would jeopardize the health of the patients. In dismissing the complaint, the court recognized that the employer must be free to hire someone who was able to manage the staff without endangering patients. The court held that a statute containing general principles pertaining to the licensing of nurses did not create a cause of action. Id. at 515–517.

[The court cited cases rejecting suits by employees discharged for attempting to correct false impressions given by the corporation to outside business associates and the public; for refusing to consent to take a psychological stress evaluation test; for participating in an unauthorized Christmas party fund; for reporting a supervisor for taking kickbacks; and for announcing an intention to attend law school at night].

Several states have declined to adopt a public policy exception to the at will doctrine. See, e.g., Martin v. Tapley, 360 So.2d 708 (Ala. 1978) (employee alleged discharge in retaliation for filing worker's compensation claim); Hinrichs v. Tranquilaire Hosp., 352 So.2d 1130 (Ala.1977) (employee alleged she was fired for refusing to falsify medical records); Segal v. Arrow Industrial Corp. 364 So.2d 89 (Fla.Ct.App. 1978) (employee alleged discharge in retaliation for filing worker's compensation claim).

This Court has long recognized the capacity of the common law to develop and adapt to current needs.... The interests of employees, employers, and the public lead to the conclusion that the common law of New Jersey should limit the right of an employer to fire an employee at will.

In recognizing a cause of action to provide a remedy for employees who are wrongfully discharged, we must balance the interests of the employee, the employer, and the public. Employees have an interest in knowing they will not be discharged for exercising their legal rights. Employers have an interest in knowing they can run their business as they see fit as long as their conduct is consistent with public policy.

The public has an interest in employment stability and in discouraging frivolous lawsuits by dissatisfied employees.

Although the contours of an exception are important to all employees at will, this case focuses on the special considerations arising out of the right to fire an employee at will who is a member of a recognized profession. . . .

Employees who are professionals owe a special duty to abide not only by federal and state law, but also by the recognized codes of ethics of their professions. That duty may oblige them to decline to perform acts required by their employers. However, an employee should not have the right to prevent his or her employer from pursuing its business because the employee perceives that a particular business decision violates the employee's personal morals, as distinguished from the recognized code of ethics of the employee's profession. . . .

We hold that an employee has a cause of action for wrongful discharge when the discharge is contrary to a clear mandate of public policy. The sources of public policy include legislation; administrative rules, regulations or decisions; and judicial decisions. In certain instances, a professional code of ethics may contain an expression of public policy. However, not all such sources express a clear mandate of public policy. For example, a code of ethics designed to serve only the interests of a profession or an administrative regulation concerned with technical matters probably would not be sufficient. Absent legislation, the judiciary must define the cause of action in case-by-case determinations. An employer's right to discharge an employee at will carries a correlative duty not to discharge an employee who declines to perform an act that would require a violation of a clear mandate of public policy. However, unless an employee at will identifies a specific expression of public policy, he may be discharged with or without cause.

. . .

We now turn to the question whether Dr. Pierce was discharged for reasons contrary to a clear mandate of public policy. . . .

The material facts are uncontroverted. In opposing the motion for summary judgment, Dr. Pierce did not contend that saccharin was harmful, but that it was controversial. Because of the controversy, she said she could not continue her work on loperamide. Her supervisor, Dr. Pasquale, disagreed and thought that research should continue.

As stated above, before loperamide could be tested on humans, an IND had to be submitted to the FDA to obtain approval for such testing. 21 U.S.C. § 355. The IND must contain complete manufacturing specifications, details of pre-clinical studies (testing on animals) which demonstrate the safe use of the drug, and a description of proposed clinical studies. The FDA then has 30 days to withhold approval of testing. 21 C.F.R. § 312.1. Since no IND had been filed here, and even giving Dr. Pierce the benefit of all doubt regarding her allegations, it is clear that clinical testing of loperamide on humans was not imminent.

Dr. Pierce argues that by continuing to perform research on loperamide she would have been forced to violate professional medical ethics expressed in the Hippocratic oath. She cites the part of the oath that reads: "I will prescribe regimen for the good of my patients according to my ability and my judgment and never do harm to anyone." Clearly, the general language of the oath does not prohibit, specifically, research that does not involve tests on humans and that cannot lead to such tests without governmental approval.

We note that Dr. Pierce did not ... allege that continuing her research would constitute an act of medical malpractice or violate any statute....

In this case, Dr. Pierce has never contended that saccharin would necessarily cause harm to anyone. She alleged that the current controversy made continued investigation an unnecessary risk. However when she stopped work on loperamide, there was no risk. Our point here is not that participation in unethical conduct must be imminent before an employee may refuse to work. The more relevant consideration is that Dr. Pierce does not allege that preparation and filing of the IND was unethical. Further Dr. Pierce does not suggest that Ortho would have proceeded with human testing without FDA approval. The case would be far different if Ortho had filed the IND, the FDA had disapproved it, and Ortho insisted on testing the drug on humans. The actual facts are that Dr. Pierce could not have harmed anyone by continuing to work on loperamide.

Viewing the matter most favorably to Dr. Pierce, the controversy at Ortho involved a difference in medical opinions. Dr. Pierce acknowledged that Dr. Pasquale was entitled to his opinion that the oath did not forbid work on loperamide. Nonetheless, implicit in Dr. Pierce's position is the contention that Dr. Pasquale and Ortho were obliged to accept her opinion. Dr. Pierce contends, in effect, that Ortho should have stopped research on loperamide because of her opinion about the controversial nature of the drug.

Dr. Pierce espouses a doctrine that would lead to disorder in drug research. Under her theory, a professional employee could redetermine the propriety of a research project even if the research did not involve a violation of a clear mandate of public policy. Chaos would result if a single doctor engaged in research were allowed to determine, according to his or her individual conscience, whether a project should continue. An employee does not have a right to continued employment when he or she refuses to conduct research simply because it would contravene his or her personal morals....

... As a matter of law, there is no public policy against conducting research on drugs that may be controversial, but potentially beneficial to mankind, particularly where continuation of the research is subject to approval by the FDA. Consequently, although we recognize an employee may maintain an action for wrongful discharge, we hold there are no issues of material fact to be resolved at trial. . . .

The legislative and regulatory framework pertaining to drug development reflects a public policy that research involving testing on humans may proceed with FDA approval. The public has an interest in the development of drugs, subject to the approval of a responsible management and the FDA, to protect and promote the health of mankind. Research on new drugs may involve questions of safety, but courts should not preempt determination of debatable questions unless the research involves a violation of a clear mandate of public policy. Where pharmaceutical research does not contravene a clear mandate of public policy, the extent of research is controlled by regulation through the FDA, liability in tort, and corporate responsibility.

. . .

PASHMAN, J., dissenting.

. . .

The majority's analysis recognizes that the ethical goals of professional conduct are of inestimable social value. By maintaining informed standards of conduct, licensed professions bring to the problems of their public responsibilities the same expertise that marks their calling. The integrity of codes of professional conduct that result from this regulation deserves judicial protection from undue economic pressure. Employers are a potential source of this pressure, for they can provide or withhold—until today, at their whim—job security and the means of enhancing a professional's reputation. Thus, I completely agree with the majority's ruling that "an employee has a cause of action for wrongful discharge when the discharge is contrary to a clear mandate of public policy" as expressed in a "professional code of ethics". . . .

The Court pronounces this rule for the first time today. One would think that it would therefore afford plaintiff an opportunity to seek relief within the confines of this newly announced cause of action. By ordering the grant of summary judgment for defendant, however, the majority apparently believes that such an opportunity would be an exercise in futility. I fail to see how the majority reaches this conclusion. There are a number of detailed, recognized codes of medical ethics that proscribe participation in clinical experimentation when a doctor perceives an unreasonable threat to human health. Any one of these codes could provide the "clear mandate of public policy" that the majority requires.

[Discussion of the Codes is omitted].

On defendant's motion for summary judgment, the majority properly assumes the truth of plaintiff's allegations that "the current controversy [regarding the carcinogenic potential of saccharin] made continued investigation an unnecessary risk." There is certainly enough evidence in the present record to create a genuine issue [of] material fact. . . . The majority notes that a safer alternative formulation of the new drug under investigation "might have been developed within approximately three months." . . . . The risks attending the formula proposed by defendant are more evident. As the majority notes, the project team developing the proposed drug formula "agreed that the formula was unsuitable for use in the United States". . . . Their agreement apparently persisted until defendant made what at present appears to have been a purely profit-motivated exercise in "corporate responsibility" . . .: to proceed with development notwithstanding the "unnecessary risk". . . .

[T]he majority . . . appears to believe that Dr. Pierce had the power to determine whether defendant's proposed development program would continue at all. . . . This is not the case, nor is plaintiff claiming the right to halt defendant's developmental efforts. [P]laintiff claims only the right to her professional autonomy. She contends that she may not be discharged for expressing her view that the clinical program is unethical or for refusing to continue her participation in the project. She has done nothing else to impede continued development of defendant's proposal; moreover, it is undisputed that defendant was able to continue its program by reassigning personnel. . . .

The second point concerns the role of governmental approval of the proposed experimental program. In apparent ignorance of the past failures of official regulation to safeguard against pharmaceutical horrors, the majority implies that the necessity for administrative approval for human testing eliminates the need for active, ethical professionals within the drug industry. . . . But we do not know whether the United States Food and Drug Administration (FDA) would be aware of the safer alternative to the proposed drug when it would pass upon defendant's application for the more hazardous formula. The majority professes no such knowledge. We must therefore assume the FDA would have been left in ignorance. This highlights the need for ethically autonomous professionals within the pharmaceutical industry, a need which the majority's approach does nothing to satisfy.

. . .

WARTHEN v. TOMS RIVER COMMUNITY MEM. HOSPITAL

Superior Court of New Jersey, 1985.
199 N.J.Super. 18, 488 A.2d 229.

The Opinion of the Court was delivered by MICHELS, P.J.A.D.

Plaintiff Corrine Warthen appeals from a summary judgment of the Law Division dismissing her action against defendant Toms River Community Memorial Hospital (Hospital). Plaintiff sought to recover damages for her allegedly wrongful discharge in violation of public policy following her refusal to dialyze a terminally ill double amputee patient because of her "moral, medical and philosophical objections" to performing the procedure.

The facts giving rise to this appeal are not in dispute and may be summarized as follows. The Hospital, where plaintiff had been employed for eleven years as a registered nurse, terminated plaintiff from its employment on August 6, 1982. For the three years just prior to her discharge, plaintiff had worked in the Hospital's kidney dialysis unit. It is undisputed that plaintiff was an at-will employee.

Plaintiff alleges that during the summer of 1982 her supervisor periodically assigned her to dialyze a double amputee patient who suffered from a number of maladies. On two occasions plaintiff claims that she had to cease treatment because the patient suffered cardiac arrest and severe internal hemorrhaging during the dialysis procedure. During the first week of 1982 plaintiff again was scheduled to dialyze this patient. She approached her head nurse and informed her that "she had moral, medical, and philosophical objections" to performing this procedure on the patient because the patient was terminally ill and, she contended, the procedure was causing the patient additional complications. At that time the head nurse granted plaintiff's request for reassignment.

On August 6, 1982, the head nurse again assigned plaintiff to dialyze the same patient. Plaintiff once again objected, apparently stating that she thought she had reached agreement with the head nurse not to be assigned to this particular patient. She also requested the opportunity to meet with the treating physician, Dr. DiBello. Dr. DiBello informed plaintiff that the patient's family wished him kept alive through dialysis and that he would not survive without it. However, plaintiff continued to refuse to dialyze the patient, and the head nurse informed her that if she did not agree to perform the treatment, the Hospital would dismiss her. Plaintiff refused to change her mind, and the Hospital terminated her.

Plaintiff subsequently instituted this action alleging that she was wrongfully discharged by the Hospital without justification and in violation of public policy....

. . .

Plaintiff ... contends that, as a matter of law, the Code for Nurses constitutes an authoritative statement of public policy which justified her conduct and that the trial court therefore improperly granted defendant's motion for summary judgment. In [Pierce v.] Ortho Pharmaceutical [Corp.,] the Supreme Court discussed the role of professional codes of ethics as sources of public policy in "at-will employment" cases: . . .

The Court carefully warned against confusing reliance on professional ethics with reliance on personal morals....

Here, plaintiff cites the Code for Nurses to justify her refusal to dialyze the terminally ill patient. She refers specifically to the following provisions and interpretive statement:

The nurse's concern for human dignity and the provision of quality nursing care is not limited by personal attitudes or beliefs. If personally opposed to the delivery of care in a particular case because of the nature of the health problem or the procedures to be used, the nurse is justified in refusing to participate. Such refusal should be made known in advance and in time for other appropriate arrangements to be made for the client's nursing care. If the nurse must knowingly enter such a case under emergency circumstances or enters unknowingly, the obligation to provide the best possible care is observed. The nurse withdraws from this type of situation only when assured that alternative sources of nursing care are available to the client. If a client requests information or counsel in an area that is legally sanctioned but contrary to the nurse's personal beliefs, the nurse may refuse to provide these services but must advise the client of sources where such service is available.

American Nurses Association, Code for Nurses with Interpretive Statements 1.4 at 5 (1981). Plaintiff contends that these provisions constitute a clear mandate of public policy justifying her conduct....

It is our view that as applied to the circumstances of this case the passage cited by plaintiff defines a standard of conduct beneficial only to the individual nurse and not to the public at large. The overall purpose of the language cited by plaintiff is to preserve human dignity; however, it should not be at the expense of the patient's life or contrary to the family's wishes. The record before us shows that the family had requested that dialysis be continued on the patient, and there is nothing to suggest that the patient had, or would have, indicated otherwise....

The position asserted by plaintiff serves only the individual and the nurses' profession while leaving the public to wonder when and whether they will receive nursing care.... Moreover, as the Hospital argues, "[i]t would be a virtual impossibility to administer a hospital if each nurse or member of the administration staff refused to carry out his or her duties based upon a personal private belief concerning the right to live...."

          . . .

[W]e conclude as a matter of law that even under the circumstances of this case the ethical considerations cited by plaintiff do not rise to the level of a public policy mandate.... Beyond this, ... we have no hesitancy in concluding on this record that plaintiff was motivated by her own personal morals, precluding application of the "public policy" exception to the "at-will employment" doctrine. [T]he very basis for plaintiff's reliance on the Code for Nurses is that she was personally opposed to the dialysis procedure. By refusing to perform the procedure she may have eased her own conscience, but she neither benefited the society-at-large, the patient, nor the patient's family.

Note on the "at will" cases: Public policy and the moral autonomy of professionals

1. The majority opinion in *Geary* not only asserts that plaintiff had no "duty" to concern himself with the safety of the product; it seems to regard his going "outside channels" as an independent basis for concluding that "public policy" was served by his discharge. Why?

Look closely at the language of Model Rule 1.13(b), dealing with the implications of the notion that "a lawyer employed or retained by an organization represents the organization...." MR 1.13(a). Were a lawyer to find himself or herself considering taking an action similar to Geary's, what would Rule 1.13(b) permit or require?

2. The Justices in *Geary* disagree over the question whether plaintiff was subject to a duty to report his concern, but seem to agree that only the existence of an obligation would suffice to ground protection. *Pierce* is explicit that only an obligatory professional norm can be the basis of a "public policy" limiting an employer's discretion.

(a) The obligations that these judges appear to recognize have two qualities that differ from "merely personal morality": First, their source is something external to the employee, in one case a professionally developed norm and in the other an employer's; second, a sanction, actual or potential, accompanies non-compliance.

- Is it the absence of one or both of these elements that makes "merely personal morality" an inadequate basis for job protection? If so, why?

- What do, or would, the opinions (in both *Geary* and *Warthen*) say about the concept of a "self-imposed obligation" (see the discussion of Senior's approach, in Note 3 of the Note on Cooper's Tale, p. 207, above)?

(b) The *Warthen* decision explicitly concludes that it does not benefit the public at large to protect the moral autonomy of professional nurses.

- In what sense is it in the public interest to discourage you (for example) from developing and applying your own moral judgment, including your own interpretation of the norms of the professional codes, in your work as a lawyer?

- In what sense might it be said to be in the public interest to encourage you to do so?

3. May one (once again) find some explanation for the views manifested in these opinions in what I have termed a "celebratory" stance toward the justness of the social order? Consider these factors:

(a) the importance given to the maintenance of a hierarchical relation in the workplace—the concern about "disruption," "chaos," and "disorder"; the relevance of the employer's need for "effective performance"; the axiomatic assertion that "doctor's orders must be carried out";

(b) the confidence with which, in *Pierce*, the majority opinion relies on the protections afforded by "the FDA, liability in tort, and corporate responsibility."

(b) *The Professional as Worker, Under the National Labor Relations Act*

The National Labor Relations Act protects "employees" as defined therein from certain employer acts interfering with their right to join or support unions, and provides for elections to be held by the National Labor Relations Board when a question arises whether a majority of employees in an appropriate unit for collective bargaining wish to have union representation. Employers are prohibited from refusing to bargain collectively with such majority representatives.

The cases in this sub-section illustrate the application of the statute, as perceived by the Supreme Court and the NLRB, to professional employees. They are presented here because of what they say, or assume, about the idea of professional employment. It is important to consider that question, however, in the broader context of the ways in which the Act as a whole has been influenced by the manner in which the law views the employment relation; at the same time, this is not the place for a capsule presentation of the law of the NLRA. Much can be gathered from a single, oft-cited passage from an early statement of the Court of Appeals in NLRB v. Montgomery Ward & Co., 157 F.2d 486 (8th Cir.1946). The Act prohibits discharge of employees for "concerted activities," including refusal to work on "struck goods," but had been construed to permit discharge of employees for concerted activities in breach of contract. In the case, however, there was no contractual "no strike" or similar provision. (There was also, at the time of the litigation, no federal prohibition of (and therefore denial of protection to) refusals to work on struck goods, which today would in most circumstances constitute an unlawful secondary boycott). The court nonetheless held unprotected a refusal to process orders from a struck facility, on the following reasoning:

> It was implied in the contract of hiring that ... employees would do the work assigned to them in a careful and workmanlike manner; that they would comply with all reasonable orders and conduct themselves so as not to work injury to the employer's business; that they would serve faithfully and be regardful of the interests of the employer during the term of their service, and carefully discharge their duties.... Any employee may, of course, be lawfully discharged for disobedience of the employer's directions in breach of his contract....

Id. at 496. In *Elk Lumber Co.*, 91 N.L.R.B. 333 (1950), the Board applied this principle to a group of employees who were discharged when they unilaterally reduced their work output in order to induce their employer to rescind a unilaterally imposed wage cut, even though in that case the employer had not specifically told the employees to restore their output to its prior level. It was sufficient, the Board reasoned, that "the men knew that the rate [of production] that they adopted was not satisfactory." Id., at 337.

Bearing in mind that there was unquestionably nothing in the language of the collective bargaining agreements or the particular setting of the employer's operations, and no written individual contracts of employment at all, what were the *sources* of the implication that the court and the Board read into these—and presumably all other—employment contracts?

NATIONAL LABOR RELATIONS BOARD
v. YESHIVA UNIVERSITY

Supreme Court of the United States, 1980.
444 U.S. 672, 100 S.Ct. 856, 63 L.Ed.2d 115.

Mr. Justice Powell delivered the opinion of the Court.

Supervisors and managerial employees are excluded from the categories of employees entitled to the benefits of collective bargaining under the National Labor Relations Act. The question presented is whether the full-time faculty of Yeshiva University fall within those exclusions.

Yeshiva is a private university which conducts a broad range of arts and sciences programs at its five undergraduate and eight graduate schools in New York City. On October 30, 1974, the Yeshiva University Faculty Association (Union) filed a representation petition with the National Labor Relations Board (Board). The Union sought certification as bargaining agent for the full-time faculty members at 10 of the 13 schools. The University opposed the petition on the ground that all of its faculty members are managerial or supervisory personnel and hence not employees within the meaning of the National Labor Relations Act (Act). A Board-appointed hearing officer held hearings over a period of five months, generating a voluminous record.

The evidence at the hearings showed that a central administrative hierarchy serves all of the University's schools. Ultimate authority is vested in a Board of Trustees, whose members (other than the President) hold no administrative positions at the University. The President sits on the Board of Trustees and serves as chief executive officer, assisted by four Vice presidents who oversee, respectively, medical affairs and science, student affairs, business affairs, and academic affairs. An Executive Council of Deans and administrators makes recommendations to the President on a wide variety of matters.

University-wide policies are formulated by the central administration with the approval of the Board of Trustees, and include general guidelines dealing with teaching loads, salary scales, tenure, sabbaticals, retirement, and fringe benefits. The budget for each school is drafted by its Dean or Director, subject to approval by the President after consultation with a committee of administrators[3]....

---

3. At Yeshiva College, budget requests prepared by the senior professor in each subject area receive the "perfunctory" approval of the Dean "99 percent" of the time and have never been rejected by the central administration.... A council of

The individual schools within the University are substantially autonomous. Each is headed by a Dean or Director, and faculty members at each school meet formally and informally to discuss and decide matters of institutional and professional concern.... Most of the schools also have faculty committees concerned with special areas of educational policy. Faculty welfare committees negotiate with administrators concerning salary and conditions of employment. Through these meetings and committees, the faculty at each school effectively determine its curriculum, grading system, admission and matriculation standards, academic calendars, and course schedules.[4]

Faculty power at Yeshiva's schools extends beyond strictly academic concerns. The faculty at each school make recommendations to the dean or director in every case of faculty hiring, tenure, sabbaticals, termination and promotion. Although the final decision is reached by the central administration on the advice of the dean or director, the overwhelming majority of faculty recommendations are implemented.[5] Even when financial problems in the early 1970's restricted Yeshiva's budget, faculty recommendations still largely controlled personnel decisions made within the constraints imposed by the administration. Indeed, the faculty of one school recently drew up new and binding policies expanding their own role in these matters. In addition, some faculties make final decisions regarding the admission, expulsion, and graduation of individual students. Others have decided questions involving teaching loads, student absence policies, tuition and enrollment levels, and in one case the location of a school.[6]

elected department chairmen at Ferkauf [Graduate School] approves the school's budget allocations when discretionary funds are available.... All of these professors were included in the bargaining unit approved by the Board.

4. For example, the Deans at Yeshiva and Erna Michael Colleges regard faculty actions as binding.... Administrators testified that no academic initiative of either faculty had been vetoed since at least 1968.... When the Stern College faculty disagreed with the Dean's decision to delete the education major, the major was reinstituted.... The Director of the Teacher's Institute for Women testified that "the faculty is the school," while the Director of the James Striar School described his position as the "executive arm of the faculty," which had overruled him on occasion.... All decisions regarding academic matters at the Yeshiva Program and Bernard Revel [Graduate School] are made by faculty consensus.... The "internal operation of [Wurzweiler] has been heavily governed by faculty decisions," according to its Dean....

5. One Dean estimated that 98% of faculty hiring recommendations were ulti-

mately given effect.... Others could not recall an instance when a faculty recommendation had been overruled.... At Stern College, the Dean in six years has never overturned a promotion decision.... The president has accepted all decisions of the Yeshiva College faculty as to promotions and sabbaticals, including decisions opposed by the Dean.... At Erna Michael [College], the Dean has never hired a full-time faculty member without the consent of the affected senior professor, ... and the Director of Teacher's Institute for Women stated baldly that no teacher had ever been hired if "there was the slightest objection, even on one faculty member's part".... The faculty at both these schools have overridden recommendations made by the deans. No promotion or grant of tenure has ever been made at Ferkauf over faculty opposition. The Dean of Belfer [Graduate School] testified that he had no right to override faculty decisions on tenure and nonrenewal....

6. The Director of Teacher's Institute for Women once recommended that the school move to Brooklyn to attract students. The faculty rejected the proposal and the school remained in Manhattan....

. . .

[T]he authority structure of a university does not fit neatly within the statutory scheme we are asked to interpret. The Board itself has noted that the concept of collegiality "does not square with the traditional authority structures with which th[e] Act was designed to cope in the typical organizations of the commercial world." Adelphi University, 195 N.L.R.B. 639, 648 (1972).

The Act was intended to accommodate the type of management-employee relations that prevail in the pyramidal hierarchies of private industry. Ibid. In contrast, authority in the typical "mature" private university is divided between a central administration and one or more collegial bodies. . . . This system of "shared authority" evolved from the medieval model of collegial decisionmaking in which guilds of scholars were responsible only to themselves. . . . At early universities, the faculty were the school. Although faculties have been subject to external control in the United States since colonial times, . . . traditions of collegiality continue to play a significant role at many universities, including Yeshiva. For these reasons, the Board has recognized that principles developed for use in the industrial setting cannot be "imposed blindly on the academic world." Syracuse University, 204 N.L.R.B. 641, 643 (1973).

The absence of explicit congressional direction, of course, does not preclude the Board from reaching any particular type of employment. . . . Acting under its responsibility for adapting the broad provisions of the Act to differing workplaces, the Board asserted jurisdiction over a university for the first time in 1970. Cornell University, 183 N.L.R.B. 329 (1970). Within a year it had approved the formation of bargaining units composed of faculty members. C. W. Post Center, 189 N.L.R.B. 904 (1971). The Board reasoned that faculty members are "professional employees" within the meaning of § 2(12) of the Act and therefore are entitled to the benefits of collective bargaining. 189 N.L.R.B., at 905; 29 U.S.C. § 152(12).[12]

Yeshiva does not contend that its faculty are not professionals under the statute. But professionals, like other employees, may be exempted from coverage under the Act's exclusion for "supervisors" who use independent judgment in overseeing other employees in the interest of the employer,[13] or under the judicially implied exclusion for "managerial employees" who are involved in developing and enforcing employer policy. Both exemptions grow out of the same concern: That an employer is entitled to the undivided loyalty of its representatives. . . . Because the Court of Appeals found the faculty to be mana-

---

12. The Act provides broadly that "employees" have organizational and other rights. . . . Section 2(3) defines "employee" in general terms . . .; § 2(12) defines "professional employee" in some detail . . .; and § 9(b)(1) prohibits the Board from creating a bargaining unit that includes both professional and nonprofessional employees unless a majority of the professionals vote for inclusion. . . .

13. An employee may be excluded if he has authority over any one of 12 enumerated personnel actions, including hiring and firing. . . .

gerial employees, it did not decide the question of their supervisory status. In view of our agreement with that court's application of the managerial exclusion, we also need not resolve that issue of statutory interpretation.

Managerial employees are defined as those who " 'formulate and effectuate management policies by expressing and making operative the decisions of their employer.' " NLRB v. Bell Aerospace Co., supra, at 288, 94 S.Ct., at 1768 (quoting Palace Laundry Dry Cleaning Corp., 75 N.L.R.B. 320, 323, n. 4 (1947). These employees are "much higher in the managerial structure" than those explicitly mentioned by Congress, which "regarded [them] as so clearly outside the Act that no specific exclusionary provision was thought necessary." 416 U.S., at 283, 94 S.Ct., at 1766. Managerial employees must exercise discretion within, or even independently of, established employer policy and must be aligned with management.... Although the Board has established no firm criteria for determining when an employee is so aligned, normally an employee may be excluded as managerial only if he represents management interests by taking or recommending discretionary actions that effectively control or implement employer policy.

The Board does not contend that the Yeshiva faculty's decision-making is too insignificant to be deemed managerial. Nor does it suggest that the role of the faculty is merely advisory and thus not managerial. Instead, it contends that the managerial exclusion cannot be applied in a straightforward fashion to professional employees because those employees often appear to be exercising managerial authority when they are merely performing routine job duties. The status of such employees, in the Board's view, must be determined by reference to the "alignment with management" criterion. The Board argues that the Yeshiva faculty are not aligned with management because they are expected to exercise "independent professional judgment" while participating in academic governance, and because they are neither "expected to conform to management policies [nor] judged according to their effectiveness in carrying out those policies." Because of this independence, the Board contends there is no danger of divided loyalty and no need for the managerial exclusion. In its view, union pressure cannot divert the faculty from adhering to the interests of the university, because the university itself expects its faculty to pursue professional values rather than institutional interests. The Board concludes that application of the managerial exclusion to such employees would frustrate the national labor policy in favor of collective bargaining.

The controlling consideration in this case is that the faculty of Yeshiva University exercise authority which in any other context unquestionably would be managerial. Their authority in academic matters is absolute. They decide what courses will be offered, when they will be scheduled, and to whom they will be taught. They debate and determine teaching methods, grading policies, and matriculation standards. They effectively decide which students will be admitted, retained, and graduated. On occasion their views have determined the size of the student body, the tuition to be charged, and the location of a school. When one considers the function of a university, it is difficult to imagine decisions more managerial than these. To the extent the industrial analogy applies, the faculty determines within each school the product to be produced, the terms upon which it will be offered, and the customers who will be served.[23]

The Board nevertheless insists that these decisions are not managerial because they require the exercise of independent professional judgment. We are not persuaded by this argument. There may be some tension between the Act's exclusion of managerial employees and its inclusion of professionals, since most professionals in managerial positions continue to draw on their special skills and training. But we have been directed to no authority suggesting that that tension can be resolved by reference to the "independent professional judgment" criterion proposed in this case....

Moreover, the Board's approach would undermine the goal it purports to serve: To ensure that employees who exercise discretionary authority on behalf of the employer will not divide their loyalty between employer and union. In arguing that a faculty member exercising independent judgment acts primarily in his own interest and therefore does not represent the interest of his employer, the Board assumes that the professional interests of the faculty and the interests of the institution are distinct, separable entities with which a faculty member could not simultaneously be aligned. The Court of Appeals found no justification for this distinction, and we perceive none. In fact, the faculty's professional interests—as applied to governance at a university like Yeshiva—cannot be separated from those of the institution.

In such a university, the predominant policy normally is to operate a quality institution of higher learning that will accomplish broadly defined educational goals within the limits of its financial resources. The "business" of a university is education, and its vitality ultimately must depend on academic policies that largely are formulated and generally are implemented by faculty governance decisions.... Faculty members enhance their own standing and fulfill their professional mission by ensuring that the university's objectives are met. But there can be no doubt that the quest for academic excellence and institutional distinction is a "policy" to which the administration expects the faculty to adhere, whether it be defined as a professional or an institutional goal. It is fruitless to ask whether an employee is "expected to conform" to one goal or another when the two are essentially the

23. The record shows that faculty members at Yeshiva also play a predominant role in faculty hiring, tenure, sabbaticals, termination and promotion.... These decisions clearly have both managerial and supervisory characteristics. Since we do not reach the question of supervisory sta-

same.[27]

The problem of divided loyalty is particularly acute for a university like Yeshiva, which depends on the professional judgment of its faculty to formulate and apply crucial policies constrained only by necessarily general institutional goals. The university requires faculty participation in governance because professional expertise is indispensable to the formulation and implementation of academic policy. It may appear, as the Board contends, that the professor performing governance functions is less "accountable" for departures from institutional policy than a middle-level industrial manager whose discretion is more confined. Moreover, traditional systems of collegiality and tenure insulate the professor from some of the sanctions applied to an industrial manager who fails to adhere to company policy. But the analogy of the university to industry need not, and indeed cannot, be complete. It is clear that Yeshiva and like universities must rely on their faculties to participate in the making and implementation of their policies.[29] The large measure of independence enjoyed by faculty members can only increase the danger that divided loyalty will lead to those harms that the Board traditionally has sought to prevent.

We certainly are not suggesting an application of the managerial exclusion that would sweep all professionals outside the Act in derogation of Congress' expressed intent to protect them. The Board has recognized that employees whose decisionmaking is limited to the routine discharge of professional duties in projects to which they have been assigned cannot be excluded from coverage even if union membership arguably may involve some divided loyalty. Only if an employee's activities fall outside the scope of the duties routinely performed by similarly situated professionals will he be found aligned with management. We think these decisions accurately capture the intent of Congress, and that they provide an appropriate starting point for analysis in cases involving professionals alleged to be managerial.[31]

tus, we need not rely primarily on these features of faculty authority.

27. At Yeshiva, administrative concerns with scarce resources and University-wide balance have led to occasional vetoes of faculty action. But such infrequent administrative reversals in no way detract from the institution's primary concern with the academic responsibilities entrusted to the faculty. The suggestion that faculty interests depart from those of the institution with respect to salary and benefits is even less meritorious. The same is true of every supervisory or managerial employee. Indeed, there is arguably a greater community of interest on this point in the university than in industry, because the nature and quality of a university depend so heavily on the faculty attracted to the institution. . . .

29. The dissent concludes, citing several secondary authorities, that the modern university has undergone changes that have shifted "the task of operating the university enterprise" from faculty to administration. . . . The shift, if it exists, is neither universal nor complete. . . . In any event, our decision must be based on the record before us. Nor can we decide this case by weighing the probable benefits and burdens of faculty collective bargaining. . . . That, after all, is a matter for Congress, not this Court.

31. We recognize that this is a starting point only, and that other factors not present here may enter into the analysis in other contexts. It is plain, for example, that professors may not be excluded merely because they determine the content of their own courses, evaluate their own stu-

...

MR. JUSTICE BRENNAN, with whom MR. JUSTICE WHITE, MR. JUSTICE MARSHALL, and MR. JUSTICE BLACKMUN join, dissenting.

...

... The Court purports to recognize that there are fundamental differences between the authority structures of the typical industrial and academic institutions which preclude the blind transplanting of principles developed in one arena onto the other; yet it nevertheless ignores those very differences in concluding that Yeshiva's faculty is excluded from the Act's coverage.

...

Unlike the purely hierarchical decisionmaking structure that prevails in the typical industrial organization, the bureaucratic foundation of most "mature" universities is characterized by dual authority systems. The primary decisional network is hierarchical in nature: Authority is lodged in the administration, and a formal chain of command runs from a lay governing board down through university officers to individual faculty members and students. At the same time, there exists a parallel professional network, in which formal mechanisms have been created to bring the expertise of the faculty into the decisionmaking process....

What the Board realized—and what the Court fails to apprehend—is that whatever influence the faculty wields in university decisionmaking is attributable solely to its collective expertise as professional educators, and not to any managerial or supervisory prerogatives.... The ... administration gives what weight and import to the faculty's collective judgment as it chooses and deems consistent with its own perception of the institution's needs and objectives.[8]

The premise of a finding of managerial status is a determination that the excluded employee is acting on behalf of management and is answerable to a higher authority in the exercise of his responsibilities....

dents, and supervise their own research. There thus may be institutions of higher learning unlike Yeshiva where the faculty are entirely or predominantly nonmanagerial. There also may be faculty members at Yeshiva and like universities who properly could be included in a bargaining unit. It may be that a rational line could be drawn between tenured and untenured faculty members, depending upon how a faculty is structured and operates. But we express no opinion on these questions, for it is clear that the unit approved by the Board was far too broad.

8. One must be careful not to overvalue the significance of the faculty's influence on academic affairs. As one commentator has noted, "it is not extraordinary for employees to seek to exert influence over matters embedded in an employment relationship for which they share a concern, or that management would be responsive to their strongly held desires." Finkin, The NLRB in Higher Education, 5 U. Toledo L.Rev. 608, 616 (1974). Who, after all, is better suited than the faculty to decide what courses should be offered, how they should be taught, and by what standards their students should be graded? Employers will often attempt to defer to their employees' suggestions, particularly where—as here—those recommendations relate to matters within the unique competence of the employees.

Yeshiva's faculty, however, is not accountable to the administration in its governance function, nor is any individual faculty member subject to personal sanction or control based on the administration's assessment of the worth of his recommendations. When the faculty, through the schools' advisory committees, participates in university decisionmaking on subjects of academic policy, it does not serve as the "representative of management." Unlike industrial supervisors and managers, university professors are not hired to "make operative" the policies and decisions of their employer. Nor are they retained on the condition that their interests will correspond to those of the university administration. Indeed, the notion that a faculty member's professional competence could depend on his undivided loyalty to management is antithetical to the whole concept of academic freedom. Faculty members are judged by their employer on the quality of their teaching and scholarship, not on the compatibility of their advice with administration policy....

It is no answer to say, as does the Court, that Yeshiva's faculty and administration are one and the same because their interests tend to coincide. In the first place, the National Labor Relations Act does not condition its coverage on an antagonism of interests between the employer and the employee. The mere coincidence of interests on many issues has never been thought to abrogate the right to collective bargaining on those topics as to which that coincidence is absent. Ultimately, the performance of an employee's duties will always further the interests of the employer, for in no institution do the interests of labor and management totally diverge. Both desire to maintain stable and profitable operations, and both are committed to creating the best possible product within existing financial constraints. Differences of opinion and emphasis may develop, however, on exactly how to devote the institution's resources to achieve those goals. When these disagreements surface, the national labor laws contemplate their resolution through the peaceful process of collective bargaining. And in this regard, Yeshiva University stands on the same footing as any other employer.

Moreover, the congruence of interests in this case ought not to be exaggerated. The university administration has certain economic and fiduciary responsibilities that are not shared by the faculty, whose primary concerns are academic and relate solely to its own professional reputation. The record evinces numerous instances in which the faculty's recommendations have been rejected by the administration on account of fiscal constraints or other managerial policies. Disputes have arisen between Yeshiva's faculty and administration on such fundamental issues as the hiring, tenure, promotion, retirement, and dismissal of faculty members, academic standards and credits, departmental budgets, and even the faculty's choice of its own departmental representative. The very fact that Yeshiva's faculty has voted for the Union to serve as its representative in future negotiations with the administration indicates that the faculty does not perceive its interests to be aligned with those of management. Indeed, on the precise topics which are specified as mandatory subjects of collective bargaining—wages, hours, and other terms and conditions of employment—the interests of teacher and administrator are often diametrically opposed.

Finally, the Court's perception of the Yeshiva faculty's status is distorted by the rose-colored lens through which it views the governance structure of the modern-day university. The Court's conclusion that the faculty's professional interests are indistinguishable from those of the administration is bottomed on an idealized model of collegial decisionmaking that is a vestige of the great medieval university. But the university of today bears little resemblance to the "community of scholars" of yesteryear. Education has become "big business," and the task of operating the university enterprise has been transferred from the faculty to an autonomous administration, which faces the same pressures to cut costs and increase efficiencies that confront any large industrial organization. The past decade of budgetary cutbacks, declining enrollments, reductions in faculty appointments, curtailment of academic programs, and increasing calls for accountability to alumni and other special interest groups has only added to the erosion of the faculty's role in the institution's decisionmaking process.

These economic exigencies have also exacerbated the tensions in university labor relations, as the faculty and administration more and more frequently find themselves advocating conflicting positions not only on issues of compensation, job security, and working conditions, but even on subjects formerly thought to be the faculty's prerogative. In response to this friction, and in an attempt to avoid the strikes and work stoppages that have disrupted several major universities in recent years, many faculties have entered into collective-bargaining relationships with their administrations and governing boards. An even greater number of schools—Yeshiva among them—have endeavored to negotiate and compromise their differences informally, by establishing avenues for faculty input into university decisions on matters of professional concern.

Today's decision, however, threatens to eliminate much of the administration's incentive to resolve its disputes with the faculty through open discussion and mutual agreement. By its overbroad and unwarranted interpretation of the managerial exclusion, the Court denies the faculty the protections of the NLRA and, in so doing, removes whatever deterrent value the Act's availability may offer against unreasonable administrative conduct. Rather than promoting the Act's objective of funneling dissension between employers and employees into collective bargaining, the Court's decision undermines that goal. . . .

CEDARS–SINAI MEDICAL CENTER

National Labor Relations Board, 1976.
223 N.L.R.B. 251.

... Cedars–Sinai is a nonprofit corporation engaged in the operation of a medical center in the Los Angeles, California, area. The Employer operates two acute general hospitals: the Cedars of Lebanon Hospital Division which is licensed to operate 530 beds, and the Mount Sinai Hospital Division which is licensed to operate 230 beds. The Petitioner seeks to represent a unit of interns, residents, and clinical fellows. The Employer contends that such a unit is inappropriate because, inter alia, these interns, residents, and clinical fellows are students, not employees. We find merit in the Employer's position, as we find that interns, residents, and clinical fellows, although they possess certain employee characteristics, are primarily students. Accordingly, for the reasons given below, we conclude that the interns, residents, and clinical fellows in the petitioned-for unit are not "employees" within the meaning of Section 2(3) of the Act.

The record shows that the medical education and training of a physician involves a progression from classroom and laboratory education in the basic and clinical sciences, through an internship, and usually then to a period of more advanced training in a specialty or subspecialty of medicine. It is the purpose of internship and residency programs to put into practice the principles of preventive medicine, diagnosis, therapy, and management of patients that the medical school graduate learned in medical school.

. . .

Graduate medical education and training programs to qualify for licensing and for certification in a specialty or subspecialty are governed by national medical organizations, such as the American Medical Association, the National Board of Medical Examiners, and the specialty boards, and by state licensing authorities. The standards for internships and residencies are contained in "Essentials of an Approved Internship" and "Essentials of Approved Residencies," hereinafter the "Essentials," prepared by the Council on Medical Education and approved by the American Medical Association. The programs are carried out in hospitals that are accredited by these various bodies and that in many instances have affiliation agreements with approved medical schools. Cedars–Sinai is such a hospital.

. . .

The placement of graduating medical students at Cedars–Sinai is governed by the National Intern and Resident Matching Program. This program is designed to place graduating medical students with a preferred graduate training institution....

The activities of interns, residents, and clinical fellows while in graduate programs such as those operated by Cedars–Sinai are prescribed by the accrediting bodies and specialty boards which govern graduate medical education, supra. The training programs consist of patient care activities coordinated with a variety of teaching and educational activities designed to develop the student's clinical judgment and proficiency in clinical skills.... These patient care activities, an integral part of a physician's educational training, are coordinated with a variety of teaching and educational activities, such as grand rounds, teaching rounds, laboratory instruction, seminars, and lectures....

During their training at Cedars–Sinai, members of the housestaff receive an annual stipend which is on a graduated basis ranging from a first-year intern to a fifth-year resident. The amount of the stipend is not determined by the nature of the services rendered or by the number of hours spent in patient care. Nor does the choice of electives or even rotations to other hospitals affect the amount of the stipend. The "Essentials" characterize the stipend as a scholarship for graduate study. The housestaff also receives a variety of fringe benefits, such as medical and dental care, an annual vacation and paid holidays, uniforms, meals while on duty, and malpractice insurance. They are not eligible for Cedars–Sinai's retirement plan. Discipline is administered by a housestaff committee.

The tenure of interns and residents at Cedars–Sinai is closely related to the length of the program which each individual pursues. The record indicates that ... the average stay of interns and residents at Cedars–Sinai is less than 2 years.... Following completion of their programs at Cedars–Sinai, the majority of the housestaff go into private practice and others go into group practices or accept positions with health organizations. Only a few interns, residents, or clinical fellows can expect to, or do, remain to establish an employment relationship with Cedars–Sinai.

From the foregoing and the entire record, we find that interns, residents, and clinical fellows are primarily engaged in graduate educational training at Cedars–Sinai and that their status is therefore that of students rather than of employees. They participate in these programs not for the purpose of earning a living; instead they are there to pursue the graduate medical education that is a requirement for the practice of medicine. An internship is a requirement for the examination for licensing. And residency and fellowship programs are necessary to qualify for certification in specialties and subspecialties. While the housestaff spends a great percentage of their time in direct patient care, this is simply the means by which the learning process is carried out. It is only through this direct involvement with patients that the graduate medical student is able to acquire the necessary diagnostic skills and experience to practice his profession. The number of hours worked or the quality of the care rendered to the patients does not result in any change in monetary compensation paid to the housestaff members. The stipend remains fixed and it seems clear that the payments are more in the nature of a living allowance than compensation for services rendered. Nor does it appear that those applying for such programs attached any great significance to the amount of the stipend. Rather their choice was based on the quality of the educational program and the opportunity for an extensive training experience. The programs themselves were designed not for the purpose of meeting the hospital's staffing requirements, but rather to allow the student to develop, in a hospital setting, the clinical judgment and the proficiency in clinical skills necessary to the practice of medicine in the area of his choice. The "Essentials," which describe the standards for approved internships and residencies, indicate that the primary function is educational. Moreover, the tenure of a member of the housestaff at Cedars–Sinai is closely related to the length of the student's training program; thus few interns, residents, or clinical fellows can expect to, or do, remain to establish an employment relationship with Cedars–Sinai following the completion of their programs.

. . .

[W]e do not find here that students and employees are antithetical entities or mutually exclusive categories under the Act. Instead, we find that the interns, residents, and clinical fellows who filed the petition herein are primarily engaged in graduate educational training at Cedars–Sinai. It is the educational relationship that exists between the housestaff and Cedars–Sinai (a teaching hospital) which leads us to conclude that the housestaff are students rather than employees, i.e., that the housestaff's relationship with Cedars–Sinai is an educational rather than an employment relationship. Thus, far from "exploiting semantic distinctions," our decision rests on the fundamental difference between an educational and an employment relationship.

MEMBER FANNING, dissenting:

Section 2(3) of the Act states that the term "employee" is meant to "include any employee.... unless the Act explicitly states otherwise," and proceeds to explicitly state those excluded from the definition, e.g., agricultural laborers, domestic servants, et al. "Students" are not among those exclusions. Recognition of an underlying Federal policy which seeks to draw a line between labor and management has further led to the exclusion, on such policy grounds, of two additional classes of "employees," namely, confidential and managerial employees. That is all. Since the statutory exclusions do not mention and the policy underlying the nonstatutory exclusions does not reach "students," the relationship between "student" and "employee" cannot be said to be mutually exclusive. The fundamental question then is always whether the individual before us, be that individual "primarily a carpenter" or "primarily a student," is, nevertheless, an "employee" under the Act.

. . .

All housestaff officers are M.D.'s. All fellows and residents are licensed physicians in every State of the Union. It is, of course, impossible to set forth the full range of services these physicians perform for the hospital and, more importantly, for the patient, but my colleagues' silence as to what these housestaff officers do cannot go unnoted. The records before us demonstrate, for example, that housestaff officers, without immediate supervision of any kind, continually deal in matters literally of the ultimate significance. That they do so is a function, no doubt, of their hours. The housestaff work round-the-clock, 7 days a week, 52 weeks a year. No other physicians do. They perform their services, on an individual basis, for periods lasting, at times, well over 100 hours a week, in shifts that often exceed 50 consecutive hours. They singly staff emergency rooms, frequently at times when their supposed "teachers" are not even in the facility. That accounts for the record facts which demonstrate that, without supervision, a housestaff officer can be called upon and, in fact, has been called upon, to open the chest wall of a 3–year–old child; hold the heart of a patient in his hands; remove breast tissues, kidneys, veins; deliver babies; insert tubes in the trachea of newborns and catheters into abdominal cavities; administer closely controlled and potentially lethal medications; and perform a host of similar procedures.

For those services and innumerable others supervised by medical staff but performed by housestaff, the hospital charges fees in amounts which have sparked national debate. In return for those services, the hospital pays that housestaff officer what my colleagues call a "stipend." It exceeds, in some cases of multiple residencies, $20,000 a year. From that "stipend," the hospital withholds Federal and state taxes, contributes to social security, and provides for health insurance. The hospital grants vacations and sick leave, laundry allowances, etc. For the negligent performance of those services the hospital can be sued. For those services the housestaff receives, absent unusual circumstances not before us, no degree, no grades, no examinations. Housestaff officers perform those services on (and in) individuals who would hardly take comfort in the notion that the individual in whose hands their life itself may repose is not primarily interested in performing that service for the hospital and patient but, rather, is primarily a student of the matter. In point of fact, according to a study initiated by the Association of American Medical Colleges itself, approximately 80 percent of a housestaff officer's time is spent "in direct patient care activities." Certainly, there is a didactic component to the work of any initiate, but simply because an individual is "learning" while performing this service cannot possibly be said to mark that individual as "primarily a student and, therefore, not an employee" for purposes of our statute.

. . .

. . . In the cases before us, there is some support for the proposition that the primary interest of the housestaff's representational aims is the improvement of patient care. There is, further, some support for the proposition that the primary value attached to an individual residency or subspecialty is the quality of the institution providing that program, and the opportunity of exposure to a wide range of medical experience. That is, hopefully, not a unique approach in any field of endeavor, particularly professional ones. There is, on the other hand, absolutely no support for a statement which implies that the so-called "stipend" (the AMA calls it "salary," the study initiated in part by AAMC calls it a "wage," the IRS calls it "payment for services rendered") is not a considerable source of concern. . . .

I fail to perceive how the fact that an individual desirous of becoming an orthopedic surgeon chooses a residency program based on its quality and the opportunity for extensive training bears relevance to the question whether, having done so, he or she is an "employee" under the Act. . . .

Note on the NLRA "employee": The job as meal-ticket

1. (a) Is the following an accurate account of the underlying presuppositions of these decisions?

Yeshiva deals with employees who, unlike most employees, have a substantial measure of autonomy, indeed, who shape the mission and actions of their employer in significant ways. To the Court majority, this can only be so because it is the employer's wish that they have such autonomy: "The university *requires* faculty participation in governance because professional expertise is necessary to the formulation and implementation of academic policy" (emphasis supplied). The idea that decisional authority over "managerial" matters is viewed by teachers themselves as an important aspect of their ability to do the kind of job they want to do as teachers and scholars, that they seek such authority in order better to carry on their life-work, is of no help, according to the Court majority, in defining their jobs. As was said to be true of Geary, Pierce, and Warthen, it is a teacher's "duties," and not his or her own priorities, that give content to the job, and the enhancement of the "managerial/professional" quality of the job only enhances a teacher's obligation to reflect management's priorities with undivided loyalty.

Cedars–Sinai, viewing a work setting with a high degree of educational value, and little correlation between compensation and the appeal of the job, sees something that is not a job at all. An employee is one who works "for the purpose of earning a living."

(b) If these statements are correct explanations of the decisions, is the truth of them related one to the other? Is there a conceptual link between the idea that it is the pay that gives work its value, and the idea that it is for the employer, and not the employee, to define the job?

(c) Consider this classic description of the traditional concept of work:

> What, then, constitutes the alienation of labor? First, the fact that labor is external to the worker, that is, it does not belong to his essential being; that in his work, therefore, he does not affirm himself. . . . The worker . . . in his work feels outside himself. . . . His labor is therefore . . . not the satisfaction of a need; it is merely a means to satisfy needs external to it. [T]he external character of labor for the worker appears in the fact that it is not his own, but someone else's, that in work he belongs, not to himself, but to another.

Karl Marx, Economic and Philosophical Manuscripts of 1844, 110–11 (D. Struik ed. 1964). The Supreme Court and the Labor Board seem to confirm, do they not, the accuracy of Marx' description of the ideology of work, but seem not to share his disapproval (only suggested in the brief excerpt above) of it.

2. These concepts of what a job is do not of course come explicitly from the statute. Nor, indeed, does the exclusion of "managerial employees" or "students" from coverage, or the idea that "disobedience" of a managerial order is a breach of contract that forfeits the protection of NLRA Section 7. What is their source?

3. Dealing with the common law, the *Restatement of Torts* (relied on by the *Geary* court, p. 246, above) does not speak of "discharging" or "dismissing" an employee, but of "refusing ... to continue a business relation," and the court refers to the discharge as the "termination of the employment relationship." Unless these locutions are simply euphemisms for the harsher-sounding terms, their use may reflect an implicit view of what the "employment relation" *is*. Viewing the employment relationship as a "contract" facilitates, does it not, answering in the negative the question whether the employer need justify its decision.

(a) Why do I say that?

(b) How, though, does the "contract model" of work guide us in deciding what obligations are "implied in the contract of hiring" (*Montgomery Ward,* p. 261, above)? Consider James Atleson's response:

> ... Contracts of employment were rarely written, let alone precise, and they almost never spelled out the range of rights or obligations that might be involved in the relationship. In fact, to the employee the arrangement is much more like the all-encompassing status agreement than the express, limited regime of contract. Traditional contract notions might suggest that all the ambiguous sections or unanticipated questions dealing, for instance, with the level of energy to be expended, working conditions, disciplinary authority, and employee integrity, could not be exclusively and authoritatively interpreted by the employer. The employer could be granted the right to make rules under the contract or by law, but the employer would not have the sole authority to determine whether these rules were arbitrary or consistent with the scope of that authority.... The legal response was the fusing of the employment contract with traditional master-servant notions....
>
> The merger of master-servant law and contract meant that the law never treated the employment contract as the result of free bargaining and mutual assent .... Instead, the contract was deemed to include "implied" terms which reserved to the employer the full authority and direction of employees.... The Webbs put the situation succinctly:
>
>> The capitalist is fond of declaring that labor is a commodity, and the wage contract a bargain of purchase and sale like any other. But he instinctively expects his wage-earners to render him, not only obedience, but also personal deference. If the wage contract is a bargain of purchase and sale like any other, why is

the workman expected to touch his hat to his employer, and to say "sir" to him without reciprocity ...?

J. Atleson, Values and Assumptions in American Labor Law 13–14 (1983).

4. (a) To what extent, if at all, do these 19th century status assumptions tend to have a continuing influence, not only on the evolution of the law, but on our thinking about work, including our own work?

(b) By what processes, if any, can the extent of that influence be made the subject of reflection and conscious decisionmaking?

The following sub-section is in part designed to provide a foundation for a response to the preceding question.

(c) *The Underlying Consciousness*

THE CONSCIOUSNESS OF WORK AND THE VALUES OF AMERICAN LABOR LAW

Howard Lesnick
32 Buff.L.Rev. 833 (1983).

I. THE DECODING OF LABOR LAW DOCTRINE

The opening sentences of Professor [James] Atleson's important new book, *Values and Assumptions in American Labor Law,* clearly express its purpose and central thesis:

> The purpose ... is to investigate the seeming incoherence of American labor law doctrine.... [Its] goal ... is to demonstrate that the decisions are incoherent only if viewed through the lens of the statute and its policies, the way in which lawyers tend to view coherency. Underlying American labor law is a set of rarely expressed values that, although illegitimate under contemporary modes of legal thought, help to explain the judicial and administrative decisions reached. These values and assumptions predate the statute and can be found in nineteenth-century judicial opinions.[1]

> . . .

What are the values and assumptions that make coherent (if illegitimate) this body of law? The many themes that Professor Atleson draws out of the decisions may be expressed, I believe, within two fundamental, mutually reinforcing propositions: (1) It is in the public interest for private management to retain discretion over the manner and goals of production; and (2) It is appropriate to view the work relation as a hierarchial one.

. . .

III. THE CONSCIOUSNESS OF WORK AND THE CONSCIOUSNESS OF FREEDOM

When we engage with the values of production, managerial discretion, and workplace hierarchy—and do so for reasons other than to consider their legitimacy as an input to adjudication—what happens?

1. J. Atleson, Values and Assumptions
in American Labor Law at ix (1983).

For many, a profound paradox arises. As Professor Atleson states, those values are deeply controversial. While many embrace them wholeheartedly, many find important aspects of them repellent, and their social consequences tragically unjust and destructive. At the same time, even to those in the latter group, there is a ring of inevitable "rightness" in many aspects of the traditional value structure. They seem to describe the world as it really is. Intermittent stirrings to act in violation of the traditional teaching seem hopelessly visionary and out of touch with reality.[40] The result is a profound sense of alienation and resignation, "when the choice between despair and illusion seems unavoidable."[41]

The dissonance suggests that the question must be addressed at a deeper level than one of the content of particular values. There is a consciousness of work that underlies and shapes our response to questions of law and questions of values. The consciousness of work is a set of ordering perceptions, priorities, and premises[42] that answers the questions: What is it to work? What is it that a person is doing when he or she works? The answers are not simply some observed phenomena, but rather a social construct—a choice of some kind that human beings have made for a reason. That quality tends to be masked, however. The answers tend to be perceived as given; their content is initially implicit, and if made explicit tends to be regarded as self-evident and uncontroversially true.[43]

40. The labor movement, and working people generally, seem increasingly to share in the general allegiance to prevailing values. See J. Atleson, supra note 1, at 158. David Trubek perceptively points out how this allegiance is part of a "complex and contradictory amalgam" with conflicting perceptions: "[W]orking class consciousness is split between a concrete realization of injustice and inequality in day-to-day matters, and an acceptance of broad propositions about the necessity and justice of existing social relations." Trubek, Where the Action Is: Critical Legal Studies and Empiricism, [36 Stan.L.Rev. 575, 614 (1984)].

41. R. Unger [Knowledge and Politics] 24 [1975].

42. Duncan Kennedy expresses the idea of consciousness in law in these terms:

The notion behind the concept of legal consciousness is that people ... can share premises ... that are so basic that actors rarely if ever bring them consciously to mind. Yet everyone, including actors who think they disagree profoundly about the substantive issues that matter, would dismiss without a second thought (perhaps as 'not a legal argu-

ment' or as 'simply missing the point') an approach appearing to deny them.

Kennedy [Toward an Historical Understanding of Legal Consciousness, 3 Research L. & Soc. 3, 6 (1980)]. Words like "world-view," "ideology," or "belief systems" are expressive of a very similar concept. See Cover, The Left, the Right and the First Amendment: 1918–1928, 40 Md. L.Rev. 349, 349–50 n. 2 (1981); Gordon, New Developments in Legal Theory, in The Politics of Law 287–89 (Kairys ed. 1983); Klare, Book Review, Contracts, Jurisprudence, and the First Year Casebook, 54 N.Y.U.L.Rev. 876, 876–77 n. 2 (1979); Trubek, supra note 40, at 21.

43. For an excellent exposition of the hypothesis that an underlying consciousness is a social construct, see Delaney, Towards a Human Rights Theory of Criminal Law: A Humanistic Perspective, 6 Hofstra L.Rev. 831, 839–42 (1978). See also Gordon, supra note 42, at 288 ("[t]hough the structures are built, piece by interlocking piece, with human intentions, people come to 'externalize' them, to attribute to them existence and control over and above human choice; and, moreover, to believe that these structures must be the way they are").

There appears to be a mutually reinforcing, mutually legitimating interaction between the prevailing consciousness of work and the law. The following discussion attempts to give content to the prevailing consciousness of work, and then to what I will call an alternative consciousness, illustrating the interaction between the consciousness of work and the law in context at several points. The purpose of this endeavor is to make explicit the reality of the existence of choice, and of its systemic masking, and to suggest further that a focus on consciousness—which underlies both values and law—might enable us to begin to engage with the process of exercising choice.[44]

The prevailing consciousness of work sees work as an exchange relation, the giving up of leisure, the expending of effort, in return for compensation (income, status). The ingredients of this consciousness cluster around three sets of qualities:

1) Since the work relation is a bilateral, consensual one, there is no right to work. A prospective worker has only the right to look for an employer.

2) The utility of work is defined by the user, initially the employer (the purchaser of labor), but ultimately the consumer of the product or service offered by the employer.

3) The meaning or value of work to the person who works is that it is a means toward self-sufficiency.

Our view of the employment relation as bilateral and consensual interacts powerfully with our notions of freedom and consent in the workplace. . . .

IV. The Implications of the Traditional Consciousness of Work

The expression of worker freedom of choice, once thus defined, is further channeled and cabined by the remaining ingredients of the exchange concept of work. First, the principle that the utility of work is defined by the user (again, initially the employer, but ultimately the consumer of the product or service made or offered by the employer) profoundly shapes our sense of what is right and proper in the job relation and in the law. Professor Atleson, in his examination of the fusing of contract and status concepts, has provided a significant historical explanation for the phenomenon that a legally equal consensual relation is usually dominated by the employer.[54] Other historical or theoretical explanations can be given.[55] But the phenomenon is

---

44. See, e.g., Klare, Labor Law as Ideology: Toward a New Historiography of Collective Bargaining Law, 4 Indus.Rel.L.J. 450, 482 (1981) ("[t]he mission of all critical social thought is to free us from the illusion of the necessity of existing social arrangements").

54. See J. Atleson, supra note 1, at 87, concluding that "there was no idyllic, free-market period when employment relation-

ships were" the product of agreement alone. Rather, the law fostered the "fusing of the employment contract with traditional master-servant notions, thereby giving a legal basis" for dominant employer power. Id. at 13.

55. For a powerful depiction of the social manipulation of "consent" to hazardous employment in the period 1870–1920, see Graebner [Doing the World's Unheal-

inherent in the concept that the utility of work is defined by the user. The employee "fills the job"; he or she has a rule defined by the job and does not own the job.

This perception is so deeply ingrained in the law that, when it is expressed at all, it is regarded as axiomatic. One modern decision that grapples with the question whether to limit the employment at will doctrine is Geary v. U.S. Steel Corp. [, 456 Pa. 171, 319 A.2d 174 (1974).] Geary was a salesperson concerned about the safety of a new product. He expressed his fears to his supervisor, who responded (truthfully) that the company engineers had cleared it. Geary was still troubled, and talked to his friend, a vice-president of the company. As a result, the product was recalled and Geary was fired. In the course of rejecting Geary's suit for wrongful discharge, the court considered Geary's argument that a strong public interest in product safety was at risk:

> Certainly the potential for abuse of an employer's power of dismissal is particularly serious when an employee must exercise independent expert judgment in matters of product safety, but Geary does not hold himself out as this sort of employee. He was involved only in the sale of products. There is no suggestion that he possessed any expert qualifications, or that his duties extended to making judgments in matters of product safety.

In other words, Geary's job was to sell the product, not to raise questions about it. But how did that get to be his job? The answer, of course, is that the company defined the job, and Geary agreed to the definition when he was hired. Geary was not hired to be an engineer. Geary was not hired to concern himself with the safety of what he was selling—whether his concern arose out of regard for the user, the company's liability or reputation, or his own self-concept. If Geary in fact had any such concern, it was a personal interest, like the contour of his lawn. He could read books on safety on Sunday, but unless his employer agreed to purchase that concern, it had nothing to do with his work.

Employer definitions of the job need not be explicit. The law attributes to an employer a definition consonant with the underlying concept of work. For example, in Elk Lumber Co., [91 N.L.R.B. 331 (1950),] one of the major exhibits adduced by Professor Atleson in support of his thesis, employees who reduced their work effort in an attempt to induce an employer to rescind a wage cut were held to have breached their employment contract, even though they had not violated any express agreement or specific direction of the employer. The National Labor Relations Board viewed it as "implied in the contract of hiring" that employees would "serve faithfully and be regardful of the interests of the employer," and that they would not be permitted to

thy Work: The Fiction of Free Choice, Hastings Center Rep. 28 (Aug. 1984)]. Graebner concludes that "the idea of choice ... was less a way of opening up options than of closing them off...." Id. [at 36].

"select what parts of their allotted tasks they cared to perform of their own volition." [60]

The final aspect of the traditional consciousness of work is the idea that the meaning of work to the person who works is that it is a means toward self-sufficiency. That perception makes it seem self-evident that there is no legitimate employee interest in the product, but only in the pay and working conditions. Professor Atleson describes the constriction of the law defining the scope of collective bargaining. For example, when unionized physicians or nurses seek to contract with their hospital employer over "quality of care" issues (sometimes by the pressure of a strike), the general response is that it is none of their business. It is the business of the board of directors, of public or private contributors, or of consumers. Residents and nurses are in their job for what they get out of it, not what they put into it.

The Geary decision also illustrates the point. The extent of an employee's autonomy is defined by the employer. The employee consents to the arrangement in taking the job. He or she legally is free to refuse to take the job on the terms offered, but that is the moment of choice. Once he or she signs on, and has not chosen to sign off, an employee continues to work on the employer's terms. The quality of the employer's product is none of the employee's business unless the employer has chosen to make it so. [62]

The idea that the meaning of work is as a means toward self-sufficiency further constrains employee free choice through the corollary notion that there is a moral obligation to render oneself employable. While there is no legal duty to work—in the sense that peonage and slavery are unlawful and delegitimated [63]—there is a moral obli-

---

60. 91 N.L.R.B. at 337–38. As Atleson observes, "the employer's expectation of work output is called a 'production standard,' a goal to be reached. Workers' attempt[s] to define the level at which they will expend energy, however, are called 'output restrictions' or 'slow-downs.' " J. Atleson, supra note 1, at 51.

62. Atleson's critique of Teamsters v. Daniel, 439 U.S. 551 (1979) (holding that noncontributory pension plans are not "securities" within the meaning of the Securities Acts) ably shows how the underlying perception comes into play even when the subject is undisputably within the zone of legitimate employee interest. Atleson observes:

The employee, says the Court, "surrenders his labor as a whole, and in return receives a compensation package that is substantially devoid of aspects resembling a security...."

... The Court, by finding it impossible to segregate an employee's investment from his noninvestment interests, over-

looks the possibility that the entire compensation package is a return for the employee's "investment" of labor.... At base, then, the Court assumes that employees sell their labor in return for a livelihood, and even if, arguably, part of this exchange could be deemed an investment interest, such an investment cannot be separated from other more predominant noninvestment interests, such as wages. Aside from pensions, then the Court assumes that workers do not invest anything in an enterprise. Their labor is purchased like other commodities; it may be treated as a commodity and the labor power purchased is not an investment by the employee in the enterprise.

63. Even this statement needs to be qualified. The law of vagrancy, only recently disappeared from our legal scene, powerfully limited the principle that there is no legal duty to work, and concededly unlawful instances of peonage have been viewed as "simply a desperate attempt to

gation to be employable, to change one's self to meet what the market may require. That duty may involve training or education, doing well in school, or developing a skill. It may involve motivation, getting up early, washing one's face and combing one's hair, and learning how to interview and prepare a resume. Some shortcomings may be a cause of scorn, others of sympathy; in either case one is obligated to do what one can to overcome them.

Personal qualities that impair employability are regarded as a "frill." This idea has manifested itself in the law through the "life-style" cases involving men with facial hair, women who wear pants, and like issues. The law struggles with the legitimacy of such personal aspects, but they are viewed as personal, and the response suggested by the prevailing concept of work is that one who really wants a job will cut his hair, wear a skirt, or take other like steps when they seem necessary in order to be hired.[64] We see in this process the commoditization of the person in a very literal sense. It is graphically manifested in school: students dressing to interview for jobs, going to "resume school," omitting from their resume or their person those qualities thought likely to be unpopular with employers.

The moral obligation to be employable implies that one unable to get the job he or she wants will take any job he or she can get. That is to say, one's willingness to take a job that is available is itself a moral test. There is much here that is central to the dispute between liberals and conservatives over work requirements in welfare law, as applied to the issue of substandard work. The conservative perspective for the most part tends to take the labor market as given, and expresses an interest in attempting to change the willingness of people to work in the labor market as it is. President Nixon said explicitly (as have other leading thinkers going back at least to ancient Greece): "[N]o work is without dignity or meaning [if it] enables an individual to feed and clothe and shelter himself, and provide for his family."[65] The liberal perspective wants to say that there is something wrong with some jobs, but that response is delegitimated by the prevailing belief that the job is more or less given and that there is something wrong with a person who does not want to take the least offensive job that he or she can get. As a result, the liberal perspective gets trapped into disputing the assertion that poor people do not want to work at menial jobs, and finds itself asserting that they do, that they are eager for work emptying

make men earn their living." Pollock v. Williams, 322 U.S. 4, 16 n. 26 (1944) (quoting A.B. Hart, The Southern South 287 (1910)).

J. Atleson, supra note 1, at 172.

64. It requires a powerful, countervailing respect for personal differences—like our tradition of religious toleration—to stand against this response. Compare Sherbert v. Verner, 374 U.S. 398 (1963) with TWA v. Hardison, 432 U.S. 53 (1977) (where the "stand" was not strong enough to prevail).

65. Statement on signing Bill Amending Social Security Act, Pub. Papers 1212 (Dec. 28, 1971). Cf. Hesiod, Works and Days, in The Homeric Hymns and Homerica (H.G. Evelyn–White trans. 1959) ("Work is no disgrace: It is idleness which is disgrace.").

other people's ash trays and cleaning their linen, a proposition that is not intuitively obvious.

The prevailing consciousness rests on a world-view that denies that work can be made to be life-affirming. The "Curse of Adam" is a metaphorical expression of this notion. It was not by being set to work that Adam was cursed: "Cursed be the ground," Genesis says [3:17–19], "for your sake; in sorrow shall you eat of it; thorns and thistles shall it bring forth all your life." In other words, humankind will be cursed by scarcity and low productivity. Work will be just barely able to sustain life. That is the way it is, that is the way it is supposed to be; the only issue is how we deal with that reality. So, we see repeatedly, in the area of safety and health, the strength of the belief that it is chimerical to expect the workplace to become truly safe. This mindset is a powerful input to the law's response to the prevalence of hazardous employment, and to our response to the law. Professor Atleson describes, in critical terms, the way that the law denies protection to employees who quit work over safety concerns. Our sense of injustice about such a law is blunted by a basic skepticism about safe work.

Finally, seeing the value of work as a means toward self-sufficiency reinforces the tendency in us to polarize—that is, to see only as antithetical—our individualist, competitive aspect and our urge toward cooperation and mutuality. It skews our response to that polarity toward the individualist pole, wherein all communitarian pulls are experienced as threats to the self, and "fellow workers" are seen largely as competitors. Within the traditional model, it seems axiomatic that one's co-workers are competing sellers of labor in a series of bilateral relationships or prospective relationships with employers. The fundamental idea of unionization was to break with that model, to substitute a collaborative for a competitive vision. And in many ways (if I may overgeneralize), the difficulty with much of what has happened to labor and to the labor movement over the past century inheres in the fact that it attempted to express a different model in the context of the prevailing concept of work. The very attempt is delegitimated by that concept.

The consciousness of union collective action, such as a picket line, is *not* that of a series of bilateral relations with an employer, but one of an interdependent relation from employee to employee, where employees pursuing their individual self-interest can choose whether to help or to hurt one another, and necessarily must do one or the other. They need not go separate ways thinking that they are necessarily competitors, and they cannot go separate ways thinking that their decisions affect only themselves. The union song, "Which Side Are You On," said this explicitly, the labor movement used to say that explicitly, and in our time Polish workers seek to call themselves by their aspiration: *Solidarity.*

The law does not recognize that consciousness....

V. THE IMPLICATIONS OF AN ALTERNATIVE CONSCIOUSNESS

An underlying consciousness shapes our notion of what is an issue—and the existence of that consciousness is not acknowledged. This is not to say that the unspoken assertions are wrong—that, for example, the relation of work is not a bilateral one—but that they are only partially expressive of reality. Their implicit quality gives them a powerful effect on our perceptions. This implicit consciousness is reflected in the law at the same time as it legitimates the law. The idea that work is a bilateral relation makes it *sensible* to view the job as belonging to the employer. Indeed, this idea makes it sensible to define work to exclude nonmarket activities such as the care of one's home or children. And the underlying "sense" seems right, not just in the way that a reasoned conclusion seems right, but in that the point seems axiomatic. It hardly seems that an issue is being decided.

The legitimating impact is reciprocal. The law made sense of by our consciousness in turn makes our consciousness make sense. I do not suggest that the law has a causal input here. It is not *because* we view work a certain way that certain things happen. It is more that there is a sense of dissonance being pushed away, of alternatives being pushed out of awareness.[69] To his great credit, Professor Atleson has not allowed himself to suppress the dissonance. It is not accidental, however, that his critique is muted, his values position largely implicit, and his "legal" position focused on perceptions regarding statutory purpose and on invocation of principles like even-handedness. Unless the dissonance is seen as reflecting a difference at the level of consciousness, and the partial quality of the traditional consciousness made the explicit subject of attention, its strictures will silently narrow the debate, in ways that predetermine the result.

The completion of the process is the reification of social reality, that is, the failure or refusal to acknowledge that our perception of social reality is a choice—a human product—that embodies a consciousness. The ultimate imprisonment is that which establishes the jail as the boundary of reality, and thereby denies its own existence.[71]

An alternative consciousness starts from the ontological reality that work is the expression of a basic human need. An alternative consciousness of work sees the prevailing concept as grounded in reality and as a *partial* view of reality. Work is more than the sale of a saleable portion of oneself in return for self-sufficiency; it is an expres-

---

69. For a useful, brief discussion of the interaction between a "system of ideas" and "the actual structure of social life," see [Gerald] Frug, The City as a Legal Concept, 93 Harv.L.Rev. 1057, 1074–80 (1980). For a succinct statement of the critical perspective on this central issue, and some penetrating questions about it, see Trubek, supra note 40, at 45–48.

71. John Delaney has ably demonstrated how the reification of social reality is itself a reinforcement of the authoritarian, hierarchical aspects of the traditional consciousness. See Delaney, supra note 43, at 843–47.

sion of one's energy, one's capacity and desire to be useful, one's responsibility and connection to fellow humans.[72]

A recent embodiment of this alternative concept is the Encyclical Letter of Pope John Paul II, *On Human Work* [(1981)]. The Encyclical speaks critically of the traditional consciousness, according to which, "work was understood and treated as a sort of 'merchandise' that the worker ... sells to the employer, who at the same time is the possessor of the capital, that is to say, of all the working tools and means that make production possible...." By contrast, the Encyclical asserts:

> [W]ork is a good thing for man.... It is not only good in the sense that it is useful or something to enjoy; it is also good as being something worthy, that is to say, something that corresponds to man's dignity, that expresses this dignity and increases it.... [T]hrough work man not only transforms nature, adapting it to his own needs, but he also achieves fulfillment as a human being and indeed, in a sense, becomes more a human being.

From the perspective of an alternative consciousness, all issues are transformed, that is, are seen in a broader context. If one without work is without an essential aspect of his or her humanity, there is a moral basis for a right to work. Marge Piercy's lines are apt here: "The pitcher cries for water to carry, and a person for work that is real." [76] In place of the dichotomization of public and private, we would think it self-evident that they are mutually reinforcing and severally responsible.[78]

Seeing the utility of work as not wholly external to the worker, and its meaning as more than a means toward self-sufficiency, would tend to legitimate the issue of work restructuring—the desire to make the workplace consonant with the values of a democratic social order and a fully enfranchised citizenry, and to make work consonant with the values of the individual worker.[79] The dissonance that regularly prompts departures from the regime of the traditional consciousness would be recognized as a response to the deepest urges of the human spirit, and alternatives would not reflexively be seen as legitimate only

---

72. See, e.g., Klare, supra note 44, at 451 ("work can and should provide dignity and meaning to life ... it can and should be a mode of expression, development and realization of the human self").

76. Piercy, To Be Of Use, in Circles on the Water: Selected Poems of Marge Piercy (1982).

78. See Klare, The Public/Private Distinction in Labor Law, 130 U.Pa.L.Rev. 1358, 1417–18 (1982) (criticizing the role that the "public/private" distinction plays in making the prevalent social order seem inevitable and unchangeable).

Pope John Paul writes of the responsibility of direct and indirect employers; of a just wage, which can be paid by the employer or through social measures such as family allowances; and of such related rights as insurance against old age or work accidents. "Among these rights there should never be overlooked the right to a working environment and to manufacturing processes which are not harmful to the workers' physical health or to their moral integrity." ... In all of this, as the Encyclical Letter presents the question, it is the actual result, and not the structuring of the bargaining process alone, which determines its justice.

79. See Klare, supra note 78, at 1387: "[T]he workplace is one of people's most important learning environments."

as they can be accommodated to the traditional concept. The effect, in short, would be to legitimate the effort to lift the Curse of Adam.

Profound as such a shift would be in its impact on legal development, an alternative consciousness of work would, most fundamentally, counteract the tendency to polarize individual and community. It would facilitate a recognition that both a legitimate self-assertive aspect and a genuine concern for others are essential attributes of our individuality. This fuller recognition of the meaning of individuality was given voice some seventeen centuries ago in the Talmudic aphorism:

"If I am not for myself, who is for me?

If I am for my own self only, what am I?" [80]

An alternative consciousness would see efficiency as seeking to maximize something more than the quantity of things that exists in the world, and freedom as something more than permission to compete with one another for scarce resources.

. . .

INSTRUCTION ON CHRISTIAN FREEDOM AND LIBERATION

Vatican Congregation for the Doctrine of the Faith.
(1986).

THE GOSPEL OF WORK

The life of Jesus of Nazareth, a real "Gopel of Work," offers us the living example and principle of the radical cultural transformation which is essential for solving the grave problems which must be faced by the age in which we live.

He, who, though He was God, became like us in all things, devoted the greater part of His earthly life to manual labor. The culture which our age awaits will be marked by the full recognition of the dignity of human work, which appears in all its nobility and fruitfulness in the light of the mysteries of creation and redemption.

In a sense, work is the key to the whole social question.

It is therefore in the domain of work that priority must be given to action of liberation on freedom.

---

80. Ethics of the Fathers 1:14, in The Babylonian Talmud, Order Nezikin, Tractate Aboth 8 (Soncino ed. 1935). A modern, secular expression of this thought eloquently concludes [Bruce] Ackerman's Social Justice and the Liberal State 378 (1980). Roberto Unger seeks to demonstrate that "a necessary implication of the self's attempt to retain its individuality" is the struggle to transcend the paradox between its individual and its social nature. R. Unger, supra note [41], at 217. As John Delaney expresses it: "The person may not be artificially abstracted from the various social contexts in which he or she achieves realization and meaning.... The individual search for fulfillment ... is inseparable from the same quest of others." Delaney, supra note 43, at 853.

Just work relationships will be a necessary precondition for a system of political community capable of favoring the integral development of every individual. . . .

A work culture such as this will necessarily presuppose and put into effect a certain number of essential values.

It will acknowledge that the person of the worker is the [principal] subject and purpose of work.

It will affirm the priority of work over capital and the fact that material goods are meant for all.

It will be animated by a sense of solidarity involving not only rights to be defended but also duties to be performed.

It will involve participation aimed at promoting the national and international good and not just defending individual or corporate interests.

It will assimilate the methods of confrontation and of frank and vigorous dialogue.

The Value of Human Work

The value of any human work does not depend on the kind of work done; it is based on the fact that the one who does it is a person. There we have an ethical criterion whose implications cannot be overlooked.

Thus every person has a right to work, and this right must be recognized in a practical way by an effective commitment to resolving the tragic problem of unemployment. The fact that unemployment keeps large sectors of the population and notably the young in a situation of marginalization is intolerable.

For this reason the creation of jobs is a primary social task facing individuals and private enterprise, as well as the state. As a general rule, in this as in other matters, the state has a subsidiary function; but often it can be called upon to intervene directly, as in the case of international agreements between different states.

Such agreements must respect the rights of immigrants and their families.

Wages, which cannot be considered as a mere commodity, must enable the worker and his family to have access to a truly human standard of living in the material, social, cultural and spiritual orders. It is the dignity of the person which constitutes the criterion for judging work, not the other way round.

Whatever the type of work, the worker must be able to perform it [as] an expression of his personality. There follows from this the necessity of a participation which, over and above a sharing in the fruits of work, should involve a truly communitarian dimension at the level of projects, undertakings and responsibilities.

The priority of work over capital places an obligation in justice upon employers to consider the welfare of the workers before the increase of profits. They have a moral obligation not to keep capital unproductive and in making investments to think first of the common good.

The latter requires a prior effort to consolidate jobs or create new ones in the production of goods that are really useful.

The right to private poverty is inconceivable without responsibilities to the common good. It is subordinated to the higher principle which states that goods are meant for all.

This teaching must inspire reforms before it is too late. Access for everyone to the goods needed for a human, personal and family life worthy of the name is a primary demand of social justice. . . .

Note on the consciousness of work: The reality of the professional ideal

1. (a) In what ways does the traditional idea of what it means to be a "professional" fit better with what I have termed, in the above essay, an "alternative," rather than a "traditional," consciousness of work?

(b) To what extent, if at all, is there a resonance between some of the qualities of professional lawyering that you thought of in response to the preceding question and the reasons that you were first attracted to a legal career?

2. (a) At the same time, as the cases in the preceding sub-section illustrate, the mutually reinforcing interaction between the law of work and the traditional consciousness of work tends to shape the prevailing view of professional work in ways that make it consistent with the traditional consciousness. Recall Justice Powell's description, p. 267, above, of a professional employee as one "whose decisionmaking is limited to the routine discharge of professional duties in projects to which they have been assigned . . ."!

(b) Beyond that, there is much, is there not, in observable emergent changes in the practice of law that seems to be eroding the distinctions between professional and other work.

(c) In what ways, if at all, does a focus on "consciousness" alter the significance of these realities? Consider this response:

> [M]uch legal reasoning exercises a profoundly repressive effect on many lay persons, law students, and lawyers, through the dual message that, first, the matter is not the contestable one of "consciousness" at all, but is determined by some legal principle that one cannot reputably dispute, and, second, that the doctrine makes deeper sense because there is an underlying consciousness that makes it coherent and just. Recognition of the salience and contingent quality of [an] underlying consciousness can help those not sharing [the prevailing] consciousness from being overawed by the gulf between their own consciousness and [that] of authoritative expositors of the law, because it helps us to desacralize their authority, to realize that the authority of judges extends to the exposition of the law, but not to the enactment of the underlying world-view that informs that exposition.

To conclude that all who expound "the law" do so from an underlying consciousness ... enable[s] us to realize that the question of underlying consciousness remains "up for grabs." No official has authority to describe the world preclusive of a like authority in any other person, for the world-view of even the most powerful, intelligent, and respected person remains a view of reality, and not reality itself.

Lesnick, The Wellsprings of Legal Responses to Inequality: A Perspective on Perspectives, 1991 Duke L.J. 431.*

6. THE POWER OF THE LEGAL SYSTEM TO REQUIRE CONFORMITY

The cases in this sub-section deal with aspects of the law governing admission to the bar and the obligation of attorneys to act respectfully toward judges. The principles and practices treated here directly affect very few lawyers or law students. However, my hypothesis is that the norms that they embody have a powerful, if unacknowledged and even unrecognized, constraining effect that goes far beyond the specific conduct giving rise to the cases, that the deference to authority that they require operates as yet another barrier to the articulation of a stance toward lawyering more responsive to internally generated norms.

The formal rules of the professional codes are innocuous enough; see MR 8.1, on knowingly false or misleading statements in connections with applications for admission, and MR 8.2(a), with respect to false statements "concerning the qualifications or integrity" of judges. (Note the change here from the earlier language of DR 1–102(A)(5), prohibiting "conduct that is prejudicial to the administration of justice"). The authority of judges and committees on character and fitness is not so cabined, however, as the following cases demonstrate.

IN RE SUMMERS
Supreme Court of the United States, 1945.
325 U.S. 561, 65 S.Ct. 1307, 89 L.Ed. 1795.

MR. JUSTICE REED delivered the opinion of the Court.

Petitioner sought a writ of certiorari ... to review the action of the Supreme Court of Illinois in denying petitioner's prayer for admission to the practice of law in that state. It was alleged that the denial was "on the sole ground that he is a conscientious objector to war" or to phrase petitioner's contention slightly differently "because of his conscientious scruples against participation in war." Petitioner challenges here the right of the Supreme Court to exclude him from the bar under the due process clause of the Fourteenth Amendment....

... From the record it appears that Clyde Wilson Summers has complied with all prerequisites for admission to the bar of Illinois

---

* The original text uses the word, "perspective," rather than "consciousness"; I have taken the liberty of revising my own words by substituting the term that I have been using in this book. For their congruence of meaning, see id. at 431 n. 3.

except that he has not obtained the certificate of the Committee on Character and Fitness.... No report appears in the record from the Committee. An unofficial letter from the Secretary gives his personal views.[1] A petition was filed in the Supreme Court on August 2, 1943, which alleged that ... the sole reason for the Committee's refusal was that petitioner was a conscientious objector to war, and averred that such reason did not justify his exclusion because of the due process clause of the Fourteenth Amendment. The denial of the petition for admission is informal....

The Justices justify their refusal to admit petitioner to practice before the courts of Illinois on the ground of petitioner's inability to take in good faith the required oath to support the Constitution of Illinois. His inability to take such an oath, the Justices submit, shows that the Committee on Character and Fitness properly refused to certify to his moral character and moral fitness.... A conscientious belief in nonviolence to the extent that the believer will not use force to prevent wrong, no matter how aggravated, and so cannot swear in good faith to support the Illinois Constitution, the Justices contend, must disqualify such a believer for admission.

Petitioner appraises the denial of admission from the viewpoint of a religionist. He said in his petition:

"The so-called 'misconduct' for which petitioner could be reproached ... consists in his attempt to act ... according to the dictates of his conscience. We respectfully submit that the profession of law does not shut its gates to persons who have qualified in all other respects even when they follow in the footsteps of that Great Teacher of mankind who delivered the Sermon on the Mount...."

... The responsibility for choice as to the personnel of its bar rests with Illinois.... Of course, under our Constitutional system, men could not be excluded from the practice of law, or indeed from following any other calling, simply because they belong to any of our religious groups, whether Protestant, Catholic, Quaker or Jewish, assuming it conceivable that any state of the Union would draw such a religious line. We cannot say that any such purpose to discriminate motivated the action of the Illinois Supreme Court.

The sincerity of petitioner's beliefs are not questioned....

---

1. In part it reads:

"I think the record establishes that you are a conscientious objector,—also that your philosophical beliefs go further. You eschew the use of force regardless of circumstances but the law which you profess to embrace and which you teach and would practice is not an abstraction observed through mutual respect. It is real. It is the result of experience of man in an imperfect world, necessary we believe to restrain the strong and protect the weak. It recognizes the right even of the individual to use force under certain circumstances and commands the use of force to obtain its observance.

. . .

"I do not argue against your religious beliefs or your philosophy of non-violence. My point is merely that your position seems inconsistent with the obligation of an attorney at law."

Illinois has constitutional provisions which require service in the militia in time of war of men of petitioner's age group.... While under § 5(g) of the Selective Training and Service Act, ..., conscientious objectors to participation in war in any form now are permitted to do non-war work of national importance, this is by grace of Congressional recognition of their beliefs. Hamilton v. Regents, 293 U.S. 245, 261–65, 55 S.Ct. 197, 203–205, 79 L.Ed. 343, and cases cited. The Act may be repealed. No similar exemption during war exists under Illinois law....

MR. JUSTICE BLACK, dissenting.

. . .

The State does not deny that petitioner possesses the following qualifications:

He is honest, moral, and intelligent, has had a college and a law school education. He has been a law professor and fully measures up to the high standards of legal knowledge Illinois has set as a prerequisite to admission to practice law in that State. He has never been convicted for, or charged with, a violation of law. That he would serve his clients faithfully and efficiently if admitted to practice is not denied. His ideals of what a lawyer should be indicate that his activities would not reflect discredit upon the bar, that he would strive to make the legal system a more effective instrument of justice. Because he thinks that "Lawsuits do not bring love and brotherliness, they just create antagonisms," he would, as a lawyer, exert himself to adjust controversies out of court, but would vigorously press his client's cause in court if efforts to adjust failed. Explaining to his examiners some of the reasons why he wanted to be a lawyer, he told them: "I think there is a lot of work to be done in the law.... I think the law has a place to see to it that every man has a chance to eat and a chance to live equally. I think the law has a place where people can go and get justice done for themselves without paying too much, for the bulk of people that are too poor." No one contends that such a vision of the law in action is either illegal or reprehensible.

The petitioner's disqualifying religious beliefs stem chiefly from a study of the New Testament and a literal acceptance of the teachings of Christ as he understands them.... The taking of human life under any circumstances he believes to be against the Law of God....

I cannot believe that a state statute would be consistent with our constitutional guarantee of freedom of religion if it specifically denied the right to practice law to all members of one of our great religious groups, Protestant, Catholic, or Jewish. Yet the Quakers have had a long and honorable part in the growth of our nation, and an amicus curiae brief filed in their behalf informs us that under the test applied to this petitioner, not one of them if true to the tenets of their faith could qualify for the bar in Illinois. And it is obvious that the same disqualification would exist as to every conscientious objector to the use of force, even though the Congress of the United States should continue its practice of absolving them from military service....

It may be, as many people think, that Christ's Gospel of love and submission is not suited to a world in which men still fight and kill one another. But I am not ready to say that a mere profession of belief in that Gospel is a sufficient reason to keep otherwise well qualified men out of the legal profession....

Nor am I willing to say that such a belief can be penalized through the circuitous method of prescribing an oath, and then barring an applicant on the ground that his present belief might later prompt him to do or refrain from doing something that might violate that oath. Test oaths, designed to impose civil disabilities upon men for their beliefs rather than for unlawful conduct, were an abomination to the founders of this nation. This feeling was made manifest in Article VI of the Constitution which provides that "no religious test shall ever be required as a Qualification to any Office or public Trust under the United States." ...

The state's denial of petitioner's application to practice law resolves itself into a holding that it is lawfully required that all lawyers take an oath to support the state constitution and that petitioner's religious convictions against the use of force make it impossible for him to observe that oath. The petitioner denies this and is willing to take the oath. The particular constitutional provision involved authorizes the legislature to draft Illinois citizens from 18 to 45 years of age for militia service. It can be assumed that the State of Illinois has the constitutional power to draft conscientious objectors for war duty and to punish them for a refusal to serve as soldiers.... But that is not to say that Illinois could constitutionally use the test oath it did in this case....

The Illinois Constitution itself prohibits the draft of conscientious objectors except in time of war.... [T]he probability that Illinois would ever call the petitioner to serve in a war has little more reality than an imaginary quantity in mathematics.

I cannot agree that a state can lawfully bar from a semi-public position a well-qualified man of good character solely because he entertains a religious belief which might prompt him at some time in the future to violate a law which has not yet been and may never be enacted. Under our Constitution men are punished for what they do or fail to do and not for what they think and believe....

MR. JUSTICE DOUGLAS, MR. JUSTICE MURPHY, and MR. JUSTICE RUTLEDGE concur in this opinion.

IN RE ANASTAPLO
Supreme Court of the United States, 1961.
366 U.S. 82, 81 S.Ct. 978, 6 L.Ed.2d 135.

MR. JUSTICE HARLAN delivered the opinion of the Court.

. . .

In 1954 petitioner, George Anastaplo, an instructor and research assistant at the University of Chicago, having previously passed his Illinois bar examinations, was denied admission to the bar of that State by the Illinois Supreme Court. The denial was based upon his refusal to answer questions of the Committee on Character and Fitness as to whether he was a member of the Communist Party.... In 1957, following this Court's decisions in the earlier Konigsberg case, 353 U.S. 252, 77 S.Ct. 722, 1 L.Ed.2d 810, and in Schware v. Board of Bar Examiners of New Mexico, 353 U.S. 232, 77 S.Ct. 752, 1 L.Ed.2d 796, ... the State Supreme Court ... directed rehearing.

The ensuing lengthy proceedings before the Committee,[4] at which Anastaplo was the only witness, are perhaps best described as a wide-ranging exchange between the Committee and Anastaplo in which the Committee sought to explore Anastaplo's ability conscientiously to swear support of the Federal and State Constitutions, as required by the Illinois attorneys' oath, and Anastaplo undertook to expound and defend, on historical and ideological premises, his abstract belief in the "right of revolution," and to resist, on grounds of asserted constitutional right and scruple, Committee questions which he deemed improper.[5] The Committee already had before it uncontroverted evidence as to Anastaplo's "good moral character," in the form of written statements or affidavits furnished by persons of standing acquainted with him, and the record on rehearing contains nothing which could properly be considered as reflecting adversely upon his character or reputation or on the sincerity of the beliefs he espoused before the Committee. Anastaplo persisted, however, in refusing to answer, among other inquiries, the Committee's questions as to his possible membership in the Communist Party or in other allegedly related organizations.

Thereafter the Committee, by a vote of 11 to 6, again declined to certify Anastaplo because of his refusal to answer such questions, the majority stating in its report to the Illinois Supreme Court:

. . .

"We draw no inference of disloyalty or subversion from applicant's continued refusal to answer questions concerning Commu-

---

4. The proceedings consumed six hearing days, and resulted in a transcript of over 400 pages.

5. More particularly: petitioner was first asked routine questions about his personal history. He refused, on constitutional grounds, to answer whether he was affiliated with any church. He answered all questions about organizational relationships so long as he did not know that the organization was "political" in character. He refused, on grounds of protected free speech and association, to answer whether he was a member of the Communist Party or of any other group named in the Attorney General's list of "subversive" organiza-

tions, including the Ku Klux Klan and the Silver Shirts of America.

Much of the ensuing five sessions was devoted to discussion of Anastaplo's reasons for believing that inquiries into such matters were constitutionally privileged, and to an unjustifiable attempt, later expressly repudiated by the Committee, to delve into the consistency of petitioner's religious beliefs with an attorney's duty to take an oath of office.

A substantial part of the proceedings revolved around Anastaplo's views as to the right to revolt against tyrannical government, and the right to resist judicial decrees in exceptional circumstances.

nist or other subversive affiliations. We do, however, hold that
there is a strong public interest in our being free to question
applicants for admission to the bar on their adherence to our basic
institutions and form of government and that such public interest
in the character of its attorneys overrides an applicant's private
interest in keeping such views to himself. By failing to respond to
this higher public interest we hold that the applicant has obstruct-
ed the proper functions of the Committee.... We cannot certify
the applicant as worthy of the trust and confidence of the public
when we do not know that he is so worthy and when he has
prevented us from finding out."

At the same time the full Committee acknowledged that Anastaplo
[had an unblemished reputation, that it had no adverse information
about his character, and that his views]

"with respect to the right to overthrow the government by force or
violence, while strongly libertarian and expressed with an intensity
and fervor not necessarily shared by all good citizens, are not
inconsistent with those held by many patriotic Americans both at
the present time and throughout the course of this country's
history and do not in and of themselves reveal any adherence to
subversive doctrines."

. . .

Two of the basic issues in this litigation have been settled by our
contemporary *Konigsberg* opinion [, 366 U.S. 36 (1960)]. We have there
held it not constitutionally impermissible for a State ... to adopt a rule
that an applicant will not be admitted to the practice of law if, and so
long as, by refusing to answer material questions, he obstructs a bar
examining committee in its proper functions of interrogating and cross-
examining him upon his qualifications....

We have also held in *Konigsberg* that the State's interest in
enforcing such a rule as applied to refusals to answer questions about
membership in the Communist Party outweighs any deterrent effect
upon freedom of speech and association, and hence that such state
action does not offend the Fourteenth Amendment. We think that in
this respect no valid constitutional distinction can be based on the
circumstance that in Konigsberg there was some, though weak, independent evidence that the applicant had once been connected with the
Communist Party, while here there was no such evidence as to Anastaplo....

Two issues, however, do arise upon this record which are not
disposed of by *Konigsberg.* The first is [omitted]. The second is
whether his exclusion from the bar on this ground was, in the circumstances of this case, arbitrary or discriminatory.

. . .

Petitioner's claim that the application of the State's exclusionary
rule was arbitrary and discriminatory in the circumstances of this case

must also be rejected. It is contended (1) that Anastaplo's refusal to answer these particular questions did not obstruct the Committee's investigation, because that body already had before it uncontroverted evidence establishing petitioner's good character and fitness for the practice of law; and (2) that the real reason why the State proceeded as it did was because of its disapproval of Anastaplo's constitutionally protected views on the right to resist tyrannical government. Neither contention can be accepted.

It is sufficient to say in answer to the first contention that even though the Committee already had before it substantial character evidence altogether favorable to Anastaplo, there is nothing in the Federal Constitution which required the Committee to draw the curtain upon its investigation at that point. It had the right to supplement that evidence and to test the applicant's own credibility by interrogating him. . . .

As to the second contention, there is nothing in the record which would justify our holding that the State has invoked its exclusionary refusal-to-answer rule as a mask for its disapproval of petitioner's notions on the right to overthrow tyrannical government.[17] While the Committee's majority report does observe that there was "a serious question" whether Anastaplo's views on the right to resist judicial decrees would be compatible with his taking of the attorney's oath, and that "certain" members of the Committee thought that such views affirmatively demonstrated his disqualification for admission to the bar,[18] it is perfectly clear that the Illinois Bar Committee and Supreme Court regarded petitioner's refusal to cooperate in the Committee's examination of him as the basic and only reason for a denial of certification.

. . . Finally, contrary to the assumption on which some of the arguments on behalf of Anastaplo seem to have proceeded, we do not understand that Illinois' exclusionary requirement will continue to operate to exclude Anastaplo from the bar any longer than he continues in his refusal to answer. We find nothing to suggest that he would not be admitted now if he decides to answer, assuming of course that no grounds justifying his exclusion from practice resulted. In short, petitioner holds the key to admission in his own hands.

17. Both the Committee's report and the State Supreme Court's opinion make it apparent that this area of Anastaplo's views played no part in his exclusion from the bar. . . .

18. This of course could hardly be so in the context of the illustrations which Anastaplo gave of his views as to when a right to resist might arise. These were: Nazi Germany; Hungary during the 1956 revolt against Russia; a hypothetical decree of this Court establishing "some dead pagan religion as the official religion of the country . . ."; a capital sentence of Jesus Christ. Asked to give a more realistic instance of when resistance would be proper, Anastaplo summarized: "I know of no decree, off hand, in the history of American government, where such a single instance has occurred. No—I grant that it is hard to find these instances. I think it is important to insist that there might be such instances." Nothing in the State Court's opinion remotely suggests its approbation of these views of "certain" Committee members.

. . .

MR. JUSTICE BLACK, with whom THE CHIEF JUSTICE [WARREN], MR. JUSTICE DOUGLAS and MR. JUSTICE BRENNAN concur, dissenting. . . .

The controversy began in November 1950, when Anastaplo, a student at the University of Chicago Law School, having two months previously successfully passed the Illinois Bar examination, appeared before the State's Committee on Character and Fitness for the usual interview preliminary to admission to the Bar. The personal history form required by state law had been filled out and filed with the Committee prior to his appearance and showed that Anastaplo was an unusually worthy applicant for admission. His early life had been spent in a small town in southern Illinois where his parents, who had immigrated to this country from Greece before his birth, still resided. After having received his precollege education in the public schools of his home town, he had discontinued his education, at the age of eighteen, and joined the Air Force during the middle of World War II— flying as a navigator in every major theater of the military operations of that war. Upon receiving an honorable discharge in 1947, he had come to Chicago and resumed his education, obtaining his undergraduate degree at the University of Chicago and entering immediately into the study of law at the University of Chicago Law School. His record throughout his life, both as a student and as a citizen, was unblemished.

The personal history form thus did not contain so much as one statement of fact about Anastaplo's past life or conduct that could have, in any way, cast doubt upon his fitness for admission to the Bar. It did, however, contain a statement of opinion which, in the minds of some of the members of the Committee at least, did cast such doubt and in that way served to touch off this controversy. This was a statement made by Anastaplo in response to the command of the personal history form: "State what you consider to be the principles underlying . . . the Constitution of the United States." Anastaplo's response to that command was as follows:

> "One principle consists of the doctrine of the separation of powers. . . . Another basic principle (and the most important) is that such government is constituted so as to secure certain inalienable rights, those rights to Life, Liberty and the Pursuit of Happiness (and elements of these rights are explicitly set forth in such parts of the Constitution as the Bill of Rights.). *And, of course, whenever the particular government in power becomes destructive of these ends, it is the right of the people to alter or to abolish it and thereupon to establish a new government.* This is how I view the Constitution." (Emphasis supplied.)

When Anastaplo appeared before a two-man Subcommittee of the Committee on Character and Fitness, one of its members almost immediately engaged him in a discussion relating to the meaning of these italicized words which were substantially taken from . . . the Declaration of Independence. . . . This discussion soon developed into an argument as Anastaplo stood by his statement and insisted that if a government gets bad enough, the people have a "right of revolution." It was at this juncture in the proceedings that the other member of the Subcommittee interrupted with the question: "Are you a member of any organization that is listed on the Attorney General's list, to your knowledge?" And this question was followed up a few moments later with the question: "Are you a member of the Communist Party?"[3] A colloquy then ensued between Anastaplo and the two members of the Subcommittee as to the legitimacy of the questions being asked, Anastaplo insisting that these questions were not reasonably related to the Committee's functions and that they violated his rights under the Constitution, and the members of the Subcommittee insisting that the questions were entirely legitimate.

The Subcommittee then refused to certify Anastaplo for admission to the Bar but, instead, set a further hearing on the matter before the

---

3. The following excerpt from the record of the first hearing indicates clearly the connection between Anastaplo's views on the "right of revolution" and the questions subsequently asked him about his "possible" political associations:

"Commissioner MITCHELL: When you say 'believe in revolution,' you don't limit that revolution to an overthrow of a particular political party or a political government by means of an election process or other political means?

"Mr. ANASTAPLO: I mean actual use of force.

"Commissioner MITCHELL: You mean to go as far as necessary?

"Mr. ANASTAPLO: As far as Washington did, for instance.

"Commissioner MITCHELL: So that would it be fair to say that you believe the end result would justify any means that were used?

"Mr. ANASTAPLO: No, the means proportionate to the particular end in sight.

. . .

"Commissioner MITCHELL: ... You believe that assuming the government should be overthrown, in your opinion, that you and others of like mind would be justified in raising a company of men with military equipment and proceed to take over the government of the United States, of the State of Illinois? . . . .

"Mr. ANASTAPLO: If you get to the point where overthrow is necessary, then overthrow is justified. It just means that you overthrow the government by force.

"Commissioner MITCHELL: And would that also include in your mind justification for putting a spy into the administrative department, one or another of the adminis-

trative departments of the United States or the government of the State of Illinois?

"Mr. ANASTAPLO: If you got to the point you think the government should be overthrown, I think that would be a legitimate means.

"Commissioner MITCHELL: There isn't any difference in your mind in the propriety of using a gun or using a spy?

"Mr. ANASTAPLO: I think spies have been used in quite honorable causes.

"Commissioner MITCHELL: Your answer is, you do think so?

"Mr. ANASTAPLO: Yes.

"Commissioner BAKER: Let me ask you a question. Are you aware of the fact that the Department of Justice has a list of what are described as subversive organizations?

"Mr. ANASTAPLO: Yes.

"Commissioner BAKER: Have you ever seen that list?

"Mr. ANASTAPLO: Yes.

"Commissioner BAKER: Are you a member of any organization that is listed on the Attorney General's list, to your knowledge? (No answer.) Just to keep you from having to work so hard mentally on it, what organizations—give me all the organizations you are affiliated with or are a member of. (No answer.) That oughtn't to be too hard.

"Mr. ANASTAPLO: Do you believe that is a legitimate question?

"Commissioner BAKER: Yes, I do. We are inquiring into not only your character, but your fitness, under Rule 58. We don't compel you to answer it. Are you a member of the Communist Party?"

full Committee. That next hearing, as well as all of the hearings that followed, have been little more than repetitions of the first. The rift between Anastaplo and the Committee has grown ever wider with each successive hearing. Anastaplo has steadfastly refused to answer any questions put by the Committee which inquired into his political associations or religious beliefs. A majority of the members of the Committee, faced with this refusal, has grown more and more insistent that it has the right to force him to answer any question it sees fit to ask. The result has been a series of hearings in which questions have been put to Anastaplo with regard to his "possible" association with scores of organizations, including the Ku Klux Klan, the Silver Shirts (an allegedly Fascist organization), every organization on the so-called Attorney General's list, the Democratic Party, the Republican Party, and the Communist Party. At one point in the proceedings, at least two of the members of the Committee insisted that he tell the Committee whether he believes in a Supreme Being and one of these members stated that, as far as his vote was concerned, a man's "belief in the Deity ... has a substantial bearing upon his fitness to practice law."

It is true, as the majority points out, that the Committee did not expressly rest its refusal to certify Anastaplo for admission to the Bar either upon his views on the "right of revolution," as that "right" is defined in the Declaration of Independence, or upon his refusal to disclose his beliefs with regard to the existence of God,[4] or upon his refusals to disclose any of his political associations other than his "possible" association with the Communist Party. But it certainly cannot be denied that the other questions were asked and, since we should not presume that these members of the Committee did not want answers to their questions, it seems certain that Anastaplo's refusal to answer them must have had some influence upon the final outcome of the hearings. In any case, when the Committee did vote, 11–6, not to certify Anastaplo for admission, not one member who asked any question Anastaplo had refused to answer voted in his favor.

The reasons for Anastaplo's position ... went much deeper than a bare reliance upon what he considered to be his legal rights. The record shows that his refusal to answer the Committee's question stemmed primarily from his belief that he had a duty, both to society and to the legal profession, not to submit to the demands of the Committee because he believed that the questions had been asked solely for the purpose of harassing him because he had expressed agreement

4. As the majority points out, the Committee eventually did expressly disavow any right to insist upon an answer to this question. This came at the end of a long disagreement between Anastaplo and certain members of the Committee with respect to the vitality of an old Illinois decision which indicated that a belief in God might be necessary in order to take an oath to testify. The Committee's abandonment of the point came only after Anastaplo produced a more recent Illinois case disapproving the earlier decision. It is interesting to note that neither of the Committee members who had expressed such a strong interest in knowing whether Anastaplo believes in God voted in favor of his certification.

with the assertion of the right of revolution against an evil government set out in the Declaration of Independence....

. . .

The reasons for the Committee's position are also clear. Its job, throughout these proceedings, has been to determine whether Anastaplo is possessed of the necessary good moral character to justify his admission to the Bar of Illinois. In that regard, the Committee has been given the benefit of voluminous affidavits from men of standing in their professions and in the community that Anastaplo is possessed of an unusually fine character....

. . .

The record also shows that the Committee supplemented the information it had obtained about Anastaplo from these affidavits by conducting informal independent investigations into his character and reputation. It sent agents to Anastaplo's home town in southern Illinois and they questioned the people who knew him there. Similar inquiries were made among those who knew him in Chicago. But these intensive investigations apparently [5] failed to produce so much as one man in Chicago or in the whole State of Illinois who could say or would say, directly, indirectly or even by hearsay, one thing derogatory to the character, loyalty or reputation of George Anastaplo, and not one man could be found who would in any way link him with the Communist Party....

In addition to the information it had obtained from the affidavits and from its independent investigations, the Committee had one more important source of information about Anastaplo's character. It had the opportunity to observe the manner in which he conducted himself during the many hours of hearings before it. That manner, as revealed by the record before us and undenied by any findings of the Committee to the contrary, left absolutely nothing to be desired. Faced with a barrage of sometimes highly provocative and totally irrelevant questions from men openly hostile to his position, Anastaplo invariably responded with all the dignity and restraint attributed to him in the affidavits of his friends. Moreover, it is not amiss to say that he conducted himself in precisely the same manner during the oral argument he presented before this Court.

Thus, it is against the background of a mountain of evidence so favorable to Anastaplo that the word "overwhelming" seems inadequate to describe it that the action of the Committee in refusing to certify Anastaplo as fit for admission to the Bar must be considered. The majority of the Committee rationalized its position on the ground that without answers to some of the questions it had asked, it could not conscientiously perform its duty of determining Anastaplo's character

---

5. The record shows that although Anastaplo repeatedly requested that the Committee allow him to see any reports that resulted from these independent investigations, the Committee, without denying that such reports existed, refused to produce them.

and fitness to be a lawyer. A minority of the Committee described this explanation as "pure sophistry." And it is simply impossible to read this record without agreeing with the minority. For, it is difficult to see what possible relevancy answers to the questions could have had in the minds of these members of the Committee after they had received such completely overwhelming proof beyond a reasonable doubt of Anastaplo's good character and staunch patriotism. I can think of no sound reason for further insistence upon these answers other than the very questionable, but very human, feeling that this young man should not be permitted to resist the Committee's demands without being compelled to suffer for it in some way.

. . .

. . . But the men who founded this country and wrote our Bill of Rights were strangers neither to a belief in the "right of revolution" nor to the urgency of the need to be free from the control of government with regard to political beliefs and associations. Thomas Jefferson was not disclaiming a belief in the "right of revolution" when he wrote the Declaration of Independence. And Patrick Henry was certainly not disclaiming such a belief when he declared in impassioned words that have come on down through the years: "Give me liberty or give me death." This country's freedom was won by men who, whether they believed in it or not, certainly practiced revolution in the Revolutionary War.

Since the beginning of history there have been governments that have engaged in practices against the people so bad, so cruel, so unjust and so destructive of the individual dignity of men and women that the "right of revolution" was all the people had left to free themselves. As simple illustrations, one government almost 2,000 years ago burned Christians upon fiery crosses and another government, during this very century, burned Jews in crematories. I venture the suggestion that there are countless multitudes in this country, and all over the world, who would join Anastaplo's belief in the right of the people to resist by force tyrannical governments like those.

In saying what I have, it is to be borne in mind that Anastaplo has not indicated, even remotely, a belief that this country is an oppressive one in which the "right of revolution" should be exercised. Quite the contrary, the entire course of his life, as disclosed by the record, has been one of devotion and service to his country—first, in his willingness to defend its security at the risk of his own life in time of war and, later, in his willingness to defend its freedoms at the risk of his professional career in time of peace. The one and only time in which he has come into conflict with the Government is when he refused to answer the questions put to him by the Committee about his beliefs and associations. And I think the record clearly shows that conflict resulted, not from any fear on Anastaplo's part to divulge his own political activities, but from a sincere, and in my judgment correct, conviction that the preservation of this country's freedom depends upon adherence to our Bill of Rights. The very most that can fairly be said against Anastaplo's position in this entire matter is that he took too much of the responsibility of preserving that freedom upon himself.

This case illustrates to me the serious consequences to the Bar itself of not affording the full protections of the First Amendment to its applicants for admission. For this record shows that Anastaplo has many of the qualities that are needed in the American Bar. It shows, not only that Anastaplo has followed a high moral, ethical and patriotic course in all of the activities of his life, but also that he combines these more common virtues with the uncommon virtue of courage to stand by his principles at any cost. It is such men as these who have most greatly honored the profession of the law—men like Malsherbes, who, at the cost of his own life and the lives of his family, sprang unafraid to the defense of Louis XVI against the fanatical leaders of the Revolutionary government of France [12]—men like Charles Evans Hughes, Sr., later Mr. Chief Justice Hughes, who stood up for the constitutional rights of socialists to be socialists and public officials despite the threats and clamorous protests of self-proclaimed superpatriots [13]—men like Charles Evans Hughes, Jr., and John W. Davis, who, while against everything for which the Communists stood, strongly advised the Congress in 1948 that it would be unconstitutional to pass the law then proposed to outlaw the Communist Party—men like Lord Erskine, James Otis, Clarence Darrow, and the multitude of others who have dared to speak in defense of causes and clients without regard to personal danger to themselves. The legal profession will lose much of its nobility and its glory if it is not constantly replenished with lawyers like these. To force the Bar to become a group of thoroughly orthodox, time-serving, government-fearing individuals is to humiliate and degrade it.

But that is the present trend, not only in the legal profession but in almost every walk of life. Too many men are being driven to become government-fearing and time-serving because the Government is being permitted to strike out at those who are fearless enough to think as they please and say what they think. This trend must be halted if we are to keep faith with the Founders of our Nation and pass on to future generations of Americans the great heritage of freedom which they

---

12. At the time of his decision to volunteer his services in defense of Louis XVI, Malsherbes, a man of more than seventy, was apparently completely safe from the post-revolutionary blood bath which then enveloped France. For, although active in public life prior to the Revolution, he had always been a friend of the people and, in any case, he had largely passed out of the public mind with his retirement some years earlier. Within a year of his unsuccessful defense of the life of France's former king, however, he, together with his entire family, was convicted by a revolutionary tribunal on the vague charge of conspiracy against "the safety of the State and the unity of the Republic." Malsherbes was then taken to the guillotine where, after being forced to witness the beheading of the other members of his family, he paid with his life for his courage as a lawyer. . . .

13. The story of Hughes' participation in the fight against the action of the New York Legislature in suspending five of its members in 1920 on the ground that they were socialists is told in John Lord O'Brian, Loyalty Tests and Guilt by Association, 61 Harv.L.Rev. 592, 593–594.

sacrificed so much to leave to us. The choice is clear to me. If we are to pass on that great heritage of freedom, we must return to the original language of the Bill of Rights. We must not be afraid to be free.

Note on Summers and Anastaplo: The refusenik as lawyer

1. In the Supreme Court, *Summers* and *Anastaplo* necessarily presented constitutional issues. For present purposes, however, the premises of the Illinois bar examiners and courts are more salient than is the Supreme Court's understanding of the Fourteenth Amendment. Consider the concept of "good moral character" that presumably underlay the examiners' and the state-court judges' negative reactions. Is the following a fair statement? *First,* a reliable allegiance to the legitimacy of prevailing political and legal institutions is a critical aspect of "good moral character." *Second,* one who cannot in good conscience take an oath that, to the bar examiners, signifies a willingness to participate in warfare in defense of one's country, or whose perception of American democracy includes a contemporary appreciation of its revolutionary origins, may well lack such allegiance.

Summers challenged the examiners' interpretation of the oath, which required only that he support the Constitution of Illinois, and stood ready to take it; the oath apart, he challenged an interpretation of "good character" that saw his fidelity to his religiously based pacifism as inconsistent with his fidelity to his country. Anastaplo challenged the examiners' right to insist on so strong a commitment to the legitimacy of the prevailing political order, and, believing his political views no more warranting scrutiny than those of the run of applicants for admission, asserted the belief that his opinions and political activities should not be laid open to special inquiry. To him, the examiners' insistence that he trust their processes and answer all questions fully was a threat to, rather than a safeguard of, democratic institutions.

2. The question then became whether adherence to these individualized views, views probably not shared by the majority of the applicants' fellow-countrymen, was inconsistent with "good moral character." The examiners and State-court judges apparently thought so; in each case, a five-Justice majority of the Supreme Court, rejecting views eloquently given voice by Justice Black,* found the Fourteenth Amendment neutral on the matter.

Another way of perceiving the question, however, is to ask whether it is not a willingness to *abandon* these sincerely held views in deference to majority sentiment, in order to be admitted to the Bar, that would be inconsistent with "good moral character." Consider, in that connection, the following:

* At Justice Black's request, portions of his *Anastaplo* dissent were read at his funeral.

(a) In a petition for rehearing, Anastaplo made this comment about the Court's observation that he "holds the key to admission in his own hands":

> Suppose . . . that petitioner should now regard this prolonged litigation merely as a "test case" and proceed to answer in the negative all unanswered questions. What more would the committee know that it does not already know? That is, what of substance would be added to the record bearing on petitioner's character and fitness that has not been available to Illinois for ten years? It is obvious that only one more item could be added, the fact of petitioner's *submission,* a selfish and even unmanly submission to what he has considered for over a decade to be dangerous and uncalled for practices. . . .

> Whether or not petitioner is correct in his evaluation of these inquiries, it is generally conceded that he has long *believed* himself to be correct about a matter so vital to the bar and to the country that he has been willing to make serious sacrifices rather than acquiesce in such practices. Thus, if petitioner follows the advice implicit in the Opinion of this Court, the committee would gain the assurance of this single additional fact, the fact that petitioner had used a "key" against what he considers the best interests of the bar and of the country and that he had done so only to preserve his own career. Should this kind of behavior make him appear in a more favorable light before a tribunal of lawyers dedicated to the moral fitness of the bar? . . . .

Petition for Rehearing, In re Anastaplo, Supreme Court of the U.S., Oct. Term 1960, No. 58. pp. 23–25 (1961).*

(b) Compare the treatment of an analogous question by the Supreme Judicial Court of Massachusetts in Matter of Hiss, 368 Mass. 447, 333 N.E.2d 429 (1975). In one of the most highly publicized trials in our history, Alger Hiss had been convicted in 1950 of perjury, for denying to a federal grand jury that he, or his wife, had many years earlier turned over secret government documents to Whittaker Chambers, his accuser at his trial. Sentenced to prison, he was disbarred in 1952.

Twenty-two years later, Hiss applied for reinstatement as an attorney, based on his activities since release from prison. The Court held, preliminarily, that conviction of perjury was not automatically disquali-

---

* The petition for rehearing was denied, and Anastaplo has never been admitted to the Bar. He is a professor of law at Loyola University, and has written extensively on the Constitution. In 1983, the Illinois State Bar Association, on its own initiative, asked the Supreme Court of the State to reconsider its decision, thirty years earlier, to deny Anastaplo admission. The President of the State Bar Association said: "We are not taking this action for Mr. Anastaplo's sake, but for the sake of the legal profession, which should be able to admit past mistakes and hold its head high." National Law Journal, Aug. 22, 1983, p. 8. Anastaplo had declined to join in the request, and the Supreme Court declined to act on the basis of a letter from the Association. "[T]here is nothing pending before the court upon which it can act." Ibid., Nov. 14, 1983, p. 19.

fying under Massachusetts law; that the readmission proceeding should proceed on the assumption that Hiss was guilty; and that his conviction was conclusive evidence of his lack of moral character at the time of his disbarment. In assessing Hiss's present fitness for reinstatement to the bar, however, the Court rejected the contention that Hiss could not be readmitted to the bar unless he admitted his guilt:

> Though we deem prior judgments dispositive of all factual issues and deny attorneys subject to disciplinary proceedings the right to relitigate issues of guilt, we recognize that a convicted person may on sincere reasoning believe himself to be innocent. We also take cognizance of Hiss's argument that miscarriages of justice are possible. Basically, his underlying theory is that innocent men conceivably could be convicted, that a contrary view would place a mantle of absolute and inviolate perfection on our system of justice, and that this is an attribute that cannot be claimed for any human institution or activity. . . .

> Simple fairness and fundamental justice demand that the person who believes he is innocent though convicted should not be required to confess guilt to a criminal act he honestly believes he did not commit. For him, a rule requiring admission of guilt and repentance creates a cruel quandry: he may stand mute and lose his opportunity; or he may cast aside his hard-retained scruples and, paradoxically, commit what he regards as perjury to prove his worthiness to practice law. . . . Honest men would suffer permanent disbarment under such a rule. [At the same time, it] might permit reinstatement of those least fit to serve. . . .

(c) Both sides of this question are stated eloquently in the brief interchange between the Duke of Norfolk and his friend, Sir Thomas More, prompted by the Duke's heart-felt appeal to More, asking him to sign the oath acknowledging the authority of the Archbishop of Canterbury to pronounce invalid the marriage of the King to Queen Catharine (and thereby denying the authority of the Pope over the Church in England), because of the stature of the many others who had done so:

NORFOLK: Oh, confound all this . . . I'm not a scholar, as Master Cromwell never tires of pointing out, and frankly I don't know whether the marriage was lawful or not. But damn it, Thomas, look at those names . . . You know those men! Can't you do what I did, and come with us, for fellowship?

MORE (moved): And when we stand before God, and you are sent to Paradise for doing according to your conscience, and I am damned for not doing according to mine, will you come with me, for fellowship?

R. Bolt, A Man for All Seasons 76–77 (1962), in Becoming a Lawyer, pp. 18–19.

3. The issue raised in this Note has implications for public policy: What meaning should the concept of "good moral character" have in a

society committed to individual liberty, especially liberty of conscience? For present purposes, however, the relevant questions are these:

(a) In light of cases like *Summers* and *Anastaplo,* to what extent, if at all, do you believe that the bar-admission process inhibits the development and articulation of your own conception of what it means to be a "good lawyer," and reinforces the tendency to look to norms set by the powerful to answer that question for you?

(b) What grounds, if any, are there for the suggestion that, to the extent any such inhibiting process is present, it survives one's admission to the Bar?

(c) Are there ways in which this inhibiting process can be lessened, by individual lawyers or law students lacking the power to influence public policy?

LAW STUDENTS CIVIL RIGHTS RESEARCH COUNCIL v. WADMOND
Supreme Court of the United States, 1971.
401 U.S. 154, 91 S.Ct. 720, 27 L.Ed.2d 749.

MR. JUSTICE STEWART delivered the opinion of the Court.

An applicant for admission to the Bar of New York must be a citizen of the United States, have lived in the State for at least six months, and pass a written examination conducted by the State Board of Law Examiners. In addition, New York requires that the Appellate Division of the State Supreme Court in the judicial department where an applicant resides must "be satisfied that such person possesses the character and general fitness requisite for an attorney and counsellor-at-law." New York Judiciary Law § 90, subd. 1, par. a (1968). To carry out this provision, the New York Civil Practice Law and Rules require the appointment, in each of the four Judicial Departments into which the Supreme Court is divided, of a Committee or Committees on Character and Fitness. Section 528.1 of the Rules of the New York Court of Appeals for the Admission of Attorneys and Counsellors-at-Law requires that the character and general fitness specified in Judiciary Law § 90 "must be shown by the affidavits of two reputable persons residing in the city or county in which [the applicant] resides, one of whom must be a practicing attorney of the Supreme Court of this State." The Committees also require the applicant himself to fill out a questionnaire.[4] After receipt of the affidavits and questionnaire, the Committees conduct a personal interview with each applicant. As a final step before actual admission to the Bar, an applicant must take an oath that he will support the Constitutions of the United States and of the State of New York.

This case involves a broad attack, primarily on First Amendment vagueness and overbreadth grounds, upon this system for screening

---

4. Answers to these questionnaires are treated as confidential.

applicants for admission to the New York Bar. The appellants, plaintiffs in the trial court, are organizations and individuals claiming to
represent a class of law students and law graduates similarly situated,
seeking or planning to seek admission to practice law in New York.
They commenced two separate actions for declaratory and injunctive
relief in the United States District Court for the Southern District of
New York, naming as defendants two Committees on Character and
Fitness and their members and two Appellate Divisions and their
judges. The complaints attacked the statutes, rules, and screening
procedures as invalid on their face or as applied in the First and Second
Departments. A three-judge court was convened and consolidated the
two suits.

In a thorough opinion, the court considered the appellants' claims
and found certain items on the questionnaires as they then stood to be
so vague, overbroad, and intrusive upon applicants' private lives as to
be of doubtful constitutional validity. It granted the partial relief
indicated by these findings, approving or further amending the revised
questions submitted by the appellees to conform to its opinion. It
upheld the statutes and rules as valid on their face and, with the
exceptions noted, sustained the validity of New York's system. This
appeal followed....

We note at the outset that no person involved in this case has been
refused admission to the New York Bar. Indeed, the appellants point
to no case in which they claim any applicant has ever been unjustifi-
ably denied permission to practice law in New York State under these
or earlier statutes, rules, or procedures. The basic thrust of the
appellants' attack is, rather, that New York's system by its very
existence works a "chilling effect" upon the free exercise of the rights
of speech and association of students who must anticipate having to
meet its requirements.

[Appellants did not challenge the constitutionality of New York's
requirement that applicants for admission possess "the character and
general fitness required for an attorney and counsellor-at-law"; be
citizens of the United States and, for six months, residents of the State;
and take an oath to support the State and Federal constitutions.]

But, the appellants contend, even though the statutory standard
may be constitutionally valid, the methods used by the Committees to
satisfy themselves that applicants meet that standard are not. Specifically, the appellants object to the terms of the third-party affidavits
attesting to an applicant's good moral character. During this litigation, the appellees revised the affidavit forms in several respects.
Whatever may have been said of the affidavits formerly used, we can
find nothing in the present forms remotely vulnerable to constitutional
attack....

... Rule 9406 of the New York Civil Practice Law and Rules
directs the Committees on Character and Fitness not to certify an
applicant for admission "unless he shall furnish satisfactory proof to

the effect" that he [among other requirements] "believes in the form of the government of the United States and is loyal to such government."

[The Court acknowledged that this requirement, as written, might well be unconstitutional. But it accepted the interpretation of it suggested by the Committee on Character and Fitness, that the requirement did not place the burden of proof on an applicant and required no more than a willingness and good faith ability to take the standard oath to support the Constitution].

As this case comes to us from the three-judge panel, the questionnaire applicants are asked to complete contains only two numbered questions reflecting the disputed provision of Rule 9406.[18] They are as follows:

> "26. . . .

> "27. (a) Is there any reason why you cannot take and subscribe to an oath or affirmation that you will support the constitutions of the United States and of the State of New York? If there is, please explain.

> "(b) Can you conscientiously, and do you, affirm that you are, without any mental reservation, loyal to and ready to support the Constitution of the United States?".

> . . . .

. . . Question 27 . . . is simply supportive of the appellees' task of ascertaining the good faith with which an applicant can take the constitutional oath. . . . [T]here is no indication that a New York Bar applicant would not be given the opportunity to explain any "mental reservation" and still gain admission to the Bar.

Finally, there emerges from the appellants' briefs and oral argument a more fundamental claim than any to which we have thus far adverted. They suggest that, whatever the facial validity of the various details of a screening system such as New York's, there inheres in such a system so constant a threat to applicants that constitutional depriva-

---

18. The district court ordered the elimination or revision of the following questions contained in the questionnaires at the time this litigation was commenced:

"26. . . .

"27 (a). Do you believe in the principles underlying the form of government of the United States of America?" [The District Court reasoned: "The phrase 'principles underlying the form of government' . . . might be understood by an applicant to include many 'principles' of a lower order than the essentials, democratic government and change by lawful methods. One who favored drastic reforms, albeit through constitutional means, might perhaps feel unable conscientiously to answer with a simple 'yes'; yet . . . the word 'prin-

ciples' is so vague as to create a problem even if opportunity for explanation were afforded." 299 F.Supp. 117, 130 (S.D.N.Y. 1969)].

"31. Is there any incident in your life not called for by the foregoing questions which has any favorable or detrimental bearing on your character or fitness? If the answer is 'Yes' state the facts." In the Second Department the words "favorable or" did not appear. [The District Court found "no interest of the state sufficiently compelling to require an applicant to engage in . . . soul-searching of his entire past life. . . ." Id. at 132].

None of the above questions is in issue here.

tions will be inevitable. The implication of this argument is that no screening would be constitutionally permissible beyond academic examination and extremely minimal checking for serious, concrete character deficiencies. The principal means of policing the Bar would then be the deterrent and punitive effects of such post-admission sanctions as contempt, disbarment, malpractice suits, and criminal prosecutions.

Such an approach might be wise policy, but decisions based on policy alone are not for us to make. We have before us a State whose agents have evidently been scrupulous in the use of the powers that the appellants attack, and who have shown every willingness to keep their investigations within constitutionally permissible limits. We are not persuaded that careful administration of such a system as New York's need result in chilling effects upon the exercise of constitutional freedoms. Consequently, the choice between systems like New York's and approaches like that urged by the appellants rests with the legislatures and other policy-making bodies of the individual States. New York has made its choice. To disturb it would be beyond the power of this Court.

APPENDIX TO OPINION OF THE COURT

. . .

AFFIDAVIT WITH RESPECT TO CHARACTER OF APPLICANT

————, being duly sworn, makes the following statement:

. . .

3. How long have you known the applicant personally?

4. State whether you are related to applicant by blood or marriage, or if there is any business, professional or similar relationship between you and the applicant or his family?

5. Describe briefly your associations with the applicant, setting forth how such associations began, and indicate in what activities (business, scholastic, cultural, recreational, athletic, social or otherwise) you have participated with applicant. It is not a sufficient answer merely to repeat the above words in parenthesis, but the particular activities should be specified.

6. How often have you come in contact with applicant during the entire period of acquaintance? ("Frequently" or "often" or other indefinite statement is not a satisfactory answer.)

7. What is your conclusion as to applicant's moral character? (Reserve details for next question.)

8. State in detail the facts upon which your knowledge or opinion as to applicant's character is based.

9. Have you visited applicant's

(a) parental home;

(b) marital home, if any;

(c) any other home or place of abode applicant may have had?

10. (a) How often have you visited the parental, marital or other home or place of abode of applicant? ("Frequently" or "often" or other indefinite statement is not a satisfactory answer. Note that in most cases visits will be less frequent than the contacts mentioned in Q. 6, above.)

(b) During what years (stating approximate dates)?

(c) At what addresses (listing them specifically)?

[The dissenting opinion of MR. JUSTICE BLACK, with whom JUSTICE DOUGLAS joined, is omitted].

MR. JUSTICE MARSHALL, whom MR. JUSTICE BRENNAN joins, dissenting.

This litigation began with a comprehensive constitutional attack by appellants on longstanding state rules and practices for screening applicants for admission to the New York Bar. During the course of the litigation some of these practices were changed by appellees; others were found wanting by the three-judge court below, and changed as a result of that court's opinion and its final order. Now we face the residuum of the appellants' original challenge, and the Court today ratifies everything left standing by the court below. I dissent from that holding because I believe that appellants' basic First Amendment complaint, transcending the particulars of the attack, retains its validity. The underlying complaint, strenuously and consistently urged, is that New York's screening system focuses impermissibly on the political activities and viewpoints of Bar applicants, that the scheme thereby operates to inhibit the exercise of protected expressive and associational freedoms by law students and others, and that this chilling effect is not justified as the necessary impact of a system designed to winnow out those applicants demonstrably unfit to practice law.

As an abstract matter I do not take issue with the proposition that some inquiry into the qualifications of Bar applicants may be made, beyond such obvious threshold qualifications as residence or success in a regularly administered written examination. Accordingly, I would not upset the general rules which charter an inquiry as to the "fitness" of applicants, absent a showing not made here, that in practice the general rules work an impermissible result. But this is hardly the end of the case. For New York is not content with a politically neutral investigation into the fitness of Bar applicants to practice law. Screening officials are specifically directed by state law to assess an applicant's political beliefs and loyalties, and to scrutinize his associational and other political activities for signs that the applicant holds certain viewpoints. Such an inquiry, in my view, flatly offends the First Amendment, and state laws or administrative rules that license such an inquiry must be struck down.

. . .

[T]he opinions below and the papers in this case reveal that these appellees, prior to the launching of this litigation, thought it their duty to make virtually unlimited inquiry into an applicant's associational, political, and journalistic activities.[7] ...

[The remainder of Justice Marshall's analysis is omitted].

For the reasons stated I would strike down the portions of Rule 9406 discussed herein, as written and construed, and also Questions 26 and 27(b). To that extent I would reverse the District Court.

Note on LSCRRC v. Wadmond: Trust the process!

1.   (a) Compare with the Court's ground for upholding Question 27(b), supra, that of Judge Friendly for the district court: "The suggestion that a prospective lawyer would fear that a declaration of loyalty to the Constitution would prevent his criticizing acts of the Government does not require discussion." 299 F.Supp. at 130.

Were you to choose to discuss the question nonetheless, what might you say?

(b) The Supreme Court did not discuss Question 32, which asked whether the applicant had read the Canons of Ethics (the litigation arose prior to the promulgation of the Code of Professional Responsibility), and then asked: "Will you conscientiously endeavor to conform your professional conduct to them?" The question was upheld by the district court:

[P]laintiffs contend that an applicant may conscientiously disagree with various Canons, ... and still deserve admission to the bar. We agree with that position but not with the conclusion plaintiffs draw from it.... If [an applicant] dissents from a particular Canon, he need only say so and explain why. We have been cited no evidence that such dissent on a reasoned basis would bar admission.

Id. at 132. To the extent that you dissent from a particular Code or Rule provision, what reassurance do you find in Judge Friendly's response?

2.   (a) Judge Motley, dissenting in the three-judge district court, made the following overall observation:

It is clear from all the questions ... that ... there has been an improper focus upon the applicant's political beliefs and associations and the improper use of a political test in determining admissions to the bar. Such an unlimited political focus and the use of a political test pursuant to a "good moral character" standard is foreclosed.... As the [Supreme] Court [has] made clear, the focus must be on the

7. Judge Motley's separate opinion below states portions of appellees' original, unrevised questionnaires that give some idea of appellees' original conception of their mission under Rule 9406. These questionnaires, utilized in the First or the Second Judicial Department, or both, asked inter alia for a list of all "unfavorable incidents in your life," a list containing "each and every club, association, society or organization of which you are or have been a member," a list of "any articles for publication" written by an applicant. An applicant was asked whether he had ever "contributed in any way or signed a petition for" any subversive organization, or had "participated in any way whatsoever" in such organization's activities. Each applicant was required to "[s]tate ... in not less than 100 words" what he thought were the "principles underlying the form of government of the United States." See 299 F.Supp., at 137–139.

...

applicant's illegal political activity, if any, and the disqualification must be on this ground, not his political beliefs or associations.

Id. at 145. The Supreme Court in effect responded that it would review the permissibility of each question separately, with a strong presumption given the good faith and fidelity to constitutional norms of the bar examiners. This is so, notwithstanding the undisputed fact that, prior to the filing of the lawsuit, many aspects of the process were substantively unconstitutional. Putting to one side the question of the merits of that response as a constitutional matter, note that such a response leaves it to potential applicants to cope with any inhibiting effect of unexpressed radiations in the questions asked or in the personnel of the examining process.

(b) Less celebratory perceptions of the character review process abound. Jerold Auerbach has documented the explicit reliance, beginning in the 1920's, on the "character" requirement as a means of limiting the admission of Jews and other "undesirable" "foreign" elements to the Pennsylvania bar, Auerbach, Unequal Justice 125–27 (1976). Deborah Rhode conducted an exhaustive contemporary study of character committee operations, and found extensive interest in the politics of applicants:

> ... Religious fanatics, suspected subversives, and "rabble rousers" have been delayed, deterred, and occasionally excluded under both administrative and disciplinary standards. Although existing caselaw constrains states' ability to deny entry solely for political associations, it has done little to curb investigation into political offenses. Responses to such activity are highly idiosyncratic. The Secretary of Arkansas' Board of Law Examiners "tend[s] to look at political dissent with a blink," while in other jurisdictions, such as Nevada, misdemeanor arrests arising out of protest activity "would raise eyebrows," and have caused some applicants to be "harried." ... So, too, avoidance of military service would be received sympathetically in some jurisdictions and found disabling in others.
>
> Although the record before the Court in *Law Students Research Council v. Wadmond* failed to persuade the majority that "careful administration of such a system as New York's need result in chilling effects upon the exercise of constitutional freedoms," certain data reviewed for this study suggest otherwise. Applicants who have denounced government policy, law school administrators, bar certification processes, or the ABA Code of Professional Responsibility have not found favor with local committees.[364] Also, since most state bars

364. Siegel v. Committee of Bar Examiners, 10 Cal.3d 156, 514 P.2d 967, 110 Cal.Rptr. 15 (1973) (reversing committee's denial of applicant who had allegedly not been candid in describing his political speeches). One basis on which the Arizona Character Committee found Edward Ronwin mentally unfit was his "irresponsible and highly derogatory untrue public accusations" against law school administrators and faculty. Application of Ronwin, 113 Ariz. 357, 359, 555 P.2d 315, 317 (1976), cert. denied, 430 U.S. 907 (1977). A New York applicant ran into problems by stating that he believed the Code of Professional Responsibility was "phony" (since lawyers did not adhere to it), and the attorneys charged too much and rendered too little public service. Chairman, N.Y. Char. and Fitness Comm., 7th Dist. (Dec. 20, 1982). Any evidence that the candidate does not share the profession's official views on unauthorized practice will almost certainly result in further investigation.... Public criticism of certification processes has also adversely affected judi-

demand disclosure of all arrests and criminal charges, and since protestors frequently run the risk of unlawful arrest, the chilling effects of certification may extend to protected political conduct. While the degree of such deterrence is difficult to assess, a third of the respondents in one law student survey reportedly had refrained from certain activities because of the impending character review. Among the activities cited were attending political rallies, signing petitions, and seeking an Army deferment on psychological grounds.

Rhode, Moral Character as a Professional Credential, 94 Yale L.J. 491, 542–43, 568–69 (1985). And a report of committees of the New York State and City Bar Associations recommended major reductions in the intrusiveness of the questionnaire, affidavit, and interviewing processes. See Committee Report, The Character and Fitness Committees in New York State, 33 The Record [of the Association of the Bar of the City of New York] 20 (1978).

IN RE SAWYER

Supreme Court of the United States, 1959.
360 U.S. 622, 79 S.Ct. 1376, 3 L.Ed.2d 1473.

MR. JUSTICE BRENNAN announced the judgment of the Court, and delivered an opinion, in which THE CHIEF JUSTICE, MR. JUSTICE BLACK, and MR. JUSTICE DOUGLAS join.

This case is here on writ of certiorari ... to review petitioner's suspension from the practice of law for one year, ordered by the Supreme Court of the Territory of Hawaii, ... and affirmed on appeal by the Court of Appeals for the Ninth Circuit....

Petitioner has been a member of the Territorial Bar in Hawaii since 1941. For many months beginning in late 1952 she participated, in the United States District Court at Honolulu, as one of the defense counsel in the trial of an indictment against a number of defendants for conspiracy under the Smith Act, 18 U.S.C. § 2385. The trial was before Federal District Judge Jon Wiig and a jury. Both disciplinary charges against petitioner had to do with the Smith Act trial. One charge related to a speech she made about six weeks after the trial began. The speech was made on the Island of Hawaii, at Honokaa, a village some 182 miles from Honolulu, Oahu, on a Sunday morning. The other charge related to interviews she had with one of the jurors after the trial concluded.

The Bar Association of Hawaii preferred the charges [2] which were referred by the Territorial Supreme Court to the Association's Legal

cial determinations. Application of Stone, 74 Wyo. 389, 288 P.2d 767 (1955)....

2. At the conclusion of the Smith Act trial, District Judge Wiig requested the local Bar Association to investigate the conduct of petitioner. The Bar Association took no action as the Attorney General of the Territory conducted an investigation. As the Rules of the Supreme Court of the

Territory then stood, only the Attorney General or a person aggrieved could file charges of unprofessional conduct against an attorney. After investigating the matter, the Attorney General did not file a complaint. A Committee of the Bar Association then proceeded to study the question of bringing charges against petitioner,

Ethics Committee for investigation. The prosecutor who represented the Government at the Smith Act trial conducted the investigation and presented the evidence before the Committee. The Committee submitted the record and its findings to the Territorial Supreme Court. Because the suspension seems to us to depend on it, ... we deal first with the charge relating to the speech. The gist of the Committee's findings was that the petitioner's speech reflected adversely upon Judge Wiig's impartiality and fairness in the conduct of the Smith Act trial and impugned his judicial integrity. The Committee concluded that petitioner "in imputing to the Judge unfairness in the conduct of the trial, in impugning the integrity of the local Federal courts and in other comments made at Honokaa, was guilty of violation of Canons 1 and 22 of the Canons of Professional Ethics of the American Bar Association [3] and should be disciplined for the same." The Territorial Supreme Court held that "... she engaged and participated in a willful oral attack upon the administration of justice in and by the said United States District Court for the District of Hawaii and by direct statement and implication impugned the integrity of the judge presiding therein ... and thus tended to also create disrespect for the courts of justice and judicial officers generally.... She has thus committed what this court considers gross misconduct." 41 Haw., at 422–423.

We think that our review may be limited to the narrow question whether the facts adduced are capable of supporting the findings that the petitioner's speech impugned Judge Wiig's impartiality and fairness in conducting the Smith Act trial and thus reflected upon his integrity in the dispensation of justice in that case.... Since no obstruction or attempt at obstruction of the trial was charged, and since it is clear to us that the finding upon which the suspension rests is not supportable by the evidence adduced, we have no occasion [to] reach or intimate any conclusion on the constitutional issues presented.

and, in the words of the then President of the Association:

"The committee subsequently made a report to the Executive Board of the Association, ruling that a complaint be filed against Mrs. Bouslog. However, under the rules then in existence—that is, the rules of the Supreme Court, the Bar Association could not be a complainant. Consequently, the matter was again referred to the Committee on Legal Ethics to study amendments to the Rules of the Supreme Court, and the Chairman of the Committee on Legal Ethics took the matter up with the Chief Justice....

"Thereafter, the chairman of the Committee on Legal Ethics submitted a proposed draft of the Complaint. The Executive Board studied the draft, recommended certain changes, and then, finally, the form of the complaint was, as filed, was [sic] agreed upon, and I, as president of the Bar Association, was authorized to file that complaint in the name of the Bar Association."

3. Canon 1 is entitled "The Duty of the Lawyer to the Courts." It reads:

"It is the duty of the lawyer to maintain towards the Courts a respectful attitude, not for the sake of the temporary incumbent of the judicial office, but for the maintenance of its supreme importance. Judges, not being wholly free to defend themselves, are peculiarly entitled to receive the support of the Bar against unjust criticism and clamor. Whenever there is proper ground for serious complaint of a judicial officer, it is the right and duty of the lawyer to submit his grievances to the proper authorities. In such cases, but not otherwise, such charges should be encouraged and the person making them should be protected."

[The Court found no issue regarding Canon 22. Its discussion of it is omitted].

Petitioner's clients included labor unions, among them the International Longshoremen's and Warehousemen's Union. Some of the defendants in the Smith Act trial were officers and members of that union and their defense was being supported by the union. The meeting at Honokaa was sponsored by the ILWU and was attended in large part by its members. The petitioner spoke extemporaneously and no transcript or recording was made of her speech. Precisely what she did say is a matter of dispute.... The version of the petitioner's speech principally relied upon by the Court of Appeals ... is derived from notes made by a newspaper reporter, Matsuoka, who attended the meeting and heard what the petitioner said. These were not Matsuoka's original notes—the originals were lost—but an expanded version prepared by him at the direction of his newspaper superiors after interest in the speech was aroused by Matsuoka's account of it in the newspaper. We ... summarize them here, as an account of what petitioner said. The summary will illumine the basis of our conclusion that the finding that the petitioner's speech impugned the integrity of Judge Wiig or reflected upon his impartiality and fairness in presiding at the Smith Act trial is without support....

Petitioner said that the Honolulu trial was really an effort to get at the ILWU. She wanted to tell about some "rather shocking and horrible things that go on at the trial." The defendants, she said, were being tried for reading books written before they were born. Jack Hall, one of the defendants, she said, was on trial because he had read the Communist Manifesto. She spoke of the nature of criminal conspiracy prosecutions, as she saw them, and charged that when the Government did not have enough evidence "it lumps a number together and says they agreed to do something." "Conspiracy means to charge a lot of people for agreeing to do something you have never done." She generally attacked the FBI, saying they spent too much time investigating people's minds, and next dwelt further on the remoteness of the evidence in the case and the extreme youth of some of the defendants at the time to which the evidence directly related. She said "no one has a memory that good, yet they use this kind of testimony. Why? Because they will do anything and everything necessary to convict." Government propaganda carried on for 10 years before the jurors entered the box, she charged, made it "enough to say a person is a communist to cook his goose." She charged that some of the witnesses had given prior inconsistent testimony but that the Government went ahead and had them "say things in order to convict." "Witnesses testify what Government tells them to." The Government, she claimed, read in evidence for two days Communist books because one of the defendants had once seen them in a duffel bag. Unless people informed on such defendants, the FBI would try to make them lose their jobs. "There's no such thing as a fair trial in a Smith Act case. All rules of evidence have to be scrapped or the Government can't make a case." She related how in another case (in the territorial courts) she was not allowed to put in evidence of a hearsay nature to exonerate a criminal defendant she was representing, but in the present case "a federal judge sitting on a federal bench permits Crouch [a witness] to testify about 27 years ago, what was said then ... here they permit a witness to tell what was said when a defendant was five years old." She then declared, "There's no fair trial in the case. They just make up the rules as they go along." She gave the example of the New York Smith Act trial before Judge Medina, see Dennis v. United States, 341 U.S. 494, 71 S.Ct. 857, 95 L.Ed. 1137 where she claimed "The Government can't make a case if it tells just what they did so they widened the rules and tell what other people did years ago, including everything including the kitchen sink." She declared, "Unless we stop the Smith trial in its tracks here there will be a new crime. People will be charged with knowing what is included in books—ideas." Petitioner said in conclusion that if things went on the freedom to read and freedom of thought and action would be subverted. She urged her auditors to go out and explain what a vicious thing the Smith Act was.

We start with the proposition that lawyers are free to criticize the state of the law. Many lawyers say that the rules of evidence relative to the admission of statements by those alleged to be co-conspirators are overbroad or otherwise unfair and unwise; that there are dangers to defendants, of a sort against which trial judges cannot protect them, in the trial of numerous persons jointly for conspiracy; and that a Smith Act trial is apt to become a trial of ideas. Others disagree. But all are free to express their views on these matters, and no one would say that this sort of criticism constituted an improper attack on the judges who enforced such rules and who presided at the trials. This is so, even though the existence of questionable rules of law might be said in a sense to produce unfair trials. Such criticism simply cannot be equated with an attack on the motivation or the integrity or the competence of the judges. And surely permissible criticism may as well be made to a lay audience as to a professional; oftentimes the law is modified through popular criticism; Bentham's strictures on the state of the common law and Dickens' novels come to mind. And needless to say, a lawyer may criticize the law-enforcement agencies of the Government, and the prosecution, even to the extent of suggesting wrongdoing on their part, without by that token impugning the judiciary....

In large part, if not entirely, Matsuoka's notes of petitioner's speech do not reveal her as doing more than this.... She said that there were "horrible" and "shocking" things going on at the trial, but this remark, introductory to the speech, of course was in the context of what she further said about conspiracy prosecutions, Smith Act trials, and the prosecution's conduct. Petitioner's statement that a fair trial was impossible in context obviously related to the state of law and to the conduct of the prosecution and the FBI, not to anything that Judge Wiig personally was doing or failing to do. It occurred immediately after an account of the FBI's alleged pressuring of witnesses. The same seems clearly the case with the remark about the necessity of scrapping the rules of evidence. The statement that if the trial went on to a conviction, new crimes—those of thought or ideas—would be created[14] could hardly be thought to reflect on the trial judge's integrity no matter how divorced from context it be considered. How any of this reflected on Judge Wiig, except insofar as he might be thought to lose stature because he was a judge in a legal system said to be full of imperfections, is not shown. To say that "the law is a ass, a idiot" is not to impugn the character of those who must administer it. To say that prosecutors are corrupt is not to impugn the character of judges who might be unaware of it, or be able to find no method under the law of restraining them....

Even if some passages can be found which go so far as to imply that Judge Wiig was taking an erroneous view of the law—perhaps the comparison made between the case in the Territorial Courts where a hearsay statement was excluded and the admission of evidence in the Smith Act case might be of this nature, and much is made of it here though the Committee and the courts below made nothing of it—we think there was still nothing in the speech warranting the findings. If Judge Wiig was said to be wrong on his law, it is no matter; appellate courts and law reviews say that of judges daily, and it imputes no disgrace. Dissenting opinions in our reports are apt to make petitioner's speech look like tame stuff indeed. Petitioner did not say Judge Wiig was corrupt or venal or stupid or incompetent. The public attribution of honest error to the judiciary is no cause for professional discipline in this country.... It may be said that some of the audience would infer improper collusion with the prosecution from a charge of error prejudicing the defense. Some lay persons may not be able to imagine legal error without venality or collusion, but it will not do to set our standards by their reactions. We can indulge in no involved speculation as to petitioner's guilt by reason of the imaginations of others.

But it is said that while it may be proper for an attorney to say the law is unfair or that judges are in error as a general matter, it is wrong for counsel of record to say so during a pending case. The verbalization is that it is impermissible to litigate by day and castigate by night.... This line seems central to the Bar Association's argument, as it appears to have been to the reasoning of the court below, and the dissent here is much informed by it, but to us it seems totally to ignore the charges made and the findings....

MR. JUSTICE STEWART, concurring in the result.

. . .

---

14. In Yates v. United States, 354 U.S. 298, 318, 77 S.Ct. 1064, 1076, this Court said: "We are thus faced with the question whether the Smith Act prohibits advocacy and teaching of forcible overthrow as an abstract principle, divorced from any effort to instigate action to that end, so long as such advocacy or teaching is engaged in with evil intent. We hold that it does not."

The convictions of petitioner's Smith Act trial clients were all reversed in the Court of Appeals on the authority of Yates, and judgment ordered entered for them. Fujimoto v. United States, 9 Cir., 251 F.2d 342.

In the present case, if it had been charged or if it had been found that the petitioner attempted to obstruct or prejudice the due administration of justice by interfering with a fair trial, this would be the kind of a case to which the language of the dissenting opinion seems largely directed. But that was not the charge here, and it is not the ground upon which the petitioner has been disciplined. Because I agree with the conclusion that there is not enough in this record to support the charge and the findings growing out of the petitioner's speech in Honokaa, I concur in the Court's judgment.

MR. JUSTICE FRANKFURTER, whom MR. JUSTICE CLARK, MR. JUSTICE HARLAN and MR. JUSTICE WHITTAKER join, dissenting.

. . .

The speech was made at a time when motions concerning the very evidence which petitioner was castigating were still sub judice. The attacks on fairness, the descriptions of the trial as horrible and shocking, were made while the jury was open and receptive to media of communication, to the impregnating atmosphere to which juries, certainly in this country, are subjected. Even though petitioner may not have had a provable desire, the specific intent, to affect the pending trial and its outcome, are we really required to attribute to the petitioner a child-like unawareness of the inevitability that her remarks would be reported and find their way to judge or jury, as they did? The very next day the speech came to the judge's attention and registered so powerfully that he felt called upon to defend his conduct of the trial in open court.

The record is thus replete with evidence to support the conclusion that virtually the entire speech constituted a direct attack on the judicial conduct of this trial during its progress by one of the lawyers for the defense. [Justice Frankfurter's extensive review of the record has been omitted].

When a lawyer attacks the fairness, the evenhandedness, and the integrity of the proceedings in a trial in which he himself is actively engaged, in the inflammatory, public fashion that this record reveals, supplemented with specific attack on the presiding judge, how can the conclusion be escaped that it was not rules of law in the abstract which were assailed, but the manner in which the processes of justice in the particular case were being conducted? More particularly, such an attack inescapably impugns the integrity of the judge. It is he who truly embodies the law as the guardian of the rights of defendants to justice under law. . . .

Having arrived at this conclusion, our task is at an end, and the order suspending Mrs. Sawyer from the practice of law for one year should be affirmed. But throughout the opinion of Mr. Justice Brennan runs the strong intimation that if the findings are supportable, a suspension based on them would be unconstitutional. This must be the import of the opinion's discussion of a lawyer's right to criticize law. . . .

The problem raised by this case—is the particular conduct in which this petitioner engaged constitutionally protected from the disciplinary proceedings of courts of law?—cannot be disposed of by general observations about freedom of speech....

... Even under the most favoring circumstances—an able, fearless, and fastidiously impartial judge, competent and scrupulous lawyers, a befittingly austere court-room atmosphere—trial by jury of a criminal case where public feeling is deeply engaged is no easy accomplishment, as every experienced lawyer knows, if due regard is to be had to the letter and spirit of the Constitution for such a trial. It is difficult enough to seal the court-room, as it were, against outside pressures. The delicate scales of justice ought not to be willfully agitated from without by any of the participants responsible for the fair conduct of the trial....

.... Here was a public meeting addressed by counsel for the defense, haranguing a crowd on the unfairness to the defendant of the proceedings in court, with the high probability indeed almost certainty under modern conditions that the goings-on of the meeting would come to the attention of the presiding judge and the jury. It took place in a case in which public interest and public tempers had been aroused. When the story of the meeting came to the attention of the judge, he felt obliged publicly to defend his conduct. It is hard to believe that this Court should hold that a member of the legal profession is constitutionally entitled to remove his case from the court in which he is an officer to the public and press, and express to them his grievances against the conduct of the trial and the judge. "Legal trials," said this Court, "are not like elections, to be won through the use of the meeting-hall, the radio, and the newspaper." Bridges v. California, 314 U.S. 252, 271, 62 S.Ct. 190, 197.

. . .

MR. JUSTICE CLARK, dissenting.

. . .

To say that there is no reasonable support in the evidence for Hawaii's conclusion, as disclosed by a fair reading of the record some six and a half years later and some 5,000 miles away, is only to say that the 12 concurring officials, all of whom are trained in the law and who under oath made and passed upon these findings at trial and on appeal, arrived at a conclusion no reasonable man could reach. By thus at this late date second-guessing those constituted authorities who in regular course have decided the facts to the contrary, the Court impugns the intelligence of the 12 individuals so participating and scatters to the winds the sincere effort of the Supreme Court of Hawaii to preserve and protect its own integrity and respect as well as that of the law....

JUSTICES OF THE APPELLATE
DIVISION v. ERDMANN

Court of Appeals of New York, 1973.
33 N.Y.2d 559, 347 N.Y.S.2d 441, 301 N.E.2d 426.

PER CURIAM.

Without more, isolated instances of disrespect for the law, Judges and courts expressed by vulgar and insulting words or other incivility, uttered, written, or committed outside the precincts of a court are not subject to professional discipline (cf. Code of Professional Responsibility, EC 8–6; . . .). Nor is the matter substantially altered if there is hyperbole expressed in the impoverished vocabulary of the street. On this view, no constitutional issue of privileged expression is involved in the conduct ascribed to appellant.

Perhaps persistent or general courses of conduct, even if parading as criticism, which are degrading to the law, the Bar, and the courts, and are irrelevant or grossly excessive, would present a different issue. No such issue is presented now.

. . .

Since appellant's out-of-court conduct was not censurable, it would not be appropriate to characterize further that conduct on the score of taste, civility, morality, or ethics.

Accordingly, the order of the Appellate Division should be reversed and the petition dismissed.

GABRIELLI, J. (dissenting). . . .

I . . . agree with the determination of the Appellate Division . . . that appellant was guilty of professional misconduct when, knowing that his statements would be published in *Life* magazine, he announced that: "There are so few trial judges who just judge, who rule on questions of law, and leave guilt or innocence to the jury. And Appellate Division judges aren't any better. They're the whores who became madams. I would like to [be a judge] just to see if I could be the kind of judge I think a judge should be. But the only way you can get it is to be in politics or buy it—and I don't even know the going price." It is appropriate to here point out that appellant admitted not only the making of these statements but also that he participated in the preparation of the magazine article which appeared in the March 12, 1971 issue of *Life*. The unabashed use of intemperate, vulgar and insulting language—certainly an offense against the integrity and dignity of the courts—tended to create disrespect for the law, the courts and judicial officers as well as lessening public confidence in the courts.

. . .

I am quick to add that as also provided by EC 8–6 of the Code of Professional Responsibility a lawyer possesses, and of course should have, the right to publicly criticize the courts provided there is merit to his complaint and he uses appropriate language. I cannot, however, find any justification for using the language of the gutter or of the brothel—as was done in this case—and condoned by the dissent at the Appellate Division as merely "a figure of speech". One who engages in making such scandalous or other improper attacks, as here, is subject to discipline.

. . .

IN RE SNYDER

Supreme Court of the United States, 1985.
472 U.S. 634, 105 S.Ct. 2874, 86 L.Ed.2d 504.

CHIEF JUSTICE BURGER delivered the opinion of the Court.

We granted certiorari to review the judgment of the Court of Appeals suspending petitioner from practice in all courts of the Eighth Circuit for six months.

In March 1983, petitioner Robert Snyder was appointed by the Federal District Court for the District of North Dakota to represent a defendant under the Criminal Justice Act. After petitioner completed the assignment, he submitted a claim for $1,898.55 for services and expenses. The claim was reduced by the District Court to $1,796.05.

Under the Criminal Justice Act, the Chief Judge of the Court of Appeals was required to review and approve expenditures for compensation in excess of $1,000. 18 U.S.C. § 3006A(d)(3). Chief Judge Lay found the claim insufficiently documented, and he returned it with a request for additional information. Because of technical problems with his computer software, petitioner could not readily provide the information in the form requested by the Chief Judge. He did, however, file a supplemental application.

The secretary of the Chief Judge of the Circuit again returned the application, stating that the proffered documentation was unacceptable. Petitioner then discussed the matter with Helen Monteith, the District Court Judge's secretary, who suggested he write a letter expressing his view. Petitioner then wrote the letter that led to this case. The letter, addressed to Ms. Monteith, read in part:

> "In the first place, I am appalled by the amount of money which the federal court pays for indigent criminal defense work. The reason that so few attorneys in Bismarck accept this work is for that exact reason. We have, up to this point, still accepted the indigent appointments, because of a duty to our profession, and the fact that nobody else will do it.
>
> "Now, however, not only are we paid an amount of money which does not even cover our overhead, but we have to go through extreme gymnastics even to receive the puny amounts which the federal courts authorize for this work. We have sent you every-

thing we have concerning our representation, and I am not sending you anything else. You can take it or leave it.

"Further, I am extremely disgusted by the treatment of us by the Eighth Circuit in this case, and you are instructed to remove my name from the list of attorneys who will accept criminal indigent defense work. I have simply had it.

"Thank you for your time and attention." ...

The District Court Judge viewed this letter as one seeking changes in the process for providing fees, and discussed these concerns with petitioner. The District Court Judge then forwarded the letter to the Chief Judge of the Circuit. The Chief Judge in turn wrote to the District Judge, stating that he considered petitioner's letter

"totally disrespectful to the federal courts and to the judicial system. It demonstrates a total lack of respect for the legal process and the courts." ...

The Chief Judge expressed concern both about petitioner's failure to "follow the guidelines and [refusal] to cooperate with the court," and questioned whether "in view of the letter" petitioner was "worthy of practicing law in the federal courts on any matter." He stated his intention to issue an order to show cause why petitioner should not be suspended from practicing in any federal court in the Circuit for a period of one year.... Subsequently, the Chief Judge wrote to the District Court again, stating that if petitioner apologized the matter would be dropped. At this time, the Chief Judge approved a reduced fee for petitioner's work of $1,000 plus expenses of $23.25.

After talking with petitioner, the District Court Judge responded to the Chief Judge as follows:

"He [petitioner] sees his letter as an expression of an honest opinion, and an exercise of his right of freedom of speech. I, of course, see it as a youthful and exuberant expression of annoyance which has now risen to the level of a cause....

"He has decided not to apologize, although he assured me he did not intend the letter as you interpreted it." ....

The Chief Judge then issued an order for petitioner to show cause why he should not be suspended for his "refusal to carry out his obligations as a practicing lawyer and officer of [the] court" because of his refusal to accept assignments under the Criminal Justice Act....

. . .

At the hearing, the Court of Appeals focused on whether petitioner's letter of October 6, 1983, was disrespectful, an issue not mentioned in the show cause order. At one point, Judge Arnold asked: "I am asking you, sir, if you are prepared to apologize to the court for the tone of your letter?" .... Petitioner answered: "That is not the basis that I am being brought forth before the court today." ....

Following the hearing, [there was a further exchange of letters, in which the Chief Judge wrote:]

> ... I would appreciate your response to Judge Arnold's specific request, and the court's request, for you to apologize for the letter that you wrote.

> "Please let me hear from you by return mail. I am confident that if such a letter is forthcoming that the court will dissolve the order." ...

Petitioner responded to the Chief Judge:

> "I cannot, and will never, in justice to my conscience, apologize for what I consider to be telling the truth, albeit in harsh terms....

> "It is unfortunate that the respective positions in the proceeding have so hardened. However, I consider this to be a matter of principle, and if one stands on a principle, one must be willing to accept the consequences." ...

After receipt of this letter, petitioner was suspended from the practice of law in the federal courts in the Eighth Circuit for six months. 734 F.2d 334 (1984). The opinion stated that petitioner "contumaciously refused to retract his previous remarks or apologize to the court." Id., at 336. It continued:

> "[Petitioner's] refusal to show continuing respect for the court and his refusal to demonstrate a sincere retraction of his admittedly 'harsh' statements are sufficient to demonstrate to this court that he is not presently fit to practice law in the federal courts. All courts depend on the highest level of integrity and respect not only from the judiciary but from the lawyers who serve in the court as well. Without public display of respect for the judicial branch of government as an institution by lawyers, the law cannot survive.... Without hesitation we find Snyder's disrespectful statements as to this court's administration of CJA contumacious conduct. We deem this unfortunate.

> " . . . ."

The opinion specifically stated that petitioner's offer to serve in Criminal Justice Act cases in the future if the panel was equitably structured had "considerable merit." ...

[Petitioner's motion] for rehearing en banc was denied. An opinion for the en banc court stated:

> "The gravamen of the situation is that Snyder in his letter [of October 6, 1983] became harsh and disrespectful to the Court. It is one thing for a lawyer to complain factually to the Court, it is another for counsel to be disrespectful in doing so.

> " ... Snyder states that his letter is not disrespectful. We disagree. In our view, the letter speaks for itself." 734 F.2d, at 343....

The en banc court opinion stayed the order of suspension for 10 days, but provided that the stay would be lifted if petitioner failed to apologize. He did not apologize, and the order of suspension took effect.

We granted certiorari.... We reverse.

. . .

Courts have long recognized an inherent authority to suspend or disbar lawyers. Ex parte Garland, 4 Wall. 333, 378–379, 71 U.S. 333, 18 L.Ed. 366 (1867); Ex parte Burr, 9 Wheat. 529, 531, 22 U.S. 529, 6 L.Ed. 152 (1824). This inherent power derives from the lawyer's role as an officer of the court which granted admission....

The phrase "conduct unbecoming a member of the bar" [the applicable criterion under F.R.A.P. 46] must be read in light of the "complex code of behavior" to which attorneys are subject. In re Bithoney, 486 F.2d 319, 324 (CA1 1973). Essentially, this reflects the burdens inherent in the attorney's dual obligations to clients and to the system of justice....

As an officer of the court, a member of the bar enjoys singular powers that others do not possess; by virtue of admission, members of the bar share a kind of monopoly granted only to lawyers. Admission creates a license not only to advise and counsel clients but also to appear in court and try cases; as an officer of the court, a lawyer can cause persons to drop their private affairs and be called as witnesses in court, and for depositions and other pretrial processes that, while subject to the ultimate control of the court, may be conducted outside courtrooms. The license granted by the court requires members of the bar to conduct themselves in a manner compatible with the role of courts in the administration of justice.

. . .

We must examine the record in light of Rule 46 to determine whether the Court of Appeals' action is supported by the evidence.... Petitioner's refusal to submit further documentation in support of his fee request could afford a basis for declining to award a fee; however, the submission of adequate documentation was only a prerequisite to the collection of his fee, not an affirmative obligation required by his duties to a client or the court. Nor, as the Court of Appeals ultimately concluded, was petitioner legally obligated under the terms of the local plan to accept Criminal Justice Act cases.

We do not consider a lawyer's criticism of the administration of the Act or criticism of inequities in assignments under the Act as cause for discipline or suspension. The letter was addressed to a court employee charged with administrative responsibilities, and concerned a practical matter in the administration of the Act. The Court of Appeals acknowledged that petitioner brought to light concerns about the administration of the plan that had "merit," 734 F.2d, at 339, and the court instituted a study of the administration of the Criminal Justice Act as a result of petitioner's complaint. Officers of the court may appropriately express criticism on such matters.

The record indicates the Court of Appeals was concerned about the tone of the letter; petitioner concedes that the tone of his letter was "harsh," and, indeed it can be read as ill-mannered. All persons involved in the judicial process—judges, litigants, witnesses, and court officers—owe a duty of courtesy to all other participants. The necessity for civility in the inherently contentious setting of the adversary process suggests that members of the bar cast criticisms of the system in a professional and civil tone. However, even assuming that the letter exhibited an unlawyerlike rudeness, a single incident of rudeness or lack of professional courtesy—in this context—does not support a finding of contemptuous or contumacious conduct, or a finding that a lawyer is "not presently fit to practice law in the federal courts." Nor does it rise to the level of "conduct unbecoming a member of the bar" warranting suspension from practice.

. . .

JUSTICE BLACKMUN took no part in the decision of this case.

SANDSTROM v. STATE
District Court of Appeal of Florida, 1975.
309 So.2d 17.

DOWNEY, JUDGE.

Appellant, a practicing member of the Florida Bar, seeks review of a judgment finding him in contempt and sentencing him to confinement in the county jail for a period of three days.

On February 6, 1974, while representing a client, appellant appeared in open court before The Honorable Robert W. Tyson, Jr., Circuit Judge, without a necktie. The judge thereupon admonished appellant that, unless they had some excuse for not doing so, all attorneys should wear a tie when appearing in court and he ordered appellant thereafter to wear a tie in court. Appellant responded: "No, sir. I am saying right now I shall not. I shall dress my mode of dress, not the dictations of the Court."

On March 12, 1974, appellant appeared once again in open court before the same judge, representing two defendants in a criminal case. He wore a white suit, a sport shirt open at the neck, and a necklace with a round gold pendant the size of a silver dollar "with the hair on his chest showing through the open shirt." Upon convening court the judge called appellant's attention to his order of February 6, 1974, and advised appellant that he was in violation thereof. After lecturing appellant on the necessity of cooperation by counsel and of decorum in the courtroom, Judge Tyson advised appellant once again that he must wear a tie in the courtroom, and that until he decided to comply with the order that he was to wear a tie, he was barred from practicing in any proceeding before Judge Tyson. The pending criminal case was then continued for one hour to afford appellant an opportunity to comply with the order relative to court attire for attorneys. The judge warned the appellant that if he returned to court without a tie, he would be held in contempt. Appellant remained intransigent. He dictated a lengthy response into the record and filed a motion to have Judge Tyson disqualify himself. Said motion was denied.

When court reconvened, the criminal case was called and appellant stepped forward to represent his clients. Judge Tyson noted that appellant was dressed exactly as he had been prior to the continuance. After appellant agreed that there was no necessity for the court to reiterate the grounds previously detailed, Judge Tyson found appellant guilty of direct criminal contempt for disobeying his order and sentenced appellant to three days in the county jail.

This appeal from the contempt conviction followed.

[W]hether an act constitutes contempt is determined by its reasonable tendencies to obstruct justice.... The contemptuous act in the present case was not appellant's failure to wear a tie but, rather, appellant's disobedience of the court's order that he wear a tie. In the absence of the trial court's order, failure to wear a tie would certainly not constitute contempt. However, wilful disobedience of the court order clearly constitutes obstruction of justice....

[T]he only question appellant may appropriately raise here is that of jurisdiction. Appellant may obtain reversal of his contempt conviction only if he shows that the order he disobeyed was void, since disobedience of an order issued without jurisdiction is not contempt....

The question we must therefore decide is whether the circuit judge whose order appellant disobeyed had jurisdiction over the subject matter (it being unquestioned that the court had jurisdiction over appellant's person), i.e., whether the judge had the power to impose dress requirements upon lawyers appearing before him in judicial proceedings. We hold that he does have such power.

To begin with, it is clear that the judicial branch of government has the inherent power to regulate the professional conduct of all lawyers.... Historically lawyers have been subject to court supervised regulation "even in matters so personal as the growth of their beard or the cut of their dress." People ex rel. Karlin v. Culkin, 248 N.Y. 465, 162 N.E. 487, 490, 60 A.L.R. 851 (1928).... Since the circuit judge clearly had jurisdiction to enter the order appellant disobeyed, this court must reject appellant's collateral attack upon the order requiring him to wear a tie in court and must affirm his conviction of contempt.

However we think it appropriate to comment upon the various arguments appellant has presented on the propriety of the trial judge's order.

. . .

As authority for his position that the contempt conviction is improper, appellant relies heavily upon Peck v. Stone, [32 A.D.2d 506, 304

N.Y.S.2d 881 (4th Dept.1969)]. In that case Ms. Peck, a young lawyer, appeared in the City Court of Syracuse, New York, to represent an indigent defendant. Ms. Peck was attired in a miniskirt, the hemline of which was approximately 5 inches above the knee and substantially higher when she was seated. Having previously admonished her about wearing a miniskirt in the courtroom, the city judge directed Ms. Peck not to appear in court before him again "until her dress is suitable, conventional and appropriate in keeping with her position as an officer of the Court." Being dissatisfied with the foregoing order, Ms. Peck filed a petition in the Supreme Court, special Term, to vacate it. Upon dismissal of said petition, she appealed to the Supreme Court, Appellate Division, which reversed the order of dismissal and held that the judge of the city court had abused his discretion.

We find a major distinguishing feature between Ms. Peck and appellant. Ms. Peck did not "take the judge on", as the saying goes, and obstinately rebuff his direction to change her attire. The appellate division found that at no time was her attitude contrary to her ethical responsibilities as an officer of the court. Whereas Ms. Peck took her grievance to a higher court for resolution, the way lawyers are trained to do, appellant chose a showdown in open court with the judge and unequivocally apprized him he would not comply with his order.

   . . .

On Petition for Writ of Certiorari

Supreme Court of Florida, 1976.

336 So.2d 572.

[The Supreme Court decided that it lacked jurisdiction to review the decision below].

ENGLAND, JUSTICE (dissenting).

   . . .

Under the Constitution of this state the people of Florida have sought to guarantee to every individual the basic right to choose his or her own lifestyle without undue governmental interference.

[P]ersonal grooming and appearance can be an integral part of a person's chosen lifestyle. An individual's manner of dress expresses and reflects ideals personal to him. I do not doubt that in many cases a sense of well-being is derived from an individual's knowledge that he is attired in a manner which is in harmony with his personal views of life, or that the opposite sense of confinement and restriction may attend required adherence to dress codes which the individual finds abhorrent. As petty as clothing might be to some, the individual liberty and free choice which our Constitution recognizes is not dependent upon either a majority or unanimous view as to the significance of any particular right.

   . . . The state here argues that control of the judicial process is a substantial, traditional and legitimate justification for restrictions on attire, and that a trial judge must be accorded complete freedom, even in the form of a dress code, to maintain the dignity of the judicial process. The state also argues that the erosion of liberty at stake here, forced fabric neckwear, is a negligible burden on practicing attorneys which is and has been borne by the vast majority of practitioners without complaint. As to the latter assertion, we have previously stated that the suppression of individual liberty frequently takes unobtrusive forms. Consequently, the slight degree of impairment may be a factor to be considered in determining whether the limitation is sufficiently justified, but it does not dispose of the issue.

There are those who will fear that small incursions on the formality of courtroom attire might lead to an erosion of our ability to perform important public work, and in time contribute to a wholly unacceptable courtroom atmosphere. This case does not in fact present an incremental change, let alone one which would inevitably lead to that situation. It is not unusual in the contemporary governmental world for men of high purpose to go about their affairs without a necktie, and it can pose no threat to our judicial system to permit attorneys freedom to adopt the reasonable clothing styles of the time. I reject any inference that respect for the judicial system is dependent upon male attorneys wearing neckties.[31] Surely the dignity of the judiciary rests on more substantial ground.

. . .

ADKINS and BOYD, JJ., concur.

---

31. Another obvious problem with the orders of the trial courts is their limited application to males, since female attorneys are not prohibited from wearing open-neck dresses or pantsuits.

III. THE CONTOURS OF AN ALTERNATIVE SYNTHESIS

1. THE EXPRESSION OF THE SELF IN LAWYERING

> MORE The Dean of St. Paul's offers you a post . . . .
> RICH What? What post?
> MORE At the new school.
> RICH (*bitterly disappointed*) A teacher!
>
> . . . .
>
> MORE Why not . . . ? You'd be a fine teacher. Perhaps even a great one.
> RICH And if I was, who would know it?
> MORE You, your pupils, your friends, God. Not a bad public, that . . . .
>
> R. Bolt, A Man for all Seasons 5–6 (1960)

THE FIVE PILLARS OF PROFESSIONALISM

Kenneth L. Penegar
49 U.Pitt.L.Rev. 307 (1988).

The ... philosophical foundation which undergirds professional ideals ... is the result of the dominant Western tradition. The core idea is that values or ends are human, that they spring from the individual's desires and that they cannot be graded because there is no common standard. This idea of subjectivity of values lies at the heart of the professional ideal of nonaccountability as seen in the Code.

... The argument against the nonaccountability principle contains an implicit reliance on a notion of values that can be objectively treated, considered, and reasoned. Indeed there is a classic idea of objective value, the very idea which liberal political thought has opposed from its beginning.

...

If values are not universal, but particular, may they nevertheless be seen as recurring or similar? Would a conception of congruent or shared values be more coherent or demonstrably valid than the theory of objective value? The search is an important one and could become the foundation for a different kind of society than the one which is the corollary or product of the theory of subjectivity of values.

The Code implicitly recognizes a common or public morality, a system of shared values. For example, EC 7–8 states,

> Advice of a lawyer to his client need not be confined to purely legal considerations.... In assisting his client to reach a proper decision, it is often desirable for a lawyer to point out those factors which may lead to a decision that is morally just as well as legally permissible.

Within the structure of the Code, then, is the suggestion that moral ideas may have sufficient common currency to be the subject of reasoned dialogue with the client. This is but the projection at least of a theory of shared values. Indeed without some shared values of some kind the social order is unthinkable. However, attorneys increasingly perceive the shared values as procedural or instrumental. Thus, it is not surprising that the Code, having barely adverted to the possibility of some decision which is inherently or substantively just, retreats again to the side of subjectivity of values. "In the final analysis ... the lawyer should always remember that the decision whether to forego legally available objectives or methods because of non-legal factors is ultimately for the client and not for himself."

The reasons for the defensiveness or vulnerability of the idea of shared values are worth pursuing in this commentary about the morality of the professional ideal of nonaccountability. [Roberto] Unger identifies two ways to conceive of a sharing of values. One view proceeds from the premises of liberal thought and treats the sharing of values as a coincidence of individual preferences. In this view the alliance of ends is precarious and unstable, lacking sufficient authority to solve problems of legislation and adjudication. Another view ... reject[s] the principle of subjectivity of value and [seeks to construct a theory of] communal value.... Constructing this theory is not as difficult as giving force to it because of our own cultural historical experience:

> The seriousness of the political premises of liberalism is a consequence of the accuracy with which they describe a form of social experience that theory alone cannot abolish. It is the experience of the precariousness and contingency of all shared values in society. This experience arises from the sense that shared values reflect the prejudices and interests of dominant groups rather than a common perception of the good. Thus, individuality remains an assertion of the private will against the conventions and traditions of the public life.

[R. Unger, Knowledge and Politics 102–03 (1975).]

. . .

The discussion of the importance of subjectivity of value ... has profound implications for professional theory....

The modern consciousness about lawyers and their roles, as expressed in such documents as the Code, reflects a larger struggle over conflicting social programs. In turn, the continuing struggle is affected by the consciousness. The struggle over social programs and the consciousness of lawyers is interactive, dynamic, and never finished. The practical difficulty is that the process by which the doctrine of professional norms is formalized, applied, reviewed, amended and restated is itself carried on in more truncated forms than the larger contest. Indeed, to anyone who participated in the ABA debates leading to the 1969 adoption of the Code, it would not be apparent that such a contest was taking place. To the contrary, the process of revision proceeds as if the elaboration of accepted principles or traditional norms simply works itself out in a new statement for modern conditions.... The result is twofold: to obscure or suppress the fundamental questions of competing social visions, and to mask the discourse in seemingly self-defining doctrinal institutional terms, such as "attorney-client privilege," "adversary system," "client autonomy," or "conflict of interest."

. . .

The dominant professional tradition of the American bar ... suggests its own larger social and philosophical context. The kind of society which this tradition appears to support or imagine may be characterized in the following ways. The society is composed of individuals whose relationships are increasingly defined by legal rights, vis-a-vis other individuals and groups, and especially the state. It is a society in which cooperation with others is based principally on contract and exchange. A sharp distinction is drawn between the public and private realms, and a very limited set of purposes is relegated to the public realm. The connection between civic virtue and private good is largely undefined. Indeed, the society scarcely reflects any discernable concept of civil virtue at all. It is a society that promotes skepticism toward human relations which are not role centered or bargained for. The standards of conduct, paradoxically, are only publicly validated ones, that is, the ones found in the legal code.

The lesser tradition of professional ethics in law, revealed only dimly and partially in the Code of Professional Responsibility, ... is, of course, more difficult to sketch very completely or confidently. Much depends upon the creative use of the mechanisms of magnification and extension. Thus, the social world of the competing professional tradition emerges as a variation of the dominant one, not a radical alternative to it. In the society of the competing visionary ideal, there is a shared consciousness wide enough to maintain the individual as primary moral agent and at the same time hold to a concrete sense of community which is more than the amorphous notion of "the public good" but less than the dominant cultural hierarchies of historic memory. Human cooperation is facilitated in a variety of ways and not predominantly through bargained exchange.[263] The definition and place of roles, especially vocational and professional ones, are tentative and less influential than within the dominant vision. The individual's moral autonomy is prominent and not obscured by role and status. The democratic ideal is prominent in discourse about the complete range of associations and not limited to merely governmental issues. The possibilities of social experiment are consciously encouraged, and the forms of society needed to shape the good are recognized as unfinished and immanent, still to be expressed, fully discovered and attempted.

. . .

Note on Penegar and the subjectivity of values: "What canst thou say?"

1. Drucilla Cornell describes in these terms the principle of the subjectivity of values:

> The severance of fact from value leads to the dissociation of truth from normative statements. Our chosen ends cannot be justified; reason can only help us develop the means to those ends. We can assess ends at all only on the basis of their strategic value within an already established value context. Reason comes to be identified with instrumental rationality. We are left with a pluralism of value systems, and those who "go to the devil" cannot be rationally condemned. The inevitable result of the acceptance of this view of reason is the belief that "all moral judgments are *nothing* but expressions of preference, expressions of attitude or feeling." [A. MacIntyre, After Virtue: A Study in Moral Theory 12 (2d ed. 1984).] The ends chosen in an individual life are no longer seen as suitable subjects for rational discussion. Without agreed-upon criteria for judgment, questions of what is good cannot be meaningfully answered. The slogan of our culture, "Do your own thing," now takes on a more sinister meaning: do your own thing because there is nothing else for you to do.

---

263. Elements of the countervision are shared in contemporary writing and thought even by those who do not share a program to transform society in these directions. Robert Bellah and his colleagues conclude their recent essay on individualism and commitment in American life in the terms:

> The morally concerned social movement, informed by republican and biblical sentiment, has stood us in good stead in the past and may still do so again. . . . Our problems today are not just political. They are moral and have to do with the meaning of life.

> Perhaps life is not a race whose only goal is being foremost. . . . There are practices of life, good in themselves, that are inherently fulfilling. Perhaps work that is intrinsically rewarding is better

for human beings than work that is only extrinsically rewarded. Perhaps enduring commitment to those we love and civil friendship toward our fellow citizens are preferable to restless competition and anxious self-defense. Perhaps common worship, in which our gratitude and wonder in the face of the mystery itself, is the most important thing of all. If so, we will have to change our lives and begin to remember what we have been happier to forget.

> We will need to remember that we did not create ourselves, that we owe what we are to the communities that formed us. . . .

R. Bellah, Habits of the Heart: Individualism and Commitment in American Life 295 (1985).

Cornell, Toward a Modern/Postmodern Reconstruction of Ethics, 113 U.Pa. L.Rev. 291, 307–08 (1985).

2. (a) Roger Cramton has summarized the polar hazards of objective and subjective approaches to values, as they are usually conceived, and has given voice in these words to his own approach to the task of transcending the dichotomy between them:

> I do not believe we are faced with a choice between objectivism and relativism. Objectivism is a term for the belief in an "ultimate reality" that is not contingent on any particular cultural or historical situation: there are permanent, immutable standards of rationality to which we can appeal when evaluating competing claims of what is good and what is real. These standards are "rational" in the strongest possible sense—they constitute a given, and hence uncontestable, framework. But given by whom? One of the legacies of the Enlightenment is skepticism that we can locate in God or anywhere else a source of valid claims that transcend subjectivity. We also justifiably worry that by accepting the possibility of such an objective form of validity, we create a serious risk that some will use objectivism to achieve and to justify domination of other members of society. . . . He who claims to have "the truth" is a person, we have learned, to be feared, unless with genuine humility he is willing fully to expose his truth to the data, arguments, and experiences of others.

> Relativism, on the other hand, is the notion that man has created a variety of moral and ethical systems and that there is no rational process by which it can be demonstrated that one of them is better than any other. You have your "values" and I have mine. Neither of us can (or, relativism implies, should) persuade the other on rational grounds that our own position is preferable. . . .

> [A]nother alternative. . . . [is that] nothing is true unless it cannot be disproved or falsified—a test so severe that most of science as well as all of ethics and morality goes out the window. . . .

> If [these] were the only alternatives, our situation would indeed be one of despair. Fortunately, they are not the only alternatives. There are methods by which we can arrive at larger and more meaningful affirmations. One's own religious and cultural tradition is a good starting point. . . .

> Now, the argument from authority is the weakest of all arguments—a good starting point, perhaps, but only that. Every belief must be tested by one's experience, evaluated for consistency with other beliefs that one has found useful and reliable, and compared with contrasting views. All great religions, including that of secular humanism, require that we use our minds to discover what is required of us. Being fully human is being rational as well as intuitive and insightful. Openness to new experiences and insights, constant reformulation of beliefs based on new knowledge, a tolerance for other views that are supported by data or rational argument—these are the basic elements of the method by which we can arrive at closer approximations of the truth. There will always be doubt. . . .

> The process I am describing ... embodies the idea that rigorous examination of our beliefs in the light of experience, data, and competing views—a dialectic process involving earnest and serious conversation with oneself and others—can produce a set of beliefs that are more consistent with one another and with what one knows, beliefs that are likely to be closer approximation to the truth.

Cramton, Beyond the Ordinary Religion, 37 J.Leg.Educ. 509, 514–15 (1987).

(b) Katherine Bartlett has articulated a stance that she terms "positionality," which likewise seeks to transcend the supposed dichotomy between relativism and absolute truth:

> The positional stance acknowledges the existence of empirical truths, values and knowledge, and also their contingency.... [P]ositionality rejects the perfectibility, externality, or objectivity of truth. Instead, the positional knower conceives of truth as situated and partial.... [T]he individual perspectives that yield and judge truth are necessarily incomplete. No individual can understand except from some limited perspective.... As a result, there will always be "knowers" who have access to knowledge that other individuals do not have, and no one's truth can be deemed total or final.

> ... Although I must consider other points of view ..., I need not accept their truths as my own. Positionality is not a strategy of process and compromise that seeks to reconcile all competing interests....

> Some "truths" ... seem to confirm the view that truth does exist ... if only I could find it.... The problem is the human inclination to make this list of "truths" too long, to be too uncritical of its contents, and to defend it too harshly and dogmatically.

Bartlett, Feminist Legal Methods, 103 Harv.L.Rev. 829, 880–84 (1990).

(c) To what extent, if at all, do you find these analyses helpful in meeting the concern over coercion or indoctrination that talk about values seems inevitably to generate?

3. (a) Apart from the correctness of these varying philosophical stances, which affect the finality of your commitment to the validity of your own values, the question remains, what is it that you believe? The concept of the subjectivity of values can easily be transmuted into an insistence that each of us have no values whatever; since our values represent nothing more than "doing our own thing," we have no substantial basis for clinging to them when they differ from prevalent ones. Although one might think that, if all values are subjective, each of us is as free to reject, as we are to accept, the prevailing values underlying the traditional concept of advocacy, the message may be that this "freedom" is nothing more than whim or caprice, a bare permission lacking the capacity to command genuine respect, from ourselves as well as others.

A premise of this book is that there is existential wisdom in Gerald Frug's insight that "answers to [fundamental] questions may be tentative and contestable, but no one, in my view, actually experiences the task of answering them as meaningless or arbitrary." Frug, Argument as Character, 40 Stan.L.Rev. 869, 876 (1988).

(b) In considering whether you share that premise, keep in mind the constraining effect of familiar patterns of thinking about "values." Consider these words of James Boyd White:

> In our world ..., even in ordinary exposition or analytic discourse we tend naturally to accept the view that ... meaning ... is propositional in character; that rationality itself consists in a certain kind of coherence, linear in nature, among its propositions; that a bright line should be drawn between propositions that are factual in kind, and hence empirically testable, and those that are logical in kind, and testable by the criteria of entailment and noncontradiction; and that propositions of value are personal in nature, inherently untestable, and thus not the subject of meaningful debate. This kind of discourse is structurally coercive, in the sense that the writer seeks to prove something even to an unwilling reader who resists with all his might until forced by factual or logical demonstration to yield. At its center is an image of language as transparent: our talk is about what is "out there" in the natural or conceptual world, to which it is the function of language to point....
>
> ...
>
> [T]his kind of discourse [has] its uses, and important ones, in the law and elsewhere. But ... it is essential to recognize that [some] texts work on a very different sense of thought and meaning indeed. They are not propositional, but experiential and performative; ...; not bound by the rule of noncontradiction but eager to embrace competing or opposing strains of thought; not purely intellectual, but affective and constitutive, and in this sense integrative, both of the composer and of the audience, indeed in a sense of the culture in which they work. Texts of this sort are not coercive of their reader, but invitational: they offer an experience, not a message, and an experience that will not merely add to one's stock of information but change one's way of seeing and being, of talking and acting.

White, What Can a Lawyer Learn from Literature?, 102 Harv.L.Rev. 2014, 2016, 2016–18 (1989).

I invite you to consider the remaining excerpts in this sub-section, not as deductions of moral truth that you are "obliged" to believe, but against your own sense of yourself as a lawyer. In the words of Professor White: "Rather than making a case that is meant to stand or fall by the degree to which the unwilling are compelled to assent to it, ... I mean to present a set of reflections ... to be tested against the reader's own." White, Economics and Law: Two Cultures in Tension, 54 Tenn.L.Rev. 161, 167 (1986).

LEGAL EDUCATION'S CONCERN WITH JUSTICE: A CONVERSATION WITH A CRITIC
Howard Lesnick
35 J.Leg.Educ. 414 (1985).

The following is a written version of a talk given at the 1984 Conference of the Society of American Law Teachers, "Looking at the

Law School Classroom," held at New York University School of Law on December 14, 1984. It retains the informality of its origins. I ask the reader to bear in mind too that the talk was given very shortly after the Bhopal disaster.

The charge is by now a familiar one: The study of law as practiced in most American law schools lacks a concern with justice.[1] The response may seem less familiar, but only because it tends to be implicit in expressions of dismay or bewilderment at the evident misunderstanding inherent in the charge: Justice is precisely what legal education has for the past half-century been principally about. Can any new growth be engendered by another effort to plow such well-worked ground? The planners of the 1984 SALT Conference evidently thought so, and asked me to focus my thoughts less on the merits of the charge and response than on the difficulties that arise for a teacher or school motivated to accept the truth and gravity of the charge and to articulate an alternative approach as a response....

... Focusing on the difficulties in expressing an alternative response can be of aid to both attackers and defenders—the former because unless they acknowledge and engage with those difficulties they will remain forever marginal, and the latter because the implicit belief that the difficulties are fundamental and irremediable is, in my judgment, at the heart of the tenacity with which the traditional faith is defended. I believe that the difficulties *are* fundamental, and are *not* irremediable.

I can develop what I want to say in the concrete context of a recent event, the disaster occasioned by the accidental release of methyl isocyanate gas at the Union Carbide plant in Bhopal, India. Let me hypothesize a colloquy several days afterward between two personified abstractions, Legal Education and a Critic, both of whom see in that colloquy a relevant manifestation of the problem each has with the other:

Critic: Well, what is your reaction to what happened at Bhopal?

Legal Education: First, I have sympathy, distress, and concern for the victims of a massive tragedy. The immediate need is for medical attention, and the mobilization of supplies and personnel in the area. Second, Union Carbide, other chemical companies and government agencies in this country and elsewhere need to review relevant safety standards and procedures, both corporate and governmental.

Third, I want the established mechanisms of our adjudicatory system to be available and effective. The victims should have access to legal representation—necessarily on a contingent-fee basis—and as prompt and full a remedy as the law can allow in so complex a matter. At the same time, we should not condemn the company without full

---

1. See my introduction to the first SALT Conference on Legal Education, Preface to Symposium, 53 N.Y.U.L.Rev. 293, 294 (1978); Jerold Auerbach, What Has the Teaching of Law to Do With Justice, id. at 457.

knowledge of the relevant facts, and their sober assessment by an impartial tribunal.

Fourth, I am concerned about the continued economic viability of Union Carbide. The bankruptcy of the company, or a substantial threat of bankruptcy, would be a major blow to the public interest, injuring as it would thousands of employees, customers and suppliers, shareholders, communities. Even a serious persisting decline in the market for Union Carbide products would be a cause for real concern. Fifth, I am conscious of the dangers to continued economic progress, in the Third World and domestically, that would attend a long-term inhibiting effect on development.

In sum, I seek a balanced appraisal of all relevant factors, aware of the complexity and elusiveness of many of them and of the great stakes involved. In a word, my critical friend, I seek Justice, exactly what you fail or refuse to see in my value system; for what is justice but the result of all of the momentous inputs I have so briefly sketched, and how else can I or anyone purport to defend or question the appropriateness of particular processes or outcomes than by reference to their justice? Of course, we all have differing ideas about particular outcomes or processes, and widely varying ideas of what is just, but my recognition of the subjectivity of those ideas in no way detracts from my acknowledgement of their centrality.

But what about you, what is your reaction to Bhopal?

Critic: OK, fair enough, but first I want to say that if *that* is what you mean by justice, no wonder we have trouble making ourselves understood to one another! I find your notion of what justice is a grotesque caricature, an unbearingly repellent caricature. I want to say more about that, but first let me try to answer your question. You asked for my reaction to the event. I do not find it easy to sort out my reactions, let alone to say them out loud. I think it is important to make the attempt.

My first reaction is to *cry.* Over 2,000 people suddenly killed in their beds, perhaps a quarter million in pain, choking and blinded, disfigured, maimed. Children, the aged, the malnourished—the more vulnerable, the more attacked. I imagine myself carrying my two-year-old daughter, stumbling to find someone safe and expert enough to treat her, or hurrying to deliver her body to an improvised communal pyre before she becomes a source, not of pleasure and pride, but of cholera. She is beautiful, precious, and innocent: except to me and to a few others, no more so than hundreds of others whose fathers were awakened to an uneradicable reality.

My second reaction is to *pray.* A silent lethal vapor, that does not exist in nature—its very function is to kill—engulfing an entire valley in minutes, leaving a slight white powder behind. Is this to be the Black Death of the Twenty–First Century? The Angel of Death, in purposeful measured coercion in the cause of human freedom, destroyed one child in each family of the Egyptian slave masters. What world lies ahead of us, and of our children? I find within me ancient words:

Holy Mary, Mother of God

Pray for us now

And at the hour of our death.

Amen.

My third reaction is to *scream*—I do not have a better word for the angry mixture of condemnation and exhortation that I want to describe:

—At the company, I want to scream, "Accept responsibility." Don't point with pride, view with alarm, cut your losses. Move, both in public and in reality, to establish (probably in collaboration with the government in India) mechanisms for prompt and real compensation to individuals, families, communities.

—At the United States, my country, I want to scream: "Is this what we have become in the world?" Over the past two centuries the principal export of the United States has been the Declaration of Independence—always of course an alloyed product, and grievously so since the end of World War II; but now, beyond the shabby record of repeated armed support of repressive elements in Third World countries, are we to come to experience the American gift to the world as an array of latter-day Trojan horses of development?

—To all of us—First, Second, and Third Worlds, whether selling or buying the ideology of the inevitability of endlessly escalating technological development—I want to scream: "Stop!" Are we really unable to consider seriously the notion that, if adequate safety measures cannot prevent what happened at Bhopal, methyl isocyanate should not exist in the world? Are our thinking and our resources so impoverished that we are indeed forced to choose between suppressing such questions by ridicule and leaving large parts of the world unable to feed itself? *

—Finally, I want to scream at the racism of it all. I simply will not presume that it was just ill luck for India that the Bhopal plant malfunctioned, that Union Carbide's West Virginia plant (for example) was as much at risk. With all of the imponderables and variables of an operation like the production of methyl isocyanate, it would take more than a few words of pompous reassurance in a corporate press release or newspaper editorial to dispel my concern that Third World countries are being subjected to, and through their leaders are subjecting themselves to, greater hazards than would be deemed tolerable in the West. . . .

My fourth reaction is want to *do something*. Law is especially oriented to solving problems, and the reactions that I have thought it important not to suppress fuel the desire to influence future events.

* [Methyl isocyanate is manufactured to   increase the productivity of agriculture].

(Lesnick)–Being a Lawyer ACB—13

What options are open to me? Shall I stop buying Prestone, Glad, or Eveready batteries? Shall I seek to organize others to do so? Shall I support (in one of a number of ways) litigation on behalf of the victims, or seeking changes in marketing or regulatory patterns? Shall I draft a statute? Shall I write an article, or a Letter to the Editor? These are not disreputable courses of action, but they foster rather than ward off my fifth reaction.

My last reaction is to *despair.* We will go on as before, convinced we have no choice. There will probably be minor regulatory changes. Years of litigation are in prospect, which will probably produce the transfer of a large sum of money from Union Carbide (and the United States Treasury) to American and Indian professionals and organizational systems, and another sum, perhaps half as large, to the victims and their families. Union Carbide might "go under" in some manner, the specific contours of the change being orchestrated most by those most responsible for what has happened and least by those—employees, customers and suppliers, communities dependent on the company's presence—who will bear the major burden of what will happen. The facility at Bhopal will stand with Three Mile Island as components of a grotesque, twentieth-century Stonehenge, to be joined inevitably by what we cannot know.

Legal Education (having listened with alternating flashes of irritated impatience and benign indulgence, now smiling broadly): *Q.E.D.* If you ever wondered why your criticism has not gotten me to change in ways responsive to it, you have provided the answer yourself, more eloquently than I ever could!

You are, first of all, completely ineffectual. Tears, prayers, screams, and despair are no one's model of effective lawyering, for any end, and when you finally seem to be gearing up to "do something," you cannot even work up any interest in the task, except to dismiss all responses as just too depressing to get involved in.

But, worse than that, you are intolerably divisive and coercive. Divisive, in more ways than I can catalogue: For one, many do not want the terms of public debate to be infused with religious thoughts, especially sectarian ones, and the fact that the sect whose words you have chosen is not your own only complicates one's reactions; for another, many will regard your indictment of half the world of racism, and of the whole world of mindless pursuit of development, as gratuitous, insulting, and half-baked. Coercive, because your tone appears to preempt the ground of moral sensibility, and does not allow others simply to disagree. You tell those who do not share your reactions that their notions of justice are—what were your words?—grotesque and repellent. Because Legal Education won't adopt your answers to the question of justice you accuse it of devaluing the question. Were it not for your incapacity to make your concerns the ground of effective action, you would be a menace; as it is, you can safely be ignored. You certainly deserve no more.

Critic: If there is one thing that Legal Education has always been able to do, it is to move in hard at the soft spots in an argument! But before you decide to ignore me or to disarm me, let me try to take what both of us have said, and relate it to where Legal Education is and can be.

First, I want to go back to what you said when you spoke initially, because even if everything you said just now about me is right, none of it makes *me* any less right about *you.* I am not Legal Education, but a Critic; if my prescription is defective, my diagnosis may be nonetheless right. And if it is right, it is your responsibility, at least as much as mine, to seek an appropriate prescription. Any failure of mine at the remedial task is not a defense to you.

Why do I call your conception of justice grotesque and repellent? It purports to espouse a nonformalist, normative view of law, and at the same time to leave each of us free, whether in academic thought or political interaction, to discern and pursue our own answers. In fact, however, it does nothing of the sort. It begs all of the crucial questions, the parameters-setting questions, asserting loudly (if implicitly) that they have only one answer. It glories in the asserted subjectivity of the idea of justice, only to legitimate a market-oriented approach by which all human needs, impulses, and values are viewed simply as commodities. It characterizes as "freedom" the exercise of choice within the constraints imposed by the power of others, and as "coercion" societal attempts to ease any of those constraints. It can hardly be an accident then that your conception of justice, for all your espousal of the subjectivity of the concept, necessarily renders existing social relations presumptively just. What is needed turns out to be no more than what is possible in any event, some fine tuning—important, difficult, intellectually challenging, but nothing more disturbing. It is of course precisely to ward off more disturbing questions that your concept of justice can and must leave out entirely such human reactions as tears, prayers, screams, and despair. *These feelings are going on around us in the world of law all the time*; yet they must be suppressed, lest they prove destabilizing.[3]

Your approach, then, has exactly the flaws of divisiveness and coercion that you attribute to me—except that, coming from an institu-

---

3. Karl Klare has written, with characteristic insight and eloquence, of an approach to scholarship that, in my view, is an application of the conception of justice described in the text:

[It] substitutes stereotyped argumentation within the accepted repertoire of legal analysis for an open-ended search for truth. It has great difficulty acknowledging the component of political and moral choice implicit in all legal decisions and arguments. It ... is hostile to any effort at fundamental reexamination or questioning of accepted

views.... [It] adheres to an unstated but pervasive belief in the inevitability of the status quo. It has difficulty imagining that history could have turned out differently but for the choices people made and the actions they took. It treats established arrangements as natural and just, and it copes poorly with evidence that prevailing arrangements may not fully serve the needs of those they are intended to serve.

Karl Klare, Traditional Labor Law Scholarship and the Crisis of Collective Bargaining Law, 44 Md.L.Rev. 737, 845 (1985).

tion in power and not merely a Critic, the coercion is tangible and effective and the divisiveness hidden, for those who would differ are cast out, channeled out, or delegitimated.

I fully acknowledge, however, in my turn that nothing I have said about *you* makes *you* wrong about *me*. The concerns that you smugly throw in my face as axiomatically unanswerable are real concerns, and present grave hazards in carrying out an alternative approach. To grapple with them is to take on the most fundamental questions of professionalism and of political theory.

First, can we respond to legal problems—that is, to human problems with legal aspects—in a way that does not deny our human reactions, without losing our ability to be effective and constructive as problem solvers? Put the other way—and it is important, if we are not to beg the question, to put it both ways—can we actualize our desire to be effective and constructive as problem solvers without suppressing our humanity?

Second, notwithstanding the teaching that has been so pervasive in the last three centuries of our heritage, can we act on the belief that there *are* values that are authentically constitutive of being a human, that values are not inherently pervasively personal and subjective, that values can be treated as something other than a subject of exchanges, without legitimating the tyranny of whoever has control of government (or of a law school)? Put the other way, again, can we avoid coercing one another without having to surrender our desire to act out of our values?

Your answer to these momentous questions is a quick and final "no." This is *your* creed. I do not subscribe to it. I shall come to subscribe to it only as a final act of surrender, an act of cosmic despair. The questions for me all begin, "*How* can we ...?" My answer is that the answer cannot be reasoned through in advance. It can be found only through a developmental process involving the interaction of thought and action. Indeed, the idea of "finding" an "answer" is too static to capture the meaning of the task. The finding is in the search, in a continually deepening unfolding of understanding.

In my view, the search for answers to the "how" is exactly what Legal Education *should be* about, indeed what the practice of law should be about. In the carrying out of that search, two conditioning thoughts seem to me to be most important to bear in mind. First, neither the question that I have called one of professionalism—the integration of human emotional responses with responsible lawyering— nor that which I have termed one of political theory—the possibility of a values-based approach that is not imposed on us—can be successfully pursued in isolation from the other. Some are naturally drawn to one of these more than the other, but I am convinced that prolonged inattention to either is a barrier to successful grappling with the other. Second, the presence in the law schools of tears, prayers, anger, despair, division, and feelings of oppression, while perhaps not symptoms of success in constructing a quality legal education, are symptoms of struggle over exactly the subjects that it is essential to struggle over. And, whether the search is for understanding or for modes of interaction, the fact that it may often seem to take place in the dark, with many stubbed toes and bumped noses, with many fingers burned trying to strike matches, is not a sign that it is misguided. Only that it is hard.

LIVING IN THE LAW
Anthony T. Kronman
54 U.Chi.L.Rev. 835 (1987).

Legal ethics is largely concerned with questions of moral permissibility. Is a lawyer morally permitted, for example, to destroy the character of an innocent witness through ruthless cross-examination or to withhold information, unknown to the authorities, regarding his client's participation in past crimes? .... [I]t is to this ... topic that ... writers on legal ethics have devoted the greatest attention....

In this article, I raise, and attempt to answer, a question of a different sort. My question does not concern the moral justifiability of what lawyers do, but the reasons a person might have for choosing the life of a practicing lawyer in the first place. What is it about the life of a lawyer that justifies the very large commitment which the decision to pursue it entails? Put differently, why should anyone care about being or becoming a lawyer, or leading the life to which the choice of law as a career confines one? ...

. . .

What sorts of reasons might one give, then, for the decision to pursue a career in the law? It is best, perhaps, to begin with the answer that many will think the least respectable, even if they also consider it the most honest. A large number of lawyers undoubtedly believe that the life they have chosen is a desirable one because it offers great opportunities for wealth and prestige, for a disproportionate share of society's material resources and high professional status. Lawyers are generally well-compensated for their work and, though as a group they are often the object of popular vilification, tend, individually, to occupy positions of distinction in their communities. This, one might think, is reason enough to choose a career in the law, and other explanations can easily seem by comparison either unnecessary or disingenuous. Many, of course, will find this view repellent and judge the lawyer who candidly admits that his or her professional goal is money and honor and nothing else irresponsibly selfish. I, too, think this conception of the worth or value of law practice deficient, but would place the deficiency at a different point.

To enter the practice of law for money and honor alone is, at bottom, to view one's professional career as a vehicle for accumulating those things that are needed in other areas of life in order to acquire or accomplish what seems intrinsically important—important, that is, for its own sake and not as a means to some yet further end. The lawyer who takes this view of his practice treats it as a means to the things he truly cares about, the things that claim his attention, so to speak, at the end of the working day. In this general respect, however, he is no different from the rest of us, for we all do certain things not because we enjoy them or find them rewarding on their own terms but because they enable us to engage in other activities that do have these characteristics. Whether the lawyer who cares only about the pecuniary and honorific benefits of his professional work, who treats his profession as an instrumental good with no intrinsic value of its own, leads a life that in an overall sense is to be admired or regarded with pity and contempt, is a question that ultimately turns on the nature of the ends he uses the external rewards of his work to pursue. The corporate lawyer, for example, who works twelve hours a day at tasks he finds dull and unchallenging may nevertheless be leading a life that not only makes sense as a whole but even has appeal or a measure of nobility. Everything depends on what happens after hours and on whether this way of accumulating the instrumental goods needed to do the important things in life is preferable to the alternatives, both in terms of what it yields and what it takes. So a lawyer should not feel deeply ashamed to say that he is in it just for the money and prestige, though, to be sure, he must give us some account of what these things are for before we can decide whether his life is one we can admire....

Still, as I have said, there is something deficient in this view. The deficiency lies, I think, in the breadth of the instrumental attitude that it endorses. No doubt, we must all take an instrumental attitude toward some of the things we do and even, in certain circumstances, toward other people (though our treatment of others as means—in the process of contractual exchange, for example—is usually circumscribed by obligations that reflect what might be called a noninstrumental conception of the other person).[9] What makes the nakedly instrumental view of law practice that I have just described so unattractive is that it takes in too much of life, or more exactly, too much of what is important in life. This should first be understood in a purely quantitative sense. The lawyer who works the kind of hours at the kind of pace necessary to achieve great wealth or fame is likely to discover he has little time or energy left in which to pursue the things for whose sake he has made his professional career the instrument or vehicle....

---

9. Consider, for example, a contract for the sale of goods. The purchaser, seeking to obtain a particular item as inexpensively as possible, looks to the seller solely for the fulfillment of his desire. The seller, wishing to maximize profit, views the buyer solely as a source of profit. The two regard each other as means, each being prepared to discard the other if a better offer comes along. Their exploitation of one another is nevertheless bounded in a number of ways, for example, by the doctrines of unconscionability and duress. These impose upon the parties a limited obligation to treat one another as ends in the context of what is otherwise a mutually instrumental transaction.

There is a second, nonquantitative sense in which the instrumental view is deficient and this, it seems to me, is more important still. The deficiency I have in mind can best be brought out if we begin by taking note of a basic fact about the nature of personal identity. Of the various things a person does, many have no bearing on who he is, on his character or personality; he would be the same person and have the same identity whether he happened to do them or not. I myself feel this way, for example, about washing the dishes and commuting to work. There are good reasons, of course, why I do these things but I am quite confident that I would be the same person if I had never done them or never did them again. To be sure, others may view these particular activities in a different light and think of them as being more directly connected with their own distinctive identities (though I must admit that I find this difficult to imagine). What seems to me indisputable, however, is the presence in every person's life of some rough division between those involvements and activities that constitute his character or personality, on the one hand, and those, on the other, that do not, between those that make someone the person he or she is and those one merely has or does.

Now the whole of a person's professional life can, in theory at least, be placed on either side of this line. There is nothing, in the nature of things, that absolutely requires that the various activities of which one's professional existence is composed be character-forming in the sense I have suggested. I believe, however, that the practice of law exerts a very strong pull in this direction. To practice law well requires not only a formal knowledge of the law (a knowledge of what the legal realists termed the "paper" rules or rules "on the books") but certain qualities of mind and temperament as well. Most lawyers recognize this and recognize, too, that the qualities in question are also the ones that experience in law practice tends to encourage and confirm.

My central claim [is that these qualities] are traits of character, permanent dispositional attitudes rooted in the realm of feeling and desire. To accept this claim, however, is to acknowledge that these are qualities a person cannot lose or acquire without experiencing a change of identity. It is to accept the idea that to be a lawyer is to be a person of a particular sort, a person with a distinctive set of character traits as well as an expertise. I believe that something like this is true, in a general way, of other professions as well and that the very notion of a profession—as distinguished from a mere technique—implies the possession of certain character-defining traits or qualities. Whatever the case may be in other professional disciplines, however, [I believe] that the dispositional habits which the practice of law both requires and encourages have a bearing not only on what a person can do (like the habit, say, of touch-typing) but on who he or she is as well (like the habits of generosity and temperance).

The instrumental view of law practice does not give adequate weight to this fact. If, in addition to requiring a large expenditure of time and energy, the practice of law also has an important influence on the kind of person one becomes, then the professional lawyer has reason to worry about the intrinsic value of his career as well as its external or instrumental worth. It is perfectly legitimate to wonder whether the sort of person one is likely to become through long immersion in the law is the sort one may reasonably take pride in being or have reason to wish to become. The problem with the instrumental view is not that it answers this question one way rather than another, but that it fails to ask it altogether and thus obscures an important dimension of the commitment entailed by the choice of law as a career.

. . .

BECOMING A LAWYER: A HUMANISTIC PERSPECTIVE ON LEGAL EDUCATION AND PROFESSIONALISM
E. Dvorkin, J. Himmelstein, & H. Lesnick
West Pub. Co., 1981.

Read pages 175–88, 197–211.

Note: "What canst thou say?" (Reprise)

Add to the excerpts you have just read John Calvin's description of the spirit in which adversary proceedings can be carried on:

[T]here are very many who boil with such a rage for litigation, that they never can be quiet with themselves unless they are fighting with others. Law-suits they prosecute with the bitterness of deadly hatred, and with an insane eagerness to hurt and revenge, and they persist in them with implacable obstinacy, even to the ruin of their adversary. Meanwhile that they may be thought to do nothing but what is legal, they use this pretext of judicial proceedings as a defence of their perverse conduct. But if it is lawful for brother to litigate with brother, it does not follow that it is lawful to hate him, and obstinately pursue him with a furious desire to do him harm.

Let such persons then understand that judicial proceedings are lawful to him who makes a right use of them; and the right use, both for the pursuer and the defender, is for the latter to sist himself on the day appointed, and, without bitterness, urge what he can in his defence, but only with the desire of justly maintaining his right; and for the pursuer ... to throw himself upon the protection of the magistrate, state his complaint, and demand what is just and good; .... [W]hen minds are filled with malevolence, corrupted by envy, burning with anger, breathing revenge, or, in fine, so inflamed by the heat of the contest, that they, in some measure, lay aside charity, the whole pleading, even of the justest case, cannot but be impious. For it ought to be an axiom among all Christians, that no plea, however equitable, can be rightly conducted by any one who does not feel as kindly toward his opponent as if the matter in dispute were amicably transacted and arranged.

Some one, perhaps, may break in and say, that such moderation in judicial proceedings is so far being seen, that an instance of it would be a kind of prodigy. I confess that in these times it is rare to meet with an example of an honest litigant; but the thing itself, untainted by the accession of evil, ceases not to be good and pure. When we hear that the assistance of the magistrate is a sacred gift from God, we ought the more carefully to beware polluting it by our fault.

J. Calvin, Institutes of the Christian Religion, Book IV, Ch. XX (Beveridge trans. 1953).

The Note preceding the last several readings asked you to "consider the remaining excerpts in this sub-section, not as deductions of moral truth that you are 'obliged' to believe, but against your own sense of yourself as a lawyer." The difficulty in reading Calvin's admonition that way is, first, embedded in the "structurally coercive" mode of discourse that James Boyd White (in the excerpt quoted in the Note) describes as the "natural" way we tend to read a text. But, beyond that, the difficulty is heightened by the fact that it is written as moral truth, obligatory on all who wish to think of themselves as good. We are used to thinking of religiously based moral insights in that way, and tend to do the same with secular ones as well.

For present purposes, however, I am less interested in what you *must* think than in what you *do* think. My invitation is that you separate out any negative response you may have had to seeming to be told what to think from the task of discerning whether any of the excerpts (Calvin included) in fact struck a responsive chord in you.

- To what extent, if at all, are you able to read and think about the excerpts in that way?

- Which, if any, of them are helpful?

IN A DIFFERENT VOICE: PSYCHOLOGICAL THEORY AND WOMEN'S DEVELOPMENT

Carol Gilligan
Pp. 25–32 (1983).

[Compare] the moral judgments of two eleven-year-old children, a boy and a girl, who see, in the same dilemma, two very different moral problems. While current theory brightly illuminates the line and the logic of the boy's thought, it casts scant light on that of the girl. The choice of a girl whose moral judgments elude existing categories of developmental assessment is meant to highlight the issue of interpretation rather than to exemplify sex differences per se....

... The two children in question, Amy and Jake, were both bright and articulate and, at least in their eleven-year-old aspirations, resisted easy categories of sex-role stereotyping, since Amy aspired to become a scientist while Jake preferred English to math. Yet their moral judgments seem initially to confirm familiar notions about differences between the sexes, suggesting that the edge girls have on moral development during the early school years gives way at puberty with the ascendance of formal logical thought in boys.

The dilemma that these eleven-year-olds were asked to resolve was one in the series devised by [Lawrence] Kohlberg to measure moral development in adolescence by presenting a conflict between moral norms and exploring the logic of its resolution. In this particular dilemma, a man named Heinz considers whether or not to steal a drug which he cannot afford to buy in order to save the life of his wife. In the standard format of Kohlberg's interviewing procedure, the description of the dilemma itself—Heinz's predicament, the wife's disease, the druggist's refusal to lower his price—is followed by the question, "Should Heinz steal the drug?" The reasons for and against stealing are then explored through a series of questions that vary and extend the parameters of the dilemma in a way designed to reveal the underlying structure of moral thought.

Jake, at eleven, is clear from the outset that Heinz should steal the drug. Constructing the dilemma, as Kohlberg did, as a conflict between the values of property and life, he discerns the logical priority of life and uses that logic to justify his choice:

> For one thing, a human life is worth more than money, and if the druggist only makes $1,000, he is still going to live, but if Heinz doesn't steal the drug, his wife is going to die. (*Why is life worth more than money?*) Because the druggist can get a thousand dollars later from rich people with cancer, but Heinz can't get his wife again. (*Why not?*) Because people are all different and so you couldn't get Heinz's wife again.

Asked whether Heinz should steal the drug if he does not love his wife, Jake replies that he should, saying that not only is there "a difference between hating and killing," but also, if Heinz were caught, "the judge would probably think it was the right thing to do." Asked about the fact that, in stealing, Heinz would be breaking the law, he says that "the laws have mistakes, and you can't go writing up a law for everything that you can imagine."

Thus, while taking the law into account and recognizing its function in maintaining social order (the judge, Jake says, "should give Heinz the lightest possible sentence"), he also sees the law as man-made and therefore subject to error and change. Yet his judgment that Heinz should steal the drug, like his view of the law as having mistakes, rests on the assumption of agreement, a societal consensus around moral values that allows one to know and expect others to recognize what is "the right thing to do."

Fascinated by the power of logic, this eleven-year-old boy locates truth in math, which, he says, is "the only thing that is totally logical." Considering the moral dilemma to be "sort of like a math problem with humans," he sets it up as an equation and proceeds to work out the solution. Since his solution is rationally derived, he assumes that anyone following reason would arrive at the same conclusion and thus that a judge would also consider stealing to be the right thing for Heinz to do. Yet he is also aware of the limits of logic. Asked whether there is a right answer to moral problems, Jake replies that "there can only be right and wrong in judgment," since the parameters of action are variable and complex. Illustrating how actions undertaken with the best of intentions can eventuate in the most disastrous of consequences, he says, "like if you give an old lady your seat on the trolley, if you are in a trolley crash and that seat goes through the window, it might be that reason that the old lady dies."

. . .

In contrast, Amy's response to the dilemma conveys a very different impression, an image of development stunted by a failure of logic, an inability to think for herself. Asked if Heinz should steal the drug, she replies in a way that seems evasive and unsure:

> Well, I don't think so. I think there might be other ways besides stealing it, like if he could borrow the money or make a loan or something, but he really shouldn't steal the drug—but his wife shouldn't die either.

Asked why he should not steal the drug, she considers neither property nor law but rather the effect that theft could have on the relationship between Heinz and his wife:

> If he stole the drug, he might save his wife then, but if he did, he might have to go to jail, and then his wife might get sicker again, and he couldn't get more of the drug, and it might not be good. So, they should really just talk it out and find some other way to make the money.

Seeing in the dilemma not a math problem with humans but a narrative of relationships that extends over time, Amy envisions the wife's continuing need for her husband and the husband's continuing concern for his wife and seeks to respond to the druggist's need in a way that would sustain rather than sever connection. Just as she ties the wife's survival to the preservation of relationships, so she considers the value of the wife's life in a context of relationships, saying that it would be wrong to let her die because, "if she died, it hurts a lot of people and it hurts her." Since Amy's moral judgment is grounded in the belief that, "if somebody has something that would keep somebody alive, then it's not right not to give it to them," she considers the problem in the dilemma to arise not from the druggist's assertion of rights but from his failure of response.

As the interviewer proceeds with the series of questions that follow from Kohlberg's construction of the dilemma, Amy's answers remain essentially unchanged, the various probes serving neither to elucidate nor to modify her initial response.... But as the interviewer conveys through the repetition of questions that the answers she gave were not heard or not right, Amy's confidence begins to diminish, and her replies become more constrained and unsure. Asked again why Heinz should not steal the drug, she simply repeats, "Because it's not right." Asked again to explain why, she states again that theft would not be a good solution, adding lamely, "if he took it, he might not know how to give it to his wife, and so his wife might still die." Failing to see the dilemma as a self-contained problem in moral logic, she does not discern the internal structure of its resolution; as she constructs the problem differently herself, Kohlberg's conception completely evades her.

Instead, seeing a world comprised of relationships rather than of people standing alone, a world that coheres through human connection rather than through systems of rules, she finds the puzzle in the dilemma to lie in the failure of the druggist to respond to the wife. Saying that "it is not right for someone to die when their life could be saved," she assumes that if the druggist were to see the consequences of his refusal to lower his price, he would realize that "he should just give it to the wife and then have the husband pay back the money later." Thus she considers the solution to the dilemma to lie in making the wife's condition more salient to the druggist or, that failing, in appealing to others who are in a position to help.

Just as Jake is confident the judge would agree that stealing is the right thing for Heinz to do, so Amy is confident that, "if Heinz and the druggist had talked it out long enough, they could reach something besides stealing." As he considers the law to "have mistakes," so she sees this drama as a mistake, believing that "the world should just share things more and then people wouldn't have to steal." Both children thus recognize the need for agreement but see it as mediated in different ways—he impersonally through systems of logic and law, she personally through communication in relationship. Just as he relies on the conventions of logic to deduce the solution to this dilemma, assuming these conventions to be shared, so she relies on a process of communication, assuming connection and believing that her voice will be heard. Yet while his assumptions about agreement are confirmed by the convergence in logic between his answers and the questions posed, her assumptions are belied by the failure of communication, the interviewer's inability to understand her response.

Although the frustration of the interview with Amy is apparent in the repetition of questions and its ultimate circularity, the problem of interpretation is focused by the assessment of her response. When considered in the light of Kohlberg's definition of the stages and sequences of moral development, her moral judgments appear to be a full stage lower in maturity than those of the boy. [H]er responses seem to reveal a feeling of powerlessness in the world, an inability to think systematically about the concepts of morality or law, a reluctance to challenge authority or to examine the logic of received moral truths, a failure even to conceive of acting directly to save a life or to consider that such action, if taken, could possibly have an effect. As her reliance on relationships seems to reveal a continuing dependence and vulnerability, so her belief in communication as the mode through

which to resolve moral dilemmas appears naive and cognitively immature.

Yet Amy's description of herself conveys a markedly different
impression. Once again, the hallmarks of the preadolescent child
depicts a child secure in her sense of herself, confident in the substance
of her beliefs, and sure of her ability to do something of value in the
world.... Yet the world she knows is a different world from that
refracted by Kohlberg's construction of Heinz's dilemma. Her world is
a world of relationships and psychological truths where an awareness of
the connection between people gives rise to a recognition of responsibility for one another, a perception of the need for response. Seen in this
light, her understanding of morality as arising from the recognition of
relationship, her belief in communication as the mode of conflict
resolution, and her conviction that the solution to the dilemma will
follow from its compelling representation seem far from naive or
cognitively immature. Instead, Amy's judgments contain the insights
central to an ethic of care, just as Jake's judgments reflect the logic of
the justice approach. Her incipient awareness of the "method of
truth," the central tenet of nonviolent conflict resolution, and her belief
in the restorative activity of care, lead her to see the actors in the
dilemma arrayed not as opponents in a contest of rights but as members of a network of relationships on whose continuation they all
depend. Consequently her solution to the dilemma lies in activating
the network by communication, securing the inclusion of the wife by
strengthening rather than severing connections.

But the different logic of Amy's response calls attention to the
interpretation of the interview itself. Conceived as an interrogation, it
appears instead as a dialogue, which takes on moral dimensions of its
own, pertaining to the interviewer's uses of power and to the manifestations of respect. With this shift in the conception of the interview, it
immediately becomes clear that the interviewer's problem in understanding Amy's response stems from the fact that Amy is answering a
different question from the one the interviewer thought had been
posed. Amy is considering not *whether* Heinz should act in this
situation ("*should* Heinz steal the drug?") but rather *how* Heinz should
act in response to his awareness of his wife's need ("Should Heinz *steal*
the drug?"). The interviewer takes the mode of action for granted,
presuming it to be a matter of fact; Amy assumes the necessity for
action and considers what form it should take. In the interviewer's
failure to imagine a response not dreamt of in Kohlberg's moral
philosophy lies the failure to hear Amy's question and to see the logic
in her response, to discern that what appears, from one perspective, to
be an evasion of the dilemma signifies in other terms a recognition of
the problem and a search for a more adequate solution.

Thus in Heinz's dilemma these two children see two very different
moral problems—Jake a conflict between life and property that can be
resolved by logical deduction, Amy a fracture of human relationship
that must be mended with its own thread. Asking different questions

that arise from different conceptions of the moral domain, the children arrive at answers that fundamentally diverge, and the arrangement of these answers as successive stages on a scale of increasing moral maturity calibrated by the logic of the boy's response misses the different truth revealed in the judgment of the girl. To the question, "What does he see that she does not?," Kohlberg's theory provides a ready response, manifest in the scoring of Jake's judgments a full stage higher than Amy's in moral maturity; to the question, "What does she see that he does not?." Kohlberg's theory has nothing to say. Since most of her responses fall through the sieve of Kohlberg's scoring system, her responses appear from his perspective to lie outside the moral domain.

. . .

These two eleven-year-old children, both highly intelligent and perceptive about life, though in different ways, display different modes of moral understanding, different ways of thinking about conflict and choice. In resolving Heinz's dilemma, Jake relies on theft to avoid confrontation and turns to the law to mediate the dispute. Transposing a hierarchy of power into a hierarchy of values, he defuses a potentially explosive conflict between people by casting it as an impersonal conflict of claims. In this way, he abstracts the moral problem from the interpersonal situation, finding in the logic of fairness an objective way to decide who will win the dispute. But this hierarchical ordering, with its imagery of winning and losing and the potential for violence which it contains, gives way in Amy's construction of the dilemma to a network of connection, a web of relationships that is sustained by a process of communication. With this shift, the moral problem changes from one of unfair domination, the imposition of property over life, to one of unnecessary exclusion, the failure of the druggist to respond to the wife.

. . .

CARING: A FEMININE APPROACH TO ETHICS AND MORAL EDUCATION

Nel Noddings
passim (1984).

Ethics, the philosophical study of morality, has concentrated for the most part on moral reasoning. Much current work, for example, focuses on the status of moral predicates and, in education, the dominant model presents a hierarchical picture of moral reasoning. This emphasis gives ethics a contemporary, mathematical appearance, but it also moves discussion beyond the sphere of actual human activity and the feeling that pervades such activity. Even though careful philosophers have recognized the difference between "pure" or logical reason and "practical" or moral reason, ethical argumentation has frequently proceeded as if it were governed by the logical necessity characteristic of geometry. It has concentrated on the establishment of principles and that which can be logically derived from them. One might say that ethics has been discussed largely in the language of the father: in principles and propositions, in terms such as justification, fairness, justice. The mother's voice has been silent. Human caring and the memory of caring and being cared for, which I shall argue form the foundation of ethical response, have not received attention except as outcomes of ethical behavior....

The view to be expressed here is a feminine view. This does not imply that all women will accept it or that men will reject it; indeed, there is no reason why men should not embrace it. It is feminine in the deep classical sense—rooted in receptivity, relatedness, and responsiveness. It does not imply either that logic is to be discarded or that logic is alien to women. It represents an alternative to present views, one that begins with the moral attitude or longing for goodness and not with moral reasoning. It may indeed be the case that such an approach is more typical of women than of men, but this is an empirical question I shall not attempt to answer.

. . .

Women, in general, ... enter the practical domain of moral action ... through a different door, so to speak. It is not the case, certainly, that women cannot arrange principles hierarchically and derive conclusions logically. It is more likely that we see this process as peripheral to, or even alien to, many problems of moral action. Faced with a hypothetical moral dilemma, women often ask for more information. We want to know more, I think, in order to form a picture more nearly resembling real moral situations. Ideally, we need to talk to the participants, to see their eyes and facial expressions, to receive what they are feeling. Moral decisions are, after all, made in real situations; they are qualitatively different from the solution of geometry problems. Women can and do give reasons for their acts, but the reasons often point to feelings, needs, impressions, and a sense of personal ideal rather than to universal principles and their application. We shall see that, as a result of this "odd" approach, women have often been judged inferior to men in the moral domain.

Because I am entering the domain through a linguistic back door of sorts, much of what I say cannot be labeled "empirical" or "logical." (Some of it, of course, can be so labeled.) Well, what is it then? It is language that attempts to capture what Wittgenstein advised we "must pass over in silence." ... We may present a coherent and enlightening picture without *proving* anything and, indeed, without claiming to present or to seek moral *knowledge* or moral *truth*. The hand that steadied us as we learned to ride our first bicycle did not provide propositional knowledge, but it guided and supported us all the same, and we finished up "knowing how."

This is an essay in practical ethics from the feminine view....

... I shall locate the very wellspring of ethical behavior in human affective response. Throughout our discussion of ethicality we shall remain in touch with the affect that gives rise to it. This does not mean that our discussion will bog down in sentiment, but it is necessary to give appropriate attention and credit to the affective foundation of existence.

I shall begin with a discussion of caring.... The relation of natural caring will be identified as the human condition that we, consciously or unconsciously, perceive as "good." It is that condition toward which we long and strive, and it is our longing for caring—to be in that special relation—that provides the motivation for us to be moral. We want to be *moral* in order to remain in the caring relation and to enhance the ideal of ourselves as one-caring.

It is this ethical ideal, this realistic picture of ourselves as one-caring, that guides us as we strive to meet the other morally. Everything depends upon the nature and strength of this ideal, for we shall not have absolute principles to guide us. Indeed, I shall reject ethics of principle as ambiguous and unstable. Wherever there is a principle, there is implied its exception and, too often, principles function to separate us from each other. We may become dangerously self-righteous when we perceive ourselves as holding a precious principle not held by the other. The other may then be devalued and treated "differently." Our ethic of caring will not permit this to happen. We recognize that in fear, anger, or hatred we will treat the other differently, but this treatment is never conducted ethically. Hence, when we must use violence or strategies on the other, we are already diminished ethically. Our efforts must, then, be directed to the maintenance of conditions that will permit caring to flourish. Along with the rejection of principles and rules as the major guide to ethical behavior, I shall also reject the notion of universalizability. Many of those writing and thinking about ethics insist that any ethical judgment—by virtue of its *being* an ethical judgment—must be universalizable; that is, it must be the case that, if under conditions X you are required to do A, then under sufficiently similar conditions, I too am required to do A. I shall reject this emphatically. First, my attention is not on judgment and not on the particular acts we perform but on how we meet the other morally. Second, in recognition of the feminine approach to meeting the other morally—our insistence on caring for the other—I shall want to preserve the uniqueness of human encounters. Since so much depends on the subjective experience of those involved in ethical encounters, conditions are rarely "sufficiently similar" for me to declare that you must do what I must do. There is, however, a fundamental universality in our ethic, as there must be to escape relativism. The caring attitude, that attitude which expresses our earliest memories of being cared for and our growing store of memories of both caring and being cared for, is universally accessible....

. . .

If we were starting out on a traditional investigation of what it means to be moral, we would almost certainly start with a discussion of moral judgment and moral reasoning.　This approach has obvious advantages.　It gives us something public and tangible to grapple with—the statements that describe our thinking on moral matters. But I shall argue that this is not the only—nor even the best—starting point.　Starting the discussion of moral matters with principles, definitions, and demonstrations is rather like starting the solution of a mathematical problem formally.　Sometimes we can and do proceed this way, but when the problematic situation is new, baffling, or especially complex, we cannot start this way.　We have to operate in an intuitive or receptive mode that is somewhat mysterious, internal, and nonsequential.　After the solution has been found by intuitive methods, we may proceed with the construction of a formal demonstration or proof.　As the mathematician Gauss put it: "I have got my result but I do not know yet how to get (prove) it."

A difficulty in mathematics teaching is that we too rarely share our fundamental mathematical thinking with our students.　We present everything ready-made as it were, as though it springs from our foreheads in formal perfection.　The same sort of difficulty arises when we approach the teaching of morality or ethical behavior from a rational-cognitive approach.　We fail to share with each other the feelings, the conflicts, the hopes and ideas that influence our eventual choices.　We share only the justification for our acts and not what motivates and touches us.

　　. . .

[T]raditional approaches to the problem of justification are mistaken.　When the ethical theorist asks, "Why should I behave thus-and-so?," his question is likely to be aimed at justification rather than motivation and at a logic that resides outside the person.　He is asking for reasons of the sort we expect to find in logical demonstration.　He may expect us to claim that moral judgments can be tested as claims to facts can be tested, or that moral judgments are derived from divine commandment, or that moral truths are intuitively apprehended. Once started on this line of discussion, we may find ourselves arguing abstractly about the status of relativism and absolutism, egoism and altruism, and a host of other positions that, I shall claim, are largely irrelevant to moral conduct.　They are matters of considerable intellectual interest, but they are distractions if our primary interest is in ethical conduct.

Moral statements cannot be justified in the way that statements of fact can be justified.　They are not truths.　They are derived not from facts or principles but from the caring attitude. . . .

The Ethical Ideal as I have described it springs from two sentiments: the natural sympathy human beings feel for each other and the longing to maintain, recapture, or enhance our most caring and tender moments.　Both sentiments may be denied, and so commitment is required to establish the ethical ideal. We must recognize our longing for relatedness and accept it, and we must commit ourselves to the openness that permits us to receive the other. The effort required to summon ethical caring is greatly reduced by renewed commitment to the sentiment from which it springs. For if we commit ourselves to receptivity, natural caring occurs more frequently, and conflicts may thereby be reduced. . . .

Note on Gilligan and Noddings: Feminist routes to self-knowledge

1. Joan Tronto has described in these terms the underlying premises of an approach to moral theory that places an "ethic of care" at its center:

> [A]n ethic of care necessarily rests on a different set of premises about what a good moral theory is. [T]he prevailing contemporary notion of what counts as a moral theory is derived from Kant. According to this view, a moral theory consists of a set of moral principles rationally chosen after consideration of competing principles. [I]t is universalizable, impartial, and concerned with describing what is right, and we would expect chosen moral principles to embody these standard notions of morality.

> An alternative model for moral theorists is contextual. . . . In any contextual moral theory, morality must be situated concretely, that is, for particular actors in a particular society. It cannot be understood by the recitation of abstract principles. By this account, morality is embedded in the norms of a given society. Furthermore, . . . morality cannot be determined by posing hypothetical moral dilemmas or by asserting moral principles. Rather, one's moral imagination, character, and actions must respond to the complexity of a given situation. . . .

> . . . . Noncontextual moral philosphers rely on rational tests to check self-interested inclinations. Hence the rational and the moral become identified. In contrast, advocates of contextual moral theories often stress moral sensitivity and moral imagination as keys to understanding moral life. . . .

> . . . . Perhaps the most important characteristics of an ethic of care is that within it, moral situations are defined not in terms of rights and responsibilities but in terms of relationships of care. The morally mature person understands the balance between caring for the self and caring for others. The perspective of care requires that conflict be worked out without damage to the continuing relationships. Moral problems can be expressed in terms of accommodating the needs of the self and of others, of balancing competition and cooperation, and of maintaining the social web of relations in which one finds oneself.

> Quite obviously, if such caretaking is the quintessential moral task, the context within which conflicting demands occur will be an important factor in determining the morally correct act. To resort to abstract, universal principles is to go outside of the web of relation-

ships. Thus, ... care may set the boundaries of when justice concerns are appropriate.

Tronto, Beyond Gender Difference to a Theory of Care, 12 Signs 644, 657–59 (1987).

2. Gilligan and Noddings identify with gender the qualities that they find lacking in the dominant patterns of thinking about ethical choice. Approaches that avowedly draw on feminist perspectives, like those that avowedly draw on religious or on Marxist perspectives, often prompt support or rejection as a response to one's belief as to the explanatory or emancipatory power of that perspective. Some find Gilligan's and Noddings' approach enormously helpful, while some find it seriously problematic. The issue is of substantial importance—see Professor Tronto's article, at pp. 646–56, for an analysis and an introduction to the literature—but for present purposes I invite you to separate your judgment on that issue from your view of the salience of the *qualities* themselves about which these authors have written.

The question I invite you to consider is the extent, if any, that the qualities of which Gilligan and Noddings (and Tronto) have written accurately describe significant aspects of your self, which were part of what motivated you to choose law as a career, aspects that you want to bring to your practice as a lawyer. In considering this question, I suggest that you think of your effort as uncovering the "feminist" aspect of your self if you find that doing so aids your inquiry, and that you leave the word behind if you find it a hindrance or a diversion. Note, too, that I am not asking merely about aspects of your personality, but about aspects of your self that are *part* of what drew you to law and inform your idea of what it is you want to be doing as a lawyer.

2. THE INTEGRATION OF CLIENT EMPOWERMENT AND LAWYER AUTONOMY

INCEST AND ETHICS: CONFIDENTIALITY'S SEVEREST TEST

Ruth Fleet Thurman
61 Denv.L.Rev. 619 (1984).

. . .

This article discusses an attorney's ethical dilemma when faced with the confidentiality requirement in light of his client's confessed incestuous relationship with the client's nine-year-old daughter. Although some states have enacted legislation and code amendments to encompass this situation, most jurisdictions have not expressed definitive guidelines for an attorney faced with this dilemma. The following is a study of an ethics committee in the mythical state of Marshall exploring three possible courses of action in an attempt to answer an inquiry from a practitioner faced with this situation.

Letter to Lawrence Sage, Esq., Chairperson, Marshall State Bar Ass'n Comm. on Professional Ethics

Dear Mr. Sage:

I would appreciate an advisory opinion from the Committee on Professional Ethics on the proper course of conduct in the following situation in which I am presently involved. Neglect proceedings have been filed against an indigent family. I have been appointed to represent the mother and father at the hearing. The petition alleges that the couple's three children, aged three, six and nine, are not receiving proper care.... I learned from the husband that he has been having sexual intercourse with their nine year old daughter for the past two years. The wife confirms this and privately tells me that she is afraid to interfere. I have reviewed the report of the child welfare investigation ordered by the court. The report, which includes interviews with the children, confirms my belief that no one except the mother has discovered the father's mistreatment of the child.

As court-appointed counsel, what are my ethical obligations? Should I disclose the father's incest? If I do not, I am afraid it will continue. I think he needs some kind of treatment or therapy. If the court does not appoint counsel for the children, should I suggest to the court that counsel be appointed? Even if counsel is appointed, he or she may not find out about the incest because apparently no one has during the past two years. I suspect that the child may be afraid to speak up against her father.

I imagine that other lawyers may have been confronted with this kind of dilemma, but I cannot find any ethics opinions addressing these questions. I would appreciate your advice.

> Sincerely yours,
> /s/
> John Barrister
> Attorney at Law

Memorandum
To: Members of the Committee on Professional Ethics
From: Lawrence Sage, Chairperson

Enclosed are copies of the above-referenced inquiry and supporting materials. The inquiring lawyer asks:

(1) Whether he should reveal confidential communications that his client, charged with child neglect, has been having sexual intercourse with his nine year old daughter for the past two years.

(2) Whether he should suggest to the court that counsel be appointed for the children.

. . .

Because of the committee's lack of familiarity with the social, medical and psychological aspects of incest, I have requested briefing reports from experts in those areas on the general problems of incest to aid the committee in reaching a decision. In addition, I have requested reports by a juvenile court judge and a legal aid attorney on judicial proceedings that might result from a charge of incest. Enclosed are [their] reports....

Please review these materials and be prepared to discuss and take a preliminary vote on this inquiry at our committee meeting on January 25.

REPORT ON SEXUAL ABUSE OF CHILDREN BY DR. HILLARY HOPE,
DIRECTOR, NATIONAL CHILDREN'S PROTECTION LEAGUE

. . .

An annual estimate of over 5,000 cases of father-daughter incest is considered the "tip of the iceberg." Only a small fraction are reported when they happen; most come to light years later. Incest occurs within the privacy of the family and is kept secret, which makes it impossible to know the real magnitude of the problem. Dr. C. Henry Kempe, pioneer researcher and a foremost authority on child abuse, described the situation: "It is usually hidden for years and only becomes known because of some dramatic change in the family situation, such as adolescent revelation of delinquent acts, pregnancy, venereal disease, a variety of psychiatric illnesses, or something as trivial as a sudden family quarrel." The acts often continue over many years and "may be carried out under actual or threatened violence or may be nonviolent or even tender, insidious, collusive, and secretive." Generally, the whole family actively or passively supports "incestuous equilibrium."

. . .

The most common form of incest is between father and daughter, however, father-son, mother-son and mother-daughter incidents have also been reported, as well as incidents between siblings. Because father-daughter incest "is potentially the most damaging to the child and family [and the] most frequently prosecuted by the courts," my remarks focus primarily on the father as abuser and the daughter as victim. In that situation the mother usually is aware of what is happening but does not protest. In fact, she often condones and even aids and abets the crime, perhaps out of fear of physical violence or of losing her husband, which would leave the family destitute. This places the victim in a vulnerable position, defenseless against paternal threats, force, or enticements. To the child, her father is a trusted authority figure who "can do no wrong." This gives him great power over her. Vincent De Francis ... described the psychodynamics in a report on a three year study of sexual abuse he directed in New York City: "The offender used the child's strong desire not to displease him, even though, to the child, the adult's request may have seemed unpleasant, or distasteful, or even bizarre.... A subtle threat underlies the compliance of the child in these circumstances." Can the child really be considered a "willing victim" under these circumstances, or "not always [an] unwilling" partner, as some commentators assert?

When the mother sides with the father against the child victim, the child feels isolated and helpless and is usually plagued by feelings of insecurity, confusion, guilt and worthlessness since she does not know where to turn for help. For older children the dilemma is staggering because they realize that the reaction to confiding this information may be disbelief, anger, ostracism or maybe even destruction of the family. Dr. Kempe said:

> They are in no way assured of ready help from anyone, but risk losing their family and feeling guilty and responsible for bringing it harm if they share their secret. Youngsters may only come to the attention of the health care system or the law through pregnancy, prostitution, venereal disease, drug abuse, or antisocial behavior.

When parents are confronted with their roles in the wrongdoings, some deny the incest, rationalize it, or even shrug it off. One mother responded that her husband "gave up smoking and needed something to help him through." Some offenders righteously defend the incest as natural, the right of a parent, or good for the child. A frequent defense is that the child seduced the parent. Although some observers give credence to this charge, recent researchers view the child's behavior as innocent affection-seeking, and place the entire responsibility for setting appropriate limits of family intimacy on the parents....

The impact of parental incest on the victim is hard to assess because many of the more serious problems do not appear until years later, and because there is a paucity of carefully controlled long-term studies of incest victims. Most clinical studies, however, have reported a variety of disturbances ranging from personality disorders, psychosomatic complaints, psychological difficulties and sexual maladjustments to full-blown psychoses. A number of studies on incest and sexual abuse of children show that the fact that the child was the victim of a trusted and respected figure causes confusion, distrust and psychiatric disorders later in life. One team of researchers said, "It is the recognition of having been exploited and uncared for as an individual human being that leads to the long-lasting residual damages of sexual abuse in development, rather than the actual physical sexual act itself." Pregnancy, vaginitis and syphilis were among the physical effects suffered by some incest victims, but the psychological effects may have been even more serious. While depression and guilt were prevalent, fatigue, loss of appetite, aches and pains, inability to concentrate and sleep disturbances were psychosomatic complaints suffered by almost all victims in one study of father-daughter incest.

Researchers ... found immediate harmful effects on personality development that varied with the developmental stages of the child. Some children showed reversion to or prolonged infantile behavior, others showed handicapped educability and social adaptations, while still others showed precocious and inappropriate development of adolescent characteristics and adjustment difficulties. The researchers also found anxiety and confusion in the victims' social relations, and concluded that incest distorted their attitudes toward family members and, later, toward society in general.

The turmoil these children endure may not, however, be recognized at the time of the incident because children frequently repress the experience. They may be emotionally withdrawn and appear unaffected . . .

. . .

REPORT ON SEXUAL ABUSE OF CHILDREN BY MS. MARY NOBLE, SUPERVISOR OF CASEWORKERS, MARSHALL DEPARTMENT OF PROTECTIVE SERVICES

The increasing child abuse caseload is placing heavy demands on community resources to provide protective and rehabilitative services to the child and the family. Ideally, the community should provide the family with support services such as caseworkers; visiting nurses; visiting homemakers; child day care; mental health services, including individual and group counseling; and short and long-term therapy for the victim, parents and siblings under social services supervision. When home-based services and treatment are not available, foster care and court action may be the only recourse. The immediate concern should be the victim's safety which may require removal, at least temporarily, to a children's shelter or foster home, particularly if the offender remains in the family home. Removal from the family, even temporarily, may cause the child to feel rejected, banished, unloved and insecure which compounds the guilt and shame already felt. The child needs competent counseling or treatment to deal with this stress and inner-turmoil.

Intervention by the state has distinct and predictable consequences for every member of the family. Examination of the victim in a hospital or clinic may be required, which can be a bewildering and frightening experience for a child. Recounting details of the assault to police and intake officers in what may be an insensitive interrogation, can make the victim feel badgered, threatened and demeaned.

For the family, state intervention invariably engenders shame, humiliation and hostility at having their private lives open to public view and censure, plus resentment toward the victim for causing this intrusion. Protective measures, viewed by professionals as helpful to a family in crisis, may seem punitive and vindictive to family members.

State intervention for the offender means community indignation and outrage, the stigma of being labeled "unfit" or "abusive" and, perhaps ultimately, the retribution of the criminal justice system. If convicted and imprisoned, the offender may be threatened and assaulted by inmates who regard child abusers as the lowest kind of criminal. Furthermore, if the offender is acquitted of criminal abuse charges, he may feel vindicated and justified in resuming the incest or punishing the victim by unreasonable chores and demands, oppressive rules, restrictions, sanctions, and other forms of blatant or subtle harassment.

If the victim remains in the home or is later restored to the family, she may be shunned, ostracized or tormented by her parents and siblings for causing so much trouble and embarrassment for the family, thus reinforcing her feelings of guilt, unworthiness and low self-esteem.

The abuse charges may be followed by proceedings to terminate parental rights. The judicial process, whether criminal or civil, makes adversaries of family members by requiring them to testify against each other. Questioning the victim about details of the assault, testifying, and being cross-examined may be as harrowing and harmful as the incest itself, if not more so.

Once the judicial process is invoked, the outcome is unpredictable. At worst, from the family's viewpoint, the offender may be imprisoned, the wife and children made destitute, the victim removed from the loved ones' home and placed with strangers, and parental rights terminated. At best, with good family support resources, a humane and enlightened program tailored to the individual family may provide the treatment and therapy necessary to stop the incest, protect the child, rehabilitate the offender, and stabilize and reunite the family, which should be the ultimate goal. When it succeeds, state intervention is vindicated, but when it fails, harm and suffering may be compounded. It is incumbent upon the community to provide the resources and upon professionals to work together to make it succeed.

CHILD ABUSE AND THE LEGAL PROCESS: A JUDGE'S PERSPECTIVE
by HONORABLE RICHARD CHANCELLOR, CIRCUIT COURT
JUDGE, JUVENILE DIVISION, STATE OF MARSHALL

Several types of laws are designed to protect children from abuse. Criminal statutes and ordinances can be invoked to punish offenders. Under juvenile or family court acts, the court may institute protective supervision or termination of parental rights when parents are found to have abused or neglected their children. Protective services are part of public child welfare laws in most states and all states have laws that require reporting known or suspected child abuse or neglect.

Criminal statutes protect children from sexual misconduct, such as statutory rape, indecent liberties, incest, and sexual battery. Once set in motion, the criminal process is "formidable, impersonal and unrelenting....; its aim is primarily punitive rather than therapeutic." The process usually begins with an information filed by a public prosecutor, followed by an arrest warrant, arraignment at which the offender receives formal notice of the charges and of his rights, including court-appointed counsel for indigent defendants, and posting bond or release on his own recognizance pending trial. After investigation by the prosecution and defense counsel, the court may accept a plea bargain. Depending on the strength or weakness of the state's evidence, the severity of the injury and the public climate, the prosecutor may agree to reduce the charge to a lesser offense in exchange for a plea of guilty, for example, from felonious assault to simple assault, a misdemeanor.

After a "guilty" plea or conviction following a trial, the defendant may apply for probation if he is not a persistent offender. A presentence or probation investigation is usually conducted and may include psychological or psychiatric evaluation, but seldom delves into the underlying cause of the abuse or proposes a positive plan for supervision or treatment of the offender. Probation services seldom have any therapeutic effect because personnel usually are not trained to understand or deal constructively with the pathology of child abuse. This deficiency and the repugnancy of the crime often result merely in punitive, restrictive surveillance, making rehabilitation improbable under the criminal justice system. Judge Delaney observed that after acquittal or release, the offender is likely to resume the conduct, but more cautiously. He described the situation in this way:

> [T]he criminal process as a solution to child abuse is usually totally ineffective. Probably it has some deterrent effect on the parent capable of controlling his conduct, but its chief value lies in satisfying the conscience of the community that the wrong to a child has been avenged. That the true causes of the battering parent's conduct have not been sought out and treated is of little concern.

Most cases of child abuse are referred to juvenile or family court and are tried as dependency cases. The proceedings involve two distinct phases: first, an adjudication of dependency upon a finding of abuse; second, the ultimate disposition. At the initial hearing the court must decide whether danger of repeated assault requires temporary removal of the child from the home. The court must weigh the risk of further abuse against the potential long-range emotional damage to the child and parents caused by temporary protective care.

When the case is tried in juvenile or family court, statutes sometimes permit limited use of written reports and other types of evidence that might not be admissible under strict evidentiary rules. The quantum of proof required to sustain a finding of abuse or neglect is usually a preponderance of the evidence, rather than proof beyond a reasonable doubt as required in criminal court. Pretrial conferences encourage full disclosure of facts and opinions and provide an opportunity to evaluate the evidence and to narrow issues in dispute which may result in a stipulation or consent decree. If not, a trial or adjudication hearing will follow.

Whether actions in juvenile or family courts are more effective than criminal actions in rehabilitating the offender, depends to a large extent on the resources available. In the absence of the needed therapeutic skills and services, "the goal of replacing punishment with treatment ... [and] incarceration with rehabilitation" may not be achieved. Recent emphasis on procedural reforms, stressing safeguards for defendants, has been described as "cheaper than providing substantive services for those who are mentally ill, engaged in deviant behavior, or are poor. Paradoxically, while adversary proceedings are becoming the fashion of the day and are resulting in dismissals of more cases, there is a growing demand for harsher sentences."

...

REPORT ON JUVENILE COURTS BY BRENDA CHALLENGER, ESQUIRE, CHIEF STAFF COUNSEL, MARSHALL CITY LEGAL SERVICES, INC.

...

My first objection to juvenile courts is that they are class-based institutions for the poor and minorities. "Certainly in the great cities of the nation the overwhelming number of children processed through the juvenile court are the children of the poor." Although abuse and neglect occur at all social and economic levels, the upper and middle classes are less likely to be observed and reported. They are also more likely to stay out of court because they have access to privately arranged corrective treatment and private care facilities not available to the poor.

...

Handicapped by poverty and lack of education, parents charged with abuse or neglect are no match for the state with its financial resources; access to records; and witnesses including caseworkers empowered to investigate and testify. Once the child is in custody, "the State even has the power to shape the historical events that form the basis for termination." As a result, "many 'voluntary' placements are in fact coerced by the threat of neglect proceedings and are not in fact voluntary in the sense of the product of informed consent."

In the dispositional stage of neglect or abuse proceedings, the "best interest of the child" standard is applied by juvenile courts in deciding whether a child should be removed from parental custody. This "allows the judge to import his personal values into the process, and leaves considerable scope for class bias.... [C]ases ... clearly reveal the risks of 'individualized' decisions under vague judicial standards."

Moreover, "foster care has been condemned as a class-based intrusion into the family life of the poor." It is also highly questionable whether these children will be better off in foster care than in their own homes. In *Santosky v. Kramer* the Court said, "Even when a child's natural home is imperfect, permanent removal from that home will not necessarily improve his welfare.... ('In fact, under current practice, coercive intervention frequently results in placing a child in a more detrimental situation than he would be in without intervention')." Said one commentator:

> For nearly two decades, noted authorities have observed that children removed from their homes and placed in 'temporary' foster care often remain there for many years, frequently until their majority. Such children often suffer serious psychological damage in foster care and are commonly subjected to numerous

moves—each of which disrupts the child's need for maintenance of continuity and stability in his relationships with parental figures.

. . .

Memorandum
To: Members of the Committee on Professional Ethics
From: Lawrence Sage, Chairperson

Enclosed are three draft opinions prepared independently by three committee members after discussion and preliminary vote at our January 25th committee meeting.

. . .

1. *Preliminary Draft of Proposed Ethics Opinion 84–1*

Proposal Number I Prepared by Veronica Truly, Esquire

. . .

(1) As to the first inquiry, the committee believes that the attorney for the parents should not reveal the information because disclosure would betray the lawyer's sacred trust to hold inviolate confidences entrusted to him by his client. Clients' confidences must be protected from disclosure because lawyers cannot properly advise or represent their clients without knowing all of the facts. Statutes, rules of evidence, and rules of ethics have codified this principle.

. . .

In addition, Canons 6 and 7 of the Marshall Code require a lawyer to represent his client competently and zealously. Voluntary disclosure of information detrimental to a client without his consent is inconsistent with zealous representation. DR 7–101(A)(3) prohibits a lawyer from prejudicing or damaging his client during the course of the professional relationship. Canon 5 requires a lawyer to exercise independent professional judgment on behalf of a client. EC 5–1 states: "The professional judgment of a lawyer should be exercised, within the bounds of the law, solely for the benefit of his client and free of compromising influences and loyalties. Neither his personal interests . . . nor the desires of third persons should be permitted to dilute his loyalty to his client."

The Comment to Model Rule 1.2 is even more specific in providing that the lawyer "should defer to the client regarding . . . concern for third persons who might be adversely affected." ABA Informal Opinion 869 (1965), applying provisions similar to the earlier Canons of Professional Ethics, advised that the wife's lawyer in divorce and custody proceedings is ethically bound not to reveal information confided to him by the client that she has become pregnant by a man other than her husband.

. . .

The committee members recognize that paternal incest is a terrible thing for a child to endure; they also recognize that maintenance of the adversary system by upholding the sanctity of confidentiality is of supreme importance. The inquiring attorney has been appointed to represent a father charged with child neglect. To reveal his confidential admission of incest might lead to criminal charges and infringe constitutionally protected rights against self-incrimination. Confidentiality must be placed above prevention of the risk of injury to individuals in particular instances. Confidentiality takes precedence, even if occasionally some people are harmed.

The inquiring lawyer in our fact situation does not know, nor should he be deemed to know, that the parent's abusive conduct will continue. Requiring disclosure under these circumstances undermines the adversary system. If clients cannot be assured that what they tell their lawyers will be held in confidence, they may withhold damaging information and lawyers will be prevented from counseling their clients to refrain from contemplated wrongful acts. The deterrent effect of lawyers' advice to clients undoubtedly forestalls many actions that would be harmful to individuals or society. In the case under consideration, the attorney may be able to deter further acts of child abuse by counseling his client. He should stress the harm and danger of the conduct and the harsh consequences that may result if he persists. The attorney may encourage his client to seek therapy or psychological counseling.

(2) As to the second inquiry, the committee believes that the parents' attorney should not suggest to the court that counsel be appointed for the children because it would not be in his clients' best interests to have counsel appointed for a child whose interests are adverse to his clients.... Suggesting appointment of counsel may also be an impermissible breach of confidence. [I]nformation indicating conflicting interests would come within the broad definition of confidences and secrets, which cannot be disclosed under Canon 4; such disclosure would also be contrary to the Canon 7 requirement of zealous representation.

[T]he attorney for a parent in child custody proceedings does not concurrently represent the child. The child need not be represented because "[p]resumably he or she is protected by the requirement of substantive law providing that custody is to be awarded 'according to the best interest of the child'." ...

2. *Preliminary Draft of Proposed Ethics Opinion 84–1*

Proposal Number II Prepared by Wellington Wright, Esquire

. . .

(1) As to the first inquiry, the committee believes that the attorney should reveal the information. Because of the helplessness of children at the hands of abusive parents, the overriding concern for welfare and protection of children must take precedence over the client's right to

confidentiality. The child may be in great jeopardy and the parents' lawyer may be the only one who knows of such danger. The child is undoubtedly too intimidated, ignorant, or embarrassed to tell anyone. She apparently has told no one in two years. The child placement process has been invoked by filing the neglect petition, and the client's disclosure is highly relevant to the issues raised. Absent the lawyer's disclosure, however, the information will almost certainly remain secret. Some intervention is necessary to assess the situation and devise protection, counseling and treatment.

It is for the courts to decide the best interest of the children and, in order to make a wise decision, courts should have all of the information available. The attorney has knowledge of activities which indicate his client's propensity for sexually abusing his young daughter, and that it may be a crime of a continuing nature. Although Canon 4 requires lawyers to maintain clients' confidences, an exception is made when the information relates to a client's intention to commit a crime. DR 4– 101(C)(3) of the Marshall CPR permits a lawyer to reveal "[t]he intention of his client to commit a crime and the information necessary to prevent the crime." In some jurisdictions (Florida, for example), the language of the Code of Professional Responsibility is mandatory and *requires* the lawyer to reveal the intention of a client to commit a crime.

Model Rule 1.6 prohibits lawyers from revealing information relating to the representation of a client unless the client consents, with the exception that "[a] lawyer may reveal such information to the extent the lawyer reasonably believes necessary: (1) to prevent the client from committing a criminal act that the lawyer believes is likely to result in imminent death or substantial bodily harm...." It is reasonable to believe that, without some type of intervention, the crime of incest will continue and will have grave consequences for the child's physical, emotional, and mental health. Such conduct is universally condemned and studies show that parental incest is a traumatic experience for a child and is likely to cause severe and long-lasting harm.

. . .

[T]he committee recognizes that DR 7–102(B) of the ABA Code and the Marshall CPR has been amended to exempt privileged communications from the requirement that the attorney reveal a client's fraud if he refuses to rectify it. Nevertheless, if not on the basis of fraud, then on the basis of continuing crime, the lawyer should disclose the information. Averting the possibility of grave harm to children should take precedence over the obligation to preserve clients' confidences.

(2) As to the second inquiry, the committee believes that if the court does not appoint counsel for the children, the attorney should suggest that counsel be appointed. The parents' lawyer does not represent the children. They are not parties to the proceedings, but will be greatly affected by the outcome and should have their own counsel appointed to represent their interests.

. . .

In the situation under consideration the children should be represented, and if the court does not appoint counsel for them, the parents' lawyer should suggest that the court do so, because no one else in the proceeding represents them. Although a petition alleging child abuse or neglect is filed on behalf of a child by the welfare department, the state attorney who represents the petitioner is a prosecutor whose goal is to prove the abuse or neglect alleged in the petition. The welfare department's responsibility is toward the entire family which may conflict with the children's best interest.

3. *Preliminary Draft of Proposed Ethics Opinion 84–1*

Proposal Number III Prepared by Wallace Good, Esquire

. . .

(1) As to the first inquiry, the committee believes that the attorney may reveal the information, but is not required to do so. Two important interests are in conflict: society's interest in protecting children versus the sanctity of the attorney-client relationship. The helplessness of children too young, frightened, and confused to escape the abuse and neglect or to communicate effectively, can create severe tensions and conflicts for the lawyer. On one hand, his duty under Canon 7 of the Marshall CPR is to represent his client zealously and under Canon 4 his duty is to preserve the client's confidences and secrets. On the other hand, EC 7–10 says, it is the duty of the lawyer "to treat with consideration all persons involved in the legal process and to avoid infliction of needless harm."

If the lawyer reasonably believes that this two-year pattern of recurring sexual abuse will continue, in spite of his client's protestations to the contrary, the lawyer may regard it as being in the nature of a continuing crime that may be revealed under DR 4–101(C)(3) of the Marshall CPR as an exception to the requirement of confidentiality of client's communications. This is consistent with modern medical and social science data recognizing a "battered child syndrome" as a recurring pattern of child abuse. Likewise, under Model Rule 1.6, a lawyer who reasonably believes disclosure is necessary to prevent a client from committing a criminal act which the lawyer believes is likely to result in "substantial bodily harm" may make such disclosure. Codes of professional responsibility in some other states are even stronger, requiring rather than permitting lawyers to reveal clients' intentions to commit crimes.

The Terminology section of the Model Rules defines "reasonably believes" (a term used in Rule 1.6) as denoting "that the lawyer believes the matter in question and that the circumstances are such that the belief is reasonable." Incest with a young child is a crime, and it is reasonable to believe that it will continue, but whether it will result in "substantial bodily harm" may be less clear. Emotional or psychological harm may be considered "mental" rather than "bodily" harm.

Even if the lawyer reasonably believes the sexual abuse will continue and that it will result in substantial bodily harm, he still has discretion under the Marshall CPR and the Model Rules as to whether or not to reveal the information. If in exercising his discretion he decides not to reveal, the child will be left unprotected from exploitation and harm by parents entrusted with her care.

Also of concern to the lawyer is his knowledge that his disclosure may lead to invocation of the criminal process, foster or institutional care for the child or children, and termination of parental rights. These are all drastic measures which some authorities believe may be even more harmful to a child than the incestuous relationship itself....

Thus, whether or not the lawyer should reveal his client's incest depends, first, on the substantive law and second, on his own judgment and assessment of the situation. Since he has discretion in the matter under the Marshall CPR, he will have to decide whether protection of the client's confidences should take precedence over the safety and welfare of children.

(2) As to the second inquiry, the committee believes that the parents' attorney should suggest to the court that counsel be appointed for the children if the court does not do so on its own initiative. This suggestion could be made without disclosing any confidential information to the court by simply suggesting appointment of counsel without specifying a reason, and would be a small intrusion on the attorney-client relationship compared to the crucial interest at stake.

Even if counsel for the children is appointed, the parents' lawyer cannot assume that counsel will learn of the incest, and this leads to another question: May the parents' lawyer disclose the information to the children's counsel? Although the question was not raised by inquiring attorney, the committee addresses it as an important related question, governed by our answer to the inquiring attorney's first question. Unfortunately, neither the Marshall CPR nor the Model Rules specifies to whom disclosure of clients' confidences should be made when required or permitted by the rules. It is the committee's opinion, however, that if the parents' lawyer determines that he may or must disclose his clients' confidences, he should make disclosure to the tribunal or other authority, but not to counsel for the children, because the parents' attorney and children's counsel represent conflicting interests.

. . .

Letter to Lawrence Sage, Esq., Chairperson, Marshall State Bar Ass'n Comm. on Professional Ethics

Dear Larry:

When we took our straw vote on this inquiry a couple of weeks ago, I didn't fully realize how complicated this "Catch–22" situation is. After studying the Truly, Wright and Good proposed opinions and the reports of the experts on child abuse, I am more perplexed than ever about how to vote. I am glad we will be able to discuss the matter further at our next meeting. Here are some random thoughts that occurred to me as I pondered the draft opinions.

(1) Allowing disclosure to be within the discretion of the parents' or children's lawyers has some obvious advantages for lawyers in general, such as providing for flexibility in assessment of the seriousness of the crime and degree of harm likely to be inflicted. A lawyer cannot be disciplined for making a bad judgment call. This is supported by a statement in the Scope section of the Model Rules, "[t]he lawyer's exercise of discretion not to disclose information under Rule 1.6 should not be subject to reexamination. Permitting such reexamination would be incompatible with the general policy of promoting compliance with law through assurances that communications will be protected against disclosure."

On the negative side, lawyers exempt from discipline for failure to make disclosure will be tempted to take the easy way out and never disclose, even when the Code of Professional Responsibility grants them discretion to reveal future crimes. They will pride themselves on their virtue in protecting their client's confidences while ignoring their callous indifference to the suffering of the weakest members of society, abused children.

(2) Another undesirable result of discretionary disclosure is that the same set of facts will produce contrary results at the hands of individual lawyers. The American public will see this as illogical and unconscionable. Respect for law and our legal system will not be enhanced by such arbitrary decision-making.

(3) If breach of confidentiality is a possibility, the question arises as to whether the lawyer should advise his client of the possibility of disclosure at the outset of representation.

. . .

(4) Another question is whether silence on the lawyer's part as to the damning information of his client's incestuous activity constitutes a deception on the court. The court needs all relevant information bearing on the best interest and welfare of young, helpless children. By remaining silent, the lawyer is allowing confidentiality to take precedence over his own humanitarian impulses to help extricate an innocent third party from a harmful and perhaps dangerous situation. Many laypersons would be shocked at the lawyer's professionally-imposed callousness in keeping the information secret.

. . .

(5) Let's assume the parents' lawyer decides that his duty is to reveal their secret; how would he go about it? For one thing, he could tell the parents that professional ethics require or permit, depending on whether the language of the pertinent ethics code is mandatory or permissive, that he reveal the information. In Marshall it is permissive. (Should he have advised them of this possibility at the outset

before he received the information, as discussed in my third question?) The lawyer could suggest in his advice to the child protection agency that the prosecutor or the court set up an appropriate treatment program for the entire family which would be supervised by the agency or the court. If the parents agree to cooperate and participate in such a program, the prosecutor or the court might agree to drop or suspend the neglect charges and to take no immediate action in regard to the incest admission. With this kind of intervention and help it might be possible to keep the family together and to spare the child the further trauma of court proceedings and possible foster home or institutional care, or permanent parental severance. If this kind of help is not available or the parents do not want it, then whether or not the lawyer should reveal, depends on which of the three proposed opinions prevails.

I look forward to comments from other committee members before we vote on these very difficult and troubling issues at our next meeting.

Cordially yours,
/s/
Frederick R. Fencestradler
Attorney at Law

. . .

Note on Thurman's tale: Caring, polarization, and lawyering

1. The concept of "empowerment" is intended to capture one approach to representation. In what ways, if at all, does the term suggest something different from the traditional concept of what it would mean to "represent" the parents in the problem situation?

Compare the issues raised in Section I, 4, (a) and (c), pp. 66–77, 117–22 above.

2. If your approach to your work as a lawyer were oriented to an "ethic of care," in what ways, if any, would you carry out your representation of the mother and father differently from the ways described in the hypothetical responses to the problem that Thurman has posed? In that connection, consider, among others that you think relevant, the following questions:

(a) Does Veronica Truly's decision manifest "care" for the father? Does Wellington Wright's decision manifest "care" for the child? For whom (or what) does Wallace Good care? What of Frederick Fencestradler?

(b) What is the relation between "caring" and "polarization"? It is easy to see Truly's and Wright's responses as polarized: In what sense, if any, may the same be said of Good? Again, what of Fencestradler?

3. (a) What light, if any, does your thinking about the preceding questions shed on the question whether an "ethic of care" is a viable model of lawyering?

(b) To the extent that you believe that it is not, what are the principal impediments to its viability?

4.   For an application of a similar approach to a problem involving the representation of a physically abusive parent, see Naomi Cahn, A Preliminary Feminist Critique of Legal Ethics, 4 Geo.J.L.Eth. 23, 39–41 (1990).

THE SOCIAL RESPONSIBILITIES OF LAWYERS: CASE STUDIES
Philip B. Heymann & Lance Liebman
Pp. 216–29 (1988).

Nancy Barrett * . . . was a third year associate working on food and drug law at the large Washington, D.C., law firm of Payne & Brewster (P & B) and had become the firm's expert on caffeine.   Barrett joined the firm in September 1978, primarily because of its reputation in the area of food and drug law.   She majored in biology in college and upon graduating from Stanford University *magna cum laude* went to work as a legislative aide to Senator John Mansfield of California, Chairman of the Committee on Health and Environment.   She worked for the Senator for three years, becoming involved in a number of public health issues including toxic chemicals, pesticides, drug regulation, and food labeling.   She was given a great deal of responsibility; however, she realized early on that a law degree was an essential credential in government work: "Most of the 'power brokers' were lawyers."

In September 1975, Barrett entered Boalt Hall School of Law at Berkeley.   She did well in her course work. . . .   She also maintained her interest in public health and wrote a paper on the history of food and drug law.   P & B, one of the largest and oldest law firms in Washington, was happy to add Nancy Barrett to its ranks. . . .   Approximately 15 attorneys practiced food and drug law on a full time basis. The firm hired only the "cream of the crop" from the top law schools, and Barrett had the right credentials plus experience.

Barrett had had several other attractive offers, including one from the U.S. Food and Drug Administration (FDA), but thought that P & B would provide her with excellent training and experience. . . .   [H]er plans were to stay at P & B for two to three years and then go back into the government.

Barrett loved the food and drug law area.   It was exciting and full of such important policy issues as public health and safety, consumer freedom of choice, and product development.   The history of food and drug law in the U.S. exemplified these conflicting policy tensions.

Congress enacted the Pure Food and Drugs Act in 1906.   The Act took a straightforward approach to food regulation.   It defined "adul-

* This case is fiction, adapted (and altered) from several experiences reported by Washington lawyers.   The information on caffeine is not comprehensive and should not be relied upon to form any conclusions about its health effects. . . .   [fn. by the authors]

terated" and "misbranded" foods and drugs and prohibited their shipment across state lines. Food was adulterated if it "contained any added poisonous or other deleterious ingredient which could render such article injurious to health." The focus was on whether the food itself, as opposed to the added substance, was injurious to health. A product was "misbranded" if it included statements that were false or misleading or failed to provide required information in labeling.

In 1938, Congress altered food and drug regulation substantially by adopting the Food, Drug, and Cosmetic Act (FDCA). In addition to food and drugs, the FDCA regulated cosmetics and therapeutic devices. It required manufacturers to provide scientific proof that new products were safe before putting them on the market, and prohibited companies from adding poisonous substances to foods unless doing so was unavoidable or required in production. To aid enforcement, the FDCA allowed false drug claims to be barred without proof of fraud and permitted federal court injunctions.

The current food and drug law, which includes the FDCA, the 1958 Food Additives Amendment, the 1960 Color Additives Amendment, and the 1962 Drug Amendments, is lengthy and complicated—the product of many forces and of legislative compromises. Its fundamentals, however, are simple and practical and reflect the framework of the 1906 law....

The 1958 Food Additives Amendment to the FDCA was particularly relevant to Barrett's work on caffeine. The amendment, enacted in response to public concern over the content of packaged foods, shifted the burden of proof to the food manufacturer to show the safety of prospective additives before marketing any food containing them. The amendment required the manufacturer to petition the FDA to establish a regulation for safe use of the additive. The petition must include health effect data, dose-response levels, and other evidence of safety investigation as established by lengthy and costly animal tests and sometimes human tests.

The amendment also expanded the definition of "adulterated" to include foods that contain either: (1) a food additive that has not been approved as "safe" by FDA, or (2) an approved food additive that is present in a quantity exceeding a tolerance level established by FDA.

One of the major issues in the ten years of congressional debate on the amendment was how additives then in use would be treated under the new law. In the end, Congress excluded a substantial portion of existing food additives from the extensive testing requirements. Specifically excluded were: (a) "prior sanctioned" substances—those that had received official approval in earlier years and had a type of "grandfather status"; (b) "generally recognized as safe" items, or the GRAS list. The GRAS list, established by regulation, included some 700 substances, among them such well known additives as ascorbic acid (vitamin C), caffeine, cinnamon, MSG, BHA, BHT, sugar, pepper, mustard, cyclamates, and saccharin.

FDA's decisions to place a substance on the original GRAS list were based on the data available at the time the lists were established and on the then current state of knowledge in the field of toxicology. Likewise, the pre–1958 approvals by FDA that qualified substances for prior-sanctioned status reflected the best safety judgments that could be made at the time. In 1970, FDA initiated a "GRAS review" program and established a select committee on GRAS substances (SCOGS) to evaluate the items on the GRAS list. The review resulted in the initiation by FDA of more than 65 rulemaking proceedings in which the agency proposed either to affirm the GRAS status of the substance under review or, where appropriate, to take action to restrict or prohibit use of the substance.

One of the most interesting GRAS substances, and one that has been the subject of much attention, is caffeine. Caffeine is a strong stimulant of the central nervous system. It occurs naturally in tea leaves and in coffee, cocoa, and kola nuts, but can also be made synthetically. It is often added to soft drinks as a flavor enhancer and because it results in something called "mouth feel" (a distinctive sensation on the tongue). Some consumer groups contend that manufacturers add caffeine to soft drinks because of its addictive qualities in order to get kids "hooked." FDA had specifically listed caffeine as GRAS as a multiple purpose ingredient in cola-type beverages, at a level not to exceed 0.02% of the beverage.

Caffeine has been under scientific study since its isolation in the laboratory in 1820. Short term effects of caffeine on the body are generally well known. The substance: (a) allays drowsiness, (b) enables one to work faster and to think more clearly, (c) stimulates the brain, heart muscle, and kidneys, (d) alters the metabolism of fat, (e) dilates the blood vessels, (f) causes insulin to be released, and (g) increases the production of stomach acid. Persons who drink large amounts of coffee (15–20 cups a day) may develop "caffeinism" which can result in insomnia, a slight fever, and irritability. What is not known is whether caffeine has long-term effects on human health.

As a result of GRAS review, in mid 1979, SCOGS determined that "while no evidence in the available information on caffeine demonstrates a hazard to the public when it is used at levels that are now current and in the manner now practiced, uncertainties exist requiring that additional studies ... be conducted."

In ... 1980, ... FDA specifically proposed to remove caffeine from the GRAS list and place it on an interim food additive list and to declare that no prior sanction existed for the use of caffeine as an added food ingredient.

Under the FDA proposal, current uses of added caffeine would be permitted under an interim food additive regulation pending the completion of studies necessary to resolve questions about the safety of caffeine added to food.... FDA proposed to require both animal and human epidemiological studies. Performance of the studies would be a condition to continued use of the substance under the interim regulation.

Due to evidence which had recently been developed concerning the capacity of caffeine to cause birth defects in rats, FDA's primary concern about caffeine was its potential teratogenicity. Although the proposed FDA regulation acknowledged the uncertainty concerning the link between caffeine and birth defects in humans, it concluded that available data from animal studies were significant enough to be of serious concern and to justify additional research to clarify the uncertainties about caffeine's potential teratogenicity in humans.

In addition to studies regarding caffeine's teratogenic effects, FDA proposed to require studies addressing the capacity of caffeine to cause adverse reproductive effects and cancer.

With regard to the teratogenic effects of caffeine, FDA reviewed animal data existing prior to 1979. Many of the studies had deficiencies (e.g., lack of proper control animals, small number of animals, insufficient information on procedures), and many of them were conducted a decade or more ago when teratology study techniques were less developed. Despite these deficiencies, the studies demonstrated that at sufficiently high levels of exposure, well above levels to which humans are normally exposed, caffeine could cause birth defects in animals. The studies were not adequate, however, to determine with any confidence a "no effect level" for the teratogenic effects of caffeine for animals, i.e., the level of exposure at which no teratogenic effects are observed.

Due to the uncertainties left by the existing animal data, the FDA in 1979 initiated two teratology studies of caffeine in laboratory animals using up-to-date teratology test methods. The results of one of the studies—the gavage study, in which mice were force-fed measured amounts of caffeine through a stomach tube—raised serious concerns about caffeine because it was the first large, well designed, and controlled teratology study on caffeine to show irreversible terata (e.g., missing digits) at levels of caffeine exposure not significantly greater than those to which humans might be exposed in the food supply. The problem, however, was whether animal teratology studies in general and rat studies on caffeine in particular were reliable indicators of human risk.

It is difficult to interpret teratology studies. No single test species can be said to predict accurately the human response to a given chemical. For example, there are physiological and biological differences between rats and humans that affect the way the body processes a substance. There is some indication that humans and experimental animals metabolize caffeine differently.

FDA also reviewed six human epidemiological studies that dealt with the teratological effects of caffeine, but most of those studies had methodological problems that made it virtually impossible to draw valid inferences from the results.

With regard to the potential carcinogenic effects of caffeine, FDA concluded in its proposed regulations that the available data were inadequate and incomplete. No lifetime feeding studies of caffeine met currently accepted toxicological testing criteria, nor were there acceptable epidemiological data linking human exposure to caffeine with a significant increase in the incidence of cancer.

Public interest groups supported FDA's efforts to regulate the use of caffeine and, in fact, urged FDA to go further in its control of the additive. The Center for Science in the Public Interest (CSPI), in Washington, D.C., submitted a petition to FDA requesting that it issue a regulation requiring all packages of tea and coffee that contain caffeine to carry a plainly visible warning advising that consumption of the product may be harmful to the unborn children of pregnant women and that FDA initiate an education campaign designed to inform pregnant women about the possibility that excessive consumption of caffeine could interfere with reproduction.

One of the most interesting projects Barrett had worked on thus far at P & B was for one of the firm's largest clients: The American Soft Drink Council (ASDC). ASDC had come to P & B five months ago, two weeks after FDA issued its proposal to tighten the regulatory grip on caffeine.

The 1,400 members of the American Soft Drink Council were concerned about FDA's proposed rule to remove caffeine from the GRAS list. Approximately 75 percent of the nation's soft drinks contained added caffeine. Although caffeine is a natural ingredient of cola drinks (as kola nuts contain caffeine), much is removed during processing, and an additional quantity is added to many colas for flavor and to give them extra "spark" or "liveliness."

. . .

The ASDC was critical of FDA's proposed rule. The trade association specifically criticized the rationale for the rule, citing weaknesses in the studies relied on and the equivocal nature of the data.

. . .

ASDC maintained that FDA's proposal was not justified under the law or under the present state of scientific knowledge and requested that FDA reaffirm that added caffeine is generally recognized as safe in soft drinks, including cola-type beverages, pepper-type beverages, and other soda water beverages.

The ASDC came to P & B to have them prepare comments on FDA's proposed regulation. Specifically, the manufacturers contended that (1) FDA sanctioned the use of caffeine in soft drinks prior to 1958, and (2) caffeine should remain on the GRAS list.

Barrett was given the task of preparing the comments for ASDC on the prior sanction issue. She immediately sent a Freedom of Information Act letter to FDA to obtain copies of all the FDA's correspondence on caffeine. Within several months, after pouring through hundreds of

FDA files, she had collected five two-inch-thick notebooks full of prior correspondence and FDA pronouncements on the substance. She reviewed the entire file, combing through the documents to determine if FDA had expressly or implicitly approved the use of caffeine as a food additive prior to 1958.

Barrett put together three lines of argument for the proposition that caffeine should be subject to a prior sanction based on FDA's course of conduct, correspondence, and other action between the enactment of the Federal Food and Drug Act of 1906 and the Food Additives Amendment of 1958.

. . .

Although she believed she had put together a strong case for prior sanction, Nancy wondered if the prior sanction route was appropriate in this case. Just one month ago—March 1981—an article had appeared in the *New England Journal of Medicine* describing research by scientists at the Harvard School of Public Health suggesting a statistical link between the drinking of coffee and cancer of the pancreas.

The researchers questioned 369 patients with cancer of the pancreas about their use of tobacco, alcohol, tea, and coffee. A control group of 644 patients, who were hospitalized for a variety of reasons unrelated to cancer of the pancreas, was asked the same set of questions. A surprisingly strong association was found between coffee consumption and pancreatic cancer in both sexes. The scientists speculated that if the association was confirmed and found to be causal, coffee might be found to contribute to more than half of the 20,000 deaths from this disease each year.

. . .

Barrett knew that the Harvard study was controversial and had some methodological problems, but she was not sure how serious they were. Just two days ago an article had appeared in the *New York Times,* criticizing the study. The story quoted a medical school dean as saying that the investigators who questioned patients on their prehospitalization coffee habits knew in advance which ones had cancer, and that this could have introduced unintentional bias in the results.

Clearly, a number of significant business interests had a stake in FDA's proposed regulation. It sounded to Barrett as if there might be some basis for concern about the link between caffeine and cancer, but she did not have the technical background to evaluate the study results. If the study results were correct, perhaps caffeine should be removed from the GRAS list and perhaps the industry should not press its legal argument that caffeine had received a prior sanction from FDA.

Prior sanction status would protect the industry by putting the burden of proof on FDA to show that caffeine is injurious to health—a difficult task given the equivocal nature of the scientific data. But Barrett started to worry that even if the industry could successfully achieve prior sanction status for its use of caffeine, doing so would impose health risks on the public. She thought that perhaps Congress had been wrong in enacting the prior sanction provision—that the provision might fail to recognize changes in technology and in the ability of modern science to detect harmful substances. If new additives could be used only after a company proved that they were safe, should a showing of safety be required as to caffeine, at least once the ingredient's safety had been challenged by reputable scientists?

Barrett knew that if FDA believed caffeine to be harmful, it could begin a regulatory proceeding and ban use of the substance under 21 C.F.R. 181.1(b). If FDA issued such a rule, the industry could persuade a court to invalidate it only by showing the rule to be "arbitrary and capricious," a difficult test to meet. But she thought the political environment—the strength of the industry and the vast public who consume caffeine daily in soft drinks and coffee—would deter the FDA from putting this particular safety issue at the top of its agenda.

While Barrett was still struggling with the soft drink issue, Donald Porter, a senior partner at the firm, asked her to attend a meeting in his office with a new client. Porter had been at P & B for almost 21 years and was one of the leading food and drug lawyers in the nation. His first assignment at P & B was working on the 1962 Drug Amendments to the FDCA in the wake of the tragic thalidomide case. He had taught about food and drug law at law schools, and had published extensively on the topic. Barrett respected him a great deal.

When Barrett arrived at Porter's office, Porter introduced her to Roger Dubarry, president of Dubarry Foods, Inc. Dubarry was a client of Benjamin Freedland, a corporate attorney at P & B....

Dubarry Foods produced a wide variety of food products in the U.S. and imported some specialty items from Europe for distribution here. Among the imported items was "Cocolait," a powdered chocolate milk drink mix. The product had been sold in France for ten years under the name "Cocaulait" and in the U.S. for five years. Dubarry Foods had been marketing Cocolait in this country without disclosure on the label that caffeine was added to the product. Although some caffeine is present naturally in cocoa, an additional amount was added to the chocolate milk drink mix to counteract the soporific effects of warm milk. Dubarry was especially nervous given the recent *New England Journal of Medicine* article on caffeine and pancreatic cancer and the FDA proposal to remove caffeine from the GRAS list.

Roger Dubarry was disturbed by the recent media focus on caffeine and wanted to know whether he was absolutely required to include caffeine on the label of his chocolate milk drink mix. He was under the impression that there were exceptions to the labeling requirements for which he might qualify. He also mentioned that some of his competitors added caffeine to their chocolate milk products and did not list caffeine on their labels. He asked Porter if he could have someone study the issue. Porter asked Barrett to research the caffeine labeling requirements and to have a response for Dubarry by the end of the week.

Barrett ... went through the possible legal arguments why Dubarry should not have to include caffeine on the label:

1. *Caffeine is a natural constituent of cocoa beans and therefore need not be declared on the label.* This argument would not hold water. Although inherent constituents of natural ingredients need not be labelled, the regulations made a clear distinction between natural and "added" ingredients. Added ingredients had to be included on the label, and Dubarry admitted that caffeine was added to the product.

2. *Compliance with the labeling requirements would result in "unfair competition."* This argument was also weak. The statute, 21 U.S.C. § 343(i), provided that a food need not include all ingredients on the label if such labeling resulted in deception or unfair competition. One might argue that because most of Dubarry's competitors were also adding caffeine and not disclosing it on the label, if he were to disclose the fact on his label he would be hurt competitively. But the statute further provided that this provision could only be used if the Secretary of Health and Human Services promulgated a regulation exempting the food from the labeling requirements. No such regulation had been promulgated for chocolate milk.

3. *Caffeine is a "flavoring" and, therefore, exempt from a requirement that it be specifically named on the label.* The statute specifies that if a food is fabricated from two or more ingredients, the label must include "the common or usual name of each such ingredient; except that spices, flavorings and colorings, other than those sold as such, may be designated as spices, flavorings, and colorings without naming each." Regulations provided that both "artificial or natural flavors" could be declared as such in the statement of ingredients. The caffeine added to Cocolait was natural caffeine as opposed to synthetic caffeine and therefore would be a natural flavoring. The regulations defined natural flavoring as any substance whose significant function in food is flavoring rather than nutritional and which is derived from plants or animals. The regulations also provided that natural flavors included the "natural essence or extractives" obtained from plants and other substances listed in the regulations. Caffeine did not appear in any of these lists, but one could argue that it fell within the broad definition of flavors in the regulations. Caffeine is used on a limited basis as an added ingredient in several categories of non-beverage foods, including baked goods, frozen dairy desserts, gelatin puddings, and fillings, in part as a flavoring agent. The "flavor" line was Dubarry's strongest argument. If he did not want to include "caffeine" on the label he might get away with adding the natural flavor wording. But knowing FDA's most

recent thinking about caffeine and its desire to have caffeine separately disclosed on the label as expressed in a recently proposed rule, Barrett did not believe this route would be sanctioned by FDA either.

4. Finally, there was another reason Dubarry might decide not to change its labels—an enforcement reason. *In small amounts it would be almost impossible to detect whether the caffeine was added or within the natural variation of cocoa.* However, Barrett did not believe this was a valid reason and did not think it appropriate to mention it to the company.

Overall, she thought the legal arguments for Dubarry were weak, but she had a difficult time thinking of reasons why it was in the interest of Dubarry Foods to comply, especially given the difficulty of distinguishing added from natural caffeine and therefore the difficulty of enforcement. If it did comply, the company might be hurt competitively. The best argument she could make was that if FDA or a consumer group discovered the company's misrepresentation, there could be serious sanctions and significant adverse publicity that would hurt sales.

On Friday, April 24, she presented the results of her research and her conclusion to Donald Porter. He basically agreed with her assessment. The meeting with Dubarry was scheduled for Monday, April 27th. Unfortunately, Porter was going to be out of town on vacation for the next three weeks so he would not be able to attend the meeting. Benjamin Freedland, who had referred Dubarry to Porter and knew quite a bit about Dubarry Foods, would take his place. Freedland had been at the firm ten years. Early in his career he practiced food and drug law but now he practiced general corporate law. Barrett had worked with him a few times and found him to be a brilliant attorney, always thorough and thoughtful.

On Monday, Barrett was prepared to present her findings. She went through the list of legal arguments one by one and shot each one down, concluding that Dubarry had no choice but to include caffeine on the label. She was somewhat taken aback, however, when Freedland quickly jumped in after she presented her conclusion: "Wait a minute, Nancy," he said. "It's not so clear to me that Dubarry must include caffeine on its Cocolait labels. I think that the company would be within the law as long as it included the phrase 'and natural flavors' on the package. There appears to be a solid basis in the law for going that route."

Barrett tried to disagree, but Roger Dubarry broke in: "I agree with Ben. It sounds like we have a pretty good legal argument. Besides, what would FDA do to me if the argument does not hold up? And how likely would it be that they would find out in the first place?"

Freedland took over at this point and answered the question as best he could. First, he explained the difficulty FDA would have in finding out whether caffeine was, in fact, added to the product given that caffeine occurs naturally in cocoa. Second, he indicated that if FDA were to find out it would probably be from a competitor and that this was unlikely since Dubarry's competitors also added caffeine to their products.

At this point Barrett interjected: "But, Mr. Freedland, there's always the possibility that one of Mr. Dubarry's competitors will develop a caffeine free chocolate milk drink mix just like many soft drink manufacturers are doing. Once that happens, the competitor is likely to go to FDA and ask them to enforce the labeling requirement."

Dubarry seemed to think this was unlikely. He asked Freedland what FDA would do if it did decide to enforce the rule.

"First of all," Freedland replied, "the agency would conduct an investigation. Field inspectors would want to collect samples of the product from your warehouses. But, as I said before, even if they analyze the powdered mix in the laboratory it will be difficult for them to determine whether caffeine has been added or is a part of the natural constituents in cocoa, especially if the amount is within the natural variation of caffeine in cocoa."

Freedland continued: "Next, FDA may ask for records of the formula for the mix from your supplier. It is much more difficult for FDA to get records for an imported product than a domestic one but it may be able to obtain them. If it did get a copy, the agency would be able to prove that the product contained added caffeine. If it were able to put together some evidence of added caffeine, the agency would send you a 'regulatory letter,' and might take some significant action such as detaining your imported supply at customs. FDA has virtually unlimited regulatory authority over imported products, much greater than it does over domestic goods. An even more drastic step it could take would be to request that you recall the product that is on the market. Arguably the agency has no legal authority to do this, but if it gets to this stage, it is usually best to comply as FDA does have the authority to take much more drastic legal actions including seizure of the product, bringing criminal suit against the president of the company, or issuing adverse publicity."

"But how likely is it that FDA would require me to recall the product?" Dubarry asked.

"Based on my experience with FDA, not very likely," Freedland responded.

At this point, Barrett broke in. She had been biting her tongue for the last 15 minutes. She was surprised at the way Freedland was handling the issue and did not agree with his assessment at all.

"I'm not so sure that's true in this case, Mr. Freedland," she said. "Given FDA's recent concern about caffeine and the susceptibility of children to caffeine in this type of product, they might request a recall. In addition," she continued, "consumer groups might bring suit for fraud or make adverse public statements about the product. Recently, several consumer groups have been analyzing soft drinks for caffeine and publishing the results. They are likely to do the same thing for chocolate milk products. Also, someone who has an allergic reaction to caffeine might bring suit for your failure to include caffeine on the label."

"But, Nancy," Freedland countered, "if the person is really sensitive to caffeine, the company would be likely to win the suit, given the fact that caffeine is a natural ingredient in chocolate products. And, as I said earlier, there is a strong legal argument that caffeine is a natural flavor, and as such need not be included by name on the label."

Before Barrett could respond, Dubarry broke in. "I agree with you, Ben. It sounds to me like we have a good legal basis for not including caffeine on the label, and I'd like a letter from your law firm on that for my files."

"Sure, Roger," he responded, and turned toward Barrett. "Nancy, I'll leave it to you to work something out with Roger. I suggest you put together a draft for him to look at sometime this week."

On that note, the meeting ended. Nancy Barrett went back to her office. She was sure when she went into the meeting that Dubarry should include caffeine on the label. Now she was less sure, especially given Freedland's response. But she still did not feel comfortable about writing the letter. She wondered if she should talk more to Freedland about it, or wait until Donald Porter got back from his vacation, or talk to Dubarry. Perhaps she should seek guidance from an expert at the FDA, she thought.

It was 12:30 p.m. She was going to meet a friend for lunch, someone she knew and trusted. She hoped her friend could help her sort through her dilemma.

Note on Heymann & Liebman's tale: Claiming, and sharing, power

1. The effort to integrate client empowerment with lawyer autonomy is seriously affected by the relative power of attorney and client vis-a-vis one another. This factor is usually not addressed openly, and if taken into account is typically regarded, *sub silentio,* as self-evidently dispositive. As with other barriers to the exercise of choice and responsibility, this book attempts to treat the question as one that is important to address frontally, and as one whose capacity to trump all other considerations needs to be evaluated situationally and not assumed *a priori.*

2. Where the power imbalance is in the client's favor—as it typically is in private practice—the problem is often whether it is possible for an attorney to succeed in practice without surrendering most of his or her autonomy. The "Cocolait" problem presents what may be the most difficult context, that where power is a pervasively dispositive factor and the

opportunities for resolving the apparent dilemma between client autonomy and lawyer autonomy seem at their weakest. Consider these questions:

- What options did Nancy Barrett have?

- What would you have done in her shoes?

- What options does she have now, against the possibility that she will be placed in a similar situation again?

- What is the lesson to be drawn from the story?

3. The easier variety of question, for the attorney, arises in those cases where the balance of power is in the lawyer's favor, where the client lacks the resources—usually, money—to command influence in decision-making. Here, the lawyer's discretion is not so evidently constrained by fear of losing the client, and his or her concept of the attorney-client relation may appear to have more of an independent role to play.

The leading presentation of a general argument for the need to revise the traditional ideas of professional autonomy, if lawyers for poor people are to serve their needs adequately, is Stephen Wexler, Practicing Law for Poor People, 79 Yale L.J. 1049 (1970). The premise of his prescription is the perception that "two major touchstones of traditional legal practice— the solving of legal problems and the one-to-one relationship between attorney and client—are either not relevant to poor people or harmful to them." Id., at 1053. His conclusion is that lawyers for the poor should devote their skills to the representation of organizations of poor people, representing individuals *only* as it aids in client organization, and that they think of their major lawyering work as the education of their clients rather than advocacy on their behalf. Failure to take these steps, he asserts, is to exalt a dysfunctional concept of professionalism over the needs of clients.

For more specific treatments of the question of the legitimacy of traditional norms of professionalism in the context of the representation of poor people, see New York County Lawyers Ass'n, Committee on Professional Ethics, Opinion No. 645 (1975), dealing with the propriety of a strike by employees of a local legal aid society over issues of lawyer pay and working conditions and the organization's system of providing legal representation, which the strikers believed deprived their clients of adequate representation; and Gary Bellow & Jeanne Kettleson, From Ethics to Politics: Confronting Scarcity and Fairness in Public Interest Practice, 58 B.U.L.Rev. 337, 362–72 (1978), asking whether the "severe systemic disadvantages," id., at 363, that poor people often face require (and justify) disregard by their attorneys of at least some of the traditional limitations on adversariness.

4. Attempts to seek an integration of client empowerment and lawyer autonomy have been portrayed in several contexts of representation in dispute settlement. The following excerpts present alternative approaches, one in the context of advocacy representation in negotiation and the other through mediation.

TOWARD ANOTHER VIEW OF LEGAL NEGOTIATION: THE STRUCTURE OF PROBLEM SOLVING

Carrie Menkel–Meadow
31 U.C.L.A. L.Rev. 754 (1984).

. . .

Much of the legal negotiation literature emphasizes an adversarial model, implying an orientation or approach that focuses on "maximizing victory." This approach is based on the assumption that the parties . . . must be in conflict and [are] bargaining for the same "scarce" items. . . . In the language of game theorists, economists, and psychologists, such negotiations become "zero-sum" or "constant-sum" games and the bargaining engaged in is "distributive" bargaining. Simply put, in the pure adversarial case, each party wants as much as he can get of the thing bargained for, and the more one party receives, the less the other party receives. . . .

Legal negotiations, at least in dispute resolution cases, are marked by another adversarial assumption. Because litigation negotiations are conducted in the "shadow of the law" [Mnookin & Kornhauser, Bargaining in the Shadow of the Law: The Case of Divorce, 88 Yale L.J. 950, 950 (1979)], that is, in the shadow of the courts, the negotiators assume that what is bargained for are the identical, but limited, items a court would award in deciding the case. Typically, it is assumed that all that is bargained for is who will get the most money and who can be compelled to do or not to do something. Indeed, it may be because litigation negotiations are so often conducted in the shadow of the court that they are assumed to be zero-sum games.

In transactional negotiation, the "common business practice" or "form provision" may serve the same limiting function. If the parties cannot resolve a particular point but still prefer to consummate the transaction, they may permit a form provision or common business practice to decide the issue. This may be true even where an unusual provision would more closely meet the parties' needs. Clauses which assign or allocate risks routinely to one side of a transaction are one example. Although transactional negotiations differ from dispute negotiations because in the former no court can force a solution, the two types of negotiation may be analogous where the shadow of the court or the "shadow of the form contract" encourage a habit of mind in the negotiators to rely on common solutions, rather than to pursue solutions which may be more tailored to the parties' particular needs.

These basic adversarial assumptions affect not only the conceptions of negotiations that their proponents asserts, but the behaviors that are recommended for successful negotiation. Indeed, a good portion of the negotiation literature focuses principally on behavioral admonitions, but never examines with any sophistication the sources or assumptions of such tactical injunctions and what their limitations might be.

. . .

The literature of negotiation presents a stylized linear ritual of struggle—planned concessions after high first offers, leading to a compromise point along a linear field of pre-established 'commitment and resistance' points. In such legal negotiations the compromise settlement point is legitimized by comparing it to the polarized demands of plaintiff and defendant and the relatively improved "joint gain" of the compromise point in comparison to the "winner take all" result achieved in court. . . .

. . .

Competitive descriptions of negotiations foster a perception of the negotiator as the principal actor in legal negotiations. Because legal negotiations are so stylized and are based on understanding of a special culture, the lawyer becomes the provider of what the court would order if the case went to trial, or what the law allows in transaction planning. The client, intimidated by these adversarial and specialized proceedings, depends on the lawyer to structure solutions that are "legal" rather than what the client might desire if the client had free rein to determine objectives. The client may also assume that the lawyer knows the only "right" way to accomplish the result and may therefore be hesitant to suggest other alternatives. Although clients generally engage lawyers to do what they cannot do themselves, they do not necessarily wish to relinquish all control over either the desired outcomes or the process by which they are achieved. This is especially true where the negotiation involves parties who will have to continue a relationship with one another, such as partnership or post-dissolution custody relationships. The client may also have an interest in how the negotiation is pursued because, if competitive processes are used, the client may have trouble enforcing the agreement or in continuing a relationship with the other party.

. . .

Certain beliefs about human and legal behavior underlie advice about appropriate and effective negotiation behavior. This section uncovers the assumptions behind the adversarial model.

The difficulty with the literature described above is that it is based on one conception of negotiation goals—maximizing individual gain of a particular kind. What the parties want and how they can best achieve it, however, may vary greatly depending on the subject matter of the dispute, the past relationship of the parties, the costs of "maximizing gain," and a number of other factors.

The adversarial paradigm is based almost exclusively on the simple negotiation over what appears to be one issue, such as price in a buy-sell transaction, or money damages in a personal injury or breach of contract lawsuit. The common assumption in these cases is that the buyer wants the lowest price, the seller the highest; the plaintiff wants the money demanded in the complaint and the defendant wants to resist paying as much as possible. Each dollar to the plaintiff is a commensurate loss to the defendant; the same is true with the buyer and seller. Given this description of the paradigmatic negotiation, the negotiator's goal is simply to maximize gain by winning as much of the material of the negotiation as possible. Underlying this general assumption are really two assumptions: first, that there is only one issue, price; and second, that both parties desire equally and exclusively the thing by which that issue is measured, in most cases, money.

The difficulty with this zero-sum approach to negotiation is not that it is necessarily wrong in all cases, but that it has become the tail that wags the dog. First, true zero-sum games are empirically quite rare. Even in game theory

> the interests of the two players have to be precisely opposed for a game to be "zero-sum." There must be no possible outcome which both would prefer, however slightly, to some other possible outcome. In other words, for every pair of outcomes if one player prefers the first the other must prefer the second.... Even in a game whose outcome is a division of a fixed sum of money between two players, the two players' interests are not generally opposed in this diametric way if there are chance elements in the game and if the players have 'risk aversion'.

[M. Bacharach, Economics and the Theory of Games 7–8, 41 (1976)].

Strictly speaking, a zero-sum game loses its zero-sum qualities and its assumptions when more than one issue is negotiated because trade-offs between issues are possible. In the paradigmatic pricing problem, if one party cares slightly more about when the payment is made (a form of risk aversion) the timing issue will have discount values that render the game less zero-sum. If a dollar is worth more to me today I will take fewer dollars to settle today than next week. This is not necessarily a loss to me and a gain to you since you may or may not have the same preferences as to the timing of payment.

While there may be some paradigmatic zero-sum games in legal negotiations, most are not zero-sum. For example, in a random search of 240 cases taken from 15 federal and state reporters most cases, in terms presented to the court, were not zero-sum disputes. Those that could be characterized as zero-sum were those which require a definitive ruling—evidentiary rulings in criminal cases, determinations that constitutional rights were infringed, or findings that contracts were applicable in particular situations. Most, however, presented multi-issue situations....

Second, at the core of the zero-sum conception is an assumption that parties value the fixed resource equally. The negotiator may assume, for example, that all parties value money equally, rather than finding out how parties value what that money can buy.... If, in a personal injury case, the plaintiff wants money to buy a new car, the defendant might be able to provide such a car directly to the plaintiff at a lower cost than the market price of a new car which defendant would have to pay in settlement.

Third, by assuming that there is only one issue, such as price, other issues or concerns of the parties may be masked and remain unresolved. In a simple "pricing" problem ..., many teachers and students of negotiation see the price ... as the only issue. More astute negotiators will recognize that in addition to price there are issues relating to quantity (with the potential for large quantity discount on price), delivery, timing, and manner of payment. There is also the potential of creating a longer term business relationship....

Finally, by assuming that the material of the negotiation is fixed or limited in some way, the parties may lose opportunities to expand the material before some division is necessary. For example, by assuming that there is a zero-sum dispute about the parties' assets to be divided in a dissolution proceeding, the parties may miss an opportunity to hold a major asset, such as the couple's residence, until such time as the market price rises. While division may be necessary at some point, both parties may increase their eventual share by deferring division and treating timing as another issue in their negotiation.

. . .

The assumption that only limited items are available in dispute resolution occurs because negotiation takes place in the shadow of the courts. Negotiators too often conclude that they are limited to what would be available if the court entered a judgment. To the extent that court resolution of problems results in awards of money damages and injunctions, negotiators are likely to limit their crafting of solutions to those remedies. To the extent that a court would not allow a particular remedy such as barter, exchange, apology, or retributory action, negotiators may reject or not even conceive of these solutions.

. . .

Problem solving is an orientation to negotiation which focuses on finding solutions to the parties' sets of underlying needs and objectives. The problem-solving conception subordinates strategies and tactics to the process of identifying possible solutions and therefore allows a broader range of outcomes to negotiation problems.

. . .

Parties to a negotiation typically have underlying needs or objectives— what they hope to achieve, accomplish, and/or be compensated for as a result of the dispute or transaction. Although litigants typically ask for relief in the form of damages, this relief is actually a proxy for more basic needs or objectives. By attempting to uncover those underlying needs, the problem-solving model presents opportunities for discovering greater numbers of and better quality solutions. It offers the possibility of meeting a greater variety of needs both directly and by trading off different needs, rather than forcing a zero-sum battle over a single item.

The principle underlying such an approach is that unearthing a greater number of the actual needs of the parties will create more possible solutions because not all needs will be mutually exclusive. As a corollary, because not all individuals value the same things in the same way, the exploitation of differential or complementary needs will produce a wider variety of solutions which more closely meet the parties' needs.

A few examples may illustrate these points. In personal injury actions courts usually award monetary damages. Plaintiffs, however, commonly want this money for specific purposes. For instance, an individual who has been injured in a car accident may desire compensation for any or all of the following items: past and future medical expenses, rehabilitation and compensation for the cost of rehabilitation, replacement of damaged property such as a car and the costs of such replacement, lost income, compensation for lost time, pain and suffering, the loss of companionship with one's family, friends and fellow employees and employer, lost opportunities to engage in activities which may no longer be possible, such as backpacking or playing basketball with one's children, vindication or acknowledgement of fault by the responsible party, and retribution or punishment of the person who was at fault. In short, the injured person seeks to be returned to the same physical, psychological, social and economic state she was in before the accident occurred. Because this may be impossible, the plaintiff needs money in order to buy back as many of these things as possible.

In the commercial context, a breach of contract for failure to supply goods might involve compensation for the following: the cost of obtaining substitute goods, psychological damage resulting from loss of a steady source of supply, lost sales, loss of goodwill, any disruption in business which may have occurred, having to lay off employees as a result of decreased business, restoration of good business relationships, and retribution or punishment of the defaulting party. In [one] case ..., the litigation model structured the parties' goals in terms of the payment of money, when in fact one party sought to purchase and own a reliable form of transportation and the other sought a profit. It may be more useful in any contract case to think of the parties' needs in terms of what originally brought them together—the purpose of their relationship. Can the parties still realize their original goals? Charles Fried describes the classic function of contracts as attempts by the parties to mutually meet each other's needs:

> You want to accomplish purpose A and I want to accomplish purpose B. Neither of us can succeed without the cooperation of the other. Thus, I want to be able to commit myself to help you achieve A so that you will commit yourself to help me achieve B. ...[161]

It is also important to recognize that both parties have such needs. For example, in the personal injury case above, the defendant may have the same need for vindication or retribution if he believes he was not responsible for the accident. In addition, the defendant may need to be compensated for his damaged car and injured body. He will also have needs with respect to how much, when and how he may be able to pay the monetary damages because of other uses for the money. A contract breaching defendant may have specific financial needs such as payroll, advertising, purchases of supplies, etc.; defendants are not always simply trying to avoid paying a certain sum of money to plaintiffs. In the commercial case, the defendant may have needs similar to those of the plaintiff: lost income due to the plaintiff's failure to pay on the contract,

---

161. Although legal negotiations tend to bring us into contact with those who seek to maximize money, there are others who seek to maximize other human goals—fame, love, power, security, maybe even altruism. These are still needs, and although they will be hard to "meet" when the other side also seems to have the same insatiable demand, it is important to understand them at their most basic level. If a demand for money is really masking a strong need for security, there may still be other ways to meet the security need....

and, to the extent the plaintiff may seek to terminate the relationship with the defendant, a steady source of future business.

[T]here may be more solutions when one takes account of both parties' needs than when one tries to evaluate the moral hierarchy of whose needs are more deserving.

. . .

To the extent that negotiators focus exclusively on "winning" the greatest amount of money, they focus on only one form of need. The only flexibility in tailoring an agreement may lie in the choice of ways to structure monetary solutions, including one shot payments, installments, and structured settlements. By looking, however, at what the parties desire money for, there may be a variety of solutions that will satisfy the parties more fully and directly. For example, when an injured plaintiff needs physical rehabilitation, if the defendant can provide the plaintiff directly with rehabilitation services, the defendant may save money and the plaintiff may gain the needed rehabilitation at lower cost. In addition, if the defendant can provide the plaintiff with a job that provides physical rehabilitation, the plaintiff may not only receive income which could be used to purchase more rehabilitation, but be further rehabilitated in the form of the psychological self-worth which accompanies such employment.[164] Admittedly, none of these solutions may fully satisfy the injured plaintiff, but some or all may be equally beneficial to the plaintiff, and the latter two may be preferable to the defendant because they are less costly.

Understanding that the other party's needs are not necessarily as assumed may present an opportunity for arriving at creative solutions. Traditionally, lawyers approaching negotiations from the adversarial model view the other side as an enemy to be defeated. By examining the underlying needs of the other side, the lawyer may instead see opportunities for solutions that would not have existed before based upon the recognition of different, but not conflicting, preferences.

. . .

In negotiation, as in counseling, the lawyer should be certain that she acts with full knowledge of the client's desires. Within the suggested framework, the lawyer ranks the client's preferences in terms of what is important to the client rather than what the lawyer assumes about the "typical" client.

In order to engage in problem-solving negotiation the lawyer must first ascertain her clients' underlying needs or objectives. In addition, the lawyer may want to explore whether there are unstated objectives, pursue those which she thinks appropriate to the situation, or probe the legitimacy and propriety of particular goals. It should be noted, however, that the lawyer's role in exploring latent concerns or discussing the propriety of objectives can come dangerously close to the role of the lawyer in the

---

164. This solution is not as far fetched as it seems. It is taken from an actual negotiation and is a relatively common solution in some types of cases. For example, both employer and employee have an interest in finding another job for a worker's compensation claimant who would like to return to work but can no longer do the original job....

adversarial model who imposes his own values or makes assumptions about what the client wants to accomplish. Finally, in order to pursue solutions that will be advantageous for both parties, the lawyer must ascertain the likely underlying needs and objectives of the other party. The client is a primary source for this information, but the lawyer should pursue other sources throughout the negotiation process.

. . .

MEDIATION AND LAWYERS

Leonard L. Riskin
43 Ohio St.L.J. 29 (1982)

A mediator helps disputants toward resolving their disagreement. Unlike a judge or arbitrator, however, the mediator lacks authority to impose a decision on the parties; he can only facilitate the process. Mediation has been and remains the dominant method of processing disputes in some quarters of the world. In parts of the Orient litigation is seen as a shameful last resort, the use of which signifies embarrassing failure to settle the matter amicably. Though it is unclear to what extent philosophy influences practice, the connection between the prominence of mediation and a Confucian heritage has been noted repeatedly by scholars. In the Confucian view,

> [a] lawsuit symbolized disruption of the natural harmony that was thought to exist in human affairs. Law was backed by coercion, and therefore tainted in the eyes of Confucianists. Their view was that the optimum resolution of most disputes was to be achieved not by the exercise of sovereign force but by moral persuasion. Moreover, litigation led to litigiousness and to shameless concern for one's own interest to the detriment of the interests of society.

This idea—that the natural and desirable condition is harmony— contrasts sharply with the predominant Western perspectives which focus on freedom as an absence of restraint and on autonomy and individual liberty as the highest goal. These Western notions, crystallized in the adversary system, pervade the American legal process and the lives of most of its citizens, including its lawyers. In recent years, though, mediation as a means of dispute processing has sent vines through the adversarial fence. They differ somewhat in purpose, orientation, and direction, but share a rapid growth rate. The development of mediation promises much that is good for American society and carries significant dangers as well.

. . .

Ten years ago, most American lawyers would have associated mediation with international or labor relations disputes, and probably confused it with arbitration. But in the last decade, mediation programs have proliferated at a breathtaking rate in this country. Most of these efforts have been directed at what the American Bar Association has called "minor disputes"—those involving "relatively small amounts of money or relatively pedestrian issues"—and were designed to provide dispute processing services for cases that the standard adversary system cannot handle. Increasingly, however, mediation is finding application in disputes that normally are processed through the adversary system.

A large number of cities have neighborhood justice centers, in which volunteers from the community mediate (or arbitrate) interpersonal, neighborhood, domestic, consumer, landlord-tenant, or minor criminal disputes. Referrals come largely from prosecutors, police, or courts, though some neighborhood justice centers have a community orientation and rely more heavily on cases brought in by the disputants themselves. These programs have delivered speedy processing with a high level of satisfaction among the disputants.

Additional efforts have been limited to cases connected with a given court or prosecutor's office that sponsored the program. Still others have sought a "community-base" with a hope of dealing with broader problems and sometimes using community leaders as mediators. For a long time, various local ethnic groups have used mediation to deal with all manner of disputes among members, and social pressure often assures compliance.

Mediation, sometimes combined with arbitration, also has been used lately in special programs established by individual businesses or by trade associations to handle consumer complaints. Prisons, schools, and other institutions have joined the movement.

New efforts at using mediation for dealing with "major" disputes of two principal types also have developed. The first includes conflicts, such as racial or environmental disputes, that concern many persons or interest groups in one locality. The second is domestic relations—primarily divorce and child custody....

. . .

Mediation is especially useful in divorce cases because the strong emotional forces at work may call for more delicately wrought measures than could be provided in a court-imposed solution. But it is not for every divorcing couple. They must have a strong commitment and the emotional and intellectual abilities to cooperate, notwithstanding their difficulties, in dividing up property and developing a framework for governing their future relationship. Each partner should be more interested in honoring the other's unique needs than hurting him. And they should be about equally powerful.

Mediation can help in other contexts in which the parties have a complex, interdependent relationship, relative equality of bargaining power, and strong incentives to work out their own relationship with minimal reliance upon others. These characteristics are often present in persons who seek lawyers' help in creating, operating, or dissolving organizations, contracts, or other relationships. And when such characteristics are weak, they can be potentiated by an urge to save time and money and avoid the possible nastiness and aggravating effects of adversary processing. Thus, many persons who now use an adversarial lawyer to handle their disputes could benefit enormously if they also could take advantage of appropriate mediation services. Savings to society in the form of reduced court costs would follow as well.

Mediation offers some clear advantages over adversary processing: it is cheaper, faster, and potentially more hospitable to unique solutions that take more fully into account nonmaterial interests of the disputants. It can educate the parties about each other's needs and those of their community. Thus, it can help them learn to work together and to see that through cooperation both can make positive gains. One reason for these advantages is that mediation is less hemmed-in by rules of procedure or substantive law and certain assumptions that dominate the adversary process. . . . [I]n mediation—as distinguished from adjudication and, usually, arbitration—the ultimate authority resides with the disputants. The conflict is seen as unique and therefore less subject to solution by application of some general principle. The case is neither to be governed by a precedent nor to set one. Thus, all sorts of facts, needs, and interests that would be excluded from consideration in an adversary, rule-oriented proceeding could become relevant in a mediation. Indeed, whatever a party deems relevant is relevant. In a divorce mediation, for instance, a spouse's continuing need for emotional support could become important, as could the other party's willingness and ability to give it. In most mediations, the emphasis is not on determining rights or interests, or who is right and who is wrong, or who wins and who loses because of which rule; these would control the typical adjudicatory proceeding. The focus, instead, is upon establishing a degree of harmony through a resolution that will work for these disputants.

A danger inheres in this alegal character: individuals who are not aware of their legal position are not encouraged by the process to develop a rights-consciousness or to establish legal rights. Thus, the risk of dominance by the stronger or more knowledgeable party is great.[52] Accordingly, for society to maximize the benefits of mediation while controlling its dangers, it must carefully adjust the role of lawyers in the mediation process.

---

52. This is a special danger when mediation is being used to support the established order. . . .

Obviously, the judicial process, as it functions in this country, is vulnerable to the same criticism. Howard Zinn gives an extreme view:

The "rule of law" in modern society is no less authoritarian than the rule of men in pre-modern society; it enforces the maldistribution of wealth and power as of old, but it does this in such complicated and indirect ways as to leave the observer bewildered. . . . In slavery, the feudal order, the colonial system, deception and patronization are the minor modes of control; force is the major one. In the modern world of liberal capitalism (and also, we should note, of state socialism), force is held in reserve while . . . "a multitude of moral teachers, counselors, and bewilderers separate the exploited from those in power." In this multitude, the books of law are among the most formidable bewilderers.

Zinn, The Conspiracy of Law, in The Rule of Law 18–19 (R. Wolff ed. 1971).

. . .

Nearly all mediators seek to help the disputants achieve an agreement. Most have educational objectives as well, especially where the parties will have a continuing relationship. There are, however, enormous differences in procedures and in roles that mediators adopt. Some will act merely as go-betweens, keeping open lines of communication. They may or may not give their own suggestions when the parties have deadlocked. Some mediators will separate the parties physically; others will insist on keeping them together. Some mediators will urge that the parties propose solutions; others will make their own proposals and try to persuade the parties to accept them and may even apply economic, social, or moral pressure to achieve a "voluntary" agreement.

One of the principal functions of the mediator is managing the communications process. He must intervene carefully at the correct moments. Accordingly, he must understand interpersonal relations and negotiations. He must be able to listen well and perceive the underlying emotional, psychological, and value orientations that may hold the keys to resolving more quantifiable issues. And he must arrange for these to be honored in the mediation process, the agreement, and the resulting relationship. A like sensitivity is essential for good lawyering as well, but it occupies a more prominent place on the list of skills required of a mediator.

. . .

Parties who have independent counsel can benefit from an adversarial look at their position. A prediction of the likely results of adversary processing is necessary for an informed, fully voluntary decision about a mediated solution. Sometimes lawyers also aid the mediation process by urging their clients to accept a reasonable compromise. There is a concomitant likelihood, however, that a lawyer's advice will work to undermine a mediation. Of course, this occasionally will be in the client's best interest. But some lawyers . . . may tend to deliver advice in a way that exaggerates the importance of the adversary perspective and the accuracy of their predictions. When this occurs, the client may be drawn away inappropriately from a mediated resolution. . . .

One way to lessen the likelihood of a lawyer's undermining a mediation is to employ an impartial attorney to advise both parties, but this raises a number of worries. . . . The most substantial concern, however, is the enormous difficulty of giving impartial or neutral legal advice if the parties have conflicting interests. This raises the spectre of breaching the requirement of Canon 5 that a lawyer exercise independent professional judgment on behalf of a client. A recent opinion imposed, inter alia, the conditions that "the issues not be of such complexity that the parties cannot prudently reach resolution of the controversy without the advice of separate and independent legal counsel," and that the lawyer advise the parties of the limitations and risks of his role and of the advantages of independent legal counsel, obtain their informed consent, give legal advice only in the presence of both, and refrain from representing either in a subsequent proceeding concerning divorce. If one lawyer advises the couple, each partner is deprived of the benefit of an adversarial look at his or her situation.

. . .

When a lawyer functions explicitly as a mediator while representing both of the parties, or just one of the parties while leaving the other unrepresented, the principal professional responsibility concern is again the Canon 5 requirement that a lawyer exercise independent professional judgment on behalf of a client. Bar associations have traditionally prohibited dual representation in matrimonial cases, but have recently shown some signs of liberalization.

. . .

The principal danger of dual representation is that one of the parties will take unfair advantage of the other, knowingly or not. With this in mind, Rule 2.2 of the proposed final draft of the American Bar Association Model Rules of Professional Conduct, which would apply where a lawyer represents both parties, provides that:

(a) A lawyer may act as intermediary between clients if:

(1) The lawyer discloses to each client the implications of the common representation, including the advantages and risks involved, and obtains each client's consent to the common representation;

(2) The lawyer reasonably believes that the matter can be resolved on terms compatible with the clients' best interests, that each client will be able to make adequately informed decisions in the matter and that there is little risk of material prejudice to the interest of any of the clients if the contemplated resolution is unsuccessful; and

(3) The lawyer reasonably believes that the common representation can be undertaken impartially and without improper effect on other responsibilities the lawyer has to any of the clients.

(b) While acting as intermediary, the lawyer shall explain fully to each client the decisions to be made and the considerations relevant in making them, so that each client can make adequately informed decisions.

(c) A lawyer shall withdraw as intermediary if any of the clients so requests, if the conditions stated in paragraph (a) cannot be met or if in the light of subsequent events the lawyer reasonably should know that a mutually advantageous resolution cannot be achieved. Upon withdrawal, the lawyer shall not continue to represent any of the clients unless doing so is clearly compatible with the lawyer's responsibilities to the other client or clients.

This model offers significant potential advantages to clients who wish to save time and money and avoid an adversarial confrontation. Yet when assets or interests that the parties consider significant are involved, they will usually want the benefit of a partisan look at their case.

The most recent development—the lawyer serving as divorce mediator but not representing either party—has earned the qualified approval of the Boston and Oregon bar ethics committees. The Oregon opinion imposed the conditions that the attorney

1.   . . . must clearly inform the parties he represents neither of them and they both must consent to this arrangement;

2.   . . . may give legal advice only to both parties in the presence of each other;

3.   . . . may draft the proposed agreement but he must advise, and encourage, the parties to seek independent legal counsel before execution of the agreement; and

4.   . . . must not represent either or both of the parties in the subsequent legal proceedings.

This model seems to offer the best possibilities for the appropriate use of law and lawyers in mediation of some matters that normally pass through the adversary process. The attorney-mediator can attempt to provide impartial legal information while making clear the risks to the clients in his doing so. The outside consultations with lawyers can defend against the possibility of bias (deliberate or not) in the lawyer-mediator's work and reduce the chances that one party will inappropriately exercise power over the other.

Another advantage is that information about what a court would do can be integrated into the mediation process in a way that suits the needs of the parties. Because he is an expert on law, the lawyer-mediator can help the parties free themselves, when appropriate, from the influence of legal norms so that they can reach for a solution that is appropriate to them. In addition, the experienced lawyer who functions as a mediator can offer a variety of business arrangements to accomplish the objectives of the parties. These options can become part and parcel of the decision process, and the law-trained mediator who is present at all the sessions and thoroughly familiar with the various needs of the parties can propose alternatives finely tuned to such needs. Moreover, the lawyer-mediator can . . . identify a myriad of legal issues that must be addressed in the final agreement, and press the disputants to reach decisions. He can incorporate the results in a draft final agreement, which—because of the lawyer-mediator's skill in identifying issues and preparing documents—would be less vulnerable to up-ending by the outside lawyers . . .

. . .

The future of mediation in this country rests heavily upon the attitudes and involvement of the legal profession. If society is to use mediation to its fullest advantage—properly employing it in minor disputes and extending its application to more major ones—and protect against the dangers of its alegal character, lawyers must be involved, but carefully. My contention is that two developments are required if mediation is to be used well. The first is that many lawyers must come to understand mediation and when it can be useful. The second is that a significant number of lawyers must begin serving explicitly as mediators, in ways that also employ their legal skills.

Unless a lawyer is familiar with mediation and when it can be useful, he will not be inclined to recommend it to his clients. Moreover, his orientation may undermine a mediation process in which his client is involved. A lawyer serving as an outside attorney to one of the parties or as an impartial advisory attorney can help the process along only if he understands it. Lawyers and judges play important roles in governing some minor disputes and community mediation programs. Unless they, too, grasp mediation's potential, they may be inclined to see these programs solely as ways of maintaining the status quo—by processing poor people's disputes so as to relieve court congestion and reduce violence in the community. The danger is that this perspective could emphasize speed over quality in mediation and might therefore exclude the possibilities that mediation holds for helping people take charge of their own lives instead of expecting elites—whether government or business, physicians or lawyers—to satisfy their needs. Each of these threats could be softened if more lawyers understood mediation.

But an expansion of lawyers' knowledge about mediation is not enough. Increased use of mediation in many cases currently processed through the adversary system will develop only if substantial numbers of lawyers begin to function *explicitly* as mediators. . . .

. . .

[I]f a cadre of lawyers who were willing and able to serve as mediators were to develop, clients and cases that were suitable for mediation would have a better chance of getting access to mediation. Some cases would be mediated because the disputants would choose a lawyer-mediator, others because the clients chanced upon a lawyer who mediated. Still others would be referred to mediation by lawyers who felt confident in the combination of legal and mediative skills possessed by the law-trained mediator and knew they could retain something like their traditional lawyer's role.

Most lawyers neither understand nor perform mediation nor have a strong interest in doing either. At least three interrelated reasons account for this: the way most lawyers, as lawyers, look at the world; the economics and structure of contemporary law practice; and the lack of training in mediation for lawyers.

. . .

The philosophical map employed by most practicing lawyers and law teachers, and displayed to the law student—which I will call the lawyer's standard philosophical map—differs radically from that which a mediator must use. What appears on this map is determined largely by the power of two assumptions about matters that lawyers handle: (1) that disputants are adversaries—*i.e.,* if one wins, the others must lose—and (2) that disputes may be resolved through application, by a third party, of some general rule of law. These assumptions, plainly, are polar opposites of those which underlie mediation: (1) that all parties can benefit through a creative solution to which each agrees; and (2) that the situation is unique and therefore not to be governed by any general principle except to the extent that the parties accept it.

The two assumptions of the lawyer's philosophical map (adversariness of parties and rule-solubility of dispute), along with the real demands of the adversary system and the expectations of many clients, tend to exclude mediation from most lawyers' repertoires. They also blind lawyers to other kinds of information that are essential for a mediator to see, primarily by riveting the lawyers' attention upon things that they must see in order to carry out their functions. The mediator must, for instance, be aware of the many interconnections between and among disputants and others, and of the qualities of these connections; he must be sensitive to emotional needs of all parties and recognize the importance of yearnings for mutual respect, equality, security, and other such non-material interests as may be present.

On the lawyer's standard philosophical map, however, the client's situation is seen atomistically; many links are not printed. The duty to represent the client zealously within the bounds of the law discourages concern with both the opponents' situation and the overall social effect of a given result.

Moreover, on the lawyer's standard philosophical map, quantities are bright and large while qualities appear dimly or not at all.[98] When one party wins, in this vision, usually the other party loses, and, most often, the victory is reduced to a money judgment. This "reduction" of nonmaterial values—such as honor, respect, dignity, security, and love—to amounts of money, can have one of two effects. In some cases, these values are excluded from the decision makers' considerations, and thus from the consciousness of the lawyers, as irrelevant. In others,

---

98. Huston Smith contrasts the modern, secular, and scientific view with the traditional, humanistic and religious. "The gist of their differences is that modernity, spawned essentially by modern science, stresses quantity (in order to get at power and control) whereas tradition stresses quality (and the participation that is control's alternative)." Smith, Excluded Knowledge: A Critique of the Modern Western Mind Set, 80 Teachers College Record 419, 421–22 (1979). Thus, the modern vision leaves out "most of the things that mankind has considered important throughout its history," including "intrinsic and normative values"; "purposes"; "global and existential meanings"; and "quality." Id. at 423–24.

The modern view clearly helps the lawyer gain and exercise power and control, and it excludes much that is important, especially for a mediator.

they are present but transmuted into something else—a justification for money damages....

The rule orientation also determines what appears on the map. The lawyer's standard world view is based upon a cognitive and rational outlook. Lawyers are trained to put people and events into categories that are legally meaningful, to think in terms of rights and duties established by rules, to focus on acts more than persons. This view requires a strong development of cognitive capabilities, which is often attended by the under-cultivation of emotional faculties. This combination of capacities joins with the practice of either reducing most nonmaterial values to amounts of money or sweeping them under the carpet, to restrict many lawyers' abilities to recognize the value of mediation or to serve as mediators.

The lawyer's standard philosophical map is useful primarily where the assumptions upon which it is based—adversariness and amenability to solution by a general rule imposed by a third party—are valid. But when mediation is appropriate, these assumptions do not fit. The problem is that many lawyers, because of their philosophical maps, tend to suppose that these assumptions are germane in nearly any situation that they confront as lawyers. The map, and the litigation paradigm on which it is based, has a power all out of proportion to its utility. Many lawyers, therefore, tend not to recognize mediation as a viable means of reaching a solution; and worse, they see the kinds of unique solutions that mediation can produce as threatening to the best interests of their clients.

"One of the central difficulties of our legal system," says John Ayer, "is its capacity to be deaf to the counsel of ordinary good sense." A law school classroom incident shows how quickly this deafness afflicts students—usually without anyone noticing. Professor Kenney Hegland writes:

> In my first year Contracts class, I wished to review various doctrines we had recently studied. I put the following:

> In a long term installment contract, Seller promises Buyer to deliver widgets at the rate of 1000 a month. The first two deliveries are perfect. However, in the third month Seller delivers only 999 widgets. Buyer becomes so incensed with this that he rejects the delivery, cancels the remaining deliveries and refuses to pay for the widgets already delivered. After stating the problem, I asked "If you were Seller, what would you say?" What I was looking for was a discussion of the various common law theories which would force the buyer to pay for the widgets delivered and those which would throw buyer into breach for cancelling the remaining deliveries. In short, I wanted the class to come up with the legal doctrines which would allow Seller to crush Buyer.

> After asking the question, I looked around the room for a volunteer. As is so often the case with the first year students, I found that they were all either writing in their notebooks or

inspecting their shoes. There was, however, one eager face, that of an eight year old son of one of my students. It seems that he was suffering through Contracts due to his mother's sin of failing to find a sitter. Suddenly he raised his hand. Such behavior, even from an eight year old, must be rewarded.

"OK," I said, "What would you say if you were the seller?"

"I'd say 'I'm sorry'."

I do not mean to imply that all lawyers see only what is displayed on the lawyer's standard philosophical map. The chart I have drawn exaggerates certain tendencies in the way many lawyers think. Any good lawyer will be alert to a range of nonmaterial values, emotional considerations, and interconnections. Many lawyers have "empathic, conciliatory" personalities that may incline them to work often in a mediative way. And other lawyers, though they may be more competitive, would recognize the value of mediation to their clients. I do submit, however, that most lawyers, most of the time, use this chart to navigate.

. . .

Mediation education for lawyers is essential if our society is to make the best use of mediation. This best use would save people time and money and a portion of the emotional turmoil that often accompanies adversary processing. It would protect the legal rights of the disputants and yield resolutions that suited their needs.... The spread of mediation could do much to improve the quality of life in our society, not only because of the savings it brings, but because it fosters interaction among people and empowers them to control their own lives.

There are similar benefits—not very certain, but profoundly important—that could follow merely from the development of mediation education for lawyers. The provision of good quality mediation-*cum*-legal services could help lawyers, the bar, and the law schools fulfill the strong impulses—frequently shaded on the lawyer's standard philosophical map—to make law more responsive to the needs of individuals and society. Properly done, mediation training can enhance the learner's awareness of his own emotional needs and value orientations and those of others. It should expand his ability to understand both sides of a case—not just with his head but with his heart as well. These sensitivities can, of course, make the lawyer better able to perceive his clients' needs and, on a purely instrumental level, to work more effectively with all manner of people.

And there is much more to it. Mediation highlights the interconnectedness of human beings. Lawyers who notice the interconnectedness are less vulnerable to the kind of over-enthusiasm with the adversary role that has brought about much of its sinister reputation. Lawyers who can experience both sides of a controversy—not merely understand the legal arguments—will have an awareness of consequences that can become a guide to their conduct which can compete with the established rules of lawyers' behavior. This may, when appropriate, blunt the edge of their adversarialness. It may also help them recognize that although their individual clients may be doing fine, in many ways the judicial system is not serving most people well.

. . .

A lawyer who has experienced the mediational perspective would have difficulty keeping on his adversarial blinders and would be more likely, therefore, to acknowledge the serious difficulties in our current adversary system. The mediation experience also may encourage the lawyer to come up with creative solutions to systemic as well as individual problems. Mediation training and practice can help lawyers question the many (often unconscious) value presuppositions that underlie normal lawyer behavior—for example, assumptions about adversariness and rules, how lawyers behave, and what clients want—from which we tend to operate automatically. Mediation training, in other words, may help lawyers break out of the "mental grooves and compartments" characteristic of the lawyer's conventional world view. This can lead not just to mediation but to legal services that are more responsive to the needs of clients and of society.

. . .

Note on Menkel–Meadow and Riskin:
Being a lawyer for the situation

1. Professors Menkel–Meadow and Riskin present the ideas of "problem-solving negotiation" and mediation largely from the perspective of their potential to serve better the client's full range of actual needs and priorities. The appeal of the authors' approaches may, however, be considered from the standpoint of the attorney as well. Consider two related but separable questions:

(a) In what ways is the authors' underlying concept of client empowerment one that is an attractive goal to some (by no means all) who decide to practice law as a career?

(b) In what ways is the stance that a lawyer, engaging in mediation or in problem-solving negotiation, has toward all of the participants in a dispute part of the attraction that a career as a practicing lawyer has for some (by no means all) people?

(c) Both Menkel–Meadow and Riskin seek, I believe—albeit in differing ways—to articulate grounds for believing that lawyer and client goals are mutually reinforcing, rather than in tension with one another.

• In what categories of cases, if any, do you think that such a belief is soundly based?

• In what is it not?

(d) Does the phrase attributed to Louis D. Brandeis, practicing as "counsel for the situation," capture this approach? (For the context in which he uttered the phrase, see John P. Frank, The Legal Ethics of Louis D. Brandeis, 17 Stan.L.Rev. 682, 702 (1965)).

2.   (a) As Riskin notes, the dominant reaction of the Code of Professional Responsibility to representational efforts, through acting as a mediator or otherwise, that attempt to look at the interests of "the situation" was one of wariness and prophylactic prohibition.   (Indeed, the instance that gave rise to Brandeis' use of the term was one of the bases on which his confirmation as a Justice of the Supreme Court was opposed by many leaders of the Bar.   See Frank, supra, at 694–703).   The idea of "independent professional judgment," Canon 5, was ordinarily taken to require a fidelity to client "interests," narrowly discerned, that seemed to view any consideration of the interests of "the other side" as a "conflict of interests." The conflict-of-interests rule of DR 5–105 prohibits representation of two or more clients with "differing interests" unless "it is obvious that [the lawyer] can adequately represent the interests of each" client, and there is consent after full disclosure of the "possible effect" of multiple representation on the lawyer's "independent professional judgment on behalf of each."

(b) Is there a sense in which the Code's view does not merely respond to conflicts of interest, but creates them as well?   Consider these thoughts:

> Clients do not have a conflict of interest simply because their interests diverge or because an intense legal dispute could arise between them.   If this were true, there would be a conflict of interest between practically everyone whose paths in life might cross.   People have conflicts of interest only if, in addition to having divergent interests, one or both wish to pursue them beyond a certain degree of aggression.   Whether they wish to do so inevitably depends on circumstances.   It also depends on the legal advice they may get, which turns the question into a circle.

Geoffrey Hazard, Ethics in the Practice of Law 78–79 (1978).

> [T]he Code does not invite the lawyer's examination of a wide range of potential client needs or latent concerns with and for others. Instead of conceding or recognizing that the situation confronting the lawyer may be one of considerable indeterminacy of objectives or deep ambivalence of feeling and attitude, the Code simply erects a concept of "interests" with which the client is inexorably identified.   "Interests" is never defined or discussed.   The term is rather like a black box into which the lawyer presumably dumps his own projections of what the client should desire, intend, feel, or anticipate.

Penegar, The Five Pillars of Professionalism, 49 U.Pitt.L.Rev. 307 (1988).

Recall, in this connection, Sub-section I(4)(a), "The identification of client priorities," pp. 66–77, above.

(c) The Model Rules are more hospitable, expressly legitimating the idea of a lawyer acting "as an intermediary between clients."   See Rule 2.2, set out by Riskin, p. 392 above.   The conflict-of-interest rule, MR 1.7, too is less guarded than DR 5–105, quoted above; it disallows representation of multiple clients only when their interests are either "directly adverse to [one] another," or when representation of one may be "materially limited" by attorney responsibility to another, and even then it permits multiple representation if the lawyer "reasonably believes" that there will not be an adverse effect and there is client consultation and consent. Consultation is required to include an explanation of the "advantages" as well as the "risks"

- Should it matter whether a mediator thinks of both parties or of neither as his or her clients? The drafters of the Model Rules seem to have thought so; Comment 2 asserts that Rule 2.2 is inapplicable to a lawyer "acting as arbitrator or mediator between or among parties who are not clients ...," but the matter is now regarded as open. For the divergent views, see Judith Maute, Public Values and Private Justice: A Case for Mediator Accountability, 4 Geo.J.Leg.Ethics 503, 510–12 (1991).

- The Rule attempts to strike a balance between inadequate safeguards and excess skepticism:

  - What are the dangers, against which there need to be safeguards?

  - Do you regard the balance struck by the Rule as responsive to the problem?

  - For an analysis suggesting a need to revise somewhat the stance toward lawyer mediation taken by MR 2.2, see Professor Maute's article, cited above.

(c) The literature on "alternative dispute resolution" is vast. For a particularly thought-provoking discussion, see David Luban, The Quality of Justice, 66 Denv.L.Rev. 381 (1989).

(d) What relevance, if any, do these issues have to the practice of problem-solving negotiation, where the lawyer has one (and only one) client and the other party and his or her lawyer are the "adversary"?

3. Very similar issues arise in the counseling context as well. An unusually gripping context for thinking about the question was the case of Rudy Linares, described in the opening paragraphs of the following excerpt.

(a) In light of the role that the hospital's lawyer played in the outcome, and the way in which Max Brown (the lawyer in question) perceived his role, how might the ideas examined in this Note, and in the readings that precede it, have affected the advice that Mr. Brown gave his client?

(b) Would such a change be for the better, or the worse, in light of your own objectives and priorities in practicing law?

LEGAL ADVICE, MORAL PARALYSIS AND THE DEATH OF SAMUEL LINARES

Lawrence J. Nelson and Ronald E. Cranford
17 Law, Medicine & Health Care 316 (1989).

Legal advice lies close to the death of Samuel Linares, closer than it usually does to the deaths of the many who die every day in American hospitals. Samuel's parents wanted the attending physician to disconnect the ventilator of their permanently unconscious son and allow him to die, something they saw as right for their son and their family. But this never happened. Samuel was not allowed to meet the death he had so narrowly avoided in August of 1988 when he accidentally swallowed a balloon and choked. He did not die uneventfully after his parents and the clinicians caring for him had carefully deliberated about the personal, ethical and professional propriety of stopping the ventilator and made a responsible decision about his fate.

Instead, Rudy Linares had to ward off nurses and security guards with a handgun until he disconnected his son's ventilator and held him in his arms until he died. According to the attending physician, Dr. Goldman, "There was no *ethical difference of opinion here.* The physicians agreed that the child was in an irreversible coma and would not recover. There was no medical opposition to removing the ventilator. *What we faced was a legal obstacle.*" (Emphasis added.)

Max Brown, in-house legal counsel for Rush–Presbyterian–St. Luke's Medical Center, the hospital in which Samuel was a patient, reportedly advised the physicians and the hospital that it was illegal to disconnect Samuel's ventilator, although he also thought disconnection was ethical. We gather this from the following statement of Mr. Brown's about the uselessness of an ethics committee consultation in the Linares case: "What we're dealing with here is a legal problem. Ethics committees are fine so long as what is ethically being contemplated is legally acceptable. *When you have an ethical alternative that is by all accounts illegal,* an ethics committee cannot do much to make it legal." (Emphasis added.)

Specifically, Mr. Brown thought that forgoing further use of the ventilator could be considered first degree murder, that is, malicious, premeditated killing. Dr. Goldman confirmed that this was the advice he received when he stated: "The father's request was that I stop the life of a child. *It's my understanding that would be murder.*" (Emphasis added.) Mr. Brown also has been reported as saying that federal law required the physicians and hospital to provide life support for the baby or risk prosecution for child neglect. We infer from this that Mr. Brown perhaps also believed that removing the ventilator would violate Illinois law regarding child abuse/neglect.

Furthermore, Mr. Brown concluded that Illinois law forbids withdrawing life support from a non-brain dead patient other than an adult who has signed a valid advance directive, but does not forbid *withholding* such support.... Dr. Goldman reported that Mr. Brown informed him that it would be legally permissible not to resuscitate Samuel, i.e., to let him die by withholding what Dr. Goldman called "extra care." When the parents asked about removing Samuel from the ventilator, Dr. Goldman told them "that was not a legal option. I *could not withdraw* life-sustaining treatment. I said they would have to obtain a court order." (Emphasis added) Given that the parents had been informed in no uncertain terms that stopping the ventilator was "not a legal option" and that it was in fact murder, no one should be surprised if they failed to grasp the point of seeking a court order to do what was illegal.

Thus, Mr. Brown's advice put the burden on the parents to secure court approval for disconnecting the ventilator. He offered at least one non-legal reason why the hospital could not be the one to seek such an order: the hospital might have suffered from bad publicity. "If we had gone to court, the court and the public might have been justified in believing we had a conflict of interest. The child was on public assistance. His case cost $600,000, and we were only expecting to get about $100,000 of that paid. A court may have believed we had another motive."

Based on these reports, we believe that Mr. Brown rendered fatally flawed substantive legal advice in the Linares case. Unfortunately, this advice apparently was never critically examined or even questioned in a serious manner by the administration or attending physicians at Rush. Furthermore, this legal advice apparently determined the medical care Samuel received and led his father to commit his desperate act with a gun, an act that we do not urge others to emulate, but that we understand. It was an act we should not say was right, but we cannot in our hearts condemn as ultimately wrong. In sum, our opinion is that the death of Samuel Linares was prefaced by distorted and defective legal advice that led his physicians and Rush to a not uncommon form of moral paralysis, namely, the abdication of responsibility for making professional decisions with primary loyalty to the best interest of the patient. Our commentary on this conclusion follows.

[The authors' legal analysis is omitted.]

Consequently, there is strong and unbroken legal precedent for the legal permissibility of stopping mechanical ventilation of permanently unconscious children at the parents' request. Indeed, there is no case that even suggests the contrary....

Of course, all of this may be beside the point to Mr. Brown because there is no Illinois appellate case or statute that expressly permits stopping ventilators on permanently unconscious children. Mr. Brown has contended that Illinois law is "less clear" than the rest of the country. We disagree and believe that Mr. Brown's legal interpretation is unnecessarily narrow. First, we can see no reasons why the Illinois courts should interpret its murder statute in a radically different manner than Georgia, Florida, Louisiana, New Jersey, or California. It is very hard to believe that stopping ventilation of a permanently unconscious child at the parents' request is fully permissible in some states and simultaneously murder in another.

Second, as described above, the evolving national jurisprudence in similar cases is unanimous in holding that stopping ventilation in a case like that of Samuel Linares is not unlawful killing. Perhaps more important, however, is the solid foundation of well-accepted medical standards and ethical values upon which this jurisprudence ultimately rests. As was plainly and correctly recognized by Dr. Goldman, forgoing further use of the ventilator in a case like Samuel's is clearly within the boundaries of accepted medical practice. Witness to this comes from recent statements of the American Academy of Neurology and the American Medical Association. Similarly, there is strong ethical consensus on the propriety of ceasing ventilation in the permanently unconscious patient. These standards and values surely apply equally in Illinois as elsewhere.

The importance of this kind of medical/ethical consensus (as well as judicial consensus) and the necessity of revising the common law to conform to it has been expressly acknowledged by the Appellate Court of Illinois. . . .

[The authors also contend that neither federal nor state child-abuse law would have been violated by removal of the ventilator.]

Mr. Brown's client was the hospital—not Dr. Goldman or the other physicians involved, not Rudy Linares, and certainly not Samuel, even though he was the hospital's patient. As the hospital lawyer, Mr. Brown's professional obligation was to protect his client's legal interests. In light of this, he appeared to have two primary goals: to minimize the hospital's exposure to legal liability and to avoid adverse publicity for the hospital. In so doing, he also attempted to protect the attending physicians' interests. After all, a murder or child abuse prosecution against one of the hospital's physicians would besmirch its reputation as well.

In our view, Mr. Brown gave the hospital and physicians incorrect legal advice on the substantive issues of liability for murder and child neglect and of the alleged impermissibility of stopping the ventilator. When rendering these flawed interpretations of the law, he adopted an ultra-conservative approach to the application of the law to Samuel's case that was based upon concern about *theoretical possibilities* of exposure to legal liability, not to *practical probabilities*. "I told the medical staff there was a *possibility* they would face criminal charges." (Emphasis added). An experienced and knowledgeable attorney, particularly one dealing with physicians and hospitals, should construct his or her advice on probabilities, not abstract possibilities. The practical probability in this case of a physician being prosecuted for murder was remote to the point of being non-existent, fundamentally because the law and the facts of the situation simply would not support even a vaguely plausible prosecution for unlawful, malicious killing. There was no practical probability of any other sort of adverse legal consequences either.

To be sure, possible legal liability lurks in almost every clinical encounter and around every corner of a hospital's halls, but then possible legal liability lies dormant in every glance away from the road while driving, every word that one utters in haste or anger, or every business decision made where large sums of money are at stake. Yet driving, speaking, and business all go on despite these risks. It is true that the applicability and meaning of the law are not always perfectly clear in every situation. Nevertheless, sound legal advice should not be based upon freak occurrences or skewed in unreasonable and improbable ways in the absence of absolutely definitive law on the matter at hand.

Hospital lawyers who dwell upon theoretical possibilities of liability are motivated to produce their fanciful legal advice by physicians (and hospital administrators) who seek absolute immunity from any possible adverse legal consequence, including the filing of a patently frivolous suit by some ill-willed person. This overwhelming fear of possible, indeed theoretical, adverse legal repercussions is pervasive in medicine today. It is a poison that can murder much of what is right, good, and even noble in medical practice. Its source is hard to pin down: extrapolation from the so-called malpractice crisis (particularly the very real problems suffered by obstetricians in "bad baby" cases), the ever-increasing litigiousness of our society, the defensiveness felt by members of a professional group unused to scrutiny from outsiders, lack of confidence that the legal system will operate with any rhyme or reason when it comes to medicine, or rumors passed among the physicians about phantom huge judgments being levied in termination of treatment cases? Whatever its source, this obsessive fear, as well as the implausible legal advice it spawns, is ugly and destructive.

. . .

As in medicine, unpredictable and freakish events occur in law. Therefore, we readily admit that Mr. Brown's advice was correct in part: it was possible that an irresponsible prosecutor would forsake a reasonable interpretation of the law and accepted values out of desire for political fame or fanaticism for a cause. Like a bolt of lightning from a blue sky, a prosecutor could theoretically come out of nowhere to wield the club of the criminal law upon an unsuspecting physician.

. . .

Anomalous actions by a prosecutor on the edge of responsible behavior notwithstanding, medicine should not be practiced out of self-interest and exaggerated fear of theoretical legal consequences, particularly when the actions generated by this fear are inconsistent with good medical practice, sound ethical values, and loyalty to the best interests of the patient—not to mention compassion, common sense, and existing legal precedent. The courts have recognized this regrettable tendency on the part of physicians to put their interests ahead of their patients' and urged them to look beyond it:

> [T]here *must* be a way to free physicians, in the pursuit of their healing vocation, from possible contamination by self-interest or self-protection concerns which would inhibit their independent medical judgments for the well-being of their dying patients. We would hope that this opinion might be serviceable to some extent in ameliorating the professional problems under discussion. (Emphasis added.)

[Matter of Quinlan, 70 N.J. 10, 355 A.2d 647, 688 (1976)].

The "contamination" of self-interest and self-protection was present in the *Linares* case: Mr. Brown's statements about the financial "conflict of interest" of the hospital if it sought a court order permitting termination of treatment makes this manifest. Mr. Brown's financial conflict of interest argument proves far too much. It is applicable to almost every decision to forgo treatment in any seriously ill Medicare, Medicaid, indigent, or uninsured patient—of which there are thousands around the country every month. If this argument were taken seriously, then any provider at financial risk, such as a capitated health plan or a hospital that accepted Medicaid patients, would be ethically or legally precluded from ever letting a patient die, assuming that Mr. Brown is considering this an ethical or legal argument. We think it is neither—it is a claim about public relations, and it really has nothing to do with what is right or wrong, or what an individual patient's best interests might be. It is not intended to do the right thing by the patient; it is meant to insulate the institution from misplaced criticism and thereby to promote its interests.

If any significant conflict of interest appears as a result of the Linares case, it is the conflict between the interests of Rush and its patients. If Mr. Brown's advice in the Linares case reigns at Rush now and into the future, this conflict is created by a de facto hospital policy that will not permit life-sustaining treatment to be withdrawn from any patient, dying or not, except in the most extreme circumstances. This policy rests upon Mr. Brown's position that it is legally impermissible to stop life-sustaining treatment unless Illinois law *explicitly* authorizes it and removes *any* possibility of criminal or civil liability. Given that such express authorization may well never exist in Illinois and there obviously are times when it is best for a patient to be rid of non-beneficial, burdensome, or ultimately futile life-sustaining treatment, this policy subordinates the interests of the patient to the legally and ethically unfounded desire of the institution and its physicians for self-protection. Perhaps Rush has a moral and legal obligation under the informed consent doctrine to alert its patients to the existence of this policy.

Advice given by lawyers excessively sensitive to the slightest, most ephemeral chance of potential legal liability can easily lead to moral paralysis in physicians or hospitals which seek the Shangri-la of total legal immunity. Moral paralysis in medicine inevitably results in the practice of bad medicine. Bad medicine led Rudy Linares to take what little was left of his son's life into his own hands and create an unnecessary and grotesque end to the story of Samuel Linares. Benevolent physicians devoted to serving their patients should never let their own interests skew their clinical care to the point that they abdicate their ethical and professional responsibility. Neither guns nor courts should ever be necessary to treat a patient in a compassionate, humane fashion.

*

APPENDIX

ABA Model Code of Professional Responsibility (1969)
(excerpts)

CANON 2

A Lawyer Should Assist the Legal Profession in Fulfilling Its Duty to Make Legal Counsel Available

DR 2–110 Withdrawal From Employment.

(A) In general.

(1) If permission for withdrawal from employment is required by the rules of a tribunal, a lawyer shall not withdraw from employment in a proceeding before that tribunal without its permission.

(2) In any event, a lawyer shall not withdraw from employment until he has taken reasonable steps to avoid foreseeable prejudice to the rights of his client, including giving due notice to his client, allowing time for employment of other counsel, delivering to the client all papers and property to which the client is entitled, and complying with applicable laws and rules.

(3) A lawyer who withdraws from employment shall refund promptly any part of a fee paid in advance that has not been earned.

(B) Mandatory withdrawal.

A lawyer representing a client before a tribunal, with its permission if required by its rules, shall withdraw from employment, and a lawyer representing a client in other matters shall withdraw from employment, if:

(1) He knows or it is obvious that his client is bringing the legal action, conducting the defense, or asserting a position in the litigation, or is otherwise having steps taken for him, merely for the purpose of harassing or maliciously injuring any person.

(2) He knows or it is obvious that his continued employment will result in violation of a Disciplinary Rule.

(3) His mental or physical condition renders it unreasonably difficult for him to carry out the employment effectively.

(4) He is discharged by his client.

(C) Permissive withdrawal.

If DR 2–110(B) is not applicable, a lawyer may not request permission to withdraw in matters pending before a tribunal, and may not withdraw in other matters, unless such request or such withdrawal is because:

(1) His client:

    (a) Insists upon presenting a claim or defense that is not warranted under existing law and cannot be supported by good faith argument for an extension, modification, or reversal of existing law.

    (b) Personally seeks to pursue an illegal course of conduct.

    (c) Insists that the lawyer pursue a course of conduct that is illegal or that is prohibited under the Disciplinary Rules.

    (d) By other conduct renders it unreasonably difficult for the lawyer to carry out his employment effectively.

    (e) Insists, in a matter not pending before a tribunal, that the lawyer engage in conduct that is contrary to the judgment and advice of the lawyer but not prohibited under the Disciplinary Rules.

    (f) Deliberately disregards an agreement or obligation to the lawyer as to expenses or fees.

(2) His continued employment is likely to result in a violation of a Disciplinary Rule.

(3) His inability to work with co-counsel indicates that the best interests of the client likely will be served by withdrawal.

(4) His mental or physical condition renders it difficult for him to carry out the employment effectively.

(5) His client knowingly and freely assents to termination of his employment.

(6) He believes in good faith, in a proceeding pending before a tribunal, that the tribunal will find the existence of other good cause for withdrawal.

CANON 3

A Lawyer Should Assist in Preventing the Unauthorized Practice of Law

DR 3–101 Aiding Unauthorized Practice of Law.

(A) A lawyer shall not aid a non-lawyer in the unauthorized practice of law.

CANON 4

A Lawyer Should Preserve the Confidences and Secrets of a Client

DR 4–101 Preservation of Confidences and Secrets of a Client.

(A) "Confidence" refers to information protected by the attorney-client privilege under applicable law, and "secret" refers to other information gained in the professional relationship that the client has requested be held inviolate or the disclosure of which would be embarrassing or would be likely to be detrimental to the client.

(B) Except when permitted under DR 4–101(C), a lawyer shall not knowingly:

(1) Reveal a confidence or secret of his client.

(2) Use a confidence or secret of his client to the disadvantage of the client.

(3) Use a confidence or secret of his client for the advantage of himself or of a third person, unless the client consents after full disclosure.

(C) A lawyer may reveal:

(1) Confidences or secrets with the consent of the client or clients affected, but only after a full disclosure to them.

(2) Confidences or secrets when permitted under Disciplinary Rules or required by law or court order.

(3) The intention of his client to commit a crime and the information necessary to prevent the crime.

(4) Confidences or secrets necessary to establish or collect his fee or to defend himself or his employees or associates against an accusation of wrongful conduct.

(D) A lawyer shall exercise reasonable care to prevent his employees, associates, and others whose services are utilized by him from disclosing or using confidences or secrets of a client, except that a lawyer may reveal the information allowed by DR 4–101(C) through an employee.

CANON 5

A Lawyer Should Exercise Independent Professional Judgment on Behalf of a Client

DR 5–105 Refusing to Accept or Continue Employment if the Interests of Another Client May Impair the Independent Professional Judgment of the Lawyer.

(A) A lawyer shall decline proffered employment if the exercise of his independent professional judgment in behalf of a client will be or is likely to be adversely affected by the acceptance of the proffered employment, or if it would be likely to involve him in representing differing interests, except to the extent permitted under DR 5–105(C).

(B) A lawyer shall not continue multiple employment if the exercise of his independent professional judgment in behalf of a client will be or is likely to be adversely affected by his representation of another client, or if it would be likely to involve him in representing differing interests, except to the extent permitted under DR 5–105(C).

(C) In the situations covered by DR 5–105(A) and (B), a lawyer may represent multiple clients if it is obvious that he can adequately represent the interest of each and if each consents to the representation after full disclosure of the possible effect of such representation on the exercise of his independent professional judgment on behalf of each.

(D) If a lawyer is required to decline employment or to withdraw from employment under a Disciplinary Rule, no partner or associate, or any other lawyer affiliated with him or his firm may accept or continue such employment.

CANON 7

A Lawyer Should Represent a Client Zealously Within the Bounds of the Law

ETHICAL CONSIDERATIONS

Duty of the Lawyer to a Client

EC 7–4 The advocate may urge any permissible construction of the law favorable to his client, without regard to his professional opinion as to the likelihood that the construction will ultimately prevail. His conduct is within the bounds of the law, and therefore permissible, if the position taken is supported by the law or is supportable by a good faith argument for an extension, modification, or reversal of the law. However, a lawyer is not justified in asserting a position in litigation that is frivolous.

EC 7–5 A lawyer as adviser furthers the interest of his client by giving his professional opinion as to what he believes would likely be the ultimate decision of the courts on the matter at hand and by informing his client of the practical effect of such decision. He may continue in the representation of his client even though his client has elected to pursue a course of conduct contrary to the advice of the lawyer so long as he does not thereby knowingly assist the client to engage in illegal conduct or to take a frivolous legal position. A lawyer should never encourage or aid his client to commit criminal acts or counsel his client on how to violate the law and avoid punishment therefor.

EC 7–6 Whether the proposed action of a lawyer is within the bounds of the law may be a perplexing question when his client is contemplating a course of conduct having legal consequences that vary according to the client's intent, motive, or desires at the time of the action. Often a lawyer is asked to assist his client in developing evidence relevant to the state of mind of the client at a particular time. He may properly assist his client in the development and preservation of evidence of existing motive, intent, or desire; obviously, he may not do anything furthering the creation or preservation of false evidence. In many cases a lawyer may not be certain as to the state of mind of his client, and in those situations he should resolve reasonable doubts in favor of his client.

EC 7-7 In certain areas of legal representation not affecting the merits of the cause or substantially prejudicing the rights of a client, a lawyer is entitled to make decisions on his own. But otherwise the authority to make decisions is exclusively that of the client and, if made within the framework of the law, such decisions are binding on his lawyer. As typical examples in civil cases, it is for the client to decide whether he will accept a settlement offer or whether he will waive his right to plead an affirmative defense. A defense lawyer in a criminal case has the duty to advise his client fully on whether a particular plea to a charge appears to be desirable and as to the prospects of success on appeal, but it is for the client to decide what plea should be entered and whether an appeal should be taken.

EC 7-8 A lawyer should exert his best efforts to insure that decisions of his client are made only after the client has been informed of relevant considerations. A lawyer ought to initiate this decision-making process if the client does not do so. Advice of a lawyer to his client need not be confined to purely legal considerations. A lawyer should advise his client of the possible effect of each legal alternative. A lawyer should bring to bear upon this decision-making process the fullness of his experience as well as his objective viewpoint. In assisting his client to reach a proper decision, it is often desirable for a lawyer to point out those factors which may lead to a decision that is morally just as well as legally permissible. He may emphasize the possibility of harsh consequences that might result from assertion of legally permissible positions. In the final analysis, however, the lawyer should always remember that the decision whether to forego legally available objectives or methods because of non-legal factors is ultimately for the client and not for himself. In the event that the client in a non-adjudicatory matter insists upon a course of conduct that is contrary to the judgment and advice of the lawyer but not prohibited by Disciplinary Rules, the lawyer may withdraw from the employment.

DISCIPLINARY RULES

DR 7-101 Representing a Client Zealously.

(A) A lawyer shall not intentionally:

> (1) Fail to seek the lawful objectives of his client through reasonably available means permitted by law and the Disciplinary Rules, except as provided by DR 7-101(B). A lawyer does not violate this Disciplinary Rule, however, by acceding to reasonable requests of opposing counsel which do not prejudice the rights of his client, by being punctual in fulfilling all professional commitments, by avoiding offensive tactics, or by treating with courtesy and consideration all persons involved in the legal process.

(2) Fail to carry out a contract of employment entered into with a client for professional services, but he may withdraw as permitted under DR 2–110, DR 5–102, and DR 5–105.

(3) Prejudice or damage his client during the course of the professional relationship except as required under DR 7–102(B).

(B) In his representation of a client, a lawyer may:

(1) Where permissible, exercise his professional judgment to waive or fail to assert a right or position of his client.

(2) Refuse to aid or participate in conduct that he believes to be unlawful, even though there is some support for an argument that the conduct is legal.

DR 7–102 Representing a Client Within the Bounds of the Law.

(A) In his representation of a client, a lawyer shall not:

(1) File a suit, assert a position, conduct a defense, delay a trial, or take other action on behalf of his client when he knows or when it is obvious that such action would serve merely to harass or maliciously injure another.

(2) Knowingly advance a claim or defense that is unwarranted under existing law, except that he may advance such claim or defense if it can be supported by good faith argument for an extension, modification, or reversal of existing law.

(3) Conceal or knowingly fail to disclose that which he is required by law to reveal.

(4) Knowingly use perjured testimony or false evidence.

(5) Knowingly make a false statement of law or fact.

(6) Participate in the creation or preservation of evidence when he knows or it is obvious that the evidence is false.

(7) Counsel or assist his client in conduct that the lawyer knows to be illegal or fraudulent.

(8) Knowingly engage in other illegal conduct or conduct contrary to a Disciplinary Rule.

(B) A lawyer who receives information clearly establishing that:

(1) His client has, in the course of the representation, perpetrated a fraud upon a person or tribunal shall promptly call upon his client to rectify the same, and if his client refuses or is unable to do so, he shall reveal the fraud to the affected person or tribunal, except when the information is protected as a privileged communication.

(2) A person other than his client has perpetrated a fraud upon a tribunal shall promptly reveal the fraud to the tribunal.

CANON 8

A Lawyer Should Assist in Improving the Legal System

EC 8–6 Judges and administrative officials having adjudicatory powers ought to be persons of integrity, competence, and suitable temperament. Generally, lawyers are qualified, by personal observation or investigation, to evaluate the qualifications of persons seeking or being considered for such public offices, and for this reason they have a special responsibility to aid in the selection of only those who are qualified. It is the duty of lawyers to endeavor to prevent political considerations from outweighing judicial fitness in the selection of judges. Lawyers should protest earnestly against the appointment or election of those who are unsuited for the bench and should strive to have elected or appointed thereto only those who are willing to forego pursuits, whether of a business, political, or other nature, that may interfere with the free and fair consideration of questions presented for adjudication. Adjudicatory officials, not being wholly free to defend themselves, are entitled to receive the support of the bar against unjust criticism. While a lawyer as a citizen has a right to criticize such officials publicly, he should be certain of the merit of his complaint, use appropriate language, and avoid petty criticisms, for unrestrained and intemperate statements tend to lessen public confidence in our legal system. Criticisms motivated by reasons other than a desire to improve the legal system are not justified.

CANON 9

A Lawyer Should Avoid Even the Appearance
of Professional Impropriety

DR 9–101 Avoiding Even the Appearance of Impropriety.

(A) A lawyer shall not accept private employment in a matter upon the merits of which he has acted in a judicial capacity.

(B) A lawyer shall not accept private employment in a matter in which he had substantial responsibility while he was a public employee.

(C) A lawyer shall not state or imply that he is able to influence improperly or upon irrelevant grounds any tribunal, legislative body, or public official.

DR 9–102 Preserving Identity of Funds and Property of a Client.

. . .

ABA MODEL RULES OF PROFESSIONAL CONDUCT (1983)
(excerpts)

Article 1. Client–Lawyer Relationship

RULE 1.2 Scope of Representation

(a) A lawyer shall abide by a client's decisions concerning the objectives of representation, subject to paragraphs (c), (d) and (e), and shall consult with the client as to the means by which they are to be pursued. A lawyer shall abide by a client's decision whether to accept an offer of settlement of a matter. In a criminal case, the lawyer shall abide by the client's decision, after consultation with the lawyer, as to a plea to be entered, whether to waive jury trial and whether the client will testify.

(b) A lawyer's representation of a client, including representation by appointment, does not constitute an endorsement of the client's political, economic, social or moral views or activities.

(c) A lawyer may limit the objectives of the representation if the client consents after consultation.

(d) A lawyer shall not counsel a client to engage, or assist a client, in conduct that the lawyer knows is criminal or fraudulent, but a lawyer may discuss the legal consequences of any proposed course of conduct with a client and may counsel or assist a client to make a good faith effort to determine the validity, scope, meaning or application of the law.

(e) When a lawyer knows that a client expects assistance not permitted by the rules of professional conduct or other law, the lawyer shall consult with the client regarding the relevant limitations on the lawyer's conduct.

Comment:

Scope of Representation

[1] Both lawyer and client have authority and responsibility in the objectives and means of representation. The client has ultimate authority to determine the purposes to be served by legal representation, within the limits imposed by law and the lawyer's professional obligations. Within those limits, a client also has a right to consult with the lawyer about the means to be used in pursuing those objectives. At the same time, a lawyer is not required to pursue objectives or employ means simply because a client may wish that the lawyer do so. A clear distinction between objectives and means sometimes cannot be drawn, and in many cases the client-lawyer relationship partakes of a joint undertaking. In questions of means, the lawyer should assume

414

responsibility for technical and legal tactical issues, but should defer to the client regarding such questions as the expense to be incurred and concern for third persons who might be adversely affected. Law defining the lawyer's scope of authority in litigation varies among jurisdictions.

RULE 1.4   Communication

(a) A lawyer shall keep a client reasonably informed about the status of a matter and promptly comply with reasonable requests for information.

(b) A lawyer shall explain a matter to the extent reasonably necessary to permit the client to make informed decisions regarding the representation.

Comment:

[1] The client should have sufficient information to participate intelligently in decisions concerning the objectives of the representation and the means by which they are to be pursued, to the extent the client is willing and able to do so. For example, a lawyer negotiating on behalf of a client should provide the client with facts relevant to the matter, inform the client of communications from another party and take other reasonable steps that permit the client to make a decision regarding a serious offer from another party. A lawyer who receives from opposing counsel an offer of settlement in a civil controversy or a proffered plea bargain in a criminal case should promptly inform the client of its substance unless prior discussions with the client have left it clear that the proposal will be unacceptable. See Rule 1.2(a). Even when a client delegates authority to the lawyer, the client should be kept advised of the status of the matter.

[2] Adequacy of communication depends in part on the kind of advice or assistance involved. For example, in negotiations where there is time to explain a proposal the lawyer should review all important provisions with the client before proceeding to an agreement. In litigation a lawyer should explain the general strategy and prospects of success and ordinarily should consult the client on tactics that might injure or coerce others. On the other hand, a lawyer ordinarily cannot be expected to describe trial or negotiation strategy in detail. The guiding principle is that the lawyer should fulfill reasonable client expectations for information consistent with the duty to act in the client's best interests, and the client's overall requirements as to the character of representation.

RULE 1.6   Confidentiality of Information

(a) A lawyer shall not reveal information relating to representation of a client unless the client consents after consultation, except for disclosures that are impliedly authorized in order to carry out the representation, and except as stated in paragraph (b).

(b) A lawyer may reveal such information to the extent the lawyer reasonably believes necessary:

(1) to prevent the client from committing a criminal act that the lawyer believes is likely to result in imminent death or substantial bodily harm; or

(2) to establish a claim or defense on behalf of the lawyer in a controversy between the lawyer and the client, to establish a defense to a criminal charge or civil claim against the lawyer based upon conduct in which the client was involved, or to respond to allegations in any proceeding concerning the lawyer's representation of the client.

Comment:

[1] The lawyer is part of a judicial system charged with upholding the law. One of the lawyer's functions is to advise clients so that they avoid any violation of the law in the proper exercise of their rights.

[2] The observance of the ethical obligation of a lawyer to hold inviolate confidential information of the client not only facilitates the full development of facts essential to proper representation of the client but also encourages people to seek early legal assistance.

[3] Almost without exception, clients come to lawyers in order to determine what their rights are and what is, in the maze of laws and regulations, deemed to be legal and correct. The common law recognizes that the client's confidences must be protected from disclosure. Based upon experience, lawyers know that almost all clients follow the advice given, and the law is upheld.

[4] A fundamental principle in the client-lawyer relationship is that the lawyer maintain confidentiality of information relating to the representation. The client is thereby encouraged to communicate fully and frankly with the lawyer even as to embarrassing or legally damaging subject matter.

[5] The principle of confidentiality is given effect in two related bodies of law, the attorney-client privilege (which includes the work product doctrine) in the law of evidence and the rule of confidentiality established in professional ethics. The attorney-client privilege applies in judicial and other proceedings in which a lawyer may be called as a witness or otherwise required to produce evidence concerning a client. The rule of client-lawyer confidentiality applies in situations other than those where evidence is sought from the lawyer through compulsion of law. The confidentiality rule applies not merely to matters communicated in confidence by the client but also to all information relating to the representation, whatever its source. A lawyer may not disclose such information except as authorized or required by the Rules of Professional Conduct or other law....

[6] The requirement of maintaining confidentiality of information relating to representation applies to government lawyers who may

disagree with the policy goals that their representation is designed to advance.

Authorized Disclosure

[7] A lawyer is impliedly authorized to make disclosures about a client when appropriate in carrying out the representation, except to the extent that the client's instructions or special circumstances limit that authority. In litigation, for example, a lawyer may disclose information by admitting a fact that cannot properly be disputed, or in negotiation by making a disclosure that facilitates a satisfactory conclusion.

[8] Lawyers in a firm may, in the course of the firm's practice, disclose to each other information relating to a client of the firm, unless the client has instructed that particular information be confined to specified lawyers.

Disclosure Adverse to Client

[9] The confidentiality rule is subject to limited exceptions. In becoming privy to information about a client, a lawyer may foresee that the client intends serious harm to another person. However, to the extent a lawyer is required or permitted to disclose a client's purposes, the client will be inhibited from revealing facts which would enable the lawyer to counsel against a wrongful course of action. The public is better protected if full and open communication by the client is encouraged than if it is inhibited.

RULE 1.7 Conflict of Interest: General Rule

(a) A lawyer shall not represent a client if the representation of that client will be directly adverse to another client, unless:

(1) the lawyer reasonably believes the representation will not adversely affect the relationship with the other client; and

(2) each client consents after consultation.

(b) A lawyer shall not represent a client if the representation of that client may be materially limited by the lawyer's responsibilities to another client or to a third person, or by the lawyer's own interests, unless:

(1) the lawyer reasonably believes the representation will not be adversely affected; and

(2) the client consents after consultation. When representation of multiple clients in a single matter is undertaken, the consultation shall include explanation of the implications of the common representation and the advantages and risks involved.

RULE 1.13 Organization as Client

(a) A lawyer employed or retained by an organization represents the organization acting through its duly authorized constituents.

(b) If a lawyer for an organization knows that an officer, employee or other person associated with the organization is engaged in action, intends to act or refuses to act in a matter related to the representation that is a violation of a legal obligation to the organization, or a violation of law which reasonably might be imputed to the organization, and is likely to result in substantial injury to the organization, the lawyer shall proceed as is reasonably necessary in the best interest of the organization. In determining how to proceed, the lawyer shall give due consideration to the seriousness of the violation and its consequences, the scope and nature of the lawyer's representation, the responsibility in the organization and the apparent motivation of the person involved, the policies of the organization concerning such matters and any other relevant considerations. Any measures taken shall be designed to minimize disruption of the organization and the risk of revealing information relating to the representation to persons outside the organization. Such measures may include among others:

(1) asking reconsideration of the matter;

(2) advising that a separate legal opinion on the matter be sought for presentation to appropriate authority in the organization; and

(3) referring the matter to higher authority in the organization, including, if warranted by the seriousness of the matter, referral to the highest authority that can act in behalf of the organization as determined by applicable law.

(c) If, despite the lawyer's efforts in accordance with paragraph (b), the highest authority that can act on behalf of the organization insists upon action, or a refusal to act, that is clearly a violation of law and is likely to result in substantial injury to the organization, the lawyer may resign in accordance with rule 1.16.

(d) In dealing with an organization's directors, officers, employees, members, shareholders or other constituents, a lawyer shall explain the identity of the client when it is apparent that the organization's interests are adverse to those of the constituents with whom the lawyer is dealing.

(e) A lawyer representing an organization may also represent any of its directors, officers, employees, members, shareholders or other constituents, subject to the provisions of rule 1.7. If the organization's consent to the dual representation is required by rule 1.7, the consent shall be given by an appropriate official of the organization other than the individual who is to be represented, or by the shareholders.

RULE 1.16 Declining or Terminating Representation

(a) Except as stated in paragraph (c), a lawyer shall not represent a client or, where representation has commenced, shall withdraw from the representation of a client if:

(1) the representation will result in violation of the rules of professional conduct or other law;

(2) the lawyer's physical or mental condition materially impairs the lawyer's ability to represent the client; or

(3) the lawyer is discharged.

(b) Except as stated in paragraph (c), a lawyer may withdraw from representing a client if withdrawal can be accomplished without material adverse effect on the interests of the client, or if:

(1) the client persists in a course of action involving the lawyer's services that the lawyer reasonably believes is criminal or fraudulent;

(2) the client has used the lawyer's services to perpetrate a crime or fraud;

(3) a client insists upon pursuing an objective that the lawyer considers repugnant or imprudent;

(4) the client fails substantially to fulfill an obligation to the lawyer regarding the lawyer's services and has been given reasonable warning that the lawyer will withdraw unless the obligation is fulfilled;

(5) the representation will result in an unreasonable financial burden on the lawyer or has been rendered unreasonably difficult by the client; or

(6) other good cause for withdrawal exists.

(c) When ordered to do so by a tribunal, a lawyer shall continue representation notwithstanding good cause for terminating the representation.

(d) Upon termination of representation, a lawyer shall take steps to the extent reasonably practicable to protect a client's interests, such as giving reasonable notice to the client, allowing time for employment of other counsel, surrendering papers and property to which the client is entitled and refunding any advance payment of fee that has not been earned. The lawyer may retain papers relating to the client to the extent permitted by other law.

Article 3. Advocate

RULE 3.1 Meritorious Claims and Contentions

A lawyer shall not bring or defend a proceeding, or assert or controvert an issue therein, unless there is a basis for doing so that is not frivolous, which includes a good faith argument for an extension, modification or reversal of existing law. A lawyer for the defendant in a criminal proceeding, or the respondent in a proceeding that could result in incarceration, may nevertheless so defend the proceeding as to require that every element of the case be established.

RULE 3.3 Candor Toward the Tribunal

(a) A lawyer shall not knowingly:

(1) make a false statement of material fact or law to a tribunal;

(2) fail to disclose a material fact to a tribunal when disclosure is necessary to avoid assisting a criminal or fraudulent act by the client;

(3) fail to disclose to the tribunal legal authority in the controlling jurisdiction known to the lawyer to be directly adverse to the position of the client and not disclosed by opposing counsel; or

(4) offer evidence that the lawyer knows to be false. If a lawyer has offered material evidence and comes to know of its falsity, the lawyer shall take reasonable remedial measures.

(b) The duties stated in paragraph (a) continue to the conclusion of the proceeding, and apply even if compliance requires disclosure of information otherwise protected by rule 1.6.

(c) A lawyer may refuse to offer evidence that the lawyer reasonably believes is false.

(d) In an ex parte proceeding, a lawyer shall inform the tribunal of all material facts known to the lawyer which will enable the tribunal to make an informed decision, whether or not the facts are adverse.

Comment:

Perjury by a Criminal Defendant

[7] Whether an advocate for a criminally accused has the same duty of disclosure has been intensely debated. While it is agreed that the lawyer should seek to persuade the client to refrain from perjurious testimony, there has been dispute concerning the lawyer's duty when that persuasion fails. If the confrontation with the client occurs before trial, the lawyer ordinarily can withdraw. Withdrawal before trial may not be possible, however, either because trial is imminent, or because the confrontation with the client does not take place until the trial itself, or because no other counsel is available.

[8] The most difficult situation, therefore, arises in a criminal case where the accused insists on testifying when the lawyer knows that the testimony is perjurious. The lawyer's effort to rectify the situation can increase the likelihood of the client's being convicted as well as opening the possibility of a prosecution for perjury. On the other hand, if the lawyer does not exercise control over the proof, the lawyer participates, although in a merely passive way, in deception of the court.

[9] Three resolutions of this dilemma have been proposed. One is to permit the accused to testify by a narrative without guidance through the lawyer's questioning. This compromises both contending principles; it exempts the lawyer from the duty to disclose false evidence but subjects the client to an implicit disclosure of information

imparted to counsel. Another suggested resolution, of relatively recent origin, is that the advocate be entirely excused from the duty to reveal perjury if the perjury is that of the client. This is a coherent solution but makes the advocate a knowing instrument of perjury.

[10] The other resolution of the dilemma is that the lawyer must reveal the client's perjury if necessary to rectify the situation. A criminal accused has a right to the assistance of an advocate, a right to testify and a right of confidential communication with counsel. However, an accused should not have a right to assistance of counsel in committing perjury. Furthermore, an advocate has an obligation, not only in professional ethics but under the law as well, to avoid implication in the commission of perjury or other falsification of evidence. See Rule 1.2(d).

Remedial Measures

[11] If perjured testimony or false evidence has been offered, the advocate's proper course ordinarily is to remonstrate with the client confidentially. If that fails, the advocate should seek to withdraw if that will remedy the situation. If withdrawal will not remedy the situation or is impossible, the advocate should make disclosure to the court. It is for the court then to determine what should be done—making a statement about the matter to the trier of fact, ordering a mistrial or perhaps nothing. If the false testimony was that of the client, the client may controvert the lawyer's version of their communication when the lawyer discloses the situation to the court. If there is an issue whether the client has committed perjury, the lawyer cannot represent the client in resolution of the issue and a mistrial may be unavoidable. An unscrupulous client might in this way attempt to produce a series of mistrials and thus escape prosecution. However, a second such encounter could be construed as a deliberate abuse of the right to counsel and as such a waiver of the right to further representation.

Article 4. Transactions with Persons Other than Clients

RULE 4.1 Truthfulness in Statements to Others

In the course of representing a client a lawyer shall not knowingly:

(a) make a false statement of material fact or law to a third person; or

(b) fail to disclose a material fact to a third person when disclosure is necessary to avoid assisting a criminal or fraudulent act by a client, unless disclosure is prohibited by rule 1.6.

Comment:

Misrepresentation

[1] A lawyer is required to be truthful when dealing with others on a client's behalf, but generally has no affirmative duty to inform an opposing party of relevant facts. A misrepresentation can occur if the

lawyer incorporates or affirms a statement of another person that the lawyer knows is false. Misrepresentations can also occur by failure to act.

Statements of Fact

[2] This Rule refers to statements of fact. Whether a particular statement should be regarded as one of fact can depend on the circumstances. Under generally accepted conventions in negotiation, certain types of statements ordinarily are not taken as statements of material fact. Estimates of price or value placed on the subject of a transaction and a party's intentions as to an acceptable settlement of a claim are in this category, and so is the existence of an undisclosed principal except where nondisclosure of the principal would constitute fraud.

Article 5. Law Firms and Associations

RULE 5.5 Unauthorized Practice of Law

A lawyer shall not:

(a) practice law in a jurisdiction where doing so violates the regulation of the legal profession in that jurisdiction; or

(b) assist a person who is not a member of the bar in the performance of activity that constitutes the unauthorized practice of law.

Article 8. Maintaining the Integrity of the Profession

RULE 8.1 Bar Admission and Disciplinary Matters

An applicant for admission to the bar, or a lawyer in connection with a bar admission application or in connection with a disciplinary matter, shall not:

(a) knowingly make a false statement of material fact; or

(b) fail to disclose a fact necessary to correct a misapprehension known by the person to have arisen in the matter, or knowingly fail to respond to a lawful demand for information from an admission or disciplinary authority, except that this rule does not require disclosure of information otherwise protected by rule 1.6.

RULE 8.2 Judicial and Legal Officials

(a) A lawyer shall not make a statement that the lawyer knows to be false or with reckless disregard as to its truth or falsity concerning the qualifications or integrity of a judge, adjudicatory officer or public legal officer, or of a candidate for election or appointment to judicial or legal office.

†